Third
BRIEF CANADIAN EDITION

Business Communication

PROCESS AND PRODUCT

MARY ELLEN GUFFEY
Professor of Business Emerita, Los Angeles Pierce College

KATHLEEN RHODES
Durham College

PATRICIA ROGIN
Durham College

NELSON EDUCATION

NELSON EDUCATION

Business Communication: Process and Product, Third Brief Canadian Edition

by Mary Ellen Guffey, Kathleen Rhodes, and Patricia Rogin

Vice-President and Editorial Director:
Evelyn Veitch

Acquisitions Editor:
Anne-Marie Taylor

Marketing Manager:
Amanda Henry

Senior Developmental Editor:
Linda Sparks

Photo Researcher and Permissions Coordinator:
Daniela Glass

Senior Content Production Manager:
Natalia Denesiuk Harris

Production Service:
Graphic World Publishing Services

Copy Editor:
Gillian Watts

Proofreader:
Graphic World Publishing Services

Indexer:
Graphic World Publishing Services

Production Coordinator:
Ferial Suleman

Design Director:
Ken Phipps

Managing Designer:
Franca Amore

Interior Design:
Imbue Design/Kim Torbeck, Cincinnati

Cover Design:
Liz Harasymczuk

Cover Images:
L to R: DAJ/Getty Images; Stockbyte/Getty Images; Blend Images/Alamy

Compositor:
Graphic World Inc.

Printer:
RR Donnelley

Printed and bound in the United States
4 5 13 12 11

For more information contact Nelson Education Ltd., 1120 Birchmount Road, Toronto, Ontario, M1K 5G4. Or you can visit our Internet site at http://www.nelson.com

Library and Archives Canada Cataloguing in Publication Data

Guffey, Mary Ellen
Business communication : process and product / Mary Ellen Guffey, Kathleen Rhodes, Patricia Rogin. — 3rd brief Canadian ed.

Includes bibliographical references and index.
ISBN 978-0-17-650046-7

1. Business communication—Textbooks. 2. Business writing—Textbooks. I. Rogin, Patricia, 1958– II. Rhodes, Kathleen, 1951– III. Title.

HF5718.3.G82 2009 651.7
C2009-900205-1

ISBN-13: 978-0-17-650046-7
ISBN-10: 0-17-650046-4

brief contents

UNIT 1	**COMMUNICATION FOUNDATIONS**	**1**
CHAPTER 1	Communicating at Work	3
CHAPTER 2	Communicating in Small Groups and Teams	27
CHAPTER 3	Workplace Listening and Nonverbal Communication	50
CHAPTER 4	Communicating Across Cultures	68
UNIT 2	**THE 3-X-3 WRITING PROCESS**	**89**
CHAPTER 5	Writing Process Phase 1: Analyze, Anticipate, Adapt	91
CHAPTER 6	Writing Process Phase 2: Research, Organize, Compose	111
CHAPTER 7	Writing Process Phase 3: Revise, Proofread, Evaluate	135
UNIT 3	**BUSINESS CORRESPONDENCE**	**153**
CHAPTER 8	Routine E-Mail Messages and Memos	155
CHAPTER 9	Routine Letters and Goodwill Messages	182
CHAPTER 10	Persuasive and Sales Messages	215
CHAPTER 11	Negative Messages	241
UNIT 4	**REPORTS AND PROPOSALS**	**269**
CHAPTER 12	Preparing to Write Business Reports	271
CHAPTER 13	Organizing and Writing Typical Business Reports	307
CHAPTER 14	Proposals and Formal Reports	339
UNIT 5	**PRESENTATIONS**	**373**
CHAPTER 15	Speaking With Confidence	375
CHAPTER 16	Employment Communication	404
APPENDIX A	Competent Language Usage Essentials (C.L.U.E.)	A-1
APPENDIX B	Documentation Formats	B-1
KEY TO C.L.U.E. REVIEW EXERCISES		Key-1
NOTES		N-1
ACKNOWLEDGMENTS		Ack-1
INDEX		I-1

detailed contents

PREFACE xiii

UNIT 1 COMMUNICATION FOUNDATIONS 1

CHAPTER 1 **Communicating at Work** **3**

Ensuring That You Succeed in the New Workplace 4
Career Coach: Understanding the Multi-generational Workforce 9
Examining the Process of Communication 10
Overcoming Interpersonal Communication Barriers 12
Communicating in Organizations 13
Improving the Flow of Information in Organizations 16
Tech Talk: Tips for Managing Your E-Mail 17
Facing Ethical Challenges 19
Strengthening Your Communication Skills 20
Summary of Learning Objectives 21
Chapter Review 23
Critical Thinking 23
Activities 23
C.L.U.E. Review 1 26

CHAPTER 2 **Communicating in Small Groups and Teams** **27**

Preparing to Work With Groups and Teams 28
Tech Talk: How to Form and Participate in Virtual Teams 29
Understanding Team Development, Roles, and Conflict 30
Characteristics of Successful Teams 33
Checklist for Developing Team Effectiveness 34
Organizing Team-Based Written and Oral Presentations 35
Planning and Participating in Productive Meetings 37
Checklist for Planning and Participating in Productive Meetings 41
Using Technology to Facilitate Collaboration 42
Strengthening Your Teamwork Skills Now 44
Summary of Learning Objectives 45
Chapter Review 47
Critical Thinking 47
Activities 47
C.L.U.E. Review 2 49

CHAPTER 3 **Workplace Listening and Nonverbal Communication** **50**
Listening in the Workplace 51
The Listening Process and Its Barriers 53
Improving Workplace Listening 55
Checklist for Improving Listening 57
Communicating Through Nonverbal Messages 57
Forms of Nonverbal Communication 58
Career Coach: Perils of Casual Apparel in the Workplace 61
Checklist of Techniques for Improving Nonverbal Communication Skills in the Workplace 62
Summary of Learning Objectives 63
Chapter Review 65
Critical Thinking 65
Activities 65
C.L.U.E. Review 3 67

CHAPTER 4 **Communicating Across Cultures** **68**
The Increasing Importance of Intercultural Communication 69
Understanding Culture 71
Tech Talk: Being Interculturally Correct on the Web 75
Achieving Intercultural Proficiency 76
Improving Communication With Intercultural Audiences 77
Checklist for Improving Intercultural Proficiency and Communication 80
Capitalizing on Workforce Diversity 80
Summary of Learning Objectives 83
Chapter Review 85
Critical Thinking 85
Activities 85
C.L.U.E. Review 4 87

UNIT 2 THE 3-X-3 WRITING PROCESS 89

CHAPTER 5 **Writing Process Phase 1: Analyze, Anticipate, Adapt** **91**
Approaching the Writing Process Systematically 92
Adapting and Altering the Writing Process 93
Writing Process Phase 1: Analyze 95
Tech Talk: Using Technology to Edit and Revise Collaborative Documents 96
Writing Process Phase 1: Anticipate 97
Writing Process Phase 1: Adapt 98
Checklist for Adapting a Message to Its Audience 104
Adapting to Legal Responsibilities 104
Summary of Learning Objectives 106

Chapter Review 108
Critical Thinking 108
Activities 108
C.L.U.E. Review 5 110

CHAPTER 6 **Writing Process Phase 2: Research, Organize, Compose** **111**

Writing Process Phase 2: Research 112
Writing Process Phase 2: Organize 114
Organizing Ideas Into Patterns 118
Tech Talk: Seven Ways Computers Can Help You Create Better Written Messages, Oral Presentations, and Web Pages 121
Writing Process Phase 2: Compose 121
Drafting Meaningful Paragraphs 125
Checklist for Composing Sentences and Paragraphs 128
Summary of Learning Objectives 129
Chapter Review 131
Critical Thinking 131
Activities 131
C.L.U.E. Review 6 134

CHAPTER 7 **Writing Process Phase 3: Revise, Proofread, Evaluate** **135**

Writing Process Phase 3: Revise 136
Revising for Conciseness 137
Revising for Vigour and Directness 139
Revising for Readability 140
Checklist for Revising Messages 143
Writing Process Phase 3: Proofread 144
Tech Talk: Using Spell Checkers and Grammar/Style Checkers Wisely 145
Writing Process Phase 3: Evaluate 146
Summary of Learning Objectives 146
Chapter Review 148
Critical Thinking 148
Activities 148
C.L.U.E. Review 7 151

UNIT 3 **BUSINESS CORRESPONDENCE** 153

CHAPTER 8 **Routine E-Mail Messages and Memos** **155**

Applying the Writing Process to Produce Effective E-Mail Messages and Memos 156
Analyzing the Structure and Format of E-Mail Messages and Memos 158
Using E-Mail Smartly and Safely 164
Writing Information and Procedure E-Mail Messages and Memos 168

Writing Request and Reply E-Mail Messages and Memos 170
Writing Confirmation E-Mail Messages and Memos 172
Checklist for Writing Routine E-Mail Messages and Memos 173
Summary of Learning Objectives 174
Chapter Review 176
Critical Thinking 176
Activities 176
C.L.U.E. Review 8 181

CHAPTER 9 **Routine Letters and Goodwill Messages** **182**

Understanding the Power of Business Letters and the Process of Writing Successful Letters 183
Applying the 3-x-3 Writing Process to Create Successful Letters 184
Analyzing the Structure and Characteristics of Business Letters 186
Analyzing the Characteristics of Good Business Letters 188
Direct Requests for Information or Action 188
Order Letters 190
Direct Claims 191
Checklist for Writing Direct Requests 194
Direct Replies 196
Adjustments 198
Checklist for Writing Positive Reply Letters 201
Goodwill Messages 202
Checklist for Writing Goodwill Messages 205
Summary of Learning Objectives 206
Chapter Review 208
Critical Thinking 208
Activities 208
C.L.U.E. Review 9 214

CHAPTER 10 **Persuasive and Sales Messages** **215**

Strategies for Making Persuasive Requests 216
Blending the Components of a Persuasive Message 218
Writing Successful Persuasive Requests 222
Planning and Composing Effective Sales Messages 228
Checklist for Writing Sales Letters 232
Developing Persuasive Press Releases 234
Summary of Learning Objectives 234
Chapter Review 236
Critical Thinking 236
Activities 236
C.L.U.E. Review 10 240

CHAPTER 11 **Negative Messages** **241**

Strategies for Delivering Bad News 242
Techniques for Delivering Bad News Sensitively 246
Refusing Routine Requests 249
Checklist for Refusing Routine Requests 252
Delivering Bad News to Customers 253
Checklist for Delivering Bad News to Customers 258
Delivering Bad News Within Organizations 259
Checklist for Delivering Bad News Within Organizations 260
Presenting Bad News in Other Cultures 262
Summary of Learning Objectives 262
Chapter Review 264
Critical Thinking 264
Activities 264
C.L.U.E. Review 11 268

UNIT 4 REPORTS AND PROPOSALS 269

CHAPTER 12 **Preparing to Write Business Reports** **271**

Understanding Report Basics 272
Applying the 3-x-3 Writing Process to Reports 278
Gathering Information From Secondary Sources 282
Comprehending the Evolving Nature of Communication Technology 286
Tech Talk: Managing Your Electronic Research Data Like a Pro 290
Gathering Information From Primary Sources 291
Documenting Data 295
Illustrating Data 298
Summary of Learning Objectives 302
Chapter Review 304
Critical Thinking 304
Activities 304
C.L.U.E. Review 12 306

CHAPTER 13 **Organizing and Writing Typical Business Reports** **307**

Interpreting Data 308
Drawing Conclusions and Making Recommendations 310
Organizing Data 314
Writing Informational Reports 317
Checklist for Writing Informational Reports 322
Writing Short Analytical Reports 324
Checklist for Writing Analytical Reports 330
Summary of Learning Objectives 333

Chapter Review 335
Critical Thinking 335
Activities 335
C.L.U.E. Review 13 338

CHAPTER 14 **Proposals and Formal Reports** **339**
Preparing Formal and Informal Proposals 340
Special Components of Formal Proposals 342
Checklist for Writing Proposals 343
Preparing an Effective Business Plan 344
Writing Formal Reports 346
Checklist for Preparing Formal Reports 365
Summary of Learning Objectives 367
Chapter Review 368
Critical Thinking 368
Activities 368
C.L.U.E. Review 14 371

UNIT 5 PRESENTATIONS 373

CHAPTER 15 **Speaking With Confidence** **375**
Preparing Effective Oral Presentations 376
Organizing the Content for a Powerful Impact 377
Career Coach: Nine Techniques for Gaining and Keeping Audience Attention 379
Building Audience Rapport Like a Pro 381
Planning Visual Aids, Handouts, and Multimedia Presentations 383
Designing a Multimedia Presentation 385
Polishing Your Delivery and Following Up 391
Career Coach: How to Avoid Stage Fright 392
Adapting to International and Cross-Cultural Audiences 394
Checklist for Preparing and Organizing Oral Presentations 395
Improving Telephone and Voice Mail Skills 397
Summary of Learning Objectives 399
Chapter Review 401
Critical Thinking 401
Activities 401
C.L.U.E. Review 15 403

CHAPTER 16 **Employment Communication** **404**
Preparing for Employment 405
The Customized Résumé 409
Arranging the Parts 414
Optimizing Your Résumé for Today's Technologies 417

Ethical Insights: Are Inflated Résumés Worth the Risk? 422
Checklist for Writing a Customized Résumé 424
The Customized Cover Letter 425
Checklist for Writing a Customized Cover Letter 430
Follow-up Letters and Other Employment Documents 431
Interviewing for Employment 434
Career Coach: Looking Good When You Answer Key Interview Questions 436
Summary of Learning Objectives 438
Chapter Review 440
Critical Thinking 440
Activities 440
C.L.U.E. Review 16 443

APPENDIX A **Competent Language Usage Essentials (C.L.U.E.)** **A-1**

APPENDIX B **Documentation Formats** **B-1**

KEY TO C.L.U.E. REVIEW EXERCISES **Key-1**

NOTES **N-1**

ACKNOWLEDGMENTS **Ack-1**

INDEX **I-1**

preface

At the request of instructors who liked *Business Communication: Process and Product* but found that it contained more material than they could cover in their courses, we introduced the first Brief Canadian Edition in 2003. Based on instructor feedback, much of the nice-to-know information, such as the case studies and career track profiles, was removed to the Instructor's Web site. In addition, the number of end-of-chapter activities was reduced. The content of the information was not compromised in any way, but was condensed to focus on key elements.

Business Communication: Process and Product, Third Brief Canadian Edition, remains true to the 3-x-3 writing process. This systematic approach provides students with a practical plan for solving communication problems and creating successful communication products. The nine-stage approach of analyzing–anticipating–adapting, researching–organizing–approaching, and revising–proofreading–evaluating makes the process understandable.

New to the Third Brief Canadian Edition

Some of the key changes in this edition include

- Up-to-date information on communication technology, including the use of wikis and blogs;

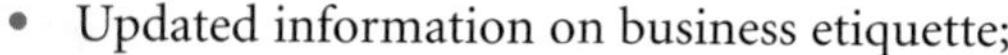

Create a slide only if it accomplishes at least one of the following purposes:
• Generates interest in what you are saying and helps the audience follow your ideas
• Highlights points you want your audience to remember
• Introduces or reviews your key points
• Provides a transition from one point to the next
• Illustrates and simplifies complex ideas
Revising, Proofreading, and Evaluating Your Slideshow. Use PowerPoint's Slide Sorter View to rearrange, insert, and delete slides during the revision process. This is the time when you will focus on making your presentation as clear as possible. If you are listing items, be sure that you use parallel grammatical form. As you are reviewing, check carefully to find spelling, grammar, punctuation, and other errors. Use PowerPoint's spell checker, but don't rely on it without careful proofing, preferably from a printed copy of the slideshow. Nothing is as embarrassing as projecting errors on a huge screen in front of an audience. Also check for consistency in how you capitalize and punctuate points throughout the presentation.
The final stage in applying the 3-x-3 process to developing a PowerPoint presentation involves evaluation. Consider whether you have done all you can to use the tools PowerPoint provides to communicate your message in a visually appealing way. In addition, test your slides on the equipment and in the room you will be using during your presentation. Do the colours you selected work in this setting? Are the font styles and sizes readable from the back of the room? Figure 15.3 shows examples of the slides that incorporate what you have learned in the discussion. The creator of the presentation varied the slide design to break the monotony of bulleted or numbered lists. Images and animated diagrams add interest and appeal to the slides.
Eight Steps to Making a Powerful Multimedia Presentation
For a powerful presentation, first write the text and then work on templates, font styles, and colours.
We have now discussed many suggestions for making effective PowerPoint presentations, but you may still be wondering how to put it all together. Here is a step-by-step process for creating a powerful multimedia presentation:
1. Start with the text. The text is the foundation of your presentation. Express your ideas using words that are clear, concise, and understandable. Once the entire content of your presentation is in place you are ready to begin adding colour and all the other elements that will make your slides visually appealing.
2. Select background and fonts. Select a template that will provide consistent font styles, font sizes, and a background for your slides. You can create your own template or use one included with PowerPoint. You cannot go wrong with selecting a basic template design with an easy-to-read font such as Times New Roman or Arial. As a general rule, use no more than two font styles in your presentation. The point size should be between 24 and 36. Title fonts should be larger than text font. The more you use PowerPoint and find out what works and does not work, the more you can experiment with bolder, more innovative background and font options that effectively convey your message.
3. Choose images that help communicate your message. Images such as clip art, photographs, and maps should complement the text. Never use an image that is not immediately relevant. Some people consider clip art amateurish, so photographs are often preferable. In addition, clip art is available to any user, so it tends to become stale fast.
UNIT 5
Presentations
388
NEL

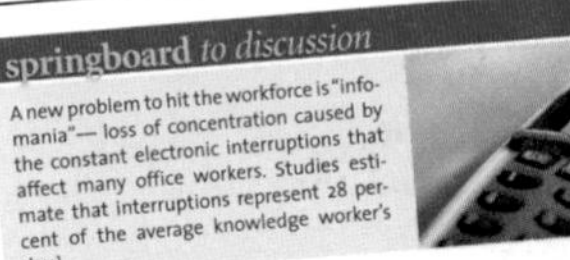

springboard to discussion
A new problem to hit the workforce is "infomania"— loss of concentration caused by the constant electronic interruptions that affect many office workers. Studies estimate that interruptions represent 28 percent of the average knowledge worker's day.[1]

- Updated information on business etiquette;
- Added coverage of guidelines for multimedia presentations to provide practical skills the student will be able to transfer to the workplace; and
- A new feature called "Springboard to Discussion" at the beginning of each chapter. These brief discussion-starters on topics such as "Infomania," human versus electronic interaction, and how different companies have handled tragic news, can be used to engage students in the traditional face-to-face classroom, as well as through discussion boards in the virtual classroom. The Instructor's Manual contains more specific suggestions for using the springboards.

Appreciation for Support

We are very pleased to present the Third Brief Canadian Edition of *Business Communication: Process and Product*. As always, we owe a huge debt of gratitude to Dr. Mary Ellen Guffey, who continues to produce timely, market-driven texts and ancillaries that form the basis of our work.

In addition, we continue to appreciate the support from the team at Nelson Education Ltd. Although the team itself seems to constantly evolve, the levels of support, enthusiasm, and professionalism remain constant.

We particularly appreciate those instructors and students who continue to choose *Business Communication: Process and Product*, especially those who provide both formal and informal feedback. Those who had a specific impact on the content of this edition include Kathryn Brillinger, Conestoga College; Chris Legebow, St. Clair College; Rhonda Malomet, George Brown College; Peter Miller, Seneca College; Kerri Shields, Centennial College; and Charlene Wyatt, Okanagan College. The support of colleagues and friends at Durham College and other institutions continues to play an important part in our work. We thank you all.

Finally, as always, we thank our families for their unswerving support.

Mary Ellen Guffey, Kathleen Rhodes, Patricia Rogin

Support Package

A rich variety of instructional resources supplement and support *Business Communication: Process and Product*, Third Brief Canadian Edition. These materials give you excellent working tools to create a dynamic, exciting, and effective course.

For the Instructor

Instructor's Manual/Test Bank (978-0-17-647408-9)

This comprehensive Instructor's Resource Manual contains both the Instructor's Manual and the Printed Test Bank.

The **Instructor's Manual** includes chapter synopses, teaching ideas, lecture enrichment material, classroom management techniques, answers for chapter review questions, suggested discussion guides for critical-thinking questions, and solution guides for case-study questions and applications.

Each chapter of the **Printed Test Bank** contains between 60 and 150 test questions. A special feature of this edition is the inclusion of feedback for the response to each question. Every chapter opens with a correlation table that identifies questions by chapter learning objective and by content: factual, conceptual, or application. Page references to the text ensure quick reference.

Instructor's Resource CD-ROM (978-0-17-647407-2)

The Instructor's CD-ROM combines popular text supplement material in one easy-to-use format. You'll have complete access to the Instructor's Manual (chapter outlines, bonus lecture material, before-and-after documents, and solutions to select chapter activities). The CD-ROM includes the following:

Microsoft® PowerPoint® Presentation Slides. This comprehensive lecture system offers summaries, explanations, and illustrations of key chapter concepts, plus lecture enrichment material not included in the text. With Microsoft® PowerPoint® software, instructors can easily customize any slide to support their lectures.

Computerized Test Bank. All items from the printed test bank are available through this automated testing program using the ExamView® testing program. Create exams by selecting provided questions, modifying existing questions, and adding questions. It is provided free to adopters of this text.

Instructor's Manual/Test Bank. You'll have complete access to the Instructor's Manual (chapter outlines, bonus lecture material, before-and-after documents, and solutions to select chapter activities) and word-processing files for the test bank.

Nelson Education Testing Advantage. In most post-secondary courses, a large percentage of student assessment is based on multiple-choice testing. Many instructors use multiple-choice reluctantly, believing that it is a methodology best used for testing what a student remembers rather than what she or he has learned.

Nelson Education Ltd. understands that a good quality multiple-choice test bank can provide the means to measure higher-level thinking skills as well as recall. Recognizing the importance of multiple-choice testing in today's classroom, we have created the Nelson Education Testing Advantage program (NETA) to ensure the value of our high quality test banks.

The test bank for *Business Communication: Process and Product*, Third Brief Canadian Edition, offers the Nelson Education Testing Advantage. NETA was created in partnership with David DiBattista, a 3M National Teaching Fellow, professor of psychology at Brock University, and researcher in the area of multiple-choice testing. NETA ensures that subject-matter experts who author test banks have had training in two areas: avoiding common errors in test construction, and developing multiple-choice test questions that "get beyond remembering" to assess higher-level thinking.

All NETA test banks include David DiBattista's guide for instructors, "Multiple Choice Tests: Getting Beyond Remembering." This guide has been designed to assist you in using Nelson test banks to achieve your desired outcomes in your course.

Book-specific Web Site http://www.guffeybrief3e.nelson.com

The book-specific Web site contains a link to Instructor's Resources, providing access to downloadable versions of the Instructor's Manual and Microsoft® PowerPoint®

slides. The book-specific site also contains links to professional organizations, media resources, online writing labs, and much more! Contact your local sales representative for a password to the Instructor Resources portion of the site.

For the Student

Student Web Site http://www.guffeybrief3e.nelson.com

This powerful site features chapter-by-chapter quizzes and Web links, career and job search information, Web media resources, online writing labs, and much more!

CengageNOW™ for *Business Communication: Process and Product*, Third Brief Canadian Edition, is an online assessment-driven and student-centred tutorial that provides students with a personalized learning plan. Based on a diagnostic Pre-Test, a customized learning path is generated for each student that targets his or her study needs and helps the student to visualize, organize, practise, and master the material in the text. Media resources enhance problem-solving skills and improve conceptual understanding.

unit 1

Communication Foundations

chapter 1

Communicating at Work

chapter 2

Communicating in Small Groups and Teams

chapter 3

Workplace Listening and Nonverbal Communication

chapter 4

Communicating Across Cultures

chapter 1

Communicating at Work

objectives

1 Identify changes in the workplace and explain the importance of communication skills.

2 Describe the process of communication.

3 Discuss barriers to interpersonal communication and the means of overcoming those barriers.

4 Analyze the functions and procedures of communication in organizations.

5 Assess the flow of communication in organizations, including barriers and methods for overcoming those barriers.

6 List the goals of ethical business communication and describe important tools for doing the right thing.

springboard *to discussion*

A new problem to hit the workforce is "info-mania"— loss of concentration caused by the constant electronic interruptions that affect many office workers. Studies estimate that interruptions represent 28 percent of the average knowledge worker's day.[1]

learning objective 1

Ensuring That You Succeed in the New Workplace

Succeeding in today's world of work demands that you read, listen, speak, and write effectively.

Employees across the country and around the world are experiencing change and upheaval. In fact, the entire work world you are about to enter is changing dramatically. The kind of work you'll do, the tools you'll use, the form of management, the environment where you'll work, the people with whom you'll interact—all are undergoing a profound transformation. Many of the changes in this dynamic workplace revolve around processing and communicating information. As a result, the most successful players in this new world of work will be those with highly developed communication skills.

The abilities to read, listen, speak, and write effectively, of course, are not inborn. Thriving in the dynamic and demanding work world depends on many factors, some of which you cannot control. But one factor that you do control is how well you communicate. The goals of this book and this course are to teach you basic business communication skills, such as how to write a memo or letter and how to make a presentation. You will also learn additional powerful communication skills that will equip you with the skills most needed in today's dynamic workplace. That's why many students decide that this is one book they will keep.

To become an effective communicator, you need practice—with meaningful feedback. You need someone such as your instructor to tell you how to modify your responses so that you can improve. This book and its supplements have been designed to provide you and your instructor with principles, processes, products, and practice—everything necessary to make you a successful business communicator in today's dynamic workplace.

Yes, the workplace is undergoing profound changes. As a businessperson and especially as a business communicator, you will undoubtedly be affected by many transformations. Some of the most significant changes include global competition, changing organizational structures, and team-based projects. Other changes reflect our constantly evolving information technology, new work environments, a diverse workforce, and the emergence of a knowledge-based economy. The following brief look at this new world of work reveals how directly your success in it will be tied to possessing excellent communication skills.

Heightened Global Competition

Small, medium, and large companies increasingly find themselves competing in global rather than local markets. Improved systems of telecommunication, advanced forms of transportation, and saturated local markets—all of these developments have encouraged companies to move beyond familiar territories to emerging markets around the world.

Doing business in far-flung countries means dealing with people who are very different from you. They have different religions, engage in different customs, live different lifestyles, and rely on different approaches in business. Now add the complications of multiple time zones, vast distances between offices, and different languages, and you can see the importance of understanding diversity.

Communication is more complicated with people who have different religions, customs, and lifestyles.

Successful communication in these new markets requires developing new skills and attitudes. These include cultural knowledge and sensitivity, flexibility, patience, and tolerance. Because these are skills and attitudes that most of us need to polish, you will receive special communication training to help you deal with intercultural business transactions.

Changing Organizational Structures

In response to intense global competition and other pressures, businesses have for years been cutting costs and flattening their management hierarchies. This flattening meant that fewer layers of managers separated decision makers from line workers. In traditional companies, information flowed through many levels of managers. In flat organizations, however, where the lines of communication are shorter, decision makers can react more quickly to market changes.

Progressive organizations have changed from "command and control" to "coordination and cultivation" management styles. This means that work is organized to let people use their own talents more wisely.[2] But flattened organizations also pose greater communication challenges. In the past, authoritarian and hierarchical management structures did not require that every employee be a skilled communicator. Managers simply passed along messages to the next level. Today, however, front-line employees as well as managers participate in decision making. Their input and commitment are necessary for their organizations to be successful in global markets. What's more, everyone has become a writer and a communicator.[3] Nearly all employees have computers and write their own messages.

Progressive organizations demand that every employee be a skilled communicator.

Expanded Team-Based Management

Along with flatter chains of command, companies are also expanding team-based operations to increase employee involvement in decision making and to improve communication. When companies form cross-functional teams, individuals must work together and share information. Working relationships can become strained when individuals don't share the same background, knowledge, or training. Some companies must hire communication coaches to help existing teams get along. They work to develop interpersonal, negotiation, and collaboration techniques. But companies would prefer to hire new workers who already possess these skills. That's why so many advertisements for new employees say "must possess good communication skills."

Innovative Communication Technologies

New electronic technologies are dramatically affecting the way workers communicate. We now exchange information and stay in touch through e-mail, instant messaging, text messaging, PDAs, fax, voice mail, wireless networking, cell phones, powerful laptop computers, and satellite communications.[4] Through teleconferencing and videoconferencing we can conduct meetings with associates around the world. We're also seeing the rapid development of social software such as weblogs, wikis (multi-user weblogs), and peer-to-peer tools, all of which make it easier for workers to communicate online almost instantaneously. Interactive software enables dozens or even hundreds of users to collaborate on projects. And no self-respecting

Smart phones, e-mail, instant messaging, voice mail, wireless networking, cell phones, and other devices are revolutionizing the way we exchange information.

businessperson today would make a presentation without using sophisticated presentation software. We rely heavily on the Internet and the Web for collecting information, serving customers, and selling products and services. Figure 1.1 illustrates many new technologies you will meet in today's workplace.

To use these new resources most effectively, you, as a skilled business communicator, must develop a tool kit of new communication skills. For example, you will want to know how to select the best communication channel, how to use each channel and medium most effectively, and how to use online search tools efficiently.

New Work Environments

Workers today are collaborating, telecommuting, working in open offices, and serving on virtual teams, all of which demand excellent communication skills.

Today's work environments are also changing. Instead of individual offices and cubicles, companies are encouraging open offices with flexible workstations, shared conference rooms, and boomerang-shaped desks that save space. Thanks largely to advances in communication and mobile technologies, many workers no longer work nine-to-five jobs that confine them to offices. They have flexible work arrangements so that they can work at home or on the road. Moreover, many workers are part of virtual teams that complete projects without ever meeting each other. Tools such as e-mail, instant and text messaging, file sharing, conferencing software, and wireless networking make it easy for employees to collaborate or complete their work in the office, at home, or on the road. As more and more employees work separately, communication skills become even more important. Staying connected involves sending messages, most of which are written. This means that your writing skills will constantly be on display.

Increasingly Diverse Workforce

Changes in today's work environments include more than innovative technology, team management, and different working arrangements. The Canadian workforce is becoming increasingly diverse, with increased immigration, equal gender labour participation, and improved access for employees with disabilities. In addition, workers 55 and over are important potential sources of labour. This age group is projected to increase to 40 percent by 2026 as baby boomers grow older, creating an aging workforce.[5] The Career Coach box on pg. 9 provides more information about generational differences in today's workforce. As a result of these and other demographic trends, businesses must create a work environment that values and supports all people.

Thriving in the Age of Knowledge

The Canadian economy is based on information and knowledge. Physical labour, raw materials, and capital are no longer the key ingredients in the creation of wealth. Tomorrow's wealth depends on the development and exchange of knowledge. And individuals entering the workforce offer their knowledge, not their muscles.

Knowledge workers generate, process, and exchange information.

What does all this mean for you? As a knowledge and information worker, you can expect to be generating, processing, and exchanging information. Whether you work in the new economy of *e-commerce* (Internet-based businesses) or the old economy of *bricks-and-mortar* companies, nearly three out of four jobs will involve some form of mind work. Jobs that require thinking, brainpower, and decision-making skills are likely to remain plentiful. To be successful in these jobs, you must be able to think critically, make decisions, and communicate those decisions.

Learning to Think Critically. Management and employees will be working together in such areas as product development, quality control, and customer satisfaction. Whether you are an executive or a subordinate, you will be asked to think

Figure 1.1 *Communication Technologies: Reshaping the World of Work*

Communication Technologies: Reshaping the World of Work
Today's workplace is changing dramatically as a result of innovative software, superfast wireless networks, and numerous technologies that allow workers to share information, work from remote locations, and be more productive in or away from the office. We're seeing a gradual progression from basic capabilities, such as e-mail and calendaring, to deeper functionality, such as remote database access, multifunctional devices, and Web-based collaborative applications. Becoming familiar with modern office and collaboration technologies can help you be successful in today's digital workplace.

Telephony: VoIP
Savvy businesses are switching from traditional phone service to Voice over Internet Protocol (VoIP). This technology allows callers to communicate using a broadband Internet connection, thus eliminating long-distance and local telephone charges. Higher-end VoIP systems now support unified voice mail, e-mail, click-to-call capabilities, and softphones (phones using computer networking). Free or low-cost Internet telephony sites, such as the popular Skype, are also increasingly used by businesses.

Multifunctional Printers
Stand-alone copiers, fax machines, scanners, and printers have been replaced with multifunctional devices. Offices are transitioning from a "print and distribute" environment to a "distribute and print" environment. Security measures include pass codes and even biometric thumbprint scanning to make sure data streams are not captured, interrupted, or edited.

Open Offices
Widespread use of laptop computers, wireless technology, and VoIP has led to more fluid, flexible, and open workspaces. Smaller computers and flat-screen monitors enable designers to save space with boomerang-shaped workstations and cockpit-style work surfaces rather than space-hogging corner work areas. Smaller breakout areas for impromptu meetings are taking over some cubicle space, and digital databases are replacing file cabinets.

Handheld Wireless Devices
A new generation of lightweight, handheld devices provides phone, e-mail, Web browsing, and calendar options anywhere there's a wireless network. Devices such as the Black-Berry and the Palm Treo now allow you to tap into corporate databases and intranets from remote locations. You can check customers' files, complete orders, and send out receipts without returning to the office.

Company Intranets
To share insider information, many companies provide their own protected Web sites, called intranets. An intranet may handle company e-mail, announcements, an employee directory, a policy handbook, frequently asked questions, personnel forms and data, employee discussion forums, shared documents, and other employee information.

Voice Recognition
Computers equipped with voice recognition software enable users to dictate up to 160 words a minute with accurate transcription. Voice recognition is particularly helpful to disabled workers and to professionals with heavy dictation loads, such as physicians and lawyers. Users can create documents, enter data, compose and send e-mails, browse the Web, and control the desktop—all by voice.

Electronic Presentations
Business presentations in PowerPoint can be projected from a laptop or PDA or posted online. Sophisticated presentations may include animations, sound effects, digital photos, video clips, or hyperlinks to Internet sites. In some industries, PowerPoint slides ("decks") are replacing or supplementing traditional hard-copy reports.

(continued)

FIGURE 1.1 *Communication Technologies: Reshaping the World of Work (Continued)*

Collaboration Technologies: Rethinking the Way We Work Together

Global competition, expanding markets, and the ever-increasing pace of business accelerate the development of exciting collaboration tools. New tools make it possible to work together without being together. Your colleagues may be down the hall, across the country, or around the world. With today's tools, you can exchange ideas, solve problems, develop products, forecast future performance, and complete team projects any time of the day or night and anywhere in the world. Blogs and wikis, part of the so-called Web 2.0 era, are social tools that create multidirectional conversations among customers and employees. Web 2.0 moves Web applications from "read only" to "read/write," thus enabling greater participation and collaboration.

Blogs, Podcasts, and Wikis

A *blog* is a Web site with journal entries usually written by one person with comments added by others. Businesses use blogs to keep customers and employees informed and to receive feedback. Company developments can be posted, updated, and categorized for easy cross-referencing. When the writer adds audio, the blog becomes a *podcast*. A *wiki* is a Web site that allows multiple users to collaboratively create and edit pages. Information gets lost in e-mails, but blogs and wikis provide an easy way to communicate and keep track of what's said.

Voice Conferencing

Telephone "bridges" allow two or more callers from any location to share the same call. *Voice conferencing* (also called *audioconferencing, teleconferencing,* or just plain *conference calling*) enables people to collaborate by telephone. Communicators at both ends use enhanced speakerphones to talk and be heard simultaneously.

Videoconferencing

Videoconferencing allows participants to meet in special conference rooms equipped with cameras and television screens. Groups see each other and interact in real time although they may be far apart. Faster computers, rapid Internet connections, and better cameras now enable 2 to 200 participants to sit at their own PCs and share applications, spreadsheets, presentations, and photos.

Web Conferencing

With services such as GoToMeeting, WebEx, or Microsoft LiveMeeting, all you need are a PC and an Internet connection to hold a meeting (*webinar*) with customers or colleagues in real time. Although the functions are constantly evolving, Web conferencing currently incorporates screen sharing, chats, slide presentations, text messaging, and application sharing.

Presence Technology

Presence technology makes it possible to locate and identify a computing device as soon as users connect to the network. This technology is an integral part of communication devices, including cell phones, laptop computers, PDAs, pagers, and GPS devices. Collaboration is possible wherever and whenever users are online.

Video Phones

Using advanced video compression technology, video phones transmit real-time audio and video so that communicators can see each other as they collaborate. With a video phone, people can videoconference anywhere in the world over a broadband IP (Internet Protocol) connection without a computer or a television screen.

career coach

Understanding the Multi-generational Workforce

For the first time in history, today's workforce has members of four generations working together. Although specific dates vary depending on individual researchers, the general trend to classify the generations is quite consistent.

The **Traditionalists** represent the longest-working generation; they have experienced world wars, the Great Depression and living within limited means. Members of this generation respect authority, follow rules, and are loyal and hard-working. This group is either approaching retirement or has retired.

The **Baby Boomers** were born after the Second World War and represent a huge growth in population. As a result of their numbers, boomers became competitive and collaborative. This group was affected by the Cold War, the space race, the civil rights movement, and women's liberation. Technological change also had an impact on this group through variety in television programming, Touch-Tone phones, calculators, and mainframe computers.

Members of **Generation X** were born between the mid-1960s and the mid-1970s; this group accounts for more than five million people who grew up dealing with change. They are considered to be pragmatic, techno-literate, and good at multitasking. After seeing their parents divorce and people being laid off after years of service, they are skeptical and distrust institutions. They have been influenced by diversity, immigration, the population explosion, sexual rights, the personal computer, e-mail, the World Wide Web, and the "50-channel universe."

Generation Y (the millennials, the net generation) was born after the late 1970s; this generation accounts for almost ten million people and rivals the baby boom in size. Members of this group are comfortable in an adult world and were encouraged to participate in family decision making. They are eager to learn, confident, and enjoy questioning things. Compared to their parents, this generation takes longer to get married, have children, or buy houses. Generation Y has been influenced by diversity, immigration, globalization, terrorism, advances in communication technology, and the "100-channel universe."[6]

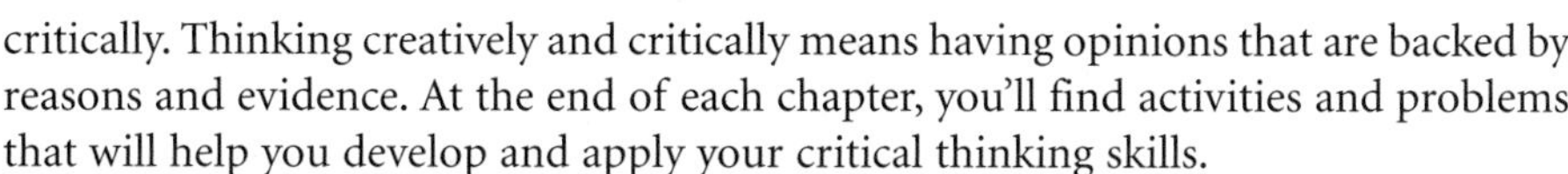

critically. Thinking creatively and critically means having opinions that are backed by reasons and evidence. At the end of each chapter, you'll find activities and problems that will help you develop and apply your critical thinking skills.

Taking Charge of Your Career. In the new world of work, you can look forward to constant training to acquire new skills that will help you keep up with evolving technologies and procedures. You can also expect to be exercising greater control over your career. Many workers today will not find nine-to-five jobs, lifetime security, predictable promotions, and even conventional workplaces. Don't presume that companies will provide you with a clearly defined career path or planned developmental experiences. And don't wait for someone to "empower" you. You have to empower yourself.[7] To thrive in the new decentralized work world, you must be flexible and continually willing to learn new skills that supplement the strong foundation of basic skills you acquire in college. The most successful businesspeople are willing to become lifelong learners.

Learning to Communicate. Probably the most important foundation skill for knowledge workers in the new environment is the ability to communicate. This means being able to listen as well as to express your ideas effectively in writing and in speech. As you advance in your career, communication skills become even more important. The number-one requirement for promotion to management is the ability to communicate.

learning objective

2

The communication process has five steps: idea formation, message encoding, message transmission, message decoding, and feedback.

Examining the Process of Communication

Since communication is a central factor in the emerging knowledge economy and a major consideration for anyone entering today's workforce, we need to look more closely at the total process of communication. Just what is communication? For our purposes communication is the *transmission of information and meaning from one individual or group to another*. The crucial element in this definition is *meaning*. Communication has as its central objective the transmission of *meaning*. The process of communication is successful only when the receiver understands an idea as the sender intended it. Both parties must agree not only on the information transmitted but also on the meaning of that information. How does an idea travel from one person to another? Despite what you may have seen in futuristic science fiction movies, we can't just glance at another person and transfer meaning directly from mind to mind. We engage in a sensitive process of communication that generally involves five steps, discussed here and depicted in Figure 1.2.

Sender Has Idea

The process of communication begins when the person with whom the message originates—the *sender*—has an idea. The form of the idea will be influenced by complex factors surrounding the sender: mood, frame of reference, background, culture, and physical makeup, as well as the context of the situation and many other factors. The way you greet people on campus or on the job, for example, depends a lot on how you feel, whom you are addressing, and what your culture has trained you to say.

FIGURE 1.2 ***The Communication Process***

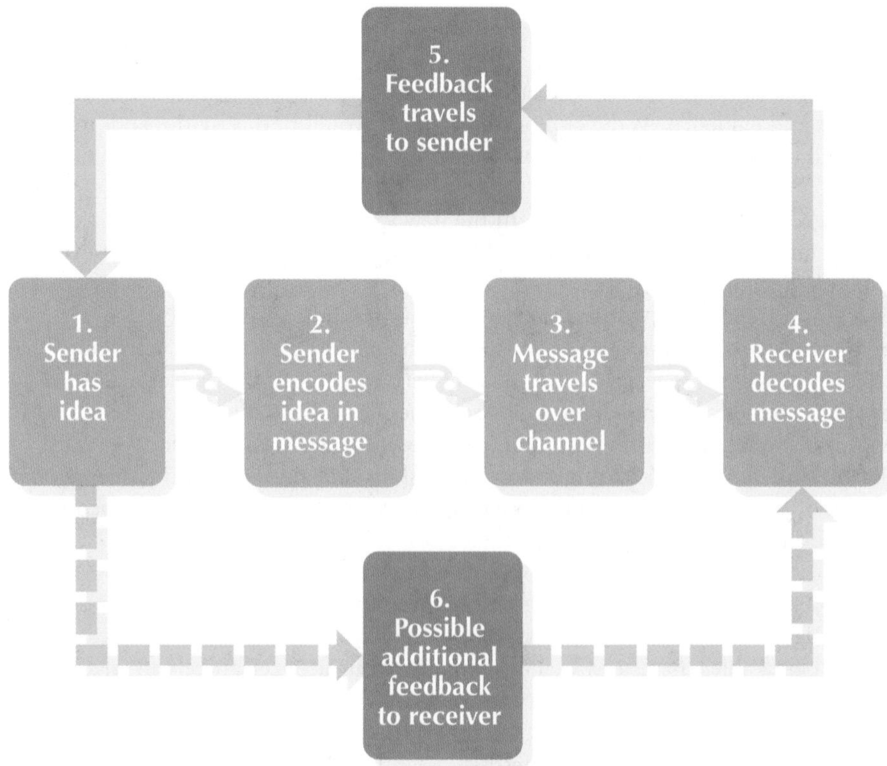

The form of the idea, whether a simple greeting or a complex idea, is shaped by assumptions based on the sender's experiences. A manager sending an e-mail announcement to employees assumes they will be receptive, whereas direct-mail advertisers assume that receivers will give only a quick glance to their message. The ability to accurately predict how a message will affect its receiver and skill in adapting that message to its receiver are key factors in successful communication.

Predicting the effect of a message and adapting the message to a receiver are key factors in successful communication.

Sender Encodes Idea in Message

The next step in the communication process involves *encoding*. This means converting the idea into words or gestures that will convey meaning. A major problem in communicating any message verbally is that words have different meanings for different people. When misunderstandings result from missed meanings, it's called *bypassing*. Recognizing how easy it is to be misunderstood, skilled communicators choose familiar words with concrete meanings on which both senders and receivers agree. In selecting proper symbols, senders must be alert to the receiver's communication skills, attitudes, background, experiences, and culture: How will the selected words affect the receiver? Because the sender initiates a communication transaction, he or she has primary responsibility for its success or failure. Choosing appropriate words or symbols is the first step.

Message Travels Over Channel

Channels are the media—computer, telephone, cell phone, letter, report, and so on—that transmit messages.

The medium over which the message is physically transmitted is the *channel*. Messages may be delivered by computer, telephone, cell phone, letter, memorandum, report, announcement, picture, spoken word, fax, pager, or Web page, or through some other channel. Because communication channels deliver both verbal and nonverbal messages, senders must choose the channel and shape the message carefully. A company may use its annual report, for example, as a channel to deliver many messages to stockholders. The verbal message lies in the report's financial and organizational news. Nonverbal messages, though, are conveyed by the report's appearance (showy versus bland), layout (ample white space versus tightly packed columns of print), and tone (conversational versus formal).

Anything that interrupts the transmission of a message in the communication process is called *noise*. Channel noise ranges from static that disrupts a telephone conversation to typographical and spelling errors in a letter or e-mail message. Such errors damage the credibility of the sender. Channel noise might even include the annoyance a receiver feels when the sender chooses an improper medium for sending a message, such as announcing a loan rejection via postcard or firing an employee by e-mail.

Receiver Decodes Message

The individual for whom the message is intended is the *receiver*. Translating the message from its symbol form into meaning involves *decoding*. Only when the receiver understands the meaning intended by the sender—that is, successfully decodes the message—does communication take place. Such success, however, is difficult to achieve, because no two people share the same life experiences and because many barriers can disrupt the process.

Decoding can be disrupted internally by the receiver's lack of attention to or bias against the sender. It can be disrupted externally by loud sounds or illegible words. Decoding can also be sidetracked by semantic obstacles, such as misunderstood words or emotional reactions to certain terms. A memo that refers to all the women in an office as "girls" or "chicks," for example, may disturb its receivers so much that they fail to comprehend the total message.

Feedback Travels to Sender

Asking questions encourages feedback that clarifies communication.

The verbal and nonverbal responses of the receiver create *feedback*, a vital part of the communication process. Feedback helps the sender know that the message was received and understood. If, as a receiver, you hear the message "How are you?", your feedback might consist of words ("I'm fine") or body language (a smile or a wave of the hand). Although the receiver may respond with additional feedback to the sender (thus creating a new act of communication), we'll concentrate here on the initial message flowing to the receiver and the resulting feedback.

Senders can encourage feedback by asking questions such as *Am I making myself clear?* and *Is there anything you don't understand?* Senders can further improve feedback by timing the delivery appropriately and by providing only as much information as the receiver can handle. Receivers can improve the process by paraphrasing the sender's message with comments, such as *Let me try to explain that in my own words.* The best feedback is descriptive rather than evaluative. For example, here's a descriptive response: *I understand you want to launch a used golf ball business.* Here's an evaluative response: *Your business ideas are always weird.* An evaluative response is judgmental and doesn't tell the sender whether the receiver actually understood the message.

learning objective 3

Overcoming Interpersonal Communication Barriers

The communication process is successful only when the receiver understands the message as intended by the sender. It sounds quite simple, yet it's not. How many times have you thought that you delivered a clear message, only to learn later that your intentions were totally misunderstood? Most messages that we send reach their destination, but many are only partially understood.

Obstacles That Create Misunderstanding

Barriers to successful communication include bypassing, differing frames of reference, lack of language or listening skills, emotional interference, and physical distractions.

You can improve your chances of communicating successfully by learning to recognize barriers that are known to disrupt the process. The most significant barriers for individuals are bypassing, differing frames of reference, lack of language skill, and distractions.

Bypassing. One of the biggest barriers to clear communication involves words. Each of us attaches a little bundle of meanings to every word, and these meanings are not always similar. *Bypassing* happens when people miss each other with their meanings.[8] Bypassing can lead to major miscommunication because people assume that meanings are contained in words. Actually, meanings are in people. For communication to be successful, the receiver and sender must attach the same symbolic meanings to their words.

Miscommunication often results when the sender's frame of reference differs markedly from the receiver's.

Differing Frames of Reference. Another barrier to clear communication is your *frame of reference*. Everything you see and feel in the world is translated through your individual frame of reference. Your unique frame is formed by a combination of your experiences, education, culture, expectations, personality, and many other elements. As a result, you bring your own biases and expectations to any communication situation. Because your frame of reference is totally different from everyone else's, you will never see things exactly as others do. Wise business communicators strive to prevent communication failure by being alert to both their own frames of reference and those of others.

Lack of Language Skill. No matter how extraordinary the idea, it won't be understood or fully appreciated unless the communicators involved have good language skills. Each individual needs an adequate vocabulary, a command of basic punctuation and grammar, and skill in written and oral expression. Moreover, poor listening skills can prevent us from hearing oral messages clearly and thus responding properly.

Distractions. Other barriers include emotional interference, physical distractions, and digital interruptions. Shaping an intelligent message is difficult when you're feeling joy, fear, resentment, hostility, sadness, or some other strong emotion. To reduce the influence of emotions on communication, both senders and receivers should focus on the content of the message and try to remain objective. Physical distractions such as faulty acoustics, noisy surroundings, or a poor cell phone connection can disrupt oral communication. Similarly, sloppy appearance, poor printing, careless formatting, and typographical or spelling errors can disrupt written messages. What's more, technology doesn't seem to be helping. Knowledge workers are increasingly distracted by multitasking, information overload, conflicting demands, and being constantly available digitally. Clear communication requires focusing on what is important and shutting out interruptions.[9]

Overcoming the Obstacles

Careful communicators can conquer barriers in a number of ways. Half the battle in communicating successfully is recognizing that the entire process is sensitive and susceptible to breakdown. Like a defensive driver anticipating problems on the road, a good communicator anticipates problems in encoding, transmitting, and decoding a message. Effective communicators also focus on the receiver's environment and frame of reference. They ask themselves questions such as *How is that individual likely to react to my message?* or *Does the receiver know as much about the subject as I do?*

To overcome obstacles, communicators must anticipate problems in encoding, transmitting, and decoding.

Misunderstandings are less likely if you arrange your ideas logically and use words precisely. But communicating is more than expressing yourself well. A large part of successful communication is listening.

Overcoming interpersonal barriers often involves questioning your preconceptions. Successful communicators continually examine their personal assumptions, biases, and prejudices. The more you pay attention to subtleties and know "where you're coming from" when you encode and decode messages, the better you'll communicate.

Effective communicators create an environment for useful feedback. In oral communication this means asking questions such as *Do you understand?* and *What questions do you have?* as well as encouraging listeners to repeat instructions or paraphrase ideas. As a listener it means providing feedback that describes rather than evaluates. And in written communication it means asking questions and providing access: *Do you have my phone numbers in case you have questions?* or *Here's my e-mail address so that you can give me your response immediately.*

Good communicators ask questions to stimulate feedback.

Communicating in Organizations

learning objective 4

Until now, you've probably been thinking about the communication you do personally. But business communicators must also be concerned with the bigger picture, and that involves sharing information in organizations. On the job you'll be exchanging information by communicating internally and externally.

Internal and External Functions

Internal communication often consists of e-mail, memos, and voice messages; external communication generally consists of letters.

Internal communication includes sharing ideas and messages with superiors, coworkers, and subordinates. When those messages must be written, you'll probably choose e-mail. When you are communicating externally with customers, suppliers, the government, and the public, you will generally send letters on company stationery.

Some of the functions of internal communication are to issue and clarify procedures and policies, inform management of progress, develop new products and services, persuade employees or management to make changes or improvements, coordinate activities, and evaluate and reward employees. External functions are to answer inquiries about products or services, persuade customers to buy products or services, clarify supplier specifications, issue credit, collect bills, respond to government agencies, and promote a positive image of the organization.

In all of these tasks, employees and managers use a number of communication skills: reading, listening, speaking, and writing. As students and workers, you probably realize that you need to improve these skills to the proficiency level required for success in today's knowledge society. This book and this course will provide you with practical advice on how to do just that.

Organizational communication has three basic functions: to inform, to persuade, and/or to promote goodwill.

Now look back over the preceding discussion of internal and external functions of communication in organizations. Although there appear to be a large number of diverse business communication functions, they can be summarized in three simple categories, as Figure 1.3 shows: (1) to inform, (2) to persuade, and/or (3) to promote goodwill.

Emphasis on Interactive, Mobile, and Instant Communication

The flattening of organizations coupled with the development of sophisticated information technology has greatly changed the way we communicate internally and externally. We are seeing a major shift away from one-sided and rather slow forms of communication, such as memos and letters, to more interactive, fast-results communication. Speeding up the flow of communication are technologies such as e-mail, instant messaging (IM), text messaging, voice mail, cell phones, and wireless fidelity ("Wi-Fi") networks. Wi-Fi lets mobile workers connect to the Internet at ultrafast speeds without cables.

FIGURE 1.3 ***Functions of Business Communication***

1. To inform
2. To persuade
3. To promote goodwill

Internal communication with
Superiors
Coworkers
Subordinates

External communication with
Customers
Suppliers
Government agencies
The public

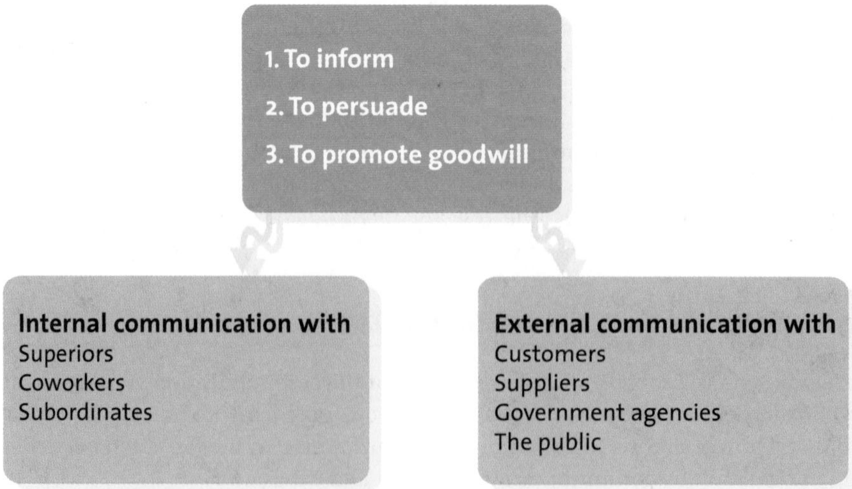

Other forms of interactive communication include intranets (company versions of the Internet), Web sites, video transmission, and videoconferencing. You'll be learning more about these forms of communication in coming chapters. Despite the range of interactive technologies, communicators are still working with two basic forms of communication: oral and written. Each has advantages and disadvantages.

Oral communication minimizes miscommunication but provides no written record.

Oral Communication. Nearly everyone agrees that the best way to exchange information is orally in face-to-face conversations or meetings. Oral communication has many advantages. For one thing, it minimizes misunderstandings because communicators can immediately ask questions to clarify uncertainties. For another, it enables communicators to see each other's facial expressions and hear voice inflections, further improving the process. Oral communication is also an efficient way to develop consensus when many people must be consulted. Finally, most of us enjoy face-to-face interpersonal communication because it's easy, feels warm and natural, and promotes friendships.

The main disadvantages of oral communication are that it produces no written record, sometimes wastes time, and may be inconvenient. When individuals meet face to face or speak on the telephone, someone's work has to be interrupted. And how many of us are able to limit a conversation to just business? Nevertheless, oral communication has many advantages. The forms and advantages of both oral and written communication are summarized in Figure 1.4.

Written communication provides a permanent record but lacks immediate feedback.

Written Communication. Written communication is impersonal in the sense that two communicators cannot see or hear each other and cannot provide immediate feedback. Most forms of business communication—including e-mail,

Figure 1.4 ***Forms of Organizational Communication***

	Forms	Advantages	Disadvantages
Oral Communication	Phone call	Immediate feedback	No permanent record
	Conversation	Nonverbal clues	Expression may be careless or imprecise
	Interview	Warm feeling	
	Meeting	Forceful impact	May be inappropriate for formal or complex ideas
	Conference	Multiple input	
Written Communication	Announcement	Permanent record	Leaves paper trail
	E-mail, memo, fax	Convenience	Requires skill
	Letter	Economy	Requires effort
	Report, proposal	Careful message	Lacks verbal cues
	Newsletter	Easy distribution	Seems impersonal
	PowerPoint presentation		
	Résumé		

announcements, memos, faxes, letters, newsletters, reports, proposals, manuals, presentations, and résumés—fall into this category.

Organizations rely on written communication for many reasons. It provides a permanent record, a necessity in these times of increasing litigation and extensive government regulation. Writing out an idea instead of delivering it orally enables communicators to develop an organized, well-considered message. Written documents are also convenient. They can be composed and read when the schedules of both communicators permit, and they can be reviewed if necessary.

Written messages have drawbacks, of course. They require careful preparation and sensitivity to audience and anticipated effects. Words spoken in conversation may soon be forgotten, but words committed to hard or soft copy become a public record—and sometimes an embarrassing or dangerous one. E-mail and text-messaging records, even deleted ones, have often become "smoking guns" in court cases, revealing insider information that was never meant for public consumption.[10]

Written messages demand good writing skills, which can be developed through training.

Another drawback to written messages is that they are more difficult to prepare. They demand good writing skills, and such skills are not inborn. But writing proficiency can be learned. Because as much as 90 percent of all business transactions may involve written messages and because writing skills are so important to your business success, you will be receiving special instruction in becoming a good writer.

Avoiding Information Overload and Productivity Meltdown

The large volume of messages and communication channel choices overwhelms many workers.

Although technology provides a myriad of communication channel choices, the sheer volume of messages is overwhelming many employees. "E-mail sending has increased more than 600 percent in the last six years. And one study reports that executives spend at least two hours a day using e-mail and employees send an average of 20 e-mails and receive about 30 e-mails a day."[11] Information overload and resulting productivity meltdown are becoming serious problems for workers and their employers. Suggestions for controlling your e-mail are shown in the accompanying Tech Talk box.

learning objective

5

Improving the Flow of Information in Organizations

Information within organizations flows through formal and informal communication channels. A free exchange of information helps organizations respond rapidly to changing markets, increase efficiency and productivity, build employee morale, serve the public, and take full advantage of the ideas of today's knowledge workers. Barriers, however, can obstruct the flow of communication.

Formal Channels

Formal communication channels follow an organization's chain of command.

Formal channels of communication generally follow an organization's hierarchy of command. Information about policies and procedures originates with executives and flows down through managers to supervisors and finally to lower-level employees. Many organizations have formulated official communication policies that encourage regular open communication, suggest means for achieving it, and spell out responsibilities. Official information among workers typically flows through formal channels in three directions: downward, upward, and horizontally.

Job plans, policies, instructions, feedback, and procedures flow downward from managers to employees.

Downward Flow. Information flowing downward generally moves from decision makers, including the CEO and managers, through the chain of command to workers. This information includes job plans, policies, and procedures. Managers

tech talk

Tips for Managing Your E-Mail

In an amazingly short time, e-mail has become one of the most powerful and useful communication channels in the workplace. But it has also produced information overload for many workers. The following techniques can help you control your e-mail:

- Send only business messages that you would have sent in a memo format. If a quick phone call or a short in-person chat could solve the problem immediately, avoid sending an e-mail.
- Check your e-mail inbox only at specific times each day, say at 9 a.m. and again at 4 p.m.
- Deal with a message only once. Answer it, delegate it to someone else, or move it to a project-specific folder for later action.
- Block unwanted incoming messages. Learn to use the filters on your mail program.
- Practise e-mail triage. Focus on the most urgent messages first. Be ruthless in deleting e-mail messages based on their headers.
- Use an alternative address when registering for anything on the Web. Avoid giving out your primary e-mail address.
- Subscribe only to mailing lists in which you are really interested.

also provide feedback about employee performance and instill a sense of mission in achieving the organization's goals. One obstacle that can impede the downward flow of information is distortion resulting from long lines of communication.

Feedback from employees forms the upward flow of communication in most organizations.

Upward Flow. Information flowing upward provides feedback from nonmanagement employees to management. Subordinate employees describe progress in completing tasks, report roadblocks encountered, and suggest methods for improving efficiency. Channels for upward communication include phone messages, e-mail, memos, reports, departmental meetings, and suggestion systems. Ideally, the heaviest flow of information should be upward, with information being fed steadily to decision makers.

Information flows upward more readily when companies provide a nonthreatening, supportive environment.

A number of obstacles, however, can interrupt the upward flow of communication. Employees who distrust their employers are less likely to communicate openly. Employees cease trusting managers if they feel they are being tricked, manipulated, criticized, or treated unfairly. Unfortunately, some employees today no longer have a strong trusting attitude toward employers. Downsizing, cost-cutting measures, the tremendous influx of temporary workers, discrimination and harassment suits, outrageous compensation packages for chief executives, and many other factors have eroded the feelings of trust and pride that employees once felt toward their employers and their jobs. Other obstacles include fear of reprisal for honest communication, lack of adequate communication skills, and differing frames of reference. Imperfect communication results when individuals are not using words or symbols with similar meanings, when they cannot express their ideas clearly, or when they come from different backgrounds.

To improve the upward flow of communication, some companies are (1) hiring communication coaches to train employees, (2) asking employees to report customer complaints, (3) encouraging regular meetings with staff, (4) providing a trusting, nonthreatening environment in which employees can comfortably share their observations and ideas with management, and (5) offering incentive programs that encourage employees to collect and share valuable feedback. Companies are also building trust by setting up hotlines for anonymous feedback to management and by installing *ombudsman* programs. An ombudsman is a mediator who hears employee complaints, investigates, and seeks to resolve problems fairly.

Workers coordinate tasks, share information, solve problems, and resolve conflicts through horizontal communication.

Horizontal Flow. Lateral channels transmit information horizontally among workers at the same level. These channels enable individuals to coordinate tasks, share information, solve problems, and resolve conflicts. Horizontal communication takes place through personal contact, telephone, e-mail, memos, voice mail, and meetings. Most traditional organizations have few established regular channels for the horizontal exchange of information. Restructured companies with flattened hierarchies and team-based management, however, have discovered that when employees combine their knowledge with that of other employees, they can do their jobs better. Much of the information in these organizations is travelling horizontally among team members.[12]

Obstacles to the horizontal flow of communication, as well as to upward and downward flow, include poor communication skills, prejudice, ego involvement, and turf wars. Some employees avoid sharing information if doing so might endanger their status or chances for promotion within the organization. Competition within units and an uneven reward system may also prevent workers from freely sharing information.

To improve horizontal communication, companies are training and rewarding employees as well as encouraging team functions.

To improve horizontal communication, companies are (1) training employees in teamwork and communication techniques, (2) establishing reward systems based on team achievement rather than individual achievement, and (3) encouraging full participation in team functions. However, employees must also realize that they are personally responsible for making themselves heard, for really understanding what other people say, and for getting the information they need. Developing those business communication skills is exactly what this book and this course will do for you.

Informal Channels

An informal communication channel, the grapevine carries organizationally relevant gossip.

Not all information within an organization travels through formal channels. The *grapevine* is an informal channel of communication that carries organizationally relevant gossip.[13] This informal but powerful channel functions through social relationships in which individuals talk about work when they are having lunch, working out, golfing, carpooling, and, more recently, blogging. Alert managers find the grapevine an excellent source of information about employee morale and problems. They have also used the grapevine as a "break it to them gently" device, planting "rumours," for example, of future layoffs or other changes.

Researchers studying communication flow within organizations know that the grapevine can be a powerful, pervasive source of information. One study found that as much as two-thirds of an employee's information comes from informal channels.[14] Is this bad? Well, yes and no. The grapevine can be a fairly accurate and speedy source of organization information. However, grapevine information is often incomplete because it travels in headlines. When employees obtain most of their company news from the grapevine, management is not releasing sufficient information through formal channels.

Employees prefer to receive vital company information through formal channels.

The truth is that most employees want to know what's going on. In fact, one study found that regardless of how much information organization members reported receiving, they wanted more.[15] Many companies today have moved away from a rigid authoritarian management structure in which only managers are privy to vital information such as product success and profit figures. Employees who know the latest buzz feel like important members of the team.[16] Through formal lines of communication, smart companies are keeping employees informed. Thus the grapevine is reduced to carrying gossip about who's dating whom and what restaurant is trendy for lunch.

Facing Ethical Challenges

learning objective

6

As a business communicator, you should understand basic ethical principles so that you can make logical decisions when faced with dilemmas in the workplace. Professionals in any field must deal with moral dilemmas on the job. However, just being a moral person and having sound personal ethics may not be sufficient to handle the ethical issues that you may face in the workplace.

On the job you will face many dilemmas, and you will want to react ethically. But what is ethical behaviour? According to Linda Crompton of Citizens Bank of Canada, "How well you stand up in a controversy—that's also what ethics are all about. People understand the effect of business on the environment or children in other countries."[17]

Goals of Ethical Business Communicators

Taking ethics into consideration can be painful in the short term. But in the long term ethical behaviour makes sense and pays off. Dealing honestly with colleagues and customers develops trust and builds stronger relationships. Many businesses today recognize that ethical practices make good business sense. Ethical companies endure less litigation, less resentment, and less government regulation. The following guidelines can help you set specific ethical goals and maintain a high ethical standard.

Abiding by the Law. Know the laws in your field and follow them. Particularly important for business communicators are issues of copyright law. Don't assume that Internet items are in the "public domain" and free to be used. Internet items are also covered by copyright laws.

Telling the Truth. Ethical business communicators do not intentionally make statements that are untrue or deceptive. We become aware of dishonesty in business when violators break laws, notably in advertising, packaging, and marketing. Half-truths, exaggerations, and deceptions constitute unethical communication. But conflicting loyalties in the workplace sometimes blur the line between right and wrong.

Facts are verifiable; opinions are beliefs held with conviction.

Labelling Opinions. Sensitive communicators know the difference between facts and opinions. Facts are verifiable and often are quantifiable; opinions are beliefs held with confidence but without substantiation. Stating opinions as if they were facts is unethical.

Being Objective. Ethical business communicators recognize their own biases and strive to keep them from distorting a message. Honest reporting means presenting the whole picture and relating all facts fairly.

"Plain English" guidelines require simple, understandable language in policies, contracts, warranties, and other documents.

Communicating Clearly. Ethical business communicators feel an obligation to write clearly so that receivers understand easily and quickly. Some organizations have even created "Plain English" guidelines that require businesses to write policies, warranties, and contracts in language comprehensible to average readers. Plain English means short sentences, simple words, and clear organization. Communicators who intentionally obscure the meaning with long sentences and difficult words are being unethical.

Using Inclusive Language. Strive to use language that includes rather than excludes. Do not use expressions that discriminate against individuals or groups on the basis of their gender, ethnicity, disability, or age. Language is discriminatory when it stereotypes, insults, or excludes people.

Giving Credit. Ethical communicators give credit for ideas by (1) referring to originators' names within the text, (2) using quotation marks, and (3) documenting sources with endnotes, footnotes, or internal references. In school or on the job, stealing ideas or words from others is unethical.

Tools for Doing the Right Thing

Acting ethically means doing the right thing—given the situation.

In composing messages or engaging in other activities on the job, business communicators can't help being torn by conflicting loyalties. Do we tell the truth and risk our jobs? Do we show loyalty to friends even if it means bending the rules? Should we be tactful or totally honest? Is it our duty to make a profit or to be socially responsible? Acting ethically means doing the right thing given the circumstances. Each set of circumstances requires analyzing issues, evaluating choices, and acting responsibly.

Business communicators can help resolve ethical issues through self-examination.

Resolving ethical issues is never easy, but the task can be made less difficult if you know how to identify key issues. The following questions may be helpful.

- **Is the action you are considering legal?** No matter who asks you to do it or how important you feel the result will be, avoid anything that is prohibited by law.
- **How would you see the problem if you were on the opposite side?** Looking at all sides of an issue helps you gain perspective. By weighing both sides of the issue, you can arrive at a more equitable solution.
- **What are alternative solutions?** Consider all dimensions of other options. Would the alternative be more ethical? Under the circumstances, is the alternative feasible? Can an alternative solution be implemented with a minimum of disruption and with a good possibility of success?
- **Can you discuss the problem with someone whose advice you trust?** Talking about your dilemma with a coworker or with a colleague in your field might give you helpful insights and lead to possible alternatives.

Discussing an ethical problem with a coworker or colleague might lead to helpful alternatives.

- **How would you feel if your family, friends, employer, or coworkers learned of your action?** If the thought of revealing your action publicly produces cold sweats, your choice is probably unwise. Losing the faith of your friends or the confidence of your customers is not worth whatever short-term gains might be realized.

Perhaps the best advice in ethical matters is contained in the Platinum Rule: "Treat others as they want to be treated." The ultimate solution to all ethics problems is treating others fairly and doing what is right to achieve what is good. In succeeding chapters you will find additional discussions of ethical questions as they relate to relevant topics.

Strengthening Your Communication Skills

You've just taken a brief look at the changing workplace, the process of communication, the flow of communication in organizations, and ethical challenges facing business communicators today. Each topic provided you not only with the latest information about an issue but also with tips and suggestions that will help you function successfully in the changing workplace. After all, it's not enough to know the problems; you also need to know some of the solutions. Our goal is to help you recognize the problems and also to equip you with techniques for overcoming the obstacles that others have faced.

Remember, communication skills are not inherent; they must be learned. Remember, too, to take advantage of the unique opportunity you now have. You have an expert who is willing to work with you to help improve your writing, speaking, and other communication skills. Many organizations pay thousands of dollars to communication coaches and trainers to teach employees the very skills that you are learning in this course. With this book as your guide and your instructor as your coach, you will find that this course, as we mentioned earlier, could very well be the most important in your entire college curriculum.

Summary of Learning Objectives

1 **Identify changes in the workplace and explain the importance of communication skills.** The workplace has undergone profound changes, such as the emergence of heightened global competition, changing organizational structures, expanded team-based management, innovative communication technologies, new work environments, and an increasingly diverse workforce. In this dynamic workplace you can expect to be a knowledge worker; that is, you will deal with words, figures, and data. The most important foundation skill for knowledge workers is the ability to communicate. You can improve your skills by studying the principles, processes, and products of communication provided in this book and in this course.

2 **Describe the process of communication.** The sender encodes (selects) words or symbols to express an idea. The message is sent verbally over a channel (such as a letter, e-mail message, or telephone call) or is expressed nonverbally, perhaps with gestures or body language. "Noise"—such as loud sounds, misspelled words, or other distractions—may interfere with the transmission. The receiver decodes (interprets) the message and attempts to make sense of it. The receiver responds with feedback, informing the sender of the effectiveness of the message. The objective of communication is the transmission of meaning so that a receiver understands a message as intended by the sender.

3 **Discuss barriers to interpersonal communication and the means of overcoming those barriers.** *Bypassing* causes miscommunication because people have different meanings for the words they use. One's *frame of reference* creates a filter through which all ideas are screened, sometimes causing distortion and lack of objectivity. *Weak language skills* as well as *poor listening skills* impair communication efforts. *Emotional interference*—joy, fear, anger, and so forth—hampers the sending and receiving of messages. *Physical distractions*—noisy surroundings, faulty acoustics, and so forth—can disrupt oral communication. You can reduce or overcome many interpersonal communication barriers if you (a) realize that the communication process is imperfect, (b) adapt your message to the receiver, (c) improve your language and listening skills, (d) question your preconceptions, and (e) plan for feedback.

4 **Analyze the functions and procedures of communication in organizations.** Internal functions of communication include issuing and clarifying procedures and policies, informing management of progress, persuading others to make changes or improvements, and interacting with employees. External functions of communication include answering inquiries about products or

services, persuading customers to buy products or services, clarifying supplier specifications, and so forth. Oral, face-to-face communication is most effective, but written communication is often more expedient. The volume of messages today is overwhelming many employees, who must institute techniques to control information overload and productivity meltdown.

5 **Assess the flow of communication in organizations, including barriers and methods for overcoming those barriers.** Formal channels of communication follow an organization's hierarchy of command. Information flows downward from management to workers. Long lines of communication tend to distort information. Many organizations are improving the downward flow of communication through newsletters, announcements, meetings, videos, and company intranets. Information flows upward from employees to management, thus providing vital feedback for decision makers. Obstacles include mistrust, fear of reprisal for honest communication, lack of adequate communication skills, and differing frames of reference. To improve upward flow, companies are improving relations with staff, offering incentive programs that encourage employees to share valuable feedback, and investing in communication training programs. Horizontal communication is among workers at the same level. Obstacles include poor communication skills, prejudice, ego involvement, competition, and turf wars. Techniques for overcoming the obstacles include (a) training employees in communication and teamwork techniques, (b) establishing reward systems, and (c) encouraging full participation in team functions. Informal channels of communication, such as the grapevine, deliver unofficial news—both personal and organizational—among friends and coworkers.

6 **List the goals of ethical business communication and describe important tools for doing the right thing.** Ethical business communicators strive to (a) tell the truth, (b) label opinions so that they are not confused with facts, (c) be objective and avoid distorting a message, (d) write clearly and avoid obscure language, and (e) give credit when using the ideas of others. When you face a difficult decision, the following questions serve as valuable tools in guiding you to do the right thing: (a) Is the action you are considering legal? (b) How would you see the problem if you were on the opposite side? (c) What are alternative solutions? (d) Can you discuss the problem with someone whose advice you trust? (e) How would you feel if your family, friends, employer, or coworkers learned of your action?

chapter review

1. How are business communicators affected by the emergence of global competition, changing organizational structures, and expanded team-based management? (Obj. 1)
2. How are business communicators affected by the emergence of innovative communication technologies, new work environments, and an increasingly diverse workforce? (Obj. 1)
3. What are knowledge workers? Why are they hired? (Obj. 1)
4. Define *communication* and explain its most critical factor. (Obj. 2)
5. Describe the five steps in the process of communication. (Obj. 2)
6. List four barriers to interpersonal communication. Be prepared to discuss each. (Obj. 3)
7. Name five specific ways you can personally reduce barriers in your communication. (Obj. 3)
8. What are the three main functions of organizational communication? (Obj. 4)
9. What are the advantages of oral, face-to-face communication? (Obj. 4)
10. What are the advantages of written communication? (Obj. 4)
11. How do formal and informal channels of communication differ within organizations? (Obj. 5)
12. Describe three directions in which communication flows within organizations and what barriers can obstruct each. (Obj. 5)
13. How can barriers to the free flow of information in organizations be reduced? (Obj. 5)
14. What are seven goals of ethical business communicators? (Obj. 6)
15. When faced with a difficult ethical decision, what questions should you ask yourself? (Obj. 6)

critical thinking

1. Why should you, as a business student and communicator, strive to improve your communication skills; and why is it difficult or impossible to do so on your own? (Obj. 1)
2. Recall a time when you experienced a problem as a result of poor communication. What were the causes of and possible remedies for the problem? (Objs. 2 and 3)
3. Some companies say that the more information provided to employees, the more employees want. How would you respond to this complaint? (Objs. 4 and 5)
4. As a channel of organizational communication, what are the advantages and disadvantages of e-mail? (Objs. 4 and 5)
5. How are the rules of ethical behaviour that govern businesses different from those that govern your personal behaviour? (Obj. 6)

activities

1.1 Communication Assessment: How Do You Stack Up? (Objs. 1–3)

You know more about yourself than anyone else. That makes you the best person to assess your present communication skills. Take an honest look at your current skills and rank them using the following chart. How well you communicate will be an important factor in your future career—particularly if you are promoted into management, as many college graduates are. For each skill, circle the number from 1 (indicating low ability) to 5 (indicating high ability) that best reflects your perception of yourself.

Writing Skills	Low				High
1. Possess basic spelling, grammar, and punctuation skills	1	2	3	4	5
2. Am familiar with proper memo, letter, and report formats for business documents	1	2	3	4	5
3. Can analyze a writing problem and quickly outline a plan for solving the problem	1	2	3	4	5
4. Am able to organize data coherently and logically	1	2	3	4	5
5. Can evaluate a document to determine its probable success	1	2	3	4	5

Reading Skills	Low				High
1. Am familiar with specialized vocabulary in my field as well as general vocabulary					
2. Can concentrate despite distractions	1	2	3	4	5
3. Am willing to look up definitions whenever necessary	1	2	3	4	5
4. Am able to move from recreational to serious reading	1	2	3	4	5
5. Can read and comprehend college-level material	1	2	3	4	5

Speaking Skills	Low				High
1. Feel at ease in speaking with friends	1	2	3	4	5
2. Feel at ease in speaking before a group of people	1	2	3	4	5
3. Can adapt my presentation to the audience	1	2	3	4	5
4. Am confident in pronouncing and using words correctly	1	2	3	4	5
5. Sense that I have credibility when I make a presentation	1	2	3	4	5

Listening Skills	Low				High
1. Spend at least half the time listening during conversations	1	2	3	4	5
2. Am able to concentrate on a speaker's words despite distractions	1	2	3	4	5
3. Can summarize a speaker's ideas and anticipate what's coming during pauses	1	2	3	4	5
4. Provide feedback, such as nodding, paraphrasing, and asking questions	1	2	3	4	5
5. Listen with the expectation of gaining new ideas and information	1	2	3	4	5

Now analyze your scores. Where are you strongest? weakest? How do you think outsiders would rate you on these skills and traits? Are you satisfied with your present skills? The first step to improvement is recognition of a need. Put check marks next to the five traits you feel you should begin working on immediately.

1.2 Getting to Know You (Objs. 1 and 2)

E-MAIL

Your instructor wants to know more about you, your motivation for taking this course, your career goals, and your writing skills.

Your Task. Send an e-mail or write a memo of introduction to your instructor. See Appendix B for memo formats and Chapter 8 for tips on preparing an e-mail message. In your message include the following:

- **a.** Your reasons for taking this class
- **b.** Your career goals (both temporary and long term)
- **c.** A brief description of your employment, if any, and your favourite activities
- **d.** An assessment and discussion of your current communication skills, including your strengths and weaknesses

1.3 Small-Group Presentation: Getting to Know Each Other (Objs. 1 and 2)

LISTENING | TEAM | SPEAKING

Many business organizations today use teams to accomplish their goals. To help you develop speaking, listening, and teamwork skills, your instructor may assign team projects. One of the first jobs in any team is selecting members and becoming acquainted.

Your Task. Your instructor will divide your class into small groups or teams. At your instructor's direction, either (a) interview another group member and introduce that person to the group or (b) introduce yourself to the group. Think of this as an informal interview for a team assignment or for a job. You'll want to make notes from which to speak. Your introduction should include information such as the following:

- **a.** Where did you grow up?
- **b.** What work and extracurricular activities have you engaged in?
- **c.** What are your interests and talents? What are you good at doing?
- **d.** What have you achieved?
- **e.** How familiar are you with various computer technologies?
- **f.** What are your professional and personal goals? Where do you expect to be five years from now?

To develop listening skills, team members should practise good listening techniques (see Chapter 2) and take notes. They should be prepared to discuss three important facts as well as remember details about each speaker.

1.4 Communication Skills: What Do Employers Really Want? (Obj. 1)

TEAM | WEB

What do employers request when they list job openings in your field?

Your Task. To learn what employers request in classified ads, check out the listings at an online job board such as Monster. Use your favourite search engine to locate the employers' sites. Follow the instructions to search job categories and locations. Study the jobs listed. Find five or more job listings in your field. If possible, print the results of your search. If you cannot print, make notes on what you find. Study the skills requested. How often do the ads mention communication, teamwork, and computer skills? What tasks do the ads mention? Discuss your findings with your team members. Prepare a list of the most frequently requested skills. Your instructor may ask you to submit your findings and/or report to the class. If you are not satisfied with the job selection at this site, choose another job board.

1.5 Workplace Writing: Separating Myths From Facts (Obj. 1)

Today's knowledge workers are doing more writing on the job than ever before. Changing organizational structures, heightened global competition, expanded team-based management, and heavy reliance on e-mail have all contributed to more written messages.

Your Task. In teams or in class, discuss the following statements. Are they myths or facts?

- **a.** Because I'm in a technical field, I'll work with numbers, not words.
- **b.** Assistants will clean up my writing problems.
- **c.** Technical writers do most of the real writing on the job.
- **d.** Computers can fix any of my writing mistakes.
- **e.** I can use form letters for most messages.

1.6 Communication Process: Analyzing the Process (Obj. 2)

TEAM

"One misspelled word and customers begin to doubt the validity of the information they are getting," warns Mary Jo Lichtenberg. She's director of training, quality, and career development at a leading computer retailer and reseller. One of her big problems is training service agents with weak communication skills. "Just because agents understand technically how to troubleshoot computers or pieces of software and can walk customers through solutions extremely well over the telephone doesn't mean they can do the same in writing," she complains. "The skill set for phone does not necessarily translate to the skill set needed for writing e-mail." As more and more customers choose e-mail and Web chat sessions to obtain service and support, service reps are doing more writing. Lichtenberg's solution to this problem is to introduce writing classes in the company's training programs.[18]

Your Task. As an intern in the training program at this organization, you and other interns have been asked to brainstorm the communication process with Mary Jo Lichtenberg. How can she best communicate her proposal to her boss? Review the entire communication process from sender to feedback. What is involved in encoding the proposal to her boss? What assumptions might she make about her audience? What communication channel should she choose and why? What noise might she expect in the transmission process and how could she overcome it? Individually or in teams, discuss your analysis in class or in a memo to your instructor.

1.7 Communication Process: Avoiding Misunderstanding (Obj. 2)

Communication is not successful unless the receiver understands the message as the sender meant it.

Your Task. Analyze the following examples of communication failures. What went wrong?

- **a.** A manager said to his assistant, "I'd sure appreciate your help in preparing a roster of volunteers." Later, the assistant was resentful when she found that she had to complete the task herself.
- **b.** A supervisor issued the following announcement: "Effective immediately the charge for copying services in Repro will be raised 1/2 to 2 cents each." Receivers scratched their heads.
- **c.** The pilot of a military airplane about to land decided that the runway was too short. He shouted to his engineer, "Takeoff power!" The engineer turned off the engines; the plane crashed.
- **d.** A China Airways flight, operating in zero visibility, crashed into the side of a mountain shortly after takeoff. The pilot's last words were, "What does *pull up* mean?" The official term is *climb.*
- **e.** The following statements appeared in letters of application for an advertised job opening. One applicant wrote, "Enclosed is my résumé in response to Sunday's *Calgary Herald.*" Another wrote, "Enclosed is my résumé in response to my search for an editorial/creative position." Still another wrote, "My experience in the production of newsletters, magazines, directories, and online data bases puts me head and shoulders above the crowd of applicants you have no doubtedly been inundated with."

1.8 Document for Analysis: Barriers to Communication (Objs. 3–5)

The following memo is from an exasperated manager to his staff. Obviously, this manager has no assistant to clean up his writing.

Your Task. Comment on the memo's effectiveness, tone, and potential barriers to communication. Your instructor may ask you to revise the memo, improving its tone, grammar, and organization.

DATE: Current
TO: All Employees
FROM: Harold Robinson, Operations Manager
SUBJECT: Cleanup!

You were all suppose to clean up your work areas last Friday, but that didn't happen. A few people cleaned their desks, but no one pitched in to clean the common areas, and you all seen what a mess they were in!

So we're going to try again. As you know, we don't hardly have a big enough custodial budget anymore. Everyone must clean up himself. This Friday I want to see action in the copy machine area, things like emptying waste baskets and you should organize paper and toner supplies. The lunch room is a disaster area. You must do something about the counters, the refrigerator, the sinks, and the coffee machine. And any food left in the refrigerator on Friday afternoon should be throwed out because it stinks by Monday. Finally, the office supply shelves should be straightened.

If you can't do a better job this Friday, I will have to assign individuals to a specific cleaning schedule. Which I don't want to do, but you may force me to.

1.9 Communicating in Organizations: Reducing Information Overload (Obj. 4)

Brad M. has been working at CoolDog Software for six months. He loved e-mail when he first joined CoolDog, but now it's overwhelming him. Every day he receives between 200 and 300 messages, some important and some junk. To keep caught up, Brad checks his e-mail every hour—sometimes more often if he's expecting a response. He joined five mailing lists because they sounded interesting and helpful. But when a topic really excites the subscribers, Brad's e-mail box is jammed with 50 or 60 postings at once. Reading all his messages prevents him from getting his real work done. If he ignores his e-mail, though, he may miss something important. What really frustrates him is what to do with messages that he must retain until he gathers the necessary information to respond.

Your Task. What suggestions can you make to lessen Brad's e-mail overload?

1.10 Information Flow: What's the Latest Buzz? (Obj. 5)

All organizations provide information to the public and to members through official channels. But information also flows through unofficial channels.

Your Task. Consider an organization to which you belong or a business where you've worked. How did members learn what was going on in the organization? What kind of information flowed through formal channels? What were those channels? What kind of information was delivered through informal channels? Was the grapevine as accurate as official channels? What barriers obstructed the flow of information? How could the flow be improved?

C.L.U.E. review 1

Each chapter includes an exercise based on Appendix A, *Competent Language Usage Essentials (C.L.U.E.)*. This appendix is a business communicator's condensed guide to language usage, covering 54 of the most used—and abused—language elements. It also includes a list of frequently misspelled words and a quick review of selected confusing words. If you are rusty on these language essentials, you should first study the guidelines and examples in Appendix A.

The following ten sentences are packed with errors based on concepts and spelling words from Appendix A. You will find the corrections for these exercises at the back of the book. On a separate sheet, edit the following sentences to correct faults in grammar, capitalization, punctuation, numbers, spelling, and word use.

1. To sucede in todays high-tech busness world you need highly-developed communication skills.
2. You especially need writting and grammer skills, because employes spend 60% of there time processing documents.
3. One organization paid three thousand dollars each for twelve employes to attend a 1 week work shop in communication training.
4. My coworker and me was serprised to learn that more information has been produced in the last thirty years then in the previous five thousand years.
5. If you work in a office with open cubicles its rude to listen to web radio streaming audio or other multimedia, without headphones.
6. When making a decision you should gather information, and than weigh the advantages and disadvantage of each alternative.
7. If you are defining communication for example, a principle element are the transmission of information and meaning.
8. Ms Johnson had 3 messages to send immediately, consequently she choose e-mail because it was definitly the most fastest comunication channel.
9. 5 elements that make up your frame of reference are the following, Experience, Education, Culture, Expectations and Personality.
10. Just between you and I; I'm sure our company President thinks that honesty and integrity is more important then increase profits.

chapter 2

Communicating in Small Groups and Teams

objectives

1 Discuss why groups and teams are formed.

2 Describe team development, team and group roles, dealing with conflict, and methods for reaching group decisions.

3 Identify the characteristics of successful teams, including an emphasis on workplace etiquette.

4 List techniques for organizing team-based written and oral presentations.

5 Discuss how to plan and participate in productive meetings.

6 Explain the usefulness of collaborative technologies such as voice conferencing, videoconferencing, Web conferencing, instant messaging, blogs, and wikis.

springboard *to discussion*

Resourceful companies are finding they can improve teamwork, share knowledge, and save money by using wikis to share important information such as documents, project information, and schedules. These collaborative tools are being used to share the knowledge base and, most important, they are free.[1]

learning objective 1

Preparing to Work With Groups and Teams

Many companies today expect employees to possess team and other soft skills. The Conference Board of Canada, in its Employability Skills 2000+, lists academic, teamwork, and personal management skills as those most sought by employers. While a good résumé and interview will get you in the door, your long-term success is greatly influenced by your ability to communicate with your boss, coworkers, and customers, as well as your ability to work as an effective and contributing team member.

To participate most effectively on a team, however, you need to learn about groups and teams. In this chapter you'll study why groups and teams are formed, how they differ and develop, typical roles members play, and how to resolve conflicts. In addition, you'll learn about workplace etiquette, how to collaborate in team-based presentations, uses of collaboration technologies, and how to plan and participate in productive meetings.

Why Form Groups and Teams?

Organizations are forming teams for better decisions, faster response, increased productivity, greater "buy-in," less resistance to change, improved morale, and reduced risks.

Today's workplace is teeming with teams. In response to intense global competition, businesses are being forced to rethink and restructure their operations. Companies are expected to compete globally, meet higher standards, and increase profits—but often with fewer people and fewer resources.[2] Striving to meet these seemingly impossible goals, organizations began developing groups and teams for the following specific reasons:[3]

- **Better decisions.** Decisions are generally more accurate and effective because group and team members contribute different expertise and perspectives.
- **Faster response.** When action is necessary to respond to competition or to solve a problem, small groups and teams can act rapidly.
- **Increased productivity.** Because they are often closer to the action and to the customer, team members can see opportunities for improving efficiencies.
- **Greater "buy-in."** Decisions derived jointly are usually better received because members are committed to the solution and are more willing to support it.
- **Less resistance to change.** People who have input into making decisions are less hostile, aggressive, and resistant to change.
- **Improved employee morale.** Personal satisfaction and job morale increase when teams are successful.
- **Reduced risks.** Responsibility for a decision is diffused, thus carrying less risk for any individual.

tech talk

How to Form and Participate in Virtual Teams

Virtual team members must overcome many obstacles not faced by intact groups. The following recommendations help members form virtual teams and interact effectively.

- **Select team members carefully.** Choose team members who are self-starters, good communicators, flexible, trusting, and experts in areas needed by the team.
- **Invest in beginnings.** If possible, meet face to face to work out procedures and to bond. Spending time together initially expedites reaching consensus about goals, tasks, and procedures.
- **Redefine "we."** Encourage behaviour that reflects unity, such as including one another in decisions and sharing information. Consider having a team photograph taken and made into something used frequently, such as a mouse pad or computer wallpaper.
- **Get the maximum benefit from technology.** Make use of speakerphones, collaborative software, e-mail, teleconferencing, videoconferencing, blogs, and wikis. But be sure that members are well trained in their use.
- **Concentrate on building credibility and trust.** Encourage team members to pay close attention to the way that others perceive them. Acting consistently, fulfilling promises, considering other members' schedules, and responding promptly to e-mail and voice messages help build credibility and trust.
- **Establish responsibilities.** Identify expectations and responsibilities for each member. Make rules about e-mail response time and sharing information with all members.
- **Keep track of information.** Capture information and decisions in a shared database, such as a wiki. Make sure all messages define expected actions, responsibilities, and time lines. Track to-do items and follow up as necessary. Expect messages to be more formal than in traditional same-time, same-place teams.
- **Avoid misinterpreting messages.** Because it's so easy to misunderstand e-mail messages, one virtual manager advises team members to always doubt their first instinct about another team member if the response is negative. Always take time to question your reactions.

Some companies rejected teams because they slowed decisions, shielded workers from responsibility, and reduced productivity.

Despite the current popularity of teams, however, they are not a panacea for all workplace problems. Some critics complain that they are the latest in a succession of management fads. Others charge that they are a screen behind which management intensifies its control over labour.[4] Some major organizations have retreated from teams, finding that they slowed decision making, shielded workers from responsibility, and created morale and productivity problems.[5] Yet in most models of future organizations, teams, not individuals, function as the primary performance unit.

Some organizations are even creating *virtual teams*, which are defined as groups of people who work interdependently with a shared purpose across space, time, and organization boundaries using technology.[6] People who work together usually see each other and can talk face to face, but virtual teams must stay connected through technology. To learn more about how to communicate effectively in digital groups, see the Tech Talk box above.

learning objective

2

Understanding Team Development, Roles, and Conflict

Small groups and teams may be formed to complete single tasks or to function as ongoing permanent bodies. Regardless of their purpose, successful teams normally go through predictable phases as they develop. In this section you'll learn about the four phases of team development. You'll see how team members can perform in functional and dysfunctional roles. You'll also study the role of conflict and how to apply a six-step plan for resolving conflict.

Four Phases of Team Development

Successful teams generally go through four phases: forming, storming, norming, and performing.

When groups are formed, they generally evolve through four phases, as identified by psychologist B. A. Tuckman. These phases include **forming**, **storming**, **norming**, and **performing**. Some groups get lucky and move quickly from forming to performing. But most struggle through disruptive, although ultimately constructive, team-building stages.

Forming. During the first stage, individuals get to know each other. They often are overly polite and feel a bit awkward. As they search for similarities and attempt to bond, they begin to develop trust in each other. Members will discuss fundamental topics such as why the team is necessary, who "owns" the team, whether membership is mandatory, how large it should be, and what talents members can contribute. A leader functions primarily as a traffic director. Groups and teams should resist the efforts of some members to sprint through the first stages and vault to the performing stage. Moving slowly through the stages is necessary in building a cohesive, productive unit.

Storming. During the second phase, members define their roles and responsibilities, decide how to reach their goals, and iron out the rules governing how they interact. Unfortunately, this stage often produces conflict, resulting in *storming*. A good leader, however, should step in to set limits, control the chaos, and offer suggestions. The leader will be most successful if she or he acts like a coach rather than a cop. Teams composed of dissimilar personality types may take longer to progress through the storming phase. Tempers may flare, sleep may be lost, leaders may be deposed. But most often the storm passes, and a cohesive group emerges.

In the norming stage, tensions subside, roles clarify, and information flows among team members.

Norming. Once the sun returns to the sky, teams and groups enter the *norming* stage. Tension subsides, roles clarify, and information begins to flow among members. The group periodically checks its agenda to remind itself of its progress toward its goals. People are careful not to shake the hard-won camaraderie and formation of a single-minded purpose. Formal leadership is unnecessary since everyone takes on leadership functions. Important data is shared with the entire group, and mutual interdependence becomes typical. The group or team begins to move smoothly in one direction. Members make sure that procedures are in place to resolve future conflicts.

Members who assume positive task roles help a team achieve its purpose.

Performing. In Tuckman's team growth model, some groups never reach the final stage of *performing*. Problems that may cause them to fail are shown in Figure 2.1. For those that survive the first three phases, however, the final stage is gratifying. Group members have established a pace and a shared language. They develop loyalty and a willingness to resolve all problems. A "can-do" mentality pervades as they

Figure 2.1 ***Why Teams Fail: Typical Problems, Symptoms, and Solutions***

Problems	Symptoms	Solutions
Confused goals	People don't know what they're supposed to do	Clarify team purpose and expected outcomes
Mismatched needs	People with private agendas working at cross-purposes	Get hidden agendas on table by asking what people personally want from team
Unresolved roles	Team members are uncertain what their jobs are	Inform team members what is expected of them
Senseless procedures	Team is at the mercy of an ineffective employee handbook	Throw away the book and develop procedures that make sense
Bad leadership	Leader is tentative, inconsistent, or foolish	Leader must learn to serve the team and keep its vision alive or give up role
Anti-team culture	Organization is not committed to the idea of teams	Team for the right reasons or don't team at all; never force people onto a team
Poor feedback	Performance is not being measured; team members are groping in the dark	Create system of free flow of useful information from all team members

Adapted from H. A. Robbins and M. Finley, *Why Teams Don't Work*. Reprinted with permission of Peterson's—a Nelnet company.

progress toward their goal. Fights are clean, and members continue working together without grudges. Best of all, information flows freely, deadlines are met, and production exceeds expectations.

Following an effective six-step procedure can help you resolve conflicts through collaboration and cooperation.

Six-Step Procedure for Dealing With Conflict. Conflict is a normal part of every workplace and every team. Although the word alone is enough to make your heart go into overdrive, conflict is not always negative. When managed properly, conflict can improve decision making, clarify values, increase group cohesiveness, stimulate creativity, decrease tensions, and undermine dissatisfaction. Unresolved conflict, however, can destroy productivity and seriously undermine morale. You will be better prepared to resolve workplace conflict if you know the five most common response patterns as well as study a six-step procedure for dealing with conflict.[7]

1. **Listen.** To be sure you understand the problem, listen carefully. If the other person doesn't seem to be listening to you, you need to set the example and be the first to listen.
2. **Understand the other's point of view.** Once you listen, it is much easier to understand the other's position. Show your understanding by asking questions and paraphrasing. This will also verify what you think the other person means.
3. **Show a concern for the relationship.** By focusing on the problem, not the person, you can build, maintain, and even improve relationships. Show an understanding of the other person's situation and needs. Show an overall willingness to come to an agreement.
4. **Look for common ground.** Identify your interests and help the other side identify its interests. Learn what you have in common, and look for a solution to which both sides can agree.

5. **Invent new problem-solving options.** Spend time identifying the interests of both sides. Then brainstorm to invent new ways to solve the problem. Be open to new options.
6. **Reach an agreement based on what's fair.** Seek to determine a standard of fairness that is acceptable to both sides. Then weigh the possible solutions, and choose the best option.

Avoiding Groupthink

Groupthink means that team members agree without examining alternatives or considering contingency plans.

Conflict is normal in team interactions, and successful teams are able to resolve it using methods you just learned. But some teams avoid conflict. They smooth things over and in doing so may fall victim to *groupthink.* This is a term coined by theorist Irving Janis to describe faulty decision-making processes by team members who are overly eager to agree with one another. Several conditions can lead to groupthink: team members with similar backgrounds, a lack of methodical procedures, a demand for a quick decision, and a strong leader who favours a specific decision. Symptoms of groupthink include pressures placed on a member who argues against the group's shared beliefs, self-censorship of thoughts that deviate from the group consensus, collective efforts to rationalize, and an unquestioned belief in the group's inherent morality. Teams suffering from groupthink fail to examine alternatives, are biased in collecting and evaluating information, and ignore the risks of the preferred choice. They may also forget to work out a contingency plan in case the preferred choice fails.[8]

Effective teams avoid groupthink by striving for team diversity—in age, gender, backgrounds, experience, and training. They encourage open discussion, search for relevant information, evaluate many alternatives, consider how a decision will be implemented, and plan for contingencies in case the decision doesn't work out.

Reaching Group Decisions

Groups may reach decisions by majority vote, consensus, minority vote, averaging of votes, or authority rule.

The way teams reach decisions greatly affects the morale and commitment of the team, as well as the implementation of any team decision. In Western culture the majority usually rules, but other methods, five of which are discussed here, may be more effective. As you study these methods, think about which methods would be best for routine decisions and which methods would be best for dealing with emergencies.

- **Majority.** Group members vote and a majority wins. This method results in a quick decision but may leave an alienated minority uncommitted to implementation.

Although time consuming, consensus decisions generally produce the most team commitment.

- **Consensus.** Discussion continues until all team members have aired their opinions and, ultimately, agree. This method is time consuming, but it produces creative, high-quality discussion and generally elicits commitment by all members to implement the decision.
- **Minority.** Typically, a subcommittee investigates and makes a recommendation for action. This method is useful when the full group cannot get together to make a decision or when time is short.
- **Averaging.** Members haggle, bargain, cajole, and negotiate to reach a middle position, which often requires compromise. With this method, the opinions of the least knowledgeable members may cancel the opinions of the most knowledgeable.

- **Authority rule with discussion.** The leader, boss, or manager listens to team members' ideas, but the final decision is his or hers. This method encourages lively discussion and results in participatory decision making. However, team members must have good communication skills. This method also requires a leader who is willing to make decisions.

Characteristics of Successful Teams

learning objective 3

The use of teams has been called the solution to many ills in the current workplace.[9] Someone even observed that as an acronym TEAM means "Together, Everyone Achieves More."[10] But many teams do not work well together. In fact, some teams can actually increase frustration, lower productivity, and create employee dissatisfaction. Experts who have studied team workings and decisions have discovered that effective teams share some or all of the following characteristics.

Small Size, Diverse Makeup. For most functions the best teams range from 2 to 25 members, although 4 or 5 is optimum for many projects. Larger groups have trouble interacting constructively, much less agreeing on actions.[11] For the most creative decisions, teams generally have male and female members who differ in age, social background, training, and experience. Members should bring complementary skills to a team. Teams with members from different ethnicities and cultures can look at projects beyond the limited view of one culture. Many organizations are finding that diverse teams can produce innovative solutions with broader applications than homogeneous teams can.

Small, diverse teams often produce more creative solutions with broader applications than homogeneous teams.

Agreement on Purpose. An effective team begins with a purpose. Working from a general purpose to specific goals typically requires a huge investment of time and effort. Meaningful discussions, however, motivate team members to buy into the project.

Agreement on Procedures. The best teams develop procedures to guide them. They set up intermediate goals with deadlines. They assign roles and tasks, requiring all members to contribute equivalent amounts of real work. They decide how they will reach decisions using one of the strategies discussed earlier. Procedures are continually evaluated to ensure movement toward the attainment of the team's goals.

Ability to Confront Conflict. Poorly functioning teams avoid conflict, preferring sulking, gossip, or backstabbing. A better plan is to acknowledge conflict and address the root of the problem openly, using the six-step plan outlined earlier. Although it may feel emotionally risky, direct confrontation saves time and enhances team commitment in the long run. To be constructive, however, confrontation must be task-oriented, not person-oriented. An open airing of differences, in which all team members have a chance to speak their minds, should centre on strengths and weaknesses of the different positions and ideas—not on personalities. After hearing all sides, team members must negotiate a fair settlement, no matter how long it takes. Good decisions are based on consensus: all members agree.

Use of Good Communication Techniques. The best teams exchange information and contribute ideas freely in an informal environment. Team members speak clearly and concisely, avoiding generalities. They encourage feedback. Listeners

Good teams exchange information freely and collaborate rather than compete.

become actively involved, read body language, and ask clarifying questions before responding. Tactful, constructive disagreement is encouraged. Although a team's task is taken seriously, successful teams are able to inject humour into their interactions.

Ability to Collaborate Rather Than Compete. Effective team members are genuinely interested in achieving team goals instead of receiving individual recognition. They contribute ideas and feedback unselfishly. They monitor team progress, including what's going right, what's going wrong, and what to do about it. They celebrate individual and team accomplishments.

Acceptance of Ethical Responsibilities. Teams as a whole have ethical responsibilities to their members, to their larger organization, and to society. Members have a number of specific responsibilities to each other. As a whole, groups have a responsibility to represent the organization's view and respect its privileged information. They should not discuss with outsiders any sensitive issues without permission. In addition, groups have a broader obligation to avoid advocating actions that would endanger members of society at large.

Shared Leadership. Effective teams often have no formal leader. Instead, leadership rotates to those with the appropriate expertise as the team evolves and moves from one phase to another. Many teams operate under a democratic approach. This approach can achieve buy-in to team decisions, boost morale, and create fewer hurt feelings and less resentment. But in times of crisis, a strong team member may need to step up as leader.

Demonstration of Good Workplace Manners. Rudeness and bad manners have become alarmingly common in the North American workplace. Successful team members treat each other and colleagues politely and respectfully. This may involve a few more *please*s and *thank you*s, as well as showing consideration for others. Good team members are aware of noise levels when colleagues are trying to concentrate. They offer support to colleagues with heavy workloads. They respect others' boundaries and need for privacy.

Checklist for Developing Team Effectiveness

- ✓ **Establish small teams.** Smaller teams are thought to function more efficiently and more effectively than larger teams.
- ✓ **Encourage diversity.** Innovative teams typically include members who differ in age, gender, and background. Team members should possess technical expertise, problem-solving skills, and interpersonal skills.
- ✓ **Determine the purpose, procedures, and roles.** Members must understand the task at hand and what is expected of them. Teams function best when operating procedures are ironed out early on and each member has a specific role.
- ✓ **Acknowledge and manage conflict.** Conflict is productive when it motivates a team to search for new ideas, increase participation, delay premature decisions, or discuss disagreements. Keep conflict centred on issues rather than on people.

- ✓ **Cultivate good communication skills.** Effective team members are willing and able to articulate ideas clearly and concisely, recognize nonverbal cues, and listen actively.

- ✓ **Advance an environment of open communication.** Teams are most productive when members trust each other and feel free to discuss all viewpoints openly in an informal atmosphere.

- ✓ **Encourage collaboration and discourage competition.** Sharing information in a cooperative effort to achieve the team purpose must be more important than competing with other members for individual achievement.

- ✓ **Share leadership.** Members with the most expertise should lead at various times during the project's evolution.

- ✓ **Create a sense of fairness in making decisions.** Effective teams resolve issues without forcing members into a win–lose situation.

- ✓ **Lighten up.** The most successful teams take their task seriously, but they are also able to laugh at themselves and inject humour to enliven team proceedings.

- ✓ **Continually assess performance.** Teams should establish checkpoints along the way to determine whether they are meeting their objectives, and adjust procedures if progress is unsatisfactory.

Organizing Team-Based Written and Oral Presentations

learning objective 4

Companies form teams for many reasons. The goal of some teams is an oral presentation to pitch a new product, to win a high-stakes contract, or to save the company money. The goal of other teams is to investigate a problem and submit recommendations to decision makers in a report. The end product of any team is often a written report or an oral presentation.

Guidelines for Team Writing and Oral Presentations

Team projects proceed more smoothly when members agree on ground rules.

Whether your team's project produces written reports or oral presentations, you generally have considerable control over how the project is organized and completed. If you've been part of any team efforts before, you also know that such projects can be very frustrating—particularly when some team members don't carry their weight or when members cannot resolve conflict. On the other hand, team projects can be harmonious and productive when members establish ground rules and follow guidelines related to preparing, planning, collecting information for, organizing, rehearsing, and evaluating team projects.

Preparing to Work Together. Before you begin talking about a specific project, it's best to discuss some of the following issues in regard to how your group will function.

- Name a meeting leader to plan and conduct meetings, a recorder to keep a record of group decisions, and an evaluator to determine whether the group is on target and meeting its goals.

Teams must decide whether they will be governed by consensus, by majority rule, or by some other method.

- Decide whether your team will be governed by consensus (everyone must agree), by majority rule, or by some other method.
- Compare schedules of team members in order to set up the best meeting times. Plan to meet often. Make team meetings a top priority. Avoid other responsibilities that might cause disruption during these meetings.
- Discuss the value of conflict. By bringing conflict into the open and encouraging confrontation, your team can prevent personal resentment and group dysfunction. Confrontation can actually create better final products by promoting new ideas and avoiding groupthink. Conflict is most beneficial when team members are allowed to air their views fully.
- Discuss how you will deal with team members who are not pulling their share of the load.

In planning a team document or presentation, develop a work plan, assign jobs, and set deadlines.

Planning the Document or Presentation. Once you've established ground rules, you're ready to discuss the final document or presentation. Be sure to keep a record of the following decisions your team makes.

- Establish the specific purpose for the document or presentation. Identify the main issues involved.
- Decide on the final format. For a report, determine what parts it will include, such as an executive summary, figures, and an appendix. For a presentation, decide on its parts, length, and graphics.
- Discuss the audience(s) for the product and what questions it would want answered in your report or oral presentation. If your report is persuasive, consider what appeals might achieve its purpose.
- Develop a work plan. Assign jobs. Set deadlines. If time is short, work backward from the due date. For oral presentations, build in time for content and creative development as well as for a series of rehearsals.
- For oral presentations, give each team member a written assignment that details his or her responsibilities for researching content, producing visuals, developing handout materials, building transitions between segments, and showing up for rehearsals.
- For written reports, decide how the final document will be composed: individuals working separately on assigned portions, one person writing the first draft, the entire group writing the complete document together, or some other method.

Unless facts are accurate, reports and presentations will fail.

Collecting Information. The following suggestions help teams generate and gather accurate information. Unless facts are accurate, the most beautiful report or the best high-powered presentation will fail.

- Brainstorm for ideas; consider cluster diagramming.
- Assign topics. Decide who will be responsible for gathering what information.
- Establish deadlines for collecting information.
- Discuss ways to ensure the accuracy of the information collected.

Organizing, Writing, and Revising. As the project progresses, your team may wish to modify some of its earlier decisions.

- Review the proposed organization of your final document or presentation and adjust it if necessary.

- Compose the first draft of a written report or presentation. If separate team members are writing segments, they should use the same word processing and/or presentation graphics program to facilitate combining files.
- Meet to discuss and revise the draft(s) or rehearse the presentation.
- If individuals are working on separate parts of a written report, appoint one person (probably the best writer) to coordinate all the parts, striving for consistent style and format. Work for a uniform look and feel to the final product.
- For oral presentations, be sure each member builds a bridge to the next presenter's topic and launches it smoothly. Strive for logical connections between segments.

For team reports, assign one person to coordinate all the parts and make the style consistent.

Editing, Rehearsing, and Evaluating. Before the presentation is made or the final document is submitted, complete the following steps.

- For a written report, give one person responsibility for finding and correcting grammatical and mechanical errors.
- For a written report, meet as a group to evaluate the final document. Does it fulfill its purpose and meet the needs of the audience? Successful group documents emerge from thoughtful preparation, clear definition of contributors' roles, commitment to a group-approved plan, and willingness to take responsibility for the final product.
- For oral presentations, assign one person the task of merging the various files, running a spell checker, and examining the entire presentation for consistency of design, format, and vocabulary.
- Schedule at least five rehearsals, say the experts.[12] Consider videotaping one of the rehearsals so that each presenter can critique his or her own performance.
- Schedule a dress rehearsal with an audience at least two days before the actual presentation. Practise fielding questions.

Schedule at least five rehearsals for a team presentation.

More information about writing business reports and making individual presentations appears in subsequent chapters of this book.

Planning and Participating in Productive Meetings

learning objective 5

As businesses become more team-oriented and management becomes more participatory, people are attending more meetings than ever. One survey of managers found that they were devoting as many as two days a week to various gatherings.[13] Yet meetings are almost universally disliked. Our task, then, as business communicators is to learn how to make meetings efficient, satisfying, and productive.

Meetings, by the way, consist of three or more individuals who gather to pool information, solicit feedback, clarify policy, seek consensus, and solve problems. But meetings have another important purpose for you—they represent opportunities. Because they are a prime tool for developing staff, they are career critical. At meetings judgments are formed and careers are made. Therefore, instead of treating them as thieves of your valuable time, try to see them as golden opportunities to demonstrate your leadership, communication, and problem-solving skills. So that you can make the most of these opportunities, here are techniques for planning and conducting successful meetings.

Because you can expect to attend many meetings, learn to make them efficient, satisfying, and productive.

Deciding Whether a Meeting Is Necessary

Call meetings only when necessary, and invite only key people.

No meeting should be called unless the topic is important, can't wait, and requires an exchange of ideas. If the flow of information is strictly one-way and no immediate feedback will result, then don't schedule a meeting. For example, if people are merely being advised or informed, send an e-mail, memo, or letter. Leave a telephone or voice mail message, but don't call a costly meeting. Remember, the real expense of a meeting is the lost productivity of all the people attending. To decide whether the purpose of the meeting is valid, it's a good idea to consult the key people who will be attending. Ask them what outcomes are desired and how to achieve those goals. This consultation also sets a collaborative tone and encourages full participation.

Selecting Participants

Problem-solving meetings should involve five or fewer people.

The number of meeting participants is determined by the purpose of the meeting, as shown in Figure 2.2. If the meeting purpose is motivational, such as an awards ceremony, then the number of participants is unlimited. But to make decisions, according to studies at 3M Corporation, the best number is five or fewer participants.[14] Ideally, those attending should be people who will make the decision and people with information necessary to make the decision. Also attending should be people who will be responsible for implementing the decision and representatives of groups who will benefit from the decision.

Distributing Advance Information

Pass out a meeting agenda showing topics to be discussed and other information.

At least two days in advance of a meeting, distribute an agenda of topics to be discussed. Also include any reports or materials that participants should read in advance. For continuing groups, you might also include a copy of the minutes of the previous meeting. To keep meetings productive, limit the number of agenda items. Remember, the narrower the focus, the greater the chances for success. A good agenda, as illustrated in Figure 2.3, covers the following information:

- Date and place of meeting
- Start time and end time
- Brief description of each topic, in order of priority, including the names of individuals who are responsible for performing actions
- Proposed allotment of time for each topic
- Any pre-meeting preparation expected of participants

Getting the Meeting Started

Start meetings on time and open with a brief introduction.

To avoid wasting time and irritating attendees, always start meetings on time—even if some participants are missing. Waiting for latecomers causes resentment and sets a bad precedent. For the same reasons, don't give a quick recap to anyone who arrives

FIGURE 2.2 ***Meeting Purpose and Number of Participants***

Purpose	Ideal Size
Intensive problem solving	5 or fewer
Problem identification	10 or fewer
Information reviews and presentations	30 or fewer
Motivational	Unlimited

FIGURE 2.3 ***Typical Meeting Agenda***

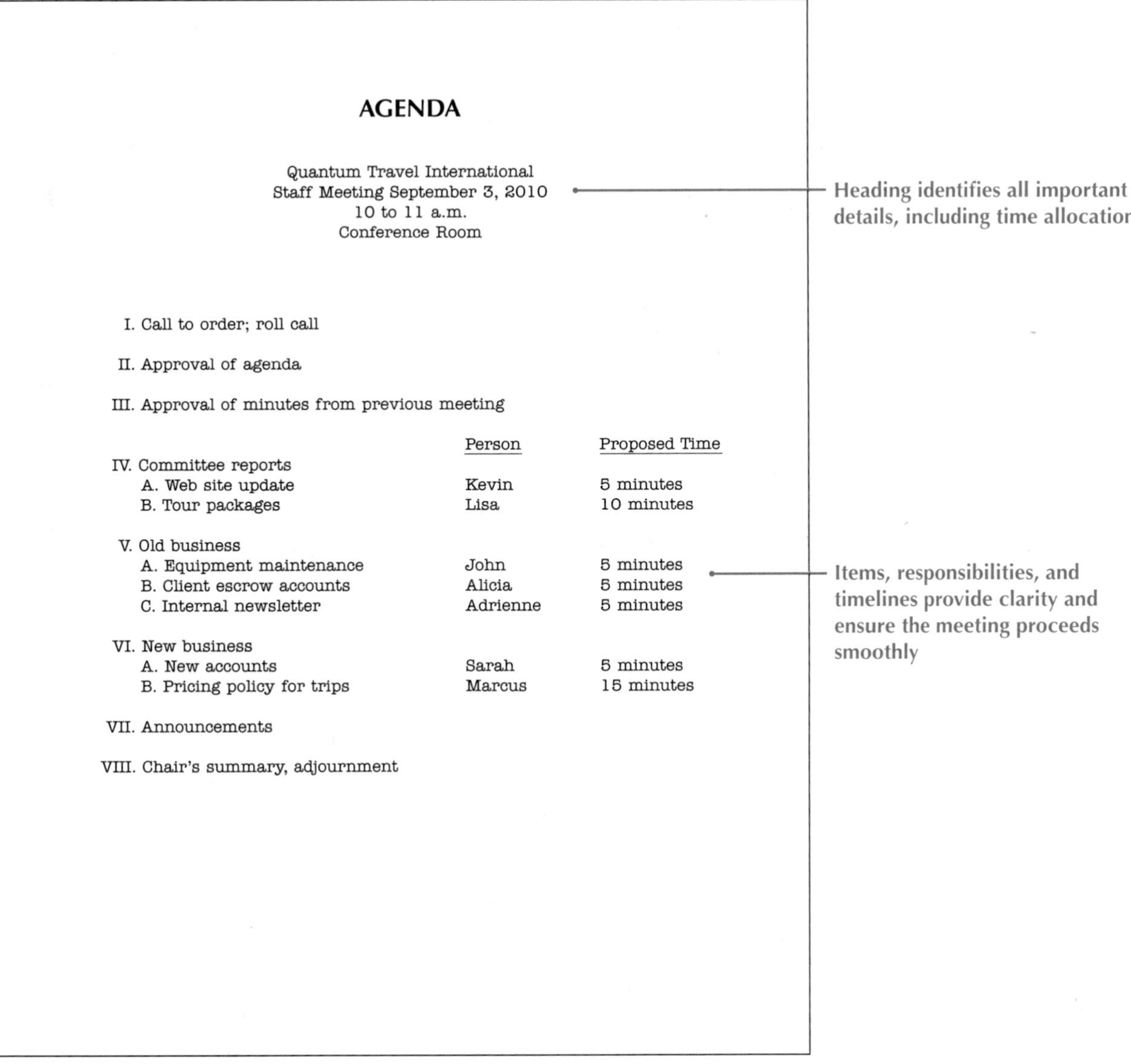

AGENDA

Quantum Travel International
Staff Meeting September 3, 2010
10 to 11 a.m.
Conference Room

I. Call to order; roll call

II. Approval of agenda

III. Approval of minutes from previous meeting

	Person	Proposed Time
IV. Committee reports		
A. Web site update	Kevin	5 minutes
B. Tour packages	Lisa	10 minutes
V. Old business		
A. Equipment maintenance	John	5 minutes
B. Client escrow accounts	Alicia	5 minutes
C. Internal newsletter	Adrienne	5 minutes
VI. New business		
A. New accounts	Sarah	5 minutes
B. Pricing policy for trips	Marcus	15 minutes

VII. Announcements

VIII. Chair's summary, adjournment

Heading identifies all important details, including time allocation
Items, responsibilities, and timelines provide clarity and ensure the meeting proceeds smoothly

late. At the appointed time, open the meeting with a three- to five-minute introduction that includes the following:

- Goal and length of the meeting
- Background of topics or problems
- Possible solutions and constraints
- Tentative agenda
- Ground rules to be followed

A typical set of ground rules might include arriving on time, communicating openly, being supportive, listening carefully, participating fully, confronting conflict frankly, and following the agenda. More formal groups follow parliamentary procedures based on *Robert's Rules of Order*. After establishing basic ground rules, the leader should ask if participants agree thus far. The next step is to assign one attendee to take minutes and one to act as a recorder. The recorder stands at a flipchart or whiteboard and lists the main ideas being discussed and agreements reached.

Moving the Meeting Along

Keep the meeting moving by avoiding issues that sidetrack the group.

After the preliminaries, the leader should say as little as possible. Remember that the purpose of a meeting is to exchange views, not to hear one person, even the leader, do all the talking. To avoid allowing digressions to sidetrack the group, try generating a "Parking Lot" list. This is a list of important but divergent issues that should be discussed at a later time. Another way to handle digressions is to say, "Folks, we are getting off track here. Forgive me for pressing on, but I need to bring us back to the central issue of ..."[15] It's important to adhere to the agenda and the time schedule. Equally important, when the group seems to have reached a consensus, is to summarize the group's position and check to see whether everyone agrees.

Recording Information

Ensure that minutes of the meeting are transcribed for consistency of information and distribution to all stakeholders. Minutes must be objective and action-oriented. Verbatim minutes are long and tedious, and may include personal and irrelevant "chatter." To capture discussion, a point-by-point summary is effective. Action-oriented minutes permit one to chair the meeting and take notes at the same time.[16]

Participating Actively and Productively

To benefit from meetings, arrive early, be prepared, contribute positively and respectfully, stay calm, give credit to others, don't use your cell phone or laptop, help summarize, express your views in the meeting (not after), and complete your assignments.

Meetings are an opportunity for you to showcase your abilities and boost your career. To get the most out of the meetings you attend, try these techniques:[17]

- Arrive early. You show respect and look well organized by arriving a little early.
- Come prepared. Bring the agenda and any distributed materials. Study the topics and be ready with questions, comments, and good ideas.
- Bring a positive attitude. Use positive body language; speak energetically.
- Contribute respectfully. Wait your turn to speak; raise your hand to be recognized.
- Wait for others to finish. Show respect and good manners by not interrupting.
- Keep your voice calm and pleasant, yet energetic. Avoid showing anger, as this focuses attention on your behaviour rather than on your ideas.
- Give credit to others. Gain allies and enhance your credibility by recognizing others in front of peers and superiors.
- Put the cell phone and laptop away. Focus your attention on the meeting, not on answering e-mail or working on your computer.
- Help summarize. Assist the meeting leader by reviewing points you have noted.
- Express your views in the meeting. Build trust by not holding post-meeting "sidebars" with criticism and judgments.
- Follow up. Send the signal that you are efficient and caring by completing the actions assigned to you.

Handling Conflict in Meetings

As you learned earlier, conflict is natural and even desirable. But it can cause awkwardness and uneasiness. In meetings, conflict typically develops when people feel unheard or misunderstood. If two people are in conflict, the best approach is to encourage each to make a complete case while group members give their full attention. Let each one question the other. Then the leader should summarize what was said and the group should offer comments. The group may modify a recommendation or suggest alternatives before reaching consensus on a direction to follow.

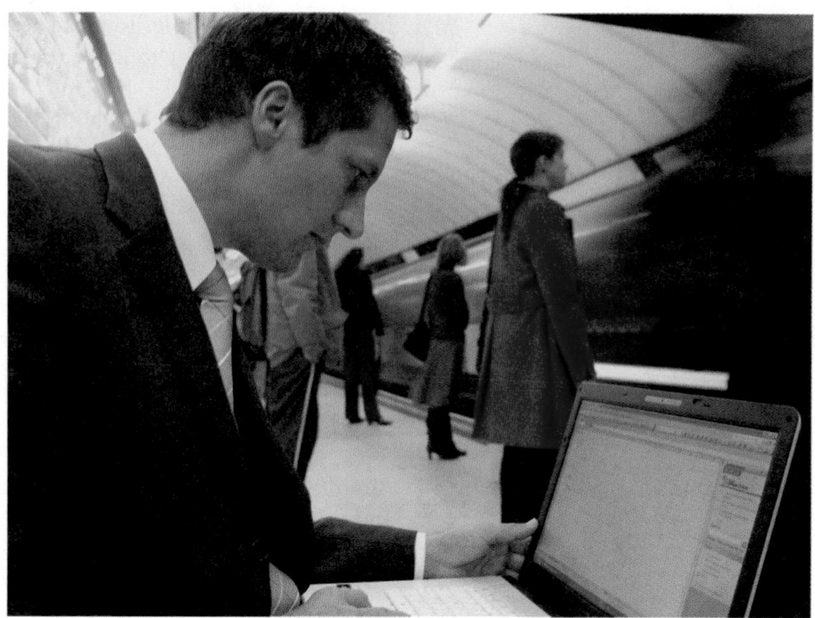

Conferencing firm WebEx Communications Inc. is finding new ways to make meetings more productive—even long after they have ended. Whereas conventional meeting follow-up revolves around handwritten notes, individuals' memories, and typed minutes, WebEx conferencing software enables businesses to record and archive entire group sessions for future retrieval.

Source: © Peter Cade/Iconica/Getty Images

Ending and Following Up

End the meeting at the agreed time. The leader should summarize what has been decided, who is going to do what, and by what time. It may be necessary to ask people to volunteer to take responsibility for completing action items agreed to in the meeting. No one should leave the meeting without a full understanding of what was accomplished. One effective technique that encourages full participation is "once around the table." Everyone is asked to summarize briefly his or her interpretation of what was decided and what happens next. Of course, this closure technique works best with smaller groups. The leader should conclude by asking the group to set a time for the next meeting. He or she should also assure the group that a report will follow, and thank participants for attending.

When a conflict develops between two members, allow each to make a complete case before the group.

Following Up Actively

If minutes were taken, they should be distributed within a couple of days after the meeting. It is up to the leader to see that what was decided at the meeting is accomplished. The leader may need to call people to remind them of their assignments and also to volunteer to help them if necessary.

End the meeting with a summary of accomplishments.

Meetings are a necessary evil for today's team-oriented workplace. The following checklist can help you use them effectively and perhaps accelerate your career.

Follow up by reminding participants of their assigned tasks.

Checklist for Planning and Participating in Productive Meetings

Before the Meeting

 **Consider alternatives.** Unless a topic is important and pressing, avoid calling a meeting. Perhaps an e-mail message, telephone call, or announcement would serve the purpose as well.

- **Invite the right people.** To make decisions, invite those people who have information and authority to make the decision and implement it.
- **Distribute an agenda.** Prepare and distribute an agenda that includes the date and the place of the meeting, the starting and ending time, a brief description of each topic, the names of people responsible for any actions, and a proposed time allotment for each topic.

During the Meeting

- **Start on time and introduce the agenda.** Discuss the goal and length of the meeting, provide the background of topics for discussion, suggest possible solutions and constraints, propose a tentative agenda, and clarify the ground rules for the meeting.
- **Appoint a secretary.** Ask one attendee to make a record of the proceedings and ask another person to record discussion topics on a flipchart or whiteboard.
- **Encourage balanced participation.** Strive to be sure that all participants' views are heard and that no one monopolizes the discussion. Avoid digressions by steering the group back to the topics on the agenda.
- **Confront conflict frankly.** Encourage people who disagree to explain their positions completely. Then restate each position and ask for group comments. The group may modify a recommendation or suggest alternatives before agreeing on a plan of action.
- **Summarize along the way.** When the group seems to reach a consensus, summarize and see whether everyone agrees.

Ending the Meeting and Following Up

- **Review meeting decisions.** At the end of the meeting, summarize what has been decided, discuss action items, and establish a schedule for completion.
- **Distribute minutes of meeting.** A few days after the meeting, arrange to have the administrative assistant distribute the minutes.
- **Remind people of action items.** Follow up by calling people to see if they are completing the actions recommended at the meeting.

learning objective 6

Using Technology to Facilitate Collaboration

Several constantly evolving technologies enable people to collaborate on projects without meeting face to face. Everyone agrees that live meetings are best to exchange ideas, brainstorm, build consensus, and develop personal relationships. But collaboration tools are becoming increasingly effective and more popular for a number of reasons. Collaboration tools make it possible for people to work together when they can't be together. These tools are fast and convenient, and can save big bucks in travel costs.

E-mail is still a major communication channel for online collaboration. Because e-mail is the first tool most people learn to use, they are often reluctant to move away from it to embrace more effective collaboration methods. Collaborators today have access to a number of efficient tools, including voice conferencing, videoconferencing, Web conferencing, instant messaging, blogs, and wikis. You may already have used many of the following tools.

Collaboration technology (sometimes called groupware) facilitates group activities.

Voice Conferencing

Among the simplest collaboration tools is *voice conferencing* (also called *audioconferencing, teleconferencing, conference calling,* or *phone conferencing*). One or more people in a work area use an enhanced speakerphone to confer with others by telephone. Voice conferencing enables people at both ends to speak and be heard simultaneously. Thanks to cell phones, people can even participate in a teleconference from an airplane or the beach. Although voice conferencing is not as rich as other collaboration tools, it is the mainstay of the entire teleconferencing industry. Because it is simple and effective, more people use it than any other of the collaboration meeting tools.

Voice conferencing enables collaborators to confer with each other by telephone.

Videoconferencing

If meeting participants need to see each other or share documents, they may use *videoconferencing.* This tool combines video, audio, and communications networking technologies for real-time interaction. Participants generally meet in special conference rooms equipped with cameras and screens for transmitting images and documents; these systems are used by scientists, researchers, and top executives for collaboration. More conventional videoconference rooms may cost \$5 000 to \$80 000 each. Whether using high- or low-end conferencing tools, participants do not have to journey to distant meetings. Organizations reduce travel expenses, travel time, and employee fatigue.

Videoconferencing combines video, audio, and software to connect collaborators in real time.

Web Conferencing

Participants can take part in "real life" meetings from the comfort of their offices. Web conferencing is similar to videoconferencing but may work with or without transmission of images of the participants. Attendees use their computers to access an online virtual meeting room where they can present PowerPoint slides or share spreadsheets or Word documents, just as they might do in a face-to-face meeting. They can even demonstrate products and make changes in real time during a meeting.

Web conferencing enables collaborators to use their computers in sharing documents, data, and slide shows.

A variety of reasonably priced commercial conferencing tools enable you to launch meetings by sending instant messages to attendees, who click on an embedded link to join the group. Participants are generally connected to a phone conference call. On their computers, attendees see the presenter's desktop and all the actions performed there—from viewing Web pages to stepping through a presentation. They can also participate with each other using instant messaging in a chat window. Constantly evolving, Web conferencing is changing the way businesspeople work together.

Instant Messaging (IM)

Once used almost exclusively by teenagers, instant messaging (IM) is now increasingly accepted as a communication tool in the workplace. In our fast-paced world, many business communicators find that even e-mail is not swift enough. Instead they rely on instant messaging to deliver messages immediately and directly to the receiver's desktop. Minor matters can be cleared up instantly. Group discussions can

Instant messaging is useful for immediate online conversations.

be easily initiated with three or more participants. Perhaps the most useful feature of this software tool is the concept of *presence*—awareness of the availability of the recipient. Colleagues may use IM to see whether someone is available for incoming calls or to have a quick online chat. Instant messaging is especially useful for back-and-forth online conversations, such as a customer communicating with a tech support person to solve a problem. Businesses use instant messaging to communicate with customers, colleagues, and vendors down the hall or across the world.

Blogs

Blogs are interactive online journals with information that team members can see and comment on.

As discussed earlier, *blogs* are a type of interactive online journal that allows collaborators to share information in one central location. A blog is a one-to-many form of communication. That is, one person speaks to an audience who can comment on, but not change, the content. Blogs are especially helpful for cross-departmental teams and when new members must get up to speed quickly. A team leader's blog can provide all project information at one central location, usually on the company's intranet. The leader can update an entire team on progress, goals, and deadlines.

Blogs reduce time spent in unnecessary meetings by allowing minor matters to be handled online. Background and preparatory information can be circulated before virtual or face-to-face meetings. Unlike e-mail messages, blogs are Web-based documents. They can be archived and searched by category, name, title, project, special interest, or authority. As a result, information remains stored, categorized, and accessible—even if the knowledge worker who posted the blog leaves the organization. Most companies use blogs behind corporate firewalls to protect company information.

Wikis

Wikis are easy-to-use collaborative Web sites where people can add, change, or delete information.

A *wiki* is a collaborative Web site that enables anyone with access to add, change, or delete information. Content can be edited more easily than in a blog. A wiki is a many-to-many form of communication, whereas blogs are a one-to-many form of communication. Blogs resemble a personal broadcasting system, whereas wikis blend many voices to produce a forum. Like blogs, wiki documents can be digitally stored, categorized, and searched. Because of their ease of use, wikis are a natural when many people are working together and updating information.

Strengthening Your Teamwork Skills Now

Developing effective teamwork skills requires study, modelling, nurturing, and practice.

At one time or another in your current or future job, and certainly in your college or university career, you will be working on a team, so you need to start developing teamwork skills now. You can't just turn them on when you want them. They need to be studied, modelled, nurtured, and practised. You've just taken a look at the inner workings of teams, including the four phases of team development, the role of conflict, the characteristics of successful teams, participating in productive meetings, and using collaboration technology. In this book, in this course, and throughout your academic career, you will have opportunities to work with teams. Begin to analyze their dynamics. Who has the power and why? Who are the most successful team members and why? What would make a team function more effectively? How can you improve your teamwork skills?

Remember, job recruiters consider team skills among the most important requirements for many of today's jobs. You can become the number-one candidate for your dream job by developing team skills and acquiring experience now.

Summary of Learning Objectives

1 **Discuss why groups and teams are formed.** Many organizations have found that groups and teams are more effective than individuals because groups make better decisions, respond faster, increase productivity, achieve greater buy-in, reduce resistance to change, improve employee morale, and result in reduced risk for individuals. Businesses are increasingly turning to *self-directed teams*, which are characterized by clearly stated goals, autonomy, decision-making authority, frequent communication, and ongoing training.

2 **Describe team development, team and group roles, dealing with conflict, and methods for reaching group decisions.** Teams typically go through four stages of development: forming, storming, norming, and performing. To resolve conflict, team members should listen, understand the other's point of view, show a concern for the relationship, look for common ground, invent new problem-solving options, and reach an agreement based on what is fair. Open discussion of conflict prevents *groupthink*, a condition that leads to faulty decisions. Methods for reaching group decisions include majority, consensus, minority, averaging, and authority rule with discussion.

3 **Identify the characteristics of successful teams, including an emphasis on workplace etiquette.** The most effective teams are usually small and diverse; that is, they are made up of people representing different ages, genders, and backgrounds. Successful teams agree on their purpose and procedures. They are able to channel conflict into constructive discussion and reach consensus. They accept their ethical responsibilities, encourage open communication, listen actively, provide feedback, and have fun. Members are able to collaborate rather than compete, and leadership is often a shared responsibility depending on the situation and expertise required. Successful team members are polite and courteous. They are aware of noise levels, they value others' time, and they respect coworkers' boundaries. They freely use *please* and *thank you*, and they praise team members for work well done.

4 **List techniques for organizing team-based written and oral presentations.** In preparing to work together, teams should limit their size, name a meeting leader, and decide whether they wish to make decisions by consensus, majority rule, or some other method. They should work out their schedules, discuss the value of conflict, and decide how to deal with team members who do not do their share. They should decide on the purpose, form, and procedures for preparing the final document or presentation. They must brainstorm for ideas, assign topics, establish deadlines, and discuss how to ensure information accuracy. In composing the first draft of a report or presentation, they should use the same software and meet to discuss drafts and rehearsals. For written reports, one person should probably compose the final draft and the group should evaluate it. For group presentations, they need to work for consistency of design, format, and vocabulary. At least five rehearsals, one of which should be videotaped, will enhance the final presentation.

5 **Discuss how to plan and participate in productive meetings.** Call a meeting only when urgent two-way communication is necessary. Limit participants to those directly involved. Distribute an agenda in advance, start the meeting on time, and keep the discussion on track. Confront conflict openly by letting each person present his or her views fully before having the group decide which direction to take. Summarize what was said and end the meeting on

time. Follow up by distributing minutes of the meeting and verifying that action items are being accomplished.

6 **Explain the usefulness of collaborative technologies such as voice conferencing, videoconferencing, Web conferencing, instant messaging, blogs, and wikis.** *Voice conferencing* enables one or more people in a work area to use an enhanced speakerphone to confer with others by telephone. *Videoconferencing* combines video, audio, and networking technologies for real-time interaction in special viewing rooms. *Web conferencing* enables participants to stay in their offices, using their computers, while presenting slides and sharing documents in a virtual real-time meeting. Participants can talk to each other through a conference call. *Instant messaging* is useful for fast back-and-forth online conversations. *Blogs* are a type of interactive online journal that allows collaborators to share information in one central location. Because blogs are Web-based documents, they can be archived and searched, thus making information permanently accessible. *Wikis* are collaborative Web sites that enable anyone with access to add, change, or delete information.

chapter review

1. List seven reasons that explain why organizations are forming groups and teams. (Obj. 1)
2. How are virtual teams different from face-to-face teams? (Obj. 1)
3. To be most successful, self-directed teams need to have what characteristics? (Obj. 1)
4. What are the four phases of team development? Is it best to move through the stages quickly? Why or why not? (Obj. 2)
5. Compare and contrast positive and negative team behaviour. (Obj. 2)
6. What is *groupthink*? (Obj. 2)
7. Why can diverse teams be more effective than homogeneous teams? (Obj. 3)
8. Why are team decisions based on consensus generally better than decisions reached by majority rule? (Obj. 3)
9. What is the best way to set team deadlines when time to complete a project is short? (Obj. 4)
10. In completing a team-written report, should all team members work together to write the report? Why or why not? (Obj. 4)
11. When groups or teams meet, what are seven ground rules they should begin with? (Obj. 5)
12. How is video conferencing different from Web conferencing? (Obj. 6)
13. What are blogs and wikis, how do they differ, and why are they valuable to collaborators? (Obj. 6)

critical thinking

1. Compare the advantages and disadvantages of using teams in today's workplace. (Objs. 1–3)
2. What kinds of conflict could erupt during the "storming" phase of team development? Should conflict be avoided? (Obj. 2)
3. How would you comment on this statement made by an executive? "If you can't orchestrate a meeting, then you are of little use to an organization." (Obj. 5)
4. Compare the advantages and disadvantages of face-to-face meetings with virtual meetings using teleconferencing and videoconferencing. (Obj. 5)

activities

2.1 Advantages of Teams: Convincing Your Boss (Obj. 1)

Your boss or organization leader comes to you and asks you to take on a big job. Use your imagination to select a task such as developing a Web site or organizing a fundraising campaign. You are flattered that your boss respects you and thinks you capable of completing the task, but you think that a team could do a better job than an individual.

Your Task. What arguments would you use to convince your boss that a team could work better than an individual?

2.2 Reaching Group Decisions: Which Method? (Objs. 1 and 2)

TEAM

Your Task. In small groups decide which decision strategy is best for the following situations:

a. Union employees numbering 600 or more must decide whether to strike or remain on the job.
b. Appointed by management, an employee team is charged with making recommendations regarding casual Fridays. Management feels that too many employees are abusing the privilege.
c. The owner of your company is meeting with all managers to decide which departments will be allowed to move into a new facility.
d. Members of a homeowners' association must decide which members will become directors.
e. An employee committee of three members (two supervisors and the manager) must decide on promotions within a department.

2.3 Analyzing Team Formation, Decision Making, and Group Roles (Objs. 1–3)

Team members of small groups play a number of different roles as their groups are formed and decisions are made. To better understand the dynamics of group formation, decision making, and group roles, you will form small groups to discuss one of the following topics.

Your Task. Decide on a team leader and a recorder. Discuss a topic for ten minutes (or as long as your instructor directs). As the discussion progresses, analyze the comments made and the group roles they represent. Then, as a group, draft an outline of the major points discussed, your team decision, and the specific roles played in the discussion. Your instructor may ask you to report to the class or prepare a group memo summarizing your discussion.

a. Should an employee be allowed to sell products such as Avon items or Girl Guide cookies at work?
b. Should an employee be allowed to send personal e-mail messages during breaks or lunch hours? How about using company computers after hours to prepare a college report? What if your supervisor gives her permission but asks you to keep quiet about it?
c. Should companies have the right to monitor e-mail messages sent by employees? If so, is it necessary for an organization to inform the employees of its policy?

2.4 Workplace Etiquette: Avoiding Shooting Yourself in the Foot (Obj. 2)

RESEARCH

When the economy slows down, business interactions seem to become more formal, according to two etiquette experts. Dining manners, greeting etiquette, and body language awareness become more important in tough times. You can learn how to avoid "shooting yourself in the foot" by reading articles on workplace etiquette.

Your Task. Using online search tools, find at least one article that addresses the following issues.

a. How have business interactions changed in the past few years?
b. What are the guidelines for effective language use?
c. In what ways are people misusing e-mail and cell phones?

2.5 Groupthink: Are We a Bit Overeager? (Obj. 2)

You are a member of the Community Service Committee, which is part of the Business Newcomers' Club in your town. Your committee must decide what local cause to support with funds earned at the Newcomers' annual celebrity auction. At the meeting, Matt, the committee chair, suggested that the group support a local literacy program. His aunt is literacy coordinator at the Davis Outreach Centre, and he knows that the group would be delighted with any contribution. Heather said that she favoured any cause that was educational. Eric announced that he had to leave for an appointment in five minutes. Mona described an article she read in the newspaper about surprisingly large numbers of people who were functionally illiterate. Kevin said that he thought they ought to consider other causes such as the homeless centre, but Matt dismissed the idea, saying, "The homeless already receive lots of funding. Besides, our contribution could make a real difference with the literacy program." The other members of the committee persuaded Kevin to agree with them, and the committee voted unanimously to support the literacy program.

Your Task. In class discussion, answer the following questions:

a. What aspects of groupthink were at work in this committee?
b. What conditions contribute to groupthink?
c. What can groups do to avoid groupthink?

2.6 Planning a Meeting: Spring Campus Event (Obj. 5)

Assume that the next meeting of your campus student organization (SO) will discuss preparations for a careers day in the spring. The group will hear reports from committees working on speakers, business recruiters, publicity, reservation of campus space, setup of booths, and any other matters you can think of.

Your Task. As president of your SO, prepare an agenda for the meeting. Compose your introductory remarks to open the meeting. Your instructor may ask you to submit these two documents or use them in staging an actual meeting in class.

2.7 Evaluating Meetings: Effective or Ineffective? (Obj. 5)

Attend a structured meeting of an academic, social, business, or other organization. Compare the way the meeting is conducted with the suggestions presented in this chapter. Why did the meeting succeed or fail? In a class discussion or in a memo to your instructor, discuss your analysis.

2.8 Videoconferencing: Using the Web for Research (Obj. 6)

Your boss wants to learn more about workplace videoconferencing because many company meetings require travelling. She thinks that the company may be able to save money and reduce employee fatigue if it could find a way to cut back travelling to meetings. Because she is a busy executive and a Web novice, she asks you to do research. She wants you to find three Web sites that will help her learn more about the terminology, functions, and costs involved in videoconferencing.

Your Task. Use a search engine such as Google (www.google.ca) to locate three helpful sites describing videoconferencing. For this purpose you should definitely consider commercial sites, including some "sponsored" sites (this means that a company paid the search engine to be listed prominently). Watch any demonstrations and evaluate what you see. In an e-mail or memo to your instructor, submit a list of the three best sites that you find. Provide a short description of each site and why you think your boss should see it.

Rich chapter resources are available on the Web site.

2.9 Webcasting: Who's Doing It? (Obj. 6)

Your company will be launching a new product shortly, and it is wondering whether webcasting is a possible way to announce it.

Your Task. Your boss asks you to use the Web or InfoTrac to find examples of three organizations that have used webcasting recently. In a class discussion or in an e-mail to your instructor, list three webcasts and explain briefly who announced what.

C.L.U.E. review 2

On a separate sheet edit the following sentences to correct faults in grammar, punctuation, spelling, numbers, proofreading, and word use.

1. Our companies management counsel had all ready decided to apoint a investigative team, however, they acted to slow.
2. Organization's are forming teams for at least 3 good reasons; better decisions, more faster response times and increase productivity.
3. Most teams go through 4 development phases, Forming, Storming, Norming, and Performing.
4. Some group members play dysfunctional rolls and they disrupt the groups progress toward it's goal.
5. Successful self directed teams are autonomous, that is they can hire fire and discipline there own member.
6. Although we tried to reach a consensus several Managers and even the Vice President opposed the hole proposal.
7. At last months Staff meeting the CEO and him complemented the teams efforts and made warm supportive comments.
8. Rather then schedule many face to face meetings the team decided to investigate a three thousand dollar desk top videoconferencing system.
9. When conflict erupted at our teams january meeting we made a conscience effort to confront the underlying issues.
10. 55 people are expected to attend the Training Session on April 15th consequently her and I must find a more larger room.

chapter 3

Workplace Listening and Nonverbal Communication

objectives

1. Explain the importance of listening in the workplace and describe three types of workplace listening.
2. Discuss the listening process and its barriers.
3. Enumerate ten techniques for improving workplace listening.
4. Define nonverbal communication and explain its functions.
5. Describe the forms of nonverbal communication and how they can be used positively in your career.
6. List specific techniques for improving nonverbal communication skills in the workplace.

springboard *to discussion*

Most people spend five times longer on electronic communications than touching other people. In fact, Canadians spend more time on nonverbal communication with their pets than they do with friends, coworkers, and acquaintances. With so much interaction happening online these days, more time is spent touching keyboards than each other.[1]

Listening in the Workplace

learning objective 1

"Companies that listen are very successful. They listen to their clients, employees, and vendors to monitor and take corrective action when necessary to maintain alignment with their business environment."[2] Today's employers are aware that listening is a critical employee and management skill. In addition, listening to customers takes on increasing importance as our economy becomes ever more service-oriented.

But, you may be thinking, everyone knows how to listen. Most of us believe that listening is an automatic response to noise. We do it without thinking. Perhaps that explains why so many of us are poor listeners. In this chapter we'll explore the importance of listening, the kinds of listening required in the workplace, the listening process, listening barriers, and how to become a better listener. You'll also study the powerful effect of nonverbal messages. These include all unwritten and unspoken messages. Although many of the tips for improving your listening and nonverbal skills will be effective in your personal life, our discussion centres primarily on workplace and employment needs.

As you learned earlier, workers are doing more communicating than ever before, largely because of the Internet, team environments, global competition, and emphasis on customer service. A vital ingredient in every successful workplace is high-quality communication. And three-quarters of high-quality communication involves listening.[3]

Listening skills are critical for career success, organization effectiveness, and worker satisfaction.

Listening skills are important for career success, organization effectiveness, and worker satisfaction. In its Employability Skills 2000+, the Conference Board of Canada lists communication skills (reading and understanding information, writing and speaking so others understand, listening and asking questions, sharing information, and using relevant knowledge and skills to explain ideas) among those fundamental skills required as a base for further development.[4]

Listening is especially important in the workplace because we spend so much time doing it. Most workers spend 30 to 45 percent of their communication time listening,[5] whereas executives spend 60 to 70 percent of their communication time listening.[6]

Poor Listening Habits

Although executives and workers devote the bulk of their communication time to listening, research suggests that they're not very good at it. In fact, most of us are poor listeners. Some estimates indicate that only half of the oral messages heard in a day are completely understood.[7] Experts say that we listen at only 25 percent

Most of us listen at only 25 percent efficiency.

We are inefficient listeners because of lack of training, competing sounds, slowness of speech, and daydreaming.

efficiency. In other words, we ignore, forget, distort, or misunderstand 75 percent of everything we hear.

Poor listening habits may result from several factors. Lack of training is one significant reason. Few schools give as much emphasis to listening as they do to the development of reading, speaking, and writing skills. In addition, our listening skills may be less than perfect because of the large number of competing sounds and stimuli in our lives that interfere with concentration. Finally, we are inefficient listeners because we are able to process speech much faster than others can speak. While most speakers talk at about 125 to 250 words per minute, listeners can think at 1000 to 3000 words per minute.[8] The resulting lag time fosters daydreaming, which clearly reduces listening efficiency.

Types of Workplace Listening

In an employment environment, you can expect to be involved in many types of listening. These include listening to superiors, listening to colleagues and team members, and listening to customers. If you are an entry-level employee, you will probably be most concerned with listening to superiors. But you must also develop skills for listening to colleagues and team members. As you advance in your career and enter the ranks of management, you will need skills for listening to subordinates. Finally, the entire organization must listen to customers to compete in today's service-oriented economy.

Listening to superiors involves hearing instructions, assignments, and explanations of work procedures.

Listening to Superiors. On the job, one of your most important tasks will be listening to instructions, assignments, and explanations about how to do your work. You will be listening to learn and to comprehend. To focus totally on the speaker, be sure you are not distracted by noisy surroundings or other tasks. Don't take phone calls, and don't try to complete another job while listening with one ear. Show your interest by leaning forward and striving for good eye contact.

Listen carefully, take selective notes, and don't interrupt.

Above all, take notes. Don't rely on your memory. Details are easy to forget. Taking selective notes also conveys to the speaker your seriousness about hearing accurately and completely. Don't interrupt. When the speaker finishes, paraphrase the instructions in your own words. Ask pertinent questions in a nonthreatening manner. And don't be afraid to ask "dumb" questions if it means you won't have to do a job twice. Avoid criticizing or arguing when you are listening to a superior. Your goals should be to hear accurately and to convey an image of competence.

Listening to colleagues and teammates involves critical listening and discriminative listening.

Listening to Colleagues and Teammates. Much of your listening will result from interactions with fellow workers and teammates. In these exchanges two kinds of listening are important. *Critical listening* enables you to judge and evaluate what you are hearing. You will be listening to decide whether the speaker's message is fact, fiction, or opinion. You will also be listening to decide whether an argument is based on logic or emotion. Critical listening requires an effort on your part. You must remain objective, particularly when you disagree with what you are hearing. Control your tendency to prejudge. Let the speaker have a chance to complete the message before you evaluate it. *Discriminative listening* is necessary when you must understand and remember. It means you must identify main ideas, understand a logical argument, and recognize the purpose of the message.

Listening to Customers. As the North American economy becomes increasingly service-oriented, the new management mantra has become "customers rule." Yet, despite 50 years of talk about customer service, the concept of "customer-centric" business is still in its infancy.[9] Many organizations are just now learning that listening to customers results in increased sales and profitability as well as improved customer acquisition and retention. The simple truth is that consumers feel better about companies that value their opinions. Listening is an acknowledgment of caring and is a potent retention tool. Customers want to be cared about; by showing that they care, companies fulfill a powerful human need.

Organizations that listen to customers improve sales and profitability.

How can organizations improve their customer listening techniques? Since employees are the eyes and ears of the organization, smart companies begin by hiring employees who genuinely care about customers. Listening organizations also train their employees to listen actively and to ask gentle, probing questions to ensure clear understanding. Employees trained in listening techniques are far more likely to elicit customer feedback and promote goodwill than untrained employees are.

The Listening Process and Its Barriers

learning objective

2

Listening takes place in four stages—perception, interpretation, evaluation, and action, as illustrated in Figure 3.1. Barriers, however, can obstruct the listening process. These barriers may be mental or physical.

The four stages of listening are perception, interpretation, evaluation, and action.

Perception

The listening process begins when you hear sounds and concentrate on them. The conscious act of listening begins when you focus on the sounds around you and select those you choose to hear. You tune in when you (1) sense that the message is important, (2) are interested in the topic, or (3) are in the mood to listen. Perception is reduced by impaired hearing, noisy surroundings, inattention, and pseudolistening. *Pseudolistening* occurs when listeners "fake it." They look as though they are listening, but their minds are wandering far off.

Figure 3.1 ***The Listening Process and Its Barriers***

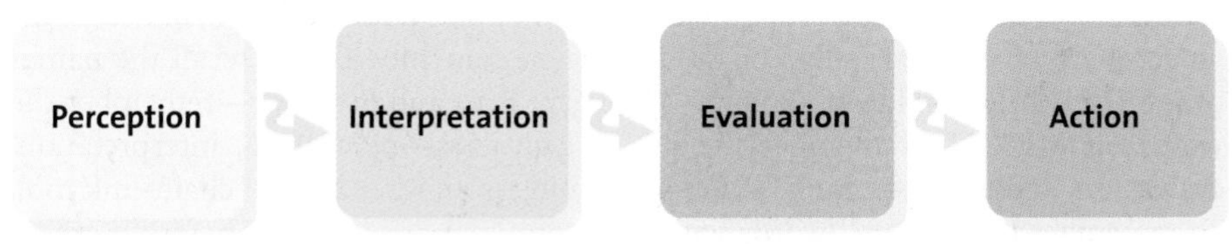

COMMON LISTENING BARRIERS

Mental Barriers	Physical and Other Barriers
Inattention	Hearing impairment
Prejudgment	Noisy surroundings
Frame of reference	Speaker's appearance
Closed-mindedness	Speaker's mannerisms
Pseudolistening	Lag time

Interpretation

Once you have focused your attention on a sound or message, you begin to interpret, or decode, it. As described in Chapter 1, interpretation of a message is coloured by your cultural, educational, and social frames of reference. The meanings you attach to the speaker's words are filtered through your expectations and total life experiences. Thus your interpretation of the speaker's meaning may be quite different from what the speaker intended, because your frame of reference is different.

Evaluation

Evaluation involves separating fact from opinion and judging messages objectively.

After interpreting the meaning of a message, you analyze its merit and draw conclusions. To do this, you attempt to separate fact from opinion. Good listeners try to be objective, and they avoid prejudging the message. Thus, to evaluate a message accurately and objectively, you should (1) consider all the information, (2) be aware of your own biases, and (3) avoid jumping to hasty conclusions.

Action

Action involves storing a message in memory, reacting, or supplying feedback.

Responding to a message may involve storing the message in memory for future use, reacting with a physical response (a frown, a smile, a laugh), or supplying feedback to the speaker. Listener feedback is essential because it helps clarify the message so that it can be decoded accurately. Feedback also helps the speaker to find out whether the message is getting through clearly. In one-to-one conversation, of course, no clear distinction exists between the roles of listener and speaker—you give or receive feedback as your roles alternate.

Enhancing Retention

Unfortunately, most of us are able to recall only 50 percent of the information we heard a day earlier and only 20 percent after two days.[10] How can we improve our retention?

Retention can be improved by deciding to remember, structuring incoming information to form relationships, and reviewing.

Memory training specialists say that effective remembering involves three factors: (1) deciding to remember, (2) structuring the incoming information to form relationships, and (3) reviewing. In the first step you determine what information is worth remembering. Once you have established a positive mindset, you look for a means of organizing the incoming information to form relationships. Chain links can help you associate the unfamiliar with something familiar. For instance, make an acronym of the first letters of the item to be remembered. To recall the names of the Great Lakes—Huron, Ontario, Michigan, Erie, and Superior—remember the word "HOMES." To remember the listening process—perception, interpretation, evaluation, and action—think "PIE-A." Rhyming is another helpful chain-link tool. To remember how to spell words with "EI" combinations, think "I before E except after C."

The world memory champion uses a device called *loci*. To remember the sequence of a pack of 52 playing cards, for example, he associates each card with a character. The queen of diamonds he might imagine covered head to foot in diamonds. Then he places each character in a location (hence, *loci*), say around the local golf course, which has 52 stages.[11]

To further improve retention, take notes and rewrite them immediately after listening.

One of the most reliable ways to improve retention is to take notes of the important ideas to be remembered. Rewriting within ten minutes of completing listening improves your notes and takes advantage of peak recall time, which immediately follows listening.

The final step in improving retention is reviewing your notes, repeating your acronym, or saying your rhyme to move the targeted information into long-term memory. Frequent reviews help strengthen your memory connections.

Improving Workplace Listening

learning objective

3

Listening on the job is more difficult than listening in classes where experienced professors present well-organized lectures and repeat important points. Workplace listening is more challenging because information is often exchanged casually. It may be disorganized, unclear, and cluttered with extraneous facts. Moreover, your coworkers are usually friends. Because they are familiar with one another, they may not be as polite and respectful as they are with strangers. Friends tend to interrupt, jump to conclusions, and take each other for granted.

Listening in groups or listening to nonnative speakers further complicates the listening process. In groups, more than one person talks at once, and topics change rapidly. Group members are monitoring both verbal and nonverbal messages to learn what relates to their group roles. Listening to nonnative speakers often creates special challenges. You'll find suggestions for communicating across cultures in Chapter 4.

You listen better when you control distractions, become actively involved, separate facts from opinion, and identify important facts.

Ten Keys to Building Powerful Listening Skills

Despite the complexities and challenges of workplace listening, good listeners on the job must remember that their goal is to listen carefully and to *understand* what is being said so that they can do their work well. The following recommendations can help you improve your workplace listening effectiveness.

1. Control External and Internal Distractions. Move to an area where you can hear without conflicting noises or conversations. Block out surrounding physical distractions. Internally, try to focus totally on the speaker. If other projects are on your mind, put them on the back burner temporarily. When you are emotionally charged, whether angry or extremely happy, it's a good idea to postpone any serious listening.

2. Become Actively Involved. Show that you are listening closely by leaning forward and maintaining eye contact with the speaker. Don't fidget or try to complete another task at the same time you are listening. Listen to more than the spoken words. How are they said? What implied meaning, reasoning, and feelings do you hear behind the spoken words? Does the speaker's body language (eye contact, posture, movements) support or contradict the main message?

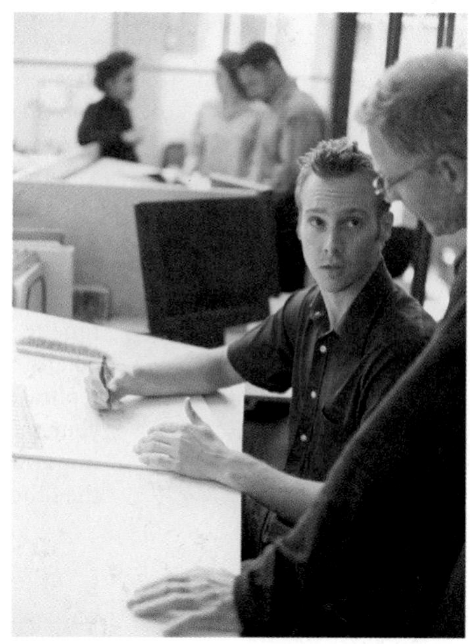

Listening on the job involves controlling external and internal distractions, becoming actively involved, identifying important facts, and taking notes. When listening to your boss, ask clarifying questions, but wait for the right moment.

Photo: © Ryan McVay/Photodisc/Getty Images

3. Separate Facts From Opinions. Facts are truths known to exist. Often, however, listeners must evaluate assertions to decide their validity. Good listeners consider whether speakers are credible and speaking within their areas of competence. They don't automatically accept assertions as facts.

4. Identify Important Facts. Speakers on the job often intersperse critical information with casual conversation. Unrelated topics pop up—ball scores, a customer's weird request, a computer glitch, the boss's extravagant new SUV. Your task is to select what's important and register it mentally. What step is next in your project? Who does what? What is your role?

You listen better when you refrain from interrupting, ask clarifying questions, paraphrase, capitalize on lag time, take notes, and observe gender differences.

5. Don't Interrupt. While someone else has the floor, don't interrupt with a quick reply or opinion. And don't show nonverbal disagreement such as head shaking, rolling eyes, sarcastic snorting, or audible sighs. Good listeners let speakers have their say. Interruptions are not only impolite but they also prevent you from hearing the speaker's complete thought. Listeners who interrupt with their opinions sidetrack discussions and cause hard feelings.

6. Ask Clarifying Questions. Good listeners wait for the proper moment and then ask questions that do not attack the speaker. Instead of saying, "But I don't understand how you can say that," a good listener seeks clarification with questions such as "Please help me understand by explaining more about ..." Because questions can put you in the driver's seat, think about them in advance. Use open questions (those without set answers) to draw out feelings, motivations, ideas, and suggestions. Use closed, fact-finding questions to identify key factors in a discussion. And, by the way, don't ask a question unless you are ready to be quiet and listen to the answer.

7. Paraphrase to Increase Understanding. To make sure you understand a speaker, rephrase and summarize a message in your own words. Be objective and nonjudgmental. Remember, your goal is to understand what the speaker has said—not to show how mindless the speaker's words sound when parroted. Remember, too, that other workplace listeners will also benefit from a clear summary of what was said.

8. Capitalize on Lag Time. While you are waiting for a speaker's next idea, use the time to review what the speaker is saying. Separate the central idea, key points, and details. Sometimes you may have to supply the organization. Use lag time to silently rephrase and summarize the speaker's message. Another effective trick for keeping your mind from drifting is to try to guess what a speaker's next point will be. Most important, keep your mind focused on the speaker and his or her ideas—not on all the other work waiting for you.

9. Take Notes to Ensure Retention. Don't trust your memory. A wise person once said that he'd rather have a short pencil than a long memory. If you have a hallway conversation with a colleague and don't have a pencil handy, make a mental note of the important items. Then write them down as soon as possible. Even with seemingly easily remembered facts or instructions, jot them down to ease your mind and also to be sure you understand them correctly. Two weeks later you'll be glad you did. Be sure you have a good place to store notes on various projects, such as file folders, notebooks, or computer files.

10. Be Aware of Gender Differences. Men tend to listen for facts, whereas women tend to perceive listening as an opportunity to connect with the other person on a personal level.[12] Men tend to use interrupting behaviour to control conversations, whereas women generally interrupt to communicate assent, to elaborate on an idea of another group member, or to participate in the topic of conversation.[13] Women listeners tend to be attentive, provide steady eye contact, remain stationary, and nod their heads.[14] Male listeners are less attentive, provide sporadic eye contact, and move around. Being aware of these tendencies will make you a more sensitive and knowledgeable listener.

Checklist for Improving Listening

- ✓ **Stop talking.** Accept the role of listener by concentrating on the speaker's words, not on what your response will be.
- ✓ **Work hard at listening.** Become actively involved; expect to learn something.
- ✓ **Block out competing thoughts.** Concentrate on the message. Don't allow yourself to daydream during lag time.
- ✓ **Control the listening environment.** Move to a quiet area where you won't be interrupted by telephone calls or visitors. Check to be certain that listeners can hear speakers.
- ✓ **Maintain an open mind.** Know your biases and try to correct for them. Be tolerant of less abled and different-looking speakers. Provide verbal and nonverbal feedback. Look alert by leaning forward.
- ✓ **Paraphrase the speaker's ideas.** Silently repeat the message in your own words, sort out the main points, and identify supporting details. In conversation sum up the main points to confirm what was said.
- ✓ **Listen between the lines.** Observe nonverbal cues and interpret the feelings of the speaker. What is really being said?
- ✓ **Distinguish between facts and opinions.** Know the difference between factual statements and opinions stated as assertions.
- ✓ **Capitalize on lag time.** Use spare moments to organize, review, anticipate, challenge, and weigh the evidence.
- ✓ **Use memory devices.** If the information is important, develop acronyms, links, or rhymes to help you remember.
- ✓ **Take selective notes.** If you are hearing instructions or important data, record the major points; then revise your notes immediately or verify them with the speaker.

Communicating Through Nonverbal Messages

learning objective

4

Understanding messages often involves more than merely listening to spoken words. Nonverbal cues also carry powerful meanings. Nonverbal communication includes all unwritten and unspoken messages, both intentional and unintentional. Eye contact, facial expression, body movements, space, time, distance, appearance—all of these nonverbal cues influence the way a message is interpreted, or decoded, by the receiver. Many of the nonverbal messages that we send are used intentionally to accompany spoken words.

Because nonverbal communication can be an important tool for you to use and control in the workplace, you need to learn more about its functions and forms.

Functions of Nonverbal Communication

Nonverbal communication functions help to convey meaning in at least five ways. As you become more aware of the following functions of nonverbal communication, you will be better able to use these silent codes to your advantage in the workplace.

- **To complement and illustrate.** Nonverbal messages can amplify, modify, or provide details for a verbal message. For example, in describing the size of a cell phone, a speaker holds his fingers apart 12 centimetres. In pumping up sales reps, the manager jams his fist into the opposite hand to indicate the strong effort required.
- **To reinforce and accentuate.** Skilled speakers raise their voices to convey important ideas, but they whisper to suggest secrecy. A grimace forecasts painful news, whereas a big smile intensifies good news. A neat, well-equipped office reinforces a message of professionalism.
- **To replace and substitute.** Many gestures substitute for words: nodding your head for *yes*, or making a V for victory. In sign language, a complex set of gestures totally replaces spoken words.
- **To control and regulate.** Nonverbal messages are important regulators in conversation. Shifts in eye contact, slight head movements, changes in posture, raising of the eyebrows, nodding of the head, and voice inflection—all of these cues tell speakers when to continue, to repeat, to elaborate, to hurry up, or to finish.
- **To contradict.** To be sarcastic, a speaker might hold his nose while stating that your new perfume is wonderful. In the workplace, individuals may send contradictory messages with words or actions.

In the workplace people may not be aware that they are sending contradictory messages. Researchers have found that when verbal and nonverbal messages contradict each other, listeners tend to believe and act on the nonverbal message.

Because nonverbal messages may speak louder than words, make sure that your nonverbal cues reinforce your spoken words.

The nonverbal messages in many situations speak louder than the words uttered. In one experiment speakers delivered a positive message but averted their eyes as they spoke. Listeners perceived the overall message to be negative. Moreover, listeners thought that gaze aversion suggested nonaffection, superficiality, lack of trust, and nonreceptivity.[15] Effective communicators must make sure that all their nonverbal messages reinforce their spoken words and their professional goals. To make sure that you're on the right track to nonverbal communication competency, let's look more carefully at the specific forms of nonverbal communication.

learning objective

5

Forms of Nonverbal Communication

Instead of conveying meaning with words, nonverbal messages carry their meaning in a number of different forms ranging from facial expressions to body language and even to clothes. Each of us sends and receives thousands of nonverbal messages daily in our business and personal lives. Although the following discussion covers all forms of nonverbal communication, we will be especially concerned with workplace applications. As you learn about the messages sent by eye contact, facial expressions, posture, and gestures, as well as the use of time, space, territory, and appearance—think about how you can use these nonverbal cues positively in your career.

Eye Contact. The eyes have been called the "windows to the soul." Even if communicators can't look directly into the soul, they consider the eyes to be the most accurate predictor of a speaker's true feelings and attitudes. Most of us cannot look another person straight in the eyes and lie. As a result, we tend to believe people who look directly at us. We have less confidence in and actually distrust those who cannot maintain eye contact. Sustained eye contact suggests trust and admiration; brief eye contact signifies fear or stress. Prolonged eye contact, however, can be intrusive and intimidating.

The eyes are thought to be the most accurate predictor of a speaker's true feelings.

Good eye contact enables the message sender to determine whether a receiver is paying attention, showing respect, responding favourably, or feeling distress. From the receiver's perspective, good eye contact reveals the speaker's sincerity, confidence, and truthfulness. Since eye contact is a learned skill, however, you must be respectful of people who do not maintain it. You must also remember that nonverbal cues, including eye contact, have different meanings in various cultures. You'll learn more about the cultural influence of nonverbal cues in Chapter 4.

Facial Expression. The expression on a communicator's face can be almost as revealing of emotion as the eyes. Researchers estimate that the human face can display over 250 000 different expressions.[16] Although a few people can control these expressions and maintain a "poker face" when they want to hide their feelings, most of us display our emotions openly. Raising or lowering the eyebrows, squinting the eyes, swallowing nervously, clenching the jaw, smiling broadly—these voluntary and involuntary facial expressions supplement or entirely replace verbal messages.

Posture and Gestures. An individual's general posture can convey anything from high status and self-confidence to shyness and submissiveness. Leaning toward a speaker suggests attraction and interest; pulling away or shrinking back denotes fear, distrust, anxiety, or disgust. Similarly, gestures can communicate entire thoughts via simple movements. But remember that these nonverbal cues may have vastly different meanings in different cultures.

Erect posture sends a message of confidence, competence, diligence, and strength.

In the workplace you can make a good impression by controlling your posture and gestures. When speaking, make sure your upper body is aligned with the person to whom you're talking. Erect posture sends a message of confidence, competence, diligence, and strength. Gestures are also important if used effectively.

Time. How we structure and use time tells observers about our personality and attitudes. For example, when someone gives a visitor a prolonged interview, she signals her respect for, interest in, and approval of the visitor or the topic being discussed. By sharing her valuable time, she sends a clear nonverbal message. Likewise, when an individual twice arrives late for a meeting, it could mean that the meeting has low priority to him, that he is a self-centred person, or that he has little self-discipline. These are assumptions that typical North Americans might make. In other cultures and regions, though, punctuality is viewed differently. In the workplace you can send positive nonverbal messages by being on time for meetings and appointments, staying on task during meetings, and giving ample time to appropriate projects and individuals.

Being on time sends a positive nonverbal message in North American workplaces.

Space. How we arrange things in the space around us tells something about ourselves and our objectives. Whether its personal space, an office, or a department, people reveal themselves in the design and grouping of furniture within that space. Generally, the more formal the arrangement, the more formal and closed the communication environment.

The way an office is arranged can send nonverbal messages about the openness of its occupant.

FIGURE 3.2 ***Four Space Zones for Social Interaction***

Intimate Zone
(30 TO 45 CM)

Personal Zone
(45 CM TO 1 M)

Social Zone
(1 TO 3.65 M)

Public Zone
(3.65 M OR MORE)

Photos L to R: © Javier Pierini/Digital Vision/Getty; © Andreas Pollok/Digital Vision/Getty; © Javier Pierini/Digital Vision/Getty; © Jacobs Stock Photography/Getty

Territory. Each of us has certain areas that we feel are our own territory, whether it's a specific spot or just the space around us. We all maintain zones of privacy in which we feel comfortable. Figure 3.2 categorizes the four zones of social interaction among North Americans, as formulated by anthropologist Edward T. Hall. Notice that we North Americans are a bit standoffish; only intimate friends and family may stand closer than about 45 centimetres. If someone violates that territory, we feel uncomfortable and defensive and may step back to reestablish our space.

Your appearance and the appearance of your documents convey nonverbal messages.

Appearance of Business Documents. The way a letter, memo, or report looks can have either a positive or negative effect on the receiver. Through their postage, stationery, and printing, envelopes can suggest routine, important, or junk mail. Letters and reports can look neat, professional, well organized, and attractive—or just the opposite. Sloppy, hurriedly written documents convey negative nonverbal messages regarding both the content and the sender. Among the worst offenders are e-mail messages.

Although they seem like conversation, e-mails are business documents that create a permanent record and often a bad impression. Sending an e-mail message full of errors conveys a damaging nonverbal message. It says that the writer doesn't care enough about this message to take the time to make it read well or look good. The sender immediately doubts the credibility of the sender. How much faith can you put in someone who can't spell, capitalize, or punctuate and won't make the effort to communicate clearly?

In succeeding chapters you'll learn how to create documents that send positive nonverbal messages through their appearance, format, organization, readability, and correctness.

Appearance of People. The way you look—your clothing, grooming, and posture—telegraphs an instant nonverbal message about you. Based on what they see, viewers make quick judgments about your status, credibility, personality, and potential. Business communicators who look the part are more likely to be successful in working with superiors, colleagues, and customers. Because appearance is such a powerful force in business, some aspiring professionals are turning for help to image consultants.

career coach

Perils of Casual Apparel in the Workplace

Your choice of work clothes sends a strong nonverbal message about you. It also affects the way you work. Some surveys suggest that the pendulum is swinging back to more conservative attire in the workplace,[17] although employers and employees have mixed feelings about what to wear to work.

What Critics Are Saying

Some employers oppose casual dress because, in their opinion, too many workers push the boundaries of what is acceptable. They contend that absenteeism, tardiness, and flirtatious behaviour have increased since dress-down policies began to be implemented. Relaxed dress codes also lead to reduced productivity and lax behaviour. Image counsellor Judith Rasband claims that the general casualization of America has resulted in an overall decline in civility. "Manners break down, you begin to feel down, and you're not as effective," she says.[18] Others fear that the authority and credibility of casually attired executives, particularly females and minorities, are undermined.[19] Moreover, customers are often turned off by casually attired employees.[20]

What Supporters Are Saying

Supporters argue that comfortable clothes and relaxed working environments lift employee morale, increase employee creativity, and improve internal communication. Employees appreciate reduced clothing-related expenses, while employers use casual dress as a recruitment and retention tool. Because employees seem to love casual dress, nine out of ten employers have adopted casual-dress days for at least part of the work week—even if it is just on Fridays during the summer.

What Employees Need to Know

The following suggestions, gleaned from surveys and articles about casual-dress trends in the workplace, can help future and current employees avoid casual-dress blunders.

- For job interviews, dress conservatively or call ahead to ask the interviewer or the receptionist what is appropriate.
- Find out what your company allows. Ask whether a dress-down policy is available. Observe what others are wearing on casual-dress days.
- If your company has no casual-dress policy, volunteer to work with management to develop relevant guidelines, including illustrations of suitable casual attire.
- Avoid wearing the following items: T-shirts, sandals, flip-flops, shoes without socks, backless dresses, tank tops, shorts, miniskirts, spandex, athletic shoes, hiking boots, baseball caps, and visors.[21]
- When meeting customers, dress as well as or better than they do.

Invest in appropriate, professional-looking clothing and accessories; quality is more important than quantity. Avoid flashy garments, clunky jewellery, garish makeup, and overpowering colognes. Pay attention to good grooming, including a neat hairstyle, body cleanliness, polished shoes, and clean nails. Project confidence in your posture, both standing and sitting.

One of the latest fashion rages is body art in the form of tattoos. Once seen primarily on bikers and sailors, inked images adorn the bodies of those who seek to be recognized. Think twice, however, before displaying "tats" at work. They may make a person feel distinctive and slightly daring, but they could derail a professional career.

A less risky trend is the movement toward one or more days per week of casual dress at work. Be aware, though, that casual clothes change the image you project and may also affect your work style. See the accompanying Career Coach box regarding the pros and cons of casual apparel.

FIGURE 3.3 ***Sending Positive Nonverbal Signals in the Workplace***

Eye contact	Maintain direct but not prolonged eye contact.
Facial expression	Express warmth with frequent smiles.
Posture	Convey self-confidence with an erect stance.
Gestures	Suggest accessibility with open-palm gestures.
Time	Be on time; use time judiciously.
Space	Maintain neat, functional work areas.
Territory	Use closeness to show warmth and to reduce status differences.
Business documents	Produce careful, neat, professional, well-organized messages.
Appearance	Be well groomed, neat, and appropriately dressed.

In the preceding discussion of nonverbal communication, you have learned that each of us gives and responds to thousands of nonverbal messages daily in our personal and work lives. You can harness the power of silent messages by reviewing Figure 3.3 and by studying the tips in the following checklist.

learning objective 6

Checklist of Techniques for Improving Nonverbal Communication Skills in the Workplace

- ✓ **Establish and maintain eye contact.** Remember that in North America appropriate eye contact signals interest, attentiveness, strength, and credibility.
- ✓ **Use posture to show interest.** Encourage communication interaction by leaning forward, sitting or standing erect, and looking alert.
- ✓ **Reduce or eliminate physical barriers.** Move out from behind a desk or lectern; shorten lines of communication; arrange meeting chairs in a circle.
- ✓ **Improve your decoding skills.** Watch facial expressions and body language to understand the complete verbal and nonverbal message being communicated.
- ✓ **Probe for more information.** When you perceive nonverbal cues that contradict verbal meanings, politely seek additional clues (*I'm not sure I understand, Please tell me more about …*, or *Do you mean that…?*).
- ✓ **Avoid assigning nonverbal meanings out of context.** Make nonverbal assessments only when you understand a situation or a culture.
- ✓ **Associate with people from diverse cultures.** Learn about other cultures to widen your knowledge and tolerance of intercultural nonverbal messages.
- ✓ **Appreciate the power of appearance.** Keep in mind that your personal appearance as well as that of your business documents and work space send immediate positive or negative messages to receivers.

- ✓ **Observe yourself on videotape.** Ensure that your verbal and nonverbal messages are in sync by taping and evaluating yourself making a presentation.

- ✓ **Enlist friends and family.** Ask them to monitor your conscious and unconscious body movements and gestures to help you become a more effective communicator.

Summary of Learning Objectives

1 **Explain the importance of listening in the workplace and describe three types of workplace listening.** A large part of the communication process involves listening. Good listeners advance more rapidly in their careers, and listening skills are increasingly important in our economy with its emphasis on customer service. Workers spend 30 to 45 percent of their communication time listening, whereas executives spend 60 to 70 percent. However, most of us listen at only 25 percent efficiency. Workplace listening involves listening to superiors, to colleagues, and to customers. When listening to superiors, take selective notes, don't interrupt, ask pertinent questions, and paraphrase what you hear. When listening to colleagues and teammates, listen critically to recognize facts and listen discriminatingly to identify main ideas and to understand logical arguments.

2 **Discuss the listening process and its barriers.** The listening process involves (a) perception of sounds, (b) interpretation of those sounds, (c) evaluation of meaning, and (d) action, which might involve a physical response or storage of the message in memory for future use. Mental barriers to listening include inattention, prejudgments, differing frames of reference, closed-mindedness, and pseudolistening. Physical and other barriers include hearing impairment, noisy surroundings, speaker's appearance, speaker's mannerisms, and lag time. Retention can be improved by developing a positive mindset, structuring the incoming information to form relationships, and reviewing.

3 **Enumerate ten techniques for improving workplace listening.** Listeners can improve their skills by controlling external and internal distractions, becoming actively involved, separating facts from opinions, identifying important facts, refraining from interrupting, asking clarifying questions, paraphrasing, taking advantage of lag time, taking notes to ensure retention, and being aware of gender differences.

4 **Define nonverbal communication and explain its functions.** Nonverbal communication includes all unwritten and unspoken messages, both intentional and unintentional. Its primary functions are to complement and illustrate, to reinforce and accentuate, to replace and substitute, to control and regulate, and to contradict. When verbal and nonverbal messages contradict each other, listeners tend to believe the nonverbal message.

5 **Describe the forms of nonverbal communication and how they can be used positively in your career.** Nonverbal communication takes many forms, including eye contact, facial expressions, posture, and gestures, as well as the use of time, space, and territory. Appearance of business documents and of people also sends silent messages. Eye contact should be direct but not prolonged; facial expression should communicate warmth with frequent smiles. Posture should convey self-confidence, and gestures should suggest

accessibility. Being on time and maintaining neat, functional work areas send positive nonverbal messages. Use closeness to show warmth and to reduce status differences. Strive for neat, professional, well-organized business messages, and be personally well groomed, neat, and appropriately dressed.

6 **List specific techniques for improving nonverbal communication skills in the workplace.** To improve your nonverbal skills, establish and maintain eye contact, use posture to show interest, reduce or eliminate physical barriers, improve your decoding skills, probe for more information, avoid assigning nonverbal meanings out of context, associate with people from diverse cultures, appreciate the power of appearance, observe yourself on videotape, and enlist friends and family to monitor your conscious and unconscious body movements and gestures.

chapter review

1. According to experts, we ignore, forget, distort, or misunderstand 75 percent of everything we hear. Why are we such poor listeners? (Obj. 1)
2. How can you improve your listening when superiors are giving instructions, assignments, and explanations? (Obj. 1)
3. What are three strategies that help you listen in team and group interactions? (Obj. 1)
4. How can employees do a better job of listening to customers? (Obj. 1)
5. Describe the four elements in the listening process. (Obj. 2).
6. How can listeners improve retention? (Obj. 2)
7. What are ten techniques for improving workplace listening? Be prepared to explain each. (Obj. 3)
8. Define *nonverbal communication.* (Obj. 4)
9. List five functions of nonverbal communication. Give an original example of each. (Obj. 4)
10. When verbal and nonverbal messages disagree, which message does the receiver consider more truthful? Give an example. (Obj. 4)
11. North Americans are said to be a little standoffish. What does this mean? (Obj. 5)
12. How can posture send nonverbal messages? (Obj. 5)
13. How can the use of space send nonverbal messages? (Obj. 5)
14. What nonverbal messages are sent by organizations with casual dress codes? (Obj. 5)
15. List ten techniques for improving nonverbal communication skills in the workplace. (Obj. 6)

critical thinking

1. Why do executives and managers spend more time listening than do workers? (Obj. 1)
2. North Americans are said to have the world's worst listening skills.[22] Why do you think North Americans get such a bad rap? (Objs. 1–3)
3. Why can two 127-kilogram professional football players slap each other on the rear end during a game, whereas two business associates in a meeting cannot? What principle of nonverbal communication can you extract from this example? (Obj. 4)
4. What arguments could you give for or against the idea that body language is a science with principles that can be interpreted accurately by specialists? (Obj. 4)

activities

LISTENING

3.1 Observing Listening Behaviour (Objs. 1–3)

You've probably never paid much attention to listening. But now that you have studied it, you have become more conscious of both good and bad listening behaviour.

Your Task. For one week focus on the listening behaviour of people around you—at work, at school, at home. Make a list of five good listening habits that you see and five bad habits. Identify the situation and participants for each item on your list. Who is the best listener you know? What makes that person a good listener? Be prepared to discuss your responses in class, with your team, or in a memo to your instructor.

3.2 Listening in the Workplace (Objs. 1 and 5)

Do the listening skills and behaviours of individuals differ depending on their careers?

Your Task. Your instructor will divide you into teams and give each team a role to discuss, such as business executive, teacher, physician, police officer, lawyer, accountant, administrative assistant, mentor, or team leader. Create a list of verbal and nonverbal cues that a member of this profession would display to indicate that he or she is listening. Would the cues and behaviour change if the person were trying to listen discriminatively versus critically? How?

3.3 Listening and Retention: How Much Can You Remember? (Objs. 2 and 3)

After studying the suggestions in this chapter for improving listening, you should be able to conduct a before-and-after study.

Your Task. Listen to a 30-minute segment of TV news using your normal listening habits. When you finish, make a list of the major items you remember, recording names, places, and figures. A day later watch the same 30-minute segment but put to use the good listening tips in this chapter, including taking selective notes and possibly using memory devices. When the segment is completed, make a list of the major items you remember. Which experience provided more information? What made a major difference for you?

3.4 Evaluating Trained and Untrained Listeners (Objs. 1–3)

Play the part of a training consultant hired to help improve customer service at a high-volume travel agency. During one training session, you hear the following comments from current customer service representatives.

Your Task. Based on what you learned in this chapter, would you characterize the speaker as a trained or an untrained listener, and what advice would you give to improve the speaker's listening skills?

a. "When the caller is upset, I try to listen carefully and occasionally give affirming comments."
b. "You know all the forms we have to fill out? The best time to do that is while you're listening to customers. I save a lot of time that way."
c. "When someone gets snippy with me, I come right back with more of the same. Works every time."
d. "I don't waste time with customers who ramble. After the first few words, I can always tell what they want."

3.5 Distinguishing Facts From Opinions (Obj. 3)

Good listeners make an effort to distinguish facts from opinions. Facts can be checked and verified through objective evidence. Opinions express beliefs, feelings, or judgments that cannot be proven.
Your Task. In teams, discuss the following statements. Decide whether they are facts or opinions. Be prepared to justify your choices.

a. Most people who learn how to listen more accurately are amazed when they find out what they have been missing.
b. Don Cherry hosts "Coach's Corner."
c. One reason Don Cherry is so successful is that he is a good listener.
d. Capital punishment is legalized murder.

3.6 Nonverbal Communication: Recognizing Functions (Obj. 4)

Most of us use nonverbal cues and react to them unconsciously. We seldom think about the functions they serve.
Your Task. To become more aware of the functions of nonverbal communication, keep a log for one week. Observe how nonverbal communication is used by friends, family, instructors, coworkers, managers, politicians, newsmakers, businesses, and others. For each of the five functions of nonverbal communication identified in this chapter, list examples illustrating that function. For example, under "To reinforce and accentuate," you might list a friend who whispers a message to you, thus suggesting that it is a secret. Under "To control and regulate," you might list the steady gaze of your instructor who has targeted a student not paying attention. Train yourself to become more observant, and begin making notes in your log. How many examples can you name for each of the five functions? Be prepared to submit your list or discuss it in class.

3.7 Nonverbal Communication: Document Appearance (Objs. 5 and 6)

How does the appearance of a document send a nonverbal message?
Your Task. Select several business letters and envelopes that you have received at home or work. Analyze the appearance and nonverbal message the letters and envelopes send. Consider the amount of postage, method of delivery, correctness of address, kind of stationery, typeface(s), format, and neatness. What assumptions did you make when you saw the envelopes and letters?

3.8 Body Language (Objs. 5 and 6)

What attitudes do the following body movements suggest to you? Do these movements always mean the same thing? What part does context play in your interpretations?

a. Whistling, wringing hands
b. Bowed posture, twiddling thumbs
c. Steepled hands, sprawling position
d. Rubbing hand through hair
e. Open hands, unbuttoned coat

3.9 Nonverbal Communication: Universal Sign for "I Goofed" (Objs. 4–6)

CRITICAL THINKING **TEAM**

In an effort to promote tranquility on the highways and reduce road rage, motorists submitted the following suggestions. They were sent to a newspaper columnist who asked for a universal nonverbal signal admitting that a driver had "goofed."[23]
Your Task. In small groups consider the pros and cons for each of the following gestures intended as an apology when a driver makes a mistake. Why would some fail?

a. Lower your head slightly and bonk yourself on the forehead with the side of your closed fist. The message is clear: "I'm stupid. I shouldn't have done that."
b. Make a temple with your hands, as if you were praying.
c. Move the index finger of your right hand back and forth across your neck—as if you are cutting your throat.
d. Flash the well-known peace sign. Hold up the index and middle fingers of one hand, making a V as in Victory.
e. Place the flat of your hands against your cheeks, as children do when they've made a mistake.
f. Clasp your hand over your mouth, raise your brows, and shrug your shoulders.

Rich chapter resources are available on the Web site. 

3.10 Role-Playing Business Casual Dress-Related Guidance (Objs. 5 and 6)

LISTENING SPEAKING

Supervisors in the workplace must occasionally deliver dress-related guidance to workers who may have dressed inappropriately for work. The following situations, written by Dr. James Calvert Scott, provide excellent opportunities for you to develop skills in applying diplomatic, positive feedback in realistic workplace contexts.[24]

Your Task. Volunteer for (or be assigned) the role of supervisor. Assume your organization has an existing business casual dress policy. Your job is to encourage an employee to comply with the dress code in the following situations:

a. A 35-year-old male systems analyst is working in his glass-walled private office wearing a T-shirt that has an obscene slogan printed on the back.

b. A 21-year-old secretary working in an open office area is wearing a tight-fitting cropped top and hip-hugger pants that expose her pierced navel.

c. A 17-year-old high school marketing intern is wearing low-riding baggy pants that expose the top 8 centimetres of his underwear as he works in the public area assigned to the marketing division.

d. A 43-year-old custodian is wearing loose-fitting sandals as he tries to move a 250-litre drum of carpet-cleaning solution from the loading dock to his supply room.

C.L.U.E. review 3

On a separate sheet edit the following sentences to correct faults in grammar, capitalization, punctuation, numbers, spelling, proofreading, and word use.

1. Every one knows how to listen but many of us listen at only twenty-five per cent effecency.

2. Its wise to avoid arguing or criticizing, when listening to a superior.

3. The 4 stages of listening are: Perception, Interpretation, Evaluation and Action.

4. To improve retention you should take notes, and rewrite it immediatley after listening.

5. While waiting for the speakers next idea you should review what was all ready spoke.

6. High-status and self-confidence is conveyed by erect posture.

7. On May 12th, the company President awarded bonuses to Tyler and I, however we didn't recieve our cheques until June first.

8. In a poll of nearly three thousand employees only 1/3 felt that there companys' valued there opinions and suggestion.

9. The appearance and mannerisms of a speaker effects a listeners evaluation of a message.

10. A list of suggestions for improving retention of a speakers ideas are found in an article titled Best Listening Habits which appeared in Fortune.

chapter 4

Communicating Across Cultures

objectives

1 Discuss three significant trends related to the increasing importance of intercultural communication.

2 Define culture. Describe five significant characteristics of culture, and compare and contrast five key dimensions of culture.

3 Explain the effects of ethnocentrism, tolerance, and patience in achieving intercultural proficiency.

4 Illustrate how to improve nonverbal and oral communication in intercultural environments.

5 Illustrate how to improve written messages in intercultural environments.

6 Explain the challenge of capitalizing on workforce diversity, including its dividends and its divisiveness. List tips for improving harmony and communication among diverse workplace audiences.

springboard *to discussion*

Ernest Biktimirov, an innovative finance professor at Brock University, found that using proverbs helped in the teaching of basic finance. When he taught the course to international students, most of them Mandarin-speaking, he translated the Chinese proverbs into Mandarin and had a class full of smiling, engaged students.[1]

The Increasing Importance of Intercultural Communication

learning objective

1

The "global village" predicted many years ago is increasingly becoming a reality. National and even local businesses push products across borders and seek customers in diverse foreign markets. Especially in North America, this movement toward a global economy has swelled to a torrent. To succeed in this global village, many organizations form multinational alliances. But many expanding companies often stumble when they are forced to confront obstacles never before encountered.

Learning more about how culture affects behaviour helps you reduce friction and misunderstandings.

Significant obstacles involve misunderstandings and contrary views resulting from intercultural differences. You may face such intercultural differences in your current or future jobs. Your employers, coworkers, or clients could very well be from other countries. You may travel abroad for your employer or on your own. Learning more about the powerful effect that culture has on behaviour will help you reduce friction and misunderstanding in your dealings with people from other cultures. Before examining strategies for helping you surmount intercultural obstacles, let's take a closer look at three significant trends: (1) the globalization of markets, (2) technological advancements, and (3) an intercultural workforce.

Globalization of Markets

National boundaries mean less as businesses expand through mergers, alliances, and acquisitions.

Doing business beyond our borders is now commonplace. Even McDonald's and Starbucks have establishments around the world. Not only are market borders blurring, but acquisitions, mergers, and alliances are obscuring the nationality of many companies. Bridgestone/Firestone is owned by a Japanese conglomerate, Sylvania is controlled by German lighting giant OSRAM, and 7-Eleven is the highest-grossing retailer in Japan.[2]

North American companies in global markets must adapt to other cultures.

To be successful in this interdependent global village, North American companies are increasingly finding it necessary to adapt to other cultures. To sell its laundry products in Europe, Unilever learned that Germans demand a product that's gentle on lakes and rivers. Spaniards want cheaper products that get shirts white and soft, and Greeks prefer small packages that are cheap and easy to carry home.[3] Domino's Pizza catered to the Japanese by adding squid to its pizza toppings.[4]

Favourable trade agreements, declining domestic markets, and the growth of the middle class fuel the expansion of global markets.

What's caused this rush toward globalization of markets and blurring of national identities? Many companies are increasingly looking overseas as domestic markets mature. They can no longer expect double-digit sales growth at home. Another significant factor is the passage of favourable trade agreements. The General Agreement on Tariffs and Trade (GATT) promotes open trade globally, and the North American Free Trade Agreement (NAFTA) expands free trade among Canada, the

United States, and Mexico. NAFTA created the largest and richest free-trade region on earth.[5] The opening of Eastern Europe and the shift away from communism in Russia have also fuelled the progress toward expanding world markets. And China's admission to the World Trade Organization unlocked its economy and suddenly provided access to a huge population.

Equally important as expanding global markets is the explosive growth of the middle class. Parts of the world formerly considered underdeveloped now boast robust middle classes. These consumers crave everything from cola to smart phones to high-definition televisions. But probably the most important factor in the rise of the global market is the development of new transportation and information technologies.

Technological Advances

Advances in transportation and information technologies contribute to global interconnectivity.

Amazing new transportation and information technologies are major contributors to the development of our global interconnectivity. Supersonic planes now carry goods and passengers to other continents overnight. Along with transportation progress, the global economy is being fuelled by incredible advances in communication technologies. The Internet now permits instantaneous oral and written communication across time zones and continents.

Companies use the Web to sell products, provide support, offer service, investigate the competition, and link to suppliers.

The Internet and the World Wide Web are changing the way we live, the way we do business, and the way we communicate. Advances in communication and transportation have made markets and jobs more accessible. They've also made the world of business more efficient and more globally interdependent. High-speed, high-capacity, and relatively low-cost communications have opened up new global opportunities and have made geographic location virtually irrelevant for many activities and services. Workers have access to company records, software programs, and colleagues whether they're working at home, in the office, or at the beach. As discussed in Chapters 1 and 2, technology is making a huge difference in the workplace. Wikis, blogs, wireless devices, and intranets streamline business processes and improve access to critical company information.

Intercultural Workforce

As world commerce mingles more and more, another trend gives intercultural communication increasing importance: people are on the move. Lured by the prospects of peace, prosperity, education, or a fresh start, persons from many cultures are moving to countries that promise to fulfill their dreams. For generations the two most popular destinations have been Canada and the United States.

Immigration makes intercultural communication skills increasingly necessary.

Because of increases in immigration, foreign-born persons are an ever-growing portion of the total population. Census results from Statistics Canada indicate that the presence of visible minorities in Canada is growing at a rate of 25 percent, or six times faster than the total Canadian population, and shows no signs of slowing.

This influx of immigrants has reshaped Canadian society. While Americans have traditionally supported the "melting pot" approach to ethnic groups, Canada has often been compared to a cultural mosaic. Although Canada's two official languages are English and French, unofficially it is a land of many languages. Instead of being the exception, cultural diversity is increasingly the norm. As we seek to accommodate multiethnic neighbourhoods, multinational companies, and an intercultural workforce, we can expect some changes to happen smoothly. Other changes will involve conflict and resentment, especially for people losing their positions of power and privilege. Learning how to manage intercultural conflict is an important part of the education of any business communicator.

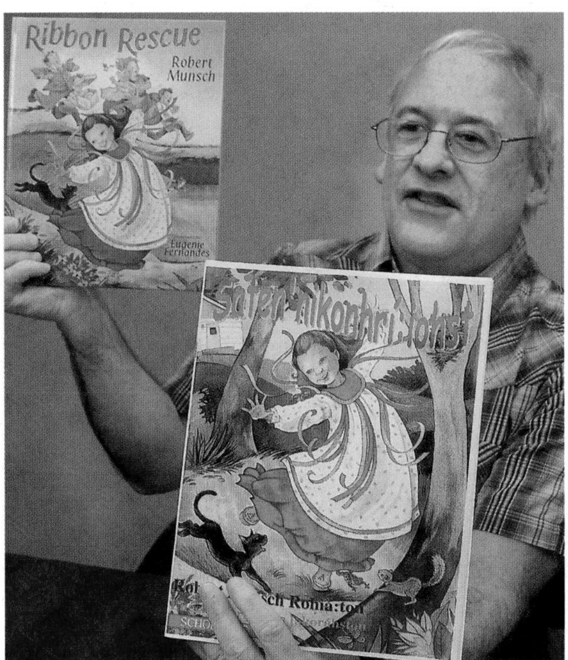

"I think having First Languages books is vital for group identity and pride," says popular children's author Robert Munsch. Munsch has become actively involved in helping First Nations preserve their aboriginal languages by allowing Native groups to use his stories at no cost. He has also written The Ocean Goes on Forever, *which is published only in Ojibway.*

Photo: © Guelph Mercury

Understanding Culture

learning objective 2

Understanding basic characteristics of culture helps us make adjustments and accommodations.

Every country or region within a country has a unique common heritage, joint experience, or shared learning. This shared background produces the culture of a region, country, or society. For our purposes, *culture* may be defined as the complex system of values, traits, morals, and customs shared by a society. Culture teaches people how to behave, and it conditions their reactions. The important thing to remember is that culture is a powerful operating force that conditions the way we think and behave. As thinking individuals, we are extraordinarily flexible and capable of phenomenal change. The purpose of this chapter is to broaden your view of culture and open your mind to flexible attitudes so that you can avoid frustration when cultural adjustment is necessary.

Characteristics of Culture

Culture is shaped by attitudes learned in childhood and later internalized in adulthood. As we enter this current period of globalization and interculturalism, we should expect to make adjustments and adopt new attitudes. Adjustment and accommodation will be easier if we understand some basic characteristics of culture.

Culture Is Learned. The rules, values, and attitudes of a culture are not inherent. They are learned and passed down from generation to generation. For example, in many Middle Eastern and some Asian cultures, same-sex people may walk hand in hand in the street, but opposite-sex people may not do so. In Arab cultures, conversations are often held in close proximity, sometimes nose to nose. Cultural rules of behaviour learned from your family and society are conditioned from early childhood.

Cultures Are Inherently Logical. The rules in any culture originated to reinforce that culture's values and beliefs. They act as normative forces. Although current cultural behaviour may sometimes seem silly and illogical, nearly all serious rules and values originate in deep-seated beliefs. Rules about how close to stand are linked to values about sexuality, aggression, modesty, and respect. Acknowledging the inherent logic of a culture is extremely important when learning to accept behaviour that differs from one's own cultural behaviour.

Culture Is the Basis of Self-identity and Community. Culture is the basis for how we tell the world who we are and what we believe. People build their identities through cultural overlays to their primary culture. North Americans, for example, make choices in education, career, place of employment, and life partner. Each of these choices brings with it a set of rules, manners, ceremonies, beliefs, language, and values. They add to one's total cultural outlook, and they represent major expressions of a person's self-identity.

Culture Combines the Visible and Invisible. To outsiders, the way we act—those things that we do in daily life and work—are the most visible parts of our culture. In Japan, for instance, harmony with the environment is important. Some actions are outward symbols of deeper values that are invisible but that pervade everything we think and do.

Culture Is Dynamic. Over time, cultures will change. Changes are caused by advances in technology and communication, as discussed earlier. Attitudes, behaviours, and beliefs change in open societies more quickly than in closed societies.

About Stereotypes, Prototypes, Prejudices, and Generalizations

Stereotypes ***are oversimplified behavioural patterns applied uncritically to groups;*** **prototypes** ***describe general characteristics that are dynamic and may change.***

Most experts recognize that it is impossible to talk about cultures without using mental categories, representations, and generalizations to describe groups. These categories are sometimes considered stereotypes. Because the term *stereotype* has a negative meaning, intercultural authors Varner and Beamer suggest that we distinguish between *stereotype* and *prototype.*

A *stereotype* is an oversimplified behavioural pattern applied uncritically to groups. The term was used originally by printers to describe identical type set in two frames, hence *stereo type.* Stereotypes are fixed and rigid. Although they may be exaggerated and overgeneralized beliefs when applied to groups of people, stereotypes are not always entirely false.[6] Often they contain a grain of truth. When a stereotype develops into a rigid attitude and when it's based on erroneous beliefs or preconceptions, then it should be called a *prejudice.*

Varner and Beamer recommend the use of the term *prototype* to describe "mental representations based on general characteristics that are not fixed and rigid, but rather are open to new definitions."[7] Prototypes, then, are dynamic and change with fresh experience. Prototypes based on objective observations usually have a considerable amount of truth in them. That's why they can be helpful in studying culture. For example, Latin businesspeople often talk about their families before getting down to business. This prototype is generally accurate, but it may not universally apply and it may change over time.

Some people object to making any generalizations whatever about cultures. Yet it is wise to remember that whenever we are confronted with something new and unfamiliar, we naturally strive to categorize the data in order to make sense out of it. In categorizing these new data, we are making generalizations. Significant intellectual discourse is impossible without generalizations. In fact, science itself would be impossible without generalizations, for what are scientific laws but valid generalizations? Much of what we teach in postsecondary courses could be called generalizations. Being able to draw generalizations from masses of data is a sign of intelligence and learning. Unfounded generalizations about people and cultures, of course, can lead to bias and prejudice. But for our purposes, when we discuss cultures, it's important to be able to make generalizations and describe cultural prototypes.

Being able to draw valid generalizations is necessary for learning and education.

Dimensions of Culture

The more you know about culture in general and your own culture in particular, the better able you will be to adapt to an intercultural perspective. A typical Canadian has habits and beliefs similar to those of other members of Western, technologically advanced societies. In our limited space in this book, it's impossible to cover fully the infinite facets of culture. But we can outline some key dimensions of culture and look at them from different views.

So that you will better understand your culture and how it contrasts with other cultures, we will describe five key dimensions of culture: context, individualism, formality, communication style, and time orientation.

Context. Context is probably the most important cultural dimension and also the most difficult to define. It's a concept developed by cultural anthropologist Edward T. Hall. In his model, context refers to the stimuli, environment, or ambiance surrounding an event. Communicators in low-context cultures (such as those in North America, Scandinavia, and Germany) depend little on the context of a situation to convey their meaning. They assume that listeners know very little and must be told practically everything. In high-context cultures (such as those in Japan, China, and Arab countries), the listener is already "contexted" and does not need to be given much background information.[8] To identify low- and high-context countries, Hall arranged them on a continuum, as shown in Figure 4.1.

Low-context cultures (such as those in North America and Western Europe) depend less on the environment of a situation to convey meaning than do high-context cultures (such as those in Japan, China, and Arab countries).

People in low-context cultures tend to be logical, analytical, and action-oriented.

Individualism. An attitude of independence and freedom from control characterizes individualism. Members of low-context cultures, particularly North Americans, tend to value individualism. They believe that initiative and self-assertion result in

Members of many low-context cultures value independence and freedom from control.

FIGURE 4.1 ***Comparing Low- and High-Context Cultures***

Low Context	High Context
Tends to prefer direct verbal interaction	Tends to prefer indirect verbal interaction
Tends to understand meaning at one level only	Tends to understand meanings embedded at many sociocultural levels
Is generally less proficient in reading nonverbal cues	Is generally more proficient in reading nonverbal cues
Values individualism	Values group membership
Relies more on logic	Relies more on context and feeling
Employs linear logic	Employs spiral logic
Says ***no*** directly	Talks around point; avoids saying ***no***
Communicates in highly structured (contexted) messages, provides details, stresses literal meanings, gives authority to written information	Communicates in simple, ambiguous, noncontexted messages; understands visual messages readily

personal achievement. They believe in individual action and personal responsibility, and they desire a large degree of freedom in their personal lives.

Members of high-context cultures are more collectivist. They emphasize membership in organizations, groups, and teams; they encourage acceptance of group values, duties, and decisions. They typically resist independence because it fosters competition and confrontation instead of consensus. In group-oriented cultures like many Asian societies, for example, self-assertion and individual decision making are discouraged. "The nail that sticks up gets pounded down" is a common Japanese saying.[9] Business decisions are often made by all who have competence in the matter under discussion. Similarly, in China, managers also focus on the group rather than on the individual, preferring a "consultative" management style over an autocratic style.[10]

Many cultures, of course, are quite complex and cannot be characterized as totally individualistic or group oriented. For example, Canadians of European descent are generally quite individualistic, while those with Asian backgrounds may be closer to the group-centred dimension.[11]

Tradition, ceremony, and social rules are more important in some cultures.

Formality. People in some cultures place less emphasis on tradition, ceremony, and social rules than do members of other cultures. North Americans, for example, tend to dress casually and are soon on a first-name basis with others. Their lack of formality is often characterized by directness. In business dealings North Americans come to the point immediately; indirectness, they feel, wastes time, a valuable commodity in Western culture.

This informality and directness may be confusing abroad. In Mexico, for instance, a typical business meeting begins with handshakes, coffee, and an expansive conversation about the weather, sports, and other light topics. An invitation to "get down to business" might offend a Mexican executive.[12] In Japan signing documents and exchanging business cards are important rituals. In Europe first names are never used without invitation. In Arab, South American, and Asian cultures, a feeling of friendship and kinship must be established before business can be transacted.

In Western cultures people are more relaxed about social status and the appearance of power.[13] Deference is not generally paid to individuals merely because of their wealth, position, seniority, or age. In many Asian cultures, however, these characteristics are important and must be respected.

Words are used differently by people in low- and high-context cultures.

Communication Style. People in low- and high-context cultures tend to communicate differently with words. To North Americans and Germans, words are very important, especially in contracts and negotiations. People in high-context cultures, on the other hand, place more emphasis on the surrounding context than on the words describing a negotiation. A Greek may see a contract as a formal statement announcing the intention to build a business for the future. The Japanese may treat contracts as statements of intention, and they assume changes will be made as a project develops. Mexicans may treat contracts as artistic exercises of what might be accomplished in an ideal world; they do not necessarily expect contracts to apply consistently in the real world. An Arab may be insulted by merely mentioning a contract; a person's word is more binding.[14]

North Americans value a direct, straightforward communication style.

North Americans tend to take words literally, whereas Latins enjoy plays on words. Arabs and South Americans sometimes speak with extravagant or poetic figures of speech that may be misinterpreted if taken literally. Nigerians prefer a quiet, clear form of expression, and Germans tend to be direct but understated.[15]

In communication style North Americans value straightforwardness, are suspicious of evasiveness, and distrust people who might have a "hidden agenda" or who

tech talk

Being Interculturally Correct on the Web

Early Web sites were almost always in English and meant for North Americans. But as online access grows around the world, multinational companies are reassessing their sites. What should companies do when they decide to go global on the Web?

- **Learn the local lingo.** Other countries have developed their own Web jargon and iconography. Home page is *page d'accueil* (welcome page) in French and *pagina inicial* (initial page) in Spanish. Experts warn against simply translating English words page by page. Hiring a proficient translator is a better idea.
- **Check icons.** North American Web surfers easily recognize the mailbox, but in Europe a more universal icon would be an envelope. Test images with local residents.
- **Relax restrictions on consistency.** Allow flexibility to meet local tastes. For example, McDonald's main site greets visitors with the golden arches and a Ronald McDonald–red background. The Japanese site, though, complements the McDonald's red and gold with pinks and browns, which are more pleasing in Japanese culture.
- **Keep the message simple.** Whether in English or the local language, use simple, easily translated words. Avoid slang, jargon, acronyms, or ambiguous expressions.
- **Customize Web content for high-context cultures.** For high-context cultures (such as those of Japan and China), Web sites often include images and wording reflecting politeness, flowery language, indirect expressions (*perhaps, probably, somewhat*), and overall humility. They may include animated images (including cartoon characters), a soft-sell approach, and appeals to harmony.[16]
- **Customize Web content for low-context cultures.** Web sites in low-context cultures (such as those in North America and Germany) use more aggressive promotions, discounts, and an emphasis on product advantages using explicit comparisons. They include superlative expressions (*We're No. 1; the world's largest; we lead the market*). Low-context Web sites often identify return policies, guarantees, and purchase conditions.[17]

"play their cards too close to the chest."[18] North Americans also tend to be uncomfortable with silence and impatient with delays. Some Asian businesspeople have learned that the longer they drag out negotiations, the more concessions impatient North Americans are likely to make.

Western cultures have developed languages that use letters describing the sounds of words. But Asian languages are based on pictographic characters representing the meanings of words. Asian language characters are much more complex than the Western alphabet; therefore, Asians are said to have a higher competence in the discrimination of visual patterns.

North Americans tend to correlate time with productivity, efficiency, and money.

Time Orientation. Punctuality is an important Western value. Most North Americans consider time a precious commodity to be conserved. They correlate time with productivity, efficiency, and money. Keeping people waiting for business appointments wastes time and is also rude. In other cultures time may be perceived as an unlimited and never-ending resource to be enjoyed.

As you can see, high-context cultures differ from low-context cultures in many dimensions. These differences can be significant for companies engaging in international business. One of the places where international business is expanding most rapidly is on the World Wide Web. Web sites give companies of all sizes global reach and the immediate ability to interact with customers all over the world. In the face of fierce competition, the most successful Web sites are built by communicators who fully understand the powerful effects of high- and low-context cultures, as discussed in the Tech Talk box above.

learning objective

3

Achieving Intercultural Proficiency

Being aware of your own culture and how it contrasts with others is an important first step in achieving intercultural proficiency. Another step involves recognizing barriers to intercultural accommodation and striving to overcome them. Some of these barriers occur quite naturally and require conscious effort to surmount. You might be thinking, Why bother? Probably the most important reasons for becoming interculturally competent are that your personal life will be more satisfying and your work life will be more productive, gratifying, and effective.

Avoiding Ethnocentrism

Ethnocentrism, *the belief in the superiority of one's own race, tends to cause us to judge others by our own values.*

The belief in the superiority of one's own race is known as *ethnocentrism*, a natural attitude inherent in all cultures. If you were raised in North America, many of the dimensions of culture described previously probably seem "right" to you.

Ethnocentrism causes us to judge others by our own values. As Professor Usha George points out, "We all try to interpret the world through our own cultural lens."[19] We expect others to react as we would, and they expect us to behave as they would. Misunderstandings naturally result. Ethnocentric reactions can be reduced through knowledge of other cultures and development of increased intercultural sensitivity.

Bridging the Gap

Because culture is learned, you can learn new attitudes and behaviours through training.

Developing cultural competence often involves changing attitudes. Remember that culture is learned. Through exposure to other cultures and through training, such as what you are receiving in this course, you can learn new attitudes and behaviours that help bridge gaps between cultures.

Tolerance. One desirable attitude in achieving intercultural proficiency is that of tolerance. Closed-minded people cannot look beyond their own ethnocentrism. But as global markets expand and as our own society becomes increasingly multiethnic, tolerance becomes especially significant. Some job descriptions now include statements such as "Must be able to interact with ethnically diverse personnel."

Empathy, *which means trying to see the world through another's eyes, helps you be more tolerant and less judgmental.*

To improve tolerance, you'll want to practise *empathy*. This means trying to see the world through another's eyes. It means being less judgmental and more eager to seek common ground. Accepting cultural differences and adapting to them with tolerance and empathy often result in a harmonious compromise.

Saving face may require indirectness to respect the feelings and dignity of others.

Saving Face. In business transactions North Americans often assume that economic factors are the primary motivators of people. It's wise to remember, though, that strong cultural influences are also at work. *Saving face*, for example, is important in many parts of the world. *Face* refers to the image a person holds in his or her social network. Positive comments raise a person's social standing, but negative comments lower it. People in low-context cultures are less concerned with face. High-context cultures, on the other hand, are more concerned with preserving social harmony and saving face. They are indirect and go to great lengths to avoid giving offence by saying *no*. The empathic listener recognizes the language of refusal and pushes no further.

Patience. Being tolerant also involves patience. If a foreigner is struggling to express an idea in English, North Americans must avoid the temptation to finish the sentence and provide the word that they presume is wanted. When we put words into their mouths, our foreign friends often smile and agree out of politeness, but our words may in fact not express their thoughts. Remaining silent is another means of exhibiting tolerance. Instead of filling every lapse in conversation, North Americans, for example, should recognize that in Asian cultures people deliberately use periods of silence for reflection and contemplation.

Tolerance sometimes involves being patient and silent.

Improving Communication With Intercultural Audiences

learning objective 4

Thus far we've discussed the increasing importance of intercultural proficiency as a result of globalization of markets, increasing migration, and technological advances. We've described characteristics and dimensions of cultures, and we've talked about avoiding ethnocentrism. Our goal was to motivate you to unlock the opportunities offered by intercultural proficiency. Remember, the key to future business success may very well lie in finding ways to work harmoniously with people from different cultures.

Adapting Messages to Intercultural Audiences

As business communicators, we need to pay special attention to specific areas of communication to enhance the effectiveness of intercultural messages. To minimize the chance of misunderstanding, we'll look more closely at nonverbal communication, oral messages, and written messages.

Nonverbal Communication. Verbal skills in another culture can generally be mastered if one studies hard enough. But nonverbal skills are much more difficult to learn. Nonverbal behaviour includes the areas described in Chapter 3, such as eye contact, facial expression, posture, gestures, and the use of time, space, and territory. The messages sent by body language and the way we arrange time and space have always been open to interpretation. Deciphering nonverbal communication is difficult for people who are culturally similar, and it is even more troublesome when cultures differ.

Understanding nonverbal messages is particularly difficult when cultures differ.

In Western cultures, for example, people perceive silence as a negative trait. It suggests rejection, unhappiness, depression, regret, embarrassment, or ignorance. However, the Japanese admire silence and consider it a key to success. Silence is equated with respect and wisdom.

Although nonverbal behaviour is ambiguous within cultures and even more problematic between cultures, it nevertheless conveys meaning. If you've ever had to talk with someone who does not share your language, you probably learned quickly to use gestures to convey basic messages. Since gestures can create very different reactions in different cultures, one must be careful in using and interpreting them.

Gestures can create different reactions in intercultural environments.

As businesspeople increasingly interact with their counterparts from other cultures, they will become more aware of these differences. Some behaviours are easy to warn against, such as touching people from the Middle East with the left hand (because it is considered unclean and is used for personal hygiene). We're also warned not to touch anyone's head (even a child's) in Thailand, as the head is considered sacred. Numerous lists of cultural dos and don'ts have been compiled. However, learning all the nuances of nonverbal behaviour in other cultures is impossible, and such lists are merely the tip of the cultural iceberg.

Becoming more aware of your own use of nonverbal cues can make you more sensitive to variations in other cultures.

Although we cannot ever hope to understand fully the nuances of meaning transmitted by nonverbal behaviour in various cultures, we can grow more tolerant, more flexible, and eventually more competent. An important part of achieving nonverbal competence is becoming more aware of our own nonverbal behaviours and their meanings. Much of our nonverbal behaviour is learned in early childhood from our families and from society, and it is largely unconscious. Once we become more aware of the meaning of our own gestures, posture, gaze, and so on, we will become more alert and more sensitive to variations in other cultures. Striving to associate with people from different cultures can further broaden our intercultural competence.

Keep your gestures to a minimum or follow the lead of native businesspeople.

From a practical standpoint, when interacting with businesspeople in other cultures, it's always wise to follow their lead. If they avoid intense eye contact, don't stare. If no one is putting his or her elbows on the table, don't be the first to do so. Until you are knowledgeable about the meaning of gestures, it's probably a good idea to keep yours to a minimum. Learning the words for *please*, *yes*, and *thank you* is even better than relying on gestures.[20] Achieving intercultural competence in regard to nonverbal behaviour may never be totally attained, but sensitivity, a nonjudgmental attitude, and tolerance go a long way toward improving interactions.

Don't assume that speakers of English as a second language understand everything you say.

Oral Messages. Although it is best to speak a foreign language fluently, many of us lack that skill. Fortunately, global business transactions are increasingly conducted in English. English has become the language of technology and the language to know in global business, even for traditionally non-English-speaking countries. English is so dominant in business that when Koreans go to China, English is the language they use to conduct business.[21] However, the level of proficiency may be limited among those for whom it is a second language. North Americans abroad make a big mistake in thinking that people who speak English always understand what is being said. Comprehension can be fairly superficial. The following suggestions are helpful for situations in which one or both communicators may be using English as a second language.

- **Learn foreign phrases.** In conversations, even when English is used, foreign nationals appreciate it when you learn greetings and a few phrases in their language. Practise the phrases phonetically so that you will be understood.

Use simple English and avoid puns, sports references, slang, and jargon when communicating with people for whom English is a second language.

- **Use simple English.** Speak in short sentences (less than 20 words) with familiar, short words. For example, use *old* rather than *obsolete* and *rich* rather than *luxurious* or *sumptuous*. Eliminate puns, sports and military references, slang, and jargon (special business terms). Be especially alert to idiomatic expressions that can't be translated, such as *burn the midnight oil* or *under the weather*.

To improve communication with those for whom English is a second language, speak slowly, enunciate clearly, observe eye messages, encourage feedback, check for comprehension, accept blame, don't interrupt, remember to smile, and follow up important conversations in writing.

- **Speak slowly and enunciate clearly.** Avoid fast speech, but don't raise your voice. Overpunctuate with pauses and full stops. Always write numbers for all to see.
- **Observe eye messages.** Be alert to a glazed expression or wandering eyes—these tell you the listener is lost.
- **Encourage accurate feedback.** Ask probing questions, and encourage the listener to paraphrase what you say. Don't assume that a yes, a nod, or a smile indicates comprehension.
- **Check frequently for comprehension.** Avoid waiting until you finish a long explanation to request feedback. Instead, make one point at a time, pausing to check for comprehension. Don't proceed to B until A has been grasped.
- **Accept blame.** If a misunderstanding results, graciously accept the blame for not making your meaning clear.

- **Listen without interrupting.** Curb your desire to finish sentences or to fill out ideas for the speaker. Keep in mind that North Americans abroad are often accused of listening too little and talking too much.
- **Smile when appropriate.** Roger Axtell, an international behaviour expert, calls the smile the single most understood and most useful form of communication in either personal or business transactions.[22] In some cultures, however, excessive smiling may be considered insincere.[23]
- **Follow up in writing.** After conversations or oral negotiations, confirm the results and agreements with follow-up letters. For proposals and contracts, engage a translator to prepare copies in the local language.

learning objective

5

Written Messages. In sending letters and other documents to businesspeople in other cultures, try to adapt your writing style and tone appropriately. For example, in cultures where formality and tradition are important, be scrupulously polite. Don't even think of sharing the latest joke. Humour translates very poorly and can cause misunderstanding and negative reactions. Familiarize yourself with accepted channels of communication. Are letters, e-mail, and faxes common? Would a direct or indirect organizational pattern be more effective? The following suggestions, coupled with the earlier guidelines, can help you prepare successful written messages for intercultural audiences.

To improve written messages, adopt local formats, use short sentences and short paragraphs, avoid ambiguous expressions, strive for clarity, use correct grammar, cite numbers carefully, and accommodate readers in organization, tone, and style.

- **Adopt local formats.** Learn how documents are formatted and addressed in the intended reader's country. Decide whether to use your organization's preferred format or adjust to local styles.
- **Observe titles and rank.** Use last names, titles, and other signals of rank and status. Send messages to higher-status people and avoid sending copies to lower-rank people.
- **Use short sentences and short paragraphs.** Sentences with fewer than 20 words and paragraphs with fewer than 8 lines are most readable.
- **Avoid ambiguous expressions.** Include relative pronouns (*that, which, who*) for clarity in introducing clauses. Stay away from contractions (especially ones like *Here's the problem*). Avoid idioms (*once in a blue moon*), slang (*my presentation really bombed*), acronyms (*ASAP* for *as soon as possible*), abbreviations (*DBA* for *doing business as*), jargon (*input, bottom line*), and sports references (*play ball, slam dunk, ballpark figure*). Use action-specific verbs (*purchase a printer* rather than *get a printer*).
- **Strive for clarity.** Avoid words that have many meanings (the word *light* has 18 different meanings!). If necessary, clarify words that may be confusing. Replace two-word verbs with clear single words (*return* instead of *bring back*; *delay* instead of *put off*; *maintain* instead of *keep up*).
- **Use correct grammar.** Be careful of misplaced modifiers, dangling participles, and sentence fragments. Use conventional punctuation.
- **Cite numbers carefully.** For international trade it's a good idea to use the metric system. In citing numbers use figures (*15*) instead of spelling them out (*fifteen*). Always convert dollar figures into local currency. Avoid using figures to express the month of the year.
- **Accommodate the reader in organization, tone, and style.** Organize your message to appeal to the reader. For example, use the indirect strategy for high-context audiences.

Making the effort to communicate with sensitivity across cultures pays big dividends. "Much of the world wants to like us," says businessman and international consultant Kevin Chambers. "When we take the time to learn about others, many will bend over backward to do business with us."[24] The following checklist summarizes suggestions for improving communication with intercultural audiences.

Checklist for Improving Intercultural Proficiency and Communication

- ✓ **Study your own culture.** Learn about your customs, biases, and views and how they differ from those in other societies. This knowledge can help you better understand, appreciate, and accept the values and behaviour of other cultures.

- ✓ **Learn about other cultures.** Education can help you alter cultural misconceptions, reduce fears, and minimize misunderstandings. Knowledge of other cultures opens your eyes and teaches you to expect differences. Such knowledge also enriches your life.

- ✓ **Curb ethnocentrism.** Avoid judging others by your personal views. Get over the idea that other cultures are incorrect, defective, or primitive. Try to develop an open mind.

- ✓ **Avoid judgmentalism.** Strive to accept other behaviour as different, rather than as right or wrong. Try not to be defensive in justifying your culture. Strive for objectivity.

- ✓ **Seek common ground.** When cultures clash, look for solutions that respect both cultures. Be flexible in developing compromises.

- ✓ **Observe nonverbal cues in your culture.** Become more alert to the meanings of eye contact, facial expression, posture, gestures, and the use of time, space, and territory. How do they differ in other cultures?

- ✓ **Use plain English.** Speak and write in short sentences, using simple words and standard English. Eliminate puns, slang, jargon, acronyms, abbreviations, and any words that cannot be easily translated.

- ✓ **Encourage accurate feedback.** In conversations ask probing questions and listen attentively without interrupting. Don't assume that a yes or a smile indicates assent or comprehension.

- ✓ **Adapt to local preferences.** Shape your writing to reflect the reader's document styles, if appropriate. Express currency in local figures. Write out months of the year for clarity.

learning objective 6

Capitalizing on Workforce Diversity

At the same time that North American businesspeople are interacting with people from around the world, the domestic workforce is becoming more diverse. This diversity has many dimensions—race, ethnicity, age, religion, gender, national origin, physical ability, and countless other qualities. No longer, say the experts, will the workplace be predominantly Anglo-oriented or male. By 2017, one in five Canadians will be part of a visible minority.[25] In addition, the size of the world's older population is seen as the century's defining demographic trend. Predictions indicate that the workplace revolution ahead will rival the gender revolution of a quarter-century ago, when women's educational levels and labour force participation soared.[26] Trends suggest that many older people will remain in the workforce. And because of technological advances, more physically challenged people are also joining the workforce.

Dividends of Diversity

A diverse workforce benefits consumers, work teams, and business organizations.

As society and the workforce become more diverse, successful interaction and communication among the various identity groups bring distinct challenges and dividends in three areas.

Consumers. A diverse staff is better able to read trends and respond to the increasingly diverse customer base in local and world markets. Diverse consumers now want specialized goods and services tailored to their needs. Teams made up of different people with different experiences are better able to create the different products that these markets require. Consumers also want to deal with companies that respect their values and reflect themselves.

Work Teams. As you learned in Chapter 2, employees today work in teams. Team members with different backgrounds may come up with more creative and effective problem-solving techniques than homogeneous teams. Chains of command, narrow job descriptions, and hierarchies are gradually becoming things of the past. Today's teams are composed of knowledgeable, diverse individuals who are concerned with sustainability, competence, and ownership within the project, team, and organization.[27]

Business Organizations. Companies that set aside time and resources to cultivate and capitalize on diversity will suffer fewer discrimination lawsuits, fewer union clashes, and less government regulatory action. Most important, though, is the growing realization among organizations that diversity is a critical bottom-line business strategy to improve employee relationships and to increase productivity. Developing a diverse staff that can work together cooperatively is one of the biggest challenges facing business organizations today.

Divisiveness of Diversity

Diversity can cause divisiveness, discontent, and clashes.

Diversity can be a positive force within organizations. But all too often diversity can also cause divisiveness, discontent, and clashes. Many of the identity groups, the so-called workforce "disenfranchised," have legitimate concerns.

The **glass ceiling** *is an invisible barrier of attitudes, prejudices, and "old boy networks" that blocks women from reaching important positions.*

Women complain of the *glass ceiling*, that invisible barrier of attitudes, prejudices, and "old boy networks" blocking them from reaching important corporate positions. Some women feel that they are the victims of sexual harassment, unequal wages, sexism, and even their style of communication. On the other hand, men, too, have gender issues. One manager described gender discrimination in his office: "My boss was a woman and was very verbal about the opportunities for women to advance in my company. I have often felt she gave much more attention to the women in the office than the men."[28]

Older employees feel that organizations favour younger employees. Minorities complain that they are discriminated against in hiring, retention, wages, and promotions. Physically challenged individuals may feel that their condition should not hold them back, and they fear that their potential is often prejudged. Individuals with different religions may feel uncomfortable working alongside each other.

Tips for Improving Communication Among Diverse Workplace Audiences

A diverse workforce may reduce productivity unless trained to value differences.

Integrating all this diversity into one seamless workforce is a formidable task and a vital one. Harnessed effectively, diversity can enhance productivity and propel a company to success well into the twenty-first century. Mismanaged, it can become a tremendous drain on a company's time and resources. How companies deal with diversity will make all the difference in how they compete in an increasingly global environment. And that means that organizations must do more than just pay lip service to these issues. Harmony and acceptance do not happen automatically when people who are dissimilar work together. The following suggestions can help you and your organization find ways to improve communication and interaction.

- **Seek training.** Especially if an organization is experiencing diversity problems, awareness-raising sessions may be helpful. Spend time reading and learning about workforce diversity and how it can benefit organizations. Look upon diversity as an opportunity, not a threat. Intercultural communication, team building, and conflict resolution are skills that can be learned in diversity training programs.
- **Understand the value of differences.** Diversity makes an organization innovative and creative. Sameness fosters an absence of critical thinking called groupthink, which you learned about in Chapter 2. Diversity in problem-solving groups encourages independent and creative thinking.
- **Don't expect conformity.** Gone are the days when businesses could say, "This is our culture. Conform or leave."[29] Paul Fireman, CEO of Reebok, stresses seeking people who have new and different stories to tell. "And then you have to make real room for them, you have to learn to listen, to listen closely, to their stories. It accomplishes next to nothing to employ those who are different from us if the condition of their employment is that they become the same as us. For it is their differences that enrich us, expand us, provide us the competitive edge."[30]
- **Learn about your cultural self.** Begin to think of yourself as a product of your culture, and understand that your culture is just one among many. Try to stand outside and look at yourself. Do you see any reflex reactions and automatic thought patterns that are a result of your upbringing? These may be invisible to you until challenged by difference. Remember, your culture was designed to help you succeed and survive in a certain environment. Be sure to keep what works and yet be ready to adapt as environments change.

Don't expect all workers to think or act alike.

- **Make fewer assumptions.** Be careful of seemingly insignificant, innocent workplace assumptions. For example, don't assume that everyone wants to observe the holidays with a Christmas party and a decorated tree. Celebrating only Christian holidays in December and January excludes those who honour Hanukkah, Kwanzaa, and the Chinese New Year. Moreover, in workplace discussions don't assume that everyone is married, or wants to be, or is even heterosexual, for that matter. In invitations, avoid phrases such as *managers and their wives. Spouses* or *partners* is more inclusive. Valuing diversity means making fewer assumptions that everyone is like you or wants to be like you.

- **Build on similarities.** Look for areas in which you and others not like you can agree or at least share opinions. Be prepared to consider issues from many perspectives, all of which may be valid. Accept that there is room for different points of view to coexist peacefully. Although you can always find differences, it's much harder to find similarities. Look for common ground in shared experiences, mutual goals, and similar values. Concentrate on your objective even when you may disagree on how to reach it.[31]

In times of conflict, look for areas of agreement and build on similarities.

Summary of Learning Objectives

1 **Discuss three significant trends related to the increasing importance of intercultural communication.** Three trends are working together to crystallize the growing need for developing intercultural proficiencies and improved communication techniques. First, the globalization of markets means that you can expect to be doing business with people from around the world. Second, technological advancements in transportation and information are making the world smaller and more intertwined. Third, more and more immigrants from other cultures are settling in North America, thus changing the complexion of the workforce. Successful interaction requires awareness, tolerance, and accommodation.

2 **Define *culture*. Describe five significant characteristics of culture, and compare and contrast five key dimensions of culture.** Culture is the complex system of values, traits, morals, and customs shared by a society. Some of the significant characteristics of culture include the following: (a) culture is learned, (b) cultures are inherently logical, (c) culture is the basis of self-identity and community, (d) culture combines the visible and invisible, and (e) culture is dynamic. Members of low-context cultures (such as those in North America, Scandinavia, and Germany) depend on words to express meaning, whereas members of high-context cultures (such as those in Japan, China, and Arab countries) rely more on context (social setting, a person's history, status, and position) to communicate meaning. Other key dimensions of culture include individualism, degree of formality, communication style, and time orientation.

3 **Explain the effects of ethnocentrism, tolerance, and patience in achieving intercultural proficiency.** *Ethnocentrism* refers to an individual's feeling that the culture you belong to is superior to all others and holds all truths. To function effectively in a global economy, we must acquire knowledge of other cultures and be willing to change attitudes. Developing tolerance often involves practising empathy, which means trying to see the world through another's eyes. Saving face and promoting social harmony are important in many parts of the world. Moving beyond narrow ethnocentric views often requires tolerance and patience.

4 **Illustrate how to improve nonverbal and oral communication in intercultural environments.** We can minimize nonverbal miscommunication by recognizing that meanings conveyed by eye contact, posture, and gestures are largely culture dependent. Nonverbal messages are also sent by the use of time, space, and territory. Becoming aware of your own nonverbal behaviour and what it conveys is the first step in broadening your intercultural competence. In improving oral messages, you can learn foreign phrases, use simple English, speak slowly and enunciate clearly, observe eye messages, encourage

accurate feedback, check for comprehension, accept blame, listen without interrupting, smile, and follow up important conversations in writing.

5 **Illustrate how to improve written messages in intercultural environments.** To improve written messages, adopt local formats, observe titles and rank, use short sentences and short paragraphs, avoid ambiguous expressions, strive for clarity, use correct grammar, and cite numbers carefully. Also try to accommodate the reader in organization, tone, and style.

6 **Explain the challenge of capitalizing on workforce diversity, including its dividends and its divisiveness. List tips for improving harmony and communication among diverse workplace audiences.** Having a diverse workforce can benefit consumers, work teams, and business organizations. However, diversity can also cause divisiveness among various identity groups. To promote harmony and communication, many organizations develop diversity training programs. As an individual, you must understand and accept the value of differences. Don't expect conformity, and create zero tolerance for bias and prejudice. Learn about your cultural self, make fewer assumptions, and seek common ground when disagreements arise.

chapter review

1. Why are North American companies expanding into overseas markets, and what developments have made such globalization possible? (Obj. 1)
2. In what ways is the Web changing the way we do business? (Obj. 1)
3. What is culture and how is culture learned? (Obj. 2)
4. Describe five major dimensions of culture. (Obj. 2)
5. Briefly, contrast high- and low-context cultures. (Obj. 2)
6. What is ethnocentrism? (Obj. 3)
7. How is a stereotype different from a prototype? (Obj. 3)
8. Why is nonverbal communication more difficult to study and learn than verbal communication? (Obj. 4)
9. Name three processes that are effective in achieving competence in dealing with nonverbal messages in other cultures. (Obj. 4)
10. Describe five specific ways you can improve oral communication with a foreigner. (Obj. 4)
11. Describe five specific ways you can improve written communication with a foreigner. (Obj. 5)
12. Name three groups who benefit from workforce diversity and explain why. (Obj. 6)
13. Describe six tips for improving communication among diverse workplace audiences. (Obj. 6)

critical thinking

1. Because English is becoming the world's business language, why should Canadians bother to learn about other cultures? (Objs. 1, 2, and 6)
2. If the rules, values, and attitudes of a culture are learned, can they be unlearned? Explain. (Obj. 2)
3. Some economists and management scholars argue that statements such as "diversity is an economic asset" or "diversity is a new strategic imperative" are unproved and perhaps unprovable assertions. Should social responsibility or market forces determine whether an organization strives to create a diverse workforce? Why? (Obj. 6)

activities

4.1 Global Interactions: What We Can Learn When Things Go Wrong (Objs. 1–3)

As business organizations become increasingly global in their structure and marketing, they face communication problems resulting from cultural misunderstandings. The following situations really happened.

Your Task. Based on what you have learned in this chapter, describe several broad principles that could be applied in helping the individuals involved understand what went wrong in the following events. What suggestions could you make for remedying the problems involved?

a. When Wal-Mart opened a store in Germany, shoppers were annoyed by the door greeters, and they regarded the ever-helpful clerks as an intrusion on their private space. They also were suspicious and wary when clerks tried to help customers carry their purchases outside.[32]

b. The employees of a large North American pharmaceutical firm became angry over the e-mail messages they received from the firm's employees in Spain. The messages weren't offensive; generally they were routine messages just explaining ongoing projects. What riled the North Americans was this: every Spanish message was copied to the hierarchy within its division. The North Americans could not understand why e-mail messages had to be sent to people who had little or nothing to do with the issues being discussed. But this was accepted practice in Spain.[33]

c. A North American businessperson guided a group of Japanese to a hospital on a business trip. The hospital director threw a handful of his business cards on a table for the Japanese to pick up. Why might the Japanese be offended?

d. A T-shirt maker in Toronto printed shirts for the Spanish market that promoted the Pope's visit. Instead of the desired "I Saw the Pope" in Spanish, the shirts proclaimed "I Saw the Potato."

4.2 Cross-Cultural Gap at Resort Hotel in Thailand (Objs. 1–4)

TEAM

The Laguna Beach Resort Hotel in Phuket, Thailand, nestled between a tropical lagoon and the sparkling Andaman Sea, is one of the most beautiful resorts in the world. (You can take a virtual tour by using Google and searching for "Laguna Beach Resort Phuket.") When Brett Peel arrived as the director of the hotel's kitchen, he thought he had landed in paradise. But only on the job for six weeks, he began wondering why his Thai staff would answer *yes* even when they didn't understand what he had said. Other foreign managers discovered that junior staff managers rarely spoke up and never expressed an opinion contrary to those of senior executives. And guests with a complaint thought that Thai employees were not taking them seriously because the Thais smiled at even the worst complaints. Thais also did not seem to understand deadlines or urgent requests.[34]

Your Task. In teams decide how you would respond to the following. If you were the director of this hotel, would you implement a training program for employees? If so, would you train only foreign managers, or would you include local Thai employees as well? What topics should a training program include? Would your goal be to introduce Western ways to the Thais? At least 90 percent of the hotel guests are non-Thai.

4.3 Interpreting Intercultural Proverbs (Objs. 2 and 3)

Proverbs, which tell truths with metaphors and simplicity, often reveal fundamental values held by a culture.

Your Task. Discuss the following proverbs and explain how they relate to some of the cultural values you studied in this chapter. What additional proverbs can you cite, and what do they mean?

North American proverbs
An ounce of prevention is worth a pound of cure.
The squeaking wheel gets the grease.
A bird in the hand is worth two in the bush.
He who holds the gold makes the rules.

Japanese proverbs
A wise man hears one and understands ten.
The pheasant would have lived but for its cry.
The nail that sticks up gets pounded down.

German proverbs
No one is either rich or poor who has not helped himself to be so.
He who is afraid of doing too much always does too little.

4.4 Negotiating Traps (Objs. 2–5)

Businesspeople often have difficulty reaching agreement on the terms of contracts, proposals, and anything that involves bargaining. They have even more difficulty when the negotiators are from different cultures.

Your Task. Discuss the causes and implications of the following common mistakes made by North Americans in their negotiations with foreigners.

a. Assuming that a final agreement is set in stone
b. Lacking patience and insisting that matters progress more quickly than the pace preferred by the locals
c. Thinking that an interpreter is always completely accurate
d. Believing that individuals who speak English understand every nuance of your meaning
e. Ignoring or misunderstanding the significance of rank

4.5 Global Economy (Obj. 1)

Fred Smith, CEO of Federal Express, said, "It is an inescapable fact that the [North] American economy is becoming much more like the European and Asian economies, entirely tied to global trade."

Your Task. Read your local newspapers for a week and peruse national newsmagazines for articles that support this assertion. Your instructor may ask you to (a) report on many articles or (b) select one article to summarize. Report your findings orally or in a memo to your instructor. This topic could be expanded into a long report for Chapter 13 or 14.

4.6 Talking Turkey: Avoiding Ambiguous Expressions (Obj. 5)

When a German firm received a message from a North American firm saying that it was "time to talk turkey," it was puzzled but decided to reply in Turkish, as requested.

Your Task. Assume you are a businessperson engaged in exporting and importing. As such, you are in constant communication with suppliers and customers around the world. In messages sent abroad, what kinds of ambiguous expressions should you avoid? In teams or individually, list three to five original examples of idioms, slang, acronyms, sports references, abbreviations, jargon, and two-word verbs.

4.7 What Makes a "Best Company for Minorities"? (Obj. 6)

SPEAKING

The Conference Board of Canada has carried out research on organizations that have made impressive strides in creating inclusive work cultures for visible minorities. The results point to several areas that employers need to focus on in order to fully maximize the talents of visible minorities. Some of the critical success factors are noted below.[35]

- Top leadership commitment
- Alignment between the organization's strategic business plan and its human resources plan
- Internal accountability frameworks
- Supplier standards
- Zero tolerance for racism

Rich chapter resources are available on the Web site.

Your Task. Assume you are someone who believes your organization would be better if it were more diverse. Because of your interest in this area, your boss says he'd like you to give a three- to five-minute informational presentation at the next board meeting. Your assignment is to provide insights on what the leading companies for minority employees are doing. You decide to prepare your comments based on the results of the Conference Board's report, using as your outline the above bulleted list. You plan to provide examples of each means of fostering diversity. Your instructor may ask you to give your presentation (a) to the entire class or (b) to small groups.

C.L.U.E. review 4

Edit the following sentences to correct faults in grammar, capitalization, punctuation, spelling, and word use.

1. The President of MainStreet Enterprises, along with other executives of local companys are considering overseas' sales.
2. International business was all ready common among big companys however even small bussinesses are now seeking global markets.
3. 3 different employees asked the Supervisor and I whether we should give gifts to our chinese business guests?
4. Gifts for the children of an arab are welcome however gifts for an arabs wife are not advisible.
5. In latin america knifes are not proper gifts, they signify cutting off an relationship.
6. When it opened it's one hundred and twenty million dollar plant in Beijing Motorola had to offer housing too attract qualety applicants.
7. On May 12th a article titled The chinese puzzle which appeared in the magazine Workforce Management described the difficultys of managing employees' world wide.
8. We invited seventy-five employees to hear the cross cultural talk that begins at four p.m..
9. Although Canadas 2 official languages are french and english:it is unofficially a land of many languages.
10. Transparency international 2,005 international global perceptions index rank's iceland as the most ethical nation.

unit 2

The 3-x-3 Writing Process

chapter 5

Writing Process Phase 1: Analyze, Anticipate, Adapt

chapter 6

Writing Process Phase 2: Research, Organize, Compose

chapter 7

Writing Process Phase 3: Revise, Proofread, Evaluate

chapter 5

Writing Process Phase 1: Analyze, Anticipate, Adapt

objectives

1 Identify three basics of business writing, summarize the 3-x-3 writing process, and explain how a writing process helps a writer.

2 Explain how the writing process may be altered and how it is affected by team projects.

3 Clarify what is involved in analyzing a writing task and selecting a communication channel.

4 Describe anticipating and profiling the audience for a message.

5 Specify six writing techniques that help communicators adapt messages to the task and audience.

6 Explain why communicators must adapt their writing in four high-risk areas.

springboard *to discussion*

RadioShack Corp. caused a stir when management at the electronics retailer used e-mail to notify 400 employees of their dismissal from the company. "The workforce reduction notification is currently in progress," the e-mail reported. "Unfortunately your position is one that has been eliminated." Management experts expressed dismay over the event, questioning whether electronic notification was proper for announcing layoffs.[1]

learning objective

1

Approaching the Writing Process Systematically

As organizations continue to evolve, their representatives must finely tune their communication skills to project a new image and capture new clients. Preparing and writing any business message—whether a letter, e-mail, memo, or sales presentation—is easier when the writer or presenter has a systematic plan to follow.

Business Writing Basics

Business writing is purposeful, economical, and reader oriented.

Business writing differs from other writing you may have done. In writing school compositions and term papers, you probably focused on discussing your feelings or displaying your knowledge. Professors wanted to see your thought processes, and they wanted assurance that you had internalized the subject matter. You may have had to meet a minimum word count. Business writers, however, have different goals. In preparing business messages and oral presentations, you'll find that your writing needs to be:

- **Purposeful.** You will be writing to solve problems and convey information. You will have a definite purpose to fulfill in each message.
- **Economical.** You will try to present ideas clearly but concisely. Length is not rewarded.
- **Reader-oriented.** You will concentrate on looking at a problem from the reader's perspective instead of seeing it from your own.

Business writers seek to express rather than impress.

These distinctions actually ease the writer's task. In writing most business documents, you won't be searching your imagination for creative topic ideas. You won't be stretching your ideas to make them appear longer; conciseness is what counts in business. Furthermore, you won't be trying to dazzle readers with your extensive knowledge, powerful vocabulary, or graceful phrasing. The goal in business writing is to *express* rather than *impress*. You will be striving to get your ideas across naturally, simply, and clearly.

In many ways business writing is easier than academic writing, but it still requires hard work, especially from beginners. However, following a process, studying models, and practising the craft can make nearly anyone a successful business writer and speaker. This book provides all three components: process, products (models), and practices. First, you'll focus on the process of writing business messages.

Figure 5.1 ***The 3-x-3 Writing Process***

1 Prewriting

Analyze: Decide on your purpose. What do you want the receiver to do or believe? What channel is best?

Anticipate: Profile the audience. What does the receiver already know? Will the receiver's response be neutral, positive, or negative?

Adapt: What techniques can you use to adapt your message to its audience and anticipated reaction?

2 Writing

Research: Gather data to provide facts. Search company files, previous correspondence, and the Internet. What do you need to know to write this message?

Organize: Group similar facts together. Decide how to organize your information. Outline your plan and make notes.

Compose: Prepare a first draft, usually writing quickly.

3 Revising

Revise: Edit your message to be sure it is clear, conversational, concise, and readable.

Proofread: Read carefully to find errors in spelling, grammar, punctuation, names, numbers, and format.

Evaluate: Will this message achieve your purpose? Have you thought enough about the audience to be sure this message is appropriate and appealing?

The 3-x-3 Writing Process for Business Messages and Oral Presentations

This book divides the writing process into three distinct phases, as shown in Figure 5.1, with each phase further divided into three major activities. This 3-x-3 process provides you with a systematic plan for developing all your business communications—from simple memos and informational reports to corporate proposals and presentations.

The phases of the 3-x-3 writing process are prewriting, writing, and revising.

The time spent on each phase varies with the deadline, purpose, and audience for the message. The first phase (prewriting) prepares you to write and involves analyzing, anticipating, and adapting. The second phase (writing) involves researching, organizing, and then composing the message. Equipped with a plan, you are ready to compose the first draft of the letter. The third phase of the writing process involves revising, proofreading, and evaluating. After writing the first draft, you will revise the message for clarity, conciseness, tone, and readability. You will proofread carefully to ensure correct spelling, grammar, punctuation, and format. Finally, you will evaluate the message to see whether it accomplishes your goal.

Collecting data, organizing it, and composing a first draft make up the second phase of the writing process.

Adapting and Altering the Writing Process

learning objective 2

Although Figure 5.1 shows the three phases equally, the time you spend on each varies. Moreover, the process is not always linear.

Scheduling the Process. One expert gives these rough estimates for scheduling a project: 25 percent worrying and planning (Phase 1), 25 percent writing (Phase 2), 45 percent revising, and 5 percent proofreading (Phase 3). These are rough guides, yet you can see that good writers spend most of their time revising. Much depends, of course, on your project, its importance, and your familiarity with it. What's critical to remember, though, is that revising is a major component of the writing process.

In the writing process, revising takes the most time.

This process may seem a bit complicated for the daily messages and oral presentations that many businesspeople prepare. Does this same process apply to memos and short letters? And how do collaborators and modern computer technologies affect the process?

Although good writers proceed through each phase of the writing process, some steps may be compressed for short, routine messages. Brief, everyday documents enlist the 3-x-3 process, but many of the steps are performed quickly, without prolonged deliberation. For example, prewriting may take the form of a few moments of reflection. The writing phase may consist of looking in the files quickly, jotting a few notes in the margin of the original document, and composing at your computer. Revising might consist of reading a printout, double-checking the spelling and grammar, and making a few changes. Longer, more involved documents—such as persuasive memos, sales letters, management reports, proposals, and résumés—require more attention to all parts of the process.

Steps in the writing process may be rearranged, shortened, or repeated.

Recursive Nature of the Process. One other point about the 3-x-3 writing process needs clarification. It may appear that you perform one step and progress to the next, always following a linear order. Most business writing, however, is not that rigid. Although writers perform the tasks described, the steps may be rearranged, abbreviated, or repeated. Some writers revise every sentence and paragraph as they go. Many find that new ideas occur after they've begun to write, causing them to back up, alter the organization, and rethink their plan. Thus the 3-x-3 writing process is more nearly recursive than linear: it sometimes curves backward before moving forward.

You should expect to follow the 3-x-3 process closely as you begin developing your business communication skills. With experience, though, you'll become like other good writers and presenters who alter, compress, and rearrange the steps as needed.

Working With Teams

As you learned in Chapter 2, many of today's workers will work with teams to deliver services, develop products, and complete projects. It's almost assumed that today's progressive organizations will employ teams in some capacity to achieve their objectives.[2] Because much of a team's work involves writing, you can expect to be putting your writing skills to work as part of the team.

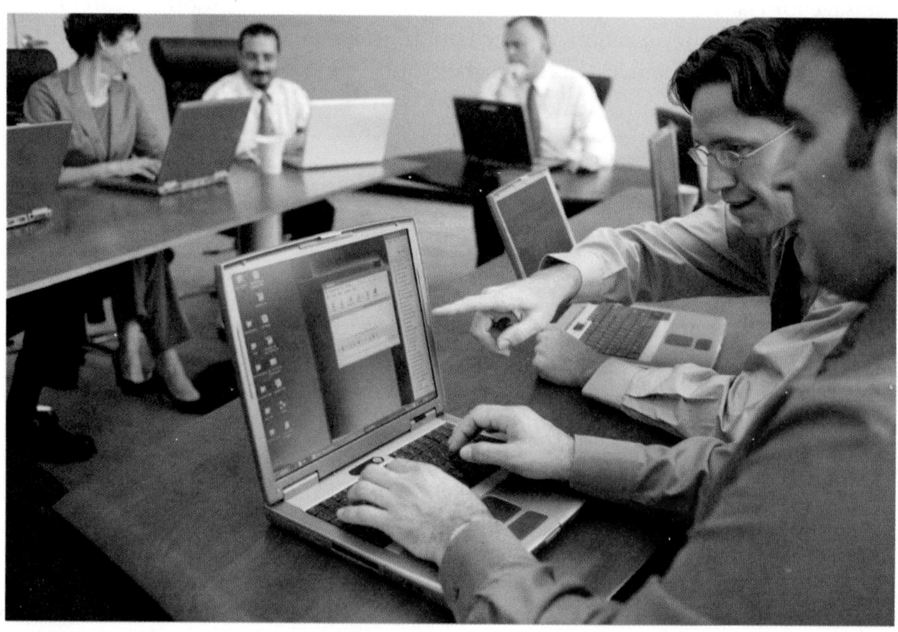

Team writing and collaboration have never been easier, thanks to the wiki. Named after the Hawaiian word for "quick" and popularized by online encyclopedia Wikipedia, wikis enable teams to create and edit shared documents using a simple Web browser.

Photo: © Purestock/Getty Images

When is writing collaboration necessary? It is especially important for (1) big tasks, (2) items with short deadlines, and (3) team projects that require the expertise or consensus of many people. Businesspeople sometimes collaborate on short documents, such as memos, letters, information briefs, procedures, and policies, but more often, teams work together on big documents and presentations.

Team-written documents and presentations are standard in most organizations because collaboration has many advantages. Most important, collaboration produces a better product. Many heads are better than one. In addition, team members and organizations benefit from team processes. Working together helps socialize members. They learn more about the organization's values and procedures. They are able to break down functional barriers, and they improve both formal and informal chains of communication. Additionally, they buy into a project when they are part of its development. Members of effective teams are eager to implement their recommendations.

Team-written documents and presentations produce better products.

In preparing big projects, teams may not actually function together for each phase of the writing process. Typically, team members gather at the beginning to brainstorm. They iron out answers to questions about purpose, audience, content, organization, and design of their document or presentation. They develop procedures for team functioning, as you learned in Chapter 2. Then they often assign segments of the project to individual members. Thus, teams work together closely in Phase 1 (prewriting) of the writing process. However, members generally work separately in Phase 2 (writing), when they conduct research, organize their findings, and compose a first draft. During Phase 3 (revising), teams may work together to synthesize their drafts and offer suggestions for revision. They might assign one person the task of preparing the final document and another the job of proofreading. The revision and evaluation phase might be repeated several times before the final product is ready for presentation.

Teams generally work closely in Phase 1, work separately in Phase 2, and synthesize their drafts in Phase 3.

One of the most frustrating tasks for teams is writing shared documents. Keeping the different versions straight and recognizing who made what comment can be confusing. Microsoft Word, however, provides a number of wonderful tools that enable team members to track changes and insert comments while editing one team document. The accompanying Tech Talk box (page 96) presents these tools.

Writing Process Phase 1: Analyze

learning objective

3

Whether you're working with a team, composing by yourself, or preparing an oral presentation, the end result of your efforts can be greatly improved by following the steps outlined in the 3-x-3 writing process. Not only are you more likely to get your message across, but you'll also feel less anxious and your writing will progress more quickly. The remainder of this chapter focuses on the prewriting phase of composition: analyzing, anticipating, and adapting. In this phase you'll first need to identify the purpose of the message and select the best channel or form in which to deliver it.

Identifying the Purpose

Most business communication has both primary purposes (to inform or persuade) and secondary purposes (to promote goodwill).

As you begin to compose a message, ask yourself two important questions: (1) Why am I sending this message? and (2) What do I hope to achieve? Your responses will determine how you organize and present your information.

Your message may have primary and secondary purposes. For academic work your primary purpose may be merely to complete the assignment; secondary purposes might be to make yourself look good and to get a good grade. The primary purposes for sending business messages are typically to inform and to persuade. A

tech talk

Using Technology to Edit and Revise Collaborative Documents

Collaborative writing and editing projects are challenging. Fortunately, Microsoft Word offers many useful tools to help team members edit and share documents electronically. Two simple but useful editing tools are *Highlight* and *Font Color*. These tools, which are found on the **Formatting** toolbar, enable reviewers to point out errors and explain problematic passages through the use of contrast. However, some projects may require more advanced editing tools such as *Track Changes* and *Insert Comments*.

Track Changes. To suggest specific editing changes to other team members, *Track Changes* is handy. The revised wording is visible onscreen, and deletions show up in call-out balloons that appear in the right-hand margin. Suggested revisions offered by different team members are identified and dated. The original writer may accept or reject these changes. In recent versions of Word, you'll find *Track Changes* on the **Tools** menu.

Insert Comments. Probably the most useful editing tool is *Insert Comments*. This tool allows users to point out problematic passages or errors, ask or answer questions, and share ideas without changing or adding text. When more than one person adds comments, the comments appear in different colours and are identified by the individual writer's name and a date/time stamp. To use this tool in newer versions of Word, each reviewer must click **Tools,** then **Options,** and fill in the **User Information** section. In older versions of Word, this collaborative tool was called *Annotation*. To facilitate adding, reviewing, editing, or deleting comments, Word now provides a special toolbar. You can activate it by using the **View** pull-down menu (click **Toolbars** and **Reviewing**). On the **Reviewing** toolbar, click **New Comment**. Then type your comment, which can be seen in the Web or print layout view (click **View** and **Print Layout** or **Web Layout**).

Completing a Document. When a document is finished, be sure to accept or reject all changes on the **Reviewing** toolbar, a step that removes the tracking information.

secondary purpose is to promote goodwill: you and your organization want to look good in the eyes of your audience.

Most business messages do nothing more than *inform*. They explain procedures, announce meetings, answer questions, and transmit findings. Some business messages, however, are meant to *persuade*. These messages sell products, convince managers, motivate employees, and win over customers. Informative messages are developed differently than persuasive messages.

Selecting the Best Channel

After identifying the purpose of your message, you need to select the most appropriate communication channel. As you learned in Chapter 1, some information is most efficiently and effectively delivered orally. Other messages should be written, and still others are best delivered electronically. Whether to set up a meeting, send a message by e-mail, or write a report depends on some of the following factors:

- Importance of the message
- Amount and speed of feedback required
- Necessity of a permanent record
- Cost of the channel
- Degree of formality desired

The foregoing factors could help you decide which of the channels shown in Figure 5.2 is most appropriate for delivering a message.

FIGURE 5.2 ***Choosing Communication Channels***

Channel	Best Use
Blog	When one person needs to present digital information easily so that it is available to others.
E-mail	When you need feedback but not immediately. Lack of security makes it problematic for personal, emotional, or private messages.
Face-to-face conversation	When you need a rich, interactive medium. Useful for delivering persuasive, bad-news, and personal messages.
Face-to-face group meeting	When group decisions and consensus are important. Inefficient for merely distributing information.
Fax	When your message must cross time zones or international boundaries, when a written record is significant, or when speed is important.
Instant message	When you are online and need a quick response. Useful for determining whether someone is available for a phone conversation.
Letter	When a written record or formality is required, especially with customers, the government, suppliers, or others outside an organization.
Memo	When you want a written record to clearly explain policies, discuss procedures, or collect information within an organization.
Phone call	When you must deliver or gather information quickly, when nonverbal cues are unimportant, and when you cannot meet in person.
Report or proposal	When you are delivering complex data internally or externally.
Voice mail message	When you wish to leave important or routine information that the receiver can respond to when convenient.
Video- or teleconference	When group consensus and interaction are important but members are geographically dispersed.
Wiki	When digital information must be made available to others. Useful for collaboration because participants can easily add, remove, and edit content.

Choosing the best channel to deliver a message depends on the importance of the message, the feedback required, the need for a permanent record, the cost, and the degree of formality needed.

Writing Process Phase 1: Anticipate

learning objective

4

By profiling your audience before you write, you can identify the appropriate tone, language, and channel.

Some messages are less successful than others. A good writer anticipates the audience for a message: What is the reader like? How will that reader react to the message? Although you can't always know exactly who the reader is, you can imagine some characteristics of the reader. By profiling your audience and shaping a message to respond to that profile, you are more likely to achieve your communication goals.

Profiling the Audience

Visualizing your audience is a pivotal step in the writing process. The questions in Figure 5.3 (page 98) will help you profile your audience. How much time you devote to answering these questions depends greatly on your message and its context. No matter how long or short your message, spend some time thinking about the audience so that you can tailor your words to your readers or listeners.

FIGURE 5.3 ***Asking the Right Questions to Profile Your Audience***

Primary Audience	Secondary Audience
Who is my primary reader or listener?	Who might see or hear this message after the primary audience?
What is my personal and professional relationship with that person?	How do these people differ from the primary audience?
What position does the individual hold in the organization?	How must I reshape my message to make it understandable and acceptable to others to whom it might be forwarded?
How much does that person know about the subject?	
What do I know about that person's education, beliefs, culture, and attitudes?	

Responding to the Profile

Anticipating your audience helps you make decisions about shaping the message. You'll discover what kind of language is appropriate, whether you're free to use specialized technical terms, whether you should explain everything, and so on. You'll decide whether your tone should be formal or informal, and you'll select the most desirable channel. Imagining whether the receiver is likely to be neutral, positive, or negative will help you determine how to organize your message.

Another result of profiling your audience will be recognizing whether a secondary audience is possible. If so, you may provide more background information and be more specific in identifying items that the secondary audience might not recognize. Analyzing the task and anticipating the audience assists you in adapting your message so that it will accomplish what you intend.

learning objective 5

Writing Process Phase 1: Adapt

After analyzing your purpose and anticipating your audience, you must convey your purpose to that audience. Adaptation is the process of creating a message that suits your audience.

One important aspect of adaptation is *tone*. Conveyed largely by the words in a message, tone reflects how a receiver feels upon reading or hearing a message. For example, think how you would react to these statements:

You must return the form by 5 p.m.
Would you please return the form by 5 p.m.

The wording of the first message establishes an aggressive or negative tone—no one likes being told what to do. The second message is reworded in a friendlier, more positive manner. Poorly chosen words may sound demeaning, condescending, discourteous, pretentious, or demanding.

Skilled communicators create a positive tone in their messages by using a number of adaptive techniques, some of which are unconscious. These include spotlighting receiver benefits; cultivating a "you" view; and avoiding gender, racial, age, and disability bias. Additional adaptive techniques include being courteous, using familiar words, and choosing precise words.

Ways to adapt to the audience include choosing the right words and tone; spotlighting reader benefits; cultivating a "you" view; and using sensitive, courteous language.

Spotlighting Receiver Benefits

Empathic communicators envision the receiver and focus on benefits to that person.

One communication consultant gives this solid advice to his business clients: "Always stress the benefit to the readers of whatever it is you're trying to get them to do. If you can show them how you're going to save them frustration or help them meet their goals, you have the makings of a powerful message."[3]

Empathy ***means being able to understand another's situation, feelings, and motives.***

Adapting your message to the receiver's needs means putting yourself in that person's shoes. It's called *empathy*. Empathic senders think about how a receiver will decode a message. They try to give something to the receiver, solve the receiver's problems, save the receiver money, or just understand the feelings and position of that person. Which of the following messages are more appealing to the receiver?

Effective communicators develop the "you" view in a sincere, not manipulative or critical, tone.

Sender-Focused	**Receiver-Focused**
Our warranty becomes effective only when we receive an owner's registration.	Your warranty begins working for you as soon as you return your owner's registration.
The Human Resources Department requires that every employee complete an online questionnaire immediately so that we can allocate our training resource funds.	You can be one of the first employees to sign up for the new career development program. Complete the online questionnaire and send it immediately.

Cultivating the "You" View

Notice how the previous receiver-focused messages included the word *you*. In concentrating on receiver benefits, skilled communicators naturally develop the "you" view. They emphasize second-person pronouns (*you, your*) instead of first-person pronouns (*I/we, us, our*). Whether your goal is to inform, persuade, or promote goodwill, the catchiest words you can use are *you* and *your*. Compare the following examples.

"I/We" View	**"You" View**
We have shipped your order by UPS, and we are sure it will arrive in time for the sales promotion January 15.	Your order will be delivered by UPS in time for your sales promotion January 15.
I'm asking all of our employees to respond to the attached survey regarding working conditions.	Because your ideas count, please complete the attached survey regarding working conditions.

Your goal is to focus on the reader, but second-person pronouns can be overused and misused. Readers appreciate genuine interest; on the other hand, they resent obvious attempts at manipulation. Some sales messages, for example, are guilty of overkill when they include *you* dozens of times in a direct-mail promotion. Furthermore, the word can sometimes create the wrong impression. Consider this statement: *You cannot return merchandise until you receive written approval. You* appears twice, but the reader feels singled out for criticism. In the following version the message is less personal and more positive: *Customers may return merchandise with written approval.* In short, avoid using *you* for general statements that suggest blame and could cause ill will.

In recognizing the value of the "you" view, however, writers do not have to sterilize their writing and avoid any first-person pronouns or words that show their feelings. Skilled communicators are able to convey sincerity, warmth, and enthusiasm by the words they choose. Don't be afraid to use phrases such as *I'm happy* or *We're delighted*, if you truly are.

When speaking face to face, communicators show sincerity and warmth with nonverbal cues such as a smile and pleasant voice tone. In letters, memos, and e-mail messages, however, only expressive words and phrases can show these feelings. These phrases suggest hidden messages that say to readers and customers, "You are important, I hear you, and I'm honestly trying to please you."

Using Bias-Free Language

Sensitive communicators avoid gender, racial or ethnic, and disability biases.

In adapting a message to its audience, be sure your language is sensitive and bias-free. Few writers set out to be offensive. Sometimes, though, we all say things that we never thought might be hurtful. The real problem is that we don't think about the words that stereotype groups of people, such as *the boys in the mailroom* or *the girls in the front office*. Be cautious about expressions that might be biased in terms of gender, race, ethnicity, age, and disability.[4]

Avoiding Gender Bias. You can defuse gender time bombs by replacing words that exclude or stereotype women (sometimes called *sexist language*) with neutral, inclusive expressions. The following examples show how sexist terms and phrases can be replaced with neutral ones.

Gender-Biased	Improved
female doctor, woman lawyer, cleaning woman	doctor, lawyer, cleaner
waiter/waitress, authoress, stewardess	server, author, cabin attendant
mankind, man-hour, man-made	humanity, working hours, artificial
office girls	office workers
the doctor ... he	doctors ... they
the teacher ... she	teachers ... they
executives and their wives	executives and their guests
foreman, flagman, workman	lead worker, flagger, worker
businessman, salesman	businessperson, sales representative
Each worker had his picture taken.	Each worker had a picture taken.
	All workers had their pictures taken.
	Each worker had his or her picture taken.

Generally, you can avoid gender-biased language by leaving out the words *man* or *woman*, by using plural nouns and pronouns, or by changing to a gender-free word (*person* or *representative*). Avoid the "his or her" option whenever possible; it's wordy and conspicuous. With a little effort, you can usually find a construction that is graceful, grammatical, and unselfconscious.

Avoiding Racial or Ethnic Bias. You need indicate racial or ethnic identification only if the context demands it.

Racially or Ethnically Biased	Improved
A Korean accountant was hired.	An accountant was hired.
James Lee, a Native Canadian, applied.	James Lee applied.

Avoiding Age Bias. Specify age only if it is relevant, and avoid expressions that are demeaning or subjective.

Age-Biased	Improved
The law applied to old people.	The law applied to people over 65.
Sally Kay, 55, was transferred.	Sally Kay was transferred.
a spry old gentleman	a man
a little old lady	a woman

Avoiding Disability Bias. Unless relevant, do not refer to an individual's disability. When necessary, use terms that do not stigmatize individuals with disabilities.

Disability-Biased	Improved
afflicted with, suffering from, crippled by	has
defect, disease	condition
confined to a wheelchair	uses a wheelchair

The preceding examples give you a quick look at a few problem expressions. The real key to bias-free communication, though, lies in your awareness and commitment. Be on the lookout to be sure that your messages do not exclude, stereotype, or offend people.

Positive language creates goodwill and gives more options to readers.

Being Conversational but Professional

Strive for conversational expression, but remember to be professional.

Most instant messages, e-mail messages, business letters, memos, and reports replace conversation. Thus, they are most effective when they convey an informal, conversational tone instead of a formal, pretentious tone. Workplace messages should not, however, become so casual that they sound low-level and unprofessional.

Instant messaging (IM) enables coworkers to have informal, spontaneous conversations. Some companies have accepted IM as a serious workplace tool. With the increasing use of instant messaging and e-mail, however, a major problem has developed. Sloppy, unprofessional expression appears in many workplace messages. You will learn more about the dangers of e-mail in Chapter 8. At this point, though, we are focusing on the tone of the language.

A professional image involves sounding educated and mature.

To project a professional image, you must sound educated and mature. Professional messages do not include IM abbreviations, slang, sentence fragments, and chitchat. We urge you to strive for a warm, conversational tone that avoids low-level diction.

Your goal is a warm, friendly tone that sounds professional. Although some writers are too casual, others are overly formal. To impress readers, they use big words, long sentences, legal terminology, and third-person constructions. Stay away from expressions such as *the undersigned, the writer*, and *the affected party*. You will sound friendlier with familiar pronouns such as *I, we*, and *you*. Study the following examples to see how to achieve a professional, yet conversational tone.

Unprofessional	**Improved**
Hey, boss, GR8 news! Firewall now installed!! BTW, check with me b4 announcing it.	Mr. Smith, our new firewall software is now installed. Please check with me before announcing it.

Overly Formal	**Conversational**
All employees are herewith instructed to return the appropriately designated contracts to the undersigned.	Please return your contracts to me.

Expressing Yourself Positively

Negative expressions can often be rephrased to sound positive.

Certain negative words create ill will because they appear to blame or accuse readers. For example, opening a letter to a customer with *You claim that* suggests that you don't believe the customer. Other loaded words that can get you in trouble are *complaint, criticism, defective, failed, mistake*, and *neglected*. Often the writer is unconscious of the effect of these words. To avoid angry reactions, restrict negative words and try to find positive ways to express ideas. You provide more options to the reader when you tell what can be done instead of what can't be done.

Negative	**Positive**
Your letter of May 2 claims that you returned a defective headset.	Your May 2 letter describes a headset you returned.
You cannot park in Lot H until April 1.	You may park in Lot H starting April 1.
You won't be sorry that ...	You will be happy that ...
Without the aid of top management, the problem can't be solved.	With the aid of top management, the problem can be solved.

Being Courteous

Even when you are justifiably angry, courteous language is the best way to achieve your objectives.

Maintaining a courteous tone involves not just guarding against rudeness but also avoiding words that sound demanding or preachy. Expressions like *you should, you must*, and *you have to* cause people to instinctively react with *Oh, yeah?* One remedy is to turn these demands into rhetorical questions that begin with *Will you please ....* Giving reasons for a request also softens the tone.

Less Courteous	**More Courteous**
You must complete this report before Friday.	Will you please complete the report by Friday.
You should organize a car pool in this department.	Organizing a car pool will reduce your transportation costs and help preserve the environment.

Even when you feel justified in displaying anger, remember that losing your temper or being sarcastic will seldom accomplish your goals as a business communicator to inform, to persuade, and to create goodwill. When you are irritated, frustrated, or infuriated, keep cool and try to defuse the situation. Concentrate on the real problem. What must be done to solve it?

You May Be Thinking This	It's Better to Say This
This is the second time I've written. Can't you get anything right?	Please credit my account for $843. My latest statement shows that the error noted in my letter of June 2 has not been corrected.
Am I the only one who can read the operating manual?	Let's review the operating manual together so that you can get your documents to print correctly next time.

Simplifying Your Language

The simpler the language, the better.

In adapting your message to your audience, whenever possible use short, familiar words that you think they will recognize. Don't, however, avoid a big word that conveys your idea efficiently and is appropriate for the audience. Your goal is to shun pompous and pretentious language. Instead, use "go" words. If you mean *begin*, don't say *commence* or *initiate*. If you mean *give*, don't write *render*.[5] By substituting everyday, familiar words for unfamiliar ones, as shown here, you help your audience comprehend your ideas quickly.

Unfamiliar	Familiar
commensurate	equal
interrogate	question
materialize	appear
obfuscate	confuse
remuneration	pay, salary
terminate	end

Using familiar but precise language helps receivers understand.

At the same time, be selective in your use of jargon. *Jargon* describes technical or specialized terms within a field. These terms enable insiders to communicate complex ideas briefly, but to outsiders they mean nothing. Human resources professionals, for example, know precisely what's meant by *cafeteria plan* (a benefits option program), but most of us would be thinking about lunch. Geologists refer to *plate tectonics*, and physicians discuss *metastatic carcinomas*. These terms mean little to most of us. Use specialized language only when the audience will understand it. And don't forget to consider secondary audiences: Will those potential readers understand any technical terms used?

Using Precise, Vigorous Words

Strong verbs and concrete nouns give readers more information and keep them interested. Don't overlook the thesaurus (or the thesaurus program on your computer) for expanding your word choices and vocabulary. Whenever possible, use specific words as shown here.

Imprecise, Dull	More Precise
a change in profits	a 25 percent increase in profits a 10 percent plunge in profits
to say	to promise, confess, understand to allege, assert, assume, judge
to think about	to identify, diagnose, analyze to probe, examine, inspect

By reviewing the tips in the following checklist, you can master the steps of writing preparation. As you review these tips, remember the three basics of prewriting: analyzing, anticipating, and adapting.

Checklist for Adapting a Message to Its Audience

- ✓ **Identify the message purpose.** Ask yourself why you are communicating and what you hope to achieve. Look for primary and secondary purposes.
- ✓ **Select the most appropriate form.** Determine whether you need a permanent record or whether the message is too sensitive to put in writing.
- ✓ **Profile the audience.** Identify your relationship with the reader and your knowledge about that individual or group. Assess how much the receiver knows about the subject.
- ✓ **Focus on reader benefits.** Phrase your statements from the reader's viewpoint, not the writer's. Concentrate on the "you" view (*Your order will arrive, You can enjoy, Your ideas count*).
- ✓ **Avoid gender and racial bias.** Use bias-free words (*businessperson* instead of *businessman*; *working hours* instead of *man-hours*). Omit ethnic identification unless the context demands it.
- ✓ **Avoid age and disability bias.** Include age only if relevant. Avoid potentially demeaning expressions (*spry old gentleman*), and use terms that do not stigmatize disabled people (*he is disabled* instead of *he is a cripple* or *he has a handicap*).
- ✓ **Be conversational but professional.** Strive for a warm, friendly tone that is not overly formal or familiar. Avoid slang and low-level diction.
- ✓ **Express ideas positively rather than negatively.** Instead of *Your order can't be shipped before June 1*, say *Your order can be shipped June 1.*
- ✓ **Use short, familiar words.** Use technical terms and big words only if they are appropriate for the audience (*end*, not *terminate*; *required*, not *mandatory*).
- ✓ **Search for precise, vigorous words.** Use a thesaurus if necessary to find strong verbs and concrete nouns (*announces* instead of *says*, *brokerage* instead of *business*).

learning objective

6

Adapting to Legal Responsibilities

One of your primary responsibilities in writing for an organization or for yourself is to avoid language that may result in litigation. Another responsibility is to be ethical. Both of these concerns revolve around the use and abuse of language. You can protect yourself and avoid litigation by knowing what's legal and by adapting your language accordingly. Be especially careful when your messages involve investments, safety, marketing, human resources, and copyright law.

Investment Information

Writers describing the sale of stocks or financial services must follow specific laws written to protect investors. Any messages—including e-mails, letters, newsletters, and pamphlets—must be free from misleading information, exaggerations, or half-truths. Experienced financial writers know that careless language and even poor timing may provoke litigation.

Safety Information

Warnings on dangerous products must be written especially clearly.

Writers describing potentially dangerous products worry not only about protecting people from physical harm but also about being sued. Although far fewer product liability cases are filed in Canada than in the United States,[6] litigation arising from these cases is an active area of tort law (tort law involves compensating those who have been injured by the wrongdoing of others).[7] Manufacturers are obligated to warn consumers of any risks in their products. These warnings must do more than suggest danger; they must also clearly tell people how to use the product safely. In writing warnings, concentrate on major points. Omit anything that is not critical. In the work area, describe a potential problem and tell how to solve it. For example, *Lead dust is harmful and gets on your clothes. Change your clothes before leaving work.*

Clearly written safety messages use easy-to-understand words, such as *doctor* instead of *physician, clean* instead of *sanitary*, and *burn* instead of *incinerate.* Technical terms are defined. For example, *Asbestos is a carcinogen (something that causes cancer).*[8] Effective safety messages also include highlighting techniques such as using headings and bullets. In coming chapters you'll learn more about these techniques for improving readability.

Marketing Information

Sales and marketing messages must not make claims that can't be verified.

Sales and marketing messages are illegal if they falsely advertise prices, performance capability, quality, or other product characteristics. Marketing messages must not deceive the buyer in any way. According to Canada's Competition Bureau, "misleading advertising occurs when representation is made to the public that is materially misleading."[9] If the consumer purchases the product or service based on the advertising, it is material. To determine whether an advertisement is misleading, the courts consider the "general impression" it conveys as well as the literal meaning.[10] Sellers of services must also be cautious about the language they use to describe what they will do. Letters, reports, and proposals that describe services to be performed are interpreted as contracts in court. Therefore, the language must not promise more than intended. Here are some dangerous words (and recommended alternatives) that have created misunderstandings leading to lawsuits.[11]

Dangerous Word	Court Interpretation	Recommended Alternative
inspect	to examine critically, to investigate and test officially, to scrutinize	to review, to study, to tour the facility
assure	to render safe, to make secure, to give confidence, to cause to feel certain	to facilitate, to provide further confidence, to enhance the reliability of

Human Resources Information

The safest employment recommendations contain positive, job-related information.

The vast number of lawsuits relating to employment makes this a treacherous area for business communicators. In evaluating employees in the workplace, avoid making unsubstantiated negative comments. It's also unwise to assess traits (*she is unreliable*) because they require subjective judgment. Concentrate instead on specific incidents (*in the last month she missed four work days and was late three times*). Defamation lawsuits have become so common that some companies no longer provide letters of recommendation for former employees. To be safe, give recommendations only when the former employee authorizes the recommendation and when you can say something positive. Stick to job-related information.

Statements in employee handbooks also require careful wording because a court might rule that such statements are "implied contracts." Companies are warned to avoid promissory phrases in writing job advertisements, application forms, and offer letters. Phrases that suggest permanent employment and guaranteed job security can be interpreted as contracts.[12]

In adapting messages to meet today's increasingly litigious business environment, be sensitive to the rights of others and to your own rights. The key elements in this adaptation process are awareness of laws, sensitivity to interpretations, and careful use of language.

Summary of Learning Objectives

1 **Identify three basics of business writing, summarize the 3-x-3 writing process, and explain how a writing process helps a writer.** Business writing differs from academic writing in that it strives to solve business problems, it is economical, and it is reader-oriented. Phase 1 of the 3-x-3 writing process (prewriting) involves analyzing the message, anticipating the audience, and considering ways to adapt the message to the audience. Phase 2 (writing) involves researching the topic, organizing the material, and composing the message. Phase 3 (revising) includes proofreading and evaluating the message. A writing process helps a writer by providing a systematic plan describing what to do in creating messages.

2 **Explain how the writing process may be altered and how it is affected by team projects.** The writing process may be compressed for short messages; steps in the process may be rearranged. Team writing, which is necessary for large projects or when wide expertise is necessary, alters the writing process. Teams often work together in brainstorming and working out their procedures and assignments. Then individual members write their portions of the report or presentation during Phase 2. During Phase 3 (revising) teams may work together to combine their drafts. Collaboration software helps teams working on shared documents.

3 **Clarify what is involved in analyzing a writing task and selecting a communication channel.** Communicators must decide why they are delivering a message and what they hope to achieve. Although many messages only inform, some must also persuade. After identifying the purpose of a message, communicators must choose the most appropriate channel. That choice depends on the importance of the message, the amount and speed of feedback required, the need for a permanent record, the cost of the channel, and the degree of formality desired.

4 **Describe anticipating and profiling the audience for a message.** A good communicator tries to envision the audience for a message. What does the receiver know about the topic? How well does the receiver know the sender? What is known about the receiver's education, beliefs, culture, and attitudes? Will the response to the message be positive, neutral, or negative? Is the secondary audience different from the primary audience? How should a document be changed if it will be read by additional readers?

5 **Specify six writing techniques that help communicators adapt messages to the task and audience.** Skilled communicators strive to (a) spotlight reader benefits; (b) look at a message from the receiver's perspective (the "you" view); (c) use sensitive language that avoids gender, racial, ethnic, and disability biases; (d) state ideas positively; (e) show courtesy; and (f) use short, familiar, and precise words.

6 **Explain why communicators must adapt their writing in four high-risk areas.** Actions and language in four information areas generate the most lawsuits: investments, safety, marketing, and human resources. In writing about investments, communicators must avoid misleading information, exaggerations, and half-truths. Safety information, including warnings, must tell people clearly how to use a product safely and motivate them to do so. In addition to being honest, marketing information must not promise more than intended. Communicators in the area of human resources must use careful wording (particularly in employment recommendations and employee handbooks) to avoid potential lawsuits. They must also avoid oral promises that can result in lawsuits.

chapter review

1. Explain how writing business messages differs from writing academic compositions and term papers. (Obj. 1)
2. Describe the components in each stage of the 3-x-3 writing process. (Obj. 1)
3. Name three instances in which collaborative writing is necessary. (Obj. 2)
4. Why is writing shared documents frustrating, and what software tools make the editing task easier? (Obj. 2)
5. List five factors to consider when selecting a communication channel. (Obj. 3)
6. Why should you profile your audience before composing a message? (Obj. 4)
7. How can a writer emphasize reader benefits? (Obj. 5)
8. When is the "you" view appropriate, and when is it inappropriate? (Obj. 5)
9. What is bias-free language? Give original examples. (Obj. 5)
10. Name replacements for the following gender-biased terms: *waitress, stewardess, foreman.* (Obj. 5)
11. Revise the following expression to show more courtesy: *For the last time I'm warning all staff members that they must use virus-protection software—or else!* (Obj. 5)
12. What is jargon, and when is it appropriate for business writing? (Obj. 5)
13. What's wrong with using words such as *commence, mandate,* and *interrogate*? (Obj. 5)
14. What four information areas generate the most lawsuits? (Obj. 6)
15. How can business communicators protect themselves against litigation? (Obj. 6)

critical thinking

1. Business communicators are encouraged to profile or "visualize" the audience for their messages. How is this possible if you don't really know the people who will receive a sales letter or who will hear your business presentation? (Obj. 4)
2. How can the 3-x-3 writing process help the writer of a business report as well as the writer of an oral presentation? (Obj. 1)
3. If adapting your tone to the receiving audience and developing reader benefits are so important, why do we see so much writing that does not reflect these suggestions? (Objs. 3–5)
4. Discuss the following statement: "The English language is a landmine—it is filled with terms that are easily misinterpreted as derogatory and others that are blatantly insulting … . Being fair and objective is not enough; employers must also appear to be so."[13] (Obj. 5)

activities

5.1 Document for Analysis (Obj. 5)

Your Task. Discuss the following memo, which is based on an actual document sent to employees. How can you apply what you learned in this chapter to improving this memo? Revise the memo to make it more courteous, positive, and precise. Focus on developing the "you" view and using familiar language. Remove any gender-biased references. Consider revising this memo as a collaboration project using Word's **Comment** feature.

TO: All Employees Using HP 5000 Computers

It has recently come to my attention that a computer security problem exists within our organization. I understand that the problem is twofold in nature:

a. You have been sharing computer passwords.
b. You are using automatic logon procedures.

Henceforth, you are prohibited from sharing passwords for security reasons that should be axiomatic. We also must forbid you to use automatic logon files because they empower anyone to have access to our entire computer system and all company data.

Enclosed please find a form that you must sign and return to the aforementioned individual, indicating your acknowledgment of and acquiescence to the procedures described here. Any computer user whose signed form is not returned will have his personal password invalidated.

5.2 Selecting Communication Channels (Obj. 3)

Your Task. Using Figure 5.2, suggest the best communication channels for the following messages. Assume that all channels shown are available. Be prepared to explain your choices.

a. You must respond to a notice from the Canada Revenue Agency insisting that you did not pay the correct amount for last quarter's employer's taxes.

Rich chapter resources are available on the Web site. 

b. Members of your task force must meet to discuss ways to improve communication among 5 000 employees at 32 branches of your large company. Task force members are from Laval, Ottawa, Winnipeg, Regina, and Victoria.
c. A prospective client in Italy wants price quotes for a number of your products—*pronto*!
d. As assistant to the vice president, you are to investigate the possibility of developing internship programs with several nearby colleges and universities.
e. As department manager, you need to inform nine staff members of a safety training session scheduled for the following month.

5.3 Analyzing Audiences (Obj. 4)

Your Task. Using the questions in Figure 5.3, write a brief analysis of the audience for each of the following communication tasks.

a. An e-mail memo to your district sales manager describing your visit to a new customer who demands special discounts.
b. A letter of application for a job advertised in your local newspaper. Your qualifications match the job description.
c. An e-mail memo to your boss persuading her to allow you to attend a computer class that will require you to leave work early two days a week for ten weeks.
d. An unsolicited sales letter promoting life insurance to a targeted group of executives.
e. A letter from a credit card organization refusing credit to an applicant.

5.4 Reader Benefits and the "You" View (Obj. 5)

Your Task. Revise the following sentences to emphasize the reader's perspective and the "you" view.

a. For just $300 per person, we have arranged a three-day trip to Las Vegas that includes deluxe accommodations, the "City Lights" show, and selected meals.
b. I give my permission for you to attend the two-day workshop.
c. We are presenting an in-house training program for employees who want to improve their writing skills.
d. We are pleased to announce an arrangement with Dell that allows us to offer discounted computers in the student bookstore.
e. Our safety policy forbids us from renting power equipment to anyone who cannot demonstrate proficiency in its use.

5.5 Language Bias (Obj. 5)

Your Task. Revise the following sentences to eliminate gender, racial, age, and disability stereotypes.

a. A skilled assistant proofreads her boss's documents and catches any errors he makes.
b. CyberSystems hired Jamal Alexander, an African Canadian, for the position of project manager.
c. Because Kevin is confined to a wheelchair, we look for restaurants without stairs.
d. Every employee must wear his ID badge on the job.
e. Some restaurants offer special discounts for old people.

5.6 Positive Expression (Obj. 5)

Your Task. Revise the following statements to make them more positive.

a. If you fail to follow each requirement, you will not receive your $50 rebate.
b. In the message you left at our Web site, you claim that you returned a printer.
c. Although you apparently failed to read the operator's manual, we are sending you a replacement blade for your food processor. Next time read page 18 carefully so that you will know how to attach this blade.
d. We can't process your application because you neglected to insert your social insurance number.
e. Construction cannot begin until the building plans are approved.

5.7 Courteous Expression (Obj. 5)

Your Task. Revise the following messages to show greater courtesy.

a. We will be forced to deactivate your debit card if you don't call this 800 number immediately to activate it.
b. This is the last time I'm writing to try to get you to record my January 6 payment of $500 to my account. Anyone who can read can see from the attached documents that I've tried to explain this to you before.
c. As departmental manager, you must organize a car pool if you expect to help us reduce air pollution.
d. To the Staff: Can't anyone around here read instructions? Page 12 of the operating manual for our copy machine very clearly describes how to remove jammed paper. But I'm the only one who ever does it, and I've had it! No more copies will be made until you learn how to remove jammed paper!
e. If you had listened to our agent more carefully, you would know that your policy does not cover accidents outside Canada.

5.8 Familiar Words (Obj. 5)

Your Task. Revise the following sentences to avoid unfamiliar words.

a. The salary we are offering is commensurate with other managers' remuneration.
b. To expedite ratification of this agreement, we urge you to vote in the affirmative.
c. In a dialogue with the manager, I learned that you plan to terminate our agreement.
d. Did the steering problem materialize subsequent to our recall effort?
e. Pursuant to your invitation, we will interrogate our agent.

5.9 Precise Words (Obj. 5)

Your Task. From the choices in parentheses, select the most precise, vigorous words.

a. When replying to e-mail, (*bring in, include, put*) enough of the old message for (*someone, the person, the recipient*) to recognize the original note.
b. For a (*hard, long, complicated*) e-mail message, (*make, create, have*) the note in your word processing program.
c. If an e-mail (*thing, catch, glitch*) interferes while writing, you can easily (*get, have, retrieve*) your message.
d. We plan to (*acknowledge, publicize, applaud*) the work of exemplary employees.
e. Ryan's excellent report has (*a lot of, many, a warehouse of*) relevant facts.

For the following sentences provide more precise alternatives for the italicized words.

f. In her e-mail memo she said that she would (a) *change* overtime hours in order to (b) *fix* the budget.
g. Our new manager (a) *said* that only (b) *the right kind of* applicants should apply.
h. After (a) *reading* the report, I decided it was (b) *bad.*
i. Rebecca said the movie was (a) *different*, but her remarks weren't very (b) *clear* to us.
j. I'm (a) *going* to Hamilton tomorrow, and I plan to (b) *find out* the real problem.

5.10 Legal Language (Obj. 6)

Your Task. To avoid possible litigation, revise the italicized words in the following sentences taken from proposals.

a. We have *inspected* the septic system and will send a complete report.
b. Our goal is to *assure* completion of the project on schedule.
c. We will *determine* the amount of stress for each supporting column.

5.11 Clear Writing

RESEARCH

Your boss has always been a stickler for clear business writing. He has preached on the subject so much that a local business organization has asked him to address its members. They want him to discuss how to write clearly. He asks you to help research the topic. He desperately needs examples and tips.

Your Task. Conduct an online search for "clear business writing." Read one or two fairly recent articles that you consider effective. In a memo to your boss (your instructor) or in a class discussion, answer the following questions:

a. What one or two articles provide effective information about clear business writing?
b. What are the advantages of clear writing? Supply specific examples of organizations that benefited from clear writing.
c. How can people learn to write more clearly? What specific tips can you list?

C.L.U.E. review 5

On a separate sheet edit the following sentences to correct faults in grammar, capitalization, punctuation, spelling, and word use.

1. In this class my friend and I learned that business writing should be: Purposeful, Economical and Reader-Oriented.
2. 5 or 6 members of our team will probly attend the writers workshop therefore be sure they recieve notices.
3. If I was you I would learn the following 3 parts of the writing process, prewriting writing and revising.
4. Experts' suggest that you spend twenty-five percent of your time planning; twenty-five percent writing; forty-five percent revising and five percent proofreading.
5. Although one of the employees are not available we proceded to schedule the meeting at three o'clock p.m. on Wednesday October 12th.
6. The Vice President was supprised to learn that a 2 day writing workshop for our companies employees would cost one thousand two hundred dollars each.
7. Were not asking the seller to altar it's proposal we are asking team members to check the proposals figures.
8. There wondering whether a list of all our customers names and addresses were inadvertently released?
9. As you begin to write you should analyse the task, and identity the purpose.
10. By replacing unfamiliar words with every day familiar ones you can make you audience comprehend your ideas more quicker.

Rich chapter resources are available on the Web site. 

chapter 6

Writing Process Phase 2: Research, Organize, Compose

objectives

1. Apply Phase 2 of the 3-x-3 writing process, which begins with formal and informal methods for researching data and generating ideas.
2. Specify how to organize data into lists and alphanumeric or decimal outlines.
3. Compare direct and indirect patterns for organizing ideas.
4. Discuss composing the first draft of a message, focusing on techniques for creating effective sentences.
5. Define a paragraph and describe three classic paragraph plans and techniques for composing meaningful paragraphs.

springboard *to discussion*

Consumers are increasingly turning to the Internet to do their research before making major purchases. As a result, Canadians are becoming more active online shoppers, comparing products, prices, and user reviews before making purchasing decisions. These online shoppers are also relying more on feedback from fellow shoppers in chat rooms and message boards than on professional reviews of products and services.[1] Research firms such as Nielsen BuzzMetrics are taking advantage of this information by viewing fan sites, blogs, and chat rooms to analyze user feedback and spot consumer trends.

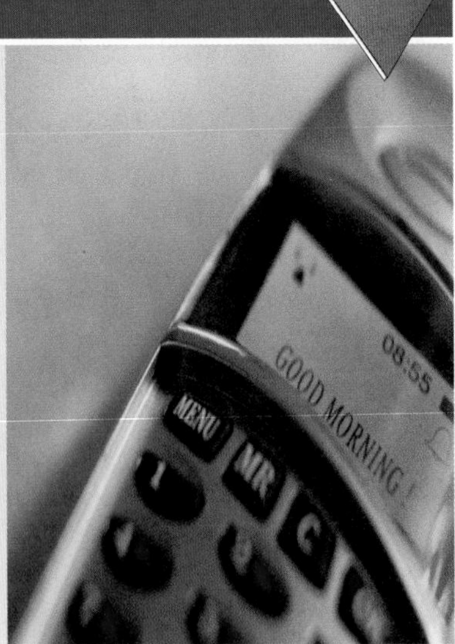

learning objective

1

Writing Process Phase 2: Research

Business communicators face daily challenges that require data collection, idea generation, and concept organization. These activities are part of the second phase of the 3-x-3 writing process: researching, organizing, and composing.

No smart businessperson would begin writing a message before collecting all the needed information. We call this collection process *research*, a rather formal-sounding term, but for simple documents the procedure can be quite informal. Research is necessary before beginning to write because the information you collect helps shape the message. Discovering significant data after a message is half completed often means starting over and reorganizing. To avoid frustration and inaccurate messages, collect information that answers a primary question:

- What does the receiver need to know about this topic?

When the message involves action, search for answers to secondary questions:

- What is the receiver to do?
- How is the receiver to do it?
- When must the receiver do it?
- What will happen if the receiver doesn't do it?

Before writing, conduct formal or informal research to collect or generate necessary data.

Whenever your communication problem requires more information than you have in your head or at your fingertips, you must conduct research. This research may be formal or informal.

Formal Research Methods

Long reports and complex business problems generally require some use of formal research methods, including:

- **Access electronically.** Like other facets of life, the research process has been changed considerably by the computer. Most businesspeople begin any research process by seeing what they can find electronically. Much of the current printed material in libraries is available from the Internet, databases, or CDs that can be accessed by computer. Database providers enable you to search millions of magazine, newspaper, and journal articles. The Internet also provides a wealth of information from public records, public and private organizations, and many other sources.

- **Search manually.** If you need background or supplementary information, you will probably conduct manual research in public or institutional libraries. These traditional resources include periodical indexes for lists of newspaper, magazine, and journal articles, along with the card catalogue for books. Other manual sources are book indexes, encyclopedias, reference books, handbooks, dictionaries, directories, and almanacs.
- **Investigate primary sources.** To develop firsthand, primary information for a project, go directly to the source. For example, you could conduct interviews, create questionnaires, or organize focus groups. Formal research includes scientific sampling methods that enable investigators to make accurate judgments and valid predictions.
- **Experiment scientifically.** Another source of primary data is experimentation. Instead of merely asking for the target audience's opinion, scientific researchers present choices with controlled variables.

Informal Research Methods

Most routine tasks—such as composing e-mail messages, memos, letters, informational reports, and oral presentations—require data that you can collect informally. For some projects, though, you rely more on your own ideas instead of—or in addition to—researching existing facts. Here are some techniques for collecting informal data and for generating ideas:

Informal research may involve looking in the files, talking with your boss, interviewing the audience, and conducting an informal survey.

- **Look in the files.** Before asking others for help, see what you can find yourself. For many routine messages you can often find previous documents to help you with content and format.
- **Talk with your boss.** Get information from the individual making the assignment. What does that person know about the topic? What slant should you take? What other sources would he or she suggest?
- **Interview the target audience.** Consider talking with individuals at whom the message is aimed. They can provide clarifying information that tells you what they want to know and how you should shape your remarks.
- **Conduct an informal survey.** Gather unscientific but helpful information via questionnaires or telephone surveys. In preparing a report predicting the success of a proposed fitness centre, for example, circulate a questionnaire asking for employee reactions.

Generating Ideas by Brainstorming

The most productive group brainstorming sessions begin with defining the problem and creating an agenda.

One popular method for generating ideas is brainstorming. We should point out, however, that some critics argue that brainstorming groups "produce fewer and poorer quality ideas than the same number of individuals working alone."[2] Proponents say that if "you've had bad luck with brainstorming, you're just not doing it right."[3] Here are suggestions for productive group brainstorming:

- Define the problem and create an agenda that outlines the topics to be covered.
- Establish time limits, remembering that short sessions are best.

- Set a quota, such as a minimum of 100 ideas. The goal is quantity, not quality.
- Require every participant to contribute ideas, accept the ideas of others, or improve on ideas.
- Encourage wild, "out of the box" thinking. Allow no one to criticize or evaluate ideas.
- Write ideas on flipcharts or on sheets of paper hung around the room.
- Organize and classify the ideas, retaining the best. Consider using cluster diagrams, which will be discussed shortly.

Collecting Information and Generating Ideas on the Job

Assume you work in the corporate offices of Gap Inc. and you have been given the task of developing a graduate recruiting brochure for all Gap stores. You think this is a great idea because many students don't know about exciting career opportunities and benefits at Old Navy and Gap. You know right away that you want the brochure to be colourful, exciting, concise, youthfully oriented, lightweight (because it has to be carried to campuses), and easily updated. Beyond that, you realize that you need ideas from others on how to develop this recruiting brochure.

To develop ideas for a recruiting brochure, use both formal and informal research.

To collect data for this project, you decide to use both formal and informal research methods. You study recruiting brochures from other companies and talk with students about information they would like to see in a brochure. You conduct more formal research among recently hired employees and among Gap division presidents and executives to learn what they think a recruiting brochure should include. Working with an outside consultant, you prepare a questionnaire to use in personal interviews with employees and executives. The interviews include some open-ended questions, such as *How did you start with the company?* It also asks specific questions about career paths, academic requirements, personality traits desired, and so forth.

Next you ask five or six coworkers and team members to help brainstorm ideas for the brochure. In a spirited session, your team comes up with the cluster diagram shown in Figure 6.1. The ideas range from the cost of the brochure to career development programs and your company's appealing locations.

From the jumble of ideas in the initial cluster diagram, you see that you can organize most of the information into three main categories relating to the brochure: development, form, and content. You eliminate, simplify, and consolidate some ideas and add other new ideas. Then you organize the ideas into subclusters, shown in Figure 6.2 on page 116. This set of subclusters could form the basis for an outline, which we will talk about shortly. Or you could make another set of subclusters, further outlining the categories.

learning objective

2

Writing Process Phase 2: Organize

Well-organized messages group similar ideas together. These groups of ideas are then sequenced in a way that helps the reader understand relationships and accept the writer's views. Unorganized messages proceed free-form, jumping from one thought to another. Such messages fail to emphasize important points. Puzzled readers can't see how the pieces fit together, and they become frustrated and irritated. Many communication experts regard poor organization as the greatest failing of business writers. Two simple techniques can help you organize data: the scratch list and the outline.

FIGURE 6.1 ***Creating a Cluster Diagram to Generate Ideas for Old Navy/Gap Recruiting Brochure***

Tips for Activating Ideas

- In the centre of a clean sheet of paper, write your topic name and circle it.
- Around that circle record any topic ideas that pop into your mind.
- Circle each separate idea.
- Avoid censoring ideas; record everything.
- If ideas seem related, join them with lines, but don't spend time on organization just yet.

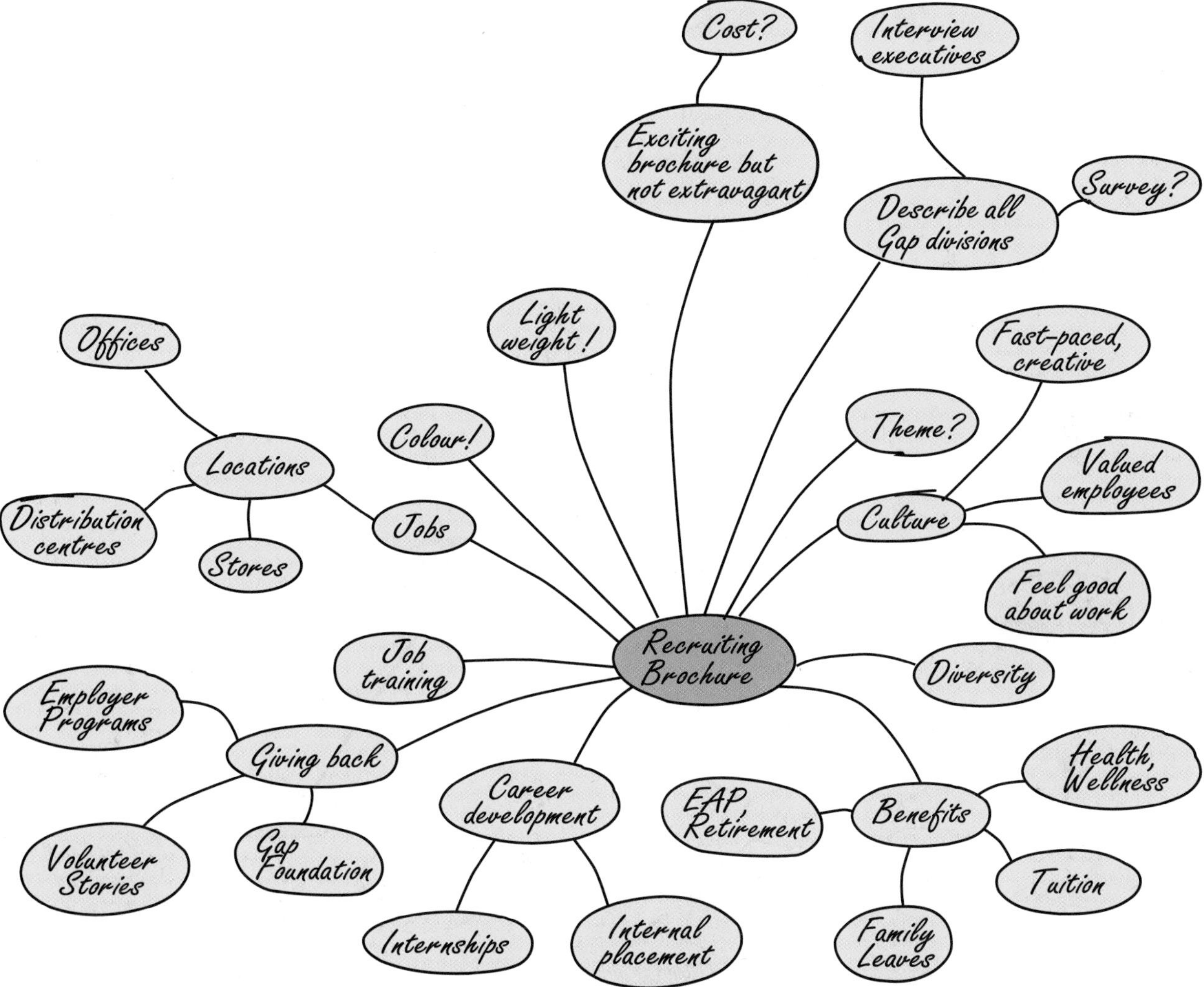

Using Lists and Outlines to Organize Ideas

Writers of well-organized messages group similar ideas together so that readers can see relationships and follow arguments.

In developing simple messages, some writers make a quick scratch list of the topics they wish to cover. Writers often jot this scratch list in the margin of the letter or memo to which they are responding (the majority of business messages are written in response to other documents). These writers then compose a message at their computers directly from the scratch list.

Most writers, though, need to organize their ideas—especially if the project is complex—into a hierarchy, such as an outline. The beauty of preparing an outline is that it gives you a chance to organize your thinking before you get bogged down in

FIGURE 6.2 ***Organizing Ideas From Cluster Diagram Into Subclusters***

Tips for Activating Ideas

- Analyze the ideas generated in the original cluster diagram.
- Cross out ideas that are obviously irrelevant; simplify and clarify.
- Add new ideas that seem appropriate.
- Study the ideas for similarities.
- Group similar ideas into classifications (such as Content, Development, and Form).
- If the organization seems clear at this point, prepare an outline.
- For further visualization, make subcluster circles around each classification.

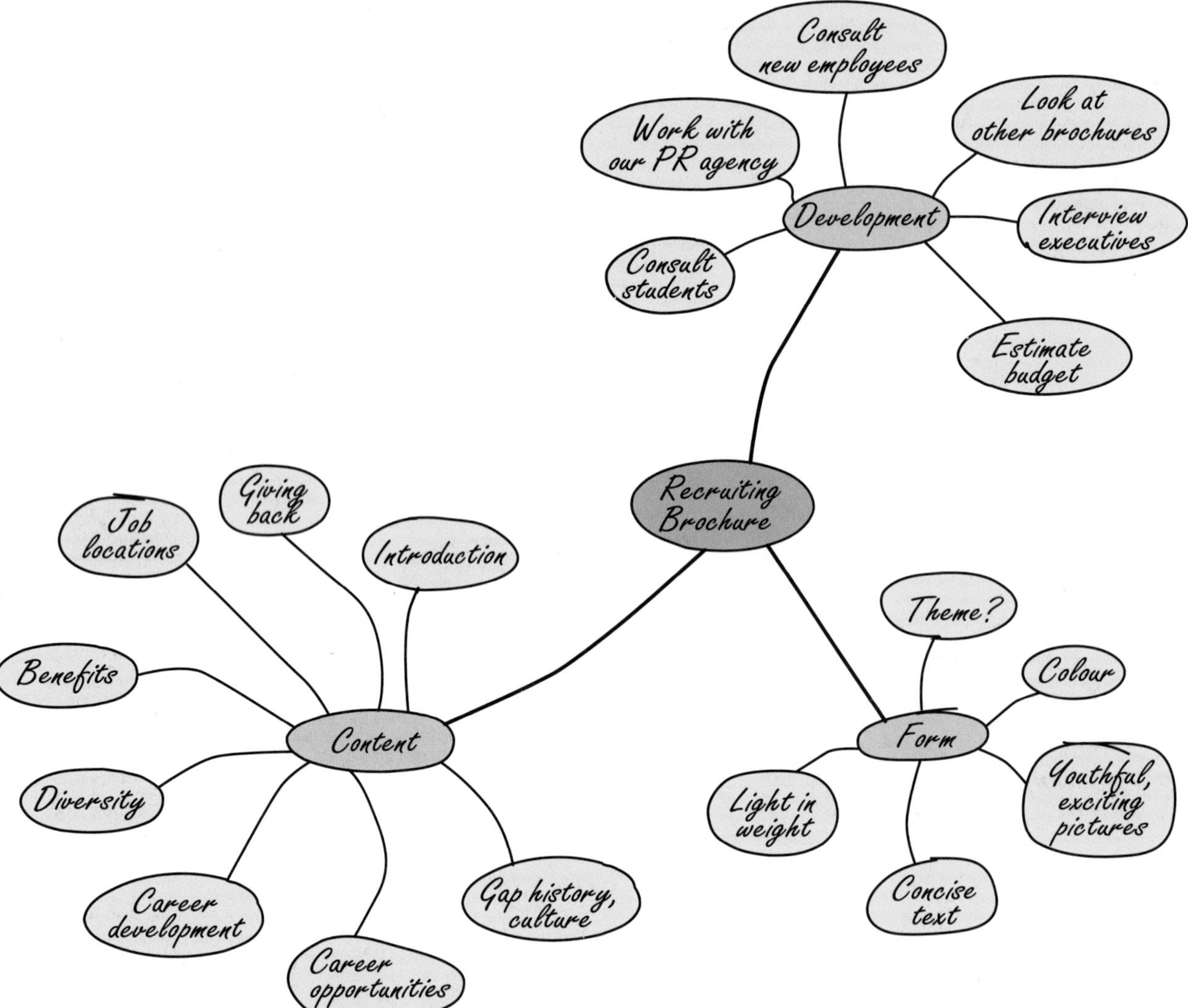

Grouping ideas into categories is the hardest part of outlining.

word choice and sentence structure.[4] Figure 6.3 shows two outline formats: alphanumeric and decimal. The familiar alphanumeric format uses Roman numerals, letters, and numbers to show major and minor ideas. The decimal format, which takes a little getting used to, has the advantage of showing how every item at every level relates to the whole. Both outlining formats force you to focus on the topic, identify major ideas, and support those ideas with details, illustrations, or evidence.

Figure 6.3 ***Two Outlining Formats***

Tips for Making Outlines

- Define the main topic (purpose of message) in the title.
- Divide the main topic into major components or classifications (preferably three to five). If necessary, combine small components into one larger category.
- Break the components into subpoints.
- Don't put a single item under a major component; if you have only one subpoint, integrate it with the main item above it or reorganize.
- Strive to make each component exclusive (no overlapping).
- Use details, illustrations, and evidence to support subpoints.

Format for Alphanumeric Outline	**Format for Decimal Outline**
Title: Major Idea, Purpose	Title: Major Idea, Purpose
I. First major component	1.0. First major component
A. First subpoint	1.1. First subpoint
1. Detail, illustration, evidence	1.1.1. Detail, illustration, evidence
2. Detail, illustration, evidence	1.1.2. Detail, illustration, evidence
B. Second subpoint	1.2. Second subpoint
1.	1.2.1.
2.	1.2.2.
II. Second major component	2.0. Second major component
A. First subpoint	2.1. First subpoint
1.	2.1.1.
2.	2.1.2.
B. Second subpoint	2.2. Second subpoint
1.	2.2.1.
2.	2.2.2.
III. Third major component	3.0. Third major component
A.	3.1.
1.	3.1.1.
2.	3.1.2.
B.	3.2.
1.	3.2.1.
2.	3.2.2.
(This method is simple and familiar.)	(This method relates every item to the overall outline.)

Many computer outlining programs now on the market make the mechanics of the process quite simple.

Alphanumeric outlines show major and minor ideas; decimal outlines show how ideas relate to one another.

The hardest part of outlining is grouping ideas into components or categories—ideally three to five in number. By the way, these major categories will become the major headings in your report. If you have more than five components, look for ways to combine smaller segments into broader topics. The following example shows how a portion of the Gap recruiting brochure subclusters (Figure 6.2) can be organized into an alphanumeric outline.[5]

An alphanumeric outline divides items into major and minor categories.

I. Introduction
    A. Brief history of Gap Inc.
        1. Founding
        2. Milestones

FIGURE 6.4 ***Typical Major Components in Business Outlines***

Letter or Memo	Procedure	Informational Report	Analytical Report	Proposal
I. Opening	I. Step 1	I. Introduction	I. Introduction/ problem	I. Introduction
II. Body	II. Step 2	II. Facts	II. Facts/findings	II. Proposed solution
III. Closing	III. Step 3	III. Summary	III. Conclusions	III. Staffing
	IV. Step 4		IV. Recommen-dations (if requested)	IV. Schedule, cost
				V. Authorization

B. Corporate culture
  1. Fast-paced, creative, feel good about work
  2. Valuing diversity, employees
  3. Social responsibility

II. Careers
  A. Opportunities
    1. Internships
    2. Management trainee programs
    3. M.B.A. programs
  B. Development
    1. Internal promotion
    2. Job training

Every major category in an outline should have at least two subcategories.

Notice that each major category is divided into at least two subcategories. These categories are then fleshed out with examples, details, statistics, case histories, and other data. In moving from major point to subpoint, you are progressing from large abstract concepts to small concrete ideas. And each subpoint could be further subdivided with more specific illustrations if you desired. You can determine the appropriate amount of detail by considering what your audience (primary and secondary) already knows about the topic and how much persuading you must do.

How you group ideas into components depends on your topic and your channel of communication. Business documents usually contain typical components arranged in traditional patterns, as shown in Figure 6.4.

Thus far, you've seen how to collect information, generate ideas, and prepare an outline. How you order the information in your outline, though, depends on what pattern or strategy you choose.

learning objective 3

Organizing Ideas Into Patterns

Two organizational patterns provide plans of action for typical business messages: the direct pattern and the indirect pattern. The primary difference between the two patterns is where the main idea is placed. In the direct pattern the main idea comes first, followed by details, explanation, or evidence. In the indirect pattern the

Figure 6.5 ***Audience Response Determines Pattern of Organization***

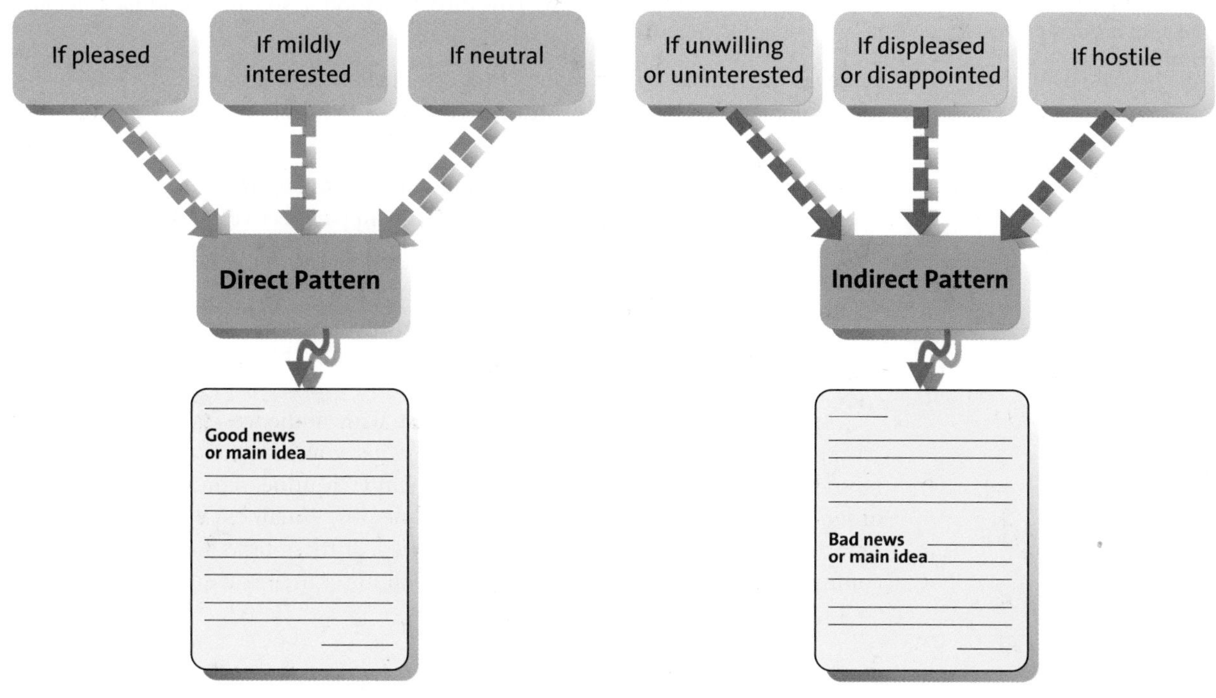

main idea follows the details, explanation, and evidence. The pattern you select is determined by how you expect the audience to react to the message, as shown in Figure 6.5.

Business messages typically follow either the (1) direct pattern, with the main idea first, or (2) the indirect pattern, with the main idea following explanation and evidence.

Direct Pattern for Receptive Audiences

In preparing to write any message, you need to anticipate the audience's reaction to your ideas and frame your message accordingly. When you expect the reader to be pleased, mildly interested, or at worst neutral—use the direct pattern. That is, put your main point—the purpose of your message—in the first or second sentence. As quickly as possible, tell why you are writing. Compare the direct and indirect patterns in the following memo openings. Notice how long it takes to get to the main idea in the indirect opening.

Indirect Opening

Our company has been concerned with attracting better-qualified prospective job candidates. For this reason, the Management Council has been gathering information about an internship program for postsecondary students. After considerable investigation, we have voted to begin a pilot program starting next fall.

Direct Opening

The Management Council has voted to begin a postsecondary internship pilot program next fall.

Frontloading saves the reader's time, establishes the proper frame of mind, and prevents frustration.

Explanations and details should follow the direct opening. What's important is getting to the main idea quickly. This direct method, also called *frontloading*, has at least three advantages:

- **Saves the reader's time.** Many of today's businesspeople can devote only a few moments to each message. Messages that take too long to get to the point may lose their readers along the way.
- **Sets a proper frame of mind.** Learning the purpose up front helps the reader put the subsequent details and explanations in perspective. Without a clear opening, the reader may be thinking, "Why am I being told this?"
- **Prevents frustration.** Readers forced to struggle through excessive verbiage before reaching the main idea become frustrated. They resent the writer. Poorly organized messages create a negative impression of the writer.

This frontloading technique works best with audiences that are likely to be receptive to or at least not to disagree with what you have to say. Typical business messages that follow the direct pattern include routine requests and responses, orders and acknowledgments, nonsensitive memos, e-mail messages, informational reports, and informational oral presentations. All these tasks have one element in common: none has a sensitive subject that will upset the reader.

Indirect Pattern for Unreceptive Audiences

The indirect pattern respects the feelings of the audience, facilitates a fair hearing, and minimizes a negative reaction.

When you expect the audience to be uninterested, unwilling, displeased, or perhaps even hostile, the indirect pattern is more appropriate. In this pattern you don't reveal the main idea until after you have offered explanation and evidence. This approach works well with three kinds of messages: (1) bad news, (2) ideas that require persuasion, and (3) sensitive news, especially when being transmitted to superiors. The indirect pattern has these benefits:

- **Respects the feelings of the audience.** Bad news is always painful, but the trauma can be lessened when the receiver is prepared for it.
- **Encourages a fair hearing.** Messages that may upset the reader are more likely to be read when the main idea is delayed. Beginning immediately with a piece of bad news or a persuasive request, for example, may cause the receiver to stop reading or listening.
- **Minimizes a negative reaction.** A reader's overall reaction to a negative message is generally improved if the news is delivered gently.

Typical business messages that could be developed indirectly include letters and memos that refuse requests, deny claims, and disapprove credit. Persuasive requests, sales letters, sensitive messages, and some reports and oral presentations also benefit from the indirect strategy. You'll learn more about how to use the indirect pattern in Chapters 10 and 11.

In summary, business messages may be organized directly, with the main idea first, or indirectly, with the main idea delayed. Although these two patterns cover many communication problems, they should be considered neither universal nor inviolate. Every business transaction is distinct. Some messages are mixed: part good news, part bad; part goodwill, part persuasion. In upcoming chapters you'll practise applying the direct and indirect patterns in typical situations. Then you'll have the skills and confidence to evaluate communication problems and vary these patterns depending on the goals you wish to achieve.

tech talk

Seven Ways Computers Can Help You Create Better Written Messages, Oral Presentations, and Web Pages

Although computers can't actually do the writing for you, they provide powerful tools that make the composition process easier and the results more professional. Here are seven ways your computer can help you improve your written documents, oral presentations, and even Web pages.

1. **Fighting writer's block.** Because word processors enable ideas to flow almost effortlessly from your brain to a screen, you can expect fewer delays resulting from writer's block. You can compose rapidly, and you can experiment with structure and phrasing, later retaining and polishing your most promising thoughts.
2. **Collecting information electronically.** As a knowledge worker in an information economy, you will need to find information quickly. Much of the world's information is now accessible in databases or on the Web. You'll learn more about these exciting electronic resources in Unit 4.
3. **Outlining and organizing ideas.** Most word processors include some form of "outliner," a feature that enables you to divide a topic into a hierarchical order with main points and subpoints. Your computer keeps track of the levels of ideas automatically so that you can easily add, cut, or rearrange points in the outline.
4. **Improving correctness and precision.** Nearly all word processing programs today provide features that catch and correct spelling and typographical errors. Grammar checkers detect many errors in capitalization, word use (such as *it's/its*), double negatives, verb use, subject–verb agreement, sentence structure, number agreement, number style, and other writing faults. But the errors are merely highlighted—not corrected. You have to do that.
5. **Adding graphics for emphasis.** Your letters, memos, and reports may be improved by the addition of graphs and artwork to clarify and illustrate data. You can import charts, diagrams, and illustrations created in database, spreadsheet, graphics, or draw-and-paint programs. Ready-made pictures, called clip art, can be used to symbolize or illustrate ideas.
6. **Designing and producing professional-looking documents, presentations, and Web pages.** Most software now includes a large selection of scalable fonts (for different character sizes and styles), italics, boldface, symbols, and styling techniques to aid you in producing consistent formatting and professional-looking results. Presentation software enables you to incorporate showy slide effects, colour, sound, pictures, and even movies into your talks for management or customers. Web document builders also help you design and construct Web pages.
7. **Using collaborative software for team writing.** Special programs with commenting and revision features, described in Chapter 5, allow you to make changes and to identify each team member's editing.

Writing Process Phase 2: Compose

learning objective 4

Once you've researched your topic, organized the data, and selected a pattern of organization, you're ready to begin composing. Most writers expect to use their computers for composition, but many are unaware of all the ways a computer can help create better written messages, oral presentations, and Web pages. See the accompanying Tech Talk box to learn how you can take full advantage of your computer.

Even with a computer, some writers have trouble getting started, especially if they haven't completed the preparatory work. Organizing your ideas and working from an outline are very helpful in overcoming writer's block. Composition is also easier if you have a quiet environment in which to concentrate. Businesspeople with messages to compose set aside a given time and allow no calls, visitors, or other interruptions. This is a good technique for students as well.

When composing the first draft, write quickly and save revision for later.

As you begin composing, keep in mind that you are writing the first draft, not the final copy. Experts suggest that you write quickly (*sprint writing*). Get your thoughts down now and refine them in later versions.[6] As you take up each idea, imagine that you are talking to the reader. Don't let yourself get bogged down. If you can't think of the right word, insert a substitute or type "find perfect word later." Sprint writing works especially well for those composing on a computer, because it's simple to make changes at any point of the composition process. If you are handwriting the first draft, double-space so that you have room for changes.

Creating Effective Sentences

As you create your first draft, you'll be working at the sentence level of composition. Although you've used sentences all your life, you may be unaware of how they can be shaped and arranged to express your ideas most effectively. First, let's review some basic sentence elements.

Sentences must have subjects and verbs and must make sense.

Complete sentences have subjects and verbs and make sense.

SUBJECT VERB
The manager of Information Technology sent an e-mail to all employees.

Clauses have subjects and verbs, but phrases do not.

Clauses and phrases, the key building blocks of sentences, are related groups of words. Clauses have subjects and verbs; phrases do not.

PHRASE PHRASE
The manager of Information Technology sent an e-mail to all employees.

PHRASE PHRASE
By reading carefully, we learned about the latest computer viruses.

CLAUSE CLAUSE
Because he is experienced, Adam knows how to repair most computer problems.

CLAUSE CLAUSE
When we have technology problems, we call a technician in our support group.

Independent clauses may stand alone; dependent clauses may not.

Clauses may be divided into two groups: independent and dependent. Independent clauses are grammatically complete. Dependent clauses depend for their meaning on independent clauses. In the two preceding examples, the clauses beginning with *Because* and *When* are dependent. Dependent clauses are often introduced by words such as *if*, *when*, *because*, and *as*.

INDEPENDENT CLAUSE
Adam solves our technology problems.

DEPENDENT CLAUSE INDEPENDENT CLAUSE
When employees need help, Adam solves our technology problems.

By learning to distinguish phrases, independent clauses, and dependent clauses, you'll be able to punctuate sentences correctly and avoid three basic sentence faults: the fragment, the run-on sentence, and the comma splice. In Guides 1–3, Appendix A, we examine these writing problems in greater detail. For now, however, let's look at some ways to make your sentences more readable.

Effective sentences are short and stress important ideas.

Preferring Short Sentences. Because your goal is to communicate clearly, you're better off limiting your sentences to about 20 or fewer words. The American Press Institute reports that reader comprehension drops off markedly as sentences become longer.[7] Thus, in crafting your sentences, think about the relationship between sentence length and comprehension:

Sentences of 20 or fewer words have the most impact.

Sentence Length	Comprehension Rate
8 words	100%
15 words	90%
19 words	80%
28 words	50%

Instead of stringing together clauses with *and*, *but*, and *however*, break some of those complex sentences into separate segments. Business readers want to grasp ideas immediately. They can do that best when thoughts are separated into short sentences. On the other hand, too many monotonous short sentences will sound "grammar school-ish" and may bore or even annoy the reader. Strive for a balance between longer sentences and shorter ones. Your computer probably can point out long sentences and give you an average sentence length.

Ensure instructions are readable by shortening sentences, emphasizing important ideas with graphic highlighting, and using active-voice verbs.

Photo: Purestock/SuperStock

Emphasizing Important Ideas. You can stress prominent ideas mechanically by underscoring, italicizing, or boldfacing. You'll learn more about these graphic highlighting devices shortly. You can also emphasize important ideas with five stylistic devices. In the bulleted items that follow, notice that each of these suggestions involves the choice of words or attention to the placement of an important idea.

Emphasize an important idea by using vivid words, labelling the main idea, placing the idea first or last in a sentence, and making it the sentence subject.

- **Use vivid words.** Vivid words are emphatic because the reader can picture ideas clearly.
- **Label the main idea.** If an idea is significant, tell the reader.
- **Place the important idea first or last in the sentence.** Ideas have less competition from surrounding words when they appear first or last in a sentence.
- **Place the important idea in a simple sentence or in an independent clause.** Don't dilute the effect of the idea by making it share the spotlight with other words and clauses.
- **Make sure the important idea is the sentence subject.** You'll learn more about active and passive voice shortly, but at this point just focus on making the important idea the subject.

Managing Active and Passive Voice. In sentences with active-voice verbs, the subject is the doer of the action. In passive-voice sentences, the subject is acted upon.

In active-voice sentences the subject is the doer; in passive-voice sentences the subject is acted upon.

Passive verb	Active verb
The tax return was completed before the April 30 deadline. (The subject, *tax return*, is acted upon.)	Brandon completed his tax return before the April 30 deadline. (The subject, *Brandon*, is the doer of the action.)

In the first sentence, the passive-voice verb emphasizes the tax return. In the second sentence, the active-voice verb emphasizes Brandon. Active-voice sentences are more direct because they reveal the performer immediately. They're easier to understand and shorter. Most business writing should be in the active voice.

Passive verbs are useful in certain instances. In sentences with passive-voice verbs, the doer of the action may be revealed or left unknown. In business writing, as well as in personal interactions, some situations demand tact and sensitivity. Instead of using a direct approach, with active verbs, we may prefer the indirectness that passive verbs allow. Rather than making a blunt announcement with an active verb (*Tyler made a major error in the estimate*), we can soften the sentence with a passive construction (*A major error was made in the estimate*).

Here's a summary of the best uses of active- and passive-voice verbs:

- **Use the active voice for most business writing.** *Our company gives drug tests to all applicants.*
- **Use the passive voice to emphasize an action or the recipient of the action.** *Drug tests are given to all applicants.*
- **Use the passive voice to de-emphasize negative news.** *Your monitor cannot be repaired.*
- **Use the passive voice to conceal the doer of an action.** *A major error was made in the estimate.*

Passive-voice sentences are useful for tact and to direct attention to actions instead of people.

How can you tell whether a verb is active or passive? Identify the subject of the sentence and decide whether the subject is doing the acting or whether it is being acted upon. For example, in the sentence *An appointment was made for January 1*, the subject is *appointment*. The subject is being acted upon; therefore the verb (*was made*) is passive. Another clue in identifying passive-voice verbs is that they generally include a *to be* helping verb, such as *is*, *are*, *was*, *were*, *being*, or *been*.

Modifiers must be close to the words they describe or limit.

Avoiding Dangling and Misplaced Modifiers. For clarity, modifiers must be close to the words they describe or limit. A dangling modifier describes or limits a word or words that are missing from the sentence. A misplaced modifier occurs when the word or phrase it describes is not close enough to be clear. In both instances, the solution is to move the modifier closer to the word(s) it describes or limits. Introductory verbal phrases are particularly dangerous; be sure to follow them immediately with the words they can logically describe or modify.

Dangling Modifier	Improved
To win the lottery, a ticket must be purchased. (The introductory verbal phrase must be followed by a logical subject.)	To win the lottery, you must purchase a ticket.
Speaking before the large audience, Lisa's knees began to knock. (Are Lisa's knees making a speech?)	Speaking before the large audience, Lisa felt her knees begin to knock.

Try this trick for detecting and remedying these dangling modifiers. Ask the question *who?* or *what?* after any introductory phrase. The words immediately following should tell the reader who or what is performing the action. Try the *who?* test on the previous danglers and on the following misplaced modifiers.

Misplaced Modifier	Improved
Seeing his error too late, the envelope was immediately resealed by Mark. (Did the envelope see the error?)	Seeing his error too late, Mark immediately resealed the envelope.
The busy personnel director interviewed only candidates who had excellent computer skills in the morning. (Were the candidates skilled only in the morning?)	In the morning the busy personnel director interviewed only candidates who had excellent computer skills.

A modifier is misplaced when the word or phrase it describes is not close enough to be clear.

Drafting Meaningful Paragraphs

learning objective

5

From composing sentences, we progress to paragraphs. A paragraph is one or more sentences designated as a separate thought group. To avoid muddled paragraphs, writers must recognize basic paragraph elements, conventional sentence patterns, and ways to organize sentences into one of three classic paragraph patterns. They must also be able to polish their paragraphs by linking sentences and using transitional expressions.

Effective paragraphs focus on one topic, link ideas to build coherence, and use transitional devices to enhance coherence.

Well-constructed paragraphs discuss only one topic. They reveal the primary idea in a main sentence that usually, but not always, appears first. Paragraphs are generally composed of three kinds of sentences:[8]

Main sentence: expresses the primary idea of the paragraph.

Supporting sentence: illustrates, explains, or strengthens the primary idea.

Limiting sentence: opposes the primary idea by suggesting a negative or contrasting thought; may precede or follow the main sentence.

These sentences may be arranged in three classic paragraph plans: direct, pivoting, and indirect.

Using the Direct Paragraph Plan to Define, Classify, Illustrate, or Describe

Paragraphs arranged in the direct plan begin with the main sentence, followed by supporting sentences. Most business messages use this paragraph plan because it clarifies the subject immediately. This plan is useful whenever you must define (a new product or procedure), classify (parts of a whole), illustrate (an idea), or describe (a process). Simply start with the main sentence; then strengthen and amplify that idea with supporting ideas, as shown here:

The direct paragraph pattern is appropriate when defining, classifying, illustrating, or describing.

Main Sentence: A social audit is a report on the social performance of a company.

Supporting Sentences: Such an audit may be conducted by the company itself or by outsiders who evaluate the company's efforts to produce safe products, engage in socially responsible activities, and protect the environment. Many companies publish the results of their social audits in their annual reports. Commitment to the environment and social responsibility have been core values for Vancouver City Savings Credit Union (Vancity) since 1993. The company conducts social audits to combine measures of financial return, social responsibility, and environmental performance.[9]

You can alter the direct plan by adding a limiting sentence if necessary. Be sure, though, that you follow with sentences that return to the main idea and support it, as shown here:

Main Sentence: Flexible work scheduling could immediately increase productivity and enhance employee satisfaction in our entire organization.

Limiting Sentence: Such scheduling, however, is impossible for all employees.

Supporting Sentences: Managers would be required to maintain their regular hours. For many other employees, though, flexible scheduling permits extra time to manage family responsibilities. Feeling less stress, employees are able to focus their attention better at work; hence they become more relaxed and more productive.

Using the Pivoting Paragraph Plan to Compare and Contrast

The pivoting paragraph pattern is appropriate when comparing and contrasting.

Paragraphs arranged in the pivoting plan start with a limiting sentence that offers a contrasting or negative idea before delivering the main sentence. Notice in the following example how two limiting sentences about drawbacks to military careers open the paragraph; only then do the main and supporting sentences describing rewards in military service appear. The pivoting plan is especially useful for comparing and contrasting ideas. In using the pivoting plan, be sure you emphasize the turn in direction with an obvious *but* or *however*.

Limiting Sentences: Military careers are certainly not for everyone.
Many are in remote countries where harsh climates, health hazards, security risks, and other discomforts exist.

Main Sentence: However, careers in the military offer special rewards for the special people who qualify.

Supporting Sentence: Military employees enjoy the pride and satisfaction of representing their country abroad. They enjoy frequent travel, enriching cultural and social experiences in living abroad, and action-oriented work.

Using the Indirect Paragraph Plan to Explain and Persuade

The indirect paragraph pattern is appropriate when delivering bad news.

Paragraphs arranged in the indirect plan start with the supporting sentences and conclude with the main sentence. This useful plan enables you to build a rationale, a foundation of reasons, before hitting the audience with a big idea—possibly one that is bad news. It enables you to explain your reasons and then in the final sentence draw a conclusion from them. In the following example the vice president of a large accounting firm begins by describing the trend toward casual dress and concludes with a recommendation that his firm change its dress code. This indirect plan works well for describing causes followed by an effect.

Supporting Sentences: According to a recent poll, more than half of all white-collar workers are now dressing casually at work. Many high-tech engineers and professional specialists have given up suits and ties, favouring khakis and sweaters instead. In our own business our consultants say they stand out like "sore thumbs" because they are attired in traditional buttoned-down styles, while the businesspeople they visit are usually wearing comfortable, casual clothing.

Main Sentence: Therefore, I recommend that we establish an optional "business casual" policy allowing consultants to dress casually, if they wish, as they perform their duties both in and out of the office.

You'll learn more techniques for implementing direct and indirect writing strategies when you prepare letters, memos, e-mail messages, reports, and oral presentations in subsequent chapters.

Linking Ideas to Build Coherence

Paragraphs are coherent when ideas are linked, that is, when one idea leads logically to the next. Well-written paragraphs take the reader through a number of steps. When the author skips from Step 1 to Step 3 and forgets Step 2, the reader is lost. You can use several techniques to keep the reader in step with your ideas.

Coherent paragraphs link ideas by sustaining the main idea, using pronouns, dovetailing sentences, and using transitional expressions.

Sustaining the Key Idea. This involves simply repeating a key expression or using a similar one. For example,

> Our philosophy holds that every customer is really a guest. All new employees to our theme parks are trained to treat guests as VIPs. These VIPs are never told what they can or cannot do.

Notice how the repetition of *guest* and *VIP* connects ideas.

Using Pronouns. Familiar pronouns, such as *we*, *they*, *he*, *she*, and *it*, help build continuity, as do demonstrative pronouns such as *this*, *that*, *these*, and *those*. These words confirm that something under discussion is still being discussed. For example,

Using pronouns strategically helps build coherence and continuity.

> All new park employees receive a two-week orientation. They learn that every staffer has a vital role in preparing for the show. This training includes how to maintain enthusiasm.

Be careful with *this*, *that*, *these*, and *those*, however. These words usually need a noun with them to make their meaning absolutely clear. In the last example, notice how confusing *this* becomes if the word *training* is omitted.

Dovetailing Sentences. Sentences are "dovetailed" when an idea at the end of one connects with an idea at the beginning of the next. For example,

Dovetailing sentences means connecting ending and beginning ideas.

> New hosts and hostesses learn about the theme park and its facilities. These facilities include telephones, food services, bathrooms, and attractions, as well as the location of offices. Knowledge of administrative offices and internal workings of the company, such as who's who in administration, ensures that staffers will be able to serve guests fully. Serving guests, of course, is our No. 1 priority.

Dovetailing of sentences is especially helpful with dense, difficult topics. This technique, however, should not be overused.

Showing Connections With Transitional Expressions. Transitional expressions are another excellent device for showing connections and achieving paragraph coherence. These words, some of which are shown in Figure 6.6, act as verbal road signs to readers and listeners. Transitional expressions enable the receiver to anticipate what's coming, to reduce uncertainty, and to speed up comprehension. They signal that a train of thought is moving forward, being developed, possibly detouring, or ending. Transitions are especially helpful in persuasive writing.

Transitional expressions help readers anticipate what's coming, reduce uncertainty, and speed comprehension.

As Figure 6.6 (page 128) shows, transitions can add or strengthen a thought, show time or order, clarify ideas, show cause and effect, contradict thoughts, and contrast ideas. Thus you must be careful to select the best transition for your

Figure 6.6 *Transitional Expressions to Build Coherence*

To Add or Strengthen	To Show Time or Order	To Clarify	To Show Cause and Effect	To Contradict	To Contrast
additionally	after	for example	accordingly	actually	as opposed to
again	before	for instance	as a result	but	at the same time
also	earlier	I mean	consequently	however	by contrast
besides	finally	in other words	for this reason	in fact	conversely
likewise	first	that is	so	instead	on the contrary
moreover	meanwhile	this means	therefore	rather	on the other hand
further	next	thus	thus	still	
furthermore	now	to put it another way	under the circumstances	though	
	previously			yet	

purpose. Look back at the examples of direct, pivoting, and indirect paragraphs to see how transitional expressions and other devices build paragraph coherence. Remember that coherence in communication rarely happens spontaneously; it requires effort and skill.

Composing Short Paragraphs for Readability

Paragraphs with eight or fewer lines are inviting and readable.

Although no rule regulates the length of paragraphs, business writers recognize that short paragraphs are more attractive and readable than longer ones. Paragraphs with eight or fewer lines look inviting, whereas long, solid chunks of print appear formidable. If a topic can't be covered in eight or fewer printed lines (not sentences), consider breaking it up into smaller segments.

The following checklist summarizes the key points of composing a first draft.

Checklist for Composing Sentences and Paragraphs

For Effective Sentences

✓ **Control sentence length.** Use longer sentences occasionally, but rely primarily on short and medium-length sentences.

✓ **Emphasize important ideas.** Place main ideas at the beginning of short sentences for emphasis.

✓ **Apply active and passive verbs carefully.** Use active verbs (*She sent the e-mail* instead of *The e-mail was sent by her*) most frequently; they immediately identify the doer. Use passive verbs to be tactful, to emphasize an action, or to conceal the performer.

✓ **Eliminate misplaced modifiers.** Be sure that introductory verbal phrases are followed by the words that can logically be modified. To check the placement of modifiers, ask *who?* or *what?* after such phrases.

For Meaningful Paragraphs

- ✓ **Develop one idea.** Use main, supporting, and limiting sentences to develop a single idea within each paragraph.
- ✓ **Use the direct plan.** Start most paragraphs with the main sentence followed by supporting sentences. This direct plan is useful in defining, classifying, illustrating, and describing.
- ✓ **Use the pivoting plan.** To compare and contrast ideas, start with a limiting sentence; then, present the main sentence followed by supporting sentences.
- ✓ **Use the indirect plan.** To explain reasons or causes first, start with supporting sentences. Build to the conclusion, with the main sentence at the end of the paragraph.
- ✓ **Build coherence by linking sentences.** Hold ideas together by repeating key words, using pronouns, and dovetailing sentences (beginning one sentence with an idea from the end of the previous sentence).
- ✓ **Provide road signs with transitional expressions.** Use verbal signals to help the audience know where the idea is going. Words such as *moreover*, *accordingly*, *as a result*, and *thus* function as idea pointers.
- ✓ **Limit paragraph length.** Remember that paragraphs with eight or fewer printed lines look inviting. Consider breaking up longer paragraphs if necessary.

Summary of Learning Objectives

1 **Apply Phase 2 of the 3-x-3 writing process, which begins with formal and informal methods for researching data and generating ideas.** The second phase of the writing process includes researching, organizing, and writing. Researching means collecting information using formal or informal techniques. Formal research for long reports and complex problems may involve searching electronically or manually, as well as conducting interviews, surveys, focus groups, and experiments. Informal research for routine tasks may include looking in company files, talking with your boss, interviewing the target audience, conducting informal surveys, brainstorming for ideas, and cluster diagramming.

2 **Specify how to organize data into lists and alphanumeric or decimal outlines.** One method for organizing data in simple messages is to list the main topics to be discussed. Organizing more complex messages usually requires an outline. To prepare an outline, divide the main topic into three to five major components. Break the components into subpoints consisting of details, illustrations, and evidence. For an alphanumeric outline arrange items using Roman numerals (I, II), capital letters (A, B), and numbers (1, 2). For a decimal outline show the ordering of ideas with decimals (1.0, 1.1, 1.1.1).

3 **Compare direct and indirect patterns for organizing ideas.** The direct pattern places the main idea first. This pattern is useful when audiences will be pleased, mildly interested, or neutral. It saves the reader's time, sets the

proper frame of mind, and prevents reader frustration. The indirect pattern places the main idea after explanations. This pattern is useful for audiences that will be unwilling, displeased, or hostile. It respects the feelings of the audience, encourages a fair hearing, and minimizes negative reactions.

4 **Discuss composing the first draft of a message, focusing on techniques for creating effective sentences.** Compose the first draft of a message in a quiet environment where you won't be interrupted. Compose quickly, preferably at a computer. Plan to revise. As you compose, remember that sentences are most effective when they are short (less than 20 words). A main idea may be emphasized by making it the sentence subject, placing it first, and removing competing ideas. Effective sentences use active verbs, although passive verbs may be necessary for tact or de-emphasis. Effective sentences avoid dangling and misplaced modifiers.

5 **Define a paragraph and describe three classic paragraph plans and techniques for composing meaningful paragraphs.** A paragraph consists of one or more sentences designated as a separate thought group. Typical paragraphs follow one of three plans. Direct paragraphs (main sentence followed by supporting sentences) are useful to define, classify, illustrate, and describe. Pivoting paragraphs (limiting sentence followed by main sentence and supporting sentences) are useful to compare and contrast. Indirect paragraphs (supporting sentences followed by main sentence) build a rationale and foundation of ideas before presenting the main idea. Paragraphs may be improved through the use of coherence techniques and transitional expressions.

chapter review

1. What are the three main activities involved in the second phase of the 3-x-3 writing process? (Obj. 1)
2. Name seven specific techniques for a productive group brainstorming session. (Obj. 1)
3. What is a cluster diagram, and when might it be useful? (Obj. 1)
4. Describe an alphanumeric outline. (Obj. 2)
5. What is the relationship between the major categories in an outline and those in a report written from the outline? (Obj. 2)
6. Distinguish between the direct and indirect patterns of organization for typical business messages. (Obj. 3)
7. Why should most messages be "frontloaded"? (Obj. 3)
8. List some business messages that should be frontloaded and some that should not be frontloaded. (Obj. 3)
9. Why should writers plan for revision? How can they do it? (Obj. 4)
10. Name three ways to emphasize important ideas in sentences. (Obj. 4)
11. Distinguish between active-voice sentences and passive-voice sentences. Give examples. (Obj. 4)
12. Give an original example of a dangling or misplaced modifier. Why are introductory verbal phrases dangerous? (Obj. 4)
13. Describe three kinds of sentences used to develop ideas in paragraphs. (Obj. 5)
14. Describe three paragraph plans. Identify the uses for each. (Obj. 5)
15. What is coherence, and how is it achieved? (Obj. 5)

critical thinking

1. Why is cluster diagramming considered an intuitive process whereas outlining is considered an analytical process? (Obj. 1)
2. Why is audience analysis so important in choosing the direct or indirect pattern of organization for a business message? (Obj. 3)
3. In what ways do you imagine that writing on the job differs from the writing you do in your academic studies? Consider process as well as product. (Obj. 1)
4. Why are short sentences and short paragraphs appropriate for business communication? (Objs. 4 and 5)

activities

6.1 Document for Analysis (Objs. 3–5)

The following interoffice memo is hard to read. It suffers from numerous writing faults discussed in this chapter.

Your Task. First, read the memo to see whether you can understand what the writer requests from all Western Division employees. Then, discuss why this memo is so hard to read. How long are the sentences? How many passive-voice constructions can you locate? How effective is the paragraphing? Can you spot four dangling or misplaced modifiers? In the next activity you'll improve the organization of this message. (Superscript numbers in the following sentences are provided to help you identify problem sentences.)

TO: All Western Division Employees

[1]Personal computers and all the software to support these computers are appearing on many desks of Western Division employees. [2]After giving the matter considerable attention, it has been determined by the Systems Development Department (SDD) that more control should be exerted in coordinating the purchase of hardware and software to improve compatibility throughout the division so that a library of resources may be developed. [3]Therefore, a plan has been developed by SDD that should be followed in making all future equipment selections and purchases. [4]To make the best possible choice, SDD should be contacted as you begin your search because questions about personal computers, word processing programs, hardware, and software can be answered by our knowledgeable staff, who can also provide you with invaluable assistance in making the best choice for your needs at the best possible cost.

[5]After your computer and its software arrive, all your future software purchases should be channelled through SDD.

[6]To actually make your initial purchase, a written proposal and a purchase request form must be presented to SDD for approval. [7]A need for the purchase must be established; benefits that you expect to derive resulting from its purchase must be analyzed and presented, and an itemized statement of all costs must be submitted. [8]By following these new procedures, coordinated purchasing benefits will be realized by all employees. [9]I may be reached at X466 if you have any questions.

6.2 Collaborative Brainstorming (Obj. 1)

Brainstorming can be a productive method for generating problem-solving ideas. You can improve your brainstorming skills through practice.

Your Task. In teams of four or five, analyze a problem on your campus such as the following: unavailable classes, unrealistic degree/diploma requirements, lack of student intern programs, poor parking facilities, inadequate registration process, lack of diversity among students on campus, and so forth. Use brainstorming techniques to generate ideas that clarify the problem and explore its solutions. Each team member should prepare a cluster diagram to record the ideas generated. Either individually or as a team, organize the ideas into an outline with three to five main points and numerous subpoints. Assume that your ideas will become part of a letter to be sent to an appropriate campus official or to your campus newspaper discussing the problem and your solution. Remember, however, your role as a student. Be polite, positive, and constructive—not negative, hostile, or aggressive.

6.3 Researching and Outlining "How-to" Techniques for Productive Brainstorming (Obj. 1)

RESEARCH

Cassandra M., your supervisor at a retail store, has been asked to lead a brainstorming group in an effort to generate new ideas for the company's product line. Although Cassandra knows a great deal about the company and its products, she doesn't know much about brainstorming. She asks you to research the topic quickly and give her a concise guide on how to brainstorm. One other thing—Cassandra doesn't want to read an entire article. She wants you to outline it.

Your Task. Conduct an online keyword search for "brainstorming." Locate an article with specific instructions for running a productive brainstorming session. Prepare an outline that tells how to (a) prepare for a brainstorming session, (b) conduct the session, and (c) follow up after the meeting. Submit your outline in a memo or an e-mail message to your supervisor (your instructor).

6.4 Using the Web to Compare Brainstorming Resources (Objs. 1 and 2)

CRITICAL THINKING | TEAM | WEB

You are part of an internship program at a large company, such as Gap Inc. Ron W., the manager in charge of interns, wants your group to use the Web to research two topics: (a) group brainstorming and (b) brainstorming software. Ron wants to know the two best Web sites that provide free advice about brainstorming, but he also wants your group to recommend two software products that teach people how to brainstorm.

Your Task. Using one or more search tools (such as Google), locate a few good Web sites that provide free advice on how to conduct brainstorming sessions. Then locate sites that sell software teaching individuals how to brainstorm. As a team, discuss which sites seemed most useful and trustworthy. How can you judge a Web software product if you have not seen it? In an e-mail or a memo to Ron, tell him what two sites you thought were best for free advice and what two software products you would recommend. Explain and defend your choices.

6.5 Collaborative Letter (Objs. 3–5)

TEAM

One of the best ways to learn about the skills required in your field is to interview individuals working in that field.

Your Task. Divide into teams of three to five people who have similar majors. Work together to compose an inquiry letter requesting career information from someone in your field. Include questions about technical and general courses to take, possible starting salaries, good companies to apply to, technical skills required, necessary interpersonal skills, computer tools currently used, and tips for getting started in the field. Although this is a small project, your team can work more harmoniously if you apply some of the suggestions from Chapter 2. For example, appoint a meeting leader, recorder, and evaluator.

6.6 Sentence Elements (Obj. 4)

Your Task. In the following sentences underscore and identify dependent clauses (DC), independent clauses (IC), and phrases (P). Circle subjects and verbs in clauses.

a. We hire talented undergraduates in our intern program.
b. If you qualify, you should send an application to us.
c. In the summer, interns appreciate a program if it offers a learning experience.

6.7 Sentence Length (Obj. 4)

Your Task. Break the following sentences into shorter sentences. Use appropriate transitional expressions.

a. If firms have a substantial investment in original research or development of new products, they should consider protecting those products with patents, although all patents eventually expire and what were once trade secrets can become common knowledge in the industry.
b. As soon as consumers recognize a name associated with a product or service, that name is entitled to legal protection as a trademark; in fact, consumers may even create a trademark where none existed or create a second trademark by using a nickname as a source indicator, such as the name "Coke," which was legally protected even before it had ever been used by the company.
c. Although no magic formula exists for picking a good trademark name, firms should avoid picking the first name that pops into someone's head; moreover, they should be aware that unique and arbitrary marks are

best, whereas descriptive terms such as "car" or "TV repair" are useless, and surnames and geographic names are weak because they lack distinction and exclusivity.

6.8 Active and Passive Voice (Obj. 4)

Your Task. In the following sentences convert passive-voice verbs to active-voice verbs. Add subjects if necessary. Be prepared to discuss which sentence version is more effective.

a. Programs were created by our board so that employees could become volunteers.
b. Employees are encouraged to take up to five hours a month of paid time to volunteer.
c. Café-style restaurants are provided for employees in our corporate buildings.
d. When it was realized that transportation was a problem, interoffice shuttles were established.
e. Our company was named in *Maclean's* magazine's "100 Best Places to Work."

Now convert active-voice verbs to passive-voice verbs, and be prepared to discuss which sentence version is more effective.

f. We cannot authorize repair of your DVD because you have allowed the warranty period to expire.
g. I cannot give you a cash refund for merchandise that you purchased 90 or more days ago.
h. ValleyView Golf Course does not accept players who are not members.
i. You must submit your résumé and cover letter by e-mail.
j. Jennifer added the two columns instead of subtracting them, thus producing the incorrect total.

6.9 Dangling and Misplaced Modifiers (Obj. 4)

Your Task. Remedy any dangling or misplaced modifiers in the following sentences. Add subjects as needed, but retain the introductory phrases. Mark *C* if correct.

a. It's hard to understand why employees would not go to our technical support staff with software problems.
b. Having found the misplaced file, the search was ended.
c. The candidate announced his intention to run for national office in his hometown of Saskatoon, Saskatchewan.
d. Ignoring the warning prompt on the screen, the computer was turned off resulting in the loss of data.
e. Using a number of creative search terms, the Web site was finally found.

6.10 Transitional Expressions (Obj. 5)

Your Task. Add transitional expressions to the following sentences to improve the flow of ideas (coherence).

a. We recognize that giving your time to important causes is just as important as giving your money. We've created several programs that make it easy and rewarding for our employees to get involved.
b. Our computerized file includes all customer data. It provides space for name, address, and other vital information. It has an area for comments, a feature that comes in handy and helps us keep our records up to date.
c. No one likes to turn out poor products. We began highlighting recurring problems. Employees make a special effort to be more careful in doing their work right the first time. It doesn't have to be returned to them for corrections.
d. In-depth employment interviews may be structured or unstructured. Structured interviews have little flexibility. All candidates are asked the same questions in the same order. Unstructured interviews allow a free-flowing conversation. Topics are prepared for discussion by the interviewer.
e. Fringe benefits consist of life, health, and dental insurance. Some fringe benefits might include paid vacations and sick pay. Other fringe benefits include holidays, funeral leave, and emergency leave. Paid lunch, rest periods, tuition reimbursement, and child care are also sometimes provided.

6.11 Paragraph Organization (Obj. 5)

Your Task. The following poorly written paragraphs follow the indirect plan. Locate the main sentence in each paragraph. Then revise each paragraph so that it is organized directly. Improve coherence by using the techniques described in this chapter.

a. Many of our customers limp through their business despite problems with their disk drives, printers, and peripherals. We cannot service their disk drives, printers, and peripherals. These customers are unable to go without this equipment long enough for the repair. We've learned that there are two times when we can get to that equipment. We can do our repairs in the middle of the night or on Sunday. All of our staff of technicians now work every Sunday. Please authorize additional budget for my department to hire technicians for night and weekend service hours.
b. Air express is one of the ways SturdyBilt power mowers and chain saws may be delivered. Air express promises two-day delivery but at a considerable cost. The cheapest method is for retailers to pick up shipments themselves at our nearest distribution centre. We have distribution centres in Regina, Winnipeg, and Thunder Bay. Another option involves having our trucks deliver the shipment from our distribution centre to the retailer's door for an additional fee. These are the options

SturdyBilt provides for the retailers purchasing our products.

C.L.U.E. review 6

Edit the following sentences to correct faults in grammar, punctuation, spelling, and word use.

1. When our Marketing Manager had to write a twenty page report she started by collecting information, and organizing it.
2. A business writters biggest problem is usually poor organization according to experts.
3. The company Vice President came to the President and I asking for help with 2 complex but seperate advertising problems.
4. Because neither of us were particularly creative we decided to organize a brainstorming session rather then work by ourself.
5. Our brain storming session included: Amanda, Rory, Rashid and Cynthia.
6. One of our principle goals were to create one hundred ideas in thirty minutes however we were prepared to meet up to 1 hour.
7. Although we knew the principals of outlining we had trouble grouping our ideas into 3 to 5 major headings.
8. Robyn Clarkes article titled A Better way to brainstorm which appeared in the magazine Black Enterprise was helpful to the President and I.
9. Frontloading a message saves a readers time therefore its worth making the effort to put the main idea first.
10. By learning to distinguish phases from clauses youll be better able to avoid 3 basic sentence faults, the fragment, the run on sentence and the comma splice.

Rich chapter resources are available on the Web site.

chapter 7

Writing Process Phase 3: Revise, Proofread, Evaluate

objectives

1. Apply Phase 3 of the 3-x-3 writing process, which begins with techniques to make a message clear and conversational.
2. Describe specific revision tactics that make a message concise.
3. Describe revision techniques that make a message vigorous and direct.
4. Discuss revision strategies that improve readability.
5. Recognize proofreading problem areas, and be able to list techniques for proofreading both routine and complex documents.
6. Evaluate a message to judge its success.

springboard *to discussion*

Language use continues to evolve, and with each new edition of a dictionary, new words are added. Canadian Mike Myers made linguistic history in the 2007 edition of the online Oxford dictionary with the inclusion of the word "shagedelic." New words are entered into a database, and in the case of the Canadian Oxford Dictionary, once it has shown up 15 times in five years, it's considered for entry.[1]

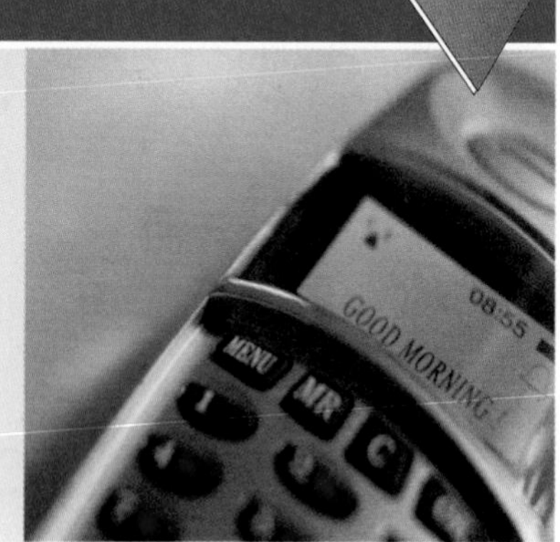

learning objective 1

Writing Process Phase 3: Revise

The final phase of the 3-x-3 writing process focuses on revising, proofreading, and evaluating. *Revising* means improving the content and sentence structure of your message. *Proofreading* involves correcting its grammar, spelling, punctuation, format, and mechanics. *Evaluating* is the process of analyzing whether your message has achieved its purpose. Many businesspeople realize that bright ideas are worth little unless they can be communicated effectively to fellow workers and to management. In the communication process, the techniques of revision can often mean the difference between acceptance or rejection of ideas.

Although the composition process differs for individuals and situations, this final phase should occupy a significant share of the total time you spend on a message. As you learned earlier, some experts recommend devoting about half the total composition time to revising and proofreading.[2]

Because few writers can produce a satisfactory copy on the first attempt, revision is an important step in the writing process.

Rarely is the first or even second version of a message satisfactory. Only amateurs expect writing perfection on the first try. The revision stage is your chance to make sure your message says what you mean. Many professional writers compose the first draft quickly without worrying about language, precision, or correctness. Then they revise and polish extensively. Other writers, however, prefer to revise as they go—particularly for shorter business documents.

Important messages—such as those you send to management or to customers or turn in to instructors for grades—deserve careful revision and proofreading. When you finish a first draft, plan for a cooling-off period. Put the document aside and return to it after a break, preferably after 24 hours or longer.

Whether you revise immediately or after a break, you'll want to examine your message critically. You should be especially concerned with ways to improve its clarity, conciseness, vigour, and readability.

The goal of business writing is to express rather than impress.

Revising for Clarity

One of the first revision tasks is assessing the clarity of your message. A clear message is one that is immediately understood. To achieve clarity, resist the urge to show off or be fancy. Remember that your goal is not to impress an instructor. Instead, the goal of business writing is to *express*, not *impress*. This involves two simple rules: (1) keep it simple and (2) keep it conversational.

Why do some communicators fail to craft simple, direct messages? Following are several reasons:

- Untrained executives and professionals worry that plain messages don't sound important.
- Subordinates fear that plain talk won't impress the boss.
- Unskilled writers create foggy messages because they haven't learned how to communicate clearly.
- Unethical writers intentionally obscure a message to hide the truth.

Whatever the cause, you can eliminate the fog by applying the familiar KISS formula: Keep It Short and Simple! One way to achieve clear writing is to use active-voice sentences that avoid foggy, indirect, and pompous language.

To achieve clarity, remember to KISS: Keep It Short and Simple!

Foggy	**Clear**
Employees have not been made sufficiently aware of the potentially adverse consequences involved regarding these chemicals.	Warn your employees about these chemicals.

Revising for Conversational Tone

Clarity is further enhanced by language that sounds like conversation. This doesn't mean that your letters and memos should be chatty or familiar. Rather, you should strive to sound professional, but not artificial or formal. This means avoiding legal terminology, technical words, and third-person constructions (*the undersigned, the writer*). Business messages should sound warm, friendly, and conversational—not stuffy. To sound friendly, include occasional contractions (*can't, doesn't*) and first-person pronouns (*I/we*). This warmth is appropriate in all but the most formal business reports. You can determine whether your writing is conversational by trying the kitchen test. If it wouldn't sound natural in your kitchen, it probably needs revision. Note how the following formal sentence was revised to pass the kitchen test.

To achieve a conversational tone, sound professional but not stilted.

Formal	**Conversational**
As per your verbal instruction, steps will be undertaken immediately to investigate your billing problem.	At your suggestion I'm investigating your billing immediately.

Revising for Conciseness

learning objective

2

In revising, be certain that a message makes its point in the fewest possible words. For instance, A. A. Milne, author of *Winnie the Pooh*, recognized the value of keeping language simple when he noted, "It is more fun to talk with someone who doesn't use long, difficult words but rather short, easy words like 'What about lunch?'"[3]

Short messages require more effort than long, flabby ones.

Messages without flabby phrases and redundancies are easier to comprehend and more emphatic because main points stand out. Efficient messages also save the reader valuable time.

But concise writing is not easy. To turn out slim sentences and lean messages, you do not have to be brusque, rude, or simple-minded. Instead, you must take time in the revision stage to "trim the fat." And before you can do that, you must learn to recognize it. Locating and excising wordiness involves eliminating (1) fillers, (2) long lead-ins, (3) redundancies, (4) compound prepositions, and (5) empty words.

Removing Fillers

Avoid fillers that fatten sentences with excess words. Beginning an idea with *There is* usually indicates that writers are spinning their wheels until they decide where the sentence is going. Used correctly, *there* indicates a specific place (*I placed the box there*). Used as fillers, *there* and occasionally *it* merely take up space. Most, but not all, sentences can be revised so that these fillers are unnecessary.

Wordy	**Concise**
There are three vice presidents who report directly to the president.	Three vice presidents report directly to the president.

Deleting Long Lead-Ins

Long lead-ins delay getting to the "meat" of the sentence.

Delete unnecessary introductory words. The meat of the sentence often follows the words *that* and *because*. In addition, many long lead-ins say what is obvious.

Wordy	**Concise**
I am sending this announcement to let you all know that the office will be closed Monday.	The office will be closed Monday.
I am writing this letter because Dr. Marcia Howard suggested that your organization was hiring trainees.	Dr. Marcia Howard suggested that your organization was hiring trainees.

Eliminating Redundancies

Redundancies convey the same meaning more than once.

Expressions that repeat meaning or include unnecessary words are redundant. To say *unexpected surprise* is like saying "surprise surprise" because *unexpected* carries the same meaning as *surprise*. Excessive adjectives, adverbs, and phrases often create redundancies and wordiness. The following list represents a tiny segment of the large number of redundancies appearing in business writing today. What word in each expression creates the redundancy?

Redundancies to Avoid

advance warning	exactly identical	perfectly clear
alter or change	few in number	personal opinion
assemble together	free and clear	potential opportunity
basic fundamentals	grateful thanks	positively certain
collect together	great majority	proposed plan
consensus of opinion	integral part	serious interest
contributing factor	last and final	refer back
dollar amount	midway between	true facts
each and every	new changes	visible to the eye
end result	past history	unexpected surprise

Reducing Compound Prepositions

Single words can often replace wordy prepositional phrases. In the following examples, notice how the shorter forms say the same thing but more efficiently.

Wordy prepositional phrases can be shortened to single words.

Wordy Compound Preposition	Shorter Form
as to whether	whether
at a later date	later
at this point in time	now
at such time, at which time	when
by means of, in accordance with	by
despite the fact that	although
due to the fact that, inasmuch as, in view of the fact that	because
for the amount of	for
in advance of, prior to	before
subsequent to	after
the manner in which	how
until such time as	until

Purging Empty Words

Familiar phrases roll off the tongue easily, but many contain expendable parts. Be alert to these empty words and phrases: *case*, *degree*, *the fact that*, *factor*, *instance*, *nature*, and *quality*. Notice how much better the following sentences sound when we remove all the empty words:

> ~~In the case of~~ *The Toronto Sun* ~~the newspaper~~ improved its readability.
>
> Because of ~~the degree of~~ active participation by our sales reps, profits soared.
>
> We are aware ~~of the fact~~ that many managers need assistance.

Also avoid saying the obvious. In the following examples notice how many unnecessary words we can omit through revision:

Good writers avoid saying what is obvious.

> ~~We need printer cartridges; therefore,~~ please send me two dozen laser cartridges. (The first clause is obvious.)
>
> ~~This is to inform you that~~ the meeting will start at 2 p.m. (Avoid unnecessary lead-ins.)

Finally, look carefully at clauses beginning with *that*, *which*, and *who*. They can often be shortened without loss of clarity. Search for phrases such as *it appears that*. Such phrases can be reduced to a single adjective or adverb such as *apparently*.

> final
> Our ^ proposal, which was slightly altered ~~in its final form~~, won approval.
>
> weekly
> We plan to schedule ^ meetings ~~on a weekly basis~~.

Revising for Vigour and Directness

learning objective

3

Much business writing has been criticized as lifeless, cautious, and "really, really boring."[4] This boredom results not so much from content as from wordiness and dull, trite expressions. You've already studied ways to improve clarity and conciseness. You can also reduce wordiness and improve vigour by (1) kicking the noun habit and (2) dumping trite business phrases.

Much business writing is plagued by wordiness and triteness.

Kicking the Noun Habit

Some writers become addicted to nouns, needlessly transforming verbs into nouns (*we make a recommendation of* instead of *we recommend*). This bad habit increases sentence length, drains verb strength, slows the reader, and muddies the thought. Notice how efficient, clean, and forceful the following verbs sound compared with their noun-phrase counterparts.

Wordy Noun Phrase	Verb
conduct a discussion of	discuss
create a reduction in	reduce
engage in the preparation of	prepare
give consideration to	consider
make an assumption of	assume
make a discovery of	discover
perform an analysis of	analyze
reach a conclusion about	conclude
take action on	act

Dumping Trite Business Phrases

Avoid trite expressions that are overused in business writing.

To sound "businesslike," many writers repeat the same stale expressions that other writers have used over the years. Your writing will sound fresher and more vigorous if you eliminate these phrases or find more original ways to convey the idea.

Trite Phrase	Improved Version
as per your request	as you request
pursuant to your request	at your request
enclosed please find	enclosed is
every effort will be made	we'll try
in accordance with your wishes	as you wish
in receipt of	have received
please do not hesitate to	please
thank you in advance	thank you
under separate cover	separately
with reference to	about

learning objective

Revising for Readability

To help receivers anticipate and comprehend ideas quickly, a number of graphic highlighting techniques are helpful. You can use (1) parallelism, which involves balanced writing; (2) lists and bullets, which facilitate quick comprehension; (3) headings, which make important points more visible; and (4) other highlighting techniques to improve readability.

Developing Parallelism for Balance

Parallelism means matching nouns with nouns, verbs with verbs, phrases with phrases, and so on.

As you revise, be certain that you express similar ideas in balanced or parallel construction. For example, the phrase *clearly, concisely, and correctly* is parallel because all the words end in *-ly*. To express the list as *clearly, concisely, and with correctness* is jarring because the last item is not what the receiver expects. Instead of an adverb, the series ends with a noun. To achieve parallelism, match nouns with nouns, verbs with verbs, phrases with phrases, and clauses with clauses. Avoid mixing active-voice verbs with passive-voice verbs.

Not Parallel
The policy affected all vendors, suppliers, and those involved with consulting.

Improved
The policy affected all vendors, suppliers, and consultants. (Series matches nouns.)

Using Numbered and Bulleted Lists for Quick Comprehension

Numbered and bulleted lists improve readability by making important ideas stand out.

One of the best ways to ensure rapid comprehension of ideas is through the use of numbered or bulleted lists. Ideas formerly buried within sentences or paragraphs stand out when listed. Readers not only understand your message more rapidly and easily but also consider you efficient and well organized. Lists provide high "skim value." This means that readers use lists to read quickly and grasp main ideas. By breaking up complex information into smaller chunks, lists improve readability, comprehension, and retention. They also force the writer to organize ideas and write efficiently. Use numbered lists for items that represent a sequence or reflect a numbering system. Use bulleted lists to highlight items that don't necessarily show a chronology.

Numbered List
Our recruiters follow these steps in hiring applicants:

1. Examine the application.
2. Interview the applicant.
3. Check the applicant's references.

Bulleted List
To attract upscale customers, we feature the following:

- Quality fashions
- Personalized service
- A generous return policy

Photo: © Robert Harding/Digital Vision/Getty

Struggling to merge cultures and regions as different as Holland, with its lighted canal bridges, and contemporary Paris and London, the European Union recently drafted a complex constitution. It was such a dense document that a reader-friendly version was posted online. Underlined sections, along with marginal comments such as those used in this textbook, improved readability and "skim value," a goal of the European Union Parliament.

Improve the skim value of a message by adding high-visibility vertical lists.

In listing items vertically, capitalize the word at the beginning of each line. Add end punctuation only if the statements are complete sentences, and be sure to use parallel construction. Notice in the numbered list that each item begins with a verb. In the bulleted list each item follows an adjective–noun sequence. In Chapter 8 you'll learn more about using lists to improve readability in e-mail messages and memos. In Chapter 15 you'll learn how to convert a paragraph into bulleted items for a PowerPoint presentation.

Be careful, however, not to overuse the list format. One writing expert warns that too many lists make messages look like grocery lists.[5]

Adding Headings for Visual Impact

Headings help writers to organize information and enable readers to absorb important ideas.

Headings are an important tool for highlighting information and improving readability. They encourage the writer to organize carefully so that similar material is grouped together. They help the reader separate major ideas from details. Moreover, headings enable a busy reader to skim familiar or less important information. They also provide a quick preview or review. Headings appear most often in reports, which you'll study in greater detail in Unit 4. But main headings, subheadings, and category headings can also improve readability in e-mail messages, memos, and letters. Here they are used with bullets to summarize categories:

Category Headings

Our company focuses on the following areas in the employment process:

- **Attracting applicants.** We advertise for qualified applicants, and we also encourage current employees to recommend good people.
- **Interviewing applicants.** Our specialized interviews include simulated customer encounters as well as scrutiny by supervisors.
- **Checking references.** We investigate every applicant thoroughly, including conversations with former employers and all listed references.

Improving Readability With Other Graphic Techniques

Graphic techniques such as capital letters, underlining, bold type, italics, and blank space spotlight ideas.

Vertical lists and headings are favourite tools for improving readability, but other graphic techniques can also focus attention.

To highlight individual words, use CAPITAL letters, underlining, **bold** type, or *italics*. Be careful with these techniques, though, because readers may feel they are being shouted at.

One final technique to enhance comprehension is blank space. Space is especially important in e-mail messages, when formatting techniques don't always work. Grouping ideas under capitalized headings with blank space preceding the heading can greatly improve readability.

Too much graphic highlighting can clutter a document and reduce comprehension.

The following chapters supply additional ideas for grouping and spotlighting data. Although highlighting techniques can improve readability, they can also clutter a message if overdone. Many of these techniques, such as listing items vertically, also require more space, so use them judiciously.

Measuring Readability

Formulas can measure how easy or difficult a message is to read. Two well-known formulas are Robert Gunning's Fog Index and the Flesch-Kincaid Index. Both measure word and sentence length to determine readability. The longer a sentence, the more difficult it is to read. If you are using a current version of Microsoft Word, the software will calculate a readability score for any passage you highlight.* Word shows a "reading ease" score as well as the Flesch-Kincaid grade-level score. A score of 10, for example, means that the passage can be easily read by a person with 10 years of schooling. Your goal should be to keep your writing between the levels of 8 and 12.

Remember that your goal as a business communicator is to make your message understood. By following the tips outlined in this chapter and occasionally using your word processor to calculate the readability of your writing, you can ensure that you stay within the appropriate range for your audience. Long words—those over two syllables—and long sentences can make your writing foggy.

Readability formulas based on word and sentence lengths do not always measure meaningfulness.

Readability formulas, however, don't always tell the full story. Although they provide a rough estimate, those based solely on word and sentence counts fail to measure meaningfulness. Even short words (such as *skew*, *onus*, and *wane*) can cause trouble if readers don't recognize them. More important than length are a word's familiarity and meaningfulness to the reader. In Chapter 5 you learned to adapt your writing to the audience by selecting familiar words. Other techniques that can improve readability include well-organized paragraphs, transitions to connect ideas, lists, and headings.

Improving readability is one of the goals of revision. As you will see in the following checklist, the task of revision has many goals, and they aren't always easy to achieve. Revision demands objectivity and a willingness to cut, cut, cut. Though painful, the process is also gratifying. It's a great feeling when you realize your finished message is clear, concise, and readable.

Checklist for Revising Messages

✓ **Keep the message simple.** Express ideas directly. Don't show off or use fancy language.

✓ **Be conversational.** Include occasional contractions (*hasn't, don't*) and first-person pronouns (*I/we*). Use natural-sounding language.

✓ **Avoid opening fillers and long lead-ins.** Omit sentence fillers such as *there is* and long lead-ins such as *this is to inform you that.*

✓ **Shun redundancies.** Eliminate words that repeat meanings, such as *mutual cooperation.* Watch for repetitious adjectives, adverbs, and phrases.

✓ **Tighten your writing.** Check phrases that include *case*, *degree*, *the fact that*, *factor*, and other words and phrases that unnecessarily increase wordiness. Avoid saying the obvious.

✓ **Don't convert verbs to nouns.** Keep your writing vigorous by avoiding the noun habit (*analyze*, not *make an analysis of*).

✓ **Avoid trite phrases.** Keep your writing fresh, direct, and contemporary by skipping such expressions as *enclosed please find* and *pursuant to your request.*

*On the **Tools** menu, click **Options,** and then click the **Spelling & Grammar** tab. Select the **Check grammar with spelling** check box. Select the **Show readability statistics** check box, and then click **OK.** When Microsoft Word finishes checking spelling and grammar, it displays information about the reading level of the highlighted passage.

- **Strive for parallelism.** Help receivers anticipate and comprehend your message by using balanced writing (*planning, drafting, and constructing*, not *planning, drafting, and construction*).
- **Highlight important ideas.** Use bullets, lists, headings, capital letters, underlining, boldface, italics, and blank space to spotlight ideas and organization.
- **Consider readability.** Strive to keep the reading level of a message between Grades 8 and 12. Remember that short, familiar words and short sentences help readers comprehend.

learning objective 5

Writing Process Phase 3: Proofread

Proofreading before a document is completed is generally a waste of time.

Once you have the message in its final form, it's time to proofread. Don't proofread earlier because you may waste time checking items that are eventually changed or omitted. Proofreading is especially difficult because most of us read what we thought we wrote. That's why it's important to look for specific problem areas.

What to Watch for in Proofreading

Careful proofreaders check for problems in these areas:

- **Spelling.** Now's the time to consult the dictionary. Is *recommend* spelled with one or two c's? Do you mean *affect* or *effect*? Use your computer spell checker, but don't rely on it totally.
- **Grammar.** Locate sentence subjects; do their verbs agree with them? Do pronouns agree with their antecedents? Review the C.L.U.E. principles in Appendix A if necessary. Use your computer's grammar checker, but be suspicious, as explained in the Tech Talk box on the next page.
- **Punctuation.** Make sure that introductory clauses are followed by commas. In compound sentences put commas before coordinating conjunctions (*and, or, but, nor*). Double-check your use of semicolons and colons.
- **Names and numbers.** Compare all names and numbers with their sources because inaccuracies are not always visible. Especially verify the spelling of the names of individuals receiving the message. Most of us immediately dislike someone who misspells our name.
- **Format.** Be sure that your document looks balanced on the page. Compare its parts and format with those of standard documents shown in Appendix B. If you indent paragraphs, be certain that all are indented.

How to Proofread Routine Documents

Routine documents need a light proofreading.

Most routine documents require a light proofreading. You may be working with a handwritten or a printed copy or on your computer screen. If you wish to print a copy, make it a rough draft (don't print it on good stationery). In time you may be able to produce a "first-time-final" message, but beginning writers seldom do.

For handwritten or printed messages, read the entire document. Watch for all of the items just described. Use standard proofreading marks, shown on the inside front cover, to indicate changes.

tech talk

Using Spell Checkers and Grammar/Style Checkers Wisely

Spell-checking and grammar-checking software are two useful tools that can save you from many embarrassing errors. They can also greatly enhance your revision techniques—if you know how to use them wisely.

Spell Checkers

Although some writers dismiss spell checkers as an annoyance, most of us are only too happy to have our typos and misspelled words detected. If you are using Microsoft Word, you need to set the options to "check spelling as you type." (Use the **Tools** menu, click **Options.** On the **Spelling & Grammar** tab choose *Check spelling as you type* and *Always suggest corrections.*) When you see a wavy red line under a word, you are being notified that the highlighted word is not in the computer's dictionary. Right-click for a list of suggested replacements and other actions.

Spell checkers are indeed wonderful, but they are far from perfect. If you mistype a word, the spell checker is not sure what you meant and the suggested replacements may be way off target. What's more, a spell checker cannot know that when you type *form*, you mean *from*. Lesson: Don't rely totally on spell checkers to find all typos and spelling errors.

Grammar and Style Checkers

Like spell checkers, today's grammar and style checkers are amazingly sophisticated. Microsoft Word marks faults in capitalization, fragments, misused words, double negatives, possessives, plurals, punctuation, subject–verb agreement, gender-specific words, wordiness, and many other problems.

How does a grammar checker work? Let's say you typed the sentence *The office and its equipment is for sale*. You would see a wavy green line appear under *is*. Right-click and a box identifies the subject–verb agreement error and suggests the verb *are* as a correction. When you click *are*, the error is corrected. You can set grammar and style options in the **Grammar** dialogue box (**Tools** menu, **Options** command, **Spelling & Grammar** tab, and **Settings**).

Before you decide that a grammar checker will solve all your writing problems, think again. Even Word's highly developed software misses plenty of errors, and it also mismarks some correct expressions.

You can read computer messages on the screen by using the down arrow to reveal one line at a time. This focuses your attention at the bottom of the screen. A safer proofreading method, however, is reading from a printed copy. You're more likely to find errors and to observe the tone.

For both routine and complex documents, it's best to proofread from a printed copy, not on a computer screen.

How to Proofread Complex Documents

Long, complex, or important documents demand more careful proofreading, using the following techniques:

- Print a copy, preferably double-spaced, and set it aside for at least a day. You'll be more alert after a breather.
- Allow adequate time to proofread carefully. A common excuse for sloppy proofreading is lack of time.
- Be prepared to find errors. Psychologically, we don't expect to find errors, and we don't want to find them. You can overcome this obstacle by anticipating errors and congratulating, not criticizing, yourself each time you find one.
- Read the message at least twice—once for word meanings and once for grammar/mechanics. For very long documents (book chapters and long articles or reports), read a third time to verify consistency in formatting.

Computer programs can help analyze writing, calculate readability, and locate some grammar and punctuation errors.

Complex documents should be proofread at least twice.

- Reduce your reading speed. Concentrate on individual words rather than ideas.
- Read aloud to hear your mistakes.
- For documents that must be perfect, enlist a proofreading buddy. Have someone read the message aloud. Spell names and difficult words, note capitalization, and read punctuation.
- Use standard proofreading marks, shown on the inside front cover of your text, to indicate changes.

Most proofreaders use standard marks to indicate revisions.

learning objective 6

Writing Process Phase 3: Evaluate

As part of applying finishing touches, take a moment to evaluate your writing. How successful will this message be? Does it say what you want it to? Will it achieve your purpose? How will you know if it succeeds?

A good way to evaluate messages is through feedback.

As you learned in Chapter 1, the best way to judge the success of your communication is through feedback. Thus, you should encourage the receiver to respond to your message. This feedback will tell you how to modify future efforts to improve your communication technique.

Your instructor will also be evaluating some of your writing. Although any criticism is painful, try not to be defensive. Look on these comments as valuable advice tailored to your specific writing weaknesses—and strengths. Many businesses today spend thousands of dollars bringing in communication consultants to improve employee writing skills. You're getting the same training in this course. Take advantage of this chance—one of the few you may have—to improve your skills. The best way to improve your skills, of course, is through instruction, practice, and evaluation.

In this class you have all three elements: instruction in the writing process, practice materials, and someone willing to guide and evaluate your efforts. Those three elements are the reasons that this book and this course may be the most valuable in your entire curriculum. Because it's almost impossible to improve your communication skills alone, grab this chance!

Summary of Learning Objectives

1 **Apply Phase 3 of the 3-x-3 writing process, which begins with techniques to make a message clear and conversational.** The final phase of the writing process involves editing, revising, and evaluating. Revising for clarity means using active-voice sentences and simple words while avoiding confusing negative expressions. Clarity is further enhanced by language that sounds conversational, including occasional contractions and first-person pronouns (*I/we*).

2 **Describe specific revision tactics that make a message concise.** Concise messages make their points in the fewest possible words. Revising for conciseness involves excluding opening fillers (*There are*), redundancies (*basic essentials*), and compound prepositions (*by means of, due to the fact that*).

3 **Describe revision techniques that make a message vigorous and direct.** Writers can achieve vigour in messages by revising wordy phrases that needlessly convert verbs into nouns. For example, instead of *we conducted a discussion of*, write *we discussed*. To make writing more direct, good writers replace trite business phrases, such as *please do not hesitate to*, with similar expressions, such as *please.*

4 **Discuss revision strategies that improve readability.** One revision technique that improves readability is the use of balanced constructions (parallelism). For example, *collecting, analyzing, and illustrating data* is balanced and easy to read. *Collecting, analysis of, and illustration of data* is more difficult to read because it is unbalanced. Parallelism involves matching nouns with nouns, verbs with verbs, phrases with phrases, and clauses with clauses. Other techniques that improve readability are bullets and lists for quick comprehension, headings for visual impact, and graphic techniques such as capital letters, underlining, italics, and bold print to highlight and order ideas. Readability can be measured by formulas that count long words and sentence length.

5 **Recognize proofreading problem areas, and be able to list techniques for proofreading both routine and complex documents.** Proofreaders must be especially alert to spelling, grammar, punctuation, names, numbers, and document format. Routine documents may be proofread immediately after completion. They may be read line by line on the computer screen or, better yet, from a printed draft copy. More complex documents, however, should be proofread after a breather. To do a good job, you must read from a printed copy, allow adequate time, reduce your reading speed, and read the document at least three times—for word meanings, for grammar/mechanics, and for formatting.

6 **Evaluate a message to judge its success.** Encourage feedback from the receiver so that you can determine whether your communication achieved its goal. Try to welcome any advice from your instructor on how to improve your writing skills. Both techniques contribute to helping you evaluate the success of a message.

chapter review

1. Approximately how much of the total composition time should be spent revising, proofreading, and evaluating? (Obj. 1)
2. What is the KISS method? In what three ways can it apply to business writing? (Obj. 1)
3. What is a redundancy? Give an example. Why should writers avoid redundancies? (Obj. 2)
4. Why should communicators avoid openings such as *there is*? (Obj. 2)
5. What shorter forms could be substituted for the expressions *at this point in time*, *for the amount of*, and *in advance of*? (Obj. 2)
6. Why should a writer avoid the opening *I am sending this e-mail because we have just hired a new manager, and I would like to introduce her.* (Obj. 2)
7. Why should a writer avoid an expression such as *We expect the executive committee to give authorization to the merger*? (Obj. 3)
8. What's wrong with businesslike expressions such as *enclosed please find* and *as per your request*? (Obj. 3)
9. What is parallelism, and how can you achieve it? (Obj. 4)
10. What is high "skim value," and how can you achieve it? (Obj. 4)
11. What factors determine whether you should use bulleted or numbered items in a list? (Obj. 4)
12. Name five specific items to check in proofreading. Be ready to discuss methods you find useful in spotting these errors. (Obj. 5)
13. In proofreading, what major psychological problem do you face in finding errors? How can you overcome this barrier? (Obj. 5)
14. List four or more effective techniques for proofreading complex documents. (Obj. 5)
15. How can you overcome defensiveness when your writing is criticized constructively? (Obj. 6)

critical thinking

1. Why is it difficult to recommend a specific process that all writers can follow in composition? (Obj. 1)
2. Would you agree or disagree with the following statement by writing expert William Zinsser? "Plain talk will not be easily achieved in corporate North America. Too much vanity is on the line." (Objs. 1 and 2)
3. Since business writing should have high "skim value," why not write everything in bulleted lists? (Objs. 2 and 4)
4. Why should the proofreading process for routine documents differ from that for complex documents? (Objs. 4 and 5)

activities

7.1 Document for Analysis: Poorly Written Letter (Objs. 1–5)

The following letter suffers from a number of weaknesses discussed in this chapter.

Your Task. Study the letter and analyze its weaknesses. In teams or in a class discussion, list at least five specific weaknesses. Then revise for clarity, tone, conciseness, readability, and correctness. As your instructor directs, use standard proofreading marks to show corrections or revise at a computer.

Current date
Mr. Gene Gorsky
702 9th Street
Meadow Lake, SK S9X 1C2
Dear Mr. Gorsky:

As per your request, the undersigned is transmitting to you the attached documents with regard to the improvement of security in your business. To ensure the improvement of your after-hours security, you should initially make a decision with regard to exactly what you contemplate must have protection. You are, in all probability, apprehensive not only about your electronic equipment and paraphernalia but also about your company records, information, and data.

Due to the fact that we feel you will want to obtain protection for both your equipment and data, we will make suggestions for taking a number of judicious steps to inhibit crime. First and foremost, we make a recommendation that you install defensive lighting. A consultant for lighting, currently on our staff, can design both outside and inside lighting, which brings me to my second point. Exhibit security signs, because of the fact that nonprofessional thieves are often as not deterred by posted signs on windows and doors. As my last and final recommendation, you should install space alarms, which are sensors that look down over the areas that are to receive protection, and activate bells or additional lights, thus scaring off intruders.

Rich chapter resources are available on the Web site.

After reading the materials that are attached, please call me to initiate a verbal discussion regarding protection of your business.

Sincerely,

7.2 Document for Analysis: Weak E-Mail Message (Objs. 1–5)

The following e-mail message suffers from a number of weaknesses discussed in this chapter.

Your Task. Study the message and analyze its weaknesses. In teams or in a class discussion, list at least five specific weaknesses. Then, revise for clarity, tone, conciseness, readability, and correctness. In this message consider using two bulleted lists and headings to improve readability. As your instructor directs, use standard proofreading marks to show corrections or revise at a computer.

TO:	Keisha Love, Sales and Marketing Manager <klove@ricco.com>
FROM:	Arthur Pentilla, CEO <apentilla@ricco.com>
DATE:	Current
SUBJECT:	IMPROVING SAFETY AND SECURITY FOR TELECOMMUTERS

This e-mail is to inform you that due to the fact that telecommuting is becoming increasingly popular, we feel that it's important and necessary for us to be more careful in planning for information security as well as for the health and personal safety of our employees.

In view of the fact that many of our employees may be considering telecommuting, we have prepared a complete guide for managers. There are structured agreements in the guide that specify space, equipment, and how you should schedule employees. Please discuss the recommendations that follow for a home workspace as well as recommendations for security with any of your staff members who may be making a consideration of telecommuting.

Preparation of a Home Workspace

In regard to the home workspace, employees should create a space that is free and clear of traffic and distractions. They should make the home workspace as comfortable as possible but also provide sufficient space for computer, printer, and for a fax. For security reasons the home workspace should be off limits to family and also to friends. Be sure to provide proper lighting and telephone service.

In regard to the matter of information security and personal security, tell your telecommuters that they should remember that a home office is an extension of the company office. They must be careful and vigilant about avoiding computer viruses and the protection of company information. On the same topic of information security, they should positively be sure to back up information that is important and it should be stored in a safe place that is off site. We do not recommend at-home meetings for telecommuters. By the same token, postal boxes are suggested rather than giving out home addresses. Smoke detectors should be installed in home work areas.

These are just a few of our recommendations. At this point in time you will find a complete guide for telecommuters at our Web site for our company. We urge you to read it carefully as soon as possible. Please do not hesitate to call Human Resources if you have questions.

7.3 Learning About Writing Techniques in Your Field (Objs. 1–6)

How much writing is required by people working in your career area? The best way to learn about on-the-job writing is to talk with someone who has a job similar to the one you hope to have one day.

Your Task. Interview someone in your field of study. Your instructor may ask you to present your findings orally or in a written report. Ask questions such as these: *What kind of writing do you do? What kind of planning do you do before writing? Where do you get information? Do you brainstorm? Make lists? Do you compose with pen and paper, a computer, or a dictating machine? How many e-mail messages do you typically write in a day? How long does it take you to compose a routine one- or two-page memo or letter? Do you revise? How often? Do you have a preferred method for proofreading? When you have questions about grammar and mechanics, what or whom do you consult? Does anyone read your drafts and make suggestions? Can you describe your entire composition process? Do you ever work with others to produce a document? How does this process work? What makes writing easier or harder for you? Have your writing methods and skills changed since you left school?*

7.4 Clarity (Objs. 1 and 2)

Your Task. Revise the following sentences to make them direct, simple, and conversational.

- **a.** There is an e-mail policy within our organization that makes a statement that management may access and monitor the e-mail activity of each and every employee.
- **b.** Due to the fact that e-mail is a valuable tool in business, we in management are pleased to make e-mail available to all employees who are authorized to use it.
- **c.** Please be advised that it is our intention to make every effort to deliver your order by the date of your request, December 1.
- **d.** Enclosed herewith please find the proposal which we have the honour to submit to your esteemed organization in regard to the acquisition and purchase of laptop computers.
- **e.** It has been established that the incontestable key to the future success of QuadCam is a deep and firm commitment to quality.

7.5 Conciseness (Obj. 2)

Your Task. Suggest shorter forms for the following expressions.

- **a.** in reference to
- **b.** without further delay
- **c.** in the event that
- **d.** a supervisor who was diligent
- **e.** a program that is intended to save time

7.6 Conciseness (Obj. 2)

Your Task. Revise and shorten the following sentences.

- **a.** As per your recommendation, we will not attempt to make alterations or changes in the proposal at this point in time.
- **b.** It is perfectly clear that meetings held on a monthly basis are most effective.
- **c.** We have received your press release, and we will be making a decision soon about whether to use it.
- **d.** There are numerous benefits that can result from a good program that focuses on customer service.
- **e.** At this point in time in the program, I wish to extend my grateful thanks to all the support staff who helped make this occasion possible.

7.7 Vigour (Obj. 3)

Your Task. Revise the following sentences to reduce noun conversions, trite expressions, and other wordiness.

- **a.** Please give consideration to our latest proposal, despite the fact that it comes into conflict with the original plan.
- **b.** Our assessment of the damages in the amount of $500 caused us to make a reduction in the amount of the claim.
- **c.** After we engage in the preparation of a report, our recommendations will be presented in their final form before the Executive Committee.
- **d.** There are three members of our staff who are making every effort to locate your lost order.
- **e.** Whether or not we make a continuation of the sales campaign is dependent upon its success in the city of Calgary.

7.8 Parallelism (Obj. 3)

Your Task. Revise the following sentences to improve parallelism. If elements cannot be balanced fluently, use appropriate subordination.

- **a.** Ensuring equal opportunities, the removal of barriers, and elimination of age discrimination are our objectives.
- **b.** The market for industrial goods includes manufacturers, contractors, wholesalers, and those concerned with the retail function.
- **c.** Last year Amanda Thomas wrote letters and was giving presentations to promote investment in her business.
- **d.** For this position we assess oral and written communication skills, how well individuals solve problems, whether they can work with teams, and we're also interested in interpersonal skills, such as cultural awareness and sensitivity.
- **e.** We have three objectives: increase the frequency of product use, introduce complementary products, and the enhancement of our corporate image.

7.9 Lists, Bullets, and Headings (Obj. 4)

Your Task. Revise the following sentences and paragraphs using techniques presented in this chapter. Improve parallel construction and reduce wordiness if necessary.

- **a.** Revise using a bulleted list.
  HR Plus specializes in pre-employment background reports. Among our background reports are ones that include professional reference interviews, criminal reports, driving records, employment verification, and credit reports.

b. Revise using a numbered list.
In writing to customers granting approval for loans, you should follow four steps that include announcing that loan approval has been granted. Then you should specify the terms and limits. Next you should remind the reader of the importance of making payments that are timely. Finally, a phone number should be provided for assistance.

c. Revise using bulleted items with category headings.
Our lawyer made a recommendation that we consider several things to avoid litigation in regard to sexual harassment. The first thing he suggested was that we should take steps regarding the establishment of an unequivocal written policy prohibiting sexual harassment within our organization. The second thing we should do is make sure training sessions are held for supervisors regarding a proper work environment. Finally, some kind of official procedure for employees to lodge complaints is necessary. This procedure should include investigation of complaints.

7.10 Proofreading (Obj. 5)

Your Task. Use proofreading marks to mark spelling, grammar, punctuation, capitalization, and other errors in the following sentences.

a. English maybe the International Language of commerce but that does not mean that every readr will have a trouble-free experience with message writen in english.

b. Be especially carful with dates. For example A message that reads "Our video conference begins at 6 p.m. on 7/10/10" would mean July 10, 2010, to north americans.

c. To europeans the time and date would be written as follows: "The video conference will begin at 18:00 on 10 July 2010.

d. Because europeans use a twenty-four-hour military clock be sure to write int'l messages in that format.

e. To avoid confusion give metric measurments followed by there imperial equivalents. For Example, "The office is 10 kilometres (6.2 miles from the TrainStation.

C.L.U.E. review 7

Edit the following sentences to correct faults in grammar, punctuation, spelling, and word use.

1. My manager tole my colleague and I that we had to be more conscience of our proofreading because our reports had to many errors.
2. Readers want to scan messages quick therefore we should use every day language and be concise.
3. Even in europe company executives are disapointed by messages that are to long an to difficult to read.
4. One managers report contained so many redundancys that it's main principals requesting Provincial and Federal funding was lost.
5. You're writing will sound more fresher, if you eliminate trite business phases such as "pursuant to you're request.
6. All 3 of our companys recruiters: Angelica Santos, Kirk Adams, and David Toms—critisized there poorly-written procedures.
7. To help recievers anticipate and comprehend ideas quick 2 special writing techniques is helpful, parallalism which involves balanced writing and bulleting which make important points more visible.
8. When I proof read a important document I all ways work with a buddy, and read from a printed copy.
9. Read a message once for word meanings, read it again for grammer and mechanics.
10. Its all most impossible to improve ones communication skills alone, therefore every one should take advantage of this educational oppertunity.

unit 3

Business Correspondence

chapter 8

Routine E-Mail Messages and Memos

chapter 9

Routine Letters and Goodwill Messages

chapter 10

Persuasive and Sales Messages

chapter 11

Negative Messages

chapter 8

Routine E-Mail Messages and Memos

objectives

1 Discuss how the 3-x-3 writing process helps you produce effective e-mail messages and memos.

2 Analyze the structure and formatting of e-mail messages and memos.

3 Describe smart e-mail practices, including getting started; content, tone, and correctness; netiquette; reading and replying to e-mail; personal use; and other practices.

4 Write information and procedure e-mail messages and memos.

5 Write request and reply e-mail messages and memos.

6 Write confirmation e-mail messages and memos.

springboard *to discussion*

A study from Glasgow and Paisley universities revealed that e-mail is causing people the greatest amount of stress at work. People feel pressured to continually check their e-mails and subsequently lower their productivity and focus in other areas of the job. The study also discovered that women feel more pressured than men to respond to e-mails.[1]

learning objective

1

Applying the Writing Process to Produce Effective E-Mail Messages and Memos

In most organizations today, an amazing change has taken place in internal communication. In the past, written messages from insiders took the form of hard-copy memorandums. A full 85 percent of online Canadians believe that e-mail has made them much more efficient, and nearly two-thirds (62 percent) prefer to communicate via e-mail than through other methods.[2] Cautious business leaders recognize the functions and benefits but also the potential dangers of e-mail.

E-mail has become the primary communication channel for internal communication.

A primary function of e-mail is exchanging messages within organizations. Such internal communication has taken on increasing importance today. Organizations are downsizing, flattening chains of command, forming work teams, and empowering rank-and-file employees. Given more power in making decisions, employees find that they need more information. They must collect, exchange, and evaluate information about the products and services they offer. Management also needs input from employees to respond rapidly to local and global market changes. This growing demand for information means an increasing use of e-mail, although hard-copy memos are still written.

Developing skill in writing e-mail messages and memos brings you two important benefits. First, well-written documents are likely to achieve their goals. They create goodwill by being cautious, caring, and clear. They do not intentionally or unintentionally create ill feelings. Second, well-written internal messages enhance your image within the organization. Individuals identified as competent, professional writers are noticed and rewarded; most often, they are the ones promoted into management positions.

This chapter focuses on routine e-mail messages and memos. These straightforward messages open with the main idea because their topics are not sensitive and require little persuasion. You will study the writing process as well as the structure and format of e-mail messages and memos. Because e-mail is such a new and powerful channel of communication, we'll devote special attention to composing smart e-mail messages and reading and responding to e-mail professionally. Finally, you'll learn to write procedure, information, request, reply, and confirmation memos.

Careful writing takes time—especially at first. By following a systematic plan and practising your skill, however, you can speed up your efforts and greatly improve the product. Bear in mind, moreover, that the effort you make to improve your communication skills can pay big dividends. Frequently your speaking and writing abilities determine how much influence you'll have in your organization. As with other writing tasks, e-mail and memo writing follow the 3-x-3 writing process.

Phase 1: Analysis, Anticipation, and Adaptation

In Phase 1, prewriting, you'll need to spend some time analyzing your task. It's amazing how many of us are ready to put our pens or computers into gear before engaging our minds. Before writing, ask yourself these important questions:

Before writing, ask questions that help you analyze, anticipate, and adapt your message.

- **Do I really need to write this e-mail or hard-copy memo?** A phone call or a quick visit to a nearby coworker might solve the problem—and save the time and expense of a written message. On the other hand, some written messages are needed to provide a permanent record.
- **Should I send an e-mail or a memo?** It's tempting to use an e-mail or a memo for all your correspondence. But a phone call or face-to-face visit is a better channel choice if you need to (a) convey enthusiasm, warmth, or other emotion; (b) supply a context; or (c) smooth over disagreements.
- **Why am I writing?** Know why you are writing and what you hope to achieve. This will help you recognize what the important points are and where to place them.
- **How will the reader react?** Visualize the reader and the effect your message will have. In writing e-mail messages, imagine that you are sitting and talking with your reader. Avoid speaking bluntly, failing to explain, or ignoring your reader's needs. Consider ways to shape the message to benefit the reader. Also remember that your message may very well be forwarded to someone else.
- **How can I save my reader's time?** Think of ways that you can make your message easier to comprehend at a glance. Use bullets, asterisks, lists, headings, and white space, as discussed in Chapter 7, to improve readability.

Phase 2: Research, Organization, and Composition

In Phase 2, writing, you'll first want to check the files, gather documentation, and prepare your message. Make an outline of the points you wish to cover. For short messages jot down notes on the document you are answering or make a scratch list at your computer. As you compose your message, avoid amassing huge blocks of text. No one wants to read endless lines of type. Instead, group related information into paragraphs, preferably short ones. Paragraphs separated by white space look inviting. Be sure each paragraph begins with the main point and is backed up by details. If you bury your main point in the middle of a paragraph, it may be missed. Be sure to prepare for revision, because excellence is rarely achieved on the first effort.

Gather background information; organize it into an outline; compose your message; and revise for clarity, correctness, and feedback.

Phase 3: Revision, Proofreading, and Evaluation

Phase 3, revising, involves putting the final touches on your message. Careful and caring writers will ask a number of questions as they do the following:

- **Revise for clarity.** Viewed from the receiver's perspective, are the ideas clear? Do they need more explanation? If the memo is passed on to others, will they need further explanation? Consider having a colleague critique your message if it is an important one.
- **Proofread for correctness.** Are the sentences complete and punctuated properly? Did you overlook any typos or misspelled words? Remember to use your spell checker and grammar checker to proofread your message before sending it.
- **Plan for feedback.** How will you know whether this message is successful? You can improve feedback by asking questions (such as *Are you comfortable with these suggestions?* or *What do you think?*). Remember to make it easy for the receiver to respond.

learning objective

2

Analyzing the Structure and Format of E-Mail Messages and Memos

E-mail messages and memos inform employees, request data, give responses, confirm decisions, and provide directions.

Because e-mail messages and memos are standard forms of communication within organizations, they will probably become your most common business communication channel. These messages perform critical tasks such as informing employees, requesting data, supplying responses, confirming decisions, and giving directions. They generally follow similar structure and formatting.

Structuring E-Mail Messages and Memos

Whether electronic or hard copy, routine memos generally contain four parts: (1) an informative subject line that summarizes the message, (2) an opening that reveals the main idea immediately, (3) a body that explains and justifies the main idea, and (4) an appropriate closing. Remember that routine messages deliver good news or standard information.

Subject lines summarize the purpose of the message in abbreviated form.

Subject Line. In e-mails and memos, an informative subject line is mandatory. It summarizes the central idea, thus providing quick identification for reading and for filing. In e-mail messages, subject lines are essential. Busy readers glance at a subject line and decide when and whether to read the message. Those without subject lines may be automatically deleted.

What does it take to get your message read? For one thing, stay away from meaningless or dangerous words. A sure way to get your message deleted or ignored is to use a one-word heading such as *Issue*, *Problem*, *Important*, or *Help*. Including a word such as *free* is dangerous because it may trigger spam filters. Try to make your subject line "talk" by including a verb. Explain the purpose of the message and how it relates to the reader (*Need You to Showcase Two Items at Our Next Trade Show* rather than *Trade Show*). Finally, update your subject line to reflect the current message (*Staff Meeting Rescheduled for May 12* rather than *Re: Re: Staff Meeting*). Remember that a subject line is usually written in an abbreviated style, often without articles (*a, an, the*). It need not be a complete sentence, and it does not end with a period.

Routine e-mails and memos open directly by revealing the main idea immediately.

Opening. Most e-mails and memos cover nonsensitive information that can be handled in a straightforward manner. Begin by frontloading; that is, reveal the main idea immediately. Even though the purpose of the memo or e-mail is summarized in the subject line, that purpose should be restated—and amplified—in the first sentence. As you learned in Chapters 5 and 6, busy readers want to know immediately why they are reading a message. Notice how the following indirect opener can be improved by frontloading.

Indirect Opening	Direct Opening
For the past six months the Human Resources Development Department has been considering changes in our employees' benefit plan.	Please review the following proposal regarding employees' benefits, and let me know by May 20 if you approve these changes.

The body explains one topic and is designed for easy comprehension.

Body. The body provides more information about the reason for writing. It explains and discusses the subject logically. Good e-mail messages and memos generally discuss only one topic. Limiting the topic helps the receiver act on the subject and file it appropriately.

Design your data for easy comprehension by using numbered lists, headings, tables, and other graphic highlighting techniques, as introduced in Chapter 6. Compare the following versions of the same message. Notice how the graphic devices of bullets, columns, headings, and white space make the main points easier to comprehend.

Hard-to-Read Paragraph Version

Effective immediately are the following air travel guidelines. Between now and December 31, only account executives may take company-approved trips. These individuals will be allowed to take a maximum of two trips, and they are to travel economy or budget class only.

Improved Version With Graphic Highlighting

Effective immediately are the following air travel guidelines:

- Who may travel: Account executives only
- How many trips: A maximum of two trips
- By when: Between now and December 31
- Air class: Economy or budget class only

Messages should close with (1) action information including dates and deadlines, (2) a summary, or (3) a closing thought.

Closing. Generally end with (1) action information, dates, or deadlines; (2) a summary of the message; or (3) a closing thought. Here again the value of thinking through the message before actually writing it becomes apparent. The closing is where readers look for deadlines and action language. An effective memo or e-mail closing might be *Please submit your report by June 15 so that we can have your data before our July planning session.*

In more complex messages, a summary of main points may be an appropriate closing. If no action request is made and a closing summary is unnecessary, you might end with a simple concluding thought (*I'm glad to answer your questions* or *This sounds like a useful project*). You needn't close messages to coworkers with goodwill statements such as those found in letters to customers or clients. However, some closing thought is often necessary to prevent a feeling of abruptness. Closings can show gratitude or encourage feedback with remarks such as *I sincerely appreciate your help* or *What are your ideas on this proposal?* Other closings look forward to what's next, such as *How would you like to proceed?* Avoid closing with overused expressions such as *Please let me know if I may be of further assistance.* This ending sounds mechanical and insincere.

Revision helps you think through a problem, clarify a solution, and express it clearly.

Putting It All Together. Now let's apply the ideas just discussed. Figure 8.1 (p. 160) shows an e-mail message that James Perkins, marketing manager, wrote to his boss, Jie Wang.

James used an informative subject line and opened directly by explaining why he was writing. His opening also outlined the two main problems so that his reader understood the background of the following recommendations. In the body of his message, James identified three corrective actions, and he highlighted them for improved readability. Notice that he listed his three recommendations using asterisks (bullets don't always transmit well in e-mail messages) with capitalized headings. Asterisks, white space, and capitalized letters work well in e-mail messages to highlight important points. Notice, too, that James closed his message with a deadline and a reference to the next action to be taken.

Formatting E-Mail Messages

Although e-mail is a new communication channel, people are beginning to agree on specific formatting and usage conventions. The following suggestions identify current formatting standards. Always check with your organization, however, to observe its practices.

FIGURE 8.1 ***E-Mail Message That Informs***

1 Prewriting

ANALYZE: The purpose of this memo is to describe database problems and recommend solutions.

ANTICIPATE: The audience is the writer's boss, who is familiar with the topic and who appreciates brevity.

ADAPT: Because the reader requested this message, the direct pattern is most appropriate.

2 Writing

RESEARCH: Gather data documenting the customer database and how to use Access software.

ORGANIZE: Announce recommendations and summarize problems. In the body, list the three actions for solving the problem. In the closing, describe reader benefits, provide a deadline, and specify the next action.

COMPOSE: Prepare the first draft.

3 Revising

REVISE: Highlight the two main problems and the three recommendations. Use asterisks, caps, and headings to improve readability. Make the bulleted ideas parallel.

PROOFREAD: Double-check to see whether *database* is one word or two. Use spell checker.

EVALUATE: Does this e-mail supply concise information the boss wants in an easy-to-read form?

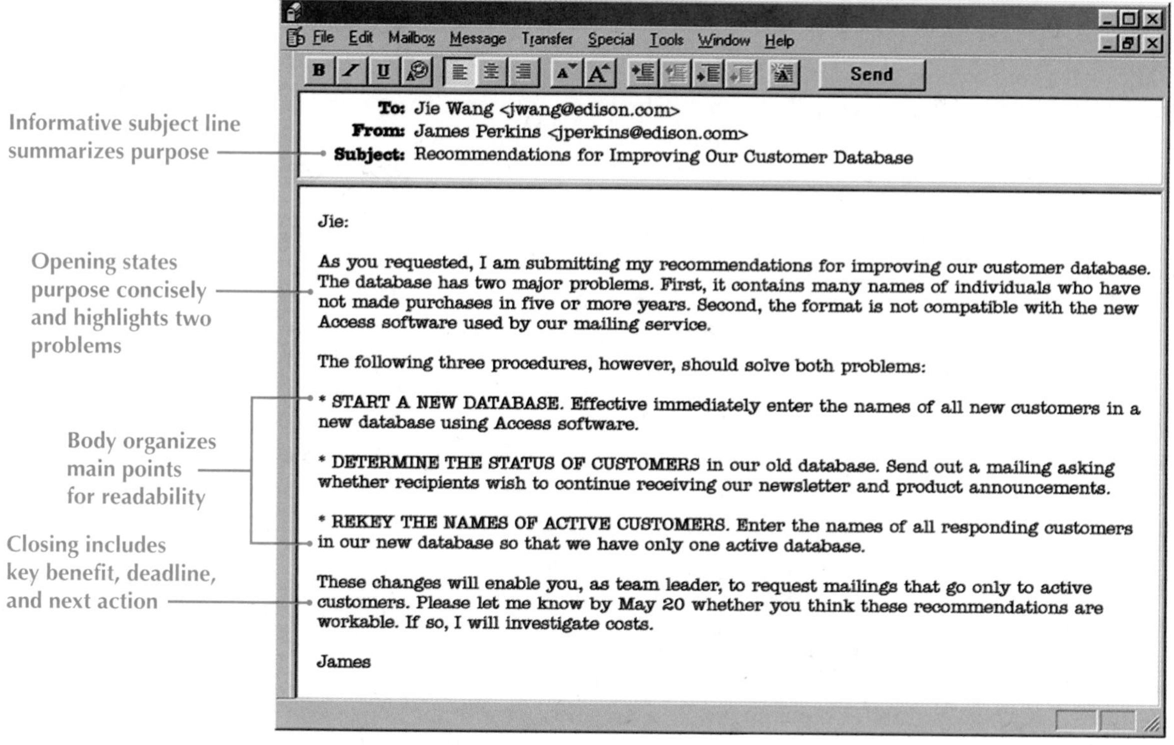

To: Jie Wang <jwang@edison.com>
From: James Perkins <jperkins@edison.com>
Subject: Recommendations for Improving Our Customer Database

Jie:

As you requested, I am submitting my recommendations for improving our customer database. The database has two major problems. First, it contains many names of individuals who have not made purchases in five or more years. Second, the format is not compatible with the new Access software used by our mailing service.

The following three procedures, however, should solve both problems:

* START A NEW DATABASE. Effective immediately enter the names of all new customers in a new database using Access software.

* DETERMINE THE STATUS OF CUSTOMERS in our old database. Send out a mailing asking whether recipients wish to continue receiving our newsletter and product announcements.

* REKEY THE NAMES OF ACTIVE CUSTOMERS. Enter the names of all responding customers in our new database so that we have only one active database.

These changes will enable you, as team leader, to request mailings that go only to active customers. Please let me know by May 20 whether you think these recommendations are workable. If so, I will investigate costs.

James

E-mails contain guide words, optional salutations, and a concise and easy-to-read message.

Guide Words. Following the guide word *To*, some writers insert just the recipient's electronic address, such as *mphilly@accountpro.com*. Other writers prefer to include the receiver's full name plus the electronic address, as shown in Figure 8.2. By including full names in the *To* and *From* slots, both receivers and senders are better able to identify the message. By the way, the order of *Date*, *To*, *From*, *Subject*, and other guide words varies depending on your e-mail program and whether you are sending or receiving the message.

Most e-mail programs automatically add the current date after *Date*. On the *CC* line (which stands for *carbon* or *courtesy copy*) you can type the address of anyone

FIGURE 8.2 *Formatting an E-Mail Request*

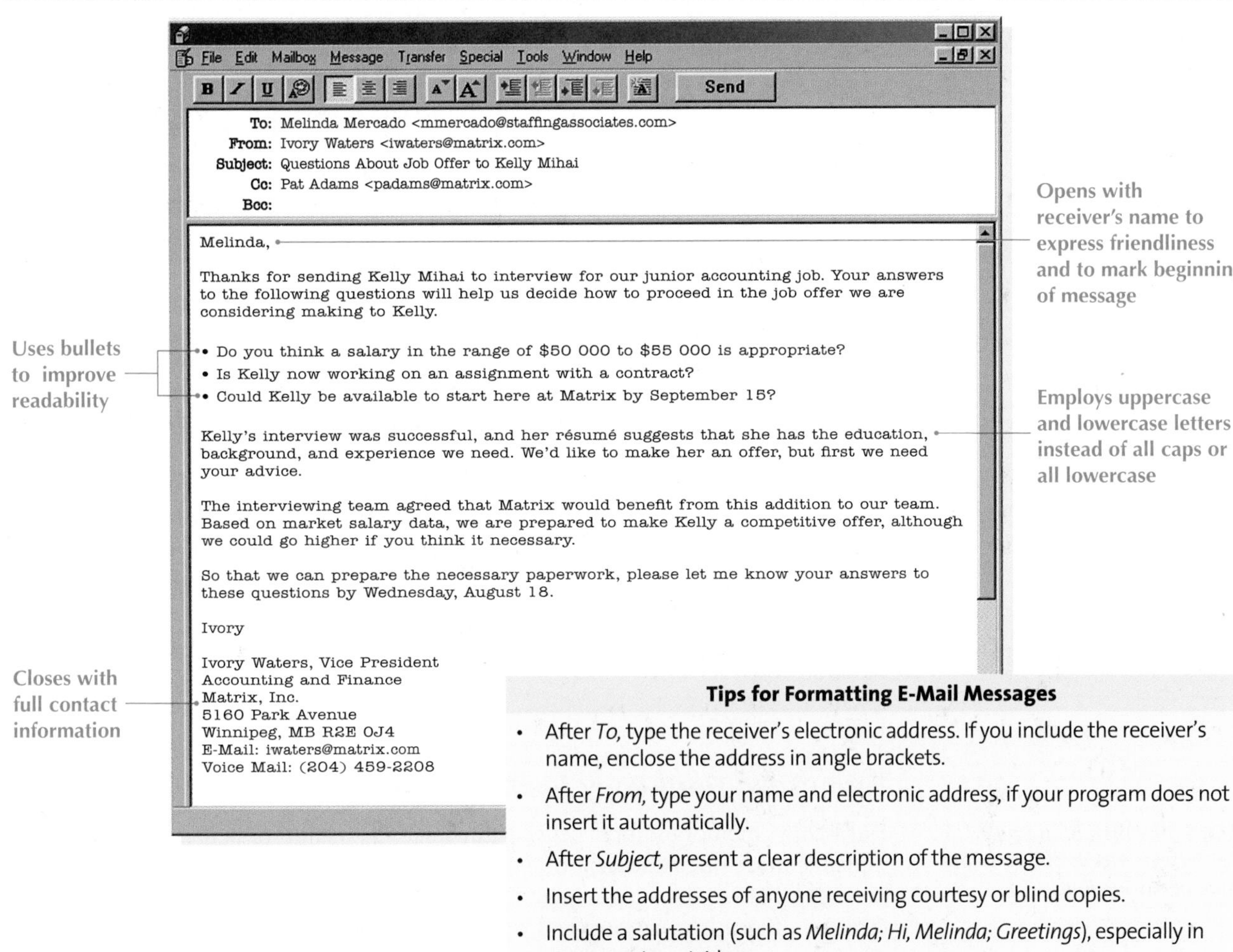

File Edit Mailbox Message Transfer Special Tools Window Help

Send

To: Melinda Mercado <mmercado@staffingassociates.com>
From: Ivory Waters <iwaters@matrix.com>
Subject: Questions About Job Offer to Kelly Mihai
Cc: Pat Adams <padams@matrix.com>
Bcc:

Melinda,

Thanks for sending Kelly Mihai to interview for our junior accounting job. Your answers to the following questions will help us decide how to proceed in the job offer we are considering making to Kelly.

- Do you think a salary in the range of $50 000 to $55 000 is appropriate?
- Is Kelly now working on an assignment with a contract?
- Could Kelly be available to start here at Matrix by September 15?

Kelly's interview was successful, and her résumé suggests that she has the education, background, and experience we need. We'd like to make her an offer, but first we need your advice.

The interviewing team agreed that Matrix would benefit from this addition to our team. Based on market salary data, we are prepared to make Kelly a competitive offer, although we could go higher if you think it necessary.

So that we can prepare the necessary paperwork, please let me know your answers to these questions by Wednesday, August 18.

Ivory

Ivory Waters, Vice President
Accounting and Finance
Matrix, Inc.
5160 Park Avenue
Winnipeg, MB R2E 0J4
E-Mail: iwaters@matrix.com
Voice Mail: (204) 459-2208

Tips for Formatting E-Mail Messages

- After *To,* type the receiver's electronic address. If you include the receiver's name, enclose the address in angle brackets.
- After *From,* type your name and electronic address, if your program does not insert it automatically.
- After *Subject,* present a clear description of the message.
- Insert the addresses of anyone receiving courtesy or blind copies.
- Include a salutation (such as *Melinda; Hi, Melinda; Greetings*), especially in messages to outsiders.
- Double-space (press *Enter*) between paragraphs.
- Do not type in all caps or in all lowercase letters.
- Include full contact information in the signature block.

who is to receive a copy of the message. Remember, though, to send copies only to those people directly involved with the message. Most e-mail programs also include a line for *BCC* (*blind carbon copy*). This sends a copy without the addressee's knowledge. Many wise writers today use *BCC* for the names and addresses of a list of receivers, a technique that avoids revealing the addresses to the entire group. On the subject line, identify the subject of the memo. Be sure to include enough information to be clear and compelling.

On messages to outsiders, salutations are important to show friendliness and to indicate the beginning of the message.

Greeting. Begin your message with a friendly greeting such as the following:

Hi Dave,	Thank you, Haley,
Greetings, Amy,	Dear Mr. Cotter, Dear Chris Cotter,
Leslie,	Dear Leslie,

In addition to being friendly, a greeting provides a visual cue marking the beginning of the message. Many messages are transmitted or forwarded with such long headers that finding the beginning of the message can be difficult. A greeting helps, as shown in Figure 8.2.

Body. When typing the body of an e-mail message, use standard caps and lowercase characters—never all uppercase or all lowercase characters. Cover just one topic, and try to keep the total message under three screens in length. To assist you, many e-mail programs have basic text-editing features, such as cut, copy, paste, and word-wrap.

E-mail messages to outsiders should include the writer's name and identification.

Complimentary Closing and Signature Block. In closing your message, you may elect to sign off with a complimentary closing such as *Cheers*, *All the best*, or *Many thanks*. Such a closing is optional. However, providing your name is mandatory. It is also smart to include full contact information as part of your signature block. Some writers prepare a number of "signatures" in their mail programs, depending on what information they want to reveal. They can choose a complete signature with all their contact information, or they can use a brief version. See Figure 8.2 for a complete signature.

Formatting Hard-Copy Memos

Hard-copy memos are typed with guide words but no salutation or closing lines.

Hard-copy memorandums deliver information within organizations. Although e-mail is more often used, hard-copy memos are still useful for important internal messages that require a permanent record or formality. For example, changes in procedures, official instructions, and organization reports are often prepared as hard-copy memos. Because e-mail is new and still evolving, we examined its formatting carefully in the previous paragraphs.

Hard-copy memos require less instruction because formatting is fairly standardized. Some offices use memo forms imprinted with the organization name and, optionally, the department or division name. Although the design and arrangement of memo forms vary, they usually include the basic elements of *Date*, *To*, *From*, and *Subject*. Large organizations may include other identifying headings, such as *File Number*, *Floor*, *Extension*, *Location*, and *Distribution*. Many business writers store memo formats in their computers and call them up when preparing memos. The guide words are then printed with the message, thus eliminating alignment problems.

If no printed or stored computer forms are available, memos may be typed on company letterhead, as shown in Figure 8.3, or typed on plain paper. On a full sheet of paper, start the guide words 5 centimetres from the top; on a half-sheet, start 2.5 centimetres from the top. Double-space and type in all caps the guide words. Align all the fill-in information 2 spaces after the longest guide word (usually *Subject:*). Leave two blank lines between the last line of the heading and the first line of the memo. Single-space within paragraphs and double-space between paragraphs. Memos are generally formatted with side margins of 2.5 to 3 centimetres, or they may conform to the printed memo form. Do not justify the right margins. Research has shown that "ragged right" margins in printed messages are easier to read. Memorandums do not end with complimentary closes or signatures. Instead, writers sign their initials after their names in the *From* line.

FIGURE 8.3 ***Hard-Copy Memo That Responds to Request***

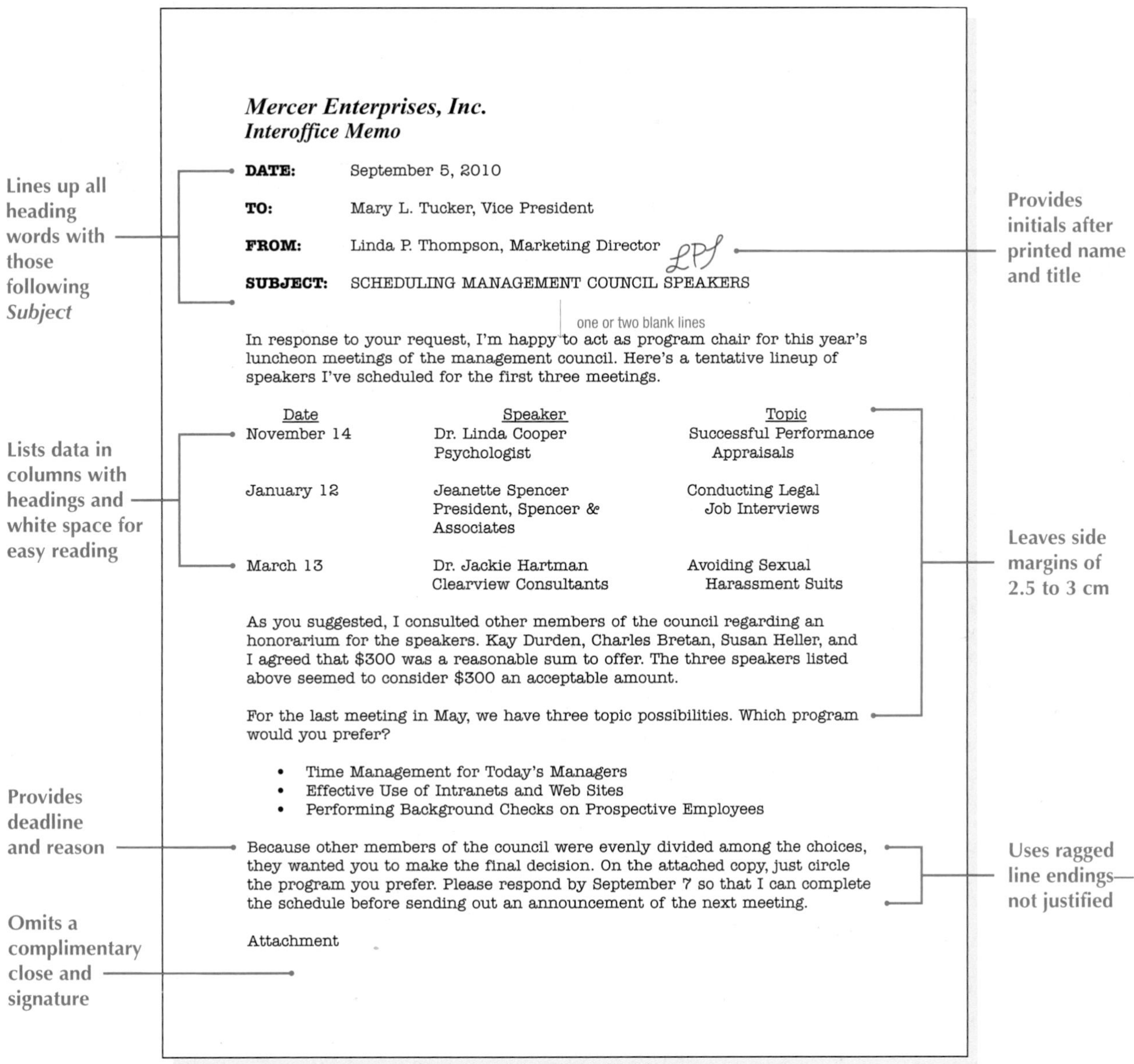

Mercer Enterprises, Inc.
Interoffice Memo

DATE: September 5, 2010

TO: Mary L. Tucker, Vice President

FROM: Linda P. Thompson, Marketing Director *LPT*

SUBJECT: SCHEDULING MANAGEMENT COUNCIL SPEAKERS

In response to your request, I'm happy to act as program chair for this year's luncheon meetings of the management council. Here's a tentative lineup of speakers I've scheduled for the first three meetings.

Date	Speaker	Topic
November 14	Dr. Linda Cooper Psychologist	Successful Performance Appraisals
January 12	Jeanette Spencer President, Spencer & Associates	Conducting Legal Job Interviews
March 13	Dr. Jackie Hartman Clearview Consultants	Avoiding Sexual Harassment Suits

As you suggested, I consulted other members of the council regarding an honorarium for the speakers. Kay Durden, Charles Bretan, Susan Heller, and I agreed that $300 was a reasonable sum to offer. The three speakers listed above seemed to consider $300 an acceptable amount.

For the last meeting in May, we have three topic possibilities. Which program would you prefer?

- Time Management for Today's Managers
- Effective Use of Intranets and Web Sites
- Performing Background Checks on Prospective Employees

Because other members of the council were evenly divided among the choices, they wanted you to make the final decision. On the attached copy, just circle the program you prefer. Please respond by September 7 so that I can complete the schedule before sending out an announcement of the next meeting.

Attachment

Tips for Formatting Hard-Copy Memos

- For full-page memos on plain paper, leave a 5-centimetre top margin.
- Set one tab to align entries evenly after ***Subject***.
- Leave one or two blank lines after the subject line.
- Single-space all but the shortest memos. Double-space between paragraphs.
- For half-page memos, leave a 2.5-centimetre top margin.
- Use 2.5- to 3-centimetre side margins.
- For a two-page memo, use a second-page heading with the addressee's name, the page number, and the date.
- Handwrite your initials after your typed name.
- Place bulleted or numbered lists flush left or indent them 1.25 centimetres.

learning objective

3

Using E-Mail Smartly and Safely

E-mail messages are becoming more proper and more professional.

Early e-mail users were encouraged to ignore stylistic and grammatical considerations. They thought that "words on the fly" required little editing or proofing. Correspondents used emoticons (such as sideways happy faces) to express their emotions. Some e-mail today is still quick and dirty. As this communication channel continues to mature, however, messages are becoming more proper and more professional. Today billions of e-mails are sent each day worldwide.

E-mail messages may be dangerous because they travel long distances and are difficult to erase.

Wise e-mail business communicators are aware of the importance as well as the dangers of e-mail as a communication channel. They know that thoughtless messages can cause irreparable harm. They also know that their messages can unintentionally reach the wrong audience. For instance, in 2007, the Ontario government had to react when a part-time employee hit the wrong button when sending an e-mail. Instead of sending it to a colleague as she intended, she sent it to a recent job applicant. The e-mail contained an inappropriate reference to the applicant's background. This accidental hitting of the Reply All button received international media attention and prompted an apology from Ontario's premier.[3]

Getting Started

Because e-mail is now a mainstream communication channel, messages should be well organized, carefully composed, and grammatically correct.

Despite its dangers and limitations, e-mail has definitely become a mainstream channel of communication. That's why it's important to take the time to organize your thoughts, compose carefully, and be concerned about correct grammar and punctuation. The following pointers will help you get off to a good start in using e-mail smartly and safely.

- **Consider composing offline.** Especially for important messages, think about using your word processing program to write offline. Then upload your message to the e-mail network. This avoids "self-destructing" (losing all your writing through some glitch or pressing the wrong key) when working online.
- **Get the address right.** E-mail addresses are sometimes complex, often illogical, and always unforgiving. Omit one character or misread the letter *l* for the number 1, and your message bounces. Solution: Use your electronic address book for people you write to frequently. And double-check every address that you key in manually. Also be sure that you don't reply to a group of receivers when you intend to answer only one.
- **Avoid misleading subject lines.** As discussed earlier, make sure your subject line is relevant and helpful. Generic tags such as *Hi!* and *Important!* may cause your message to be deleted before it is opened.
- **Apply the top-of-screen test.** When readers open your message and look at the first screen, will they see what is most significant? Your subject line and first paragraph should convey your purpose.

Content, Tone, and Correctness

Avoid sending sensitive, confidential, inflammatory, or potentially embarrassing messages, because e-mail is not private.

Although e-mail seems as casual as a telephone call, it's not. Because it produces a permanent record, think carefully about what you say and how you say it.

- **Be concise.** Don't burden readers with unnecessary information. Remember that monitors are small and typefaces are often difficult to read. Organize your ideas tightly.
- **Don't send anything you wouldn't want published.** Because e-mail seems like a telephone call or a person-to-person conversation, writers sometimes send sensi-

tive, confidential, inflammatory, or potentially embarrassing messages. Beware! E-mail creates a permanent record that does not go away even when deleted. And every message is a corporate communication that can be used against you or your employer. Don't write anything that you wouldn't want your boss, your family, or a judge to read.

- **Don't use e-mail to avoid contact.** E-mail is inappropriate for breaking bad news or for resolving arguments. For example, it's improper to fire a person by e-mail. It's also not a good channel for dealing with conflict with supervisors, subordinates, or others. If there's any possibility of hurt feelings, pick up the telephone or pay the person a visit.
- **Care about correctness.** People are still judged by their writing, whether electronic or paper-based. Sloppy e-mail messages (with missing apostrophes, haphazard spelling, and stream-of-consciousness writing) make readers work too hard. They resent not only the information but also the writer.
- **Care about tone.** Your words and writing style affect the reader. Avoid sounding curt, negative, or domineering.
- **Resist humour and tongue-in-cheek comments.** Without the nonverbal cues conveyed by your face and your voice, humour can easily be misunderstood.

Netiquette

Although e-mail is a new communication channel, a number of rules of polite online interaction are emerging.

- **Limit any tendency to send blanket copies.** Send copies only to people who really need to see a message. It is unnecessary to document every business decision and action with an electronic paper trail.
- **Never send "spam."** Sending unsolicited advertisements ("spam") either by fax or e-mail wastes valuable time and electronic resources.
- **Consider using identifying labels.** When appropriate, add one of the following labels to the subject line: *Action* (action required, please respond); *FYI* (for your information, no response needed); *Re* (this is a reply to another message); *Urgent* (please respond immediately); *REQ* (required).
- **Use capital letters only for emphasis or for titles.** Avoid writing entire messages in all caps, which is like SHOUTING.
- **Don't forward without permission.** Obtain approval before forwarding a message.
- **Reduce attachments.** Because attachments may carry viruses, some receivers won't open them. Consider including short attachments within an e-mail message. If you must send a longer attachment, explain it.

Reading and Replying to E-Mail

The following tips can save you time and frustration when reading and answering messages:

Skim all messages before responding, paste in relevant sections, revise the subject if the topic changes, provide a clear first sentence, and never respond when angry.

- **Scan all messages in your inbox before replying to each individually.** Because subsequent messages often affect the way you respond, skim all messages first (especially all those from the same individual).
- **Print only when necessary.** Generally, read and answer most messages online without saving or printing. Use folders to archive messages on special topics.

Print only those messages that are complex or controversial or involve significant decisions and follow-up.

- **Acknowledge receipt.** If you can't reply immediately, tell when you can (*Will respond Friday*).
- **Don't automatically return the sender's message.** When replying, cut and paste the relevant parts. Avoid irritating your recipients by returning the entire "thread" (sequence of messages) on a topic.
- **Revise the subject line if the topic changes.** When replying or continuing an e-mail exchange, revise the subject line as the topic changes.
- **Provide a clear, complete first sentence.** Avoid fragments such as *Fine with me* or *Sounds good!* Busy respondents forget what was said in earlier messages, so be sure to fill in the context and your perspective when responding.
- **Never respond when you're angry.** Always allow some time to cool off before shooting back a response to an upsetting message. You often come up with different and better alternatives after thinking about what was said. If possible, iron out differences in person.

Personal Use

Remember that office computers are meant for work-related communication.

- **Don't use company computers for personal matters.** Unless your company specifically allows it, never use your employer's computers for personal messages, personal shopping, or entertainment.
- **Assume that all e-mail is monitored.** Employers legally have the right to monitor e-mail, and many do.

Other Smart E-Mail Practices

Design your messages to enhance readability, and double-check before sending.

Depending on your messages and audience, the following tips promote effective electronic communication.

- **Improve the readability of longer messages with graphic highlighting.** When a message requires several screens, help the reader with headings, bulleted listings, side headings, and perhaps an introductory summary that describes what will follow. Although these techniques lengthen a message, they shorten reading time.
- **Consider cultural differences.** When using this borderless tool, be especially clear and precise in your language. Remember that figurative clichés (*pull up stakes, playing second fiddle*), sports references (*hit a home run, play by the rules*), and slang (*cool, stoked*) cause confusion abroad.
- **Double-check before hitting the Send button.** Have you included everything? Avoid the necessity of sending a second message, which makes you look careless. Use spell-check and reread for fluency before sending. It's also a good idea to check your incoming messages before sending, especially if several people are involved in a rapid-fire exchange. This helps avoid "passing"—sending out a message that might be altered depending on an incoming note.
- **Use instant messaging professionally to expand your communication channel choices.** As more knowledge workers turn to instant messaging on the job, be sure you are using it effectively as a business tool.

Writers of e-mail are sometimes tempted to take shortcuts. Figure 8.4 illustrates bad and good e-mail messages so that you can avoid the confusing shortcuts.

FIGURE 8.4 ***Bad and Good E-Mail Messages***

Bad E-Mail Subject	Good E-Mail Subject	Tips
To: Peyton Moss **From:** Gina Jones **Subject:** Need Help!	**To:** Peyton Moss **From:** Gina Jones **Subject:** Need Help in Writing Job Placement Ad	Expand subject with more information.
Bad E-Mail Response	**Good E-Mail Response**	**Tips**
To: Peyton Moss **From:** Gina Jones **Subject:** Re: Re: Re: Advertising Our Job Opening Yes, I agree totally!	**To:** Peyton Moss **From:** Gina Jones **Subject:** Re: Re: Re: Advertising Our Job Opening Yes, I agree that our first choice should be an online listing at Monster.ca.	Provide context to orient reader, which is especially helpful in messages with many replies and multiperson conversations.
Bad E-Mail Instructions	**Good E-Mail Instructions**	**Tips**
To: Haley Krebs, Brandon Kim, Nicole Sanchez **From:** Gina Jones **Subject:** Relocation Options Ready for Your Analysis Please analyze the four possible relocation sites recommended by our consultants in the attached file. Your written reactions by May 1 will enable us to make a presentation to management by the middle of the month.	**To:** Haley Krebs, Brandon Kim, Nicole Sanchez **From:** Gina Jones **Subject:** Relocation Options Ready for Your Analysis Please analyze the four possible relocation sites recommended by our consultants in the attached file. Your written reactions by May 1 will enable us to make a presentation to management by the middle of the month. HALEY: DECISION NEEDED. Check the footage available for office space in each option. BRANDON: FYI, if we move forward, your project will be delayed. NICOLE: PLEASE CONFIRM. Do these four locations meet all the specifications you submitted?	Send general message to coworkers but include individual action requests to be sure everyone understands specific assignment or ramifications of message.

(continued)

FIGURE 8.4 ***Bad and Good E-Mail Messages (Continued)***

Bad Use of BCC	Good E-Mails	Tips
To: Peyton Moss **From:** Gina Jones **Subject:** Conference Thursday at 2 p.m. **Bcc:** Sabrina Please attend the conference tomorrow	**To:** Peyton Moss **From:** Gina Jones **Subject:** Conference Thursday at 2 p.m. Peyton, please attend the conference tomorrow (Thursday) at 2 p.m. **To:** Sabrina **From:** Gina **Subject:** Reserve Conference Room Thursday at 2 p.m. Please reserve the conference room for Peyton and me tomorrow (Thursday) at 2 p.m.	Send two messages because naming someone in a "bcc" may not sufficiently explain why that person is being copied.

Writing Information and Procedure E-Mail Messages and Memos

learning objective 4

Thus far in this chapter we've reviewed the writing process, analyzed the structure and format of e-mail messages and memos, and presented a number of techniques for using e-mail smartly and safely. Now we're going to apply those techniques to three categories of messages that you can expect to be writing as a business communicator: (1) information and procedure messages, (2) request and reply messages, and (3) confirmation messages.

Information and procedure messages generally flow downward from management to employees.

Let's focus first on techniques that will help you write information and procedure messages quickly and efficiently. These messages distribute standard information, describe procedures, and deliver instructions. They typically flow downward from management to employees and relate to the daily operation of an organization. In writing these messages, you have one primary function: conveying your idea so clearly that no further explanation (return message, telephone call, or personal visit) is necessary.

As you compose information and procedure messages, follow the writing process and organization plan outlined earlier. That includes an informative subject line, a direct opening, a body that explains, and an appropriate closing.

When writing messages that describe procedures, be particularly careful about clarity and readability. Figure 8.5 shows the first draft of a hard-copy memo written by Troy Bell. His memo was meant to announce a new procedure for employees to follow in advertising open positions. However, the tone was negative, the explanation of the problem rambled, and the new procedure was unclear. Notice, too, that Troy's first draft told readers what they *shouldn't* do *(Do not submit advertisements for new employees directly to an Internet job bank or a newspaper).* It's more helpful to tell readers what they *should* do. Finally, Troy's memo closed with a threat instead of showing readers how this new procedure will help them.

In the revision Troy improved the tone considerably. The subject line contains a *please*, which is always pleasant to see even if one is giving an order. The subject line

FIGURE 8.5 ***Memo That Describes a New Procedure***

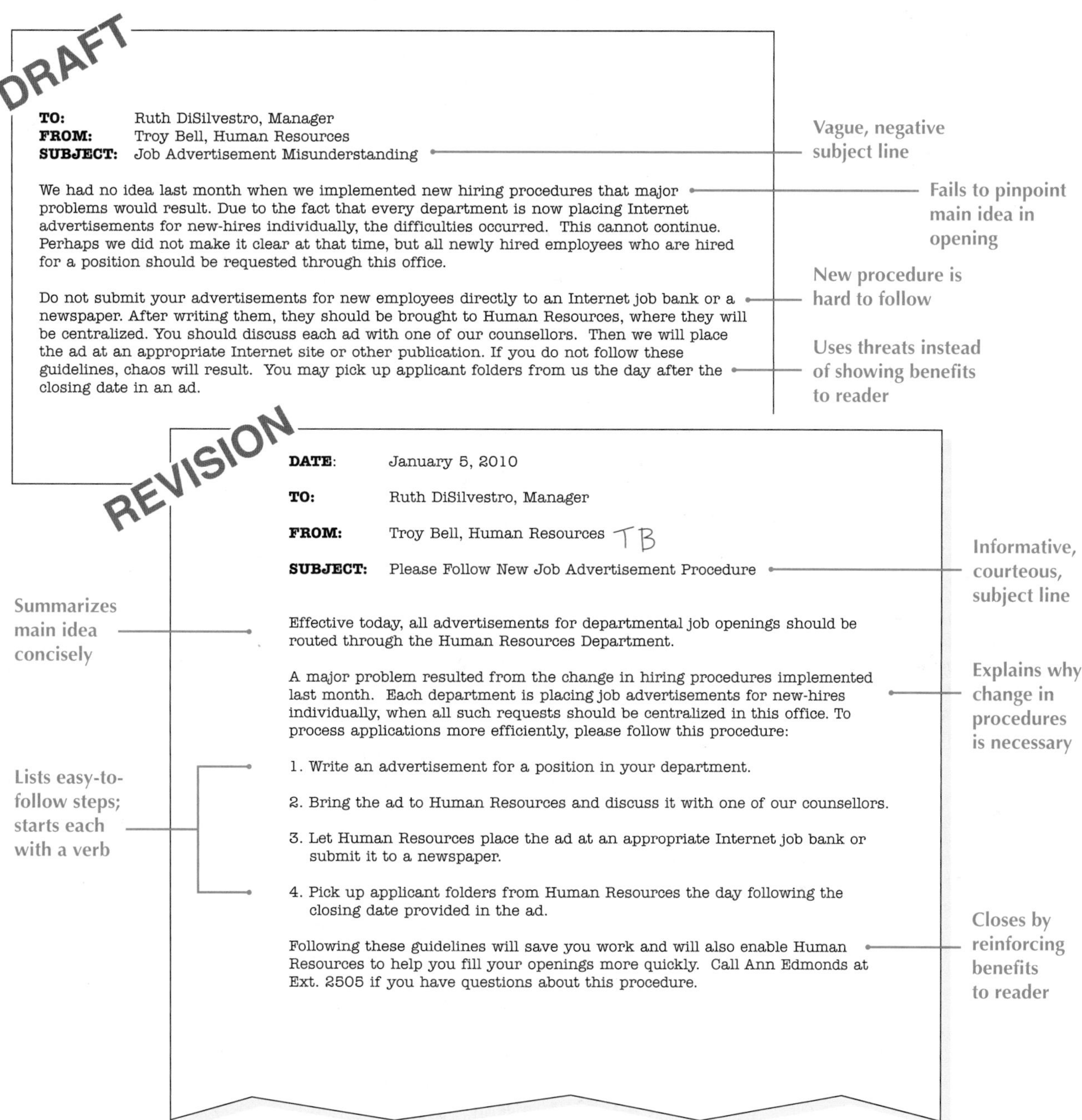
DRAFT

TO: Ruth DiSilvestro, Manager
FROM: Troy Bell, Human Resources
SUBJECT: Job Advertisement Misunderstanding

We had no idea last month when we implemented new hiring procedures that major problems would result. Due to the fact that every department is now placing Internet advertisements for new-hires individually, the difficulties occurred. This cannot continue. Perhaps we did not make it clear at that time, but all newly hired employees who are hired for a position should be requested through this office.

Do not submit your advertisements for new employees directly to an Internet job bank or a newspaper. After writing them, they should be brought to Human Resources, where they will be centralized. You should discuss each ad with one of our counsellors. Then we will place the ad at an appropriate Internet site or other publication. If you do not follow these guidelines, chaos will result. You may pick up applicant folders from us the day after the closing date in an ad.

REVISION

DATE: January 5, 2010
TO: Ruth DiSilvestro, Manager
FROM: Troy Bell, Human Resources TB
SUBJECT: Please Follow New Job Advertisement Procedure

Effective today, all advertisements for departmental job openings should be routed through the Human Resources Department.

A major problem resulted from the change in hiring procedures implemented last month. Each department is placing job advertisements for new-hires individually, when all such requests should be centralized in this office. To process applications more efficiently, please follow this procedure:

1. Write an advertisement for a position in your department.
2. Bring the ad to Human Resources and discuss it with one of our counsellors.
3. Let Human Resources place the ad at an appropriate Internet job bank or submit it to a newspaper.
4. Pick up applicant folders from Human Resources the day following the closing date provided in the ad.

Following these guidelines will save you work and will also enable Human Resources to help you fill your openings more quickly. Call Ann Edmonds at Ext. 2505 if you have questions about this procedure.

also includes a verb and specifies the purpose of the memo. Instead of expressing his ideas with negative words and threats, Troy revised his message to explain objectively and concisely what went wrong.

Troy realized that his original explanation of the new procedure was vague. Messages explaining procedures are most readable when the instructions are broken down into numbered steps listed chronologically. Each step should begin with an action verb in the command mode. Notice in Troy's revision in Figure 8.5 that num-

***Procedures and instructions are often written in numbered steps using command language* (Do this, don't do that).**

bered items begin with *Write*, *Bring*, *Let*, and *Pick up*. It's sometimes difficult to force all the steps in a procedure into this kind of command language.

Why should you go to so much trouble to make lists and achieve parallelism? Because readers can comprehend what you have said much more quickly. Parallel language also makes you look professional and efficient.

In writing information and procedure messages, be careful of tone. Today's managers and team leaders seek employee participation and cooperation. These goals can't be achieved, though, if the writer sounds like a dictator or an autocrat. Avoid making accusations and fixing blame. Rather, explain changes, give reasons, and suggest benefits to the reader. Assume that employees want to contribute to the success of the organization and to their own achievement.

learning objective

5

Writing Request and Reply E-Mail Messages and Memos

Business organizations require information as their fuel. To make operations run smoothly, managers and employees request information from each other and then respond to those requests. Knowing how to write those requests and responses efficiently and effectively can save you time and make you look good.

Making Requests

Use the direct approach in routine requests for information or action, opening with the most important question, a polite command, or a brief introductory statement.

When requesting routine information or action within an organization, the direct approach works best. Generally this means asking for information or making the request without first providing elaborate explanations and justifications. Remember that readers are usually thinking, "Why me? Why am I receiving this?" Readers can understand the explanation better once they know what you are requesting.

If you are seeking answers to questions, you have three options for opening the message: (1) ask the most important question first, followed by an explanation and then the other questions, (2) use a polite command (*Please answer the following questions regarding*), or (3) introduce the questions with a brief statement (*Your answers to the following questions will help us . . .*).

In the body of the memo, explain and justify your request or reply. When you must ask many questions, list them, being careful to phrase them similarly. Be courteous and friendly. In the closing include an end date (with a reason, if possible) to promote a quick response.

The e-mail message shown in Figure 8.6 requests information. It opens with a polite command followed by a brief explanation. Notice that the questions are highlighted with asterisks to provide the high "skim value" that is important in business messages. The reader can quickly see what is being asked. The message concludes with an end date and a reason. Providing an end date helps the reader know how to plan a response so that action is completed by the date given. Expressions such as *do it whenever you can* or *complete it as soon as possible* make little impression on procrastinators or very busy people. It's always wise to provide a specific date for completion. Dates can be entered on calendars to serve as reminders.

Replying to Requests

Much business correspondence reacts or responds to previous messages. When responding to an e-mail, memo, or other document, be sure to follow the 3-x-3 writing process. Analyze your purpose and audience, collect whatever information is necessary, and organize your thoughts. Make a brief outline of the points you plan to cover.

FIGURE 8.6 ***E-Mail Message That Makes a Request***

1 Prewriting

ANALYZE: The purpose of this e-mail is to solicit feedback regarding a casual-dress policy.

ANTICIPATE: The message is going to a subordinate who is busy but probably eager to be consulted in this policy matter.

ADAPT: Use a direct approach beginning with the most important question. Strive for a positive, professional tone rather than an autocratic, authoritative tone.

2 Writing

RESEARCH: Collect secondary information about dress-down days in other organizations. Collect primary information by talking with company managers.

ORGANIZE: Begin with the main idea followed by a brief explanation and questions. Conclude with an end date and a reason.

COMPOSE: Prepare the first draft, remembering that the receiver is busy and appreciates brevity.

3 Revising

REVISE: Rewrite questions to ensure that they are parallel and readable.

PROOFREAD: Decide whether to hyphenate *casual-dress policy* and *dress-down days*. Be sure commas follow introductory clauses. Check question marks.

EVALUATE: Does this memo encourage participatory management? Will the receiver be able to answer the questions and respond easily?

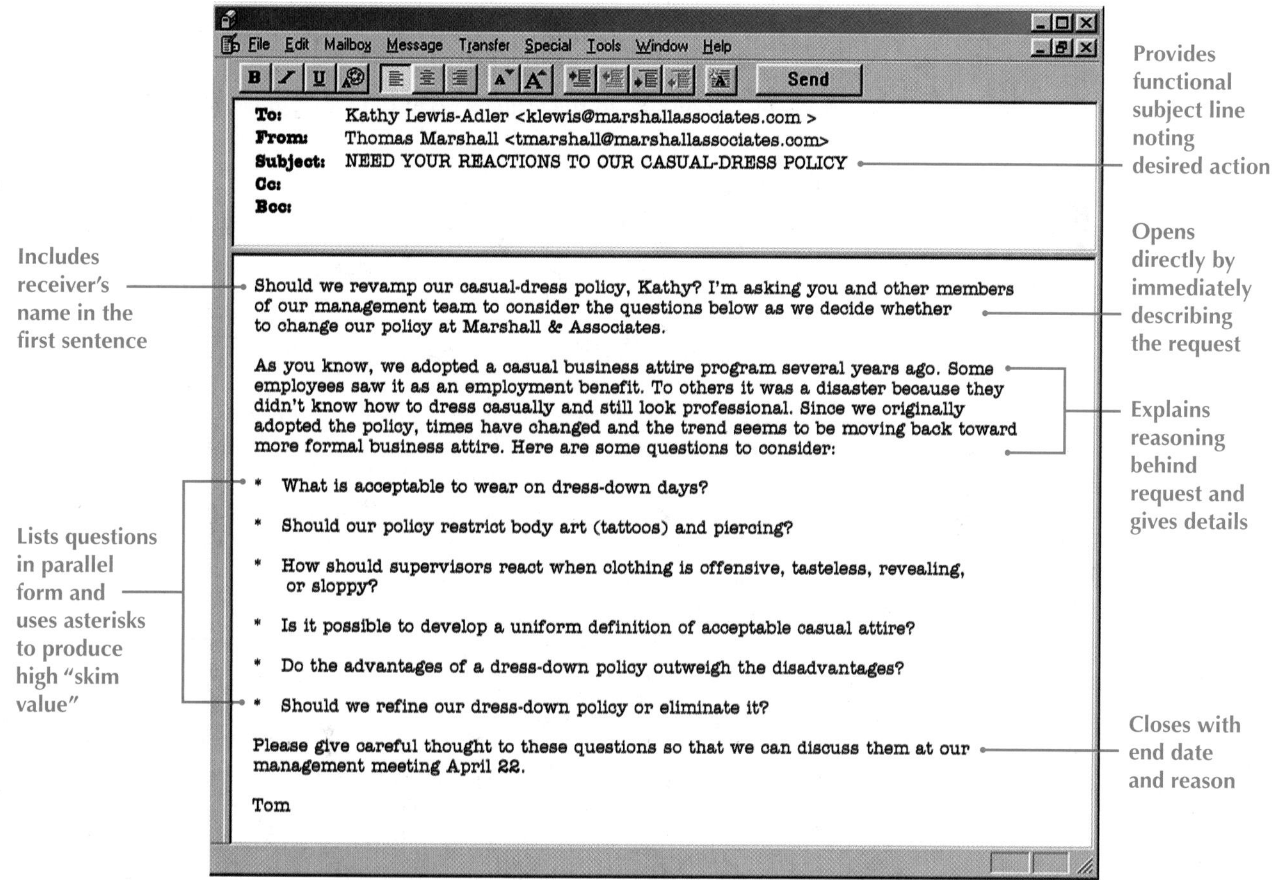

File Edit Mailbox Message Transfer Special Tools Window Help

Send

To: Kathy Lewis-Adler <klewis@marshallassociates.com >
From: Thomas Marshall <tmarshall@marshallassociates.com>
Subject: NEED YOUR REACTIONS TO OUR CASUAL-DRESS POLICY
Cc:
Bcc:

Should we revamp our casual-dress policy, Kathy? I'm asking you and other members of our management team to consider the questions below as we decide whether to change our policy at Marshall & Associates.

As you know, we adopted a casual business attire program several years ago. Some employees saw it as an employment benefit. To others it was a disaster because they didn't know how to dress casually and still look professional. Since we originally adopted the policy, times have changed and the trend seems to be moving back toward more formal business attire. Here are some questions to consider:

* What is acceptable to wear on dress-down days?
* Should our policy restrict body art (tattoos) and piercing?
* How should supervisors react when clothing is offensive, tasteless, revealing, or sloppy?
* Is it possible to develop a uniform definition of acceptable casual attire?
* Do the advantages of a dress-down policy outweigh the disadvantages?
* Should we refine our dress-down policy or eliminate it?

Please give careful thought to these questions so that we can discuss them at our management meeting April 22.

Tom

Writers sometimes fall into bad habits in replying to messages. Here are some trite and long-winded openers that are best avoided:

Overused and long-winded openers bore readers and waste their time.

In response to your message of the 15th … (States the obvious.)
Thank you for your memo of the 15th in which you … (Suggests the writer can think of nothing more original.)
Pursuant to your request of the 15th … (Sounds old-fashioned.)
This is to inform you that … (Delays getting to the point.)

Business discussions may take place casually in hotel lobbies, in office hallways, or over coffee in the lunchroom. When significant oral decisions and commitments are made, it's always a good idea to write a confirmation memo that creates a permanent record of the facts.

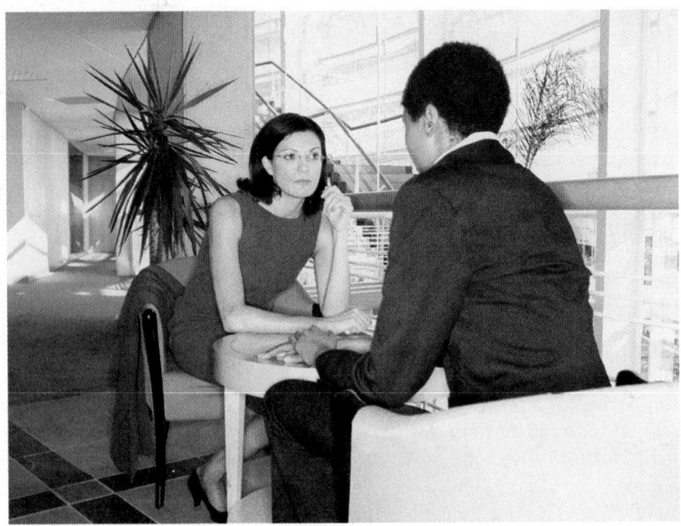

Source: Image Source/Corbis

Direct opening statements can also be cheerful and empathic.

Instead of falling into the trap of using one of the preceding shopworn openings, start directly by responding to the writer's request. If you agree to the request, show your cheerful compliance immediately. Consider these good-news openers:

Here are answers to the questions you asked about . . . (Sounds straightforward, businesslike, and professional.)
We are happy to assist you in . . . (Shows writer's helpful nature and goodwill.)
As you requested, I am submitting . . . (Gets right to the point.)

After a direct and empathic opener, provide the information requested in a logical and coherent order. If you are answering a number of questions, arrange your answers in the order of the questions. In providing additional data, use familiar words, short sentences, short paragraphs, and active-voice verbs. When alternatives exist, make them clear.

If further action is required, be specific in spelling it out. What may be clear to you (because you have been thinking about the problem) is not always immediately apparent to a reader with limited time and interest.

learning objective 6

Writing Confirmation E-Mail Messages and Memos

Confirmation messages provide a permanent record of oral discussions, decisions, and directives.

Confirmation messages—also called *to-file reports* or *incident reports*—record oral decisions, directives, and discussions. They create a concise, permanent record that could be important in the future. Because individuals may forget, alter, or retract oral commitments, it's wise to establish a written record of significant happenings. Such records are unnecessary, of course, for minor events. The confirmation e-mail message shown in Figure 8.7 reviews the significant points of a sales agreement discussed in a telephone conversation. When you write to confirm an oral agreement, remember these tips:

- Include the names and titles of involved individuals.
- Itemize major issues or points concisely.
- Request feedback regarding unclear or inaccurate points.

FIGURE 8.7 ***Confirmation E-Mail***

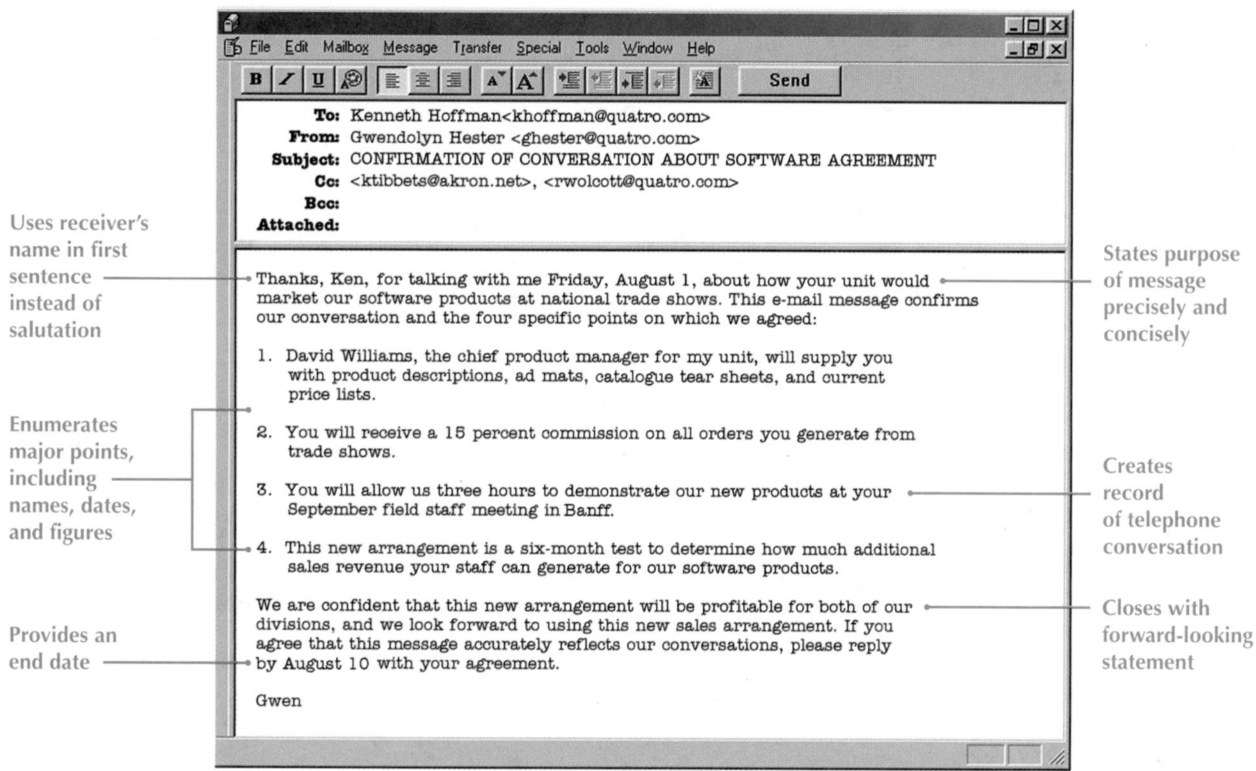

To: Kenneth Hoffman<khoffman@quatro.com>
From: Gwendolyn Hester <ghester@quatro.com>
Subject: CONFIRMATION OF CONVERSATION ABOUT SOFTWARE AGREEMENT
Cc: <ktibbets@akron.net>, <rwolcott@quatro.com>
Bcc:
Attached:

Thanks, Ken, for talking with me Friday, August 1, about how your unit would market our software products at national trade shows. This e-mail message confirms our conversation and the four specific points on which we agreed:

1. David Williams, the chief product manager for my unit, will supply you with product descriptions, ad mats, catalogue tear sheets, and current price lists.

2. You will receive a 15 percent commission on all orders you generate from trade shows.

3. You will allow us three hours to demonstrate our new products at your September field staff meeting in Banff.

4. This new arrangement is a six-month test to determine how much additional sales revenue your staff can generate for our software products.

We are confident that this new arrangement will be profitable for both of our divisions, and we look forward to using this new sales arrangement. If you agree that this message accurately reflects our conversations, please reply by August 10 with your agreement.

Gwen

Another type of confirmation message simply verifies the receipt of materials or a change of schedule. It is brief and often kept on file to explain your role in a project. Be sure to print a copy if you are using e-mail.

Some critics complain that too many "cover-your-tail" messages are written, thus creating excessive and unnecessary paperwork.[4] However, legitimate messages that confirm and clarify events have saved many thoughtful workers from being misunderstood or blamed unfairly.

Confirmation messages can save employees from being misunderstood or blamed unfairly.

Sometimes taken lightly, e-mail messages and office memos, like other business documents, should be written carefully. Once they leave the author's hands, they are essentially published. They can't be retrieved, corrected, or revised. Review the following checklist for tips in writing memos that accomplish what you intend.

Checklist for Writing Routine E-Mail Messages and Memos

Subject Line

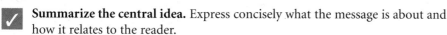

Summarize the central idea. Express concisely what the message is about and how it relates to the reader.

Make the subject line "talk." Particularly if action is involved, include a verb.

Avoid empty or dangerous words. Don't write one-word subject lines such as *Help*, *Problem*, or *Free*.

Opening

- ✓ **State the purpose for writing.** Include the same information that's in the subject line, but expand it.

- ✓ **Highlight questions.** If you are requesting information, begin with the most important question, use a polite command (*Please answer the following questions about . . .*), or introduce your request courteously.

- ✓ **Supply information directly.** If responding to a request, give the reader the requested information immediately in the opening. Explain later.

Body

- ✓ **Explain details.** Arrange information logically. For complex topics use separate paragraphs developed coherently.

- ✓ **Enhance readability.** Use short sentences, short paragraphs, and parallel construction for similar ideas.

- ✓ **Supply graphic highlighting.** Provide bulleted and/or numbered lists, tables, or other graphic devices to improve readability and comprehension.

- ✓ **Be cautious.** Remember that memos and e-mail messages often travel far beyond their intended audiences.

Closing

- ✓ **Request action.** If appropriate, state specifically what you want the reader to do. Include a deadline, with reasons, if possible.

- ✓ **Summarize the memo or provide a closing thought.** For long memos provide a summary of the important points. If neither an action request nor a summary is necessary, end with a closing thought.

- ✓ **Avoid cliché endings.** Use fresh remarks rather than overused expressions such as *If you have additional questions, please do not hesitate to call* or *Thank you for your cooperation.*

Summary of Learning Objectives

1 **Discuss how the 3-x-3 writing process helps you produce effective e-mail messages and memos.** The 3-x-3 writing process helps you analyze your purpose and audience before writing. E-mail and memos are appropriate for routine business messages, but they shouldn't be used if you need to convey enthusiasm, warmth, or some other emotion; if you need to supply a context; or if you need to smooth over a disagreement. The 3-x-3 process helps you decide how the reader will react and makes you consider how you can save the reader's time. Before writing routine e-mails and memos, collect information and organize your thoughts into a brief outline. After composing the first draft, revise for clarity, proofread for correctness, and plan for feedback.

2 **Analyze the structure and formatting of e-mail messages and memos.** Routine e-mails and memos begin with a subject line that summarizes the central idea. The opening repeats that idea and amplifies it. The body explains and provides more information. The closing includes (1) action information, dates, and deadlines; (2) a summary of the memo; and/or (3) a closing thought. E-mail messages should be formatted with a meaningful subject line, an optional salutation, a single-spaced body that is typed with a combination of upper- and lowercase letters, and optional closing lines. Hard-copy memos are formatted similarly but without a salutation or closing. Writers place their initials next to their names on the *From* line.

3 **Describe smart e-mail practices, including getting started; content, tone, and correctness; netiquette; reading and replying to e-mail; personal use; and other practices.** Careful e-mail users compose offline, get the address right, avoid misleading subject lines, and apply the top-of-the-screen test. They write concisely and don't send anything they wouldn't want published. They don't use e-mail to avoid contact. They care about correctness, resist humour, never send spam, use identifying labels when appropriate, and use attachments sparingly. In reading and responding, they employ a number of efficient practices such as scanning all incoming messages, limiting printing, and revising the subject line as the message thread changes. They don't use company computers for personal use unless specifically allowed to do so, and they realize that e-mail may be monitored. They strive to improve readability through design, they consider cultural differences, and they double-check before hitting the Send button.

4 **Write information and procedure e-mail messages and memos.** Messages delivering information or outlining procedures follow the direct plan, with the main idea stated immediately. Ideas must be explained so clearly that no further explanation is necessary. The tone of the memo or e-mail message should be positive and encourage cooperation. Procedures should enumerate steps in command language (*Do this, don't do that*) and should be written in parallel form.

5 **Write request and reply e-mail messages and memos.** Messages requesting action or information open with a specific request, followed by details. Messages that reply to requests open with information the reader most wants to learn. The body contains details, and the closing may summarize the important points or look forward to a subsequent event or action.

6 **Write confirmation e-mail messages and memos.** Sometimes called *to-file reports* or *incident reports*, confirmation messages create a permanent record of oral decisions, directives, and discussions. They should include the names and titles of involved individuals, the major issues discussed, and a request for approval by the receiver.

chapter review

1. List five questions you should ask yourself before writing an e-mail or memo. (Obj. 1)
2. Briefly describe the standard structure of e-mail messages and memos. (Obj. 2)
3. What can writers do to improve the readability and comprehension of e-mails and memos? (Obj. 2)
4. What are three ways in which a routine e-mail or memo may be closed? (Obj. 2)
5. How are the structure and formatting of e-mail messages and memos similar and different? (Obj. 2)
6. What are some of the dangers of e-mail in the workplace? (Obj. 3)
7. Suggest at least ten pointers that you could give to a first-time e-mail user. (Obj. 3)
8. Name at least five rules of e-mail etiquette that show respect for others. (Obj. 3)
9. What are three possibilities in handling the salutation for an e-mail message? (Obj. 3)
10. What tone should managers avoid in writing procedure or information e-mail messages and memos? (Obj. 4)
11. Why should writers of information e-mail messages and memos strive to express ideas positively instead of negatively? (Obj. 4)
12. Should a request e-mail message or memo open immediately with the request or with an explanation? Why? (Obj. 5)
13. What's wrong with a message opener such as *This is to inform you that…*? (Obj. 5)
14. What is a confirmation e-mail message or memo? What other names could it be given? (Obj. 6)
15. What three elements should most confirmation e-mail messages and memos include? (Obj. 6)

critical thinking

1. How can the writer of a business e-mail message or memo develop a conversational tone and still be professional? Why do e-mail writers sometimes forget to be professional? (Objs. 1–3)
2. What factors would help you decide whether to write a memo, send an e-mail, make a telephone call, leave a voice mail message, or deliver a message in person? (Objs. 1 and 2)
3. Why are lawyers and technology experts warning companies to store, organize, and manage computer data, including e-mail, with sharper diligence? (Obj. 3)
4. Discuss the ramifications of the following statement: Once a memo or any other document leaves your hands, you have essentially published it. (Objs. 2–6)

activities

8.1 Document for Analysis: Information E-Mail (Objs. 1–4)

Your Task. Analyze the following e-mail message. It suffers from many writing faults. List its specific weaknesses. If your instructor directs, revise it.

To:	Ceresa Rothery <crothery@rancho.com>
From:	Paul Rouse <prouse@rancho.com>
Subject:	REPORT
Cc:	

Ceresa:

I went to the Workplace Issues conference on November 3, as you suggested. The topic was how to prevent workplace violence, and I found it very fascinating. Although we have been fortunate to avoid serious incidents at our company, it's better to be safe than sorry. Since I was the representative from our company and you asked for a report, here it is. Susan Sloan was the presenter, and she made suggestions in three categories, which I will summarize here.

Ms. Sloan cautioned organizations to prescreen job applicants. As a matter of fact, wise companies do not offer employment until after a candidate's background has been checked. Just the mention of a background check is enough to make some candidates withdraw. These candidates, of course, are the ones with something to hide.

A second suggestion was that companies should prepare a good employee handbook that outlines what employees should do when they suspect potential workplace violence. This handbook should include a way for informers to be anonymous.

A third recommendation had to do with recognizing red-flag behaviour. This involves having companies train managers to recognize signs of potential workplace violence. What are some of the red flags? One sign is an increasing number of arguments (most of them petty) with coworkers. Another sign is extreme changes in behaviour or statements indicating depression over family or financial problems. Another sign is bullying or harassing behaviour. Bringing a firearm to work or displaying an extreme fascination with firearms is another sign.

By the way, the next Workplace Issues conference is in January, and the topic is employee e-mail monitoring.

I think that the best recommendation is prescreening job candidates. This is because it is most feasible. If you want me to do more research on prescreening techniques, do not hesitate to let me know. Let me know by November 18 if you want me to make a report at our management meeting, which is scheduled for December 3.

Paul

8.2 Document for Analysis: Request Memo (Objs. 1–5)

Your Task. Analyze the following memo. List its weaknesses. If your instructor directs, revise it.

DATE: Current
TO: All Employees
FROM: Kim Albano, Human Resources
SUBJECT: NEW PLAN

In the past we've offered all employees 11 holidays (starting with New Year's Day in January and proceeding through Christmas Day the following December). Other companies offer similar holiday schedules.

In addition, we've given all employees one floating holiday. As you know, we've determined that day by a companywide vote. As a result, all employees had the same day off. Now, however, management is considering a new plan that we feel would be better. This new plan involves a floating holiday that each individual employee may decide for herself or himself. We've given it considerable thought and decided that such a plan could definitely work. We would allow each employee to choose a day that he or she wants. Of course, we would have to issue certain restrictions. Selections would have to be subject to our staffing needs within individual departments. For example, if everyone wanted the same day, we could not allow everyone to take it. In that case, we would allow the employee with the most seniority to have the day off.

Before we institute the new plan, though, we wanted to see what employees thought about this. Is it better to continue our current companywide uniform floating holiday? Or should we try an individual floating holiday? Please let us know what you think as soon as possible.

8.3 Document for Analysis: Confirmation E-Mail (Objs. 1–6)

Your Task. Analyze the following e-mail message. List its weaknesses. If your instructor directs, revise it.

To: David Ricci <dricci@commercial.com>
From: Jillian Ann Brody <JillianAnnBrody@aol.com>
Subject: OUR RECENT TALK
Cc:

Dear Mr. Ricci:

It was good to talk to you on the telephone yesterday (December 2) after exchanging letters with you and after reading so much about Bermuda. I was very interested in learning about the commercials you want me to write. As I understand it, Mr. Ricci, you want a total of 240 one-minute radio commercials. These commercials are intended to rejuvenate the slumping tourist industry in Bermuda. You said that these commercials would be broadcast from March 30 through June 30. You said these commercials would be played on three radio stations. These stations are in five major cities on the East Coast. The commercials would be aimed at morning and evening drive time, for drivers who are listening to their radios, and the campaign would be called "Radio Bermuda."

I am sure I can do as you suggested in reminding listeners that Bermuda is less than three hours away. You expect me to bring to these commercials the colour and character of the island. You want me to highlight the attractions and the civility of Bermuda, at least as much as can be done in one-minute radio commercials. In my notes I wrote that you also mentioned that I should include references to tree frogs and royal palm trees. Another item you suggested that I include in some of the commercials was special Bermuda food, such as delicacies like shark on toast, conch fritters, and mussel stew.

I wanted to be sure to write these points down so that we both agreed on what we said in our telephone conversation. I am eager to begin working on these commercials immediately, but I would feel better if you looked over these points to see if I have it right. I look forward to working with you.

Jillian Ann Brody

8.4 Openers for E-Mail Messages and Memos (Objs. 1–3)

Your Task. Revise the following e-mail and memo openers so that they are more direct.

a. I enjoyed talking with you at our last committee meeting. I told you that I didn't believe in electronic monitoring of employees, but just yesterday we discovered that one of our employees printed out several pages from a porn site and forgot to retrieve them from the printer. Now we realize that we need to crack down. You said you were pleased with your organization's written Internet policy and that you would be willing to share it. I would be very happy if you would send me a copy of that policy.[5]

b. I appreciate your asking me for my ideas on selling soft drinks in schools. Some local school officials and consumer groups say that guidelines established by the Coca-Cola Company and other bottlers do not go far enough to combat childhood obesity and commercialism in schools. I've worked out six suggestions for school boards to consider in regard to practices for all current and future deals regarding vending machine sales. My suggestions are described below.

c. I have before me your memo of the 16th in which you request permission to attend the Web Site Design Seminar sponsored by Presentation Planners. As I understand it, this is a two-day seminar scheduled for February 25 and 26. Your reasons for attending were well stated and convincing. You have my permission to attend.

d. As you are aware, the document specialists in our department have been unhappy about their chairs and their inability to adjust the back height. The chairs are uncomfortable and cause back fatigue. As a result, I looked into the possibility of purchasing new adjustable chairs that I think will be just right for these employees. New chairs have been ordered for all these employees. The new chairs should be arriving in about three weeks.

8.5 Subject Lines (Objs. 1–3)

Your Task. Write effective subject lines for the messages represented by the openings in Activity 8.4.

8.6 Graphic Highlighting Techniques (Objs. 1 and 3)

Your Task. Revise the following hard-to-read paragraphs. Include an introductory statement or a title before presenting the data in bulleted or numbered lists.

a. The personal computer has become indispensable for many workers. A recent North American survey revealed interesting information about how the computer is used. Of the 72.3 million workers who use a computer on the job, 72 percent said that they used the computer to connect to the Internet or to their e-mail. At the lowest end of the scale were 32 percent who used it for graphics and design, while 15 percent reported using computers for programming. A fairly large number (67 percent) said that they used the computer for word processing. Close to that number were 62 percent who worked with spreadsheets or databases. Slightly more than half (53 percent) said they used the computer in calendar-related or scheduling activities.

b. Our employee leasing program has proven to be an efficient management tool for business owners because we take care of everything. Our program will handle your payroll preparation. Moreover, benefits for employees are covered. We also know what a chore calculating workers' compensation premiums can be, so we do that for you. And we make all the necessary provincial and federal reports that are required today.

8.7 Information E-Mail or Memo: Driving Less and Breathing Easier (Obj. 4)

E-MAIL

The air in your city has been getting progressively worse over the years. Your company, Mercer Enterprises, wants to contribute to local air quality programs by encouraging a significant number of employees to share rides, take the bus, or ride a bicycle to work.

After studying what other large companies were doing, Mercer developed a number of incentives to entice employees to leave their cars at home. One incentive offers employees who maintain a 75 percent rate of participation in the rideshare program for a period of six months one full workday off with pay. This incentive begins May 1. Other incentives include preferential parking near building entrances. These special parking places are for car pools only, and a parking pass is required. Another incentive involves bus passes. Employees who use public transportation will receive a subsidy of $25 per month. Employees will also get a free round-trip transit pass for the first month. This pass applies only to workplace commuting, of course.

Employees receiving this memo might want more information about the program. They may also want to sign up for the incentives mentioned here. If so, they should contact Jennifer O'Toole (Jennifer.Otoole@mercer.com) before June 1.

Another incentive is the provision of a subsidy for van pools. The company will help obtain a van and will provide a $150 per month subsidy to the van pool. What's even more terrific is that the van-pool driver will have unlimited personal use of the vehicle off company time. A final subsidy involves bicycles. Employees who bicycle to work will receive $25 per month as a subsidy. And Mercer Enterprises will provide bicycle racks, locks, and chains.

Your Task. As employee transportation coordinator for your company, send an e-mail or memo to all employees describing the incentives offered by Mercer. You can improve readability of your message by using graphic highlighting for the incentives.

8.8 Information E-Mail or Memo: What I Do on the Job (Obj. 4)

E-MAIL

Some employees have remarked to the boss that they are working more than other employees. Your boss has decided to study the matter by collecting information from everyone.
Your Task. He asks you to write an e-mail or memo describing your current duties and the skills required for your position. If some jobs are found to be overly demanding, your boss may redistribute job tasks or hire additional employees. Based on your own work or personal experience, write a well-organized message describing your duties, the time you spend on each task, and the skills needed for what you do. Provide enough details to make a clear record of your job. Use actual names and describe actual tasks. Report to the head of the organization. The organization could be a campus club or committee on which you serve. Don't make your message a list of complaints. Just describe what you do in an objective tone. By the way, your boss appreciates brevity. Keep your message under one page.

8.9 Information E-Mail or Memo: Party Time (Obj. 4)

E-MAIL

Staff members in your office were disappointed that no holiday party was given last year. They don't care what kind of party it is, but they do want some kind of celebration this year.
Your Task. You have been asked to draft a message to the office staff about the upcoming December holiday party. Decide what kind of party you would like. Include information about where the party will be held, when it is, what the cost will be, what kind of food will be served, whether guests are allowed, and with whom to make reservations.

8.10 Procedure E-Mail or Memo: Parking Guidelines With a Smile (Obj. 4)

E-MAIL

As Adelle Justice, director of Human Resources, you must remind both day-shift and swing-shift employees of the company's parking guidelines. Day-shift employees must park in Lots A and B in their assigned spaces. If they have not registered their cars and received their white stickers, the cars will be ticketed.

Day-shift employees are forbidden to park at the curb. Swing-shift employees may park at the curb before 3:30 p.m. Moreover, after 3:30 p.m., swing-shift employees may park in any empty space—except those marked Tandem, Handicapped, Van Pool, Car Pool, or Management. Day-shift employees may loan their spaces to other employees if they know they will not be using them.

One serious problem is lack of registration (as evidenced by white stickers). Registration is done by Employee Relations. Any car without a sticker will be ticketed. To encourage registration, Employee Relations will be in the cafeteria May 12 and 13 from 11:30 a.m. to 1:30 p.m. and from 3 p.m. to 5 p.m. to take applications and issue white parking stickers.
Your Task. Write a procedure e-mail or memo to employees that reviews the parking guidelines and encourages them to get their cars registered. Use itemization techniques, and strive for a tone that fosters a sense of cooperation rather than resentment.

8.11 Procedure Memo: Managing Your Time More Wisely (Obj. 4)

RESEARCH

You work with a group of engineers who are constantly putting in 60- and 70-hour work weeks. The vice president worries that major burnout will occur. Personally, he believes that some of the engineers simply manage their time poorly. He asks you to look into the topic of time management and put together a list of procedures that might help these professionals use their time more wisely. Your suggestions may become the basis for an in-service training program.
Your Task. Conduct a keyword search for articles about time management. Read several articles. Summarize five or six procedures that might be helpful to employees. Write a memo to Thomas Sawicky, Vice President, with your suggestions.

8.12 Request Memo or E-Mail: Dress-Down Day for Us? (Obj. 5)

E-MAIL

According to a poll funded by Levi Strauss & Co., more than half of all white-collar workers now can dress casually at work. The dress-down trend reflects larger changes in work patterns. Top-down management is less prevalent, and more people work at home or have flexible hours. Even John Molloy, the guru of the 1980s "dress for success" movement, now works with "befuddled executives" teaching them what to wear in a casual world.[6]

As Thomas Marshall, CEO of Marshall & Associates, a sedate accountancy firm, you have had some inquiries from your accountants and other employees about the possibility of dressing casually—not all the time, but occasionally.

You decide to ask a few key people what they think about establishing a casual-dress day. It sounds like a good idea, especially if it makes people feel more at ease in the office. But you worry that it might look unprofessional and encourage sloppy work and horsing around. Moreover, you are concerned about what people might wear, such as shorts, tank tops, T-shirts with slogans, baseball caps, and dirty athletic clothes. Would a dress-down policy make the office atmosphere less professional? Perhaps a written dress code will be necessary if a casual-dress policy is allowed.

Your Task. To solicit feedback, you write the same memo to two partners and your office manager. Ask for their opinions, but do so with specific questions. Be sure to include an end date so that you can decide on a course of action before the next management council meeting. Address the same memo or e-mail to Mary E. Leslie <mel@marsh.com>, Sam W. Miller <sam@marsh.com>, and Jonathon Galston <jon@marsh.com>.

8.13 Reply E-Mail or Memo: Cross-cultural Dilemma (Obj. 5)

E-MAIL | TEAM | WEB

After seeing an article in the newspaper stating that women are required to wear neck-to-toe robes in Saudi Arabia, your boss began to worry about sending female engineers there. Your company has been asked to submit a proposal to develop telecommunications within that country, and some of the company's best staff members are female. If your company wins the contract, it will undoubtedly need women to be in Saudi Arabia to complete the project. Because your boss knows little about the country, he asks you, his assistant, to do some research to find out what is appropriate business dress.

Your Task. Visit two or three Web sites and learn about dress expectations in Saudi Arabia. Is Western-style clothing acceptable for men? for women? Are there any clothing taboos? Should guest workers be expected to dress like natives? In teams discuss your findings. Individually or collectively, prepare a memo or e-mail addressed to J. E. Rivers, your boss. Summarize your most significant findings.

8.14 Reply Memo or E-Mail: Scheduling Appointments to Interview a New Project Manager (Obj. 5)

E-MAIL

You're frustrated! Your boss, Paul Rosenberg, has scheduled three appointments to interview applicants for the position of project manager. All of these appointments are for Thursday, May 5. However, he now must travel to Halifax on that weekend. He asks you to reschedule all the appointments for one week later. He also wants a brief summary of the background of each candidate.

Despite your frustration, you call each person and are lucky enough to arrange these times. Carol Chastain, who has been a project manager for nine years with Piedmont Corporation, agrees to come at 10:30 a.m. Richard Emanuel, who is a systems analyst and a consultant to many companies, will come at 11:30. Lara Lee, who has an M.A. degree and six years of experience as senior project coordinator at High Point Industries, will come at 9:30 a.m. You're wondering whether Mr. Rosenberg forgot to include Hilary Iwu, operations personnel officer, in these interviews. Ms. Iwu usually is part of the selection process.

Your Task. Write an e-mail or memo to Mr. Rosenberg including all the vital information he needs.

8.15 Confirmation Memo or E-Mail: Did I Hear This Correctly? (Obj. 6)

E-MAIL

At lunch one day you had a stimulating discussion with Jayne Moneysmith, a lawyer specializing in employment risk management. You are a manager with a growing brokerage firm that has more than 250 employees. All employees except top managers are "at will" employees without employment contracts. Your company has an extensive set of procedures and policies regarding sexual harassment, but it has no e-mail policies.

Ms. Moneysmith told you that in certain instances e-mail transmissions can constitute hostile-environment sexual harassment. Although an e-mail message is not a "verbal statement" uttered by an alleged harasser face to face, it can cross the legal line. If the message is severe and adversely affects the receiver's work environment, the message could constitute actionable sexual harassment. Even deleted messages can come back to haunt the company in employment discrimination cases. E-mails leave a "metadata" trail revealing attachments, dates and times of edits and transmissions, file size, conversation threads, and document file paths. These attributes ensure that any inappropriate behaviour conducted via an employer's digital technology will leave a permanent record. She said that "at will" employees who send inappropriate messages or pornographic materials can legally be terminated if the circumstances suggest an outright dismissal is appropriate.[7]

Your Task. You would like to report Ms. Moneysmith's remarks at the next management council meeting. Before you do, however, you want to be sure that you heard her accurately. Write a memo or e-mail to Ms. Moneysmith condensing and confirming the major points she covered.

8.16 What to Do About the Junk E-Mail Epidemic? (Obj. 3)

SPEAKING

The modern-day epidemic of unsolicited electronic messages sent over the Internet, popularly known as "spam," is estimated to cost $25 billion a year worldwide and is expected to soon represent as much as 86 percent of electronic messaging traffic. Hundreds of millions of junk e-mails sent each day cause problems for communications systems and rack up financial losses and productivity losses for both companies and individual users.

In Geneva, Switzerland, the International Telecommunication Union (ITU) organized a meeting to discuss ways to combat the epidemic. Representatives from 60 countries—mostly officials from telecommunication regulatory agencies and industry executives—discussed four response avenues:

- Legislation
- Public education
- Industry actions by Internet service providers
- Software solutions[8]

Your Task. As a member in your group of three to five students, assume the role of one of the delegates at the Geneva meeting. Discuss specific strategies you would suggest under each of the four methods for combating the junk e-mail epidemic. Submit the results of your group's discussion either in a written format specified by your instructor or during a class discussion.

8.17 Reply Memo or E-Mail: What Is a FICO Credit Rating Score? (Obj. 5)

CONSUMER | E-MAIL | WEB

For years the credit industry hushed up a consumer's credit score. Credit bureaus would reveal a consumer's credit rating only to a lender when an applicant wanted a loan. Customers could not learn their scores unless credit was denied. Now all that has changed. Using the Internet, consumers can check their credit files and even obtain specific credit scores, which are key factors in obtaining loans, renting property, and protecting against identity theft. Although the three national credit bureaus (Equifax, Northern Credit Bureaus, Inc., and TransUnion Canada) may use different scoring systems, many lenders now mention FICO scores as the favoured ranking to estimate the risk involved in an individual's loan application.

Your Task. As an intern in architect Eric Larson's office, you must do some Internet research. Mr. Larson recently had to reject two potentially lucrative house construction jobs because the clients received low FICO scores from their credit bureaus. They could not qualify for construction loans. He wants you to learn exactly what "FICO" means and how this score is determined. Mr. Larson also wants to know how consumers can raise their FICO scores. Go to http://www.myfico.com and study its information (use a search engine with the term "My Fico" if this URL fails). Summarize your findings in your own words in a well-organized, concise memo or e-mail addressed to Eric Larson <elarson@arnet.com>. Use bulleted lists for some of the information.

C.L.U.E. review 8

Edit the following sentences to correct all language faults, including grammar, punctuation, spelling, and word use.

1. More then ninety percent of companys now use e-mail therefore employees must become more knowlegable about it's dangers.
2. Most e-mails and memos delivery straight-forward information that is not sensitive, and require little persuasion.
3. If I was you I would check all in coming e-mail and attachments that was sent to you and he.
4. Memos typically contain 4 nesessary parts; subject line, opening, body and action closing.
5. Fear of inappropriate e-mail use, and the need to boost productivity, has spurred employee monitoring programs.
6. When you respond too a e-mail message you should not automaticly return the senders message.
7. Wasnt it Dr Rivers and Ms Johnson who allways wrote there e-mails in all capitol letters.
8. A list of the names' and addresses' of e-mail recipients were sent using the "bcc" function.
9. Our information technology department which was formerally in room 35 has moved it's offices to room 5.
10. The Evening news press our local newspaper featured as its principle article a story entitled, Cyber-slacking is killing productivity!

chapter 9

Routine Letters and Goodwill Messages

objectives

1 Explain why business letters are important and how the three phases of the 3-x-3 writing process relate to creating successful business letters.

2 Analyze the structure and characteristics of good business letters.

3 Write direct letters that request information and action as well as place orders for products and services.

4 Write letters that make direct claims.

5 Write letters that comply with requests.

6 Write letters that make adjustments.

7 Write messages that generate goodwill.

springboard *to discussion*

Letter writing is still alive and well, according to letters sent to the North Pole. In 2001, when children first had the opportunity to send their requests via e-mail, using a link on the Canada Post web page, 18 530 e-mails were sent to Santa. That number grew to 34 039 in 2005. However, these numbers are low compared to the more than one million pieces of regular mail that Santa receives annually.[1]

Understanding the Power of Business Letters and the Process of Writing Successful Letters

learning objective

1

This chapter concentrates on positive, straightforward letters through which we conduct everyday business and convey goodwill to outsiders. Such letters go to suppliers, government agencies, other businesses, and, most important, customers. The letters to customers receive a high priority because these messages encourage product feedback, project a favourable image of the company, and promote future business.

Letters sent to customers are a primary channel of communication for delivering messages outside an organization.

This chapter teaches you what engages readers. We will begin by discussing the importance of business letters and analyzing the structure and characteristics of letters. Then you will learn to apply this information in writing routine letters that request information, require action, place orders, and make straightforward claims. You will also learn to grant claims, comply with requests, write letters of recommendation, and compose goodwill messages.

Why Business Letters Are Still Necessary

Business letters are necessary (a) when a permanent record is required, (b) when formality is important, and (c) when a message is sensitive and requires an organized, well-considered presentation.

Even with the new media available today, a letter remains one of the most powerful and effective ways to get your message across. Although e-mail is incredibly successful for both internal and external communication, many important messages still call for letters. Business letters are necessary when (a) a permanent record is required; (b) confidentiality is paramount; (c) formality and sensitivity are essential; and (d) a persuasive, well-considered presentation is important.

Business Letters Produce a Permanent Record. Many business transactions require a permanent record. Business letters fulfill this function. For example, when a company enters into an agreement with another company, business letters introduce the agreement and record decisions and points of understanding. Although telephone conversations and e-mail messages may be exchanged, important details are generally recorded in business letters that are kept in company files. Business letters deliver contracts, explain terms, exchange ideas, negotiate agreements, answer vendor questions, and maintain customer relations. Business letters are important for any business transaction that requires a permanent written record.

Business Letters Can Be Confidential. Carefree use of e-mail was once a sign of sophistication. Today, however, communicators know how dangerous it is to entrust confidential and sensitive information to digital channels, since letters are less likely to be misdirected, forwarded, or retrieved by an unintended audience.

Business Letters Convey Formality and Sensitivity. Business letters presented on company stationery carry a sense of formality and importance not possible with e-mail. They look important. They carry a nonverbal message saying that the communication was considered to be so significant and the receiver so prestigious that the writer was moved to send a real letter. Business letters deliver more information than e-mail because they are written on stationery that is usually printed with company information such as logos, addresses, titles, and contact details.

Business Letters Deliver Persuasive, Well-Considered Messages. When a business communicator must be persuasive and can't do it in person, a business letter is more effective than other communication channels. Letters can persuade people to change their actions, adopt new beliefs, make donations, contribute their time, and try new products. Direct-mail letters remain a powerful tool to promote services and products, boost online and retail traffic, and solicit contributions. Business letters represent deliberate communication. They give you a chance to think through what you want to say, organize your thoughts, and write a well-considered argument. You will learn more about writing persuasive and marketing messages in Chapter 10.

Applying the 3-x-3 Writing Process to Create Successful Letters

In this book, we will divide letters into three groups: (1) routine letters communicating straightforward requests, replies, and goodwill messages, covered in this chapter; (2) persuasive messages, including sales pitches, covered in Chapter 10; and (3) negative messages delivering refusals and bad news, covered in Chapter 11.

Although routine letters may be short and straightforward, they benefit from attention to the composition process. Taking the time to think through what you want to achieve and how the audience will react makes writing much easier.[2] Here's a quick review of the 3-x-3 writing process to help you think through its application to routine letters.

Phase 1: Analysis, Anticipation, and Adaptation

In Phase 1 of the writing process, analyze your purpose, visualize the audience, and anticipate the response.

Before writing, spend a few moments analyzing your task and audience. Your key goals here are (1) determining your purpose, (2) visualizing the audience, and (3) anticipating the reaction to your message. Too often, letter writers start a message without enough preparation.

In the Booster Juice letter in Figure 9.1, the writer responds to the request of a young student. The writer first thought about the receiver and tried to personalize what could have been a form letter.

Phase 2: Research, Organization, and Composition

In Phase 2 of the writing process, gather information, make notes or prepare an outline, and compose the first draft.

In the second phase, collect information and make a list of the points you wish to cover. For short messages such as an answer to a customer's inquiry, you might jot your notes down on the document you are answering. For longer documents that require formal research, use a cluster diagram or the outlining techniques discussed in Chapter 6. When business letters carry information that won't upset the receiver, you can organize them in the direct manner with the main idea expressed immediately.

FIGURE 9.1 ***Reply to Customer Request***

1 Prewriting

ANALYZE: The purpose of this letter is to build goodwill and promote Booster Juice products.

ANTICIPATE: The reader is young, enthusiastic, and eager to hear from Booster Juice. She will appreciate personalized comments.

ADAPT: Use short sentences, cheerful thoughts, and plenty of references to the reader, her school, and her request.

2 Writing

RESEARCH: Reread the customer's letter. Decide on which items to enclose and locate them.

ORGANIZE: Write the first draft quickly. Realize that revision will improve it.

ORGANIZE: Open directly with a positive response. Explain the enclosed items. Find ways to make the reader feel a special connection with Booster Juice.

3 Revising

REVISE: Revise the message striving for a warm tone. Use the receiver's name. Edit long paragraphs and add bulleted items.

PROOFREAD: Check the address of the receiver.

EVALUATE: Consider how you would feel if you received this letter.

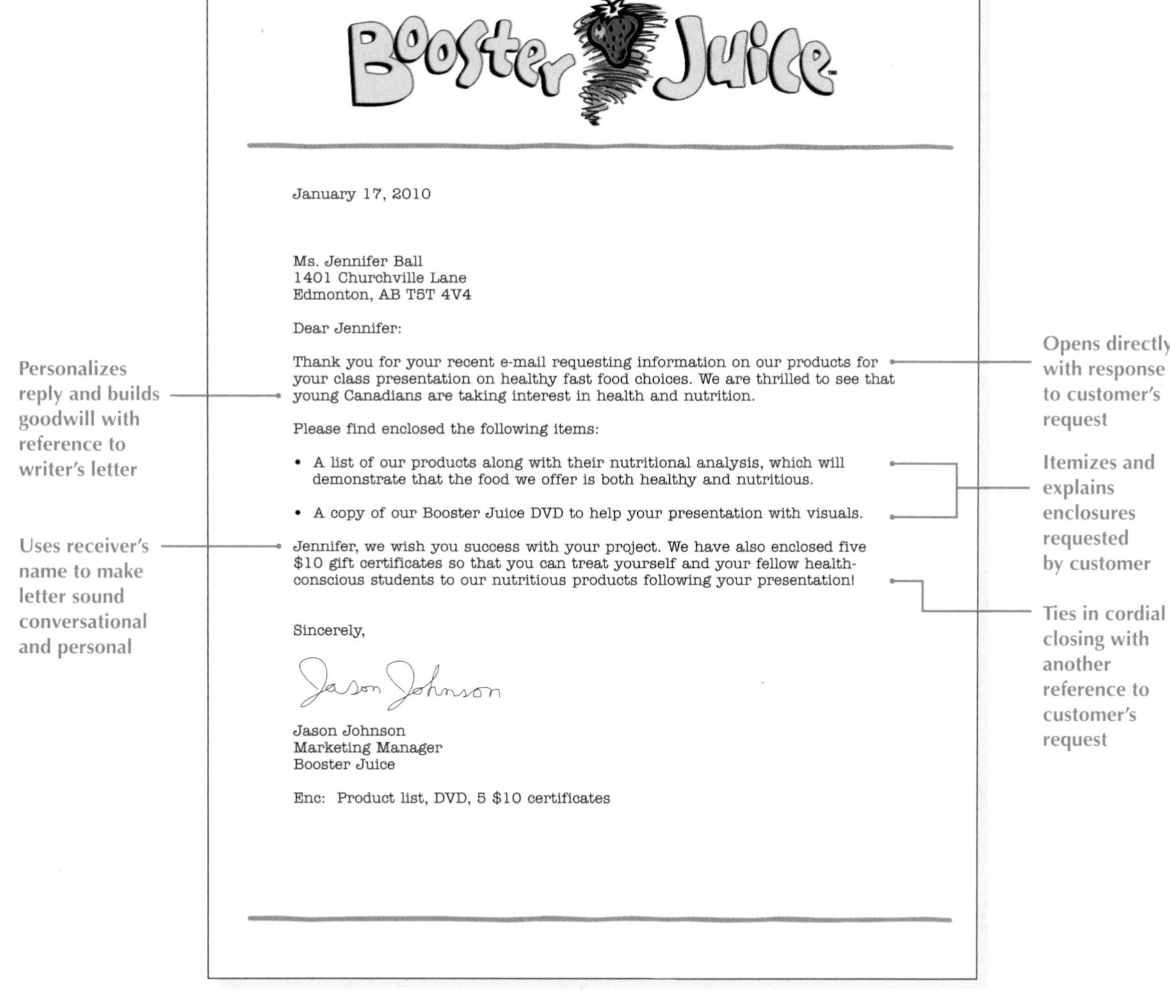

January 17, 2010

Ms. Jennifer Ball
1401 Churchville Lane
Edmonton, AB T5T 4V4

Dear Jennifer:

Thank you for your recent e-mail requesting information on our products for your class presentation on healthy fast food choices. We are thrilled to see that young Canadians are taking interest in health and nutrition.

Please find enclosed the following items:

- A list of our products along with their nutritional analysis, which will demonstrate that the food we offer is both healthy and nutritious.
- A copy of our Booster Juice DVD to help your presentation with visuals.

Jennifer, we wish you success with your project. We have also enclosed five $10 gift certificates so that you can treat yourself and your fellow health-conscious students to our nutritious products following your presentation!

Sincerely,

Jason Johnson

Jason Johnson
Marketing Manager
Booster Juice

Enc: Product list, DVD, 5 $10 certificates

Logo courtesy of Booster Juice.

Phase 3: Revision, Proofreading, and Evaluation

In Phase 3 of the writing process, revise for clarity, add graphic highlighting if possible, and proofread for correctness.

When you finish the first draft, revise for clarity. The receiver should not have to read the message twice to grasp its meaning. Proofread for correctness. Check for punctuation irregularities, typos, misspelled words, or other mechanical problems. Also be sure to look for ways to create high "skim value." *Always* take time to examine the words highlighted by your spell checker. Finally, evaluate your product. Before any letter leaves your desk, always reread it and put yourself in the shoes of the reader, asking yourself, "How would I feel if I were receiving it?"

learning objective 2

Analyzing the Structure and Characteristics of Business Letters

The everyday transactions of a business consist mainly of routine requests and responses. Because you expect the reader's response to be positive or neutral, you won't need special techniques to be convincing, to soften bad news, or to be tactful. Use the direct strategy, outlined in Chapter 6. In composing routine letters, you can structure your message, as shown in Figure 9.2, into three parts:

- **Opening:** a statement that announces the purpose immediately
- **Body:** details that explain the purpose
- **Closing:** a request for action or a courteous conclusion

Frontload in the Opening

Everyday business messages "frontload" by presenting the main idea or purpose immediately.

You should use the direct strategy for routine, everyday messages. This means developing ideas in a straightforward manner and frontloading the main idea. State immediately why you are writing so that the reader can anticipate and comprehend what follows. Remember, every time a reader begins a message, he or she is thinking, "Why was this sent to me?" "What am I to do?"

Some writers make the mistake of organizing a message as if they were telling a story or solving a problem. They start at the beginning and follow the same sequence in which they thought through the problem. This means reviewing the background, discussing the reasons for action, and then requesting an action. Most business letters, though, are better written "backwards." Start with the action desired or the main idea. Don't get bogged down in introductory material, history, justifications, or old-fashioned "business" language.[3] Instead, reveal your purpose immediately. Compare the following indirect and direct openers to see the differences:

Indirect Opening
Our company is experiencing difficulty in retaining employees. We also need help in screening job applicants. Our current testing program is unsatisfactory. I understand that you offer employee testing materials, and I have a number of questions to ask.

Direct Opening
Please answer the following questions about your personnel testing materials.

Most simple requests should open immediately with a statement of purpose (*Please answer these questions about . . .*). Occasionally, however, requests may require a sentence or two of explanation or background before the purpose is revealed.

FIGURE 9.2 *Three-Part Structure for Routine Requests and Responses*

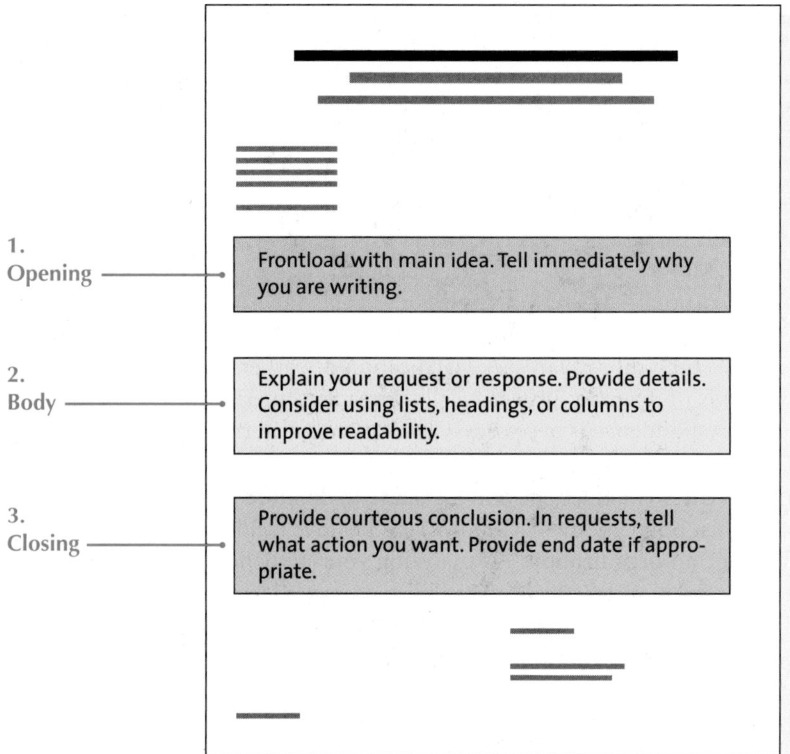

1. Opening
Frontload with main idea. Tell immediately why you are writing.
2. Body
Explain your request or response. Provide details. Consider using lists, headings, or columns to improve readability.
3. Closing
Provide courteous conclusion. In requests, tell what action you want. Provide end date if appropriate.

What you want to avoid, though, is delaying the purpose of the letter beyond the first paragraph.

Explain in the Body

The body explains the purpose for writing, perhaps using graphic devices to highlight important ideas.

After a direct opening that tells the reader why you are writing, present details that explain your request or response. This is where your planning pays off, allowing you to structure the information for maximum clarity and readability. Here you should consider using some graphic devices to highlight the details: a numbered or bulleted list, headings, columns, or boldface or italic type.

If you have considerable information, you'll want to develop each idea in a separate paragraph with effective transitions to connect them. The important thing to remember is to keep similar ideas together. The biggest problem in business writing is poor organization, and the body of a letter is where that failure becomes apparent.

Be Specific and Courteous in the Closing

The closing courteously specifies what the receiver is to do.

In the last paragraph of direct letters, readers look for action information: schedules, deadlines, activities to be completed. Thus, at this point, you should specify what you want the reader to do. If appropriate, include an end date—a date for completion of the action. If possible, give reasons for establishing the deadline. Research shows that people want to know why they should do something—even if the reasons seem obvious. Moreover, people want to be treated courteously (*Please answer these questions before April 1, when we must make a final decision*), not bossed around (*Send this information immediately*).

Analyzing the Characteristics of Good Business Letters

Although routine letters deliver straightforward facts, they don't have to sound and look dull or mechanical. At least three characteristics distinguish good business letters: clear content, a tone of goodwill, and correct form.

Clear letters feature short sentences and paragraphs, transitional expressions, familiar words, and active-voice verbs.

Clear Content. A clearly written letter separates ideas into paragraphs, uses short sentences and paragraphs, and guides the reader through the ideas with transitional expressions. Moreover, a clear letter uses familiar words and active-voice verbs. In other words, it incorporates the writing techniques you studied in Chapters 5, 6, and 7.

But many business letters are not written well. As many as one third of business letters do nothing more than seek clarification of earlier correspondence. Clear letters avoid this problem by answering all the reader's questions or concerns so that no further correspondence is necessary. Clear letters speak the language of the receiver.

Goodwill Tone. Good letters, however, have to do more than deliver clear messages; they also must build goodwill. Goodwill is a positive feeling the reader has toward an individual or an organization. By analyzing your audience and adapting your message to the reader, your letters can establish an overall tone of goodwill.

To achieve goodwill, look for ways to present the message from the reader's perspective. In other words, emphasize the "you" view and point out benefits to the reader. In addition, be sensitive to words that might suggest gender, racial, age, or disability bias. Finally, frame your ideas positively because they will sound more pleasing and will give more information than negative constructions.

Appropriate letter formats send silent but positive messages.

Correct Form. A business letter conveys silent messages beyond that of its printed words. The letter's appearance and format reflect the writer's carefulness and experience. A short letter bunched at the top of a sheet of paper, for example, looks as though it were prepared in a hurry or by an amateur.

For your letters to make a good impression, you need to select an appropriate format. The block style shown in Figure 9.3 is a popular format. Other letter formats are illustrated later in this chapter. In the block style the parts of your letter—dateline, inside address, body, and so on—are set flush left on the page. Also, the letter is formatted so that it is centred on the page and framed by white space. Most letters will have margins of 2.5 to 4 centimetres.

Finally, be sure to use ragged-right margins; that is, don't allow your computer to justify the right margin and make all lines end evenly. Unjustified margins improve readability, say experts, by providing visual stops and by making it easier to tell where the next line begins. Although book publishers use justified right margins, as you see on this page, your letters should be ragged right. Study Figure 9.3 for more tips on making your letters look professional.

learning objective 3

Direct Requests for Information or Action

Because business letters are costly, don't write if a phone call or e-mail message might solve the problem.

The majority of your business letters will involve routine messages organized directly. Before you write any letter, though, consider its costs in terms of your time and workload. Whenever possible, don't write! Instead of asking for information, could you find it yourself? Would a telephone call, an e-mail message, or a brief visit to a coworker solve the problem quickly? If not, use the direct pattern to present your request efficiently.

FIGURE 9.3 ***Business Letter Formatting—Block Style***

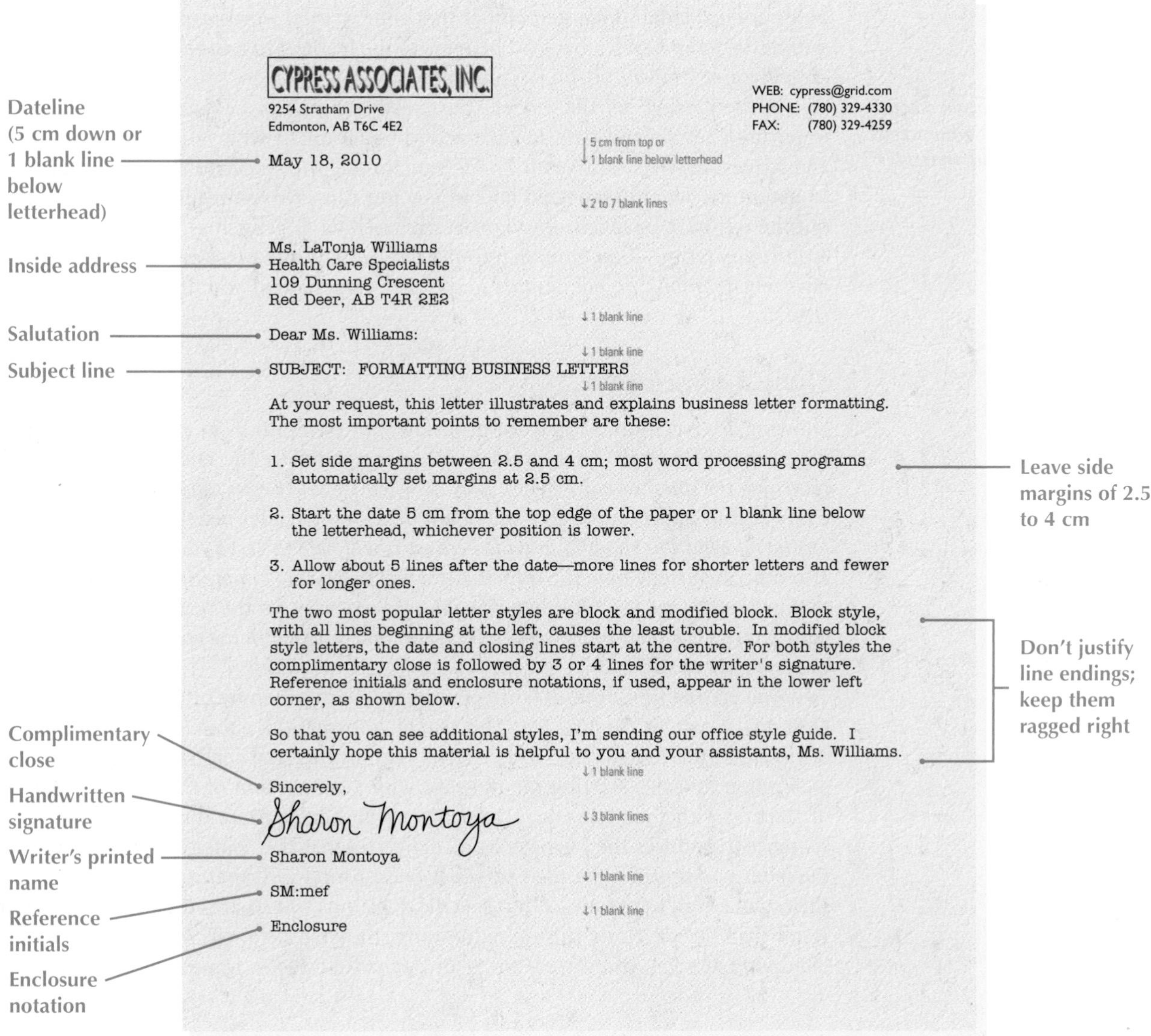

CYPRESS ASSOCIATES, INC.
9254 Stratham Drive
Edmonton, AB T6C 4E2

WEB: cypress@grid.com
PHONE: (780) 329-4330
FAX: (780) 329-4259

May 18, 2010

Ms. LaTonja Williams
Health Care Specialists
109 Dunning Crescent
Red Deer, AB T4R 2E2

Dear Ms. Williams:

SUBJECT: FORMATTING BUSINESS LETTERS

At your request, this letter illustrates and explains business letter formatting. The most important points to remember are these:

1. Set side margins between 2.5 and 4 cm; most word processing programs automatically set margins at 2.5 cm.
2. Start the date 5 cm from the top edge of the paper or 1 blank line below the letterhead, whichever position is lower.
3. Allow about 5 lines after the date—more lines for shorter letters and fewer for longer ones.

The two most popular letter styles are block and modified block. Block style, with all lines beginning at the left, causes the least trouble. In modified block style letters, the date and closing lines start at the centre. For both styles the complimentary close is followed by 3 or 4 lines for the writer's signature. Reference initials and enclosure notations, if used, appear in the lower left corner, as shown below.

So that you can see additional styles, I'm sending our office style guide. I certainly hope this material is helpful to you and your assistants, Ms. Williams.

Sincerely,

Sharon Montoya

Sharon Montoya

SM:mef

Enclosure

Many of your messages will request information or action. Suppose you have questions about a payroll accounting service your company is considering or you need to ask a customer to supply missing data from an order. If your request involves several questions, you could open with a polite request, such as *Will you please answer the following questions about your payroll service.* Note that although this request sounds like a question, it's actually a disguised command. Because you expect an action rather than a reply, punctuate this polite command with a period instead of a question mark. Or, to avoid this punctuation problem, just omit *Will you* and start with *Please answer.*

A direct letter may open with a question or a polite request.

Clarify Requests

In the body of your letter, explain your purpose and provide details. If you have questions, express them in parallel form so that you balance them grammatically. To elicit the most information, pose open-ended questions (*What computer lock-down device can you recommend?*) instead of yes-or-no questions (*Do you carry computer lock-down devices?*). If you are asking someone to do something, be sure your tone is polite and undemanding. Remember that your written words cannot be softened by a smile. When possible, focus on benefits to the reader (*To ensure that you receive the exact sweater you want, send us your colour choice*).

Request letters maintain a courteous tone, spell out what needs to be done, and focus on reader benefits.

In the closing tell the reader courteously what is to be done. If the timing is important, set an end date to take action and explain why. Some careless writers end request letters simply with *Thank you*, forcing the reader to review the contents to determine what is expected and when. You can save the reader time by spelling out the action to be taken. Avoid other overused endings such as *Thank you for your cooperation* (trite), *Thank you in advance for . . .* (trite and presumptuous), and *If you have any questions, do not hesitate to call me* (suggests that you didn't make yourself clear).

Show Appreciation

Showing appreciation is always appropriate, but try to do so in a fresh and efficient manner. For example, you could hook your thanks to the end date (*Thanks for returning the questionnaire before May 5, when we will begin tabulation*). You might connect your appreciation to a statement developing reader benefits (*We are grateful for the information you will provide because it will help us serve you better*). You could also describe briefly how the information will help you (*I appreciate this information that will enable me to . . .*). When possible, make it easy for the reader to comply with your request (*Note your answers on this sheet and return it in the postage-paid envelope* or *Here's my e-mail address so that you can reach me quickly*).

Analyze the first draft of a direct request letter written by office manager Deana Godfrey, shown in Figure 9.4. She wants information about computer security devices, but the first version of her letter is confusing and inefficient. Deana makes a common mistake: starting the message with a description of the problem instead of starting with the main idea. Deana's revision begins more directly. The opening sentence introduces the purpose immediately so that the reader quickly knows why the letter was sent. Deana then provides background information. Most important, she organizes all her requests into specific questions, which are sure to bring a better result than her previous, diffuse request. By studying the 3-x-3 writing process outlined in Figure 9.4, you can see the plan Deana followed in improving her letter.

learning objective

Order Letters

You may occasionally need to write a letter that orders supplies, merchandise, or services. Generally, such purchases are made by web page, telephone, catalogue order form, or fax. Sometimes, however, you may not have a telephone number, order form, or web address—only a street address. Other times you may want to have a written record of your order. To order items by letter, supply the same information that an order blank would require. In the opening let the reader know immediately that this is a purchase authorization and not merely an information inquiry. Instead of *I saw a number of interesting items in your catalogue*, begin directly with order language such as *Please send me by UPS the following items from your fall merchandise catalogue.*

Letters placing orders specify items or services, quantities, dates, prices, and payment method.

If you're ordering many items, list them vertically in the body of your letter. Include as much specific data as possible: quantity, order number, complete description, unit price, and total price. Show the total amount, and figure the tax and shipping costs if possible. The more information you provide, the less likely that a mistake will be made.

FIGURE 9.4 ***Direct Request Letter***

1 Prewriting

ANALYZE: The purpose of this letter is to ask specific questions about computer devices.

ANTICIPATE: The audience is expected to be a busy but receptive service representative.

ADAPT: Because the reader will react positively, the direct pattern is best.

2 Writing

RESEARCH: Determine equipment needs and what questions must be answered.

ORGANIZE: Open with a general inquiry. In the body give details; arrange any questions logically. Close by courteously providing a specific deadline.

COMPOSE: Write the first draft.

3 Revising

REVISE: Improve the clarity by grouping similar ideas. Improve readability by numbering questions.

PROOFREAD: Look for typos and spelling errors. Check punctuation, placement, and format.

EVALUATE: Is this message attractive and easily comprehended?

DRAFT

Opens with background information instead of request

Our insurance rates will be increased soon if we don't install security devices on our computer equipment. We have considered some local suppliers, but none had exactly what we wanted.

Fails to organize information logically

We need a device that can be used to secure separate computer components at a workstation including a computer, keyboard, and monitor. We currently own 18 computers, keyboards, and monitors, along with six printers.

Ends with cliché; fails to reveal what to do and when

We wonder if professionals are needed to install your security devices. We're also interested in whether the devices can be easily removed when we need to move equipment around. We are, of course, very interested in prices and quantity discounts, if you offer them. Thank you for your attention to this matter.

(continued)

In the closing tell how you plan to pay for the merchandise. Enclose a cheque, provide a credit card number, or ask to be billed. Many business organizations have credit agreements with their regular suppliers that enable them to send goods without prior payment. In addition to payment information, tell when the merchandise should be sent and express appreciation. The order letter from Michael Walker of Wilkenson Industries, shown in Figure 9.5 on page 193, illustrates the pattern of an order letter.

Direct Claims

In business many things can go wrong—promised shipments are late, warranted goods fail, or service is disappointing. When you as a customer must write to identify or correct a wrong, the letter is called a *claim*. Straightforward claims are those to which you expect the receiver to agree readily. But even these claims often require a letter. Your first action may be a telephone call or a visit to submit your claim, but you may not be satisfied with the result. Written claims are often taken more seriously, and they also establish a record of what happened. Straightforward claims use a direct approach. Claims that require persuasion are presented in Chapter 10.

Claim letters are written by customers to identify or correct a wrong.

FIGURE 9.4 *Direct Request Letter (Continued)*

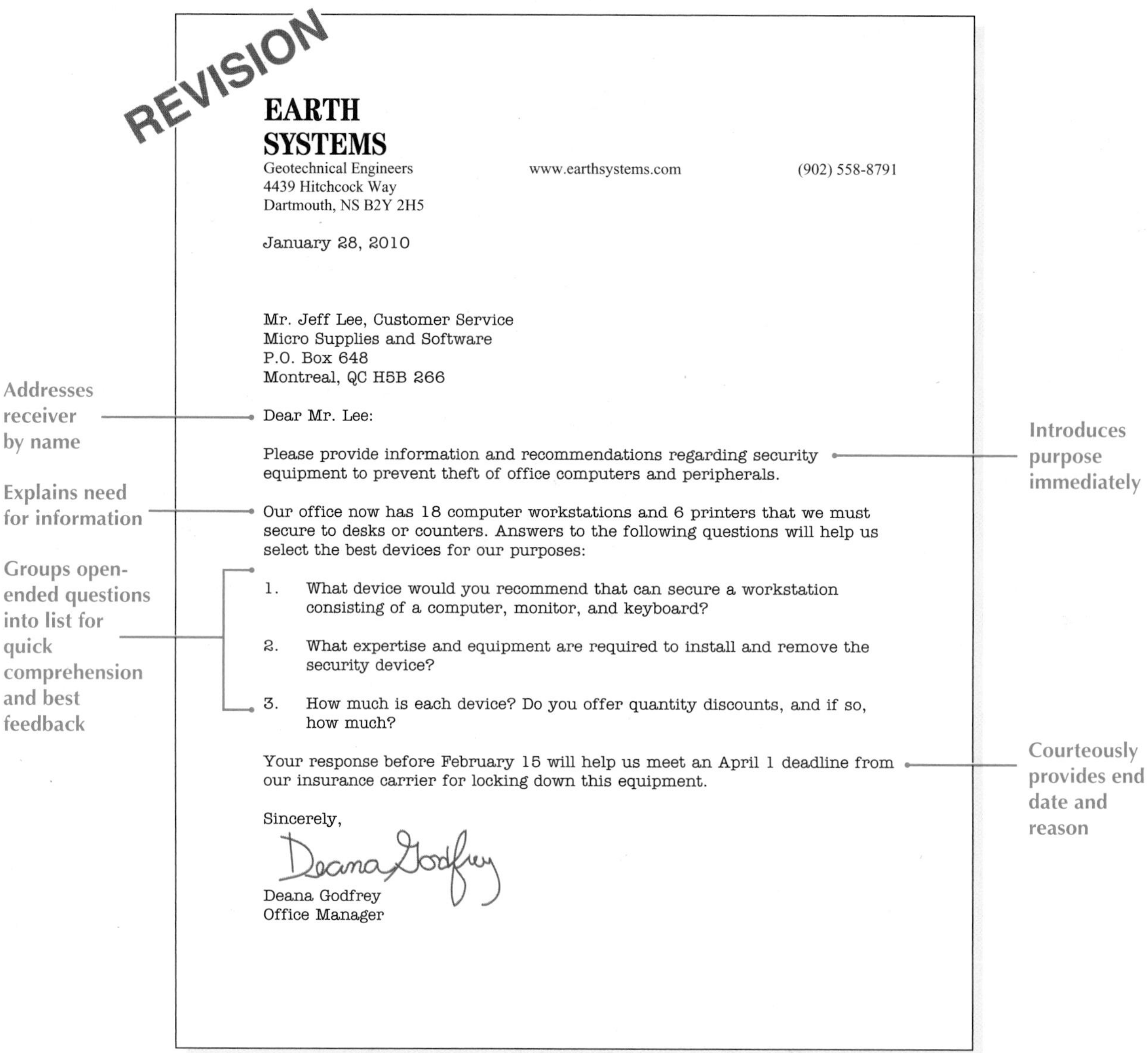

EARTH SYSTEMS
Geotechnical Engineers
4439 Hitchcock Way
Dartmouth, NS B2Y 2H5

www.earthsystems.com

(902) 558-8791

January 28, 2010

Mr. Jeff Lee, Customer Service
Micro Supplies and Software
P.O. Box 648
Montreal, QC H5B 266

Dear Mr. Lee:

Please provide information and recommendations regarding security equipment to prevent theft of office computers and peripherals.

Our office now has 18 computer workstations and 6 printers that we must secure to desks or counters. Answers to the following questions will help us select the best devices for our purposes:

1. What device would you recommend that can secure a workstation consisting of a computer, monitor, and keyboard?

2. What expertise and equipment are required to install and remove the security device?

3. How much is each device? Do you offer quantity discounts, and if so, how much?

Your response before February 15 will help us meet an April 1 deadline from our insurance carrier for locking down this equipment.

Sincerely,

Deana Godfrey

Deana Godfrey
Office Manager

Open With a Clear Statement

Claim letters open with a clear problem statement or with an explanation of the action necessary to solve the problem.

When you, as a customer, have a legitimate claim, you can expect a positive response from a company. Smart businesses want to hear from their customers. They know that retaining a customer is far less costly than recruiting a new customer. That's why you should open a claim letter with a clear statement of the problem or with the action you want the receiver to take. You might expect a replacement, a refund, a new order, credit to your account, correction of a billing error, free repairs, free inspection, or cancellation of an order. When the remedy is obvious, state it immediately (*Please send us 25 Sanyo digital travel alarm clocks to replace the Sanyo analogue travel alarm clocks sent in error with our order shipped January 4*). When the remedy is less obvious, you might ask for a change in policy or procedure or simply for an explana-

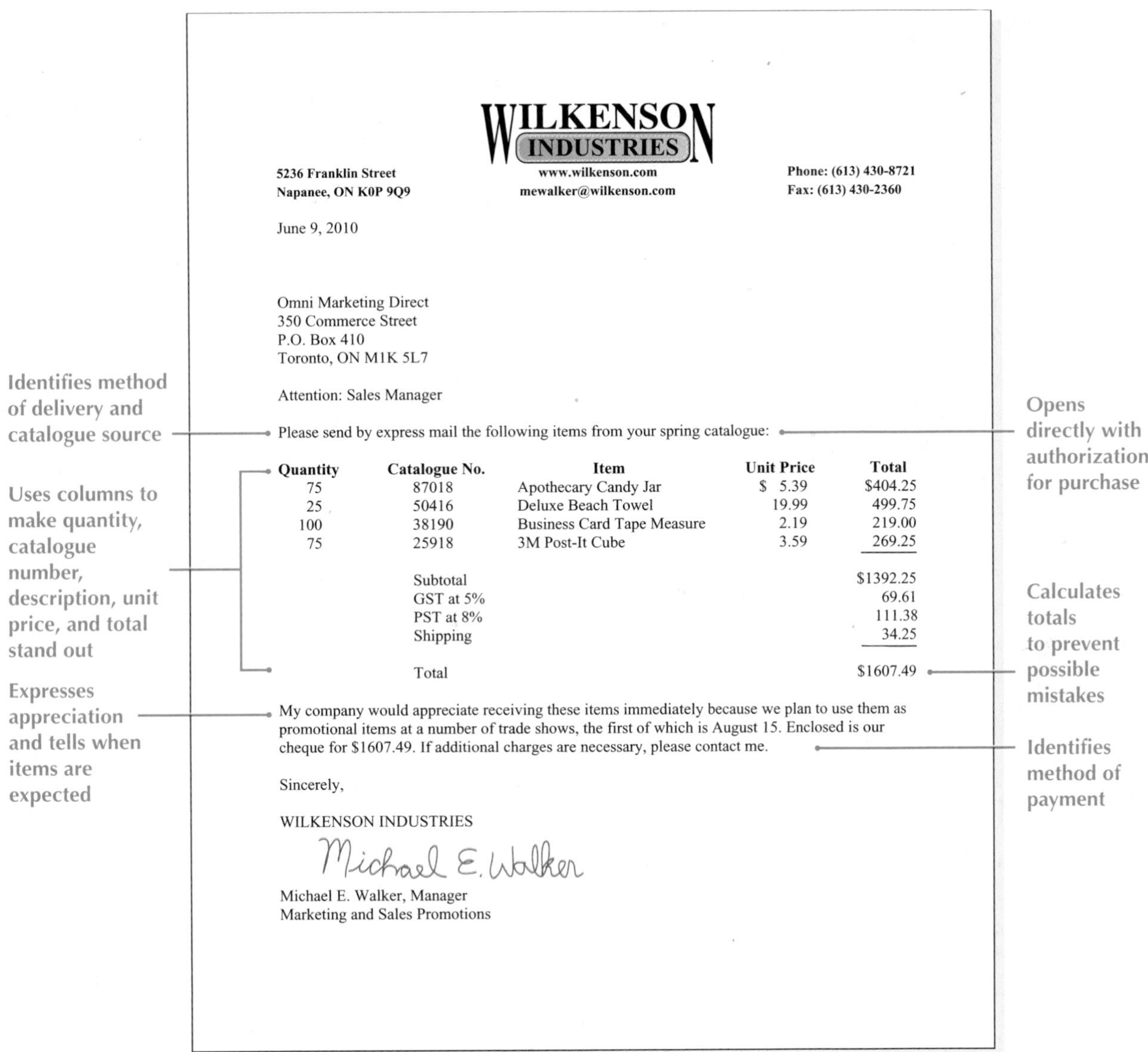
WILKENSON INDUSTRIES

5236 Franklin Street
Napanee, ON K0P 9Q9

www.wilkenson.com
mewalker@wilkenson.com

Phone: (613) 430-8721
Fax: (613) 430-2360

June 9, 2010

Omni Marketing Direct
350 Commerce Street
P.O. Box 410
Toronto, ON M1K 5L7

Attention: Sales Manager

Please send by express mail the following items from your spring catalogue:

Quantity	Catalogue No.	Item	Unit Price	Total
75	87018	Apothecary Candy Jar	$ 5.39	$404.25
25	50416	Deluxe Beach Towel	19.99	499.75
100	38190	Business Card Tape Measure	2.19	219.00
75	25918	3M Post-It Cube	3.59	269.25
	Subtotal			$1392.25
	GST at 5%			69.61
	PST at 8%			111.38
	Shipping			34.25
	Total			$1607.49

My company would appreciate receiving these items immediately because we plan to use them as promotional items at a number of trade shows, the first of which is August 15. Enclosed is our cheque for $1607.49. If additional charges are necessary, please contact me.

Sincerely,

WILKENSON INDUSTRIES

Michael E. Walker

Michael E. Walker, Manager
Marketing and Sales Promotions

tion (*Because three of our employees with confirmed reservations were refused rooms September 16 in your hotel, would you please clarify your policy regarding reservations and late arrivals*).

Explain and Justify

In the body of a claim letter, explain the problem and justify your request. Provide the necessary details so that the difficulty can be corrected without further correspondence. Avoid becoming angry or trying to fix blame. Bear in mind that the person reading your letter is seldom responsible for the problem. Instead, state the facts logically, objectively, and unemotionally; let the reader decide on the causes. Include

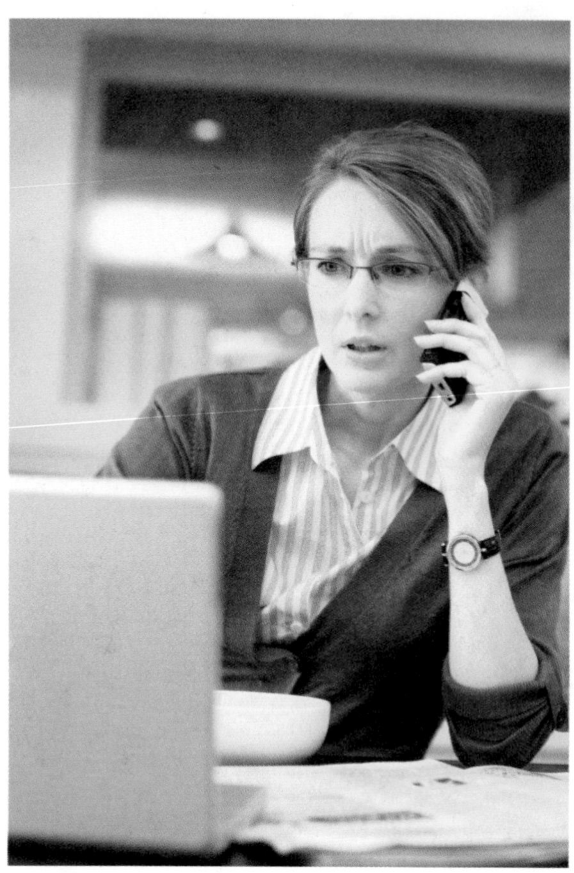

copies of all pertinent documents such as invoices, sales slips, catalogue descriptions, and repair records. (By the way, be sure to send copies and NOT your originals, which could be lost.) When service is involved, cite names of individuals spoken to and dates of calls. Assume that a company honestly wants to satisfy its customers—because most do. When an alternative remedy exists, spell it out (*If you are unable to send 25 Sanyo digital travel alarm clocks immediately, please credit our account now and notify us when they become available*).

Conclude With an Action Request

End a claim letter with a courteous statement that promotes goodwill and summarizes your action request. If appropriate, include an end date (*We realize that mistakes in ordering and shipping sometimes occur. Because we've enjoyed your prompt service in the past, we hope that you will be able to send us the Sanyo digital travel alarm clocks by January 15*). Finally, in making claims, act promptly. Delaying claims makes them appear less important. Delayed claims are also more difficult to verify. By taking the time to put your claim in writing, you indicate your seriousness. A written claim starts a record of the problem, should later action be necessary. Be sure to keep a copy of your letter.

Customers who call to complain may not reach the right person at the best time. To register a serious claim, always write a letter. A letter creates a paper trail and is taken more seriously than a telephone call. Use the direct strategy for straightforward claims.

Photo: © Radius Images/Alamy

When Keith Cortez received a statement showing a charge for a three-year service warranty that he did not purchase, he was furious. He called the store but failed to get satisfaction on his complaint. Then he decided to write. You can see the first draft of his direct claim letter in Figure 9.6. This draft gave him a chance to vent his anger, but it accomplished little else. The tone was belligerent, and it assumed that the company intentionally mischarged him. Furthermore, it failed to tell the reader how to remedy the problem. The revision, also shown in Figure 9.6, tempered the tone, described the problem objectively, and provided facts and figures. Most important, it specified exactly what Keith wanted to be done.

Close a claim letter with a summary of the action requested and a courteous goodwill statement.

Notice in Figure 9.6 that Keith used the personal business letter style, which is appropriate for you to use in writing personal messages. Your return address, but not your name, appears above the date. Keith used modified block style, in which the return address, date, and closing lines start at the centre. Full block style, however, is also appropriate for personal business letters.

To sum up, use the direct pattern with the main idea first when you expect little resistance to letters making requests. The following checklist reviews the direct strategy for information and action requests, orders, and claim letters.

Checklist for Writing Direct Requests

Information or Action Request Letters

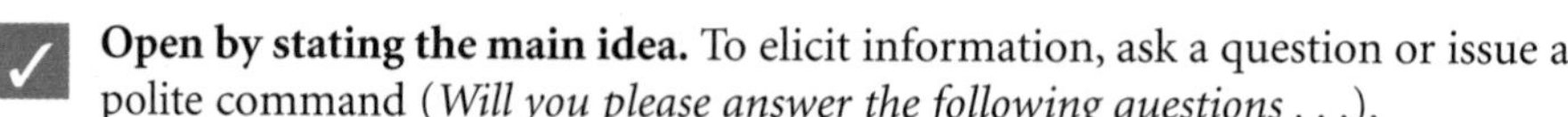

- ✓ **Open by stating the main idea.** To elicit information, ask a question or issue a polite command (*Will you please answer the following questions . . .*).

- ✓ **Explain and justify the request.** In seeking information, use open-ended questions structured in parallel, balanced form.

FIGURE 9.6 ***Direct Claim Letter***

DRAFT

Dear Premier Quality Systems, Inc.:

You call yourselves Premier Quality, but all I'm getting from your service is garbage! I'm furious that you have your salespeople slip in unwanted service warranties to boost your sales.

When I bought my Panatronic DVD from PQS, Inc., in August, I specifically told the salesperson that I did NOT want a three-year service warranty. But there it is on my VISA statement this month! You people have obviously billed me for a service I did not authorize. I refuse to pay this charge.

How can you hope to stay in business with such fraudulent practices? I was expecting to return this month and look at CD players, but you can be sure I'll find an honest dealer this time.

Sincerely,

Sounds angry; jumps to conclusions

Forgets that mistakes happen

Fails to suggest solution

REVISION

2352 Hall Avenue
Windsor, ON N8X 3L9

September 3, 2010

Mr. Sam Lee, Customer Service
Premier Quality Systems, Inc.
41 Bricker Avenue
Waterloo, ON N2L 3B6

Dear Mr. Lee:

Please credit my VISA account, No. 0000-0046-2198-9421, to correct an erroneous charge of $99.

On August 8 I purchased a Panatronic DVD from PQS, Inc. Although the salesperson discussed a three-year extended warranty with me, I decided against purchasing that service for $99. However, when my credit card statement arrived this month, I noticed an extra $99 charge from PQS, Inc. I suspect that this charge represents the warranty I declined.

Enclosed is a copy of my sales invoice along with my VISA statement on which I circled the charge. Please authorize a credit immediately and send a copy of the transaction to me at the above address.

I'm enjoying all the features of my Panatronic DVD and would like to be shopping at PQS for a CD player shortly.

Sincerely,

Keith Cortez

Keith Cortez

Enclosure

Personal business letter style

States simply and clearly what to do

Explains objectively what went wrong

Does not blame or accuse

Requests action

Suggests continued business once problem is resolved

Uses friendly tone

- ✓ **Request action in the closing.** Express appreciation, and set an end date if appropriate. Avoid clichés (*Thank you for your cooperation*).

Order Letters

- ✓ **Open by authorizing the purchase.** Use order language (*Please send me . . .*), designate the delivery method, and state your information source (such as a catalogue, advertisement, or magazine article).
- ✓ **List items in the body.** Include quantity, order number, description, unit price, total price, tax, shipping, and total costs.
- ✓ **Close with the payment data.** Tell how you are paying and when you expect delivery. Express appreciation.

Direct Claim Letters

- ✓ **Begin with the purpose.** Present a clear statement of the problem or the action requested—such as a refund, replacement, credit, explanation, or correction of an error.
- ✓ **Explain objectively.** In the body tell the specifics of the claim. Provide copies of necessary documents.
- ✓ **End by requesting action.** Include an end date if important. Add a pleasant, forward-looking statement. Keep a copy of the letter.

learning objective 5

Direct Replies

Often, your messages will reply directly and favourably to requests for information or action. A customer wants information about a product. A supplier asks to arrange a meeting. Another business inquires about one of your procedures or about a former employee. In complying with such requests, you'll want to apply the same direct pattern you used in making requests.

Letters responding to requests may open with a subject line to identify the topic immediately.

The opening of a customer reply letter might contain a subject line, as shown in Figure 9.7. A subject line helps the reader recognize the topic immediately. Usually appearing two lines below the salutation, the subject line refers in abbreviated form to previous correspondence and/or summarizes a message (*Subject: Your July 12 Inquiry About WorkZone Software*). It often omits articles (*a, an, the*), is not a complete sentence, and does not end with a period. Knowledgeable business communicators use a subject line to refer to earlier correspondence so that in the first sentence, the most emphatic spot in a letter, they are free to emphasize the main idea.

Open Directly

Announce the good news promptly.

In the first sentence of a direct reply letter, deliver the information the reader wants. Avoid wordy, drawn-out openings such as *I have before me your letter of August 5, in which you request information about . . . .* More forceful and more efficient is an opener that answers the inquiry (*Here is the information you wanted about . . .*). When agreeing to a request for action, announce the good news promptly (*Yes, I will be happy to speak to your business communication class on the topic of . . .*).

FIGURE 9.7 *Customer Reply Letter*

1 Prewriting

ANALYZE: The purpose of this letter is to provide helpful information and to promote company products.

ANTICIPATE: The reader is the intelligent owner of a small business who needs help with personnel administration.

ADAPT: Because the reader requested this data, he will be receptive to the letter. Use the direct pattern.

2 Writing

RESEARCH: Gather facts to answer the business owner's questions. Consult brochures and pamphlets.

ORGANIZE: Prepare a scratch outline. Plan for a fast, direct opening. Use numbered answers to the business owner's three questions.

COMPOSE: Write the first draft on a computer. Strive for short sentences and paragraphs.

3 Revising

REVISE: Eliminate jargon and wordiness. Look for ways to explain how the product fits the reader's needs. Revise for "you" view.

PROOFREAD: Double-check the form of numbers (July 12, page 6, 8 to 5 PST).

EVALUATE: Does this letter answer the customer's questions and encourage an order?

KELOWNA SOFTWARE, INC.
777 Raymer Road
Kelowna, BC V1W 1H7
www.kelownaasoft.ca

July 15, 2010 — *Chooses modified block style with date and closing lines starting at the centre*

Mr. Jeffrey M. White
White-Rather Enterprises
220 Telford Court
Leduc, AB T9E 5M6

Dear Mr. White:

SUBJECT: YOUR JULY 12 INQUIRY ABOUT WORKZONE SOFTWARE — *Identifies previous correspondence and subject*

Puts most important information first — Yes, we do offer personnel record-keeping software specially designed for small businesses like yours. Here are answers to your three questions about this software:

Lists answers to sender's questions in order asked / *Emphasizes "you" view*

1. Our WorkZone software provides standard employee forms so that you are always in compliance with current government regulations.

2. You receive an interviewer's guide for structured employee interviews, as well as a scripted format for checking references by telephone.

3. Yes, you can update your employees' records easily without the need for additional software, hardware, or training.

Our WorkZone software was specially designed to provide you with expert forms for interviewing, verifying references, recording attendance, evaluating performance, and tracking the status of your employees. We even provide you with step-by-step instructions and suggested procedures. You can treat your employees as if you had a professional human resources specialist on your staff. — *Links sales promotion to reader benefits*

Helps reader find information by citing pages — On page 6 of the enclosed pamphlet, you can read about our WorkZone software. To receive a preview copy or to ask questions about its use, just call 1-800-354-5500. Our specialists are eager to help you weekdays from 8 to 5 PST. If you prefer, visit our Web site to receive more information or to place an order. — *Makes it easy to respond*

Sincerely,

Linda DeLorme

Linda DeLorme
Senior Marketing Representative

Enclosure

In the body of your reply, supply explanations and additional information. Because a letter written on company stationery is considered a legally binding contract, be sure to check facts and figures carefully. If a policy or procedure needs authorization, seek approval from a supervisor or executive before writing the letter.

Arrange Information Logically

Responding to customer inquiries provides a good opportunity to promote your business.

When answering a group of questions or providing considerable data, arrange the information logically and make it readable by using lists, tables, headings, boldface, italics, or other graphic devices. When customers or prospective customers inquire about products or services, your response should do more than merely supply answers. You'll also want to promote your organization and products. Often companies have particular products and services they want to spotlight. Thus, when a customer writes about one product, provide helpful information that satisfies the inquiry, but consider using the opportunity to introduce another product as well. Be sure to present the promotional material with attention to the "you" view and to reader benefits (*You can use our standardized tests to free you from time-consuming employment screening*). You'll learn more about special techniques for developing sales and persuasive messages in Chapter 10.

In concluding, make sure you are cordial and personal. Refer to the information provided or to its use. If further action is required, describe the procedure and help the reader with specifics.

Emphasize the Positive in Mixed Messages

In mixed-news messages the good news should precede the bad.

The direct pattern is also appropriate for messages that are mostly good news but may have some negative elements. For example, a return policy has time limits; an airfare may contain holiday restrictions; a speaker can come but not at the time requested; an appliance can be repaired but not replaced. When the message is mixed, emphasize the good news by presenting it first (*Yes, I would be happy to address your marketing class on the topic of . . .*). Then, explain why a problem exists (*My schedule for the week of October 10, however, takes me to Ottawa and Montreal, where I am . . .*). Present the bad news in the middle (*Although I cannot meet with your class during the week of October 10, perhaps we can schedule a date during the week of . . .*). End the message cordially by returning to the good news (*Thanks for the invitation. I'm looking forward to arranging a date in October when I can talk with your students about careers in marketing*).

Your goal is to present the negative news clearly without letting it become the focus of the message. Thus, you want to spend more time talking about the good news; and by placing the bad news in the middle of the letter, you deemphasize it. You'll learn other techniques for presenting bad news in Chapter 11.

learning objective 6

Adjustments

Even the best-run and best-loved businesses occasionally receive claims or complaints from consumers. When a company receives a claim and decides to respond favourably, the letter is called an *adjustment letter*. Most businesses make adjustments promptly—they replace merchandise, refund money, extend discounts, send coupons, and repair goods. Businesses make favourable adjustments to legitimate claims for two reasons. First, consumers are protected by law for recovery of damages. Consumer protection is a joint effort of both federal and provincial legislation.[4] Second, and more obviously, most organizations genuinely want to satisfy their customers and retain their business.

When a company responds favourably to a customer's claim, the response is called an adjustment.

Customer goodwill and retention have an important effect on profits. One study showed that losing a customer reduces profits by $118. Keeping that customer satisfied, however, costs only $20.[5] When customers are unhappy, they don't return. A staggering 91 percent of disgruntled customers swear they will never do business again with a company that does not resolve their complaints.[6]

Favourable responses to customer claims follow the direct pattern; unfavourable responses follow the indirect pattern.

In responding to customer claims, you must first decide whether to grant the claim. Unless the claim is obviously fraudulent or represents an excessive sum, you'll probably grant it. When you say *yes*, your adjustment letter will be good news to the reader, so you'll want to use the direct pattern. When your response is *no*, the indirect pattern might be more appropriate. Chapter 11 discusses the indirect pattern for conveying negative news.

Adjustment letters seek to right wrongs, regain customer confidence, and promote further business.

You have three goals in adjustment letters:

- Rectifying the wrong, if one exists
- Regaining the confidence of the customer
- Promoting further business

Open With the Good News

Opening sentences reveal the good news quickly.

The opening of a positive adjustment letter should approve the customer's claim immediately. Notice how quickly the following openers announce the good news:

> You're right! We agree that the warranty on your Standard Model UC600 dishwasher should be extended for six months.
>
> Please take your portable Admiral microwave oven to A-1 Appliance Service, 220 Orange Street, Saskatoon, where it will be repaired at no cost to you.

Occasionally, customers merely want to lodge a complaint and know that something is being done about it. Here's the opening from a bank responding to such a complaint:

> We agree with you completely. Some of our customers have recently spent too much time "on hold" while waiting to speak to a customer service representative. These delays are unacceptable, and we are taking strong measures to eliminate such delays.

Most businesses comply with claims because they want to promote customer goodwill.

In making an adjustment, avoid sounding resentful or grudging. Once you decide to grant a claim, do so willingly. Remember that a primary goal in adjustments is retaining customer loyalty. Statements that sound reluctant (*Although we generally refuse to extend warranties, we're willing to make an exception in this case*) may cause greater dissatisfaction than no response at all.

Explain the Reasons

In responding to claims, most organizations sincerely want to correct a wrong. They want to do more than just make the customer happy. They want to stand behind their products and services; they want to do what's right.

In the body of the letter, explain how you are complying with the claim. In all but the most routine claims, you should seek to regain the confidence of the customer. You might reasonably expect that a customer who has experienced difficulty with a product, with delivery, with billing, or with service has lost faith in your organization. Rebuilding that faith is important for future business. How to rebuild lost confidence depends on the situation and the claim. If procedures need to be revised, explain what changes will be made. If a product has defective parts, tell how the product is being improved. If service is faulty, describe genuine efforts to improve it.

Sometimes the problem is not with the product but with the way it is being used. In other instances customers misunderstand warranties or inadvertently cause delivery and billing mix-ups by supplying incorrect information. Remember that rational and sincere explanations will do much to regain the confidence of unhappy customers.

Because negative words suggest blame and fault, avoid them in letters that attempt to build customer goodwill.

In your explanation avoid emphasizing negative words such as *trouble, regret, misunderstanding, fault, defective, error, inconvenience* and *unfortunately.* Keep your message positive and upbeat.

Decide Whether to Apologize

Apologize if it seems natural and appropriate.

Whether to apologize is a debatable issue. Studies of adjustment letters received by consumers show that a majority do contain apologies, either in the opening or in the closing.[7] Some business writing experts advise against apologies, contending that they are counterproductive and merely remind the customer of unpleasantness related to the claim. If, however, it seems natural to you to apologize, do so. Don't, however, fall back on the familiar phrase *I'm sorry for any inconvenience we may have caused.* It sounds mechanical and totally insincere. Instead try something like this: *We understand the frustration our delay has caused you. We're sorry you didn't receive better service,* or *You're right to be disappointed.* If you feel that an apology is appropriate, do it early and briefly.

Focus on complying with the request, explaining reasons, and preventing recurrence.

The primary focus of your letter is on how you are complying with the request, how the problem occurred, and how you are working to prevent its recurrence.

Use Sensitive Language

The language of adjustment letters must be particularly sensitive, since customers are already upset. Here are some don'ts:

- Don't use negative words (*trouble, regret, misunderstanding, fault, error, inconvenience, you claim*).
- Don't blame customers—even when they may be at fault.
- Don't blame individuals or departments within your organization; it's unprofessional.
- Don't make unrealistic promises; you can't guarantee that the situation will never recur.

Avoiding negative language retains customer goodwill, and resale information rebuilds customer confidence.

To regain the confidence of your reader, consider including resale information. Describe a product's features and any special applications that might appeal to the reader. Promote a new product if it seems appropriate.

Close Positively

End positively by expressing confidence that the problem has been resolved and that continued business relations will result. You might mention the product in a favourable light, suggest a new product, express your appreciation for the customer's business, or anticipate future business. It is often appropriate to refer to a desire to be of service and to satisfy customers. Notice how the following closings illustrate a positive, confident tone:

Close an adjustment letter with appreciation, thanks for past business, a desire to be of service, or promotion of a new product.

> You were most helpful in informing us of this situation and permitting us to correct it. We appreciate your thoughtfulness in writing to us.
>
> Your flat-panel Inspiron 1200 Notebook will come in handy whether you're working at home or on the road. What's more, you can upgrade to a 17-inch display for only $100. Take a look at the enclosed booklet detailing the big savings for essential technology on a budget. We value your business and look forward to future orders.

Although the direct pattern works for many requests and replies, it obviously won't work for every situation. With more practice and experience, you'll be able to alter the pattern and apply the writing process to other communication problems.

Checklist for Writing Positive Reply Letters

Letters That Comply With Requests

✓ **Use a subject line.** Identify previous correspondence and the topic of this letter.

✓ **Open directly.** In the first sentence deliver the information the reader wants (*Yes, I can meet with your class* or *Here is the information you requested*). If the message is mixed, present the best news first.

✓ **In the body, provide explanations and additional information.** Arrange this information logically, perhaps using a bulleted list, headings, or columns. For prospective customers, build your company image and promote your products.

✓ **End with a cordial, personalized statement.** If further action is required, tell the reader how to proceed and give helpful details.

Letters That Make Adjustments

✓ **Open with approval.** Comply with the customer's claim immediately. Avoid sounding grudging or reluctant.

✓ **In the body, win back the customer's confidence.** Explain the cause of the problem or describe your ongoing efforts to avoid such difficulties. Focus on your efforts to satisfy customers. Apologize if you feel that you should, but do so early and quickly. Avoid negative words, accusations, and unrealistic promises. Consider including resale and sales promotion information.

✓ **Close positively.** Express appreciation to the customer for writing, extend thanks for past business, anticipate continued patronage, refer to your desire to be of service, and/or mention a new product if it seems appropriate.

learning objective

7

Goodwill Messages

Written goodwill messages carry more meaning than ready-made cards.

Many communicators are intimidated when they must write messages expressing thanks, recognition, and sympathy. Finding the right words to express feelings is often more difficult than writing ordinary business documents. That's why writers tend to procrastinate when it comes to goodwill messages. Sending a ready-made card or picking up the telephone is easier than writing a message. Remember, though, that the personal sentiments of the sender are always more expressive and more meaningful to readers than are printed cards or oral messages. Taking the time to write gives more importance to our well-wishing. Personal notes also provide a record that can be reread, savoured, and treasured.

In expressing thanks, recognition, or sympathy, you should always do so promptly. These messages are easier to write when the situation is fresh in your mind. They also mean more to the recipient. And don't forget that a prompt thank-you note carries the hidden message that you care and that you consider the event to be important. The best goodwill messages—whether thanks, congratulations, praise, or sympathy—concentrate on the five Ss. Goodwill messages should be

- **Selfless.** Be sure to focus the message solely on the receiver, not the sender. Don't talk about yourself; avoid such comments as *I remember when I . . ..*
- **Specific.** Personalize the message by mentioning specific incidents or characteristics of the receiver. Telling a colleague *Great speech* is much less effective than *Great story about McDonald's marketing in Moscow*. Take care to verify names and other facts.
- **Sincere.** Let your words show genuine feelings. Rehearse in your mind how you would express the message to the receiver orally. Then transform that conversational language to your written message. Avoid pretentious, formal, or flowery language (*It gives me great pleasure to extend felicitations on the occasion of your firm's twentieth anniversary*).
- **Spontaneous.** Keep the message fresh and enthusiastic. Avoid canned phrases (*Congratulations on your promotion, Good luck in the future*). Strive for directness and naturalness, not creative brilliance.
- **Short.** Although goodwill messages can be as long as needed, try to accomplish your purpose in only a few sentences. What is most important is remembering an individual. Such caring does not require documentation or wordiness. Individuals and business organizations often use special note cards or stationery for brief messages.

Thanks

When someone has done you a favour or when an action merits praise, you need to extend thanks or show appreciation. Letters of appreciation may be written to customers for their orders, to hosts and hostesses for their hospitality, to individuals for kindnesses performed, and especially to customers who complain. After all, complainers are actually providing you with "free consulting reports from the field." Complainers who feel that they were listened to often become the greatest promoters of an organization.[8]

Because the receiver will be pleased to hear from you, you can open directly with the purpose of your message. The letter in Figure 9.8 thanks a speaker who addressed a group of marketing professionals. Although such thank-you notes can

FIGURE 9.8 ***Thank-You Letter for a Favour***

1 Prewriting ◀▶ 2 Writing ◀▶ 3 Revising

ANALYZE: The purpose of this letter is to express appreciation to a business executive for presenting a talk before professionals.

ANTICIPATE: The reader will be more interested in personalized comments than in general statements showing gratitude.

ADAPT: Because the reader will be pleased, use the direct pattern.

RESEARCH: Consult notes taken during the talk.

ORGANIZE: Open directly by giving the reason for writing. Express enthusiastic and sincere thanks. In the body provide specifics. Refer to facts and highlights in the talk. Supply sufficient detail to support your sincere compliments. Conclude with appreciation. Be warm and friendly.

COMPOSE: Write the first draft.

REVISE: Revise for tone and warmth. Use the reader's name. Include concrete detail but do it concisely. Avoid sounding gushy or phony.

PROOFREAD: Check the spelling of the receiver's name; verify facts. Check the spelling of *gratitude, patience, advice, persistence,* and *grateful.*

EVALUATE: Does this letter convey sincere thanks?

Hamilton–Wentworth Chapter
North American Marketing Association
P.O. Box 3598
Hamilton, ON L8V 4X2

March 20, 2010

Mr. Bryant Huffman
Marketing Manager, Western Division
Toys "R" Us, Inc.
2777 Langstaff Avenue
Thornhill, ON L3T 3M8

Dear Bryant:

You have our sincere gratitude for providing the Hamilton-Wentworth chapter of the NAMA with one of the best presentations our group has ever heard. — *Tells purpose and delivers praise*

Personalizes the message by using specifics rather than generalities — Your description of the battle Toys "R" Us waged to begin marketing products in Japan was a genuine eye-opener for many of us. Nine years of preparation establishing connections and securing permissions seems an eternity, but obviously such persistence and patience pays off. We now understand better the need to learn local customs and nurture relationships when dealing in Japan.

In addition to your good advice, we particularly enjoyed your sense of humour and jokes—as you must have recognized from the uproarious laughter. What a great routine you do on faulty translations! — *Spotlights the reader's talents*

Concludes with compliments and thanks — We're grateful, Bryant, for the entertaining and instructive evening you provided our marketing professionals. Thanks!

Cordially,

Joyce Barnes

Joyce Barnes
Program Chair, NAMA

JRB:grw

be quite short, this one is a little longer because the writer wants to lend importance to the receiver's efforts. Notice that every sentence relates to the receiver and offers enthusiastic praise. By using the receiver's name along with contractions and positive words, the writer makes the letter sound warm and conversational.

Written notes that show appreciation and express thanks are significant to their receivers. In expressing thanks, you generally write a short note on special notepaper or heavy card stock. The following messages provide models for expressing thanks for a gift, for a favour, and for hospitality.

Identify the gift, tell why you appreciate it, and explain how you will use it.

To Express Thanks for a Gift

Thanks, Laura, to you and the other members of the department for honouring me with the elegant Waterford crystal vase at the party celebrating my twentieth anniversary with the company.

The height and shape of the vase are perfect to hold roses and other bouquets from my garden. Each time I fill it, I'll remember your thoughtfulness in choosing this lovely gift for me.

Tell what the favour means using sincere, simple statements.

To Send Thanks for a Favour

I sincerely appreciate your filling in for me last week when I was too ill to attend the planning committee meeting for the spring exhibition.

Without your participation much of my preparatory work would have been lost. It's comforting to know that competent and generous individuals like you are part of our team, Mark. Moreover, it's my very good fortune to be able to count you as a friend. I'm grateful to you.

Compliment the fine food, charming surroundings, warm hospitality, excellent host and hostess, and/or good company.

To Extend Thanks for Hospitality

Jeffrey and I want you to know how much we enjoyed the dinner party for our department that you hosted Saturday evening. Your charming home and warm hospitality, along with the lovely dinner and sinfully delicious chocolate dessert, combined to create a truly memorable evening.

Most of all, though, we appreciate your kindness in cultivating togetherness in our department. Thanks, Jennifer, for being such a special person.

Response

Take the time to respond to any goodwill message you may receive.

Should you respond when you receive a congratulatory note or a written pat on the back? By all means! These messages are attempts to connect personally; they are efforts to reach out, to form professional and/or personal bonds. Failing to respond to notes of congratulations and most other goodwill messages is like failing to say "You're welcome" when someone says "Thank you." Responding to such messages is simply the right thing to do. Do avoid, though, minimizing your achievements with comments that suggest you don't really deserve the praise or that the sender is exaggerating your good qualities.

To Answer a Congratulatory Note

Thanks for your kind words regarding my award, and thanks, too, for sending me the newspaper clipping. I truly appreciate your thoughtfulness and warm wishes.

To Respond to a Pat on the Back

Your note about my work made me feel good. I'm grateful for your thoughtfulness.

Sympathy

Most of us can bear misfortune and grief more easily when we know that others care. Notes expressing sympathy, though, are probably more difficult to write than any other kind of message. Commercial "In sympathy" cards make the task easier, but they are far less meaningful. Grieving friends want to know what you think—not what Hallmark's card writers think. To help you get started, you can always glance through cards expressing sympathy. They will supply ideas about the kinds of thoughts you might wish to convey in your own words. In writing a sympathy note, (a) refer to the death or misfortune sensitively, using words that show you understand what a crushing blow it is; (b) in the case of a death, praise the deceased in a personal way; (c) offer assistance without going into excessive detail; and (d) end on a reassuring, forward-looking note. Sympathy messages may be typed, although handwriting seems more personal. In either case, use notepaper or personal stationery.

Sympathy notes should refer to the misfortune sensitively and offer assistance.

To Express Condolences

We are deeply saddened, Gayle, to learn of the death of your husband. Warren's kind nature and friendly spirit endeared him to all who knew him. He will be missed.

Although words seem empty in expressing our grief, we want you to know that your friends at QuadCom extend their profound sympathy to you. If we may help you or lighten your load in any way, you have but to call.

We know that the treasured memories of your many happy years together, along with the support of your family and many friends, will provide strength and comfort in the months ahead.

Mention the loss tactfully; recognize good qualities of the deceased; assure the receiver of your concern; offer assistance; and conclude on a positive, reassuring note.

Checklist for Writing Goodwill Messages

General Guidelines: The Five Ss

- ✓ **Be selfless.** Discuss the receiver, not the sender.
- ✓ **Be specific.** Instead of generic statements (*You did a good job*), include special details (*Your marketing strategy to target key customers proved to be outstanding*).
- ✓ **Be sincere.** Show your honest feelings with conversational, unpretentious language (*We're all very proud of your award*).
- ✓ **Be spontaneous.** Strive to make the message natural, fresh, and direct. Avoid canned phrases (*If I may be of service, please do not hesitate . . .*).
- ✓ **Keep the message short.** Remember that, although they may be as long as needed, most goodwill messages are fairly short.

Giving Thanks

- ✓ **Cover three points in gift thank-yous.** Identify the gift, tell why you appreciate it, and explain how you will use it.
- ✓ **Be sincere in sending thanks for a favour.** Tell what the favour means to you. Avoid superlatives and gushiness. Maintain credibility with sincere, simple statements.

- ☑ **Offer praise in expressing thanks for hospitality.** Compliment, as appropriate, the fine food, charming surroundings, warm hospitality, excellent host and/or hostess, and good company.

Answering Congratulatory Messages

- ☑ **Respond to congratulations.** Send a brief note expressing your appreciation. Tell how good the message made you feel.
- ☑ **Accept praise gracefully.** Don't make belittling comments (*I'm not really all that good!*) to reduce awkwardness or embarrassment.

Extending Sympathy

- ☑ **Refer to the loss or tragedy directly but sensitively.** In the first sentence mention the loss and your personal reaction.
- ☑ **For a death, praise the deceased.** Describe positive personal characteristics (*Howard was a forceful but caring leader*).
- ☑ **Offer assistance.** Suggest your availability, especially if you can do something specific.
- ☑ **End on a reassuring, positive note.** Perhaps refer to the strength the receiver finds in friends, family, colleagues, or religion.

Summary of Learning Objectives

1 **Explain why business letters are important and how the three phases of the 3-x-3 writing process relate to creating successful business letters.** Although many e-mail messages are written today, business letters are important when a permanent record is necessary, when formality is required, and when a message is sensitive and needs an organized, well-considered presentation. In Phase 1 of the writing process for straightforward letters, you should determine your purpose, visualize the audience, and anticipate the reaction of the reader to your message. In Phase 2 you should collect information, make an outline of the points to cover, and write the first draft. In Phase 3 you should revise for clarity, proofread for correctness, and look for ways to apply graphic highlighting techniques so that the message has high "skim value." Finally, you should decide whether the message accomplishes its goal.

2 **Analyze the structure and characteristics of good business letters.** Most straightforward business letters are structured into three parts: (a) an opening that announces the purpose immediately, (b) a body with details explaining the purpose, and (c) a closing that includes a request for action or a courteous conclusion. Letters that make requests close by telling what action is desired and establishing a deadline (end date) for that action. Good letters are characterized by clear content, a tone of goodwill, and correct form. Letters carrying positive or neutral messages should be organized directly. That means introducing the main idea (the purpose for writing) immediately in the opening.

3 **Write direct letters that request information and action as well as place orders for products and services.** In a letter requesting information and action, the opening immediately states the purpose of the letter, perhaps asking a question. The body explains and justifies the request. The closing tells the reader courteously what to do and shows appreciation. In letters that place orders, the opening introduces the order and authorizes a purchase (*Please send me the following items . . .*). The body lists the desired items, including quantity, order number, description, unit price, and total price. The closing describes the method of payment, tells when the merchandise should be sent, and expresses appreciation.

4 **Write letters that make direct claims.** When a customer writes to identify and correct a wrong, the message is called a claim. A direct claim is one in which the receiver is expected to readily agree. A well-written claim begins by describing the problem clearly or telling what action is to be taken. The body explains and justifies the request without anger or emotion. The closing summarizes the request or action to be taken. It includes an end date if appropriate and courteously looks forward to continued business if the problem is resolved. Copies of relevant documents should be enclosed.

5 **Write letters that comply with requests.** In a letter that complies with a request, a subject line identifies previous correspondence and the opening immediately delivers the good news. If the message is mixed, the best news comes first. The body explains and provides additional information. The closing is cordial and personalized. If action is necessary, the ending tells the reader how to proceed and gives helpful details.

6 **Write letters that make adjustments.** When a company grants a customer's claim, it is called an adjustment. An adjustment letter has three goals: (a) rectifying the wrong, if one exists; (b) regaining the confidence of the customer; and (c) promoting further business. The opening immediately grants the claim without sounding grudging. To regain the confidence of the customer, the body may explain what went wrong and how the problem will be rectified. However, it may avoid accepting responsibility for any problems. The closing expresses appreciation, extends thanks for past business, refers to a desire to be of service, and/or mentions a new product. If an apology is offered, it should be presented early and briefly.

7 **Write messages that generate goodwill.** Goodwill messages deliver thanks, praise, or sympathy. They should be selfless, specific, sincere, spontaneous, and short. Gift thank-yous should identify the gift, tell why you appreciate it, and explain how you will use it. Thank-yous for favours should tell, without gushing, what they mean to you. Expressions of sympathy should mention the loss tactfully, recognize good qualities in the deceased (in the case of a death), offer assistance, and conclude on a positive, reassuring note.

chapter review

1. Under what conditions is it important to send business letters rather than e-mail messages? (Obj. 1)
2. What three activities should you perform in Phase 1 of the writing process for a business letter? (Obj. 1)
3. Describe the three-part structure of a routine business letter. (Obj. 2)
4. What is frontloading, and why is it useful in routine business letters? (Obj. 2)
5. Why is it best to write most business letters "backwards"? (Obj. 2)
6. What is goodwill? Briefly describe five ways to develop goodwill in a letter. (Obj. 2)
7. For order letters, what information goes in the opening? in the body? in the closing? (Obj. 3)
8. What is a claim? When is it straightforward? (Obj. 4)
9. In complying with requests, why is it especially important that all facts are correct on letters written on company stationery? (Obj. 5)
10. What is an adjustment letter, and what are a writer's three goals in writing adjustment letters? (Obj. 6)
11. Name four things to avoid in adjustment letters. (Obj. 6)
12. Name five characteristics of goodwill messages. (Obj. 7)

critical thinking

1. A recent article in a professional magazine carried this headline: "Is Letter Writing Dead?"[9] How would you respond to such a question? (Obj. 1)
2. In promoting the value of letter-writing, a well-known columnist recently wrote, "To trust confidential information to email is to be a rube."[10] What did he mean? Do you agree?
3. Is it insensitive to include resale or sales promotion information in an adjustment letter? (Obj. 6)
4. Why is it important to regain the confidence of a customer in an adjustment letter? How can it be done? (Obj. 6)

activities

9.1 Direct Openings (Objs. 1–7)

Your Task. Revise the following openings so that they are more direct. Add information if necessary.

a. I seem to have lost your order blank, so I have to write this letter. I hope that it is acceptable to place an order this way. I am interested in ordering a number of items from your winter catalogue, which I still have although the order blank is missing.

b. Your letter of March 4 has been referred to me. Pursuant to your inquiry, I have researched your question in regard to whether or not we offer our European-style patio umbrella in colours. This unique umbrella is one of our most popular items. Its 3 m canopy protects you when the sun is directly overhead, but it also swivels and tilts to virtually any angle for continuous sun protection all day long. It comes in two colours: cream and forest green.

c. Pursuant to your inquiry of June 14, which was originally sent to *Classic Motorcycle Magazine*, I am happy to respond to you. In your letter you ask about the tire choices for the Superbike and Superstock teams competing at the Honda Superbike Classic in Mosport. As you noted, the track temperatures reached above 52°C, and the new asphalt surface had an abrasive effect on tires. With the added heat and reduced grip, nearly all of the riders in the competition selected Dunlop Blue Groove hard-compound front and rear tires.

d. Thank you for your recent order of February 4. We are sure your customers and employees will love the high-quality Colour-Block Sweatshirts in an 80/20 cotton/polyester blend that you ordered from our spring catalogue. Your order is currently being processed and should leave our warehouse in Montreal in mid-February. We use UPS for all deliveries. Because you ordered sweatshirts with your logo embroidered in a two-tone combination, your order cannot be shipped until February 18. You should not expect it until about February 20.

e. We have just received your letter of October 3 regarding the unfortunate troubles you are having with your Premier DVD. In your letter you ask if you may send the flawed DVD to us for inspection. It is our normal practice to handle all service requests through our local dealers. However, in your circumstance we are willing to take a look at your unit here at our St. Catharines plant. Therefore, please send it to us so that we may determine what's wrong.

Rich chapter resources are available on the Web site.

9.2 Subject Lines (Objs. 1–7)

Your Task. Write efficient subject lines for each of the messages in Activity 9.1. Add dates and other information if necessary.

9.3 Letter Formatting (Obj. 2v)

Your Task. On a sheet of paper draw two rectangles about 10 by 15 centimetres. Within these rectangles show where the major parts of letters go: letterhead, dateline, inside address, salutation, body, complimentary close, signature, and writer's name. Use lines to show how much space each part would occupy. Illustrate two different letter formats, such as block and modified block style. Be prepared to discuss your drawings.

9.4 Document for Analysis: Information Request (Obj. 3)

Your Task. Analyze the following letter. It suffers from many writing faults. List its weaknesses. If your instructor directs, revise the letter. Where mailing information is not provided, create your own.

Dear Sir:

As a recently hired member of the Marketing and Special Events Division of my company, Cynergy, I have been given the assignment of making initial inquiries in regard to our next marketing meeting. Pursuant to this assignment, I am writing to you. We would like to find a resort hotel with conference facilities, and we have heard wonderful things about your resort.

Our marketing meeting will require banquet facilities where we can all be together, but we will also need at least four smaller meeting rooms. Each of these rooms should accommodate about 75. We hope to arrange our conference October 23–27, and we expect about 250 sales associates. Most of our associates will be flying in, so I'm interested in transportation to and from the airport.

Does your resort have public address systems in the meeting rooms? How about audiovisual equipment and computer facilities for presentations? Thank you for your cooperation.

Sincerely,

9.5 Document for Analysis: Adjustment (Obj. 6)

Your Task. Analyze the following letter. It suffers from many writing faults. List its weaknesses. If your instructor directs, revise the letter.

Dear Mr. Thomas:

Your letter has been referred to me for reply. You claim that the painting recently sent by Central Park Gallery arrived with sags in the canvas and that you are unwilling to hang it in your executive offices. I have examined your complaint carefully, and, frankly, I find it difficult to believe because we are so careful about shipping, but if what you say is true, I suspect that the shipper may be the source of your problem. We give explicit instructions to our shippers that large paintings must be shipped standing up, not lying down. We also wrap every painting in two layers of convoluted foam and one layer of Perf-Pack foam, which we think should be sufficient to withstand any bumps and scrapes that negligent shipping may cause. We will certainly look into this.

Although it is against our policy, we will in this instance allow you to take this painting to a local framing shop for restretching. We are proud that we can offer fine works of original art at incredibly low prices, and you can be sure that we do not send out sagging canvases.

Sincerely,

9.6 Direct Request: Going to the Source (Obj. 3)

You feel fortunate to have found a manager in your field who is willing to talk to you about careers. Your purpose is to learn more about your career area so that you can train for the occupation and also find a job when you finish your schooling. The manager you selected is a busy person, and he will try to work a personal interview into his schedule. But in case he can't meet you in person, he would like to have your questions in letter form so that he could answer them in a telephone conversation if necessary. Seeing the questions arranged in a logical order will also help him be best prepared.

Your Task. Write an information request to a real or hypothetical person in a company where you would like to work. If you want to start your own business, write to someone who has done it. Assume that the person has agreed to talk with you, but you haven't set a date. Use your imagination in creating five to eight interview questions. Be sure to show appreciation!

9.7 Direct Request: Conference at the Fabulous Paris Las Vegas (Obj. 3)

Your company, Vortex Enterprises, has just had an enormously successful two-year sales period. CEO Kenneth Richardson has asked you, as marketing manager, to arrange a fabulous conference/retreat. "This will be a giant thank-you gift for all 75 of our engineers, product managers, and salespeople," he says. Warming up to the idea, he says, "I want the company to host a four-day combination sales conference/vacation/retreat at some spectacular location. Let's begin by inquiring at Paris Las Vegas. I hear it's awesome!" You check its Web site and find some general information. However, you decide to write a letter so that you can have a permanent, formal record of all the resorts you investigate. You estimate that your company will require about 75 rooms—preferably with a view of the Strip. You'll also need about three conference rooms for one and a half days. You want to know room rates, conference facilities, and entertainment possibilities for families. The CEO gave you two possible times: July 8–12 or August 18–22. You know that these are off-peak times, and you wonder whether you can get a good room rate. What entertainment will be showing at Paris Las Vegas during these times? One evening the CEO will want to host a banquet for about 140 people. Oh yes, he wants a report from you by March 1.

Your Task. Write a well-organized information request to Ms. Nancy Mercado, Manager, Convention Services, Paris Las Vegas, 281 Paris Drive, Las Vegas, NV 87551. Spell out your needs and conclude with a logical end date.

9.8 Direct Request: Computer Code of Conduct (Obj. 3)

WEB

As an assistant in the campus computer laboratory, you have been asked by your boss to help write a code of conduct for use of the laboratory facilities. This code will spell out what behaviour and activities are allowed in your lab. The first thing you are to do is conduct a search of the Internet to see what other college or university computing labs have written as conduct codes.

Your Task. Using at least two search engines, search the Web employing variations of the keywords "computer code of conduct." Print two or three codes that seem appropriate. Write a letter (or an e-mail message, if your instructor agrees) to the director of an educational computer laboratory asking for further information about its code and its effectiveness. Include at least five significant questions. Attach your printouts to your letter.

9.9 Direct Request: Checking on Fats and Carbs (Obj. 3)

As Patrick Clark, manager of a health spa and also an ardent backpacker, you are organizing a group of hikers for a wilderness trip to northern Saskatchewan. One item that must be provided is freeze-dried food for the three-week trip. You are unhappy with the taste and quality of the backpacking food products currently available. You expect to have a group of hikers who are older, affluent, and natural-food enthusiasts. Some are concerned about products containing preservatives, sugar, and additives. Others are on diets restricting carbohydrates, cholesterol, fat, and salt. It's a rather finicky group!

You've heard that Northface Outfitters offers a new line of freeze-dried products. You want to know what they offer and whether they have sufficient variety to serve all the needs of your group. You need to know where their products can be purchased and what the cost range is. You'd also like to try a few of their items before placing a large order. You are interested in how they produce the food products and what kinds of ingredients they use. If you have any items left over, you wonder how long they can be kept and still be usable.

Your Task. Write an information request letter to Robin Smith, Northface Outfitters, 2380 Westside Drive, Vancouver, BC V5P 1W8.

9.10 Order Letter: Office Supply Jumble (Obj. 3)

Your Task. Study the following poorly written request for merchandise. Revise the letter and place your return address above the date. Address the letter to Office Central, 200 Main Street, Mississauga, ON L5B 3X3. Add any necessary information.

Dear Sir:

A number of office supplies items in your winter catalogue interested me for my home office. I've lost the catalogue order form, so I hope I can submit my order by letter. Please send me 5 stackable letter trays, No. 648291-J4. They cost $3.39 each. Also send 3 Premier recycled easel pads, Item No. 247411-J4. Each one costs $24.49. I could also use a box (100 to the box) of your Top-load sheet protectors at $14.95 for the box of 100. The item number is 489130-J4. And I need a box of Avery self-laminating sheets (Item 262981-J4) at the price of $21.99, with 50 to a box.

I am interested in having these items charged to my credit card. Please send them quickly because I'm about to run out.

Sincerely,

9.11 Direct Claim: Headaches From "No Surprise" Offer (Obj. 4)

As vice president of Breaktime Travel Service, you are upset with Virtuoso Enterprises. Virtuoso is a catalogue company that provides imprinted promotional products for companies. Your travel service was looking for something special to offer in promoting its cruise ship travel packages. Virtuoso offered free samples of its promotional merchandise under its "No Surprise" policy.

You figured, what could you lose? So on February 5 you placed a telephone order for a number of samples. These included an insulated lunch sack, an AM-FM travel radio, and a square-ended barrel bag with fanny pack, as well as a deluxe canvas attaché case and two colours of garment-dyed sweatshirts. All items were supposed to be free. You did think it odd that you were asked for your company's MasterCard credit number, but Virtuoso promised to bill you only if you kept the samples.

When the items arrived, you were not pleased, and you returned them all on February 11 (you have a postal receipt showing the return). But your March credit card statement showed a charge of $229.13 for the sample items. You called Virtuoso in March and spoke to Rachel, who assured you that a credit would be made on your next statement. However, your April statement showed no credit. You called again and received a similar promise. It's now May and no credit has been made. You decide to write and demand action.

Your Task. Write a claim letter that documents the problem and states the action that you want taken. Add any information you feel is necessary. Address your letter to Ms. Paula Loveday, Customer Services, Virtuoso Enterprises, 420 Ninth Street South, Langley, BC V2Y 2R1.

9.12 Direct Claim: This Desk Is Going Back (Obj. 4)

As the founder and president of a successful consulting firm, you decided to splurge and purchase a fine executive desk for your own office. You ordered an expensive desk described as "North American white oak embellished with hand-inlaid walnut cross-banding." Although you would not ordinarily purchase large, expensive items by mail, you were impressed by the description of this desk and by the money-back guarantee promised in the catalogue.

When the desk arrived, you knew that you had made a mistake. The wood finish was rough, the grain looked splotchy, and many of the drawers would not pull out easily. The advertisement had promised "full suspension, silent ball-bearing drawer slides."

Your Task. Because you are disappointed with the desk, you decide to send it back, taking advantage of the money-back guarantee. Write a claim letter to Patrick Dwiggens, Operations Manager, Premier Wood Products, P.O. Box 528, Sydney, NS B1S 1A9, asking for your money back. You're not sure whether the freight charges can be refunded, but it's worth a try. Supply any details needed.

9.13 Direct Claim: The Real Thing (Obj. 4)

Let's face it. Like most consumers, you've probably occasionally been unhappy with service or with products you have used.

Your Task. Select a product or service that has disappointed you. Write a claim letter requesting a refund, replacement, explanation, or whatever seems reasonable. Generally, such letters are addressed to customer service departments. For claims about food products, be sure to include bar-code identification from the package, if possible. Your instructor may ask you to actually mail this letter. Remember that smart companies want to know what their customers think, especially if a product could be improved. Give your ideas for improvement. When you receive a response, share it with your class.

9.14 Direct Reply: McDonald's Recycles and Reduces Waste (Obj. 5)

TEAM

Danielle Turner, director of Customer Service for McDonald's Corporation, has received a letter from Nedra Lowe, an environmentalist. Ms. Lowe wants to know what McDonald's is doing to reduce the huge amounts of waste products that its restaurants generate. She argues that these wastes not only deplete world resources but also clog our already overburdened landfills. Danielle Turner thinks that this is a good opportunity for her student interns to sharpen their reasoning and writing skills on the job. She asks you and the other interns to draft a response to the inquiry telling how McDonald's is cleaning up its act. Here are some of the facts that your boss supplies your group.

Actually, McDonald's has been quite active in its environmental efforts. Working with environmental groups, McDonald's has initiated a series of 42 resolutions that are cutting by more than 80 percent the huge waste stream from its 12 000 restaurants. McDonald's efforts meant making changes in packaging, increasing its recycling campaign, trying more composting, and retraining employees.

McDonald's was one of the food industry leaders in abandoning the polystyrene "clamshell" box for hamburgers and sandwiches. Formerly using an average of 9 kilograms of polystyrene a day per restaurant, McDonald's now uses only 10 percent of that figure. Moreover, McDonald's is increasing the postconsumer recycled content of its napkins and using lighter-weight paperboard for its fry cartons. Other environmental efforts include testing a starch-based material for consumer cutlery to replace plastic forks, knives, and spoons. Many restaurants have also begun trial composting of eggshells, coffee grounds, and food scraps, and McDonald's is starting a nationwide program for recycling corrugated boxes. In addition, the company is testing reusable salad lids and shipping pallets, pump-style bulk dispensers for condiments, and refillable coffee mugs.

McDonald's has retrained its restaurant crews to give waste reduction equal weight with other priorities such as quickness, cleanliness, and quality service. The company is trying to reduce the waste both behind the counter (which accounts for 80 percent of the total waste) and over the counter.[11]

Your Task. Prepare a letter that can be used for inquiries. To promote goodwill, you might wish to throw in a few coupons for free sandwiches. Send this letter to Nedra Lowe, 2591 Evergreen Road, Waterloo, ON N2A 3G6.

9.15 Direct Reply: Explaining How to Send Résumés (Obj. 5)

You've worked at CyberSoft in the Ottawa Valley for a couple of years. It's a great place to work, and it receives many letters from job applicants. Some of them inquire about the company's résumé-scanning techniques. You generally send out the following form letter that has been in the files for some time.

Dear Sir or Madam:

Your letter of April 11 has been referred to me for a response. We are pleased to learn that you are considering employment here at CyberSoft, and we look forward to receiving your résumé, should you decide to send same to us.

You ask if we scan incoming résumés. Yes, we certainly do. Actually, we use SmartTrack, an automated résumé-tracking system. SmartTrack is incredible! We sometimes receive as many as 300 résumés a day, and SmartTrack helps us sort, screen, filter, and separate the résumés. It also processes them, helps us organize them, and keeps a record of all of these résumés. Some of the résumés, however, cannot be scanned, so we have to return those—if we have time.

The reasons that résumés won't scan may surprise you. Some applicants send photocopies or faxed copies, and these can cause misreading, so don't do it. The best plan is to send an original copy. Some people use coloured paper. Big mistake! White letter-sized paper printed on one side is the best bet. Another big problem is unusual type fonts, such as script or fancy gothic or antique fonts. They don't seem to realize that scanners do best with plain, readable fonts such as Arial or Universe in a 10- to 14-point size.

Other problems occur when applicants use graphics, shading, italics, underlining, horizontal and vertical lines, parentheses, and brackets. Scanners like plain "vanilla" résumés! Oh yes, staples can cause misreading. And folding of a résumé can also cause the scanners to foul up. To be safe, don't staple or fold, and be sure to use wide margins and a quality printer.

When a hiring manager within CyberSoft wants to look for an appropriate candidate, he is told to submit keywords to describe the candidate he has in mind for his opening. We tell him (or sometimes her) to zero in on nouns and phrases that best describe what they want. Thus, my advice to you is to try to include those words that highlight your technical and professional areas of expertise.

If you do decide to submit your résumé to CyberSoft, be sure you don't make any of the mistakes described herein that would cause the scanner to misread it.

Sincerely,

Your Task. Your boss saw this letter one day and thought it was miserable. She asks you and your team to produce an informative and effective letter that can be sent to anyone who inquires. As a team, (1) discuss how this letter could be improved; (2) decide what information is necessary to send to potential job applicants; (3) search the Web for additional information that might be helpful; and (4) develop a better letter. Address your first letter to Mr. Oliver Chase, 1101 Copeland Street, Winnipeg, MB R2C 3H8.

9.16 Direct Reply: Tell Me About Your Major (Obj. 5)

A friend in a distant city is considering moving to your area for more education and training in your field. This individual wants to know about your program of study.

Your Task. Write a letter describing a program in your field (or any field you wish to describe). What courses must be taken? Toward what degree/diploma, certificate, or employment position does this program lead? Why did you choose it? Would you recommend this program to your friend? How long does it take? Add any information you feel would be helpful.

9.17 Direct Reply: Sharing Customer Information (Obj. 5)

CRITICAL THINKING TEAM

You work as an assistant to the vice president of West Bank, a medium-sized bank with 65 branch offices. With so many recent news stories about companies revealing private customer information, some of the bank's customers are beginning to inquire about its privacy policy. Like many financial organizations (including insurance companies and brokerage firms), West Bank does share some customer information within the West Bank family of branches, as well as with selected subsidiaries outside the family. Companies are legally allowed to share information such as names, addresses, social insurance numbers, account balances, and spending habits of individuals—unless the customer specifically asks them to stop. But at West Bank, privacy is one of its highest priorities.

West Bank has a privacy policy based on three principles. First, information security is extremely important. The bank regularly reviews its security standards and practices to protect customers from any unauthorized access to information. But the bank also feels that privacy is a shared responsibility. This is the second point. Customers trust the bank to take care of their financial needs. They should feel confident that the bank is managing customers' accounts responsibly. However, customers also have a responsibility. They can help the bank protect their privacy by knowing what information is on their credit reports, understanding the choices they have about the use of their information, and protecting their passwords. Finally, the bank feels that responsible use of information is beneficial. Information is important for meeting customer needs and providing consistent service quality. The more the bank understands about customers and their needs, the better the bank can suggest products and services, create new opportunities, and help customers manage their financial assets. By being able to share information, banks are better able to service accounts and protect against fraud.

West Bank's privacy policy provides for "opting out." If customers don't want any of their information shared within the bank or with selected companies outside the bank, customers should call 1-800-848-7632.

Your Task. The vice president wants you to draft a response letter to customers who inquire about West Bank's privacy policy. In teams, discuss the content of the letter. Should it reveal that West Bank already shares customer information? Would it be smarter business practice to emphasize the privacy policy and not say anything about the "opt out" toll-free line? The bank has prepared a booklet that provides helpful tips on how to protect privacy. You'll probably want to include it. Address your first letter to Valeria MacCammon, 4529 Evergreen Drive, High River, AB T1V 1M5. Be sure that your letter could also be sent to other customers who inquire.

9.18 Adjustment: Backing Out of a Project Management Seminar (Obj. 6)

Ace Executive Training Institute offered a seminar titled "Enterprise Project Management Protocol" for June 1–2 and was delighted to receive reservations for four attendees from Raintree Manufacturing. But six weeks before the seminar, Ace receives a letter from Raintree asking for a refund because three of the four cannot attend. Ace has already hired the instructor and made arrangements for the seminar based on the projected attendance, so is disappointed to see this cancellation. However, it wants to retain good relations with Raintree in anticipation of future business, so it will return the registration fees of $6600. Because Raintree is having difficulty freeing up its employees to get away for training, it may be interested in Ace's AccuVision Series with on-site training modules. These modules bring the seminar to the client. They teach team building, situational interaction style, initiative, and analysis/problem solving—right on the client's premises. Ace's Web site provides all the details.

Your Task. As assistant to Addison O'Neill, registrar for Ace Executive Training Institute, write an adjustment letter to Kit Adkins, Raintree Manufacturing, 491 South Emerald Road, St. John's, NL A1N 3Y1. Take advantage of this opportunity to promote your company's on-site programs.

9.19 Adjustment: Cure for "No Surprise" Headache (Obj. 6)

Virtuoso Enterprises prides itself on its "No Surprise" offer. This means that anything ordered from its catalogue of promotional products may be returned for a full refund within two weeks of purchase. The claim from Breaktime Travel Service (see Activity 9.11) describes an order placed February 5 and returned February 11. As assistant to Paula Loveday, manager of Customer Services, you check the return files and see that the items were received February 16. You speak with service agent Rachel, who agrees with you—the credit of $229.13 should have been granted to Breaktime Travel. She reminds you that a new system for handling credits was implemented in March. Perhaps the Breaktime return slipped through the cracks. Regardless of the reason, you decide to tell Accounting to issue the credit immediately.

Your Task. In an adjustment letter, try to regain the confidence and the business of Breaktime Travel Service. Include a sample imprinted travel mug in a gift box and a Coleman jug cooler. You know that you are the most reliable source for the lowest-priced imprinted promotional products in the field, and this travel agency should be able to find something suitable in your catalogue. Address your letter to Leila Chambers.

9.20 Thanks for a Favour: Got the Job! (Obj. 7)

Congratulations! You completed your degree or diploma and got a terrific job in your field. One of your instructors was especially helpful to you when you were a student. This instructor also wrote an effective letter of recommendation that was instrumental in helping you obtain your job.

Your Task. Write a letter thanking your instructor.

9.21 Thanks for the Hospitality: Holiday Entertaining (Obj. 7)

You and other members of your staff or organization were entertained at an elegant dinner during the winter holiday season.

Your Task. Write a thank-you letter to your boss (supervisor, manager, vice president, president, or chief executive officer) or to the head of an organization to which you belong. Include specific details that will make your letter personal and sincere.

9.22 Sending Good Wishes: Personalizing Group Greeting Cards (Obj. 7)

TEAM | WEB

When a work colleague has a birthday, gets promoted, or retires, someone generally circulates a group greeting card. In the past it wasn't a big deal. Office colleagues just signed their names and passed the store-bought card along to others. But the current trend is toward personalization with witty, oh-so-clever quips. And that presents a problem. What should you say—or not say? You know that people value special handwritten quips, but you realize that you're not particularly original and you don't have a store of *bons mots* (clever sayings, witticisms). You're tired of the old standbys such as *This place won't be the same without you* and *You're only as old as you feel.*

Your Task. To be prepared for the next greeting card that lands on your desk at work, you decide to work with some friends to make a list of remarks appropriate for business occasions. Use the Web to research witty sayings appropriate for promotions, birthdays, births, weddings, illnesses, or personal losses. Use a search term such as "birthday sayings," "retirement quotes," or "cool sayings." You may decide to assign each category (birthday, retirement, promotion, and so forth) to a separate team. Submit the best sayings in a memo to your instructor.

C.L.U.E. review 9

Edit the following sentences to correct faults in grammar, punctuation, spelling, and word use.

1. Business letters, despite the enormous popularity of e-mail must still be wrote when a permenent record is neccessary.
2. If you follow a writing process organizing the content and composing the first draft is easier.
3. Chelsea acts as if she was the only person who ever received a complement about their business writting.
4. Chelseas letter which she sent to the manager and I was distinguished by 3 characteristics. Clear content, a goodwill tone, and correct form.
5. Davonne Jordan whom I think is our newly-appointed Vice President wants everyone in the Company to beware of computer viruses.
6. When the Office Manager writes business letters or memos he allways ends it with the same "Do not hesitate" phrase.
7. The manager and myself realized an item was missing from the April 1st shipment consequently we sent a claim letter for one hundred thirty-one dollars.
8. After our supervisor and her returned from there meeting at two P.M. we were able to sort the customers names and addresses more quick.
9. If you must write an order letter be sure to include: the quantity order number description unit price tax shipping and total costs.
10. Matthew enclosed a cheque for two hundred dollars, however he worried that it was insufficient to regain the confidence of the customer.

chapter 10

Persuasive and Sales Messages

objectives

1 Apply the 3-x-3 writing process to persuasive messages.

2 Explain the components of a persuasive message and how to blend them effectively.

3 Write successful persuasive messages, including requesting favours and actions, persuading within organizations, and writing complaint letters.

4 Plan and compose outstanding sales messages.

5 Describe the basic elements in persuasive press releases.

springboard *to discussion*

Since 75 percent of North American shoppers subscribe to some form of loyalty program, from airlines to coffee shops, businesses realize the benefits of such incentives. The programs do more than create goodwill; they allow companies to reward loyal customers as well as attract new ones. And the benefits seem to pay off.[1] Shoppers Drug Mart indicates that customers who take advantage of the Optimum loyalty card spend 56 percent more at its stores than customers without the card.[2]

learning objective 1

Strategies for Making Persuasive Requests

The art of convincing others that your point of view is the right one is a critical business communication skill. You have already studied techniques for writing routine request messages that require subtle forms of persuasion. This chapter focuses on messages with the goal of deliberate and skilled persuasion.

What Is Persuasion?

Persuasion is defined as the ability to use argument or discussion in attempting to change an individual's beliefs or actions. A team member uses persuasion to convince her technology-averse manager that instant messaging is an excellent tool to keep all team members informed about a project. Or you might want to persuade your boss to allow you to work at home part of the time.

Some people think that persuasion involves coercion or trickery. They think that you can achieve what you seek only if you twist an arm or deceive someone. Such negative tactics are ineffective and unethical. What's more, these tactics don't truly represent persuasion. To persuade is to present information that enables others to see the benefits of what you are offering without tricking them into agreement.

Successful persuasion depends largely on the reasonableness of your request, your credibility, and the ability to make your request attractive to the receiver. Many techniques can help you be effective in getting your ideas accepted by your fellow workers, superiors, and clients.

Effective Persuasion Techniques

Successful persuasion results from a reasonable request, a credible source, and a well-presented argument.

When you want your ideas to prevail, spend some time thinking about how to present them. Readers and listeners will be more inclined to accept what you are offering if you focus on the following important strategies.

- Establish credibility.
- Make a reasonable, precise request.
- Tie facts to benefits.

- Recognize the power of loss.
- Expect and overcome resistance.
- Share solutions and compromise.

You will be more persuasive if you are credible, make a reasonable request, tie facts to benefits, recognize the power of loss, overcome resistance, share solutions, and are ready to compromise.

The Importance of Tone

Tone is particularly important in persuasion today because the workplace has changed. Gone are the days when managers could simply demand compliance. Today's managers and team leaders strive to generate cooperation and buy-in instead of using intimidation, threats, and punishment to gain compliance.[3] Team members no longer accept unquestioned authority. How can persuaders improve the tone of their requests?

The tone of effective persuasive business requests invites cooperation and avoids intimidation, lecturing, and excessive authoritarianism.

- Avoid sounding preachy or parental.
- Don't pull rank.
- Avoid making threats.
- Soften your words when persuading upward.
- Be enthusiastic.
- Be positive and likeable.

Applying the 3-x-3 Writing Process to Persuasive Messages

Persuasion means changing people's views, and that's a difficult task. Pulling it off demands planning and perception. The 3-x-3 writing process provides you with a helpful structure for laying a foundation for persuasion. Of particular importance here are (a) analyzing the purpose, (b) adapting to the audience, (c) collecting information, and (d) organizing the message.

Persuasive messages require careful analysis of the purpose for writing.

Analyzing the Purpose. The purpose of a persuasive message is to convert the receiver to your ideas or to motivate action. A message without a clear purpose is doomed. Not only must you know what your purpose is and what response you want, but you must know these things when you start writing the letter or planning the presentation. Too often, ineffective communicators reach the end of a message before discovering exactly what they want the receiver to do. Then they must start over, giving the request a different "spin" or emphasis. Because your purpose establishes the strategy of the message, determine it first.

By identifying your purpose up front, you can shape the message to point toward it. This planning effort saves considerable rewriting time and produces the most successful persuasive messages.

Effective persuasive messages focus on audience needs or goals.

Adapting to the Audience. While you're considering the purpose of a persuasive message, you also need to concentrate on the receiver. How can you adapt your request to that individual so that your message is heard? In a broad sense, you will be seeking to show how your request helps the receiver achieve some of life's major goals or fulfills key needs, such as money, power, comfort, confidence, importance, friends, peace of mind, and recognition, to name a few. On a more practical level, you want to show how your request solves a problem, achieves a personal or work objective, or just makes life easier for your audience.

Figure 10.1 ***Four-Part Indirect Pattern for Sales or Persuasion***

Gaining Attention	Building Interest	Reducing Resistance	Motivating Action
Free offer	Rational appeals	Testimonials	Gift
Promise	Emotional appeals	Satisfied users	Incentive
Question	Dual appeals	Guarantee	Limited offer
Quotation	Product description	Free trial	Deadline
Product feature	Reader benefits	Sample	Guarantee
Testimonial	Cold facts mixed with warm feelings	Performance tests	Repetition of selling feature
Action setting		Polls, awards	

To adapt your request to the receiver, consider these questions, which receivers will very likely be asking themselves:

Why should I?	What's in it for you?
What's in it for me?	Who cares?

Adapting to your audience means being ready to answer these questions. It means learning about audience members and analyzing why they might resist your proposal. It means searching for ways to connect your purpose with their needs. If completed before you begin writing, such analysis goes a long way toward overcoming resistance and achieving your goal.

Researching and Organizing Data. Once you have analyzed the audience and considered how to adapt your message to its needs, you are ready to collect data and organize it. You might brainstorm and prepare cluster diagrams to provide a rough outline of ideas.

The next step in a persuasive message is organizing your data into a logical sequence. If you are asking for something that you know will be approved, little persuasion is required. Thus you would make a direct request, as you studied in Chapters 8 and 9. But when you expect resistance or when you need to educate the receiver, the indirect pattern often works better. Use the components of a persuasive message listed below and shown graphically in Figure 10.1:

1. Gain attention.
2. Build interest.
3. Reduce resistance.
4. Motivate action.

learning objective

2

The key components of a persuasive request are gaining attention, showing the worth of the proposal, overcoming resistance, and motivating action.

Blending the Components of a Persuasive Message

Although the indirect pattern appears to contain separate steps, successful persuasive messages blend these steps into a seamless whole. However, the sequence of the components may change depending on the situation and the emphasis. Regardless of where they are placed, the key elements in persuasive requests are (a) gaining your audience's attention, (b) building interest by convincing your audience that your proposal is worthy, (c) reducing resistance, and (d) motivating action.

Gaining Attention

To grab attention, the opening statement in a persuasive request should be brief, relevant, and engaging. When only mild persuasion is necessary, the opener can be low-key and factual. If, however, your request is substantial and you anticipate strong resistance, provide a thoughtful, provocative opening. Following are some examples.

Successful openers to persuasive requests should be brief, relevant, and engaging.

- **Problem description.** In a recommendation to hire temporary employees: *Last month legal division staff members were forced to work 120 overtime hours, costing us $6000 and causing considerable employee unhappiness.* With this opener you've presented a capsule of the problem your proposal will help solve.
- **Unexpected statement.** In a memo to encourage employees to attend an optional sensitivity seminar: *Men and women draw the line at decidedly different places in identifying what behaviour constitutes sexual harassment.* Note how this opener gets readers thinking immediately.
- **Reader benefit.** In a letter promoting Clear Card, a service that helps employees make credit card purchases without paying interest: *The average employee carries nearly $9000 in revolving debt and pays $1800 in interest and late fees. The Clear Card charges zero percent interest. You can't beat it!* Employers immediately see this offer as a benefit it can offer employees.
- **Compliment.** In a letter inviting a business executive to speak: *Because our members admire your success and value your managerial expertise, they want you to be our speaker.* In offering praise or compliments, however, be careful to avoid obvious flattery.
- **Related fact.** In a message to company executives who are considering restricting cell phone use by employee drivers: *A recent study revealed that employers pay an average of $16 500 each time an employee is in a traffic accident.* This relevant fact sets the scene for the interest-building section that follows.

Photo: © Todd Pitt/Imagebox

When Subway began promoting its low-fat sandwiches as healthier options for take-out, it gained attention by showing Lanette Kovach, its chief nutritionist, with a platter of mouth-watering menu options. The first step in developing a sales or persuasive message is gaining attention and shaping the message to the receiver's interests and benefit.

- **Stimulating question.** In a plea for funds to support environmental causes: *What do golden tortoise beetles, bark spiders, flounders, and Arctic foxes have in common?* Readers will be curious to find the answer to this intriguing question. (They all change colour according to their surroundings.)

Building Interest

The body of a persuasive request may require several paragraphs to build interest and reduce resistance.

After capturing attention, a persuasive request must retain that attention and convince the audience that the request is reasonable. To justify your request, be prepared to invest in a few paragraphs of explanation. Persuasive requests are likely to be longer than direct requests because the audience must be convinced rather than simply instructed. You can build interest and conviction through the use of the following:

- Facts, statistics
- Examples
- Expert opinion
- Specific details
- Direct benefits
- Indirect benefits

Showing how your request can benefit the audience directly or indirectly is a key factor in persuasion. A *direct benefit* can be a tax write-off for the contribution. An *indirect benefit* comes from feeling good about helping others who will benefit from the gift. Nearly all charities rely in large part on indirect benefits—the selflessness of givers—to promote their causes.

Reducing Resistance

Persuasive requests reduce resistance by addressing what-if questions and establishing credibility.

One of the biggest mistakes in persuasive requests is failure to anticipate and offset audience resistance. How will the receiver object to your request? In brainstorming for clues, try what-if scenarios. For each of these what-if scenarios, you need a counterargument.

Unless you anticipate resistance, you will give the receiver an easy opportunity to dismiss your request. Countering this resistance is important, but you must do it with finesse. You can minimize objections by presenting your counterarguments in sentences that emphasize benefits. However, don't spend too much time on counterarguments, as that will make them seem overly important. Finally, avoid bringing up objections that might never have occurred to the receiver in the first place.

Another factor that reduces resistance is credibility. Receivers are less resistant if your request is reasonable and if you are believable. When the receiver does not know you, you may have to establish your expertise, refer to your credentials, or demonstrate your competence. Even when you are known, you may have to establish your knowledge in a given area. Some charities establish their credibility by displaying on their stationery the names of famous people who serve on their board. The credibility of speakers making presentations is usually confirmed by someone who introduces them.

Motivating Action

After gaining attention, building interest, and reducing resistance, you'll want to inspire the receiver to act. This is where your planning pays dividends. Knowing exactly what action you favour before you start to write enables you to point your arguments toward this important final paragraph. Here you will make your

Figure 10.2 ***Techniques for Crafting Successful Persuasive Messages***

Gaining Attention	Building Interest	Reducing Resistance	Motivating Action
Summary of problem	Facts, figures	Anticipate objections	Describe specific request
Unexpected statement	Expert opinion	Offer counterarguments	Sound confident
Reader benefit	Examples	Use what-if scenarios	Make action easy to take
Compliment	Specific details	Establish credibility	Offer incentive
Related fact	Direct benefits	Demonstrate competence	Don't provide excuses
Stimulating question	Indirect benefits	Show value of proposal	Repeat main benefit

recommendation as specifically and confidently as possible—without seeming pushy. Compare the following closings for a persuasive memo recommending training seminars in communication skills.

Too General
We are certain we can develop a series of training sessions that will improve the communication skills of your employees.

Too Timid
If you agree that our training proposal has merit, perhaps we could begin the series in June.

Too Pushy
Because we're convinced that you will want to begin improving the skills of your employees immediately, we've scheduled your series to begin in June.

Effective
You will see decided improvement in the communication skills of your employees. Please call me at 439-2201 by May 1 to give your approval so that training sessions may start in June, as we discussed.

Note how the last opening suggests a specific and easy-to-follow action. Figure 10.2 summarizes techniques for overcoming resistance and crafting successful persuasive messages.

Persuasive requests motivate action by specifying exactly what should be done.

Being Persuasive but Ethical

Business communicators may be tempted to make their persuasion even more forceful by fudging on the facts, exaggerating a point, omitting something crucial, or providing deceptive emphasis. A persuader is effective only when he or she is believable. If receivers suspect that they are being manipulated or misled or if they find any part of the argument untruthful, the entire argument fails. Persuaders can also fall into traps of logic without being aware of it. Avoid the common logical fallacies of circular reasoning, begging the question, and post hoc (after, thus, because).

Persuasion becomes unethical when facts are distorted, overlooked, or manipulated with intent to deceive. Of course, persuaders naturally want to put forth their strongest case, but that argument must be based on truth, objectivity, and fairness. In prompting ethical and truthful persuasion, two factors act as powerful motivators. The first is the desire to preserve your reputation and credibility. Once lost, a good name is difficult to regain. An equally important force prompting ethical behaviour, though, is your opinion of yourself.

Ethical business communicators maintain credibility and respect by being honest, fair, and objective.

learning objective

3

Writing Successful Persuasive Requests

The indirect pattern is appropriate when requesting favours and action.

Convincing someone to change a belief or to perform an action when that individual is reluctant requires planning and skill—and sometimes a little luck. If the request is in writing, rather than face to face, the task is a bit harder. However, persuasion is often more precise and controlled when you can think through your purpose and prepare a thoughtful message in writing. The indirect pattern gives you an effective structure.

Requesting Favours and Actions

Persuading someone to do something that largely benefits you may not be the easiest task. Fortunately, many individuals and companies are willing to grant requests for time, money, information, special privileges, and cooperation. They grant these favours for a variety of reasons. They may just happen to be interested in your project, or they may see goodwill potential for themselves. Often, though, they comply because they see that others will benefit from the request. Professionals sometimes feel obligated to contribute their time or expertise to "pay their dues."

You may find that you have few direct benefits to offer in your efforts to persuade. Instead, you'll be focusing on indirect benefits, as the writer does in Figure 10.3. In asking a manager to speak before a restaurant industry meeting, the writer has little to offer as a direct benefit other than a $200 honorarium. But indirectly, the writer offers enticements such as an enthusiastic audience and a chance to help other restaurateurs solve common problems. This persuasive request appeals primarily to the reader's desire to serve her profession—although a receptive audience and an opportunity to function as an expert among one's peers have a certain ego appeal as well. Together, these appeals—professional, egoistic, monetary—make a persuasive argument rich and effective.

An offer to work as an intern, at no cost to a company, would seem to require little persuasion. Many companies, however, hesitate to participate in internship programs because student interns require supervision, desk space, and equipment. They also pose an insurance liability threat.

In Figure 10.4 college student Melanie Harris seeks to persuade Software Enterprises to accept her as an intern. In the analysis process before writing, Melanie thought long and hard about what benefits she could offer the reader and how she could present them strategically. She decided that the offer of a trained college student's free labour was her strongest benefit. Thus she opens with it, as well as mentioning the same benefit in the letter body and in the closing. After opening with the main audience benefit, she introduces the actual request ("Could you use the part-time services of a college senior . . . ?").

In the interest section, Melanie tells why she is making the request and describes its value in terms of direct and indirect benefits. Notice how she transforms obstacles (lack of equipment or desk space) into helpful suggestions about how her services would free up other staff members to perform more important tasks. She delays mentioning a negative (being able to work only 15 hours a week and only in the afternoon) until she builds interest and reduces resistance. And she closes confidently and motivates action with reference to both direct and indirect benefits.

Persuading Within Organizations

Instructions or directives moving downward from superiors to subordinates usually require little persuasion. Employees expect to be directed how to perform their jobs. These messages (such as information about procedures, equipment, or customer

FIGURE 10.3 ***Persuasive Favour Request***

1 Prewriting

ANALYZE: The purpose of this letter is to persuade the reader to speak at a dinner meeting.

ANTICIPATE: Although the reader is busy, she may respond to appeals to her ego (describing her previous excellent presentation) and to her professionalism.

ADAPT: Because the reader may be uninterested at first and require persuasion, use the indirect pattern.

2 Writing

RESEARCH: Study the receiver's interests and find ways to relate this request to her interests.

ORGANIZE: Gain attention by opening with praise or a stimulating remark. Build interest with explanations and facts. Show how compliance benefits the reader and others. Reduce resistance by providing ideas for the dinner talk.

COMPOSE: Prepare a first draft with the intention to revise.

3 Revising

REVISE: Revise to show direct and indirect benefits more clearly.

PROOFREAD: Check spelling of *restaurateur.* In the fourth paragraph, use a semicolon in the compound sentence. Start all lines at the left for a block-style letter.

EVALUATE: Will this letter convince the reader to accept the invitation?

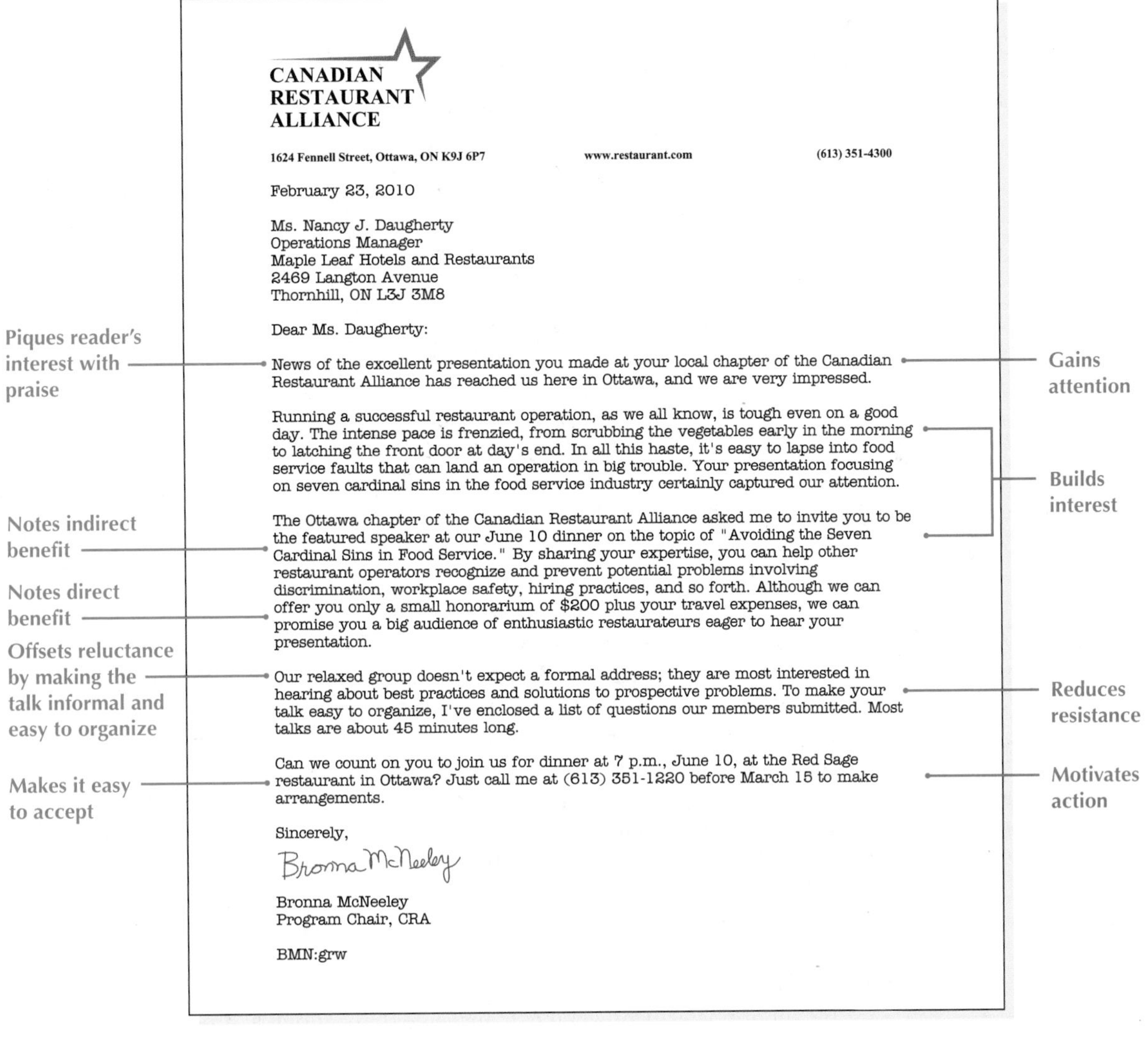

CANADIAN RESTAURANT ALLIANCE

1624 Fennell Street, Ottawa, ON K9J 6P7 www.restaurant.com (613) 351-4300

February 23, 2010

Ms. Nancy J. Daugherty
Operations Manager
Maple Leaf Hotels and Restaurants
2469 Langton Avenue
Thornhill, ON L3J 3M8

Dear Ms. Daugherty:

News of the excellent presentation you made at your local chapter of the Canadian Restaurant Alliance has reached us here in Ottawa, and we are very impressed.

Running a successful restaurant operation, as we all know, is tough even on a good day. The intense pace is frenzied, from scrubbing the vegetables early in the morning to latching the front door at day's end. In all this haste, it's easy to lapse into food service faults that can land an operation in big trouble. Your presentation focusing on seven cardinal sins in the food service industry certainly captured our attention.

The Ottawa chapter of the Canadian Restaurant Alliance asked me to invite you to be the featured speaker at our June 10 dinner on the topic of "Avoiding the Seven Cardinal Sins in Food Service." By sharing your expertise, you can help other restaurant operators recognize and prevent potential problems involving discrimination, workplace safety, hiring practices, and so forth. Although we can offer you only a small honorarium of $200 plus your travel expenses, we can promise you a big audience of enthusiastic restaurateurs eager to hear your presentation.

Our relaxed group doesn't expect a formal address; they are most interested in hearing about best practices and solutions to prospective problems. To make your talk easy to organize, I've enclosed a list of questions our members submitted. Most talks are about 45 minutes long.

Can we count on you to join us for dinner at 7 p.m., June 10, at the Red Sage restaurant in Ottawa? Just call me at (613) 351-1220 before March 15 to make arrangements.

Sincerely,

Bronna McNeeley

Bronna McNeeley
Program Chair, CRA

BMN:grw

FIGURE 10.4 ***Persuasive Action Request***

4320 North Dinosaur Trail
Drumheller, AB T0J 0Y1

January 8, 2010

Ms. Nancy Ashley, Director
Human Resources Department
Software Enterprises, Inc.
268 Redmond Avenue
Calgary, AB T3B 6W7

Dear Ms. Ashley:

How often do college-trained specialists offer to work for nothing?

Very infrequently, I imagine. But that's the offer I'm making to Software Enterprises. During the next 14 weeks, could you use the part-time services of a college senior with communication and computer skills?

To gain work experience and to earn three units of credit, I would like to become an intern at Software Enterprises. My skills in Word and Excel, as well as training in letter and report writing, could be put to use in your Customer Service, Human Resources, Legal, Documentation, or other departments.

By granting this internship, your company not only secures the skills of an enthusiastic and well-trained college student, but it also performs a valuable service to Edmonds College. Your cooperation provides an opportunity for students to acquire the kind of job training that college classrooms simply cannot give.

If equipment and desk space at Software Enterprises are limited, you may want me to fill in for employees who can then be freed up for other projects, training, or release time. In regard to supervision you'll find that I require little direction once I start a project. Moreover, you don't need to worry about insurance, as our college provides liability coverage for all students at internship sites.

Although I'm taking classes in the mornings, I'm available to work afternoons for 15 hours a week. Please examine the attached résumé to confirm my preparation and qualifications.

Do you have any questions about my proposal to become an intern? To talk with me about it, please call 893-2155. I could begin working for you as early as February 1. You gain a free employee, and you also provide an appreciative local college student with much-needed job training.

Sincerely,

Melanie E. Harris

Melanie E. Harris

Enclosure

Starts with date and address in personal business style

Introduces request after presenting main benefit

Uses strongest benefit for stimulating opener

Notes direct benefit

Notes indirect benefit

Anticipates three obstacles and answers each

Introduces a negative in a positive way

Refers to enclosure only after presenting main points

Couples action request with reference to direct and indirect benefits

Internal persuasive memos present honest arguments detailing specific reader benefits.

service) follow the direct pattern, with the purpose immediately stated. However, employees are sometimes asked to perform in a capacity outside their work roles or to accept changes that are not in their best interests—such as pay cuts, job transfers, or reduced benefits. In these instances, a persuasive memo using the indirect pattern may be most effective.

The goal is not to manipulate employees or to seduce them with trickery. Rather, the goal is to present a strong but honest argument, emphasizing points that are important to the receiver. In business, honesty is not just the best policy—it's the *only* policy. Especially within your own organization, people see right through puffery and misrepresentation. For this reason, the indirect pattern is effective only when supported by accurate, honest evidence.

Another form of persuasion within organizations centres on suggestions made by subordinates. Convincing management to adopt a procedure or invest in a product or new equipment generally requires skilful communication. Managers are just as resistant to change as others. Providing evidence is critical when subordinates submit recommendations to their bosses. Be ready to back up your request with facts, figures, and evidence. A request that emphasizes how the proposal saves money or benefits the business is more persuasive than one that simply announces a good deal or tells how a plan works.

When selling an idea to management, writers often are successful if they make a strong case for saving money.

In Figure 10.5 (page 226), you see the draft copy of a persuasive memo that needs revision. The writer lacked organization and did not sell the benefits. When revising, it was apparent that a little more time spent on developing the persuasive argument would increase the chance of approval.

Notice that although the revision is longer, it is far more effective. Remember that a successful persuasive message will typically take more space than a direct message because proving a case requires evidence. Notice that the subject line in Figure 10.5 tells the purpose of the memo without disclosing the actual request. By delaying the request until she's had a chance to describe the problem and discuss a solution, the writer prevents the reader's premature rejection.

The strength of this revision, though, is in the clear presentation of comparison figures showing how much money can be saved by purchasing a remanufactured copier. Although the organization pattern is not obvious, the revised memo begins with an attention-getter (frank description of problem), builds interest (with easy-to-read facts and figures), provides benefits, and reduces resistance. Notice that the conclusion tells what action is to be taken, makes it easy to respond, and repeats the main benefit to motivate action.

Complaint Letters: Writing Persuasive Claims

Persuasive claim letters typically involve damaged products, mistaken billing, inaccurate shipments, warranty problems, return policies, insurance mix-ups, faulty merchandise, and so on. Generally, the direct pattern is best for requesting straightforward adjustments (see Chapter 9). When you feel your request is justified and will be granted, the direct strategy is most efficient. But if a past request has been refused or ignored or if you anticipate reluctance, then the indirect pattern is appropriate.

In a sense, a claim letter is a complaint letter. Someone is complaining about something that went wrong. Some complaint letters just vent anger; the writers are mad, and they want to tell someone about it. But if the goal is to change something (and why bother to write except to motivate change?), then persuasion is necessary. Effective claim letters make a reasonable request, present a logical case with clear facts, and adopt a moderate tone. Anger and emotion are not effective persuaders.

Effective complaint/adjustment letters make reasonable claims backed by solid evidence.

Logical Development. Strive for logical development in a claim letter. You might open with sincere praise, an objective statement of the problem, a point of agreement, or a quick review of what you have done to resolve the problem. Then you can explain precisely what happened or why your claim is legitimate. Don't provide a blow-by-blow chronology of details; just hit the highlights. Be sure to enclose copies of relevant invoices, shipping orders, warranties, and payments. And close with a clear statement of what you want done: refund, replacement, credit to your account, or other action. Be sure to think through the possibilities and make your request reasonable.

Moderate Tone. The tone of the letter is important. Don't suggest that the receiver intentionally deceived you or intentionally created the problem. Rather, appeal to the receiver's sense of responsibility and pride in its good name. Calmly express your disappointment in view of your high expectations of the product and the company. Communicating your feelings, without malice, is often your strongest appeal.

Adjustment requests should adopt a moderate tone, appeal to the receiver's sense of responsibility, and specify needed actions.

Janet Walker's letter, shown in Figure 10.6 (page 227), follows the persuasive pattern as she seeks to return three answering machines. Notice that she uses simplified

FIGURE 10.5 *Persuasive Memo*

DRAFT

TO: Kenneth Richardson, Vice President

Although you've opposed the purchase of additional copiers in the past, I think I've found a great deal on a copier that's just too good to pass up but we must act before May 1! Copy City has reconditioned copiers that are practically being given away. If we move fast, they will provide many free incentives—like a free copier stand, free starter supplies, free delivery, and free installation.

We must find a way to reduce copier costs in my department. Our current copier can't keep up with our demand. We're sending secretaries or sales reps to Copy Quick for an average of 10 000 copies a month. These copies cost 7 cents a page and waste a lot of time. We're making at least eight trips a week, adding up to a considerable expense in travel time and copy costs.

Please give this matter your immediate attention and get back to me as soon as possible. We don't want to miss this great deal!

Begins poorly with reminder of past negative feelings

Sounds high-pressured

Fails to compare costs and emphasize savings in logical, coherent presentation

Does not request or motivate specific action

REVISION

DATE: April 18, 2010

TO: Kenneth Richardson, Vice President

FROM: Mona Massey, Marketing

SUBJECT: Saving Time and Money on Copying

Describes topic without revealing request

Summarizes problem

We're losing money on our current copy services and wasting the time of employees as well. Because our Canon copier is in use constantly, we find it increasingly necessary to send major jobs out to Copy Quick. Just take a look at how much we spend each month for outside copy service:

Copy Costs: Outside Service

10 000 copies/month made at Copy Quick	$700.00
Salary costs for assistants to make 32 trips to drop off originals and pick up copies	384.00
Total	$1084.00

Uses headings and columns for easy comparison

When sales reps make the trips, the costs are even greater. Because this expense must be reduced, I've been considering alternatives. New copiers with collating capability and automatic multidrawer paper feeding are very expensive. But reconditioned copiers with all the features we need are available—and at attractive prices and terms. From Copy City we can get a fully remanufactured copier that is guaranteed to work like new. After we make an initial payment of $219, our monthly costs would look like this:

Copy Costs: Remanufactured Copier

Paper supplies for 10 000 copies	$130.00
Toner and copy supplies	95.00
Labour of assistants to make copies	130.00
Monthly financing charge for copier (purchase price of $1105 amortized at 10% with 29 payments)	34.52
Total	$389.52

Proves credibility of request with facts and figures

As you can see, **a remanufactured copier saves us nearly $700 per month.**

Highlights most important benefit

Provides more benefits

For a limited time Copy City is offering a free 15-day trial offer, a free copier stand (worth $165), free starter supplies, and free delivery and installation. We have office space available, and my staff is eager to add a second machine.

Counters possible resistance

Makes it easy to grant approval

Call me at Ext. 630 if you have questions. This copier is such a good opportunity that I've attached a purchase requisition authorizing the agreement with Copy City. With your approval before May 1, we can have our machine by May 10 and start saving time and nearly $700 every month. Fast action will also take advantage of Copy City's free start-up incentives.

Repeats main benefit with motivation to act quickly

Attachment

FIGURE 10.6 ***Claim (Complaint) Letter***

Tips for Writing Claim Letters and Making Complaints

- Begin with a compliment, point of agreement, statement of the problem, or brief review of action you have taken to resolve the problem.
- Provide identifying data.
- Prove that your claim is valid; explain why the receiver is responsible.
- Enclose document copies supporting your claim.
- Appeal to the receiver's fairness, ethical and legal responsibilities, and desire for customer satisfaction.
- Describe your feelings and your disappointment.
- Avoid sounding angry, emotional, or irrational.
- Close by telling exactly what you want done.

CHAMPION AUTOMOTIVES
141 Rue Champlain, Gatineau, QC J8T 3H9 (819) 690-3500

November 21, 2010

Customer Service
Raytronic Electronics
57 Emile Simard Avenue
Edmunston, NB E3V 3N9

SUBJECT: CODE-A-PHONE MODEL 100S

Uses simplified letter style when name of receiver is unknown

Your Code-A-Phone Model 100S answering unit came well recommended. We liked our neighbour's unit so well that we purchased three for different departments in our business.

Begins with compliment

After the three units were unpacked and installed, we discovered a problem. Apparently our office fluorescent lighting interferes with the electronics in these units. When the lights are on, heavy static interrupts every telephone call. When the lights are off, the static disappears.

Describes problem calmly

We can't replace the fluorescent lights, so we tried to return the Code-A-Phones to the place of purchase (Office Mart, 2560 Hastings Street, Ottawa, ON K1N 5A2). A salesperson inspected the units and said they could not be returned because they were not defective and they had been used.

Because the descriptive literature and instructions for the Code-A-Phones say nothing about avoiding use in rooms with fluorescent lighting, we expected no trouble. We were quite disappointed that this well-engineered unit—with its time/date stamp, room monitor, and auto-dial features—failed to perform as we hoped it would.

Suggests responsibility

Stresses disappointment

If you have a model with similar features that would work in our offices, give me a call. Otherwise, please authorize the return of these units and refund the purchase price of $519.45 (see enclosed invoice). We're confident that a manufacturer with your reputation for excellent products and service will want to resolve this matter quickly.

Tells what action to take

Appeals to company's desire to preserve good reputation

Janet Walker
JANET WALKER, PRESIDENT

JPW:ett
Enclosure

letter style (skipping the salutation and complimentary close) because she doesn't have a person's name to use in addressing the letter. Note also her positive opening, her calm and well-documented claims, and her request for specific action.

The following checklist reviews pointers for helping you make persuasive requests of all kinds.

Checklist for Making Persuasive Requests

- ✓ **Gain attention.** In requesting favours, begin with a compliment, statement of agreement, unexpected fact, stimulating question, reader benefit, summary of the problem, or candid plea for help. For claims and complaints, also consider opening with a review of actions you have taken to resolve the problem.

- ✓ **Build interest.** Prove the accuracy and merit of your request with solid evidence, including facts, figures, expert opinion, examples, and details. Suggest direct and indirect benefits for the receiver. Avoid sounding high-pressured, angry, or emotional.

- ✓ **Reduce resistance.** Identify what factors will be obstacles to the receiver; offer counterarguments. Demonstrate your credibility by being knowledgeable. In requesting favours or making recommendations, show how the receiver or others will benefit. In making claims, appeal to the receiver's sense of fairness and desire for goodwill. Express your disappointment.

- ✓ **Motivate action.** Confidently ask for specific action. For favours, include an end date (if appropriate) and try to repeat a key benefit.

learning objective

4

Write effective yet ethical sales and marketing messages.

Planning and Composing Effective Sales Messages

Sales messages involve using persuasion to promote specific products and services. In our coverage we will be most concerned with sales messages delivered by mail. Many of the concepts you will learn about marketing persuasion, however, can be applied to online, wireless, TV, print, radio, and other media. The best sales messages, whether delivered by e-marketing or direct mail, have much in common. In this section you will study how to apply the 3-x-3 writing process to sales messages. Then you will learn techniques developed by experts to draft effective sales messages, both in print and online.

Direct-Mail Sales Letters

Our main focus in this section will be on writing sales letters as part of direct-mail marketing. Traditional sales letters are a powerful means to make sales, generate leads, boost retail traffic, solicit donations, and direct consumers to Web sites. Mail allows a personalized, tangible, three-dimensional message that is less invasive than telephone solicitations and less reviled than unsolicited e-mail.

Professionals who specialize in traditional direct-mail services have made it a science. They analyze a market, develop an effective mailing list, study the product, prepare a sophisticated campaign aimed at a target audience, and motivate the reader to act. You have probably received many direct-mail packages, often called "junk mail." These packages typically contain a sales letter, a brochure, a price list, illustrations of the product, testimonials, and other persuasive appeals.

We are most concerned here with the sales letter: its strategy, organization, and evidence. Because sales letters are generally written by specialists, you may never write one on the job. Why, then, learn how to write a sales letter? In many ways, every letter we create is a form of sales letter. We sell our ideas, our organizations, and ourselves. Learning the techniques of sales writing will help you be more successful in any communication that requires persuasion and promotion. Furthermore, you'll recognize sales strategies, thus enabling you to become a more perceptive consumer of ideas, products, and services.

Studying marketing messages helps consumers become more perceptive in understanding sales strategies.

Applying the 3-x-3 Writing Process to Sales Messages

Marketing professionals analyze every aspect of a sales message because consumers reject most direct-mail offers. Like the experts, you'll want to pay close attention to the preparatory steps of analysis and adaptation before writing the actual message.

Analyzing the Product and Purpose. Before sitting down to write a sales letter, you must study the product carefully. What can you learn about its design, construction, raw materials, and manufacturing process, and about its ease of use, efficiency, durability, and applications? Be sure to consider warranties, service, price, premiums, exclusivity, and special appeal. At the same time, evaluate the competition so that you can compare your product's strengths against the competitor's weaknesses. Now you're ready to identify your central selling points. Analyzing your product and studying the competition help you determine what to emphasize in your sales letter.

Successful sales messages require research on the product or service offered and analysis of the purpose for writing.

Another important decision in the preparatory stage involves the specific purpose of your letter. Before you write the first word of your message, know what response you want and what central selling points you will emphasize to achieve that purpose.

Adapting to the Audience. Blanket mailings sent "cold" to occupants generally produce a low response—typically less than 2 percent. That means that 98 percent of the receivers usually toss direct-mail sales letters directly into the wastebasket. But the response rate can be increased dramatically by targeting the audience through selected database mailing lists. These lists can be purchased or compiled. By directing your message to a selected group, you can make certain assumptions about the receivers. You would expect similar interests, needs, and demographics (age, income, and other characteristics). With this knowledge you can adapt the sales letter to a specific audience.

Crafting a Winning Sales Message

Your primary goal in writing a sales message is to get someone to devote a few moments of attention to it.[4] You may be promoting a product, a service, an idea, or yourself. In each case the most effective messages will (a) gain attention, (b) build interest, (c) reduce resistance, and (d) motivate action. This is the same recipe we studied earlier, but the ingredients are different.

Openers for sales messages should be brief, honest, relevant, and provocative.

Gaining Attention. One of the most critical elements of a sales letter is its opening paragraph. This opener should be short (one to five lines), honest, relevant, and stimulating. Marketing pros have found that eye-catching typographical arrangements or provocative messages, such as the following, can hook a reader's attention:

- **Offer:** *A free trip to Hawaii is just the beginning!*
- **Promise:** *Now you can raise your sales income by 50 percent or even more with the proven techniques found in . . . .*
- **Question:** *Do you yearn for an honest, fulfilling relationship?*
- **Quotation or proverb:** *Necessity is the mother of invention.*
- **Fact:** *The Greenland Inuit ate more fat than anyone in the world. And yet . . . they had virtually no heart disease.*
- **Product feature:** *Volvo's snazzy new convertible ensures your safety with a roll bar that pops out when the car tips 40 degrees to the side.*
- **Testimonial:** *My name is Sheldon Schultz. I am a medical doctor. I am also a multimillionaire. I didn't make my millions by practising medicine, though; I made them by investing in my spare time.*
- **Startling statement:** *Let the poor and hungry feed themselves! For just $100 they can.*
- **Personalized action setting:** *It's 4:30 p.m. and you've got to make a decision. You need everybody's opinion, no matter where they are. Before you pick up your phone to call them one at a time, pick up this card: Bell Canada Teleconference Services.*

Other openings calculated to capture attention might include a solution to a problem, an anecdote, a personalized statement using the receiver's name, or a relevant current event.

Building Interest. In this phase of your sales message, you should describe clearly the product or service. In simple language emphasize the central selling points that you identified during your prewriting analysis. Those selling points can be developed using rational or emotional appeals.

Rational appeals reflect reason and intellect.

Emotional appeals reflect status, ego, and sensual feelings.

Dual appeals combine reason and emotion.

Rational appeals are associated with reason and intellect. They translate selling points into references to making or saving money, increasing efficiency, or making the best use of resources. In general, rational appeals are appropriate when a product is expensive, long-lasting, or important to health, security, or financial success. Emotional appeals relate to status, ego, and sensual feelings. Appealing to the emotions is sometimes effective when a product is inexpensive, short-lived, or nonessential. Many clever sales messages, however, combine emotional and rational strategies for a dual appeal. Consider these examples:

Rational Appeal

You can buy the things you need and want, pay household bills, and pay off higher-cost loans and credit cards—as soon as you're approved and your Credit-Line account is opened.

Emotional Appeal

Leave the urban bustle behind and escape to sun-soaked Bermuda! To recharge your batteries with an injection of sun and surf, all you need are your bathing suit, a little suntan lotion, and your Credit-Line card.

Dual Appeal
New Credit-Line cardholders are immediately eligible for a $200 travel certificate and additional discounts at fun-filled resorts. Save up to 40 percent while lying on a beach in picturesque, sun-soaked Bermuda, the year-round resort island.

However, a physical description is not enough. Zig Ziglar, thought by some to be America's greatest salesperson, points out that no matter how well you know your product, no one is persuaded by cold, hard facts alone. In the end, he contends, people buy because of product benefits.[5] Your job is to translate those cold facts into warm feelings and reader benefits.

Reducing Resistance. Marketing pros use a number of techniques to overcome resistance and build desire. When price is an obstacle, consider these suggestions:

- Delay mentioning price until after you've created a desire for the product.
- Show the price in small units, such as the price per issue of a magazine.
- Demonstrate how the reader saves money by, for instance, subscribing for two or three years.
- Compare your prices with those of a competitor.

In addition, you need to anticipate other objections and questions the receiver may have. When possible, translate these objections into selling points (*If you're worried about training your staff members on the new software, remember that our offer includes $1000 worth of on-site one-on-one instruction*). Other techniques to overcome resistance and prove the credibility of the product include the following:

- **Testimonials:** *"I never stopped eating, yet I lost 50 kilograms." — Tina Rivers, Woodstock, Ontario*
- **Names of satisfied users (with permission, of course):** *Enclosed is a partial list of private pilots who enthusiastically subscribe to our service.*
- **Money-back guarantee or warranty:** *We offer the longest warranties in the business—all parts and service on-site for five years!*
- **Free trial or sample:** *We're so confident that you'll like our new accounting program that we want you to try it absolutely free.*
- **Performance tests, polls, or awards:** *Our TP-3000 was named Best Web Phone, and Etown.com voted it Cell Phone of the Year.*

Techniques for motivating action include offering a gift or incentive, limiting an offer, and guaranteeing satisfaction.

Motivating Action. All the effort put into a sales message is wasted if the reader fails to act. To make it easy for readers to act, you can provide a reply card, a stamped and preaddressed envelope, a toll-free telephone number, an easy-to-scan Web site, or a promise of a follow-up call. Because readers often need an extra push, consider including additional motivators, such as the following:

- **Offer a gift:** *You'll receive a free cell phone with the purchase of any new car.*
- **Promise an incentive:** *With every new, paid subscription, we'll plant a tree in one of Canada's national parks.*
- **Limit the offer:** *Only the first 100 customers receive free cheques.*
- **Set a deadline:** *You must act before June 1 to get these low prices.*
- **Guarantee satisfaction:** *We'll return your full payment if you're not entirely satisfied—no questions asked.*

The final paragraph of the sales letter carries the punchline. This is where you tell readers what you want them to do and give them reasons for doing it. Most sales letters also include postscripts because they make irresistible reading. Even readers who might skim over or bypass paragraphs are drawn to a P.S. Therefore, use a postscript to reveal your strongest motivator, to add a special inducement for a quick response, or to reemphasize a central selling point.

Because direct mail is an expensive way to advertise, messages should present complete information in a personalized tone for specific audiences.

Putting It All Together. Sales letters are a preferred marketing medium because they can be personalized, directed to target audiences, and filled with a more complete message than other advertising media. But direct mail is expensive. That's why the total sales message is crafted so painstakingly.

Figure 10.7 shows a sales letter addressed to a target group of small-business owners. To sell the new magazine *Small Business Monthly*, the letter incorporates all four components of an effective persuasive message. Notice that the personalized action-setting opener places the reader in a familiar situation (getting into an elevator) and draws an analogy between failing to reach the top floor and failing to achieve a business goal. The writer develops a rational central selling point (a magazine that provides valuable information for a growing small business) and repeats this selling point in all the components of the letter. Notice, too, how a testimonial from a small-business executive lends support to the sales message, and how the closing pushes for action. Because the cost of the magazine is not a selling feature, price is mentioned only on the reply card. This sales letter saves its strongest motivator—a free booklet—for the high-impact P.S. line.

Whether you actually write sales letters on the job or merely receive them, you'll better understand their organization and appeal by reviewing this chapter and the tips in the following checklist.

Checklist for Writing Sales Letters

- ✓ **Gain attention.** Offer something valuable, promise the reader a result, pose a stimulating question, describe a product feature, present a testimonial, make a startling statement, or show the reader in an action setting. Other attention-getters are a solution to a problem, an anecdote, a statement using the receiver's name, or a relevant current event.

- ✓ **Build interest.** Describe the product in terms of what it does for the reader: saves or makes money, reduces effort, improves health, produces pleasure, boosts status. Connect cold facts with warm feelings and needs.

- ✓ **Reduce resistance.** Counter reluctance with testimonials, money-back guarantees, attractive warranties, trial offers, or free samples. Build credibility with results of performance tests, polls, or awards. If price is not a selling feature, describe it in small units (*only 99 cents an issue*), show it as savings, or tell how it compares favourably with the competition's.

- ✓ **Motivate action.** Close with a repetition of the central selling point and clear instructions for an easy action to be taken. Prompt the reader to act immediately with a gift, incentive, limited offer, deadline, and/or guarantee of satisfaction. Put the strongest motivator in a postscript.

FIGURE 10.7 ***Sales Letter***

1 Prewriting

ANALYZE: The purpose of this letter is to persuade the reader to return the reply card and subscribe to *Small Business Monthly*.

ANTICIPATE: The targeted audience consists of small-business owners. The central selling point is providing practical business data that will help their businesses grow.

ADAPT: Because readers will be reluctant, use the indirect pattern.

2 Writing

RESEARCH: Gather facts to promote your product, including testimonials.

ORGANIZE: Gain attention by opening with a personalized action picture. Build interest with an analogy and a description of magazine features. Use a testimonial to reduce resistance. Motivate action with a free booklet and an easy-reply card.

COMPOSE: Prepare first draft for pilot study.

3 Revising

REVISE: Use short paragraphs and short sentences. Replace words like *malfunction* with *glitch*.

PROOFREAD: Indent long quotations on the left and right sides. Italicize or underscore titles of publications. Hyphenate *hard-headed* and *first-of-its-kind*.

EVALUATE: Monitor the response rate to this letter to assess its effectiveness.

small business monthly
160 Duncan Mills Road • Toronto, ON M38 1Z5

April 15, 2010

Mr. James Wehrley
1608 Montlieu Avenue
Listowel, ON N4W 3A2

Dear Mr. Wehrley:

Puts reader into action setting

You walk into the elevator and push the button for the top floor. The elevator glides upward. You step back and relax.

Gains attention

But the elevator never reaches the top. A glitch in its electronics prevents it from processing the information it needs to take you to your destination.

Suggests analogy

Do you see a similarity between your growing company and this elevator? You're aiming for the top, but a lack of information halts your progress. Now you can put your company into gear and propel it toward success with a new publication—*Small Business Monthly*.

Emphasizes central selling point

This first-of-its-kind magazine brings you marketing tips, hard-headed business pointers, opportunities, and inspiration. This is the kind of current information you need today to be where you want to be tomorrow. One executive wrote:

Builds interest

Uses testimonial for credibility

> As president of a small manufacturing company, I read several top business publications, but I get my "bread and butter" from *Small Business Monthly*. I'm not interested in a lot of "pie in the sky" and theory. I find practical problems and how to solve them in *SBM*.
> —Mitchell M. Perry, Oshawa, ON

Mr. Perry's words are the best recommendation I can offer you to try *SBM*. In less time than you might spend on an average business lunch, you learn the latest in management, operations, finance, taxes, business law, compensation, and advertising.

Reduces resistance

Repeats central sales pitch in last sentence

To evaluate *Small Business Monthly* without cost or obligation, let me send you a free issue. Just initial and return the enclosed card to start receiving a wealth of practical information that could keep your company travelling upward to its goal.

Motivates action

Cordially,

Cheryl Owings

Cheryl Owings
Vice President, Circulation

Spotlights free offer in P.S. to prompt immediate reply

P.S. Act before May 15 and I'll send you our valuable booklet *Managing for Success*, revealing more than 100 secrets for helping small businesses grow.

Enclosure

learning objective 5

Developing Persuasive Press Releases

Press (news) releases announce information about your company to the media: new products, new managers, new facilities, participation in community projects, awards given or received, joint ventures, donations, or seminars and demonstrations. Naturally, you hope that this news will be published and provide good publicity for your company. But this kind of largely self-serving information is not always appealing to magazine and newspaper editors or to TV producers. To get them to read beyond the first sentence, try these suggestions:

- Open with an attention-getting lead or a summary of the important facts.
- Include answers to the five Ws and one H (*who, what, when, where, why,* and *how*) in the article—but not all in the first sentence!
- Appeal to the audience of the target media. Emphasize reader benefits in the style of the focus publication or newscast.
- Present the most important information early, followed by supporting information. Don't put your best ideas last because they may be chopped off or ignored.
- Make the release visually appealing. Limit the text to one or two double-spaced pages with attractive formatting.
- Look and sound credible—no typos, no imaginative spelling or punctuation, no factual errors.

Effective press releases feature an attention-getting opener, place key information up front, appeal to the target audience, and maintain visual interest.

The most important ingredient of a press release, of course, is *news*. Articles that merely plug products end up in the circular file. Newspapers and magazines will be most likely to publish a release that is both informative and interesting. Many companies provide readily available press information, including releases and photos, on their Web sites.

Summary of Learning Objectives

1 **Apply the 3-x-3 writing process to persuasive messages.** Persuasion may be defined as the ability to use argument or discussion to change an individual's beliefs or actions. The first step in the writing process for a persuasive message is analysis of the audience and purpose. Writers must know exactly what they want receivers to do or think. The second step involves thinking of ways to adapt the message to the audience. Particularly important is expressing the request so that it may benefit the reader. Next, the writer must collect data and organize it into an appropriate strategy. An indirect strategy is probably best if the audience will resist the request.

2 **Explain the components of a persuasive message and how to blend them effectively.** The most effective persuasive messages gain attention by opening with a problem, unexpected statement, reader benefit, compliment, related fact, stimulating question, or similar device. They build interest with facts, expert opinions, examples, details, and additional reader benefits. They reduce resistance by anticipating objections and presenting counterarguments. They conclude by motivating a specific action and making it easy for the reader to respond. Skilled communicators avoid distortion, exaggeration, and deception when making persuasive arguments.

3 **Write successful persuasive messages, including requesting favours and actions, persuading within organizations, and writing complaint letters.** When you ask for a favour or action, the indirect pattern is appropriate. This means delaying the request until after logical reasons have been presented. Such messages should emphasize, if possible, benefits to the reader. Appeals to professionalism are often a useful technique. Writers should counter any anticipated resistance with explanations and motivate action in the closing. Use the same indirect method when writing internal messages that require persuasion. These messages might begin with a frank discussion of a problem. They build interest by emphasizing points that are important to the readers. They support the request with accurate, honest evidence. When writing about damaged products, mistaken billing, or other complaints and claims, the indirect pattern is appropriate. These messages might begin with a sincere compliment or an objective statement of the problem. They explain concisely why a claim is legitimate. Copies of relevant documents should be enclosed. The message should conclude with a clear statement of the action to be taken.

4 **Plan and compose outstanding sales messages.** Before writing a sales message, it's necessary to analyze the product and purpose carefully. The letter begins with an attention-getting statement that is short, honest, relevant, and stimulating. It builds interest by describing the product or service clearly in simple language, incorporating appropriate appeals. Testimonials, a money-back guarantee, a free trial, or some other device can reduce resistance. A gift, incentive, deadline, or other device can motivate action.

5 **Describe the basic elements in persuasive press releases.** Effective press releases usually open with an attention-getting lead or summary of the important facts. They attempt to answer the questions *who*, *what*, *when*, *where*, *why*, and *how*. They are written carefully to appeal to the audience of the target media. The best press releases present the most important information early, make the release visually appealing, and look and sound credible.

chapter review

1. List the four key elements in a persuasive request. (Objs. 1 and 2)
2. List six or more techniques for opening a persuasive request for a favour. (Obj. 2)
3. List techniques for building interest in a persuasive request for a favour. (Obj. 3)
4. Describe ways to reduce resistance in persuasive requests. (Obj. 3)
5. How should a persuasive request end? (Objs. 2 and 3)
6. When does persuasion become unethical? (Obj. 2)
7. What are the differences between direct and indirect reader benefits? Give an original example of each (other than those described). (Obj. 3)
8. When would persuasion be necessary in messages moving downward in organizations? (Obj. 3)
9. Why are persuasive messages usually longer than direct messages? (Objs. 1–4)
10. When is it necessary for a subordinate to be persuasive in addressing a superior on the job? (Obj. 3)
11. What is an appropriate tone for a claim letter? (Obj. 3)
12. Name eight or more ways to attract attention in opening a sales message. (Obj. 4)
13. How do rational appeals differ from emotional appeals? Give an original example of each. (Obj. 4)
14. Name five or more ways to motivate action in closing a sales message. (Obj. 5)
15. List five or more topics that an organization might feature in a press release. (Obj. 5)

critical thinking

1. How are requests for action and sales letters similar and how are they different? (Objs. 3 and 4)
2. What are some of the underlying motivations that prompt individuals to agree to requests that do not directly benefit them or their organizations? (Objs. 2–4)
3. In view of the burden that "junk mail" places on society (depleted landfill capacity, declining timber supplies, overburdened postal system), how can it be justified? (Obj. 4)
4. Why is it important to know your needs and have documentation when you make requests of superiors? (Obj. 3)

activities

10.1 Document for Analysis: Weak Persuasive Memo (Obj. 3)

Your Task. Analyze the following memo, which suffers from many writing faults. List its weaknesses. If your instructor directs, revise the letter.

DATE: Current
TO: Candace Daly, Vice President, Marketing
FROM: Robert Forsythe, Exhibit Manager
SUBJECT: TRADE BOOTH

Trade shows are a great way for us to meet customers and sell our Life Fitness equipment. But instead of expanding our visits to these trade shows, we continue to cut back the number that we attend. And we send fewer staff members. I know that you've been asking us to find ways to reduce costs, but perhaps we're not going about it right.

With increased air fares and hotel charges, my staff has tried to find ways to live within our very tight budget. Yet, we're being asked to find other ways to reduce our costs. I'm currently thinking ahead to the big Toronto trade show coming up in September.

One area where we could make a change is in the gift that we give away. In the past we have presented booth visitors with a nine-colour T-shirt that is silk-screened and gorgeous. But it comes at a cost of $15 for each and every one of these beauties from a top-name designer. To save money, I suggest that we try a $4 T-shirt made in China, which is reasonably presentable. It's got our name on it, and, after all, folks just use these shirts for workouts. Who cares if it is a fancy silk-screened T-shirt or a functional Chinese one that has "Life Fitness" plastered on the chest? Since we give away 2 000 T-shirts at our largest show, we could save big bucks by dumping the designer shirt. But we have to act quickly. I've enclosed a cheap one for you to see.

Let me know what you think.

Rich chapter resources are available on the Web site.

10.2 Document for Analysis: Poor Claim Letter (Obj. 3)

Your Task. Analyze the following poorly written claim letter. List its weaknesses. If your instructor directs, revise it and include mailing information.

Dear Sir:

Three months ago we purchased four of your E-Studio 120 photocopiers, and we've had nothing but trouble ever since.

Our salesperson, Julia Franks, assured us that the E-Studio 120 could easily handle our volume of 3 000 copies a day. This seemed strange since the sales brochure said that the E-Studio 120 was meant for 500 copies a day. But we believed Ms. Franks. Big mistake! Our four E-Studio 120 copiers are down constantly; we can't go on like this. Because they're still under warranty, they eventually get repaired. But we're losing considerable business in downtime.

Your Ms. Franks has been less than helpful, so I telephoned the district manager, Ron Rivera. I suggested that we trade in our E-Studio 120 copiers (which we got for $2500 each) on two E-Studio 600 models (at $13 500 each). However, Mr. Rivera said he would have to charge 50 percent depreciation on our E-Studio 120 copiers. What a ripoff! I think that 20 percent depreciation is more reasonable since we've had the machines only three months. Mr. Rivera said he would get back to me, and I haven't heard from him since.

I'm writing to your headquarters because I have no faith in either Ms. Franks or Mr. Rivera, and I need action on these machines. If you understood anything about business, you would see what a sweet deal I'm offering you. I'm willing to stick with your company and purchase your most expensive model—but I can't take such a steep loss on the E-Studio 120 copiers. The E-Studio 120 copiers are relatively new; you should be able to sell them with no trouble. And think of all the money you'll save by not having your repair technicians making constant trips to service our 120 copiers! Please let me hear from you immediately.

Sincerely yours,

10.3 Sales Letter Analysis (Obj. 4)

Your Task. Select a one- or two-page sales letter received by you or a friend. Study the letter and then answer these questions:

a. What techniques capture the reader's attention?
b. Is the opening effective? Explain.
c. What are the central selling points?
d. Does the letter use rational or emotional appeals, or a combination of both? Explain.
e. What reader benefits are suggested?
f. How does the letter build interest in the product or service?
g. How is price handled?
h. How does the letter anticipate reader resistance and offer counterarguments?
i. What action is the reader to take? How is the action made easy?
j. What motivators spur the reader to act quickly?

10.4 Persuasive Request: A Helping Hand for College Expenses (Obj. 3)

CRITICAL THINKING | TEAM

After working a few years, you would like to extend your college education on a part-time basis. You know that your further education can benefit your employer, but you can't really afford the fees for tuition and books. You've heard that many companies offer reimbursement for fees and books when employees complete approved courses with a grade of C or higher.

Your Task. In teams discuss the best way to approach an employer whom you wish to persuade to start a tuition/books reimbursement program. How could such a program help the employer? Remember that the most successful requests help receivers see what's in it for them. What objections might your employer raise? How can you counter them? After discussing strategies in teams, write a team memo or individual memos to your boss (for a company where you now work or one with which you are familiar). Persuade her or him to act on your action request.

10.5 Persuasive Favour/Action Request: How About Mandatory Tipping? (Obj. 3)

TEAM

As a server at the Tejas Grill, you have occasionally been "stiffed" by a patron who left no tip. You know your service is excellent, but some customers just don't get it. They seem to think that tips are optional, a sign of appreciation. For servers, however, tips are 80 percent of their income.

In a recent newspaper article, you learned that some restaurants—like the famous Coach House Restaurant in Victoria—automatically add a 15 percent tip to the bill. In Montreal the Porte Rouge restaurant prints "gratuity guidelines" on bills, showing customers what a 15 or 20 percent tip would be. You also know that American Express recently developed a gratuity calculation feature on its terminals. This means that diners don't even have to do the math!

Your Task. Because they know you are studying business communication, your fellow servers have asked you to write a serious letter to Nicholas Ruiz, General Manager, Tejas Grill, 3150 Signal Drive SW, Calgary, AB T3H 3T2. Persuade him to adopt mandatory tipping guidelines in the restaurant. Talk with fellow servers (your classmates) to develop logical persuasive arguments.

10.6 Persuasive Action Request: Asking Your Member of Parliament to Listen and Act (Obj. 3)

WEB | CRITICAL THINKING

Assume you are upset about an issue, and you want your Member of Parliament to know your position. Choose a national issue about which you feel strongly: student loans, social insurance depletion, human rights in other countries, federal safety regulations for employees, environmental protection, employment equity, gun control, Aboriginal issues, the federal deficit, or some other area regulated by government.

Your Task. Obtain your MP's address and appropriate title by visiting the Government of Canada Web site (**www.parl.gc.ca**). You'll find e-mail and postal addresses, along with fax and telephone numbers. Remember that although e-mail and fax messages are fast, they don't have as much influence as personal letters. And MPs are having trouble responding to the overload of e-mail messages they receive. Decide whether it's better to send an e-mail message or a letter to your representative outlining your feelings. For best results, consider these tips: (1) Use the proper form of address (*The Honourable John Smith, Dear Mr. Smith* or *The Honourable Joan Doe, Dear Ms. Doe*). (2) Identify yourself as a resident of his or her province or territory. (3) Immediately state your position (*I urge you to support/oppose . . . because . . .*). (4) Present facts and illustrations and how they affect you personally. If legislation were enacted, how would you or your organization be better off or worse off? Avoid generalities. (5) Offer to provide further information. (6) Keep the message polite, constructive, and brief (one page maximum).

10.7 Persuasive Internal Memo or E-Mail: Dear Boss (Obj. 3)

CRITICAL THINKING | E-MAIL

In your own work or organization experience, identify a problem for which you have a solution. Should a procedure be altered to improve performance? Would a new or different piece of equipment help you perform your work better? Could some tasks be scheduled more efficiently? Are employees being used most effectively? Could customers be better served by changing something? Do you want to work other hours or perform other tasks? Do you deserve a promotion? Do you have a suggestion to improve profitability?

Your Task. Once you have identified a situation requiring persuasion, write a memo or an e-mail to your boss or organization head. Use actual names and facts. Employ the concepts and techniques in this chapter to help you convince your boss that your idea should prevail. Include concrete examples, anticipate objections, emphasize reader benefits, and end with a specific action to be taken.

10.8 Persuasive Internal Request: Supporting Project H.E.L.P. (Obj. 3)

E-MAIL

As employee relations manager of the Prudential Insurance Company, one of your tasks is to promote Project H.E.L.P. (Higher Education Learning Program), an on-the-job learning opportunity. Project H.E.L.P. is a combined effort of major corporations and the Bruce County District School Board. You must recruit 12 employees who will volunteer as instructors for 50 or more students. The students will spend four hours a week at the Prudential's Bruce County facility earning an average of five units of credit a semester.

This semester the students will be serving in the Claims, Word Processing, Corporate Media Services, Marketing, Communications, Library, and Administrative Support departments. Your task is to convince employees in these departments to volunteer. They will be expected to supervise and instruct the students. In return, employees will receive two hours of release time per week to work with the students. The program has been very successful thus far. School officials, students, and employees alike express satisfaction with the experience and the outcomes.

Your Task. Write a persuasive memo or e-mail message with convincing appeals that will bring you 12 volunteers to work with Project H.E.L.P.

10.9 Persuasive Internal Request: Revising a Miserable Memo (Obj. 3)

The following memo (with names changed) was actually sent.

Your Task. Based on what you have learned in this chapter, improve the memo. Expect the staff to be somewhat resistant because they've never before had meeting restrictions.

TO: All Managers and Employees
FROM: Nancy Nelson, CEO
SUBJECT: SCHEDULING MEETINGS

Please be reminded that travel in the greater Toronto area is time consuming. In the future we're asking that you set up meetings that

1. Are of critical importance
2. Consider travel time for the participants
3. Consider phone conferences (or video or e-mail) in lieu of face-to-face meetings

4. Should be at the location where most of the participants work and at the most opportune travel times
5. Travelling together is another way to save time and resources.

We all have our traffic stories. A recent one is that a certain manager was asked to attend a one-hour meeting in Guelph. This required one hour of travel in advance of the meeting, one hour for the meeting, and two-and-a-half hours of travel through Toronto afterward. This meeting was scheduled for 4 p.m. Total time consumed by the manager for the one-hour meeting was four-and-a-half hours.

Thank you for your consideration.

10.10 Persuasive Claim: Legal Costs for Sharing a Slice of Heaven (Obj. 3)

A small prairie town is best known for Tumbleweed Pizza, a bustling local pizzeria where customers line up on the sidewalk waiting to taste its pizza.

Assume that you are the business manager for Tumbleweed Pizza's owners. They were approached by an independent vendor who wants to use the Tumbleweed Pizza name and secret recipes to distribute frozen pizza through grocery and convenience stores. As business manager, you worked with a law firm, Lancombe, Pereigni, and Associates. This firm was to draw up contracts regarding the use of Tumbleweed Pizza's name and quality standards for the product. When you received the bill from Louis Lancombe, you were flabbergasted. It itemized 38 hours of lawyer preparation at $400 per hour, and 55 hours of paralegal assistance at $100 per hour. The bill also showed $415 for telephone calls, which might be accurate because Mr. Lancombe had to talk with the owners, who were vacationing in Italy at the time. You seriously doubt, however, that an experienced lawyer would require 38 hours to draw up the contracts in question. When you began checking, you discovered that excellent legal advice could be obtained for $200 an hour.

Your Task. Decide what you want to request, and then write a persuasive request to Louis Lancombe, LLB, Lancombe, Pereigni, and Associates, 1675 Croydon Avenue, Winnipeg, MB R3N OS8. Include an end date and a reason for it.

10.11 Sales Letter: Promoting Your Product or Service (Obj. 4)

Your Task. Identify a situation in your current job or a previous one in which a sales letter is/was needed. Using suggestions from this chapter, write an appropriate sales letter that promotes a product or service. Use actual names, information, and examples. If you have no work experience, imagine a business you'd like to start: word processing, pet grooming, car detailing, tutoring, specialty knitting, balloon decorating, delivery service, child care, gardening, lawn care, or something else. Write a letter selling your product or service to be distributed to your prospective customers. Be sure to tell them how to respond.

10.12 Press Release: Fast-Food Wraps That Decompose Like Grass and Leaves (Obj. 5)

INFOTRAC WEB

You have been interviewed for a terrific job in corporate communications at EarthShell. It produces biodegradable packaging materials for traditional food service items. Its clamshell sandwich containers and food wraps are made from potato starch, limestone, and other biodegradable materials that actually decompose like leaves and grass. At this writing its newest customer is Hood Packaging, which plans to market EarthShell's food service wraps. These are the papers used to cover tacos, burritos, hamburgers, and other take-out sandwiches.

You're excited about the job for many reasons; however, EarthShell wants you to submit a press release as a writing sample. EarthShell features some rather long press releases at its Web site. Many articles about its products have also appeared in periodicals. The EarthShell recruiter wants you to submit a press release that would appeal to the publisher of your local newspaper.[6]

Your Task. Using electronic tools, search for information on EarthShell. Read several articles. Also go to its Web site (use a search engine to find it) and look at its current press releases. Select one event or product that you think would be of interest to your local newspaper. Although you can use the information from current EarthShell press releases, don't copy the exact wording because it will be obvious to EarthShell. Use a name from a current EarthShell press release as a contact person.

10.13 Press Release: Finding the Best (Obj. 5)

INFOTRAC

One of the best ways to learn about press releases is to study them on the Web.

Your Task. Using a search engine, search for "news releases." You'll find some that are boring and self-serving and others that are entertaining and instructive. Study many recent releases looking for those that are good enough to appear in your local newspaper. Select the best three. In a message to your instructor or in a class discussion, identify your selections and describe at least six elements that make them outstanding.

C.L.U.E. review 10

Edit the following sentences to correct faults in grammar, punctuation, spelling, and word use.

1. Persuasion requires learning about you're audience, and analysing why they might resist your goal.
2. An especialy effective arguement includes 2 indespensable elements; a reasonable request, and a well presented line of reasoning.
3. If you're goal is to persuade a lending institution to give you fifty thousand dollars you would probably use rational appeal.
4. Our President and Senior Sales Manager decided to send a sales letter to all current customers therefore they analyzed the product, purpose and audience.
5. There sales letter focuses on the following 4 parts (1) Gaining the audiences attention (2) Convincing them that the purpose is worthy (3) Overcoming resistance and (4) Motivating action.
6. Experts agree that one of the biggest mistakes in persuasive request's are the failure to anticipate, and off set audience resistance.
7. Because the Manager and him builded interest with easy to read facts and figures they're letter will undoubtably suceed.
8. A claim letter is a form of complaint consequently its wise to use the indirect strategy.
9. Anger and emotion is not effective in persuasion but many writers can not controll there temper.
10. Our latest press release which was written in our corporate communication department announces the opening of 3 canadian office.

chapter 11

Negative Messages

objectives

1 Describe the goals and strategies of business communicators in delivering bad news, including knowing when to use the direct and indirect patterns, applying the writing process, and avoiding legal problems.

2 Explain techniques for delivering bad news sensitively.

3 Identify routine requests and describe a strategy for refusing such requests.

4 Explain techniques for delivering bad news to customers.

5 Explain techniques for delivering bad news within organizations.

6 Compare strategies for revealing bad news in different cultures.

springboard *to discussion*

In the summer of 2008, two Canadian companies were faced with serious health and safety concerns. While Maple Leaf Foods handled its listeria outbreak by publically acknowledging the problem and explaining next steps, Sunrise Propane was criticized for maintaining a low profile after an explosion forced approximately 12 000 people from their homes.

learning objective

1

Strategies for Delivering Bad News

In all businesses things sometimes go wrong. Goods are not delivered, a product fails to perform as expected, service is poor, billing gets fouled up, or customers are misunderstood. You may have to write messages ending business relationships, declining proposals, announcing price increases, refusing requests for donations, terminating employees, turning down invitations, or responding to unhappy customers. You might have to apologize for mistakes in orders, errors in pricing, rude employees, overlooked appointments, substandard service, pricing errors, faulty accounting, defective products, or jumbled instructions.

Receivers of bad news are less disappointed if they (a) know the reason for the rejection, (b) feel that the news was revealed sensitively, (c) think the matter was treated seriously, and (d) believe the decision was fair.

Everyone occasionally must deliver bad news. Because bad news disappoints, irritates, and sometimes angers the receiver, such messages must be written carefully. The bad feelings associated with disappointing news can generally be reduced if the receiver (a) knows the reasons for the rejection, (b) feels the bad news was revealed with sensitivity, (c) thinks the matter was treated seriously, and (d) believes that the decision was fair.

In this chapter you will learn when to use the direct pattern and when to use the indirect pattern to deliver bad news. You will study the goals of business communicators in working with bad news and you will examine the three causes for legal concerns. The major focus of this chapter, however, is on developing the indirect strategy and applying it to situations in which you must refuse typical requests, decline invitations, and deliver negative news to employees and customers. You will also learn how other cultures handle bad news.

Goals in Communicating Bad News

When you communicate bad news, your primary goals are to make the receiver understand and accept the bad news and to maintain a good image of you and your organization.

Delivering bad news is not the happiest writing task you may have, but it can be gratifying if you do it effectively. As a business communicator working with bad news, you will have many goals, the most important of which are these:

Primary Goals

- Make the reader understand the bad news.
- Have the reader accept the bad news.
- Maintain a positive image of you and your organization.

Figure 11.1 *Four-Part Indirect Pattern for Bad News*

Buffer	Reasons	Bad News	Closing
Open with a neutral but meaningful statement that does not mention the bad news.	Explain the causes of the bad news before disclosing it.	Reveal the bad news without emphasizing it. Provide an alternative or compromise, if possible.	End with a personalized, forward-looking, pleasant statement. Avoid referring to the bad news.

Secondary Goals

- Reduce bad feelings.
- Convey fairness.
- Eliminate future correspondence.
- Avoid creating legal liability or responsibility for you or your organization.

These are ambitious goals, and we're not always successful at achieving them all. The patterns you're about to learn, however, provide the beginning communicator with strategies and tactics that many writers have found successful in conveying disappointing news sensitively and safely. With experience, you'll be able to vary these patterns and adapt them to your organization's specific writing tasks.

Using the Indirect Pattern to Prepare the Reader

Revealing bad news slowly and indirectly shows sensitivity to your reader. By preparing the reader, you tend to soften the impact. A blunt announcement of disappointing news might cause the receiver to stop reading and toss the message aside. The indirect strategy enables you to keep the reader's attention until you have been able to explain the reasons for the bad news. In fact, the most important part of a bad-news letter is the explanation, which you'll learn about shortly. The indirect plan consists of four parts, as shown in Figure 11.1.

The indirect pattern softens the impact of bad news by giving reasons and explanations first.

When to Use the Direct Pattern

Many bad-news letters are best organized indirectly, beginning with a buffer and reasons. The direct pattern, with the bad news first, may be more effective, though, in situations such as the following:

The direct pattern is appropriate when the receiver might overlook the bad news, when directness is preferred, when firmness is necessary, and when the bad news is not damaging.

- **When the receiver may overlook the bad news.** With the crush of mail today, many readers skim messages, looking only at the opening. If they don't find substantive material, they may discard the message. Rate increases, changes in service, new policy requirements—these critical messages may require boldness to ensure attention.
- **When organization policy suggests directness.** Some companies expect all internal messages and announcements—even bad news—to be straightforward and presented without frills.
- **When the receiver prefers directness.** Busy managers may prefer directness. Such shorter messages enable the reader to get in the proper frame of mind immediately. If you suspect that the reader prefers the facts to be presented straightaway, use the direct pattern.

- **When firmness is necessary.** Messages that must demonstrate determination and strength should not use delaying techniques. For example, the last in a series of collection letters that seek payment of overdue accounts may require a direct opener.
- **When the bad news is not damaging.** If the bad news is insignificant (such as a small increase in cost) and doesn't personally affect the receiver, then the direct strategy certainly makes sense.

Applying the 3-x-3 Writing Process

The 3-x-3 writing process is especially important in crafting bad-news messages because of the potential consequences of poorly written messages.

Thinking through the entire process is especially important in bad-news letters. Not only do you want the receiver to understand and accept the message, but you want to be careful that your words say only what you intend. Thus, you'll want to apply the familiar 3-x-3 writing process to bad-news letters.

Analysis, Anticipation, and Adaptation. In Phase 1 (prewriting) you need to analyze the bad news so that you can anticipate its effect on the receiver. If the disappointment will be mild, announce it directly. If the bad news is serious or personal, consider techniques to reduce the pain. Adapt your words to protect the receiver's ego. Choose words that show you respect the reader as a responsible, valuable person.

Research, Organization, and Composition. In Phase 2 (writing) you can gather information and brainstorm for ideas. Jot down all the reasons you have that explain the bad news. If four or five reasons prompted your negative decision, concentrate on the strongest and safest ones. Avoid presenting any weak reasons; readers may seize on them to reject the entire message. After selecting your best reasons, outline the four parts of the bad-news pattern: buffer, reasons, bad news, closing. Flesh out each section as you compose your first draft.

Revision, Proofreading, and Evaluation. In Phase 3 (revising) you're ready to switch positions and put yourself in the receiver's shoes. Have you looked at the problem from the receiver's perspective? Is your message too blunt? too subtle? Does the message make the refusal, denial, or bad-news announcement clear? Prepare the final version, and proofread for format, punctuation, and correctness.

Avoiding Three Causes of Legal Problems

Before we examine the components of a bad-news message, let's look more closely at how you can avoid exposing yourself and your employer to legal liability in writing negative messages. Although we can't always anticipate the consequences of our words, we should be alert to three causes of legal difficulties: (a) abusive language, (b) careless language, and (c) the "good-guy syndrome."

Abusive language becomes legally actionable when it is false, harmful to the person's good name, and "published."

Abusive Language. Calling people names (such as *deadbeat*, *crook*, or *quack*) can get you into trouble. *Defamation* is the legal term for any false statement that harms an individual's reputation. When the abusive language is written, it is called *libel*; when spoken, it is *slander*.

To be actionable (likely to result in a lawsuit), abusive language must be (a) false, (b) damaging to one's good name, and (c) "published"—that is, spoken within the presence of others or written. Thus, if you were alone with Jane Doe and accused her of accepting bribes and selling company secrets to competitors, she couldn't sue because the defamation wasn't published. Her reputation was not damaged. But if anyone heard the words or if they were written, you might be legally liable.

In a new wrinkle, you may now be prosecuted if you transmit a harassing or libellous message by e-mail or post it on a bulletin board. Such electronic transmissions are considered to be published. Moreover, a company may incur liability for messages sent through its computer system by employees. That's why many companies are increasing their monitoring of both outgoing and internal messages. "Off-the-cuff, casual e-mail conversations among employees are exactly the type of messages that tend to trigger lawsuits and arm litigators with damaging evidence," says e-mail guru Nancy Flynn.[1] Instant messaging adds another danger for companies. Whether in print or electronically, competent communicators avoid making unproven charges and letting their emotions prompt abusive language.

Careless language includes statements that could be damaging or misinterpreted.

Avoid statements that make you feel good but may be misleading or inaccurate.

Use organizational stationery for official business only, and beware of making promises that can't be fulfilled.

Careless Language. As the marketplace becomes increasingly litigious, we must be certain that our words communicate only what we intend. First, be careful in making statements that are potentially damaging or that could be misinterpreted. Be wary of explanations that convey more information than you intend. Second, be careful about what documents you save. Lawyers may demand, in pursuing a lawsuit, all company files pertaining to a case. Even documents marked "Confidential" or "Personal" may be used.

Remember, too, that e-mail messages are especially risky. You may think that a mere tap of the Delete key makes a file disappear; however, messages continue to exist on backup storage devices in the files of the sender and the recipient.

The Good-Guy Syndrome. Most of us hate to have to reveal bad news—that is, to be the bad guy. To make ourselves look better, to make the receiver feel better, and to maintain good relations, we are tempted to make statements that are legally dangerous.

Business communicators act as agents of their organizations. Their words, decisions, and opinions are assumed to represent those of the organization. If you want to communicate your personal feelings or opinions, use your home computer or write on plain paper (rather than company letterhead) and sign your name without title or affiliation. Volunteering extra information can lead to trouble. Thus, avoid supplying data that could be misused, and avoid making promises that can't be fulfilled. Don't admit or imply responsibility for conditions that caused damage or injury. Even apologies (*We're sorry that a faulty bottle cap caused damage to your carpet*) may suggest liability.

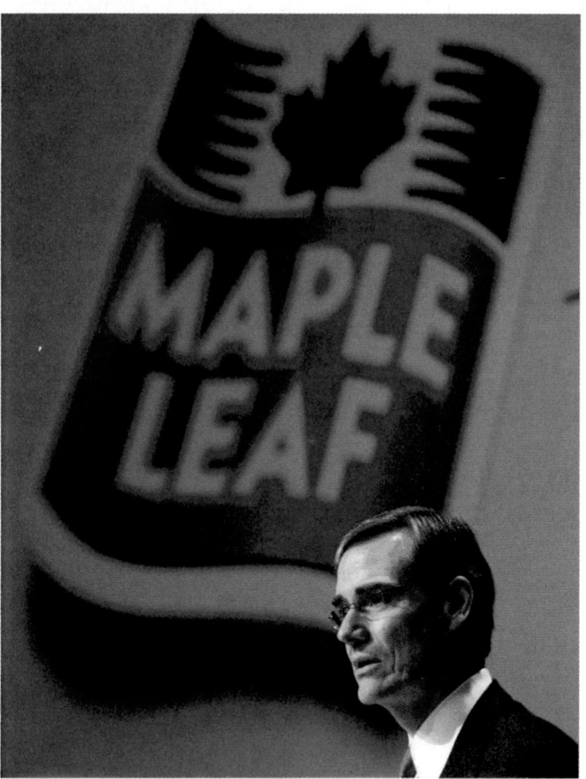

Maple Leaf Foods has been cited for effectively handling crisis communication by having CEO Michael McCain issue a public apology.

Photo: CP Picture Archive/Adrian Wyld

In Chapter 5 we discussed four information areas that generate the most lawsuits: investments, safety, marketing, and human resources. In this chapter we'll make specific suggestions for avoiding legal liability in writing responses to claim letters, credit letters, and personnel documents. You may find that in the most critical areas (such as collection letters or hiring/firing messages) your organization provides language guidelines and form letters approved by legal counsel. As the business environment becomes more perilous, we must not only be sensitive to receivers but also keenly aware of risks to ourselves and to the organizations we represent.

FIGURE 11.2 ***Delivering Bad News Sensitively***

Buffer	Reasons	Bad News	Closing
Best news	Cautious explanation	Embedded placement	Forward look
Compliment	Reader or other benefits	Passive voice	Information about alternative
Appreciation	Company policy explanation	Implied refusal	Good wishes
Agreement	Positive words	Compromise	Freebies
Facts	Evidence that matter was considered fairly and seriously	Alternative	Resale
Understanding			Sales promotion
Apology			

learning objective

2

Techniques for Delivering Bad News Sensitively

Legal matters aside, let's now study specific techniques for using the indirect pattern in sending bad-news messages. In this pattern the bad news is delayed until after explanations have been given. The four components of the indirect pattern, shown in Figure 11.2, include buffer, reasons, bad news, and closing.

Buffering the Opening

A buffer is a device to reduce shock or pain. To buffer the pain of bad news, begin with a neutral but meaningful statement that makes the reader continue reading. The buffer should be relevant and concise and provide a natural transition to the explanation that follows. The individual situation, of course, will help determine what you should put in the buffer. Avoid trite buffers such as *Thank you for your letter*. Here are some possibilities for opening bad-news messages.

Openers can buffer the bad news with compliments, appreciation, agreement, relevant facts, and understanding.

- **Best news.** Start with the part of the message that represents the best news.
- **Compliment.** Praise the receiver's accomplishments, organization, or efforts, but do so with honesty and sincerity.
- **Appreciation.** Convey thanks to the reader for doing business, for sending something, for conveying confidence in your organization, for expressing feelings, or simply for providing feedback. Avoid thanking the reader, however, for something you are about to refuse.
- **Agreement.** Make a relevant statement with which both reader and receiver can agree.
- **Facts.** Provide objective information that introduces the bad news.
- **Understanding.** Show that you care about the reader. You may want to express concern.
- **Apology.** As you learned in Chapter 9, a carefully worded apology may be appropriate. Apologize if you or your company erred, apologize sincerely, and accept responsibility.

Good buffers avoid revealing the bad news immediately, and they do not convey a false impression that good news follows. Additionally, they provide a natural transition to the next bad-news letter component—the reasons.

Presenting the Reasons

The most important part of a bad-news letter is the section that explains why a negative decision is necessary. Without sound reasons for denying a request or refusing a claim, a letter will fail, no matter how cleverly it is organized or written. As part of your planning before writing, you analyzed the problem and decided to refuse a request for specific reasons. Before disclosing the bad news, try to explain those reasons. Providing an explanation reduces feelings of ill will and improves the chances that the reader will accept the bad news.

Bad-news messages should explain reasons before stating the negative news.

Explaining Clearly. If the reasons are not confidential and if they will not create legal liability, you can be specific. Don't, however, make unrealistic or dangerous statements in an effort to be the good guy.

Citing Reader or Other Benefits If Plausible. Readers are more open to bad news if in some way, even indirectly, it may help them. Readers also accept bad news better if they recognize that someone or something else benefits, such as other workers or the environment. Avoid trying to show reader benefits, though, if they appear insincere.

Readers accept bad news more readily if they see that someone else benefits.

Explaining Company Policy. Readers resent blanket policy statements prohibiting something: *Company policy prevents us from making cash refunds* or *Contract bids may be accepted from local companies only* or *Company policy requires us to promote from within.* Instead of hiding behind company policy, gently explain why the policy makes sense: *We prefer to promote from within because it rewards the loyalty of our employees. In addition, we've found that people familiar with our organization make the quickest contribution to our team effort.* By offering explanations, you demonstrate that you care about readers and are treating them as important individuals.

Choosing Positive Words. Because the words you use can affect a reader's response, choose carefully. Remember that the objective of the indirect pattern is holding the reader's attention until you've had a chance to explain the reasons justifying the bad news. To keep the reader in a receptive mood, avoid expressions with punitive, demoralizing, or otherwise negative connotations. Stay away from such words as *cannot, claim, denied, error, failure, fault, impossible, mistaken, misunderstand, never, regret, rejected, unable, unwilling, unfortunately,* and *violate.*

Showing That the Matter Was Treated Seriously and Fairly. In explaining reasons, demonstrate to the reader that you take the matter seriously, have investigated carefully, and are making an unbiased decision. Receivers are more accepting of disappointing news when they feel that their requests have been heard and that they have been treated fairly. Avoid blaming others within your organization. Such unprofessional behaviour makes the reader lose faith in you and your company.

Cushioning the Bad News

Although you can't prevent the disappointment that bad news brings, you can reduce the pain somewhat by breaking the news sensitively. Be especially considerate when the reader will suffer personally from the bad news. A number of thoughtful techniques can cushion the blow.

Techniques for cushioning bad news include positioning it strategically, using the passive voice, implying the refusal, and suggesting alternatives or compromises.

Positioning the Bad News Strategically. Instead of spotlighting it, sandwich the bad news between other sentences, perhaps among your reasons. Don't let the refusal begin or end a paragraph—the reader's eye will linger on these high-visibility spots. Another technique that reduces shock is putting a painful idea in a subordinate clause, which often begins with words such as *although, as, because, if,* and *since.*

Using the Passive Voice. Passive-voice verbs enable you to depersonalize an action. Whereas the active voice focuses attention on a person, the passive voice highlights the action. Use the passive voice for the bad news. In some instances you can combine passive-voice verbs and a subordinate clause.

Accentuating the Positive. As you learned earlier, messages are far more effective when you describe what you can do instead of what you can't do.

Implying the Refusal. It's sometimes possible to avoid a direct statement of refusal. Often, your reasons and explanations leave no doubt that a request has been denied. Explicit refusals may be unnecessary and at times cruel. The danger of an implied refusal, of course, is that it is so subtle that the reader misses it. Be certain that you make the bad news clear, thus preventing the need for further correspondence.

Suggesting a Compromise or Alternative. A refusal is not so depressing—for the sender or the receiver—if a suitable compromise, substitute, or alternative is available. You can further reduce the impact of the bad news by refusing to dwell on it. Present it briefly (or imply it), and then move on to your closing.

Closing Pleasantly

Closings to bad-news messages might include a forward look, an alternative, good wishes, freebies, or resale or sales promotion information.

After explaining the bad news sensitively, close the message with a pleasant statement that promotes goodwill. The closing should be personalized and may include a forward look, an alternative, good wishes, freebies, resale information, or an off-the-subject remark.

- **Forward look.** Anticipate future relations or business.
- **Alternative.** If an alternative exists, end your letter with follow-through advice.
- **Good wishes.** End with a positive. For example, a letter rejecting a job candidate may conclude with good-luck wishes.
- **Freebies.** When customers complain—primarily in the case of food products or small consumer items—companies often send coupons, samples, or gifts to restore confidence and to promote future business.
- **Resale or sales promotion.** When the bad news is not devastating or personal, references to resale information or promotion may be appropriate.

Avoid endings that sound canned, insincere, inappropriate, or self-serving. Don't invite further correspondence (*If you have any questions, do not hesitate . . .*), and don't refer to the bad news. To review these suggestions for delivering bad news sensitively, refer to Figure 11.2.

Refusing Routine Requests

learning objective

3

Every business communicator will occasionally have to say no to a request. Depending on how you think the receiver will react to your refusal, you can use the direct or the indirect pattern. If you have any doubts, use the indirect pattern.

Rejecting Requests for Favours, Money, Information, or Action

Most of us prefer to be let down gently when we're being refused something we want. That's why the reasons-before-refusal pattern works well when you must turn down requests for favours, money, information, action, and so forth.

The reasons-before-refusal pattern works well when turning down requests for favours, money, information, or action.

Saying No to Requests From Outsiders. Requests for contributions to charity are common. Many big and small companies receive requests for contributions of money, time, equipment, and support. Although the causes may be worthy, resources are usually limited. In a letter from Forest Financial Services, shown in Figure 11.3, the company must refuse a request for a donation to a charity. Following the indirect strategy, the letter begins with a buffer acknowledging the request. It also praises the good works of the charity and uses those words as a transition to the second paragraph. In the second paragraph the writer explains why the company cannot donate. Notice that the writer reveals the refusal without actually stating it. This gentle refusal makes it unnecessary to be blunter in stating the denial. In some donation refusal letters, the reasons may not be fully explained. In the letter shown in Figure 11.3, the writer felt a connection to the charity. Thus he wanted to give a fuller explanation.

Internal request refusals focus on explanations and praise, maintaining a positive tone, and offering alternatives.

Refusing Internal Requests. Just as managers must refuse requests from outsiders, they must also occasionally refuse requests from employees. In Figure 11.4 you see the first draft and revision of a message responding to a request from a key manager, Mark Stevenson. He wants permission to attend a conference. However, he can't attend the conference because the timing is bad; he must be present at budget planning meetings scheduled for the same two weeks. Normally this matter would be discussed in person, but Mark has been travelling among branch offices, and he just hasn't been in the office recently.

Compliments can help buffer the impact of request refusals.

The vice president's first inclination was to send a quick memo, as shown in the draft version in Figure 11.4, and "tell it like it is." In revising, the vice president realized that this message was going to hurt and that it had possible danger areas. Moreover, the memo missed a chance to give Mark positive feedback. An improved version of the memo starts with a buffer that delivers honest praise. By the way, don't be stingy with compliments; they cost you nothing. The buffer also includes the date of the meeting, used strategically to connect the reasons that follow. You will recall from Chapter 6 that repetition of a key idea is an effective transitional device to provide smooth flow between components of a message.

The middle paragraph provides reasons for the refusal. Notice that they focus on positive elements: Mark is the specialist, the company relies on his expertise, and everyone will benefit if he passes up the conference. In this section it becomes obvious that the request will be refused. The writer is not forced to say, *No, you may not attend.* Although the refusal is implied, the reader gets the message.

The closing suggests a qualified alternative (*if our workloads permit, we'll try to send you then*). It also ends positively with gratitude for Mark's contributions to the organization and with another compliment (*You're a valuable player*). Notice that the improved version focuses on explanations and praise rather than on refusals and apologies.

FIGURE 11.3 ***Refusing Donation Request***

1 Prewriting

ANALYZE: The purpose of this letter is to reject the request for a monetary donation without causing bad feelings.

ANTICIPATE: The reader is proud of his or her organization and the good work it pursues.

ADAPT: The writer should strive to cushion the bad news and explain why it is necessary.

2 Writing

RESEARCH: Collect information about the receiver's organization as well as reasons for the refusal.

ORGANIZE: Use the indirect strategy. Begin with complimentary comments, present reasons, reveal the bad news gently, and close pleasantly.

COMPOSE: Write the message and consider keeping a copy to serve as a form letter.

3 Revising

REVISE: Be sure that the tone of the message is positive and that it suggests that the matter was taken seriously.

PROOFREAD: Check the receiver's name and address to be sure they are accurate. Check the letter's format.

EVALUATE: Will this message retain the goodwill of the receiver despite its bad news?

FOREST FINANCIAL SERVICES
3410 Willow Grove Boulevard
London, ON N5Z 2Z7
519.593.4400
www.forestfinancial.com

November 14, 2010

Mr. Alan Gee, Chair
Oxford-Wellington County Chapter
National Reye's Syndrome Foundation
RR #2
Kerwood, ON NOM 2B0

Dear Mr. Gee:

We appreciate your letter describing the good work your Oxford-Wellington County chapter of the National Reye's Syndrome Foundation is doing in preventing and treating this serious affliction. Your organization is to be commended for its significant achievements resulting from the efforts of dedicated members.

Supporting the good work of your organization and others, although unrelated to our business, is a luxury we have enjoyed in past years. Because of sales declines and organizational downsizing, we're forced to take a much harder look at funding requests that we receive this year. We feel that we must focus our charitable contributions on areas that relate directly to our business.

We're hopeful that the worst days are behind us and that we'll be able to renew our support for worthwhile projects like yours next year.

Sincerely,

Paul Rosenberg

Paul Rosenberg
Vice President

Opens with praise and compliments

Doesn't say yes or no

Transitions with repetition of key idea *(good work)*

Explains sales decline and cutback in gifts

Reveals refusal without actually stating it

Closes graciously with forward look

Figure 11.4 ***Refusing an Internal Request***

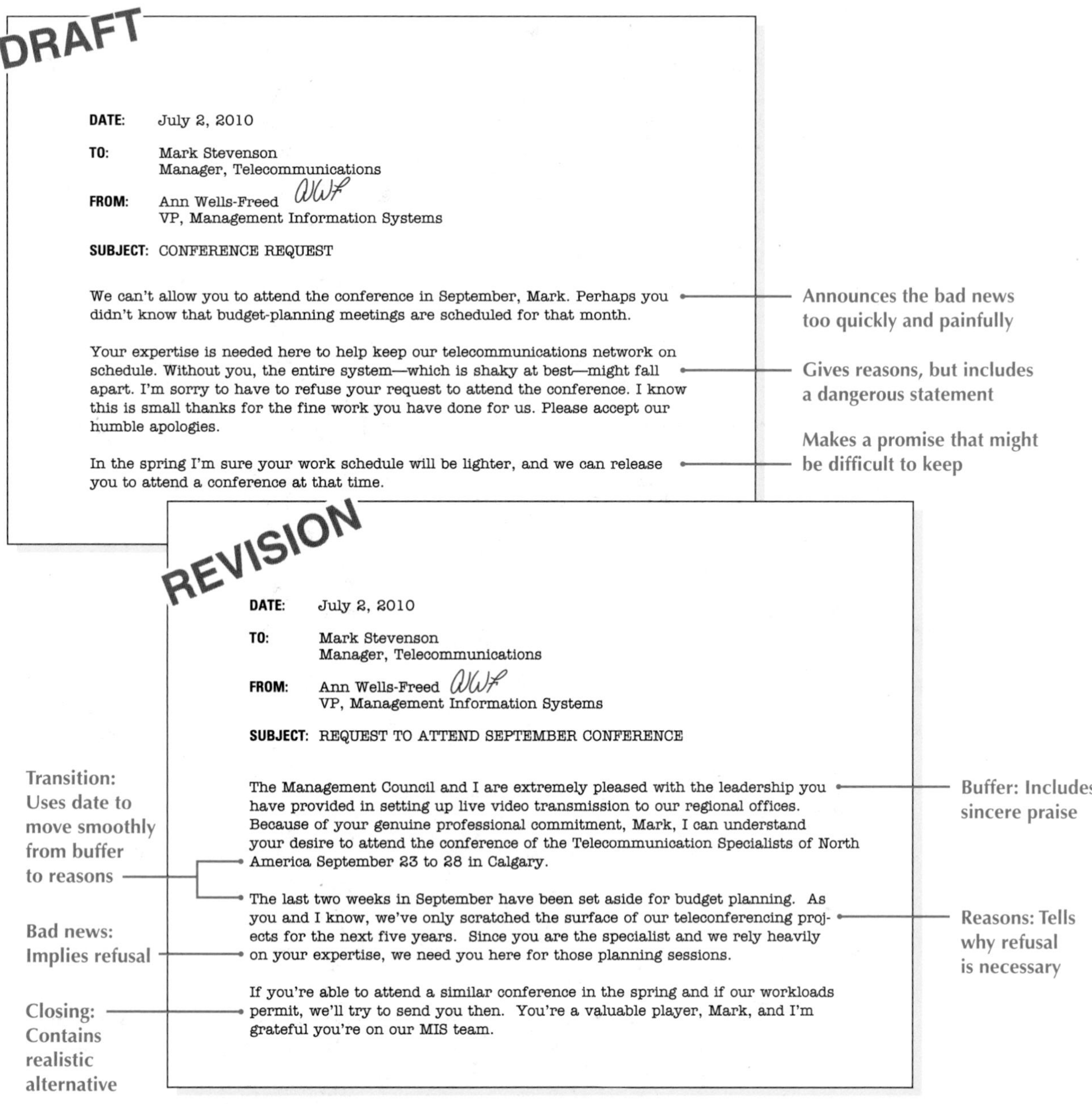
DRAFT

DATE: July 2, 2010

TO: Mark Stevenson
Manager, Telecommunications

FROM: Ann Wells-Freed
VP, Management Information Systems

SUBJECT: CONFERENCE REQUEST

We can't allow you to attend the conference in September, Mark. Perhaps you didn't know that budget-planning meetings are scheduled for that month.

Your expertise is needed here to help keep our telecommunications network on schedule. Without you, the entire system—which is shaky at best—might fall apart. I'm sorry to have to refuse your request to attend the conference. I know this is small thanks for the fine work you have done for us. Please accept our humble apologies.

In the spring I'm sure your work schedule will be lighter, and we can release you to attend a conference at that time.

REVISION

DATE: July 2, 2010

TO: Mark Stevenson
Manager, Telecommunications

FROM: Ann Wells-Freed
VP, Management Information Systems

SUBJECT: REQUEST TO ATTEND SEPTEMBER CONFERENCE

The Management Council and I are extremely pleased with the leadership you have provided in setting up live video transmission to our regional offices. Because of your genuine professional commitment, Mark, I can understand your desire to attend the conference of the Telecommunication Specialists of North America September 23 to 28 in Calgary.

The last two weeks in September have been set aside for budget planning. As you and I know, we've only scratched the surface of our teleconferencing projects for the next five years. Since you are the specialist and we rely heavily on your expertise, we need you here for those planning sessions.

If you're able to attend a similar conference in the spring and if our workloads permit, we'll try to send you then. You're a valuable player, Mark, and I'm grateful you're on our MIS team.

The success of this message depends on attention to the entire writing process, not just on using a buffer or scattering a few compliments throughout.

Declining Invitations

When we must decline an invitation to speak or attend a program, we generally try to provide a response that says more than *I can't* or *I don't want to*. Unless the reasons are confidential or business secrets, try to explain them. Because responses to invitations are often taken personally, make a special effort to soften the refusal. In the letter shown in Figure 11.5, an accountant must say no to an invitation from a

Figure 11.5 ***Refusing an Invitation***

GALLAGHER, BRACIO, CASAGRANDE, L.L.P.
Certified General Accountants
942 Lascelles Boulevard
Toronto, ON M4P 2B9
(416) 435-9800

E-mail: cpa@gbcllp.com www.gbcllp.com

April 14, 2010

Mr. Tyler Simpson
4208 Collins Avenue
Toronto, ON M3H 1A5

Dear Tyler:

News of your leadership position in your campus student association fills me with delight and pride. Your father must be proud also of your educational and extracurricular achievements.

You honour me by asking me to speak to your group in the spring about codes of ethics in the accounting field. Because our firm has not yet adopted such a code, we have been investigating the codes developed by other accounting firms. I am decidedly not an expert in this area, but I have met others who are. Although your invitation must be declined, I would like to recommend Dr. Carolyn S. Marshall, who is a member of the ethics subcommittee of the Institute of Internal Auditors. Dr. Marshall is a professor who often addresses groups on the subject of ethics in accounting. I spoke with her about your group, and she indicated that she would be happy to consider your invitation.

It's good to learn that you are guiding your organization toward such constructive and timely program topics. Please call Dr. Marshall at (416) 389-2210 if you would like to arrange for her to address your group.

Sincerely,

Joan F. Gallagher

Joan F. Gallagher, CGA

JFG:mhr

Opens cordially with praise

Focuses attention on alternative

Reduces impact of refusal by placing it in subordinate clause

Ends positively with compliments and offer of assistance

friend's son to speak before the young man's student association. This refusal starts with conviviality and compliments. The writer then explains why she cannot accept. The refusal is embedded in a long paragraph and deemphasized in a subordinate clause. The reader naturally concentrates on the main clause that follows. If no alternative is available, focus on something positive about the situation. Overall, the tone of this refusal is warm, upbeat, and positive.

The following checklist reviews the steps in composing a letter refusing a routine request.

Checklist for Refusing Routine Requests

✓ **Open indirectly with a buffer.** Pay a compliment to the reader, show appreciation for something done, or mention some mutual understanding. Avoid raising false hopes or thanking the reader for something you will refuse.

- ✓ **Provide reasons.** In the body explain why the request must be denied—without revealing the refusal. Avoid negativity (*unfortunately, unwilling, impossible*) and potentially damaging statements. Show how your decision benefits the reader or others, if possible.

- ✓ **Soften the bad news.** Reduce the impact of bad news by using a subordinate clause, the passive voice, a long sentence, or a long paragraph. Consider implying the refusal, but be certain it is clear. Suggest an alternative, if a suitable one exists.

- ✓ **Close pleasantly.** Supply more information about an alternative, look forward to future relations, or offer good wishes and compliments. Maintain a bright, personal tone. Avoid referring to the refusal.

Delivering Bad News to Customers

learning objective 4

Businesses must occasionally respond to disappointed customers. In Chapter 9 you learned to use the direct strategy in granting claims and making adjustments because these were essentially good-news messages. But in some situations you have little good news to share. Sometimes your company is at fault, in which case an apology is generally in order. Other times the problem is with orders you can't fill, claims you must refuse, or credit you must deny. Messages with bad news for customers generally follow the same pattern as other negative messages. Customer letters, though, differ in one major way: they usually include resale or sales promotion emphasis.

Damage Control: Dealing With Disappointed Customers

All companies occasionally disappoint their customers. Merchandise is not delivered on time, a product fails to perform as expected, service is deficient, charges are erroneous, or customers are misunderstood. All businesses offering products or services must sometimes deal with troublesome situations that cause unhappiness to customers. Whenever possible, these problems should be dealt with immediately and personally. A majority of business professionals strive to control the damage and resolve such problems in the following manner.[2]

- Call the individual involved.
- Describe the problem and apologize.
- Explain why the problem occurred, what you are doing to resolve it, and how you will prevent it from happening again.
- Follow up with a letter that documents the phone call and promotes goodwill.

When a customer problem arises and the company is at fault, many businesspeople call and apologize, explain what happened, and follow up with a goodwill letter.

Dealing with problems immediately is very important in resolving conflict and retaining goodwill. Written correspondence is generally too slow for problems that demand immediate attention. But written messages are important (a) when personal contact is impossible, (b) to establish a record of the incident, (c) to formally confirm follow-up procedures, and (d) to promote good relations.

A written follow-up letter is necessary when personal contact is impossible, to establish a record, to formally confirm follow-up procedures, and to promote good relations.

A bad-news follow-up letter is shown in Figure 11.6 (page 254). Consultant Maris Richfield found herself in the embarrassing position of explaining why she

FIGURE 11.6 ***Bad-News Follow-up Message***

Tips for Resolving Problems and Following Up

- Whenever possible, call or see the individual involved.
- Describe the problem and apologize.
- Explain why the problem occurred.
- Describe what you are doing to resolve the problem.
- Explain how it will not happen again.
- Follow up with a letter that documents the personal contact.
- Look forward to positive future relations.

RICHFIELD CONSULTING SERVICES

1642 Sherbrooke St. W.
Montreal, QC H3E 1H6

Voice: (514) 499-8224
Web: www.richfieldconsulting.com

October 23, 2010

Ms. Angela Ranier
Vice President, Human Resources
Data.com, Inc.
21067 Lacombe Avenue
Montreal, QC H5B 2G6

Dear Angela:

Opens with agreement and apology

You have every right to expect complete confidentiality in your transactions with an independent consultant. As I explained in yesterday's telephone call, I am very distressed that you were called by a salesperson from Payroll Services, Inc. This should not have happened, and I apologize to you again for inadvertently mentioning your company's name in a conversation with a potential vender, Payroll Services, Inc.

Explains what caused the problem and how it was resolved

Promises to prevent recurrence

All clients of Richfield Consulting are assured that their dealings with our firm are held in the strictest confidence. Because your company's payroll needs are so individual and because you have so many contract workers, I was forced to explain how your employees differed from those of other companies. The name of your company, however, should never have been mentioned. I can assure you that it will not happen again. I have informed Payroll Services that it had no authorization to call you directly and its actions have forced me to reconsider using its services for my future clients.

Closes with forward look

A number of other payroll services offer excellent programs. I'm sure we can find the perfect partner to enable you to outsource your payroll responsibilities, thus allowing your company to focus its financial and human resources on its core business. I look forward to our next appointment when you may choose from a number of excellent payroll outsourcing firms.

Sincerely yours,

Maris Richfield

Maris Richfield

had given out the name of her client to a salesperson. The client, Data.com, Inc., had hired her firm, Richfield Consulting Services, to help find an appropriate service for outsourcing its payroll functions. Without realizing it, Maris had mentioned to a potential vendor (Payroll Services, Inc.) that her client was considering hiring an outside service to handle its payroll. An overeager salesperson from Payroll Services immediately called on Data.com, thus angering the client. The client had hired the consultant to avoid this very kind of intrusion. Data.com did not want to be hounded by vendors selling their payroll services.

When she learned of the problem, the first thing consultant Maris Richfield did was call her client to explain and apologize. She was careful to control her voice and rate of speaking. A low-pitched, deliberate pace gives the impression that you are thinking clearly, logically, and reasonably—not emotionally, and certainly not irrationally. She followed up with the letter shown in Figure 11.6. The letter not only confirms the telephone conversation but also adds the right touch of formality. It sends the nonverbal message that the matter is being taken seriously and that it is important enough to warrant a written letter.

When situations involve many unhappy customers, companies may need to write personalized form letters. The following specific strategies are effective in dealing with unhappy customers.

- Apologize if your organization is to blame.
- Identify the problem and take responsibility.
- Explain the steps being taken to prevent recurrence.
- Offer gifts, benefits, or bonuses to offset disappointment and to reestablish a relationship.
- Thank customers for their past business and patience.
- Look forward to future warm relations.

Handling Problems With Orders

Not all customer orders can be filled as received. Suppliers may be able to send only part of an order or none at all. Substitutions may be necessary, or the delivery date may be delayed. Suppliers may suspect that all or part of the order is a mistake; the customer may actually want something else. In writing to customers about problem orders, it's generally wise to use the direct pattern if the message has some good-news elements. But when the message is disappointing, the indirect pattern may be more appropriate.

In handling problems with orders, writers use the indirect pattern unless the message has some good-news elements.

Let's say you represent Live and Learn Toys, a large toy manufacturer, and you're scrambling for business in a slow year. A big customer, Child Land, calls in August and asks you to hold a block of your best-selling toy, Space Station. Like most vendors, you require a deposit on large orders. September rolls around, and you still haven't received any money from Child Land. You must now write a tactful letter asking for the deposit—or else you will release the toys to other buyers. The problem, of course, is delivering the bad news without losing the customer's order and goodwill. Another challenge is making sure the reader understands the bad news. An effective letter might begin with a positive statement that also reveals the facts:

> You were smart to reserve a block of 500 Space Stations, which we have been holding for you since August. As the holidays approach, the demand for all our learning toys, including the Space Station, is rapidly increasing.

Next, the letter should explain why the payment is needed and what will happen if it is not received:

> Toy stores from St. John's to Victoria are asking us to ship these Space Stations. One reason the Space Station is moving out of our warehouses so quickly is its assortment of gizmos that children love, including a land-rover vehicle, a shuttle craft, a hovercraft, astronauts, and even a robotic arm. As soon as we receive your deposit of $4000, we'll have this popular item on its way to your stores. Without a deposit by September 20, though, we must release this block to other retailers.

The closing makes it easy to respond and motivates action:

> Use the enclosed envelope to send us your cheque immediately. You can begin showing this fascinating Live and Learn toy in your stores by November 1.

Denying Claims

Customers occasionally want something they're not entitled to or that you can't grant. They may misunderstand warranties or make unreasonable demands. Because these customers are often unhappy with a product or service, they are emotionally involved. Letters that say no to emotionally involved receivers will probably be your most challenging communication task.

In denying claims, the reasons-before-refusal pattern sets an empathic tone and buffers the bad news.

Fortunately, the reasons-before-refusal plan helps you be empathic and artful in breaking bad news. Obviously, in denial letters you'll need to adopt the proper tone. Don't blame customers, even if they are at fault. Avoid "you" statements that sound preachy (*You would have known that cash refunds are impossible if you had read your contract*). Use neutral, objective language to explain why the claim must be refused. Consider offering resale information to rebuild the customer's confidence in your products or organization. In Figure 11.7 the writer denies a customer's claim for the difference between the price the customer paid for speakers and the price he saw advertised locally (which would have resulted in a cash refund of $151). Although the catalogue service does match any advertised lower price, the price-matching policy applies only to exact models. This claim must be rejected because the advertisement the customer submitted showed a different, older speaker model.

The letter to Matthew Tyson opens with a buffer that agrees with a statement in the customer's letter. It repeats the key idea of product confidence as a transition to the second paragraph. Next comes an explanation of the price-matching policy. The writer does not assume that the customer is trying to pull a fast one, nor does he suggest that the customer is a dummy who didn't read or understand the price-matching policy. The safest path is a neutral explanation of the policy along with precise distinctions between the customer's speakers and the older ones. The writer also gets a chance to resell the customer's speakers and demonstrate what a quality product they are. By the end of the third paragraph, it's evident to the reader that his claim is unjustified.

Refusing Credit

When customers apply for credit, they must be notified if the application is rejected. Credit applications, from individuals or from businesses, are generally approved or disapproved on the basis of the applicant's credit history. This record is supplied by a credit-reporting agency such as Northern Credit Bureau, Equifax, or TransUnion. The business then makes a decision whether to grant credit based on the information supplied.

FIGURE 11.7 ***Denying a Claim***

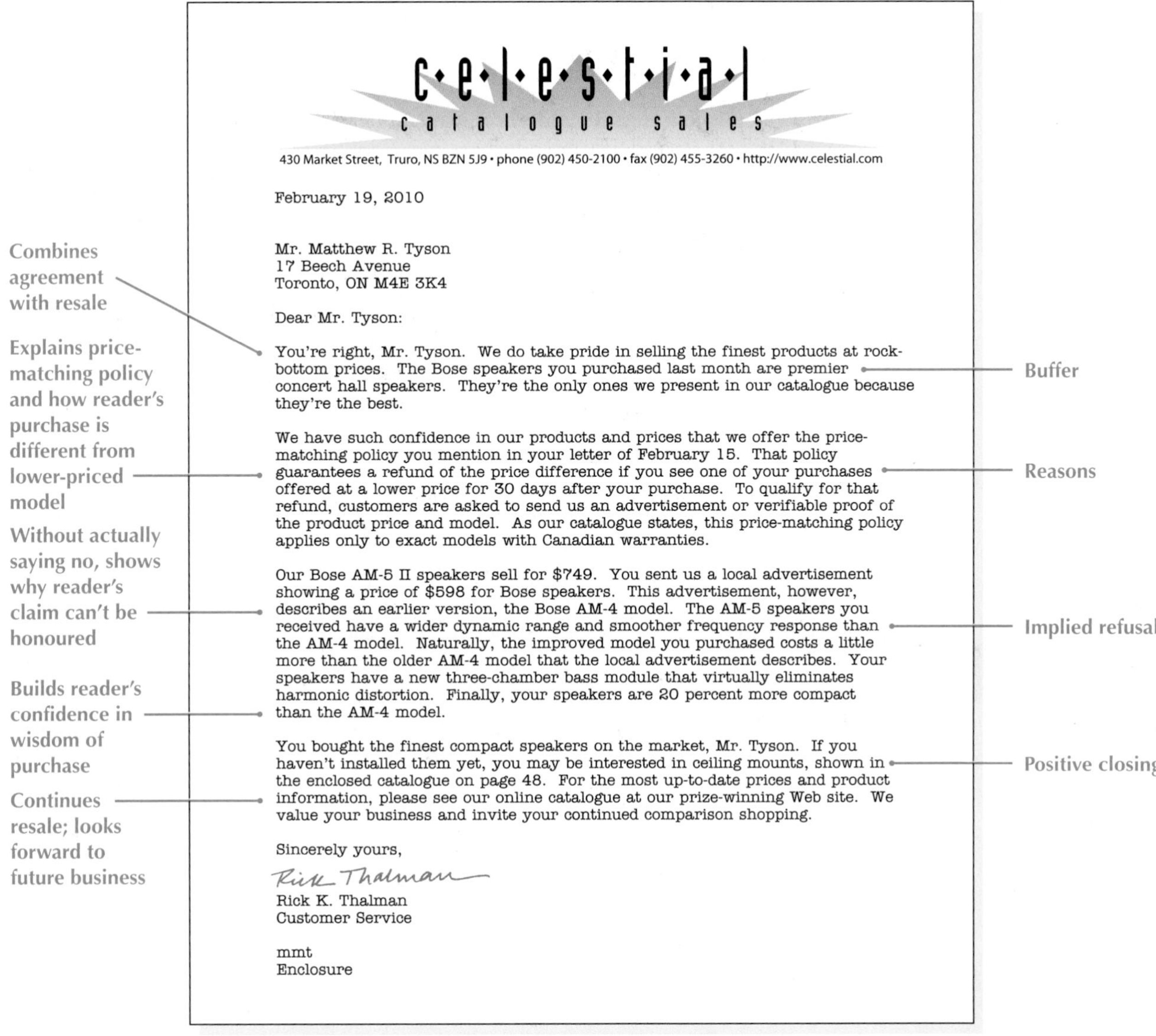

c·e·l·e·s·t·i·a·l
catalogue sales
430 Market Street, Truro, NS BZN 5J9 • phone (902) 450-2100 • fax (902) 455-3260 • http://www.celestial.com

February 19, 2010

Mr. Matthew R. Tyson
17 Beech Avenue
Toronto, ON M4E 3K4

Dear Mr. Tyson:

You're right, Mr. Tyson. We do take pride in selling the finest products at rock-bottom prices. The Bose speakers you purchased last month are premier concert hall speakers. They're the only ones we present in our catalogue because they're the best.

We have such confidence in our products and prices that we offer the price-matching policy you mention in your letter of February 15. That policy guarantees a refund of the price difference if you see one of your purchases offered at a lower price for 30 days after your purchase. To qualify for that refund, customers are asked to send us an advertisement or verifiable proof of the product price and model. As our catalogue states, this price-matching policy applies only to exact models with Canadian warranties.

Our Bose AM-5 II speakers sell for $749. You sent us a local advertisement showing a price of $598 for Bose speakers. This advertisement, however, describes an earlier version, the Bose AM-4 model. The AM-5 speakers you received have a wider dynamic range and smoother frequency response than the AM-4 model. Naturally, the improved model you purchased costs a little more than the older AM-4 model that the local advertisement describes. Your speakers have a new three-chamber bass module that virtually eliminates harmonic distortion. Finally, your speakers are 20 percent more compact than the AM-4 model.

You bought the finest compact speakers on the market, Mr. Tyson. If you haven't installed them yet, you may be interested in ceiling mounts, shown in the enclosed catalogue on page 48. For the most up-to-date prices and product information, please see our online catalogue at our prize-winning Web site. We value your business and invite your continued comparison shopping.

Sincerely yours,

Rick Thalman

Rick K. Thalman
Customer Service

mmt
Enclosure

Combines agreement with resale
Explains price-matching policy and how reader's purchase is different from lower-priced model
Without actually saying no, shows why reader's claim can't be honoured
Builds reader's confidence in wisdom of purchase
Continues resale; looks forward to future business
Buffer
Reasons
Implied refusal
Positive closing

If you must write a letter to a customer denying credit, you have four goals in conveying the refusal:

Goals when refusing credit include maintaining customer goodwill and avoiding actionable language.

- Avoiding language that causes hard feelings
- Retaining customers on a cash basis
- Preparing for possible future credit without raising false expectations
- Avoiding disclosures that could cause a lawsuit

Because credit applicants are likely to continue to do business with an organization even if they are denied credit, you'll want to do everything possible to encourage that patronage. Thus, keep the refusal respectful, sensitive, and upbeat. A letter to a customer denying her credit application might begin as follows:

> We genuinely appreciate your application of January 12 for a Fashion Express credit account.

To avoid possible litigation, many companies offer no explanation of the reasons for a credit refusal. Instead they provide the name of the credit-reporting agency and suggest that inquiries be directed to it. In the following example, notice the use of the passive voice (*credit cannot be extended*) and a long sentence to deemphasize the bad news:

> After we received a report of your current credit record from Equifax, it is apparent that credit cannot be extended at this time. To learn more about your record, you may call an Equifax credit counsellor at (800) 356-0922.

The cordial closing looks forward to the possibility of a future reapplication:

> Thanks, Ms. Love, for the confidence you've shown in Fashion Express. We invite you to continue shopping at our stores, and we look forward to your reapplication in the future.

Some businesses do provide reasons explaining credit denials (*Credit cannot be granted because your firm's current and long-term credit obligations are nearly twice as great as your firm's total assets*). They may also provide alternatives, such as deferred billing or cash discounts. When the letter denies a credit application that accompanies an order, the message may contain resale information. The writer tries to convert the order from credit to cash. For example, if a big order cannot be filled on a credit basis, perhaps part of the order could be filled on a cash basis.

Whatever form the bad-news letter takes, it is a good idea to have the message reviewed by legal counsel because of the litigation landmines awaiting unwary communicators in this area. The following checklist provides tips on how to craft effective bad-news letters.

Checklist for Delivering Bad News to Customers

- ✓ **Begin indirectly.** Express appreciation (but don't thank the reader for requesting something you're about to refuse), show agreement on some point, review facts, or show understanding. Consider apologizing if your organization was responsible for disappointing its customers.

- ✓ **Provide reasons.** Except in credit denials, justify the bad news with objective reasons. Use resale, if appropriate, to restore the customer's confidence. Avoid blaming the customer or hiding behind company policy. Look for reader benefits.

- ✓ **Present the bad news.** State the bad news objectively or imply it. Although resale or sales promotion is appropriate in order letters, it may offend in claim or credit refusals.

- ✓ **Offer gifts, benefits, or tokens of appreciation.** When appropriate, look for ways to offset your customers' disappointment.

- ✓ **Close pleasantly.** Look forward to future business, suggest action on an alternative, offer best wishes, refer to gifts, or use resale sensitively. Don't mention the bad news.

Delivering Bad News Within Organizations

learning objective

5

A tactful tone and a reasons-first approach help preserve friendly relations with customers. These same techniques are useful when delivering bad news within organizations. Interpersonal bad news might involve telling the boss that something went wrong or confronting an employee about poor performance. Organizational bad news might involve declining profits, lost contracts, harmful lawsuits, public relations controversies, or changes in policy. Whether you use a direct or an indirect pattern in delivering that news depends primarily on the anticipated reaction of the audience. Generally, bad news is better received when reasons are given first. Within organizations, you may find yourself giving bad news in person or in writing.

Giving Bad News Personally

When delivering bad news within organizations, strive to do so tactfully, professionally, and safely.

Whether you are an employee or a supervisor, you may have the unhappy responsibility of delivering bad news. First, decide whether the negative information is newsworthy. For example, trivial, noncriminal mistakes or one-time bad behaviours are best left alone. But fraudulent travel claims, consistent hostile behaviour, or failing projects must be reported.[3] For example, you might have to tell the boss that the team's computer crashed with all its important files. As a team leader or supervisor, you might be required to confront an underperforming employee. If you know that the news will upset the receiver, the reasons-first strategy is most effective. When the bad news involves one person or a small group nearby, you should generally deliver that news in person. Here are pointers on how to do so tactfully, professionally, and safely.[4]

- **Gather all the information.** Cool down and have all the facts before marching in on the boss or confronting someone. Remember that every story has two sides.
- **Prepare and rehearse.** Outline what you plan to say so that you are confident, coherent, and dispassionate.
- **Explain past, present, and future.** If you are telling the boss about a problem such as the computer crash, explain what caused the crash, the current situation, and how and when you plan to fix it.
- **Consider taking a partner.** If you fear a "shoot the messenger" reaction, especially from your boss, bring a colleague with you. Each person should have a consistent and credible part in the presentation. If possible, take advantage of your organization's internal resources. To lend credibility to your view, call on auditors, inspectors, or human resources experts.
- **Think about timing.** Don't deliver bad news when someone is already stressed or grumpy. Experts also advise against giving bad news on Friday afternoon, since people have the weekend to dwell on it.
- **Be patient with the reaction.** Give the receiver time to vent, think, recover, and act wisely.

Delivering Workplace Bad News

Many of the same techniques used to deliver bad news personally are useful when organizations face a crisis or must deliver bad news in the workplace. Smart organizations involved in a crisis prefer to communicate the news openly to employees, customers, and stockholders. A crisis might involve serious performance problems, a major relocation, massive layoffs, a management shakeup, or public controversy. Instead of letting rumours distort the truth, they explain the organization's side of the story honestly and early. Morale can be destroyed when employees learn of major events that affect their jobs through the grapevine or from news accounts, rather than from management.

Organizations can sustain employee morale by communicating bad news openly and honestly.

When bad news must be delivered to employees, management may want to deliver the news personally. With large groups, however, this is generally impossible. Instead, organizations deliver bad news through hard-copy memos. Organizations are experimenting with other delivery channels such as e-mail, videos, webcasts, and voice mail. Still, hard-copy memos seem to function most effectively because they are more formal and make a permanent record.

The draft of the memo shown in Figure 11.8 announces a substantial increase in the cost of employee health care benefits. However, the draft suffers from many problems. It announces jolting news bluntly in the first sentence. Worse, it offers little or no explanation for the steep increase in costs. It also sounds insincere (*We did everything possible . . .*) and arbitrary. In a final miscue, the writer fails to give credit to the company for absorbing previous health cost increases.

Saying No to Job Applicants

Being refused a job is one of life's major rejections. The blow is intensified by tactless letters (*Unfortunately, you were not among the candidates selected for . . .*).

Letters that deny applications for employment should be courteous and tactful but free of specifics that could trigger lawsuits.

You can reduce the receiver's disappointment somewhat by using the indirect pattern—with one important variation. In the reasons section it's wise to be vague in explaining why the candidate was not selected. First, giving concrete reasons may be painful to the receiver (*Your grade point average of 2.7 was low compared with the GPAs of other candidates*). Second, and more important, providing extra information may prove fatal in a lawsuit. Hiring and firing decisions generate considerable litigation today. To avoid charges of discrimination or wrongful actions, legal advisors warn organizations to keep employment rejection letters general, simple, and short.

The following checklist gives tips on how to communicate bad news within organizations.

Checklist for Delivering Bad News Within Organizations

- ✓ **Start with a relevant, upbeat buffer.** Open with a small bit of good news, praise, appreciation, agreement, understanding, or a discussion of facts leading to the reasons section.
- ✓ **Discuss reasons.** Except in job refusal letters, explain what caused the decision necessitating the bad news. Use objective, nonjudgmental, and nondiscriminatory language. Show empathy and fairness.
- ✓ **Reveal the bad news.** Make the bad news clear but don't accentuate it. Avoid negative language.
- ✓ **Close harmoniously.** End on a positive, friendly note. For job refusals, extend good wishes.

FIGURE 11.8 ***Announcing Bad News to Employees***

1 Prewriting

ANALYZE: The purpose of this memo is to tell employees that they must share with the company the increasing costs of health care.

ANTICIPATE: The audience will be employees who are unaware of health care costs and, most likely, reluctant to pay more.

ADAPT: Because the readers will probably be unhappy and resentful, use the indirect pattern.

2 Writing

RESEARCH: Collect facts and statistics that document health care costs.

ORGANIZE: Begin with a buffer describing the company's commitment to health benefits. Provide an explanation of health care costs. Announce the bad news. In the closing, focus on the company's major share of the cost.

COMPOSE: Draft the first version with the expectation to revise.

3 Revising

REVISE: Remove negativity (*unfortunately, we can't, extra cost, we were forced, inadvisable*). Explain the increase with specifics.

PROOFREAD: Use a semicolon before *however*. Use quotes around *defensive* to show its special sense. Spell out *percent* after 300.

EVALUATE: Is there any other way to help readers accept this bad news?

DRAFT

Beginning January 1 your monthly payment for health care benefits will be increased to $119 (up from $52 last year). — Hits readers with bad news without any preparation

Every year health care costs go up. Although we considered dropping other benefits, Midland decided that the best plan was to keep the present comprehensive package. Unfortunately, we can't do that unless we pass along some of the extra cost to you. Last year the company was forced to absorb the total increase in health care premiums. However, such a plan this year is inadvisable. — Offers no explanation

We did everything possible to avoid the sharp increase in costs to you this year. A rate schedule describing the increases in payments for your family and dependants is enclosed. — Fails to take credit for absorbing previous increases

REVISION

DATE: October 2, 2010

TO: Fellow Employees

FROM: Lawrence R. Romero, President *LRR*

SUBJECT: Maintaining Quality Health Care

Begins with positive buffer — Health care programs have always been an important part of our commitment to employees at Midland, Inc. We're proud that our total benefits package continues to rank among the best in the country.

Offers reasons explaining why costs are rising — Such a comprehensive package does not come cheaply. In the last decade health care costs alone have risen over 300 percent. We're told that several factors fuel the cost spiral: inflation, technology improvements, increased cost of outpatient services, and "defensive" medicine practised by doctors to prevent lawsuits.

Reveals bad news clearly but embeds it in paragraph — Just two years ago our monthly health care cost for each employee was $515. It rose to $569 last year. We were able to absorb that jump without increasing your contribution; however, this year's hike to $639 forces us to ask you to share the increase. To maintain your current health care benefits, you will be paying $119 a month. The enclosed rate schedule describes the costs for families and dependants.

Ends positively by stressing the company's major share of the costs — Midland continues to pay the major portion of your health care program ($520 each month). We think it's a wise investment.

Enclosure

learning objective

6

Communicating bad news in other cultures may require different strategies.

Presenting Bad News in Other Cultures

To minimize disappointment, North Americans generally prefer to present negative messages indirectly. Other cultures may treat bad news differently.

In Germany, for example, business communicators occasionally use buffers but tend to present bad news directly. British writers also tend to be straightforward with bad news, seeing no reason to soften its announcement. In Latin countries the question is not how to organize negative messages but whether to present them at all. It's considered disrespectful and impolite to report bad news to superiors. Thus, reluctant employees may fail to report accurately any negative messages to their bosses.

In Asian cultures, harmony and peace are sought in all relationships. Disrupting the harmony with bad news is avoided. To prevent discord, Japanese communicators use a number of techniques to indicate *no*—without being forced to say it. In conversation they may respond with silence or with a counter-question such as "Why do you ask?" They may change the subject or tell a white lie to save face for themselves and for the questioner. Sometimes the answer sounds like a qualified *yes*: "I will do my best, but if I cannot, I hope you will understand"; "Yes, but . . . "; or "yes" followed by an apology. All of these responses should be recognized as *no*.

In China, Westerners often have difficulty understanding the "hints" given by communicators.

"I agree" might mean "I agree with 15 percent of what you say."
"We might be able to" could mean "Not a chance."
"We will consider" could mean "*We* will, but the real decision maker will not."
"That is a little too much" might equate to "That is outrageous."[5]

In Thailand the negativism represented by a refusal is completely alien: the word *no* does not exist. In many cultures negative news is offered with such subtleness or in such a positive light that it may be overlooked or misunderstood by literal-minded low-context cultures.

In many high-context cultures, saving face is important. A refusal is a potential loss of face for both parties. To understand the meaning of what's really being communicated, we must look beyond an individual's actual words and consider the communication style, the culture, and especially the context.

Conveying bad news in any culture is tricky and requires sensitivity to and awareness of cultural practices.

Summary of Learning Objectives

1 **Describe the goals and strategies of business communicators in delivering bad news, including knowing when to use the direct and indirect patterns, applying the writing process, and avoiding legal problems.** All businesses will occasionally deal with problems. Good communicators have several goals in delivering bad news: (a) making the reader understand and accept the bad news, (b) promoting and maintaining a good image of themselves and their organizations, (c) making the message so clear that additional correspondence is unnecessary, and (d) avoiding creating legal liability or responsibility. The indirect pattern involves delaying the bad news until reasons have been presented. The direct pattern reveals the main idea immediately. The direct pattern is preferable when the receiver may overlook the bad news, when the organization's policy suggests directness, and for other reasons. Careful communicators will avoid careless and abusive language, which is actionable when it is false, damages a person's reputation, and is "published" (spoken within the presence of others or written). Messages written on company stationery represent that company and can be legally binding.

2 **Explain techniques for delivering bad news sensitively.** Begin with a buffer, such as a compliment, appreciation, a point of agreement, objective information, understanding, or some part of the message that represents good news. Then explain the reasons that necessitate the bad news, trying to cite benefits to the reader or others. Choose positive words, and clarify company policy if necessary. Announce the bad news strategically, mentioning a compromise or alternative if possible. Close pleasantly with a forward-looking goodwill statement.

3 **Identify typical requests and describe a strategy for refusing such requests.** Typical requests ask for favours, money, information, action, or other items. When the answer will be disappointing, use the reasons-before-refusal pattern. Open with a buffer, provide reasons, announce the refusal sensitively, suggest possible alternatives, and end with a positive, forward-looking comment.

4 **Explain techniques for delivering bad news to customers.** When a company disappoints its customers, most organizations (a) call the individual involved, (b) describe the problem and apologize (when the company is to blame), (c) explain why the problem occurred and what is being done to prevent its recurrence, and (d) follow up with a letter that documents the phone call and promotes goodwill. Some organizations also offer gifts or benefits to offset customers' disappointment and to reestablish the business relationship. In denying claims or refusing credit, begin indirectly, provide reasons for the refusal, and close pleasantly, looking forward to future business. When appropriate, resell a product or service.

5 **Explain techniques for delivering bad news within organizations.** When delivering bad news personally to a superior, gather all the information, prepare and rehearse, explain what happened and how the problem will be repaired, consider taking a colleague with you, think about timing, and be patient with the reaction. In delivering workplace bad news to employees, use the indirect pattern but be sure to provide clear, convincing reasons that explain the decision. In refusing job applicants, however, keep letters short, general, and tactful.

6 **Compare strategies for revealing bad news in different cultures.** North American communicators often prefer to break bad news slowly and indirectly. In other low-context cultures, such as Germany and Britain, however, bad news is revealed directly. In high-context cultures, straightforwardness is avoided. In Latin cultures, bad news may be totally suppressed. In Asian cultures, negativism is avoided and hints may suggest bad news. Subtle meanings must be interpreted carefully.

chapter review

1. Why is the indirect strategy appropriate for some bad-news messages? (Obj. 1)
2. What are four goals when a business communicator delivers bad news? (Obj. 1)
3. Describe the four parts of the indirect message pattern. (Obj. 1)
4. Name five situations in which the direct pattern should be used for bad news. (Obj. 1)
5. Name five or more techniques to buffer the opening of a bad-news message. (Obj. 2)
6. Name four or more techniques to deemphasize bad news when it is presented. (Obj. 2)
7. Name four kinds of routine requests that businesses must frequently refuse. (Obj. 3)
8. Why should you be especially careful in cushioning a refusal to an invitation? (Obj. 3)
9. What is the major difference between bad-news messages for customers and those for other people? (Obj. 4)
10. Identify a process used by a majority of business professionals in resolving problems with disappointed customers. (Obj. 4)
11. List four goals a writer seeks to achieve in writing messages that deny credit to prospective customers. (Obj. 4)
12. Why should a writer be somewhat vague in the reasons section of a letter rejecting a job applicant? (Obj. 4)
13. Why is the reasons-before-refusal strategy appropriate for customers who are unhappy with a product or service? (Obj. 4)
14. What actions are tactful, professional, and safe when a subordinate must personally deliver upsetting news to a superior? (Obj. 5)
15. In Latin countries, why may employees sometimes fail to report accurately any negative messages to management? (Obj. 6)

critical thinking

1. Does bad news travel faster and farther than good news? Why? What implications would this have for companies responding to unhappy customers? (Objs. 1–5)
2. Some people feel that all employee news, good or bad, should be announced directly. Do you agree or disagree? Why? (Objs. 1–5)
3. Consider times when you have been aware that others have used the indirect pattern in writing or speaking to you. How did you react? (Objs. 1–5)
4. How effective is the following advice for supervisors? "Most bad news doesn't have to be given to employees. Instead, ask your employee two open-ended questions: 'How do you think you performed?' and 'How could you do better next time?'"[6] (Obj. 5)

activities

11.1 Organizational Patterns (Objs. 1–5)

Your Task. Identify which organizational pattern you would use for the following messages: direct or indirect.

a. A letter refusing a request by a charitable organization to use your office equipment on the weekend.
b. A memo from the manager denying an employee's request for special parking privileges. The employee works closely with the manager on many projects.
c. An announcement to employees that a financial specialist has cancelled a scheduled lunchtime talk and cannot reschedule.
d. A letter from a bank refusing to fund a company's overseas expansion plan.
e. A form letter from an insurance company announcing new policy requirements that many policyholders may resent. If policyholders do not indicate the plan they prefer, they may lose their insurance coverage.

11.2 Passive-Voice Verbs (Obj. 2)

Your Task. Revise the following sentences to present the bad news with passive-voice verbs.

a. Company policy forbids us to give performance reviews until an employee has been on the job for 12 months.
b. Because management now requires more stringent security, we are postponing indefinitely requests for company tours.
c. We do not examine patients until we have verified their insurance coverage.
d. Your car rental insurance coverage does not cover large SUVs.

Rich chapter resources are available on the Web site.

11.3 Subordinating Bad News (Obj. 2)

Your Task. Revise the following sentences to position the bad news in a subordinate clause. (Hint: Consider beginning the clause with *Although.*) Use passive-voice verbs for the bad news.

- **a.** Unfortunately, we no longer print a complete catalogue. However, we now offer all of our catalogue choices at our Web site, which is always current.
- **b.** We appreciate your interest in our organization, but we are unable to extend an employment offer to you at this time.
- **c.** It is impossible for us to ship your complete order at this time. However, we are able to send the four oak desks now; you should receive them within five days.
- **d.** Provincial law does not allow smoking within 1.5 metres of a public building. But the college has set aside 16 outdoor smoking areas.

11.4 Implying Bad News (Obj. 2)

Your Task. Revise the following statements to imply the bad news. If possible, use passive-voice verbs and subordinate clauses to further deemphasize the bad news.

- **a.** Unfortunately, we find it impossible to contribute to the fund-raising campaign this year. At present all the funds of my organization are needed to lease new equipment and offices for our new branch in Richmond. We hope to be able to support this endeavour in the future.
- **b.** Because of the holiday period, all our billboard space was used this month. Therefore, we are sorry to say that we could not give your charitable group free display space. However, next month, after the holidays, we hope to display your message as we promised.
- **c.** We cannot ship our fresh fruit baskets C.O.D. Your order was not accompanied by payment, so we are not shipping it. We have it ready, though, and will rush it to its destination as soon as you call us with your credit card number.

11.5 Evaluating Bad-News Statements (Obj. 2)

Your Task. Discuss the strengths or weaknesses of the following bad-news statements.

- **a.** It's impossible for us to ship your order before May 1.
- **b.** Frankly, we like your résumé, but we were hoping to hire someone a little younger who might be able to stay with us longer.
- **c.** I'm thoroughly disgusted with this entire case, and I will never do business with shyster lawyers like you again.
- **d.** We can assure you that on any return visit to our hotels, you will not be treated so poorly.
- **e.** We must deny your credit application because your record shows a history of late payments, nonpayment, and irregular employment.
- **f.** *In a confidential company memo*: I cannot recommend that we promote this young lady into any position where she will meet the public. Her colourful facial decoration, which is part of her religion, may offend our customers.

11.6 Document for Analysis: Favour Refusal (Objs. 1–3)

Your Task. Analyze the following letter. List its weaknesses. If your instructor directs, revise it.

Dear Ms. Lazarovich:

I have before me your unusual request inviting my company to participate in your research for a proposed article about "sales stars who are ascending." Unfortunately, your request involves salaries of young salespeople. As must be apparent to any clear-thinking executive, we cannot accept your invitation to release salary information. Exposing the salaries of our salespeople—regardless of how outstanding they are—would violate their privacy, jeopardize their careers, and reveal insider information. Doing so might even violate the law.

We do, however, have many outstanding young salespeople who command top salaries, and we are proud of their success. Unfortunately, during salary negotiations several years ago we reached an agreement. Both sales staff members and management agreed to keep the terms of individual contracts confidential. We could not possibly reveal specific salaries and commission rates.

Since your article is to focus on star performers, you might be interested in our ranked list of top salespeople for the past five years. As I glance over the list, I see that three of our current top salespeople are under the age of 35. We have a fact sheet about all of our top salespeople, and I will include that sheet.

Perhaps you can include some of this information in your article because we would like to see our company represented.

Cordially,

11.7 Document for Analysis: Saying No to a Job Applicant (Objs. 1, 2, and 5)

Your Task. Analyze the following letter. List its weaknesses. If your instructor directs, revise it.

Dear Mr. Margolies:

Ms. Martineau and I wish to thank you for the pleasure of allowing us to interview you last Thursday. We were delighted to learn about your superb academic record, and we also appreciated your attentiveness in listening to our description of the operations of Vortec Enterprises.

However, we had many well-qualified applicants who were interested in the advertised position of human resources assistant. As you may have guessed, we were particularly eager to find a minority individual who could help us fill out our employment equity goals. Although you did not fit one of our goal areas, we enjoyed talking with you. We hired a female graduate of Ryerson University who had most of the qualities we sought.

Although we realize that the job market is difficult at this time, you have our heartfelt wishes for good luck in finding precisely what you are looking for.

Sincerely,

11.8 Bad News for Customers—Stop Trashing Canada, Tim Hortons! (Obj. 4)

When Tim Hortons introduced its "Roll Up the Rim to Win" contest in 1986, "rolling to win" became a national pastime. This contest, which takes place annually from March to May, rewards loyal Tim's customers with opportunities to win prizes that include cars, plasma TVs, and Tim Hortons products. However, environmentalists claim that this contest increases waste and littering since people are motivated to buy more cups of coffee, and if they don't win, they just throw out the cup.

When a new Tim Hortons opened in St. Andrews, New Brunswick, a local resident brought the littering problem to light. He began a daily pickup of litter, noting, "Everywhere I've been, I've seen Tim Hortons cups all over the place. You'll see them in Iqaluit, you'll see them on Pelee Island." The prevalence of Tim Hortons cups is no secret in Atlantic Canada, where a Nova Scotia study found that 22 percent of identifiable trash in the province's roadways and ditches could be credited to Tim Hortons. McDonald's was a distant second at 10 percent. Needless to say, environmentalists are concerned. With over 2 470 restaurants in Canada, Tim Hortons cups seem to be a favourite throwaway item of litterbugs, and the problem is only intensified during the annual contest. Ronald Colman, executive director of GPI Atlantic, a nonprofit group that researches environmental and quality of life issues, asserts, "I don't think it's socially responsible to have a promotion which creates massive waste." Obviously, many other people agree, since in response to customer concerns, Tim Hortons provides information on its Web site that addresses the measures it takes to deal with the environmental concerns caused by the cups.[7]

Your Task. Assume you are part of an intern team in the public relations office at Tim Hortons in Oakville, Ontario. As a learning experience, your group has been asked to draft a message that can be used in response to the negative incoming mail about container waste and litter. Your intern supervisor tells you to go to the company Web site (**www.timhortons.com**) and read its environment/waste management statements (Hint: Look under FAQs). Locate other useful articles or information on the Web or with InfoTrac. Discuss an appropriate response based on the information you found and your training in writing bad-news messages. Individually or as a team, draft a message that could be used as a letter or an e-mail responding to inquiries requesting Tim Hortons to stop trashing Canada. You should produce a polite but responsive message, not a long, data-filled defence. For the signature of Newton M. Haynes, prepare a letter draft addressed to Mrs. Dorothy King, 118 Market Street, Hamilton, ON L8R 3P9.

11.9 Damage Control for Disappointed Customers: Costly SUV Upgrade to a Ford Excursion (Obj. 4)

CRITICAL THINKING

Steven Yule, a consultant from Calgary, Alberta, was surprised when he picked up his rental car from Budget over Easter weekend. He had reserved a full-size car, but the rental agent told him he could upgrade to a Ford Excursion for an additional $25 a day. "She told me it was easy to drive," Mr. Yule reported. "But when I saw it, I realized it was huge—like a tank. You could fit a full-size bed inside."

On his trip Mr. Yule managed to scratch the paint and damage the rear doorstep. He didn't worry, though, because he thought the damage would be covered, since he had charged the rental on his American Express card. He knew that the company offered backup car rental insurance coverage. To his dismay, he discovered that its car rental coverage excluded large SUVs. "I just assumed they'd cover it," he confessed. He wrote to Budget to complain about not being warned that certain credit cards may not cover damage to large SUVs or luxury cars.

Budget agents always encourage renters to sign up for Budget's own "risk product." But they don't feel that it is their responsibility to study the policies of customers' insurance carriers and explain what may or may not be covered. Moreover, they try to move customers into their rental cars as quickly as possible and avoid lengthy discussions of insurance coverage. Customers who do not purchase insurance are at risk. Mr. Yule does not make any claim against Budget, but he is upset about being "pitched" to upgrade to the larger SUV, which he didn't really want.[8]

Your Task. As a member of the communication staff at Budget, respond to Mr. Yule's complaint. Budget obviously is not going to pay for the SUV repairs, but it does want to salvage his goodwill and future business. Offer him a coupon worth two days' free rental of any full-size sedan. Write to Steven Yule, 5300 Park Ridge, Apt. 4A, Calgary, AB T2P 2M5.

11.10 Damage Control for Disappointed Customers: Late Delivery of Printing Order (Obj. 4)

LISTENING SPEAKING

Kevin Kearns, a printing company sales manager, must tell one of his clients that the payroll cheques his company ordered are not going to be ready by the date Kearns had promised. The printing company's job scheduler overlooked the job and didn't get the cheques into production in time to meet the deadline. As a result, Kearns's client, a major insurance company, is going to miss its pay run.

Kearns meets with internal department heads. They decide on the following plan to remedy the situation: (1) move the cheque order to the front of the production line; (2) make up for the late production date by shipping some of the cheques—enough to meet their client's immediate payroll needs—by air freight; and (3) deliver the remaining cheques by truck.[9]

Your Task. Form groups of three to four students. Discuss the following issues about how to present the bad news to Andrew Tyra, Kearns's contact person at the insurance company.

- **a.** Should Kearns call Tyra directly or delegate the task to his assistant?
- **b.** When should Tyra be informed of the problem?
- **c.** What is the best procedure for delivering the bad news?
- **d.** What follow-up would you recommend to Kearns?

Be prepared to share your group's responses during a class discussion. Your instructor may ask two students to role-play the presentation of the bad news.

11.11 Credit Refusal: No Hawaiian Luaus on the Beach (Obj. 4)

Your Task. Revise the following ineffective letter that refuses credit.

Current date

Mr. Stefano Romano
Creative Catering
225 Stafford Road South
Lethbridge, AB T1J 4R5

Dear Mr. Romano:

This is to inform you that we have received your recent order for our fine restaurant supplies. However, we are unable to fill this order because of the bad credit record you have on file at Equifax Credit Services.

We understand that at this point in time you are opening a new gourmet catering business called Creative Catering. Our sales rep told us about your plans to serve Hawaiian-style barbecue and luaus in urban settings. He said your firm will also cater corporate events, box lunches, theme parties, and fund-raising events. I must say that we were all impressed with your plan to provide elegant yet economical catering in the Regina area. Although we are sure your catering business will be a success, we cannot extend credit because of your current poor credit rating.

You might be interested in investigating what is in your credit file. The Consumer Reporting Act guarantees you the right to see the information contained in your file. If you would like to see what prevented you from obtaining credit from us, you should call 1-888-EQUIFAX1.

We are truly sorry that we cannot fill your initial order, totalling $1430, for our superior restaurant supplies. We pride ourselves on serving most of Western Canada's finest restaurants and catering services. We would be proud to add Creative Catering to our list of discerning customers. Perhaps the best way for you to join that select list is with a smaller order to begin with. We would be happy to serve you on a cash basis. If this plan meets with your approval, do let me know.

Sincerely,

11.12 Bad News to Employees: Suit Up or Ship Out (Obj. 5)

During the feverish dot-com boom days, "business casual" became the workplace norm. Many companies loosened their dress policies and allowed employees to come to work in polo shirts, khaki pants, and loafers for two important reasons: They had to compete with Internet companies in a tight employment market, and they wanted to fit in with their casual dot-com customers. But when the dot-com bubble burst and the economy faltered, the casual workplace environment glorified by failed Internet companies fell out of favour.

Managers at one securities firm decided to reverse course and cancel the casual dress code that had been in effect for two years. Company spokesperson Elizabeth Ventura said, "Our employees should reflect the professionalism of our business." Some observers felt that relaxed dress codes carried over into relaxed work attitudes.

Particularly in difficult economic times, the company believed that every aspect of the business, including dress, should reflect the serious attitude and commitment it had toward relations with clients. After the securities market plunged, the company slashed 830 jobs, amounting to 7.5 percent of its workforce. This was the biggest cut in its history, and officials vowed to get serious about regaining market share.

To put into effect its more serious business tone, the organization decided to return to a formal dress code. For men, suits and ties would be required. For women, dresses, suits with skirts or slacks, or "equivalent attire" would be expected. Although the company decided to continue to allow casual dress on Fridays, sports jackets would be required for men.

Despite the policy reversal, company officials downplayed the return to traditional, more formal attire. Spokesperson Ventura noted that the company's legal, administrative, and private client services departments had never adopted the casual dress code. In addition, she said, "We've always had a formal dress policy for meetings with clients."

To ease the transition, a nearby conservative clothing store offered a special invitation. On September 20 it would stay open an extra hour to host an evening of wine, cheese, and shopping, with discounts of 20 percent for staffers.[10]

Your Task. As an assistant to John Jones, chairman of the Management and Compensation Committee, you have the challenging task of drafting a message to employees announcing the return to a formal dress code. He realizes that this is going to be a tough sell, but he's hoping that employees will recognize that difficult economic times require serious efforts and sacrifices. In the message to employees, he wants you to tell supervisors that they must speak to employees who fail to adhere to the new guidelines. You ask Mr. Jones whether he wants the message to open directly or indirectly. He says that the organization generally prefers directness in messages to employees, but he wants you to prepare two versions and he will choose one.

C.L.U.E. review 11

Edit the following sentences to correct all language faults, including grammar, punctuation, spelling, and word confusions.

1. Bad news is generaly disapointing, however the negative feelings can be reduced.
2. 2 ways to reduce the disapointment of bad news is to: (1) give reasons first, and (2) reveal the news sensitively.
3. When delivering bad news its important that you make sure the reciever understands and excepts it.
4. The indirect pattern consists of 4 parts, buffer, reasons, bad news, and closing.
5. Although the indirect pattern is not apropriate for every situation it is usualy better then a blunt announcement of bad news.
6. On June 1st, our company President and Vice President revealed a four million dollar drop in profits which was bad news for every one.
7. Because of declining profits and raising Health costs the Director of our Human Resources Department announced a increase in each employees contribution to Health Benefits.
8. Most of us prefer to be let down gentle, when were being refused something, thats why the reasons before refusal pattern is effective.
9. When a well known Tire company recalled 100s of thousands of tires it's President issued a apology to the public, and all injured customers'.
10. If I was you I would begin the bad news message with a complement not a blunt rejection.

unit 4

Reports and Proposals

chapter 12

Preparing to Write Business Reports

chapter 13

Organizing and Writing Typical Business Reports

chapter 14

Proposals and Formal Reports

chapter 12

Preparing to Write Business Reports

objectives

1 Describe business report basics, including functions, patterns (indirect or direct), writing style, and formats.

2 Apply the 3-x-3 writing process to business reports.

3 Understand where to find and how to use print and electronic sources of secondary data.

4 Comprehend the evolving nature of communication technology: the Web, electronic databases, and other resources for business writers and researchers.

5 Understand where to find and how to use sources of primary data.

6 Recognize the purposes and techniques of documentation in business reports and avoid plagiarism.

7 Illustrate reports with graphics that create meaning and interest.

springboard *to discussion*

Technology has changed the way that researchers are getting information. Many researchers are finding that telephone surveys are yielding response rates in North America of less than 30 percent, since more people are relying on screening tools, using cell phones, and becoming reluctant to speak to strangers. As an alternative, online surveys are being used since they are more convenient for the respondent and less disruptive and intrusive. Participants can choose the place and time for completing surveys. Additionally, response rates range from 45 to 65 percent and higher, depending on the desired target group.[1]

learning objective 1

Understanding Report Basics

Reports are common in North American business. In this low-context culture, our values and attitudes seem to prompt us to write reports. We analyze problems, gather and study the facts, and then assess the alternatives. We pride ourselves on being practical and logical as we apply scientific procedures. When we must persuade a client that our services can add value, we generally write a report outlining our case.

Management decisions in many organizations are based on information submitted in the form of reports. Reports help us understand and study systematically the challenges that we encounter in business before we can outline the steps toward solving them. Business solutions are unthinkable without a thorough examination of the problems that prompted them. This chapter examines the functions, patterns, writing style, and formats of typical business reports. It also introduces the report-writing process and discusses methods of collecting, documenting, and illustrating data.

Business reports range from informal half-page trip reports to formal 200-page financial forecasts. Reports may be presented orally in front of a group or electronically on a computer screen. Some reports appear as words on paper in the form of memos and letters. Others are primarily numerical data, such as tax reports or profit-and-loss statements. Increasingly, reports are delivered and presented digitally, for instance, as PDF (portable digital format) documents or as electronic "slide decks." These files can then be e-mailed or distributed on the company intranet or posted on the Internet. Hyperlinks tie together content within the document, between associated files, and with Web site sources. Such linking adds depth and flexibility to traditional linear texts. Some provide information only; others analyze and make recommendations. Although reports vary greatly in length, content, form, and formality level, they all have one common purpose: *to answer questions and solve problems.*

Effective business reports answer questions and solve problems systematically.

FIGURE 12.1 ***Audience Analysis and Report Organization***

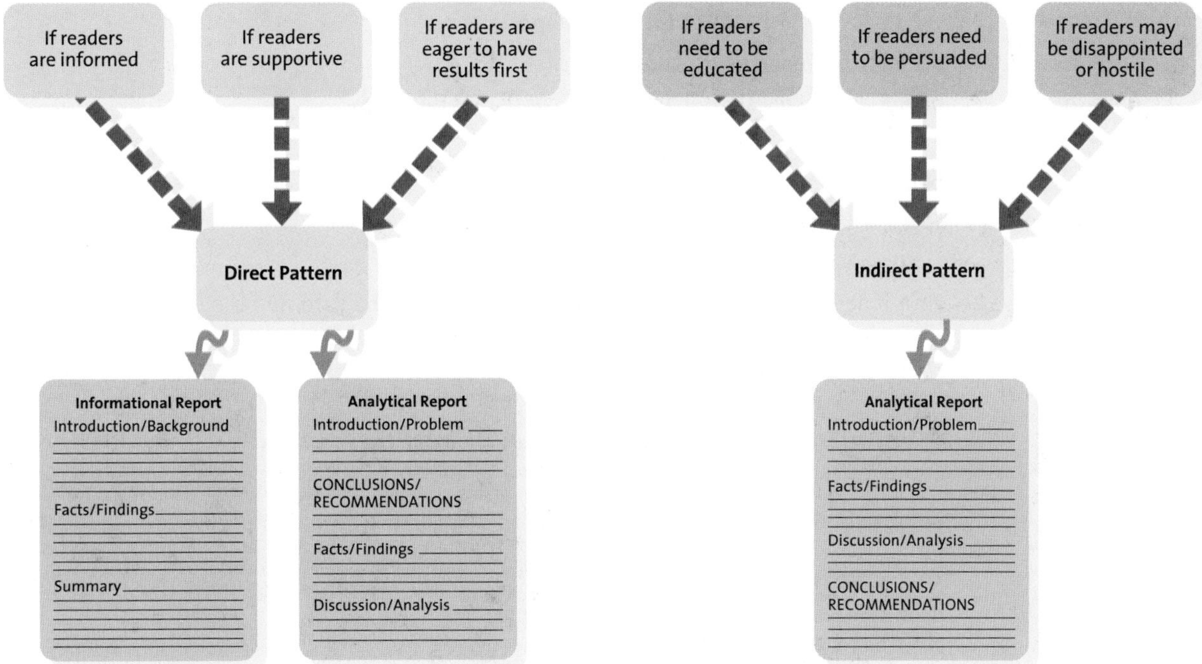

Functions

In terms of what they do, most reports fit into two broad categories: informational reports and analytical reports.

Informational reports present data without comment or recommendations. Analytical reports provide data, analyses, conclusions, and, if requested, recommendations.

Informational Reports. Reports that present data without analysis or recommendations are primarily informational. For such reports, writers collect and organize facts but they do not analyze the facts for readers. A trip report describing an employee's visit to a trade show, for example, presents information. Other reports that present information without analysis involve routine operations, compliance with regulations, and company policies and procedures.

Analytical Reports. Reports that provide data, analyses, and conclusions are analytical. If requested, writers also supply recommendations. Analytical reports may intend to persuade readers to act or change their beliefs. For example, if you were writing a feasibility report that compared several potential locations for a fast-food restaurant, you might conclude by recommending one site. Your report, an analysis of alternatives and a recommendation, attempts to persuade readers to accept that site.

Organizational Patterns

Like letters and memos, reports may be organized directly or indirectly. The reader's expectations and the content of a report determine its pattern of development, as illustrated in Figure 12.1. In long reports, such as corporate annual reports, some parts may be developed directly whereas other parts are arranged indirectly.

Direct Pattern. When the purpose for writing is presented close to the beginning, the organizational pattern is direct. Informational reports, such as the letter report shown in Figure 12.2 (page 274), are usually arranged directly. They open with an

FIGURE 12.2 ***Informational Report—Letter Format***

Tips for Letter Reports

- Use letter format for short informal reports sent to outsiders.
- Organize the facts section into logical divisions identified by consistent headings.
- Single-space the body.
- Double-space between paragraphs.
- Leave two blank lines above each side heading.
- Create side margins of 2.5 to 3 centimetres.
- Add a second-page heading, if necessary, consisting of the addressee's name, the date, and the page number.

Centre for Consumers of Legal Services
P.O. Box 260
Kitchener, ON N2K 2V5

Uses letterhead stationery for an informal report addressed to an outsider

September 7, 2010

Ms. Lisa Burgess, Secretary
Westwood Homeowners
3902 Westwood Drive
Guelph, ON N1H 6Y7

Dear Ms. Burgess:

As executive director of the Centre for Consumers of Legal Services, I'm pleased to send you this information describing how your homeowners' association can sponsor a legal services plan for its members. After an introduction with background data, this report will discuss three steps necessary for your group to start its plan.

Presents introduction and facts without analysis or recommendations

Introduction

A legal services plan promotes preventive law by letting members talk to lawyers whenever problems arise. Prompt legal advice often avoids or prevents expensive litigation. Because groups can supply a flow of business to the plan's lawyers, groups can negotiate free consultation, follow-up, and discounts.

Two kinds of plans are commonly available. The first, a free plan, offers free legal consultation along with discounts for services when the participating groups are sufficiently large to generate business for the plan's lawyers. These plans actually act as a substitute for advertising for the lawyers. The second common type is the prepaid plan. Prepaid plans provide more benefits, but members must pay annual fees, usually of $200 or more per year.

Since you inquired about a free plan for your homeowners' association, the following information describes how to set up such a program.

Arranges facts of report into sections with descriptive headings

Determine the Benefits Your Group Needs

The first step in establishing a free legal services plan is to meet with the members of your group to decide what benefits they want. Typical benefits include the following:

Emphasizes benefits in paragraph headings with boldface type

Free consultation. Members may consult a participating lawyer—by phone or in the lawyer's office—to discuss any matter. The number of consultations is unlimited, provided each is about a separate matter. Consultations are generally limited to 30 minutes, but they include substantive analysis and advice.

Free document review. Important papers—such as leases, insurance policies, and installment sales contracts—may be reviewed with legal counsel. Members may ask questions and receive an explanation of terms.

Ms. Lisa Burgess Page 2 September 7, 2010

Discount on additional services. For more complex matters, participating lawyers will charge members 75 percent of the lawyer's normal fee. However, some organizations choose to charge a flat fee for commonly needed services.

Select the Lawyers for Your Plan

Groups with geographically concentrated memberships have an advantage in forming legal plans. These groups can limit the number of participating lawyers and yet provide adequate service. Generally, smaller panels of lawyers are advantageous.

Assemble a list of candidates, inviting them to apply. The best way to compare prices is to have candidates submit their fee schedules. Your group can then compare fee schedules and select the lowest bidder, if price is important. Arrange to interview lawyers in their offices.

After selecting a lawyer or a panel, sign a contract. The contract should include the reason for the plan, what the lawyer agrees to do, what the group agrees to do, how each side can end the contract, and the signatures of both parties. You may also wish to include references to malpractice insurance, assurance that the group will not interfere with the lawyer–client relationship, an evaluation form, a grievance procedure, and responsibility for government filings.

Publicize the Plan to Your Members

Members won't use a plan if they don't know about it, and a plan will not be successful if it is unused. Publicity must be vocal and ongoing. Announce it in newsletters, meetings, bulletin boards, and flyers.

Persistence is the key. All too frequently, leaders of an organization assume that a single announcement is all that's needed. They expect members to see the value of the plan and remember that it's available. Most organization members, though, are not as involved as the leadership. Therefore, it takes more publicity than the leadership usually expects in order to reach and maintain the desired level of awareness.

Summary

A successful free legal services plan involves designing a program, choosing the lawyers, and publicizing the plan. To learn more about these steps or to order a $25 how-to manual, call me at (519) 884-9901.

Sincerely,

Richard M. Ramos

Richard M. Ramos
Executive Director

pas

Identifies second and succeeding pages with headings

Uses parallel side headings for consistency and readability

Includes complimentary close and signature

introduction, which is followed by the facts and a summary. In Figure 12.2 the writer explains a legal services plan using a letter report. The report begins with an introduction. The facts, divided into three subtopics and identified by descriptive headings, follow. The report ends with a summary and a complimentary close.

Analytical reports may also be organized directly, especially when readers are supportive of or familiar with the topic. Many busy executives prefer this pattern because it gives them the results of the report immediately. They don't have to spend time wading through the facts, findings, discussion, and analyses to get to the two items they are most interested in—the conclusions and recommendations. Figure 12.3 on page 276 illustrates such an arrangement. This analytical memo report describes environmental hazards of a property that a realtor has just listed. The realtor is familiar with the investigation and eager to find out the recommendations.

The direct pattern places conclusions and recommendations near the beginning of a report.

FIGURE 12.3 ***Analytical Report—Memo Format***

Tips for Memo Reports

- Use memo format for most short (ten or fewer pages) informal reports within an organization.
- Leave side margins of 2.5 to 3 centimetres.
- Sign your initials on the *From* line.
- Use an informal, conversational style.
- For direct analytical reports, put recommendations first.
- For indirect analytical reports, put recommendations last.

Atlantic Environmental, Inc.

Interoffice Memo

Applies memo format for short, informal internal report

DATE: March 7, 2010

TO: Kermit Fox, President

FROM: Cynthia M. Rashid, Environmental Engineer CMR

SUBJECT: INVESTIGATION OF MOUNTAIN PARK COMMERCIAL SITE

Uses first paragraph as introduction

For Laurentian Realty, Inc., I've completed a preliminary investigation of its Mountain Park property listing. The following recommendations are based on my physical inspection of the site, official records, and interviews with officials and persons knowledgeable about the site.

Presents recommendations first (direct pattern) because reader is supportive and familiar with topic

Recommendations

To reduce its potential environmental liability, Laurentian Realty should take the following steps in regard to its Mountain Park listing:

- Conduct an immediate asbestos survey at the site, including inspection of ceiling insulation material, floor tiles, and insulation around a gas-fired heater vent pipe at 2539 Mountain View Drive.
- Prepare an environmental audit of the generators of hazardous waste currently operating at the site, including Mountain Technology.
- Obtain lids for the dumpsters situated in the parking areas and ensure that the lids are kept closed.

Combines findings and analyses in short report

Findings and Analyses

My preliminary assessment of the site and its immediate vicinity revealed rooms with damaged floor tiles on the first and second floors of 2539 Mountain View Drive. Apparently, in recent remodelling efforts, these tiles had been cracked and broken. Examination of the ceiling and attic revealed further possible contamination from asbestos. The insulation for the hot-water tank was in poor condition.

Located on the property is Mountain Technology, a possible hazardous waste generator. Although I could not examine its interior, this company has the potential for producing hazardous material contamination.

In the parking area large dumpsters collect trash and debris from several businesses. These dumpsters were uncovered, thus posing a risk to the general public.

In view of the construction date of the structures on this property, asbestos-containing building materials might be present. Moreover, this property is located in an industrial part of the city, further prompting my recommendation for a thorough investigation. Laurentian Realty can act immediately to eliminate one environmental concern: covering the dumpsters in the parking area.

FIGURE 12.4 *Report-Writing Styles*

	Formal Writing Style	Informal Writing Style
Use	Theses	Short, routine reports
	Research studies	Reports for familiar audiences
	Controversial or complex reports (especially to outsiders)	Noncontroversial reports
Effect	Impression of objectivity, accuracy, professionalism, fairness	Most reports for company insiders
	Distance created between writer and reader	Feeling of warmth, personal involvement, closeness
Characteristics	Absence of first-person pronouns; use of third-person *(the researcher, the writer)*	Use of first-person pronouns *(I, we, me, my, us, our)*
	Absence of contractions *(can't, don't)*	Use of contractions
	Use of passive-voice verbs *(the study was conducted)*	Emphasis on active-voice verbs *(I conducted the study)*
	Complex sentences; long words	Shorter sentences; familiar words
	Absence of humour and figures of speech	Occasional use of humour, metaphors
	Reduced use of colourful adjectives and adverbs	Occasional use of colourful speech
	Elimination of "editorializing" (author's opinions, perceptions)	Acceptance of author's opinions and ideas

Therefore, the memo is organized directly. You should be aware, though, that unless readers are familiar with the topic, they may find the direct pattern confusing. Many readers prefer the indirect pattern because it seems logical and mirrors the way they solve problems.

Indirect Pattern. When the conclusions and recommendations, if requested, appear at the end of the report, the organizational pattern is indirect. Such reports usually begin with an introduction or description of the problem, followed by facts and interpretations from the writer. They end with conclusions and recommendations. This pattern is helpful when readers are unfamiliar with the problem. It's also useful when readers must be persuaded or when they may be disappointed in or hostile toward the report's findings. The writer is more likely to retain the reader's interest by first explaining, justifying, and analyzing the facts and then making recommendations. This pattern also seems most rational to readers because it follows the normal thought process: problem, alternatives (facts), solution.

The indirect pattern is appropriate for analytical reports that seek to persuade or that convey bad news.

Writing Style

Like other business messages, reports can range from informal to formal, depending on their purpose, audience, and setting. Research reports from consultants to their clients tend to be rather formal. Such reports must project an impression of objectivity, authority, and impartiality. But a report to your boss describing a trip to a conference would probably be informal. Figure 12.4, which compares characteristics of formal and informal report-writing styles, can help you decide the writing style that's appropriate for your reports.

Reports can be formal or informal depending on the purpose, audience, and setting.

Formats

A report's format depends on its length, audience, topic, and purpose.

The format of a report is governed by its length, topic, audience, and purpose. After considering these elements, you'll probably choose from among the following formats.

Letter Format. Use letter format for short (usually eight or fewer pages) informal reports addressed outside an organization. Prepared on office stationery, a letter report contains a date, inside address, salutation, and complimentary close, as shown in Figure 12.2. Although they may carry information similar to that found in correspondence, letter reports usually are longer and show more careful organization than most letters. They also include headings.

Memo Format. For short informal reports that stay within organizations, the memo format is appropriate. Memo reports begin with essential background information, using standard headings: *Date*, *To*, *From*, and *Subject*, as shown in Figure 12.3. Like letter reports, memo reports differ from regular memos in length, use of headings, and deliberate organization.

Manuscript Format. For longer, more formal reports, use the manuscript format. These reports are usually printed on plain paper instead of letterhead stationery or memo forms. They begin with a title followed by systematically displayed headings and subheadings. You will see examples of proposals and formal reports using the manuscript format in Chapter 14.

Printed Forms. Prepared forms are often used for repetitive data, such as monthly sales reports, performance appraisals, merchandise inventories, and personnel and financial reports. Standardized headings on these forms save time for the writer. Preprinted forms also make similar information easy to locate and ensure that all necessary information is provided.

Digital Format. Digital media allow writers to produce and distribute reports in electronic form, not in hard copy. With Adobe Acrobat, any report can be converted into a PDF document that retains its format and cannot be changed. In addition, today's communicators can use programs such as PowerPoint to create electronic presentations that often double as a "slide deck" to concisely display the content of a report. Such presentations are meant not so much for verbal delivery (because they are more text-heavy than typical PowerPoint slides) as they are for posting online and e-mailing. They are called slide decks because, when printed out, the stacks of slides resemble decks of playing cards. Digital delivery has also changed Microsoft Word documents. This popular program lets users hyperlink multimedia content within the document or with associated text or media files. Such digital documents create a nonlinear reading experience similar to that of browsing Web pages.

learning objective 2

Applying the 3-x-3 Writing Process to Reports

Because business reports are systematic attempts to answer questions and solve problems, the best reports are developed methodically. That same process is even more necessary in helping you prepare longer projects such as reports and proposals. Let's channel the writing process into seven specific steps:

- **Step 1:** Analyze the problem and purpose.
- **Step 2:** Anticipate the audience and issues.

- **Step 3:** Prepare a work plan.
- **Step 4:** Implement your research strategy.
- **Step 5:** Organize, analyze, interpret, and illustrate the data.
- **Step 6:** Compose the first draft.
- **Step 7:** Revise, proofread, and evaluate.

The best reports grow out of a seven-step process beginning with analysis and ending with proofreading and evaluation.

How much time you spend on each step depends on your report task. A short informational report on a familiar topic might require a brief work plan, little research, and no data analysis. A complex analytical report, on the other hand, might demand a comprehensive work plan, extensive research, and careful data analysis. In this section we will consider the first three steps in the process: (1) analyzing the problem and purpose, (2) anticipating the audience and issues, and (3) preparing a work plan.

To illustrate the planning stages of a report, we will watch Diane Camas develop a report she's preparing for her boss, Mike Rivers, at Mycon Pharmaceutical Laboratories. Mike asked Diane to investigate the problem of transportation for sales representatives. Currently, some Mycon reps visit customers (mostly doctors and hospitals) using company-leased cars. A few reps drive their own cars, receiving reimbursements for use. In three months Mycon's leasing agreement for 14 cars expires, and Mike is considering a major change. Diane's task is to investigate the choices and report her findings to Mike.

Analyzing the Problem and Purpose

The first step in writing a report is understanding the problem or assignment clearly. For complex reports it's wise to prepare a written problem statement. In analyzing her report task, Diane had many questions: Is the problem that Mycon is spending too much money on leased cars? Does Mycon wish to invest in owning a fleet of cars? Is Mike unhappy with the paperwork involved in reimbursing sales reps when they use their own cars? Does he suspect that reps are submitting inflated mileage figures? Before starting research for the report, Diane talked with Mike to define the problem. She learned several dimensions of the situation and wrote the following statement to clarify the problem—both for herself and for Mike.

Before beginning a report, identify the problem to be solved in a clear statement.

> **Problem Statement:** The leases on all company cars will be expiring in three months. Mycon must decide whether to renew them or develop a new policy regarding transportation for sales reps. Expenses and paperwork for employee-owned cars seem excessive.

Diane further defined the problem by writing a specific question that she would try to answer in her report:

> **Problem Question:** What plan should Mycon follow in providing transportation for its sales reps?

Now Diane was ready to concentrate on the purpose of the report. Again she had questions: Exactly what did Mike expect? Did he want a comparison of costs for buying and leasing cars? Should she conduct research to pinpoint exact reimbursement costs when employees drive their own cars? Did he want her to do all the legwork, present her findings in a report, and let him make a decision? Or did he want her to evaluate the choices and recommend a course of action? After talking with Mike, Diane was ready to write a simple purpose statement for this assignment.

A simple purpose statement defines the focus of a report.

Simple Statement of Purpose: To recommend a plan that provides sales reps with cars to be used in their calls.

Preparing a written purpose statement is a good idea because it defines the focus of a report and provides a standard that keeps the project on target. In writing useful purpose statements, choose action verbs telling what you intend to do: *analyze, choose, investigate, compare, justify, evaluate, explain, establish, determine,* and so on. Notice that Diane's statement begins with the action verb *recommend.*

Some reports require only a simple statement of purpose: to investigate expanded teller hours, to select a manager from among four candidates, to describe the position of accounts supervisor. Many assignments, though, demand additional focus to guide the project. An expanded statement of purpose considers three additional factors: scope, significance, and limitations.

Setting boundaries on a project helps determine its scope.

Scope. What issues or elements will be investigated? To determine the scope, Diane brainstormed with Mike and others to pin down her task. She learned that Mycon currently had enough capital to consider purchasing a fleet of cars outright. Mike also told her that employee satisfaction was almost as important as cost-effectiveness. Moreover, he disclosed his suspicion that employee-owned cars were costing Mycon more than leased cars. Diane had many issues to sort out in setting the boundaries of her report.

Significance. Why is the topic worth investigating at this time? Some topics, after initial examination, turn out to be less important than originally thought. Others involve problems that cannot be solved, making a study useless. For Diane and Mike the problem had significance because Mycon's leasing agreement would expire shortly and decisions had to be made about a new policy for transportation of sales reps.

Limitations. What conditions affect the generalizations and utility of a report's findings? For this report Diane realized that her conclusions and recommendations might apply only to reps in her Edmonton sales district. Her findings would probably not be reliable for reps in Rimouski, Windsor, or Brandon. Another limitation for Diane was time. She had to complete the report in four weeks, thus restricting the thoroughness of her research.

An expanded purpose statement considers scope, significance, and limitations.

Diane decided to expand her statement of purpose to define the scope, significance, and limitations of the report.

Expanded Statement of Purpose: The purpose of this report is to recommend a plan that provides sales reps with cars to be used in their calls. The report will compare costs for three plans: outright ownership, leasing, and compensation for employee-owned cars. It will also measure employee reaction to each plan. The report is significant because Mycon's current leasing agreement expires April 1 and an improved plan could reduce costs and paperwork. The study is limited to costs for sales reps in the Edmonton district.

After preparing the statement of purpose, Diane checked it with Mike Rivers to be sure she was on target.

Anticipating the Audience and Issues

After defining the purpose of a report, a writer must think carefully about who will read it. Concentrating solely on a primary reader is a major mistake. Although one individual may have solicited the report, others within the organization may eventually read it, including upper management and people in other departments. A report to an outside client may first be read by someone who is familiar with the problem and then distributed to others less familiar with the topic. Moreover, candid statements to one audience may be offensive to another audience. Diane could make a major blunder, for instance, if she mentioned Mike's suspicion that sales reps were padding their mileage statements. If the report were made public—as it probably would be to explain a new policy—the sales reps could feel insulted that their integrity was being questioned.

As Diane considered her primary and secondary readers, she asked herself these questions:

- *What do my readers need to know about this topic?*
- *What do they already know?*
- *What is their educational level?*
- *How will they react to this information?*
- *Which sources will they trust?*
- *How can I make this information readable, believable, and memorable?*

Answers to these questions help writers determine how much background material to include, how much detail to add, whether to include jargon, what method of organization and presentation to follow, and what tone to use.

In the planning stages a report writer must also break the major investigative problem into subproblems. This process, sometimes called factoring, identifies issues to be investigated or possible solutions to the main problem. In this case Mycon had to figure out the best way to transport sales reps. Each possible "solution" or issue that Diane considered became a factor or subproblem to be investigated. Diane came up with three tentative solutions to providing transportation for sales reps: (1) purchase cars outright, (2) lease cars, or (3) compensate employees for using their own cars. These three factors formed the outline of Diane's study.

Diane continued to factor these main points into the following subproblems for investigation:

What plan should Mycon use to transport its sales reps?

I. Should Mycon purchase cars outright?
  A. How much capital would be required?
  B. How much would it cost to insure, operate, and maintain company-owned cars?
  C. Do employees prefer using company-owned cars?
II. Should Mycon lease cars?
  A. What is the best lease price available?
  B. How much would it cost to insure, operate, and maintain leased cars?
  C. Do employees prefer using leased cars?
III. Should Mycon compensate employees for using their own cars?
  A. How much has it cost in the past to operate employee-owned cars?
  B. How much paperwork is involved in reporting expenses?
  C. Do employees prefer being compensated for using their own cars?

Each subproblem could probably be further factored into additional subproblems. These issues may be phrased as questions, as Diane's were, or as statements. In factoring a complex problem, prepare an outline showing the initial problem and its breakdown into subproblems. Make sure your divisions are consistent (don't mix issues), exclusive (don't overlap categories), and complete (don't skip significant issues).

An outline in question form shows the factoring of a problem and highlights possible solutions.

Preparing a Work Plan

A good work plan provides an overview of a project: resources, priorities, course of action, and schedule.

After analyzing the problem, anticipating the audience, and factoring the problem, you're ready to prepare a work plan. A good work plan includes the following:

- Statement of the problem (based on key background/contextual information)
- Statement of the purpose, including scope, significance, and limitations
- Research strategy, including a description of potential sources and methods of collecting data
- Tentative outline that factors the problem into manageable chunks
- Work schedule

Preparing a plan encourages you to evaluate your resources, set priorities, outline a course of action, and establish a time schedule. Having a plan keeps you on schedule and provides management with a means of measuring your progress.

A work plan gives a complete picture of a project. Because the usefulness and quality of any report rest primarily on its data, you'll want to develop a clear research strategy, which includes allocating plenty of time to locate sources of information. For firsthand information you might interview people, prepare a survey, or even conduct a scientific experiment. For secondary information you'll probably search printed materials such as books and magazines as well as electronic materials on the Internet. Your work plan describes how you expect to generate or collect data. Because data collection is a major part of report writing, the next section of this chapter treats the topic more fully.

Figure 12.5 shows a complete work plan for a proposal presented to Lee Jeans. This work plan is particularly useful because it outlines the issues to be investigated. Notice that considerable thought and discussion and even some preliminary research are necessary to be able to develop a useful work plan.

Although this tentative outline guides investigation, it does not determine the content or order of the final report. You may, for example, study five possible solutions to a problem. If two prove to be useless, your report may discuss only the three winners. Moreover, you will organize the report to accomplish your goal and satisfy the audience. Remember that a busy executive who is familiar with a topic may prefer to read the conclusions and recommendations before a discussion of the findings. If someone authorizes the report, be sure to review the work plan with that individual (your manager, client, or professor, for example) before proceeding with the project.

learning objective 3

Gathering Information From Secondary Sources

A report is only as good as its foundation, which is based on data.

One of the most important steps in the process of writing a report is that of gathering information (research). Because a report is only as good as its foundation—the questions you ask and the data you gather to answer those questions—the remainder of this chapter describes the foundational work of finding, documenting, and illustrating data.

As you analyze a report's purpose and audience and prepare your research strategy, you will identify and assess the data you need to support your argument or explain your topic. As you analyze a report's purpose and audience, you will assess the kinds of data needed to support your argument and explain your topic. Do you need statistics, background data, expert opinions, group opinions, or organization data? Figure 12.6 (page 284) lists five forms of data and provides questions to guide you in making your research accurate and productive.

FIGURE 12.5 *Work Plan for a Formal Report*

Tips for Preparing a Work Plan

- Start early; allow plenty of time for brainstorming and preliminary research.
- Describe the problem motivating the report.
- Write a purpose statement that includes the report's scope, significance, and limitations.
- Describe the research strategy, including data collection sources and methods.
- Divide the major problem into subproblems stated as questions to be answered.
- Develop a realistic work schedule citing dates for completion of major tasks.
- Review the work plan with whoever authorized the report.

Statement of Problem

Many women between the ages of 22 and 35 have trouble finding jeans that fit. Lee Jeans hopes to remedy that situation with its One True Fit line. We want to demonstrate to Lee that we can create a word-of-mouth campaign that will help it reach its target audience.

Defines purpose, scope, limits, and significance of report

Statement of Purpose

The purpose of this report is to secure an advertising contract from Lee Jeans. We will examine published accounts about the jeans industry and Lee Jeans in particular. In addition, we will examine published results of Lee's current marketing strategy. We will conduct focus groups of women in our company to generate campaign strategies for our pilot study of 100 BzzAgents. The report will persuade Lee Jeans that word-of-mouth advertising is an effective strategy to reach women in this demographic group and that BzzAgent is the right company to hire. The report is significant because an advertising contract with Lee Jeans would help our company grow significantly in size and stature.

Describes primary and secondary data

Research Strategy (Sources and Methods of Data Collection)

We will gather information about Lee Jeans and the product line by examining published marketing data and conducting focus group surveys of our employees. In addition, we will gather data about the added value of word-of-mouth advertising by examining published accounts and interpreting data from previous marketing campaigns, particularly those with similar age groups. Finally, we will conduct a pilot study of 100 BzzAgents in the target demographic.

Factors problem into manageable chunks

Tentative Outline

I. How effectively has Lee Jeans marketed to the target population (women, ages 22 to 35)?
   A. Historically, who has typically bought Lee Jeans products? How often? Where?
   B. How effective are the current marketing strategies for the One True Fit line?
II. Is this product a good fit for our marketing strategy and our company?
   A. What do our staff members and our sample survey of BzzAgents say about this product?
   B. How well does our pool of BzzAgents correspond to the target demography in terms of age and geographic distribution?
III. Why should Lee Jeans engage BzzAgent to advertise its One True Fit line?
   A. What are the benefits of word of mouth in general and for this demographic in particular?
   B. What previous campaigns have we engaged in that demonstrate our company's credibility?
   C. What are our marketing strategies, and how well did they work in the pilot study?

Estimates time needed to complete report tasks

Work Schedule

Investigate Lee Jeans and the One True Fit line's current marketing strategy	July 15–25
Test product using focus groups	July 15–22
Create campaign materials for BzzAgents	July 18–31
Run a pilot test with a selected pool of 100 BzzAgents	August 1–21
Evaluate and interpret findings	August 22–25
Compose draft of report	August 26–28
Revise draft	August 28–30
Submit final report	September 1

FIGURE 12.6 ***Gathering and Selecting Report Data***

Form of Data	Questions to Ask
Background or historical	How much do my readers know about the problem?
	Has this topic/issue been investigated before?
	Are those sources current, relevant, and/or credible?
	Will I need to add to the available data?
Statistical	What or who is the source?
	How recent are the data?
	How were the figures derived?
	Will these data be useful in this form?
Expert opinion	Who are the experts?
	What are their biases?
	Are their opinions in print?
	Are they available for interviewing?
	Do we have in-house experts?
Individual or group opinion	Whose opinion(s) would the readers value?
	Have surveys or interviews been conducted on this topic?
	If not, do questionnaires or surveys exist that I can modify and/or use?
	Would focus groups provide useful information?
Organizational	What are the proper channels for obtaining in-house data?
	Are permissions required?
	How can I learn about public and private companies?

Primary data come from firsthand experience and observation; secondary data, from reading.

Data fall into two broad categories, primary and secondary. Primary data result from firsthand experience and observation. Secondary data come from reading what others have experienced and observed. Secondary data are easier and cheaper to develop than primary data, which might involve interviewing large groups or sending out questionnaires.

We are going to discuss secondary data first because that is where nearly every research project should begin. Often something has already been written about your topic. Reviewing secondary sources can save time and effort and prevent you from reinventing the wheel. Most secondary material is available either in print or electronically.

Print Resources

Print sources are still the most visible part of libraries.

Although we're seeing a steady movement away from print to electronic data, print sources are still the most visible part of most libraries. Much information is available only in print, and you may want to use some of the following print resources.

By the way, if you are an infrequent library user, begin your research by talking with a reference librarian about your project. These librarians won't do your research for you, but they will steer you in the right direction. Many librarians help you understand their computer, cataloguing, and retrieval systems by providing advice, brochures, handouts, and workshops.

Books provide historical, in-depth data; periodicals focus on up-to-date information.

Books. Although quickly outdated, books provide excellent historical, in-depth data on subjects. Books can be located through print or online listings.

- **Card catalogues.** Some libraries still maintain card catalogues with all the books indexed on file cards alphabetized by author, title, or subject.
- **Online catalogues.** Most libraries today have computerized their card catalogues. Some systems are fully automated, thus allowing users to learn not only whether a book is located in the library but also whether it is currently available. Moreover, online catalogues can help you trace and retrieve items from other area libraries if your institution does not own them.

Periodicals. Magazines, pamphlets, and journals are called periodicals because of their recurrent or periodic publication. Journals are compilations of scholarly articles. Articles in journals and other periodicals will be extremely useful because they are concise, limited in scope, and current, and can supplement information in books.

Exploration of secondary data includes searching both electronic and print periodicals.

- **Print indexes.** Most post-secondary libraries now offer online access to the *Readers' Guide to Periodical Literature*. In small libraries you may still find print copies of this valuable index of article titles from general-interest magazines. It includes such magazines as *Time*, *Newsweek*, *Maclean's*, and *The Canadian Forum*. However, business writers today rely almost totally on electronic indexes and databases.
- **Electronic indexes.** Online indexes are stored in digital databases. Most libraries now provide such databases to help you locate references, abstracts, and full-text articles from magazines, journals, and newspapers such as *The Globe and Mail*. When using Web-based online indexes, follow the on-screen instructions or ask for assistance from a librarian. It's a good idea to begin with a subject search because it generally turns up more relevant citations than keyword searches, especially when searching for names of people or companies. Once you locate usable references, either print a copy of your findings, save them to a portable memory device, or send them to your e-mail address.

Electronic Databases

Most researchers begin by looking in electronic databases.

As a writer of business reports today, you will probably begin your secondary research with electronic resources. Online databases have become the staple of secondary research. Most writers turn to them first because they are fast and easy to use. This means that you can conduct detailed searches without ever leaving your office, home, or residence room.

A database is a collection of information stored electronically so that it is accessible by computer and digitally searchable. Databases provide both bibliographic (titles of documents and brief abstracts) and full-text documents. Most researchers today prefer full-text documents because they are convenient. Various databases contain a rich array of magazine, newspaper, and journal articles, as well as newsletters, business reports, company profiles, government data, reviews, and directories. The four databases most useful to business writers for general searches are ABI/INFORM (ProQuest), Factiva (Dow Jones), LexisNexis Academic, and Academic Search Elite (EBSCO). Your school library and many businesses probably subscribe to these expensive resources and perhaps to other, more specialized commercial databases.

Developing a search strategy and narrowing your search can save time. As you develop your strategy, think about the time frame for your search, the language of publication, and the types of materials you will need. Most databases enable you to focus a search easily. All databases and search engines allow you to refine your search and increase the precision of your hits. In addition, for research in international business, don't limit yourself to English-language articles only; some Web sites, most notably Yahoo!'s Babel Fish, offer rough but free translations. What's more, many organizations overseas present their Web content in multiple languages. Electronic resources may take time to master. Therefore, before wasting time and retrieving lots of useless material, talk to your librarian.

learning objective 4

Comprehending the Evolving Nature of Communication Technology

The World Wide Web

If you are like most students today, you probably use the Web every day. You stay in touch with your friends by e-mail and instant messaging, and perhaps exchange text messages and pictures using increasingly more capable cell phones. Chances are you have a personal page on a social networking site such as MySpace or Facebook, and perhaps you play one of the countless free online games. You have probably looked up directions on MapQuest and may have bid on or sold items on eBay. You are likely to download ring tones for your cell phone and perhaps you obtain your favourite music from iTunes (not some illegal file-sharing site). Your generation is much more likely to follow the news online than in the daily paper or even on TV. In short, you rely on the Internet daily for information and entertainment. You are part of a vast virtual community that, in turn, consists of many smaller communities all over the world. The Web and the Internet as a whole are referred to as a "global village" for a reason.

Information on the Web grows and changes constantly and is available on the go with handheld devices.

The Web is an amazing resource. It started as a fast but exclusive network linking scientists, academics, military people, and other "tech heads." In the beginning information travelled purely in text form. Today the Web is user-friendly, with multimedia content ranging from digital sound files to vivid images and video files. More important, the Web is considered to be an ever-expanding democratic medium, where anyone can be a publisher and everyone can consume most of its boundless content free of charge. Armed with camera phones, average citizens post their videos on the hugely popular YouTube, acting as virtual reporters. Interest groups of all stripes gather in Usenet communities or newsgroups (digital bulletin boards and discussion forums), exchanging news, opinions, and other information. The fastest-growing sector of the Internet is blogs (short for weblogs); this sector is sometimes called the "blogosphere." These online journals allow users to comment on any imaginable topic or event and post their views instantly. Corporate blogs are also growing as companies begin to understand their marketing potential. In short, the Web is an invaluable resource—but report writers must approach it with caution and sound judgment.

Virtual Communities. The Web has fostered virtual communities and encourages teamwork among strangers all over North America and globally. One such democratic, free-access tool is the wiki. This group communication software enables users to create and change Web pages. Perhaps the best known is Wikipedia, a free online reference that can be edited even by a layperson. Behind company firewalls, many wikis help technical experts and other specialists to collaborate.

Information Mobility. Digital content on the Web has also become more mobile in recent years. Thanks to browser-enabled smart phones and wireless personal digital assistants (PDAs), businesspeople can surf Web pages and write e-mail on the go with devices that fit into their pockets. Similarly, users can listen to podcasts, digital recordings of radio programs, and other audio files on demand; podcasts are distributed for downloading to a portable media player such as the iPod.

To a business researcher, the Web offers a wide range of organizational and commercial information. You can expect to find such items as product and service facts, public relations material, mission statements, staff directories, press releases, current company news, government information, selected article reprints, collaborative scientific project reports, and employment information.

Learning to navigate the full extent of the Web will enable you to become a critical consumer of its information.

Although a wealth of information is available on the Web, finding exactly what you need can be frustrating and time-consuming. The constantly changing contents of the Web and its lack of organization make it more problematic for research than commercial databases such as LexisNexis. Moreover, Web content is uneven, and often the quality is questionable. The problem of gathering information is complicated by the fact that the number of Web sites increases on a regular basis.

To succeed in your search for information and answers, you need to understand the search tools available to you. You also need to understand how to evaluate the information you find.

Search tools such as Google, Yahoo!, and MSN help you locate specific Web sites and information.

Identifying Search Tools. Finding what you are looking for on the Web is hopeless without powerful specialized search tools such as Google, Yahoo!, MSN, AOL, and Ask. These search tools can be divided into two types: subject (or Web) directories and search engines. In addition, some search engines specialize in "metasearching." This means that they combine several powerful search engines into one (e.g., Dogpile). Large search sites such as Yahoo! and Google Directory are actually search engines and subject directories combined. Subject directories fall into two categories: commercial (e.g., Yahoo!, About, and others) and academic ones (e.g., InfoMine). Organized into subject categories, these human-compiled directories contain a collection of links to Internet resources submitted by site creators or evaluators.

Search engines differ in the way they trawl the vast amount of data on the Web. Google uses automated software "spiders" that crawl through the Web at regular intervals to collect and index the information from each location visited. Clusty, by Vivísimo, not only examines several search engines but also groups results into topics called clusters. Some search tools (e.g., Ask) use natural language–processing technology to enable you to ask questions to gather information. Both search engines and subject directories will help you find specific information.

No search engine or directory indexes all Web pages.

Even though search engines such as Google boast about the numbers of items they have indexed, no single search engine or directory can come close to indexing all the pages on the Internet. However, if you try a multiple-search site such as Dogpile, you can save much time; its metasearch technology compares the results of at least seven major search engines, eliminates duplicates, and then ranks the best hits.[2] To help you search for data effectively, consider using the search tools listed in Figure 12.7 on page 288.

Web research is often time-consuming and frustrating unless you know special techniques.

Internet Search Tips and Techniques. To conduct a thorough search for the information you need, build a (re)search strategy by understanding the tools available.

- **Use two or three search tools.** Begin by conducting a topic search. Use a subject directory such as Yahoo!, About, or Open Directory Project. Once you have narrowed your topic, switch to a search engine or metasearch engine.

FIGURE 12.7 ***Web Search Tools for Business Writers***

Business Databases (subscription-based, commercial)	**Features**
ABI/INFORM Complete (ProQuest)	Best database for reliable, scholarly sources; recommended first stop for business students
LexisNexis Academic	Database of over 5 000 newspapers, magazines, etc.; very current; forces users to limit their search to fewer than 1 000 hits
Factiva	Stores over 5 000 periodicals; very current; best with narrow search subject or to add results to other searches (unlimited results)
JSTOR	Scholarly articles; best for historical, not current information
Search Engines (open-access business information)	
Business.com http://www.business.com	Search engine and subject directory/portal in one; features any business-related subject
BRINT BizTech Network http://www.brint.com/interest.html	Huge search portal; business research in information and technology; 20 main business subject categories
CEO Express http://www.ceoexpress.com	Human-selected directories of subjects relevant to business executives and researchers
Google Scholar http://scholar.google.com	Scholarly articles in various disciplines—business, administration, finance, and economics among them
Search Engines (general)	
Google http://www.google.com http://www.google.ca	Relevance ranking; most popular search site or portal; advanced search options and subject directories
Yahoo! http://www.yahoo.com http://ca.yahoo.com	Search engine and directory; popular free e-mail site; relevance ranking
All the Web http://www.alltheweb.com	Advanced search option; searches for audio and video files
Ask http://www.ask.com	Plain English (natural language) questions
Metasearch Engines (results from several search sites)	
Vivísimo/Clusty http://www.vivisimo.com http://clusty.com	Metasearch function clusters results into categories; offers advanced search options and help
InfoSpace http://www.infospace.com http://dogpile.com http://www.webcrawler.com http://www.metacrawler.com	Metasearch technology; searches Google, Yahoo!, MSN Search, Ask, and more; owns other metasearch engines: Dogpile, WebCrawler, MetaCrawler, etc.
Search http://www.search.com	Searches Google, Ask, LookSmart, and dozens of other leading search engines
Subject Directories or Portals	
About http://www.about.com	Directory that organizes content from over 1.2 million sites, with commentary from 500 "guides"—chosen experts on 57 000+ topics
InfoMine http://infomine.ucr.edu	Directory of over 100 000 sites, grouped into nine indexed and annotated categories for scholarly research
Librarian's Internet Index http://lii.org	Over 20 000 entries; maintained by librarians and organized into 14 main topics and nearly 300 related topics

- **Know your search tool.** When connecting to a search service for the first time, always read the description of its service, including its FAQs (Frequently Asked Questions), Help, and How to Search sections. Often there are special features (e.g., the News, Images, Video, Books, and other categories on Google) that can speed up the search process.
- **Understand case sensitivity.** Generally use lowercase for your searches, unless you are searching for a term that is usually written in upper- and lowercase, such as a person's name.
- **Use nouns as search words and up to six to eight words in a query.** The right key words—and more of them—can narrow the search effectively.
- **Combine keywords into phrases.** Phrases, indicated by using quotation marks (e.g., "business ethics"), will limit results to specific matches.
- **Omit articles and prepositions.** Known as "stop words," articles and prepositions do not add value to a search. Instead of *request for proposal*, use *proposal request.*
- **Use wild cards.** Most search engines support wild cards such as asterisks. For example, the search term *cent** will retrieve *cents*, while *cent*** will retrieve both *center* and *centre.*
- **Learn basic Boolean search strategies.** You can save yourself a lot of time and frustration by narrowing your search with the following Boolean operators:

  AND Identifies only documents containing all of the specified words: **employee AND productivity AND morale**

  OR Identifies documents containing at least one of the specified words: **employee OR productivity OR morale**

  NOT Excludes documents containing the specified word: **employee productivity NOT morale**

  NEAR Finds documents containing target words or phrases within a specified distance, for instance, within ten words: **employee NEAR productivity**
- **Bookmark the best.** To keep track of your favourite Internet sites, save them as bookmarks or favourites.
- **Keep trying.** If a search produces no results, check your spelling. If you are using Boolean operators, check the syntax of your queries. Try synonyms and variations on words. Try to be less specific in your search term. If your search produces too many hits, try to be more specific. Think of words that uniquely identify what you're looking for. Use as many relevant keywords as possible.
- **Repeat your search a week later.** For the best results, return to your search a couple of days or a week later. The same keywords will probably produce additional results. That's because millions of new pages are being added to the Web every day.

Search engines vary in their ability to retrieve data. Learn about their advanced features, and then practise using them.

Remember, subject directories and search engines vary in their contents, features, selectivity, accuracy, and retrieval technologies. Only through clever cybersearching can you uncover the jewels hidden in the Internet.

Evaluating Web Sources. Most of us using the Web have a tendency to assume that any information turned up via a search engine has somehow been evaluated as part of a valid selection process. Wrong! The truth is that the Internet is rampant

tech talk

Managing Your Electronic Research Data Like a Pro

In amassing electronic data, you can easily lose track of Web sites and articles you quoted. To document Web data that may change as well as to manage all of your electronic data, you need a specific plan for saving sources. At the very least, you will want to create a *working bibliography* in which you record the URL of each electronic source and its access date. Here are techniques that can help you build your bibliography as well as manage your electronic data like a pro:

- **Saving sources to disk** has advantages, including being able to open the document in a browser even if you don't have access to the Internet. More important, saving sources to disk ensures that you will have access to information that may or may not be available later. Using either the **File** and **Save As** or the **File** and **Save Page As** menu command in your browser, you will be able to store the information permanently. Saving images and other kinds of media can be accomplished with your mouse by either right-clicking or command-clicking on the item, followed by a command such as **Save Picture As** or **Save Image As** from a pop-up window.
- **Copying and pasting** information you find on the Web into word processing documents is an easy way to save and store it. Remember to copy and paste the URL into the file as well, and record the URL in your working bibliography.
- **Printing** pages is a handy way to gather and store information. Doing so enables you to have copies of important data that you can annotate or highlight. Make sure the URL prints with the document (usually on the bottom of the page). If not, write it on the page.
- **Bookmarking favourites** is an option within browsers to enable users to record and store the URLs for important sources. The key to using these options is learning to create folders with names that are relevant and to use names for bookmarks that make sense and are not redundant. Pay attention or the browser will provide the information for you, relying on the name the Web page creator gave it. If no name is provided, the browser will default to the URL.
- **E-mailing** documents, URLs, or messages to yourself is another useful strategy. Many databases and online magazines permit you to e-mail information and sometimes the entire article to your account. If you combine the copy-and-paste function with e-mail, you can send yourself nearly any information you find on the Web.

with unreliable sites that reside side by side with reputable sites. Anyone with a computer and an Internet connection can publish anything on the Web. Unlike library-based research, information at many sites has not undergone the editing or scrutiny of scholarly publication procedures. The information we read in journals and most reputable magazines is reviewed, authenticated, and evaluated. That's why we have learned to trust these sources as valid and authoritative.

Information on the Web is much less reliable than data from traditional sources. Wikis, blogs, and discussion forum entries are a case in point. Although they turn up in many Internet searches, they are mostly useless because they are short-lived. They change constantly and may disappear fast, so your source can't be verified. Academic researchers prefer lasting, scholarly sources. Many professors will not allow you to cite from Wikipedia, for example, because this collaborative tool and online reference can be edited by any contributor and is considered to be unreliable. Moreover, citing from an encyclopedia shows poor research skills. Some sites exist to propagandize;

others want to sell you something. To use the Web meaningfully, you must scrutinize what you find. Here are specific questions to ask as you examine a site:

Evaluate the currency, authority, content, and accuracy of Web sites carefully.

- **Currency.** What is the date of the Web page? When was it last updated? Is some of the information obviously out of date? If the information is time-sensitive and the site has not been updated recently, the site is probably not reliable.
- **Authority.** Who publishes or sponsors this Web page? What makes the presenter an authority? Is information about the author or creator available? Is a contact address available for the presenter? Learn to be skeptical about data and assertions from individuals whose credentials are not verifiable.
- **Content.** Is the purpose of the page to entertain, inform, convince, or sell? How would you classify this page (e.g., news, personal, advocacy, reference)? Who is the intended audience, based on content, tone, and style? Can you judge the overall value of the content compared with the other resources on this topic? Web presenters with a slanted point of view cannot be counted on for objective data. Be particularly cautious with blogs; they often abound in grandstanding and ranting but lack factual information. Read them side by side with reputable news sources.
- **Accuracy.** Do the facts that are presented seem reliable to you? Do you find errors in spelling, grammar, or usage? Do you see any evidence of bias? Are footnotes provided? If you find numerous errors and if facts are not referenced, you should be alerted that the data may be questionable.

Gathering Information From Primary Sources

learning objective

5

Up to this point, we've been talking about secondary data. You should begin nearly every business report assignment by evaluating the available secondary data. However, you will probably need primary data to give a complete picture. Business reports that solve specific current problems typically rely on primary, firsthand data. Providing answers to business problems often means generating primary data through surveys, interviews, observation, or experimentation.

Business reports often rely on primary data from firsthand experience.

Surveys

Surveys collect data from groups of people. When companies develop new products, for example, they often survey consumers to learn their needs. The advantages of surveys are that they gather data economically and efficiently. Mailed surveys reach big groups nearby or at great distances. Moreover, people responding to mailed surveys have time to consider their answers, thus improving the accuracy of the data.

Surveys yield efficient and economical primary data for reports.

Mailed questionnaires, of course, have disadvantages. Most of us rank them with junk mail, so response rates may be no higher than 5 percent. Furthermore, those who do respond may not represent an accurate sample of the overall population, thus invalidating generalizations from the group. A final problem with surveys has to do with truthfulness. Some respondents exaggerate their incomes or distort other facts, thus causing the results to be unreliable. Nevertheless, surveys may be the best way to generate data for business and student reports. In preparing print or electronic surveys, consider these pointers:

Although mailed surveys may suffer low response rates, they are still useful for generating primary data.

- **Select the survey population carefully.** Many surveys question a small group of people (the sample) and project the findings onto a larger population. To be able to generalize from a survey, you need to make the sample as large as possible.

Effective surveys target appropriate samples and ask a limited number of specific questions.

In addition, you need to determine whether the sample is like the larger population. For important surveys you will want to consult books on or experts in sampling techniques.

- **Explain why the survey is necessary.** In a cover letter or an opening paragraph, describe the need for the survey. Suggest how someone or something other than you will benefit. If appropriate, offer to send recipients a copy of the findings.
- **Consider incentives.** If the survey is long, persuasive techniques may be necessary. Response rates can be increased by offering money (such as a loonie), coupons, gift certificates, free books, or other gifts.
- **Limit the number of questions.** Resist the temptation to ask for too much. Request only information you will use. Don't, for example, include demographic questions (income, gender, age, and so forth) unless the information is necessary to evaluate responses.
- **Use questions that produce quantifiable answers.** Check-off, multiple-choice, yes/no, and scale (or rank-order) questions, illustrated in Figure 12.8, provide quantifiable data that are easily tabulated. Responses to open-ended questions (*What should the bookstore do about plastic bags?*) reveal interesting but difficult-to-quantify perceptions.[3] To obtain workable data, give interviewees a list of possible responses, as shown in items 5 through 8 of Figure 12.8. For scale and multiple-choice questions, try to present all the possible answer choices. To be safe, add an "Other" or "Don't know" category in case the choices seem insufficient to the respondent. Many surveys use scale questions because they capture degrees of feelings. Typical scale headings are "agree strongly," "agree somewhat," "neutral," "disagree somewhat," and "disagree strongly."

The way a question is stated influences its response.

- **Avoid leading or ambiguous questions.** The wording of a question can dramatically affect responses to it.[4] When respondents were asked, "Are we spending too much, too little, or about the right amount on *assistance to the poor*?" [emphasis added], 13 percent responded "too much." When the same respondents were asked, "Are we spending too much, too little, or about the right amount on *welfare*?" [emphasis added], 44 percent responded "too much." Because words have different meanings for different people, you must strive to use objective language and pilot-test your questions with typical respondents. Stay away from questions that suggest an answer (*Do you agree that the salaries of CEOs are obscenely high?*). Instead, ask neutral questions (*Do CEOs earn too much, too little, or about the right amount?*). Also avoid queries that really ask two or more things (*Should the salaries of CEOs be reduced or regulated by government legislation?*). Instead, break them into separate questions (*Should the salaries of CEOs be reduced by government legislation? Should the salaries of CEOs be regulated by government legislation?*).
- **Make it easy for respondents to return the survey.** Provide a stamped, return-addressed envelope, a handy collection box, or some other means for respondents to submit the survey.
- **Conduct a pilot study.** Try the questionnaire with a small group so that you can remedy any problems. For example, in the survey shown in Figure 12.8, a pilot study revealed that female students generally favoured cloth book bags and were willing to pay for them. Male students opposed purchasing cloth bags. By adding a gender category, researchers could verify this finding. The pilot study also revealed the need to ensure an appropriate representation of male and female students in the survey.

FIGURE 12.8 *Preparing a Survey*

1 Prewriting

ANALYZE: The purpose is to help the bookstore decide if it should replace plastic bags with cloth bags for customer purchases.

ANTICIPATE: The audience will be busy students who will be initially uninterested.

ADAPT: Because students will be unwilling to participate, the survey must be short and simple. Its purpose must be significant and clear.

2 Writing

RESEARCH: Ask students how they would react to cloth bags. Use their answers to form question response choices.

ORGANIZE: Open by explaining the survey's purpose and importance. In the body ask clear questions that produce quantifiable answers. Conclude with appreciation and instructions.

COMPOSE: Write the first draft of the questionnaire.

3 Revising

REVISE: Try out the questionnaire with a small, representative group. Revise unclear questions.

PROOFREAD: Read for correctness. Be sure that answer choices do not overlap and that they are complete. Provide an "other" category if appropriate (as in item 9).

EVALUATE: Is the survey clear, attractive, and easy to complete?

North Shore College Bookstore
STUDENT SURVEY

The North Shore College Bookstore wants to do its part in protecting the environment. Each year we give away 45 000 plastic bags for students to carry off their purchases. We are considering changing from plastic to cloth bags or some other alternative, but we need your views.

[Explains need for survey (use cover letter for longer surveys)]

Please place checks below to indicate your responses.

[Uses groupings that do not overlap (not 9 to 15 and 15 or more)]

1. How many units are you presently carrying?
   ___ 15 or more units
   ___ 9 to 14 units
   ___ 8 or fewer units

   ___ Male
   ___ Female

2. How many times have you visited the bookstore this semester?
   ___ 0 times ___ 1 time ___ 2 times ___ 3 times ___ 4 or more times

3. Indicate your concern for the environment.
   ___ Very concerned ___ Concerned ___ Unconcerned

4. To protect the environment, would you be willing to change to another type of bag when buying books?
   ___ Yes
   ___ No

Indicate your feeling about the following alternatives.

[Uses scale questions to channel responses into quantifiable alternatives, as opposed to open-ended questions]

For major purchases the bookstore should	Agree	Undecided	Disagree
5. Continue to provide plastic bags.	___	___	___
6. Provide no bags; encourage students to bring their own bags.	___	___	___
7. Provide no bags; offer cloth bags at reduced price (about $3).	___	___	___
8. Give a cloth bag with each major purchase, the cost to be included in registration fees.	___	___	___

[Allows respondent to add an answer in case choices provided seem insufficient]

9. Consider another alternative, such as
____

Please return the completed survey form to your instructor or to the survey box at the North Shore College Bookstore exit. Your opinion counts.

[Tells how to return survey form]

Thanks for your help!

Interviews

Some of the best report information, particularly on topics about which little has been written, comes from individuals. These individuals are usually experts or veterans in their fields. Consider both in-house and outside experts for business reports. Tapping these sources will call for in-person, telephone, or online interviews. To elicit the most useful data, try these techniques:

Interviews with experts yield useful report data, especially when little has been written about a topic.

- **Locate an expert.** Ask managers and individuals whom they consider to be most knowledgeable in their areas. Check membership lists of professional organizations and consult articles about the topic or related topics. Most people enjoy being experts, or at least recommending them. You could also post an inquiry to an Internet newsgroup. An easy way to search newsgroups in a topic area is through the "Browse all groups" category indexed by the popular search tool Google.
- **Prepare for the interview.** Learn about the individual you're interviewing, and make sure you can pronounce his or her name. Research the background and terminology of the topic. In addition, prepare by making a list of questions that pinpoint your focus on the topic. Ask the interviewee if you may record the talk.
- **Maintain a professional attitude.** Call before the interview to confirm the arrangements, and then arrive on time. Be prepared to take notes if your recorder fails (and remember to ask permission beforehand if you want to record). Use body language to convey respect.
- **Make your questions objective and friendly.** Adopt a courteous and respectful attitude. Don't get into a debating match with the interviewee. Remember that you are there to listen, not to talk! Use open-ended rather than yes-or-no questions to draw experts out.
- **Watch the time.** Tell the interviewee in advance how much time you expect to need for the interview. Don't overstay your appointment.
- **End graciously.** Conclude the interview with a general question such as "Is there anything you'd like to add?" Express your appreciation, and ask permission to telephone later if you need to verify points.

Observation and Experimentation

Some of the best report data come from firsthand observation and investigation.

Some kinds of primary data can be obtained only through firsthand observation and investigation. If you determine that the questions you have require observational data, then you need to plan the observations carefully. One of the most important questions to ask is what or whom you're observing and how often those observations are necessary to provide reliable data.

Before you observe, plan ahead. Arrive early enough to introduce yourself and set up whatever equipment you think is necessary. Make sure that you've received permissions beforehand, particularly if you are recording. In addition, take notes, not only of the events or actions but also of the settings. Changes in environment often have an effect on actions.

Experimentation produces data that suggests causes and effects. Informal experimentation might be as simple as a pretest and post-test in a college course. Did students expand their knowledge as a result of the course? More formal experimentation is undertaken by scientists and professional researchers who control variables to test their effects. Assume, for example, that Cadbury Chocolate Canada Inc. wants to test the hypothesis (a tentative assumption) that chocolate lifts people out of the doldrums. An experiment testing the hypothesis would separate depressed individuals into two groups: those who ate chocolate (the experimental group) and those who did not (the control group). What effect did chocolate have? Such experiments are not done haphazardly, however. Valid experiments require sophisticated research design and careful attention to matching the experimental and control groups.

Documenting Data

learning objective

6

In writing business and other reports, you will often build on the ideas and words of others. In Western culture, whenever you "borrow" the ideas of others, you must give credit to your information sources. This is called *documentation.*

Purposes of Documentation

As a careful writer, you should take pains to properly document report data for the following reasons:

Documenting data lends credibility, protects the writer from charges of plagiarism, and aids the reader.

- **To strengthen your argument.** Including good data from reputable sources will convince readers of your credibility and the logic of your reasoning.
- **To protect yourself against charges of plagiarism.** Acknowledging your sources keeps you honest. Plagiarism, which is illegal and unethical, is the act of using others' ideas without proper documentation.
- **To instruct the reader.** Citing references enables readers to pursue a topic further and make use of the information themselves.

Academic Documentation vs. Business Documentation

Business writers may not follow the same strict documentation standards as academic writers do.

In the academic world, documentation is critical. Especially in the humanities and sciences, students are taught to cite sources by using quotation marks, parenthetical citations, footnotes, and bibliographies. Academic term papers require full documentation to demonstrate that a student has become familiar with respected sources and can cite them properly in developing an argument. Giving credit to the author is extremely important. Students who plagiarize risk a failing grade in a class and even expulsion from school.

In the business world, however, documentation is often viewed differently. Business communicators on the job may find that much of what is written does not follow the standards they learned in school.[5] In many instances, individual authorship is unimportant. For example, employees may write for the signature of their bosses; the writer receives no credit. Similarly, team projects turn out documents written by many people, none of whom receives individual credit. Internal business reports, which often include chunks of information from previous reports, also fail to acknowledge sources or give credit. Even information from outside sources may lack proper documentation. Yet, if facts are questioned, business writers must be able to produce their source materials.

Although both internal and external business reports are not as heavily documented as school assignments or term papers, business communication students are well advised to learn proper documentation methods. Your instructor may use a commercial plagiarism detection service such as Turnitin.com, which can cross-reference much of the information on the Web, looking for documents with similar phrasing. The result, an "originality report," will provide the instructor with a clear idea of whether you've been accurate and honest.

Plagiarism of words or ideas is a serious offence and can lead to loss of a job. You can avoid charges of plagiarism as well as add clarity to your work by knowing what to document and by developing good research habits.

Learning What to Document

When you write reports, especially in college and university, you are continually dealing with other people's ideas. You are expected to conduct research, synthesize ideas, and build on the work of others. But you are also expected to give proper credit for borrowed material. To avoid plagiarism, you must give credit whenever you use the following:[6]

Give credit when you use another's ideas, when you borrow facts that are not common knowledge, and when you quote or paraphrase another's words.

- Another person's ideas, opinions, examples, or theory
- Any facts, statistics, graphs, and drawings that are not common knowledge
- Quotations of another person's actual spoken or written words
- Paraphrases of another person's spoken or written words

Information that is common knowledge requires no documentation. For example, this statement—*Canadian Business is a popular business magazine*—would require no citation. Statements that are not common knowledge, however, must be documented. For example, *In 2008, 12 783 university students responded to the Canadian Undergraduate Survey Consortium's questions about their learning environments* would require a citation because most people do not know this fact. Cite sources for proprietary information such as statistics organized and reported by a newspaper or magazine. Also use citations to document direct quotations and ideas that you summarize in your own words.

Developing Research Habits

Report writers who are gathering information have two methods available for recording the information they find. The time-honoured manual method of notetaking works well because information is recorded on separate cards, which can then be arranged in the order needed to develop a thesis or argument. Today, though, writers rely heavily on electronic researching. Traditional notetaking methods may seem antiquated and laborious in comparison. Let's explore both methods.

Handwritten note cards help writers identify sources and organize ideas.

Manual Notetaking. To make sure you know whose ideas you are using, train yourself to take excellent notes. If possible, know what you intend to find before you begin your research so that you won't waste time on unnecessary notes. Here are some pointers on taking good notes:

- Record all major ideas from various sources on separate note cards.
- Include all publication information (author, date, title, and so forth) along with precise quotations.
- Consider using one card colour for direct quotes and a different colour for your paraphrases and summaries.
- Put the original source material aside when you are summarizing or paraphrasing.

Electronic Notetaking. Instead of recording facts on note cards, wise researchers today take advantage of electronic tools, as noted in the earlier Tech Talk box (page 290). Beware, though, not to cut and paste your way into plagiarism. Here are some pointers on taking good electronic notes:

- Begin your research by setting up a folder on your hard drive. On the go, you can use a storage device such as a USB flash drive, CD, DVD, or portable hard drive to carry your data.
- Create subfolders for major sections, such as introduction, body, and closing.
- When you find facts on the Web or in electronic databases, highlight the material you want to record, copy it, and paste it into a document in an appropriate folder.
- Be sure to include all publication data.
- As discussed in the section on managing research data, consider archiving on a CD, DVD, or external hard drive those Web pages or articles used in your research in case the data must be verified.

Set up a folder for electronic notes, but be careful not to cut and paste excessively in writing reports.

Developing the Fine Art of Paraphrasing

In writing reports and using the ideas of others, you will probably rely heavily on *paraphrasing*, which means restating an original passage in your own words and in your own style. To do a good job of paraphrasing, follow these steps:

Paraphrasing involves putting an original passage into your own words.

- Read the original material intently to comprehend its full meaning.
- Write your own version without looking at the original.
- Do not repeat the grammatical structure of the original, and do not merely replace words with synonyms.
- Reread the original to be sure you covered the main points but did not borrow specific language.

To better understand the difference between plagiarizing and paraphrasing, study the following examples. Notice that the writer of the plagiarized version uses the same grammatical construction as the source and often merely replaces words with synonyms. Even the acceptable version, however, requires a reference to the source author.

Source
While the BlackBerry has become standard armour for executives, a few maverick leaders are taking action to reduce e-mail use. . . . The concern, say academics and management thinkers, is misinterpreted messages, as well as the degree to which e-mail has become a substitute for the nuanced conversations that are critical in the workplace.[7]

The plagiarized version uses the same sentence structure as the original and makes few changes other than replacing some words.

Plagiarized Version
Although smart phones are standard among business executives, some pioneering bosses are acting to lower e-mail usage. Business professors and management experts are concerned that messages are misinterpreted and that e-mail substitutes for nuances in conversations that are crucial on the job (Brady 2006).

The acceptable paraphrase presents ideas from a different perspective and uses a different sentence structure than the original.

Acceptable Paraphrase
E-mail on the go may be all the rage in business. However, some executives are rethinking its use, as communication experts warn that e-mail triggers misunderstandings. These specialists believe that e-mail should not replace the more subtle face-to-face interaction needed on the job (Brady 2006).

Knowing When and How to Quote

Use quotations only to provide background data, to cite experts, to repeat precise phrasing, or to duplicate exact wording before criticizing.

On occasion you will want to use the exact words of a source. But beware of overusing quotations. Documents that contain pages of spliced-together quotations suggest that the writers have few ideas of their own. Wise writers and speakers use direct quotations for three purposes only:

- To provide objective background data and establish the severity of a problem as seen by experts
- To repeat identical phrasing because of its precision, clarity, or aptness
- To duplicate exact wording before criticizing

When you must use a long quotation, try to summarize and introduce it in your own words. Readers want to know the gist of a quotation before they tackle it. For example, to introduce a quotation discussing the shrinking staffs of large companies, you could precede it with your words: *In predicting employment trends, Charles Waller believes the corporation of the future will depend on a small core of full-time employees.* To introduce quotations or paraphrases, use wording such as the following:

According to Waller, . . .
Waller argues that . . .
In his recent study, Waller reported . . .

Use quotation marks to enclose exact quotations, as shown in the following: "The current image," says Charles Waller, "of a big glass-and-steel corporate headquarters on landscaped grounds directing a worldwide army of tens of thousands of employees may soon be a thing of the past." (51)

Using Citation Formats

You can direct readers to your sources with parenthetical notes inserted into the text and with bibliographies. The most common citation formats are those presented by the Modern Language Association (MLA) and the American Psychological Association (APA). Learn more about how to use these formats in Appendix B.

learning objective

7

Illustrating Data

After collecting and interpreting information, you need to consider how best to present it. If your report contains complex data and numbers, you may want to consider using graphics such as tables and charts. These graphics clarify data, create visual interest, and make numerical data meaningful. By simplifying complex ideas and emphasizing key data, well-constructed graphics make key information easier to remember. However, the same data can be shown in many different forms, for example, in a chart, table, or graph. That's why you need to recognize how to match the appropriate graphic with your objective and incorporate it into your report.

Effective graphics clarify numerical data and simplify complex ideas.

Matching Graphics and Objectives

In developing the best graphics, you must decide what data you want to highlight and which graphics are most appropriate to your objectives. Tables? Bar charts? Pie charts? Line charts? Surface charts? Flow charts? Organization charts? Pictures? Figure 12.9 summarizes appropriate uses for each type of graphic. The following text discusses each visual in more detail.

FIGURE 12.9 ***Matching Graphics to Objectives***

Graphic	Objective
Table	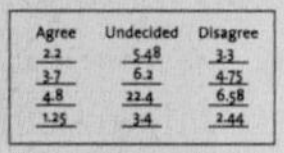 To show exact figures and values
Bar chart	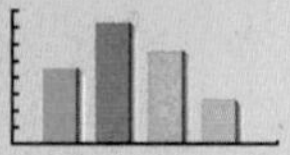 To compare one item with others
Line chart	 To demonstrate changes in quantitative data over time
Pie graph	 To visualize a whole unit and the proportions of its components
Flow chart	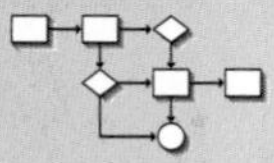 To display a process or procedure
Organization chart	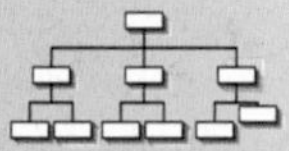 To define a hierarchy of elements
Photograph, map, illustration	 To create authenticity, to spotlight a location, and to show an item in use

Tables permit the systematic presentation of large amounts of data, whereas charts and graphs enhance visual comparisons.

Tables. Probably the most frequently used graphic in reports is the table. Because a table presents quantitative or verbal information in systematic columns and rows, it can clarify large quantities of data in small spaces. The disadvantage is that tables do not readily display trends. You may have made rough tables to help you organize the raw data collected from questionnaires or interviews. In preparing tables for your readers or listeners, though, you'll need to pay more attention to clarity and emphasis. Here are tips for making good tables:

- Place titles and labels at the top of the table.
- Arrange items in a logical order (alphabetical, chronological, geographical, highest to lowest), depending on what you need to emphasize.
- Provide clear headings for the rows and columns.
- Identify the units in which figures are given (percentages, dollars, units per worker hour, and so forth) in the table title, in the column or row heading, with the first item in a column, or in a note at the bottom.
- Use *N/A* (not available) for missing data.
- Make long tables easier to read by shading alternate lines or by leaving a blank line after each group of five.
- Place tables as close as possible to the place where they are mentioned in the text.

Selecting an appropriate graphic depends on the purpose that it serves.

Figure 12.9 shows how various graphics are effective in serving different purposes. Tables are especially suitable for illustrating exact figures in systematic rows and columns.

Bar Charts. Although they lack the precision of tables, bar charts enable you to make emphatic visual comparisons by using horizontal or vertical bars of varying lengths. Bar charts are useful to compare related items, illustrate changes in data over time, and show segments as a part of the whole. Many techniques for constructing tables also hold true for bar charts. Here are a few additional tips:

- Keep the length and width of each bar and segment proportional.
- Include a total figure in the middle of the bar or at its end if the figure helps the reader and does not clutter the chart.
- Start dollar or percentage amounts at zero.
- Place the first bar at some distance (usually half the amount of space between bars) from the *y* axis.
- Avoid showing too much information, thus producing clutter and confusion.
- Place each bar chart as close as possible to the place where it is mentioned in the text.

Line charts illustrate trends and changes in data over time.

Line Charts. The major advantage of line charts is that they show changes over time, thus indicating trends. The vertical axis is typically the dependent variable and the horizontal axis the independent one. Simple line charts show just one variable. Multiple line charts compare items, such as two or more data sets, using the same variable. Segmented line charts, also called surface charts, illustrate how the components of a whole change over time. To prepare a line chart, remember these tips:

- Begin with a grid divided into squares.
- Arrange the time component (usually years) horizontally across the bottom; arrange values for the other variable vertically.
- Draw small dots at the intersections to indicate each value at a given year.
- Connect the dots and add colour if desired.
- To prepare a segmented (surface) chart, plot the first value across the bottom; add the next item to the first figures for every increment; for the third item, add its value to the total for the first two items. The top line indicates the total of the three values.

Pie charts are most useful for showing the proportion of parts to a whole.

Pie Charts. Pie, or circle, charts enable readers to see a whole and the proportion of its components, as wedges. Although less flexible than bar or line charts, pie charts are useful for showing percentages. They are very effective for lay or nonexpert audiences. Notice that a wedge can be "exploded" or popped out for special emphasis. For the most effective pie charts, follow these suggestions:

- Make the biggest wedge appear first. Remember that, beginning at the 12 o'clock position, computer spreadsheet programs correctly assign the biggest wedge first and arrange the others in decreasing size, as long as you list the data representing each wedge on the spreadsheet in descending order.
- Include, if possible, the actual percentage or absolute value for each wedge.
- Use four to six segments for best results; if necessary, group small portions into a wedge called "other."
- Draw radii from the centre.

- Distinguish wedges with colour, shading, or cross-hatching.
- Keep all the labels horizontal.

Flow Charts. Procedures are simplified and clarified by diagramming them in a flow chart. Whether you need to describe the procedure for handling a customer's purchase order or outline steps in solving a problem, flow charts help the reader visualize the process. Traditional flow charts use the following symbols:

- Ovals to designate the beginning and end of a process
- Diamonds to designate decision points
- Rectangles to represent major activities or steps

Organization Charts. Many large organizations are so complex that they need charts to show the chain of command, from the boss down to the line managers and employees. Organization charts provide such information as who reports to whom, how many subordinates work for each manager (the span of control), and what channels of official communication exist. These charts may illustrate a company's structure, for example, by function, customer, or product. They may also be organized by the work being performed in each job or by the hierarchy of decision making.

Organization charts show the line of command and thus the flow of official communication from management to employees.

Photographs, Maps, and Illustrations. Some business reports include photographs, maps, and illustrations to serve specific purposes. Photos, for example, add authenticity and provide a visual record. Maps enable report writers to depict activities or concentrations geographically, such as dots indicating sales reps in provinces across the country. Illustrations and diagrams are useful in indicating how an object looks or operates. A drawing showing the parts of a printer with labels describing their functions, for example, is more instructive than a photograph or verbal description. With today's computer technology, photographs, maps, and illustrations can be scanned directly into business reports, or they can be accessed through hyperlinks within an electronically delivered document.

Computer technology permits photographs, maps, and illustrations to be scanned directly into reports.

Incorporating Graphics in Reports

Used appropriately, graphics make reports more interesting and easier to understand. In putting graphics into your reports, follow these suggestions for best effects:

- **Evaluate the audience.** Consider the reader, the content, your schedule, and your budget. Graphics take time and money to prepare, so think carefully before deciding how many graphics to use. Six charts in an internal report to an executive may seem like overkill, but in a long technical report to outsiders, six may be too few.
- **Use restraint.** Don't overuse colour or decorations. Although colour can effectively distinguish bars or segments in charts, too much colour can be distracting and confusing. Remember, too, that colours themselves sometimes convey meaning: red suggests deficits or negative values, blue suggests calmness and authority, and yellow may suggest warning.
- **Be accurate and ethical.** Double-check all graphics for accuracy of figures and calculations. Be certain that your visuals aren't misleading—either accidentally or intentionally. Manipulation of a chart scale can make trends look steeper and more dramatic than they really are. Also be sure to cite sources when you use someone else's facts.

Effective graphics are accurate and ethical, they do not overuse colour or decorations, and they include titles.

Graphics should be introduced by statements that help readers interpret them.

- **Introduce a graphic meaningfully.** Refer to every graphic in the text, and place the graphic close to the point where it is mentioned. Most important, though, help the reader understand the significance of the graphic. You can do this by telling the reader what to look for or by summarizing the main point of the graphic. Don't assume the reader will automatically draw the same conclusions you reached from a set of data. Instead of *The findings are shown in Figure 3*, tell the reader what to look for: *Two-thirds of the responding employees, as shown in Figure 3, favour a flextime schedule.* The best introductions for graphics interpret them for readers.
- **Choose an appropriate caption or title style.** Like reports, graphics may use "talking" titles or generic descriptive titles. Talking titles are more persuasive; they tell the reader what to think. Descriptive titles describe the facts more objectively.

Talking Title
Average Annual Health Care Costs per Worker Rise Steeply as Workers Grow Older

Descriptive Title
Average Annual Health Care Costs per Worker as Shown by Age Groups

Summary of Learning Objectives

1 **Describe business report basics, including functions, patterns (indirect or direct), writing style, and formats.** Business reports generally function either as informational reports (without analysis or recommendations) or as analytical reports (with analysis, conclusions, and possibly recommendations). Reports organized directly present the purpose immediately. This pattern is appropriate when the audience is supportive and familiar with the topic. Reports organized indirectly provide the conclusions and recommendations last. This pattern is helpful when the audience is unfamiliar with the problem or when they may be disappointed or hostile. Reports written in a formal style use third-person constructions, avoid contractions, and include many passive-voice verbs, complex sentences, and long words. Reports written informally use first-person constructions, contractions, shorter sentences, familiar words, and active-voice verbs. Reports may be formatted as letters, memos, manuscripts, prepared forms, or electronic slides.

2 **Apply the 3-x-3 writing process to business reports.** Report writers begin by analyzing a problem and writing a problem statement, which may include the scope, significance, and limitations of the project. Writers then analyze the audience and define major issues. They prepare a work plan, including a tentative outline and work schedule. They collect, organize, interpret, and illustrate their data. Then they compose the first draft. Finally, they revise (often many times), proofread, and evaluate.

3 **Understand where to find and how to use print and electronic sources of secondary data.** Secondary data may be located by searching for books, periodicals, and newspapers through print or electronic indexes. Look for information using electronic databases such as ABI/Inform and LexisNexis. You may also find information on the Internet, but searching for it requires knowledge of search tools and techniques. Popular search tools such as

Google, Yahoo!, and MSN will help you. Once found, however, information obtained on the Internet should be scrutinized for currency, authority, content, and accuracy.

4 **Comprehend the evolving nature of communication technology: the Web, electronic databases, and other resources for business writers and researchers.** The World Wide Web is used every day by individuals and organizations for business and pleasure. A vast resource, the Web offers a wealth of varied and often uneven secondary data. It is a complex network of information from private citizens, businesses, and other institutions that form a global virtual community. At the same time, these users also announce and advertise their local presence. As a business communicator, you must be aware that information online changes rapidly and is not considered as lasting as scholarly sources. To make the most of Web sites, you must be a critical consumer of the information you retrieve. You need to understand the function of Web search tools and the reliability of the results they present. As an honest researcher, you must kept track of the retrieved data and incorporate them ethically into your documents.

5 **Understand where to find and how to use sources of primary data.** Researchers generate firsthand, primary data through surveys (in-person, print, and online), interviews, observation, and experimentation. Surveys are most economical and efficient for gathering information from large groups of people. Interviews are useful when working with experts in a field. Firsthand observation can produce rich data, but it must be objective. Experimentation produces data suggesting causes and effects. Valid experiments require sophisticated research designs and careful attention to matching the experimental and control groups.

6 **Recognize the purposes and techniques of documentation in business reports and avoid plagiarism.** Documentation means giving credit to information sources. Careful writers document data to strengthen an argument, protect against charges of plagiarism, and instruct readers. Although documentation is less stringent in business reports than in academic reports, business writers should learn proper techniques to be able to verify their sources and to avoid charges of plagiarism. Report writers should document others' ideas, facts that are not common knowledge, quotations, and paraphrases. Good notetaking, either manual or electronic, enables writers to give accurate credit to sources. Paraphrasing involves putting another's ideas into your own words. Quotations may be used to provide objective background data, to repeat identical phrasing, and to duplicate exact wording before criticizing.

7 **Illustrate reports with graphics that create meaning and interest.** Good graphics improve reports by clarifying, simplifying, and emphasizing data. Tables organize precise data into rows and columns. Bar and line charts enable data to be compared visually. Line charts are especially helpful in showing changes over time. Pie charts show a whole and the proportion of its components. Organization charts, pictures, maps, and illustrations serve specific purposes. In choosing or crafting graphics, effective communicators evaluate their audience, purpose, topic, and budget to determine the number and kind of graphics. They write "talking" titles (telling readers what to think about the graphic) or descriptive titles (summarizing the topic objectively). Finally, they work carefully to avoid distorting visual aids.

chapter review

1. What purpose do most reports serve? (Obj. 1)
2. How do informational and analytical reports differ? (Obj. 1)
3. How do the direct and indirect patterns of report development differ? (Obj. 1)
4. Name five common report formats. (Obj. 1)
5. List the seven steps in the report-writing process. (Obj. 2)
6. What questions should you ask to anticipate your audience's reaction? (Obj. 2)
7. How do primary data differ from secondary data? Give an original example of each. (Obj. 3)
8. Discuss five techniques that you think are most useful for enhancing a Web search. (Obj. 3)
9. Why are your professors likely to discourage your use of Wikipedia, blogs, and many other resources found on the Web as sources in your reports? (Obj. 4)
10. What are four major sources of primary information? (Obj. 5)
11. Why is a pilot study necessary before conducting a survey? (Obj. 5)
12. What is documentation, and why is it necessary in reports? (Obj. 6)
13. List two strategies for managing your research data. (Obj. 6)
14. Briefly compare the advantages and disadvantages of illustrating data with charts (bar and line) versus tables. (Obj. 7)
15. What is the major advantage of using a pie chart to illustrate data? (Obj. 7)

critical thinking

1. When you are engaged in the planning process of a report, what is the advantage of factoring (the process of breaking problems into subproblems)?
2. For long reports, why is a written work plan a wise idea? (Obj. 2)
3. Is information obtained on the Web as reliable as information obtained from journals, newspapers, and magazines? (Obj. 3)
4. Some people say that business reports never contain footnotes. If you were writing your first report for a business and were doing considerable research, what would you do about documenting your sources? (Obj. 5)

activities

12.1 Report Functions, Writing Styles, and Formats (Obj. 1)

Your Task. For the following reports, (a) name the report's primary function (informational or analytical), (b) recommend a direct or indirect pattern of development, and (c) select a report format (memo, letter, or manuscript).

a. A persuasive proposal from a group of citizens to their town council to turn the old elementary school, which is no longer in use, into a multipurpose building for citizen education, community action meetings, and a low-cost daycare centre.
b. A report prepared by an outside consultant examining whether a sports franchise should refurbish its stadium or look to relocate to another city.
c. A report from a national moving company telling provincial authorities how it has improved its safety program so that its trucks now comply with provincial regulations. The report describes but doesn't interpret the program.

12.2 Collaborative Project: Report Portfolio (Obj. 1)

TEAM

Your Task. In teams of three or four, collect four or more sample business reports illustrating various types of reports. Don't forget corporate annual reports. For each report identify and discuss the following characteristics:

a. Function (informational or analytical)
b. Pattern (primarily direct or indirect)
c. Writing style (formal or informal)
d. Format (memo, letter, manuscript, preprinted form)
e. Effectiveness (clarity, accuracy, expression)

In an informational memo report to your instructor, describe your findings.

12.3 Problem and Purpose Statements (Obj. 2)

Your Task. The following situations require reports. For each situation write (1) a concise problem question and (2) a simple statement of purpose.

a. Last winter a severe ice storm damaged well over 50 percent of the pear trees lining the main street in the small town of Somerset. The local university's experts believe that well over 70 percent of the damaged trees will die in the next two years and that this variety is not the best one for providing shade (one of the major goals behind planting the trees eight years ago).

Rich chapter resources are available on the Web site. 

b. Health Canada's new food and drug regulations have changed the definitions of common terms such as *fresh, fat-free, low in cholesterol*, and *light*. The Big Deal Bakery worries that it must rewrite all its package labels. Big Deal doesn't know whether to hire a laboratory or a consultant for this project.
c. Customers placing telephone orders for clothing with James River Enterprises typically order only one or two items. JRE wonders whether it can train telephone service reps to motivate customers to increase the number of items ordered per call.

12.4 Problem and Purpose Statements (Obj. 2)

Your Task. Identify a problem in your current job or a previous job, such as inadequate equipment, inefficient procedures, poor customer service, poor product quality, or personnel problems. Assume your boss agrees with your criticism and asks you to prepare a report. Write (a) a two- or three-sentence statement describing the problem, (b) a problem question, and (c) a simple statement of purpose for your report.

12.5 Factoring and Outlining a Problem (Obj. 2)

CRITICAL THINKING

Japan Airlines has asked your company, Connections International, to prepare a proposal for a training school for tour operators. JAL wants to know whether Victoria would be a good spot for its school. Victoria interests JAL but only if nearby entertainment facilities can be used for tour training. The airline also needs an advisory committee consisting, if possible, of representatives of the travel community and perhaps executives of other major airlines. The real problem is how to motivate these people to cooperate with JAL.

You've heard that CBC Studios in Victoria offers training seminars, guest speakers, and other resources for tour operators. You wonder whether Magic Mountain in Vancouver would also be willing to cooperate with the proposed school. And you remember that Griffith Park is nearby and might make a good tour training spot. Before JAL will settle on Victoria as its choice, it wants to know whether access to air travel is adequate. It's also concerned about available school-building space. Moreover, JAL wants to know whether city officials in Victoria would be receptive to this tour training school proposal.
Your Task. To guide your thinking and research, factor this problem into an outline with several areas to investigate. Further divide the problem into subproblems, phrasing each entry as a question. For example, *Should the JAL tour training program be located in Victoria?* (See the work plan model in Figure 12.5.)

12.6 Developing a Work Plan (Obj. 2)

Any long report project requires a structured work plan.
Your Task. Select a report topic provided by your instructor or from those listed at the student Web site. For that report prepare a work plan that includes the following:

a. Statement of the problem
b. Expanded statement of purpose (including scope, limitations, and significance)
c. Research strategy to answer the questions
d. Tentative outline of key questions to answer
e. Work schedule (with projected completion dates)

12.7 Using Secondary Sources (Obj. 3)

Secondary sources can provide quite different information depending on your mode of inquiry.
Your Task. Select a topic in your field and conduct research in your school's library. Then research the same topic using the Internet. Write a short memo to your instructor comparing the results, focusing on the strengths and weaknesses of each search strategy.

12.8 Documenting the Best Resources in Your Field (Obj. 3)

Business and professional people should know what publications are most significant in their career fields.
Your Task. Prepare a bibliography of the most important magazines and professional journals in your major field of study. Your instructor may ask you to list the periodicals and briefly describe their content, purpose, and audience. In a cover memo to your instructor, describe your bibliography and your research sources (manual or electronic indexes, Web, databases, CD-ROM, and so on).

12.9 Developing Primary Data: Collaborative Survey (Obj. 4)

TEAM

Parking on campus has always been a problem. Students complain bitterly about the lack of spaces for them, the distance of parking lots from classrooms, and the poor condition of the lots. Some solutions have been proposed: limiting parking to full-time students, using auxiliary parking lots farther away and offering a shuttle bus to campus, encouraging bicycle and moped use, and reducing the number of spaces for visitors.
Your Task. In teams of three to five, design a survey for your associated student body council. The survey seeks student feedback in addressing the parking problem on campus. Discuss these solutions and add at least three other possibilities. Then prepare a questionnaire to be distributed on campus. If possible, pilot test the questionnaire before submitting it to your instructor. Be sure to consider how the results will be tabulated and interpreted.

12.10 Selecting Graphics (Obj. 6)

Your Task. Identify the best kind of graphic to illustrate the following data.

a. Figures showing the process of delivering electricity to a metropolitan area

b. Data showing the academic, administrative, and operation divisions of a college, from the president to department chairs and division managers

c. Figures showing the distribution of West Nile virus in humans by province

d. Percentages showing the causes of forest fires (lightning, 73 percent; arson, 5 percent; campfires, 9 percent; and so on) in the Rocky Mountains

e. Figures comparing the costs of cable, DSL, and satellite Internet service in ten major metropolitan areas of Canada for the past ten years (for a parliamentary investigation)

12.11 Evaluating Graphics (Obj. 6)

Your Task. Select four graphics from newspapers or magazines. Look in *The Globe and Mail, The Economist, Canadian Business,* the *Financial Post*, or other business news publications. In a memo to your instructor, critique each graphic based on what you have learned in this chapter. What is correctly shown? What is incorrectly shown? How could the graphic be improved?

12.12 Drawing a Bar Chart (Obj. 6)

Your Task. Prepare a bar chart comparing the tax rates of eight industrial countries in the world: Canada, 34 percent; France, 42 percent; Germany, 39 percent; Japan, 26 percent; Netherlands, 48 percent; Sweden, 49 percent; United Kingdom, 37 percent; United States, 28 percent. These figures represent a percentage of the gross domestic product for each country. The sources of the figures are the International Monetary Fund and the Japanese Ministry of Finance. Arrange the entries logically. Write two titles: a talking title and a descriptive title. What should be emphasized in the chart and title?

12.13 Drawing a Line Chart (Obj. 6)

Your Task. Prepare a line chart showing the sales of Sidekick Athletic Shoes, Inc., for these years: 2010, $6.7 million; 2009, $5.4 million; 2008, $3.2 million; 2007, $2.1 million; 2006, $2.6 million; 2005, $3.6 million. In the chart title, highlight the trend you see in the data.

12.14 Studying Graphics in Annual Reports (Obj. 6)

Your Task. In a memo to your instructor, evaluate the use and effectiveness of graphics in three to five corporation annual reports. Critique their readability, clarity, and effectiveness in visualizing data. How were they introduced in the text? What suggestions would you make to improve them?

C.L.U.E. review 12

On a separate sheet edit the following sentences to correct faults in grammar, punctuation, spelling, numbers, and word use.

1. Reports are a Fact of Life in canadian business consequently businesswriters must learn to prepare it.
2. Although reports vary in length content form and formality level they all have 1 purpose.
3. The primary purpose of reports, are to answer questions and solve problems systemly.
4. Letter reports usualy have side margins of two and one half to three and one half centimetres.
5. The format of a report is determined by it's: length topic audience and purpose.
6. The CEO and Manager who had went to a conference in the west delivered a report to Jeff and I when they returned.
7. If you're report is authorized by someone be sure to review it's workplan with them before proceding.
8. Ilia was offerred five hundred dollars to finish Maxs report but she said it was "to little and to late."
9. To search the internet you need a browser such as microsoft internet explorer.
10. If you wish to illustrate report data; you may chose from among the following visual aids, tables, charts, graphs and pictures.

Rich chapter resources are available on the Web site.

chapter 13

Organizing and Writing Typical Business Reports

objectives

1 Use tabulating and statistical techniques to sort and interpret business report data.

2 Draw meaningful conclusions and make practical report recommendations based on prior logical analysis.

3 Organize report data logically and provide cues to aid readers' comprehension.

4 Prepare short informational reports.

5 Prepare short analytical reports that solve business problems.

springboard *to discussion*

Canadian companies such as Loblaws realize the value of reports. When Dave Nichol introduced the highly successful *Insider's Report*—half advertising and half food discussion—by its second issue, readers were asking for more.[1] More than fifteen years later, Loblaws announced the release of its first *Corporate Social Responsibility Report*. According to Galen G. Weston, Executive Chairman, Loblaw, "In the past year we embarked on an ambitious turnaround with a simple, yet powerful objective—Making Loblaw the Best Again. One area that remained constant was our commitment to social responsibility. This first Loblaw report is an important early milestone in the enduring and integrated way of doing business at Loblaw."[2]

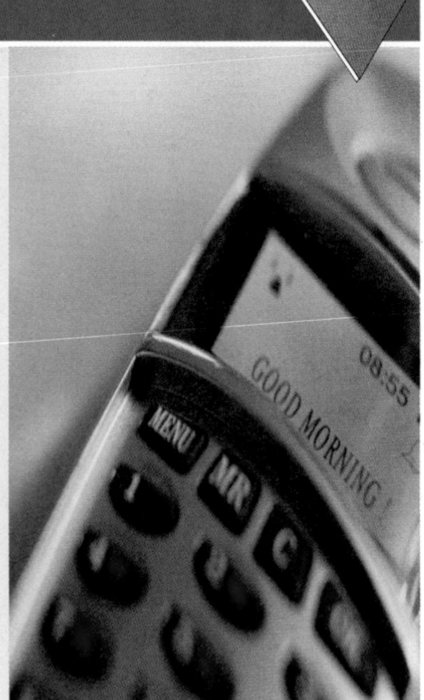

learning objective

1

Interpreting Data

Interpreting data means sorting, analyzing, combining, and recombining to yield meaningful information.

All organizations need information to stay abreast of what's happening inside and outside their firms. Much of that information will be presented to decision makers in the form of reports. This chapter will focus on interpreting and organizing data, drawing conclusions, providing reader cues, and writing typical business reports.

Unprocessed data become meaningful information through sorting, analysis, combination, and recombination. You will be examining each item to see what it means by itself and what it means when connected with other data. You are looking for meanings, relationships, and answers to the research questions posed in your work plan.

Tabulating and Analyzing Responses

Numerical data must be tabulated and analyzed statistically to bring order out of chaos.

If you have collected considerable numerical and other information, you must tabulate and analyze it. Fortunately, several tabulating and statistical techniques can help you create order from the chaos. These techniques simplify, summarize, and classify large amounts of data into meaningful terms. From the condensed data you're more likely to be able to draw valid conclusions and make reasoned recommendations. The most helpful summarizing techniques include tables, statistical concepts (mean, median, and mode), correlations, and grids.

Tables. Numerical data from questionnaires or interviews are usually summarized and simplified in tables. Using systematic columns and rows, tables make quantitative information easier to comprehend. After assembling your data, you'll want to prepare preliminary tables to enable you to see what the information means.

Sometimes data become more meaningful when cross-tabulated. This process allows analysis of two or more variables together. By cross-tabulating the findings, you sometimes uncover data that may help answer your problem question or that may prompt you to explore other possibilities. Don't, however, undertake cross-tabulation unless it serves more than mere curiosity.

Tables also help you compare multiple data collected from questionnaires and surveys. Figure 13.1 (page 310) shows, in raw form, responses to several survey items. To convert these data into a more usable form, you need to calculate percentages for each item. Then you can arrange the responses in some rational sequence, such as largest percentage to smallest.

Once the data are displayed in a table, you can more easily draw conclusions. As Figure 13.1 shows, Midland College students apparently are not interested in public transportation or shuttle buses from satellite lots. They want to park on campus, with restricted visitor parking; and only half are willing to pay for new parking lots.

Three statistical concepts—mean, median, and mode—help you describe data.

The mean is the arithmetic average; the median is the midpoint in a group of figures; the mode is the most frequently occurring figure.

Grids permit analysis of raw verbal data by grouping and classifying.

The Three Ms: Mean, Median, Mode. Tables help you organize data, and the three Ms help you describe it. These statistical terms—mean, median, and mode—are all occasionally used loosely to mean "average." To be safe, though, you should learn to apply these statistical terms precisely.

When people say *average*, they usually intend to indicate the *mean*, or arithmetic average. Means are very useful to indicate central tendencies of figures, but they have one major flaw: extremes at either end cause distortion. Because means can be misleading, you should use them only when extreme figures do not distort the result.

The *median* represents the midpoint in a group of figures arranged from lowest to highest (or vice versa). The median is useful when extreme figures may warp the mean.

The *mode* is simply the value that occurs most frequently. The mode has the advantage of being easily determined—just a quick glance at a list of arranged values reveals it. Although mode is infrequently used by researchers, knowing the mode is useful in some situations. To remember the meaning of *mode*, think about fashion: the most frequent response—the mode—is the most fashionable.

Mean, median, and mode figures are especially helpful when the range of values is also known. *Range* represents the span between the highest and lowest values. To calculate the range, you simply subtract the lowest figure from the highest. Knowing the range enables readers to put mean and median figures into perspective. This knowledge also prompts researchers to wonder why such a range exists, thus stimulating hunches and further investigation to solve problems.

The annual Canadian Vehicle Survey allows Transport Canada to understand developments in national vehicle use to improve road safety, monitor fuel consumption, and deal with the impact of vehicle usage on the environment. The survey provides the sole national source of road vehicle use information for researchers and interested members of the public.

Correlations. In tabulating and analyzing data, you may see relationships among two or more variables that help explain the findings. Intuition suggests correlations that may or may not prove to be accurate. Although one event may not be said to cause another, the business researcher who sees a correlation begins to ask why and how the two variables are related. In this way, apparent correlations stimulate investigation and present possible problem solutions to be explored.

In reporting correlations, you should avoid suggesting that a cause-and-effect relationship exists when none can be proved. Only sophisticated research methods can statistically prove correlations. Instead, present a correlation as a possible relationship. Cautious statements followed by explanations gain you credibility and allow readers to make their own decisions.

Grids. Another technique for analyzing raw data—especially verbal data—is the grid. Complex verbal information is transformed into concise, manageable data; readers can see immediately which points are supported and which are opposed. Arranging data in a grid also works for projects such as feasibility studies that compare many variables. *Consumer Reports* often uses grids to show information.

FIGURE 13.1 ***Converting Survey Data into Finished Tables***

Tips for Converting Raw Data

- Tabulate the responses on a copy of the survey form.
- Calculate percentages (divide the score for an item by the total for all responses to that item; for example, for item 1, divide 331 by 663 times 100).
- Round off figures to one decimal point or to whole numbers.
- Arrange items in a logical order, such as largest to smallest percentage.
- Prepare a table with a title that tells such things as who, what, when, where, and why.
- Include the total number of respondents.

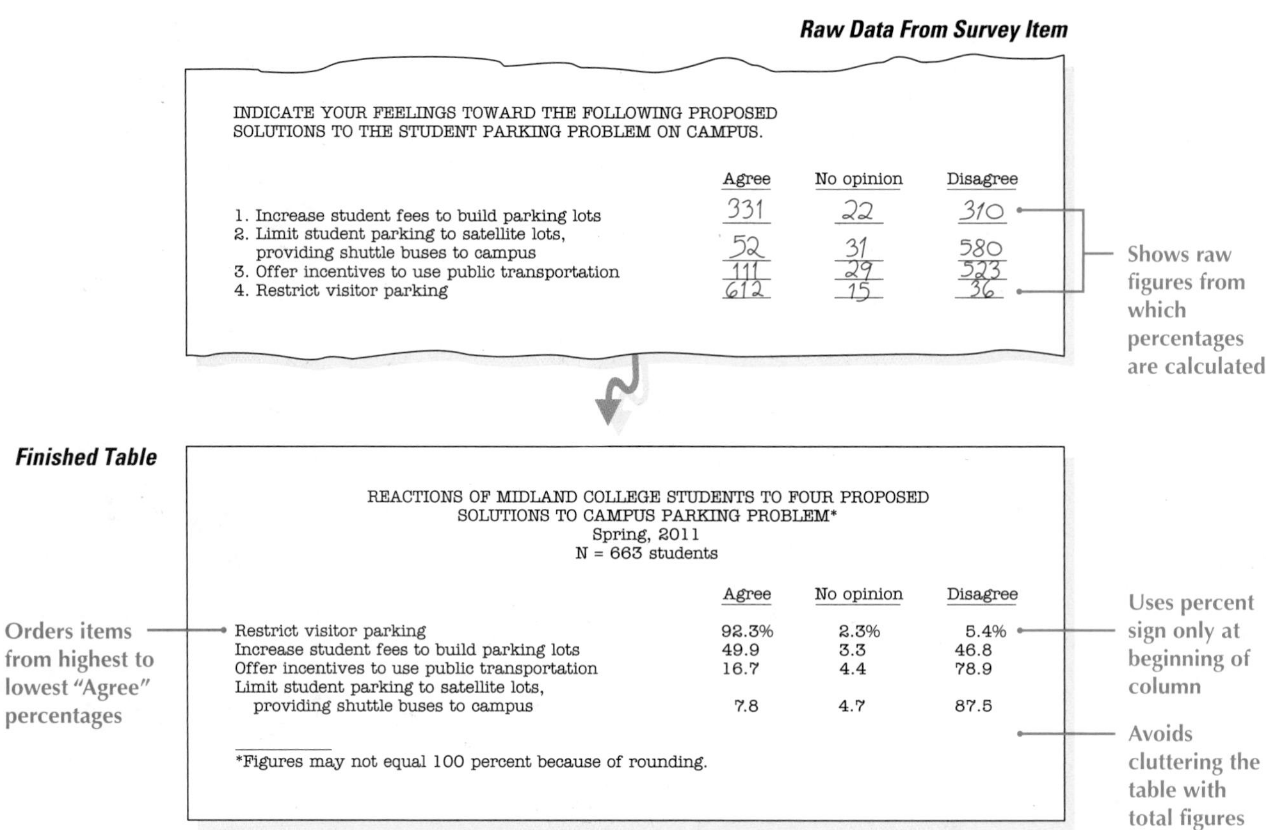

Raw Data From Survey Item
Shows raw figures from which percentages are calculated
Finished Table
Orders items from highest to lowest "Agree" percentages
Uses percent sign only at beginning of column
Avoids cluttering the table with total figures

INDICATE YOUR FEELINGS TOWARD THE FOLLOWING PROPOSED SOLUTIONS TO THE STUDENT PARKING PROBLEM ON CAMPUS.

	Agree	No opinion	Disagree
1. Increase student fees to build parking lots	331	22	310
2. Limit student parking to satellite lots, providing shuttle buses to campus	52	31	580
3. Offer incentives to use public transportation	111	29	523
4. Restrict visitor parking	612	15	36

REACTIONS OF MIDLAND COLLEGE STUDENTS TO FOUR PROPOSED SOLUTIONS TO CAMPUS PARKING PROBLEM*
Spring, 2011
N = 663 students

	Agree	No opinion	Disagree
Restrict visitor parking	92.3%	2.3%	5.4%
Increase student fees to build parking lots	49.9	3.3	46.8
Offer incentives to use public transportation	16.7	4.4	78.9
Limit student parking to satellite lots, providing shuttle buses to campus	7.8	4.7	87.5

*Figures may not equal 100 percent because of rounding.

Drawing Conclusions and Making Recommendations

learning objective 2

Conclusions summarize and explain the findings in a report.

The most widely read portions of a report are the sections devoted to conclusions and recommendations. Knowledgeable readers go straight to the conclusions to see what the report writer thinks the data mean. Because conclusions summarize and explain the findings, they represent the heart of a report. Your value in an organization rises considerably if you can draw conclusions that analyze information logically and show how the data answer questions and solve problems.

Analyzing Data to Arrive at Conclusions

Any set of data can produce a variety of conclusions. Always bear in mind, though, that the audience for a report wants to know how these data relate to the problem being studied. What do the findings mean in terms of solving the original report problem?

For example, the Marriott Corporation recognized a serious problem among its employees. Conflicting home and work requirements seemed to be causing excessive employee turnover and decreased productivity. To learn the extent of the problem and to consider solutions, Marriott surveyed its staff.[3] It learned, among other things, that nearly 35 percent of its employees had children under age twelve, and 15 percent had children under age five. Other findings, shown in Figure 13.2, indicated that one-third of its staff with young children took time off because of child-care difficulties. Moreover, many current employees had left previous jobs because of work and family conflicts. The survey also showed that managers did not consider child-care or family problems to be appropriate topics for discussion at work.

A sample of possible conclusions that could be drawn from these findings is shown in Figure 13.2. Notice that each conclusion relates to the initial report problem. Although only a few possible findings and conclusions are shown here, you can see that the conclusions try to explain the causes for the home/work conflict among employees. Many report writers would expand the conclusions section by explaining each item and citing supporting evidence. Even for simplified conclusions, such as those shown in Figure 13.2, you will want to number each item separately and use parallel construction (balanced sentence structure).

Although your goal is to remain objective, drawing conclusions naturally involves a degree of subjectivity. Your goals, background, and frame of reference all colour the inferences you make. All writers interpret findings from their own perspective, but they should not manipulate them to achieve a preconceived purpose.

Effective report conclusions are objective and bias-free.

You can make your report conclusions more objective if you use consistent evaluation criteria. Let's say you are comparing computers for an office equipment purchase. If you evaluate each by the same criteria (such as price, specifications, service, and warranty), your conclusions are more likely to be bias-free.

You also need to avoid the temptation to sensationalize or exaggerate your findings or conclusions. Be careful of words like *many*, *most*, and *all*. Instead of *many of the respondents felt . . .*, you might more accurately write *some of the respondents . . . .* Examine your motives before drawing conclusions. Don't let preconceptions or wishful thinking colour your reasoning.

Preparing Report Recommendations

Conclusions explain what the problem is, whereas the recommendations tell how to solve it. Typically, readers prefer specific recommendations. They want to know exactly how to implement the suggestions. The specificity of your recommendations depends on your authorization. What are you commissioned to do, and what does the reader expect? In the planning stages of your report project, you anticipate what the reader wants in the report. Your intuition and your knowledge of the audience determine how far your recommendations should be developed.

The best recommendations offer practical suggestions that are feasible and agreeable to the audience.

In the recommendations section of the Marriott employee survey, shown in Figure 13.2 on page 313, many of the suggestions are summarized. In the actual report each recommendation could have been backed up with specifics and ideas for implementing them. For example, the child-care resource recommendation would be explained: it provides parents with names of agencies and professionals who specialize in locating child care across the country.

FIGURE 13.2 *Report Conclusions and Recommendations*

Tips for Writing Conclusions

- Interpret and summarize the findings; tell what they mean.
- Relate the conclusions to the report problem.
- Limit the conclusions to the data presented; do not introduce new material.
- Number the conclusions and present them in parallel form.
- Be objective; avoid exaggerating or manipulating the data.
- Use consistent criteria in evaluating options.

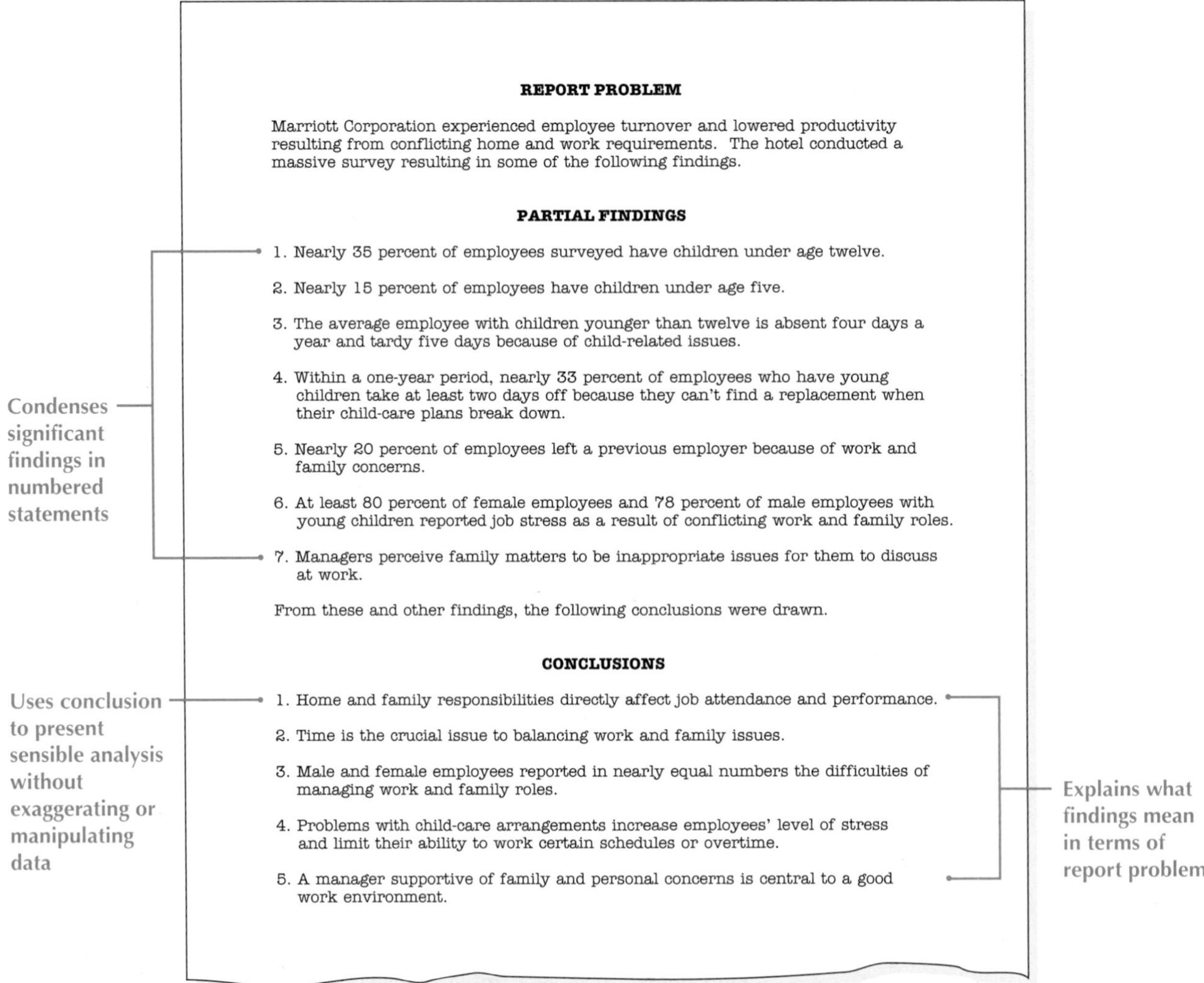
REPORT PROBLEM

Marriott Corporation experienced employee turnover and lowered productivity resulting from conflicting home and work requirements. The hotel conducted a massive survey resulting in some of the following findings.

PARTIAL FINDINGS

1. Nearly 35 percent of employees surveyed have children under age twelve.
2. Nearly 15 percent of employees have children under age five.
3. The average employee with children younger than twelve is absent four days a year and tardy five days because of child-related issues.
4. Within a one-year period, nearly 33 percent of employees who have young children take at least two days off because they can't find a replacement when their child-care plans break down.
5. Nearly 20 percent of employees left a previous employer because of work and family concerns.
6. At least 80 percent of female employees and 78 percent of male employees with young children reported job stress as a result of conflicting work and family roles.
7. Managers perceive family matters to be inappropriate issues for them to discuss at work.

From these and other findings, the following conclusions were drawn.

CONCLUSIONS

1. Home and family responsibilities directly affect job attendance and performance.
2. Time is the crucial issue to balancing work and family issues.
3. Male and female employees reported in nearly equal numbers the difficulties of managing work and family roles.
4. Problems with child-care arrangements increase employees' level of stress and limit their ability to work certain schedules or overtime.
5. A manager supportive of family and personal concerns is central to a good work environment.

Condenses significant findings in numbered statements
Uses conclusion to present sensible analysis without exaggerating or manipulating data
Explains what findings mean in terms of report problem

A good report provides practical recommendations that are agreeable to the audience. In the Marriott survey, for example, report researchers knew that the company wanted to help employees cope with conflicts between family and work obligations. Thus, the report's conclusions and recommendations focused on ways to resolve the conflict. If Marriott's goal had been merely to save money by reducing employee absenteeism, the recommendations would have been quite different.

Tips for Writing Recommendations

- Make specific suggestions for actions to solve the report problem.
- Prepare practical recommendations that will be agreeable to the audience.
- Avoid conditional words such as *maybe* and *perhaps*.
- Present each suggestion separately as a command beginning with a verb.
- Number the recommendations for improved readability.
- If requested, describe how the recommendations may be implemented.
- When possible, arrange the recommendations in an announced order, such as most important to least important.

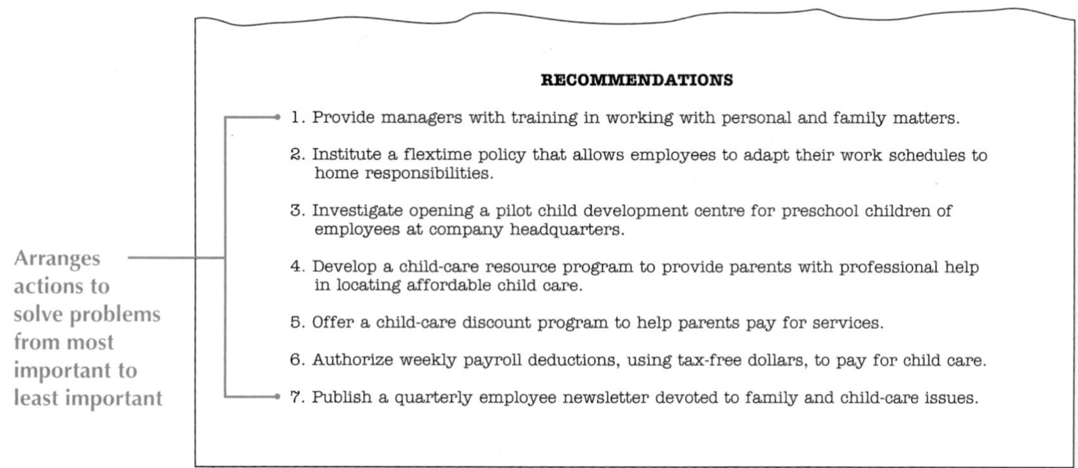

RECOMMENDATIONS

1. Provide managers with training in working with personal and family matters.
2. Institute a flextime policy that allows employees to adapt their work schedules to home responsibilities.
3. Investigate opening a pilot child development centre for preschool children of employees at company headquarters.
4. Develop a child-care resource program to provide parents with professional help in locating affordable child care.
5. Offer a child-care discount program to help parents pay for services.
6. Authorize weekly payroll deductions, using tax-free dollars, to pay for child care.
7. Publish a quarterly employee newsletter devoted to family and child-care issues.

Arranges actions to solve problems from most important to least important

If possible, make each recommendation a command. Note in Figure 13.2 that each recommendation begins with a verb. This structure sounds forceful and confident and helps the reader comprehend the information quickly. Avoid words such as *maybe* and *perhaps*; they suggest conditional statements that reduce the strength of recommendations.

Conclusions explain a problem; recommendations offer specific suggestions for solving the problem.

Experienced writers may combine recommendations and conclusions. In short reports writers may omit conclusions and move straight to recommendations. An important point about recommendations is that they include practical suggestions for solving the report problem. Furthermore, they are always the result of prior logical analysis.

Moving From Findings to Recommendations

Recommendations evolve from interpretation of the findings and conclusions. Consider the following examples from the Marriott survey:

Finding
Managers perceive family matters to be inappropriate issues for them to discuss at work.

Conclusion
Managers are neither willing nor trained to discuss family troubles that may cause employees to miss work.

Recommendation
Provide managers with training in recognizing and working with personal and family troubles that affect work.

Finding
Within a one-year period, nearly 33 percent of employees who have young children take at least two days off because they can't find a replacement when their child-care plans break down.

Conclusion
Problems with child-care arrangements increase employees' level of stress and limit their ability to work certain schedules or overtime.

Recommendation
Develop a child-care resource program to provide parents with professional help in locating affordable child care.

learning objective 3

Organizing Data

After collecting sets of data, interpreting them, drawing conclusions, and thinking about the recommendations you will make, you're ready to organize the parts of the report into a logical framework. Poorly organized reports lead to frustration. Readers will not understand, remember, or be persuaded. Wise writers know that reports rarely just "organize themselves." Instead, organization must be imposed on the data.

The direct pattern is appropriate for informed or receptive readers; the indirect pattern is appropriate when educating or persuading.

Informational reports, as you learned in Chapter 12, generally present data without interpretation. As shown in Figure 13.3, informational reports are typically organized in three parts: (1) introduction/background, (2) facts/findings, and (3) summary/conclusion. Analytical reports, which generally analyze data and draw conclusions, typically contain four parts: (1) introduction/problem, (2) facts/findings, (3) discussion/analysis, and (4) conclusions/recommendations. However, the parts in analytical reports do not always follow the same sequence. For readers who know about the project, are supportive, or are eager to learn the results quickly, the direct method is appropriate. Conclusions and recommendations, if requested, appear up front. For readers who must be educated or persuaded, the indirect method works better. Conclusions/recommendations appear last, after the findings have been presented and analyzed.

Although every report is different, the overall organizational patterns described here typically hold true. The real challenge, though, lies in (a) organizing the facts/findings and discussion/analysis sections and (b) providing reader cues.

Ordering Information Logically

Organization by time, component, importance, criteria, or convention helps readers comprehend data.

Whether you are writing informational or analytical reports, the data you've collected must be structured coherently. Five common organizational methods are by time, component, importance, criteria, or convention. Regardless of the method you choose, be sure that it helps the reader understand the data. Reader comprehension, not writer convenience, should govern organization.

Time. Ordering data by time means establishing a chronology of events. Agendas, minutes of meetings, progress reports, and procedures are usually organized by time. Beware of overusing time chronologies, however. Although this method is easy and

FIGURE 13.3 *Organizational Patterns for Informational and Analytical Reports*

Informational Reports	Analytical Reports Direct Pattern	 Indirect Pattern
I. Introduction/background	I. Introduction/problem	I. Introduction/problem
II. Facts/findings	II. Conclusions/recommendations	II. Facts/findings
III. Summary/conclusion	III. Facts/findings	III. Discussion/analysis
	IV. Discussion/analysis	IV. Conclusions/recommendations

often mirrors the way data are collected, chronologies tend to be boring, repetitious, and lacking in emphasis. Readers can't always pick out what's important.

Component. Especially for informational reports, data may be organized by components such as location, geography, division, product, or part. Organization by components works best when the classifications already exist.

Importance. Organization by importance involves beginning with the most important item and proceeding to the least important—or vice versa. The Marriott report describing work/family conflicts might begin by discussing child care, if the writer considered it the most important issue. Using importance to structure findings involves a value judgment. The writer must decide what is most important, always keeping in mind the readers' priorities and expectations. Busy readers appreciate seeing important points first; they may skim or skip other points. On the other hand, building to a climax by moving from least important to most important enables the writer to focus attention at the end. Thus the reader is more likely to remember the most important item. Of course, the writer also risks losing the attention of the reader along the way.

Organizing by level of importance saves the time of busy readers and increases the odds that key information will be retained.

Criteria. Establishing criteria by which to judge helps writers to treat topics consistently. Organizing a report around criteria helps readers make comparisons instead of forcing them to search through the report for similar data.

To evaluate choices or plans fairly, apply the same criteria to each.

Convention. Many operational and recurring reports are structured according to convention. That is, they follow a prescribed plan that everyone understands. Like operating reports, proposals are often organized conventionally. They might use such groupings as background, problem, proposed solution, staffing, schedule, costs, and authorization. As you might expect, following these conventional prescribed structures greatly simplifies the task of organization.

Organizing by convention simplifies the organizational task and yields easy-to-follow information.

Providing Reader Cues

When you finish organizing a report, you probably see a neat outline in your mind: major points, supported by subpoints and details. Readers, however, don't know the material as well as you do; they cannot see your outline. To guide them through the data, you need to provide the equivalent of a map and road signs. For both formal and informal reports, devices such as introductions, transitions, and headings prevent readers from getting lost.

Good openers tell readers what topics will be covered in what order and why.

Introduction. One of the best ways to point a reader in the right direction is to provide a report introduction that does three things:

- Tells the purpose of the report
- Describes the significance of the topic
- Previews the main points and the order in which they will be developed

The following paragraph includes all three elements in introducing a report on computer security:

> This report examines the security of our current computer operations and presents suggestions for improving security. Lax computer security could mean loss of information, loss of business, and damage to our equipment and systems. Because many former employees released during recent downsizing efforts know our systems, major changes must be made. To improve security, three recommendations will be presented: (1) begin using smart cards that limit access to our computer system; (2) alter sign-on and log-off procedures; (3) move central computer operations to a more secure area.

This opener tells the purpose (examining computer security), describes its significance (loss of information and business, damage to equipment and systems), and outlines how the report is organized (three recommendations). Good openers in effect set up a contract with the reader. The writer promises to cover certain topics in a specified order. Readers expect the writer to fulfill the contract. They want the topics to be developed as promised—using the same wording and presented in the order mentioned. For example, if in your introduction you state that you will discuss the use of *smart cards*, don't change the heading for that section to *access cards*. Remember that the introduction provides a map to a report; switching the names on the map will ensure that readers get lost. To maintain consistency, delay writing the introduction until after you have completed the report. Long, complex reports may require introductions for each section.

Transitional expressions inform readers where ideas are headed and how they relate.

Transitions. Expressions such as *on the contrary*, *at the same time*, and *however* show relationships and help reveal the logical flow of ideas in a report. These transitional expressions enable writers to tell readers where ideas are headed and how they relate.

The following expressions (see Chapter 6, Figure 6.6, for a complete list) enable you to show readers how you are developing your ideas.

To present additional thoughts: additionally, again, also, moreover, furthermore

To suggest cause and effect: accordingly, as a result, consequently, therefore

To contrast ideas: at the same time, but, however, on the contrary, though, yet

To show time and order: after, before, first, finally, now, previously, then, to conclude

To clarify points: for example, for instance, in other words, that is, thus

In using these expressions, recognize that they don't have to sit at the head of a sentence. Listen to the rhythm of the sentence, and place the expression where a natural pause occurs. Used appropriately, transitional expressions serve readers as guides; misused or overused, they can be as distracting and frustrating as too many road signs on a highway.

Headings. Good headings are another structural cue to assist readers in comprehending the organization of a report. They highlight major ideas, allowing busy readers to see the big picture in a glance. Moreover, headings provide resting points for the mind and for the eye, breaking up large chunks of text into manageable and inviting segments.

Good headings provide organizational cues and spotlight key ideas.

Report writers may use functional or talking heads. Functional heads (for example, *Background*, *Findings*, *Personnel*, and *Production Costs*) describe functions or general topics. They show the outline of a report but provide little insight for readers. Functional headings are useful for routine reports. They're also appropriate for sensitive topics that might provoke emotional reactions. By keeping the headings general, experienced writers hope to minimize reader opposition or response to controversial subjects. Talking heads (for example, *Two Sides to Campus Parking Problem* or *Survey Shows Support for Parking Fees*) provide more information and interest. Unless carefully written, however, talking heads can fail to reveal the organization of a report. With some planning, though, headings can be both functional and talking, such as *Parking Recommendations: Shuttle and New Structures.* To create the most effective headings, follow a few basic guidelines:

Headings should be brief, parallel, and ordered in a logical hierarchy.

- **Use appropriate heading levels.** The position and format of a heading indicate its level of importance and relationship to other points. Figure 13.4 (page 318) illustrates and discusses a commonly used heading format for business reports.
- **Capitalize and underline carefully.** Most writers use all capital letters (without underlines) for main titles, such as the report, chapter, and unit titles. For first- and second-level headings, they capitalize only the first letter of main words. For additional emphasis, they use a bold font, as shown in Figure 13.4.
- **Balance headings within levels.** All headings at a given level should be grammatically similar. For example, *Developing Product Teams* and *Presenting Plan to Management* are balanced, but *Development of Product Teams* and *Presenting Plan to Management* are not.
- **For short reports use first- or second-level headings.** Many business reports contain only one or two levels of headings. For such reports use first-level headings (centred, bolded) and/or second-level headings (flush left, bolded). See Figure 13.4.
- **Include at least one heading per report page.** Headings increase the readability and attractiveness of report pages. Use at least one per page to break up blocks of text.
- **Keep headings short but clear.** One-word headings are emphatic but not always clear. For example, the heading *Budget* does not adequately describe figures for a summer project involving student interns for an oil company in Alberta. Try to keep your headings brief (no more than eight words), but make sure they are understandable. Experiment with headings that concisely tell who, what, when, where, and why.

Writing Informational Reports

learning objective 4

Now that we have covered the basics of gathering, interpreting, and organizing data, we are ready to put it all together into typical informational or analytical reports. Informational reports often describe periodic, recurring activities (such as monthly sales or weekly customer calls) as well as situational, nonrecurring events (such as trips, conferences, and progress on special projects). What they have in common is

FIGURE 13.4 ***Levels of Headings in Reports***

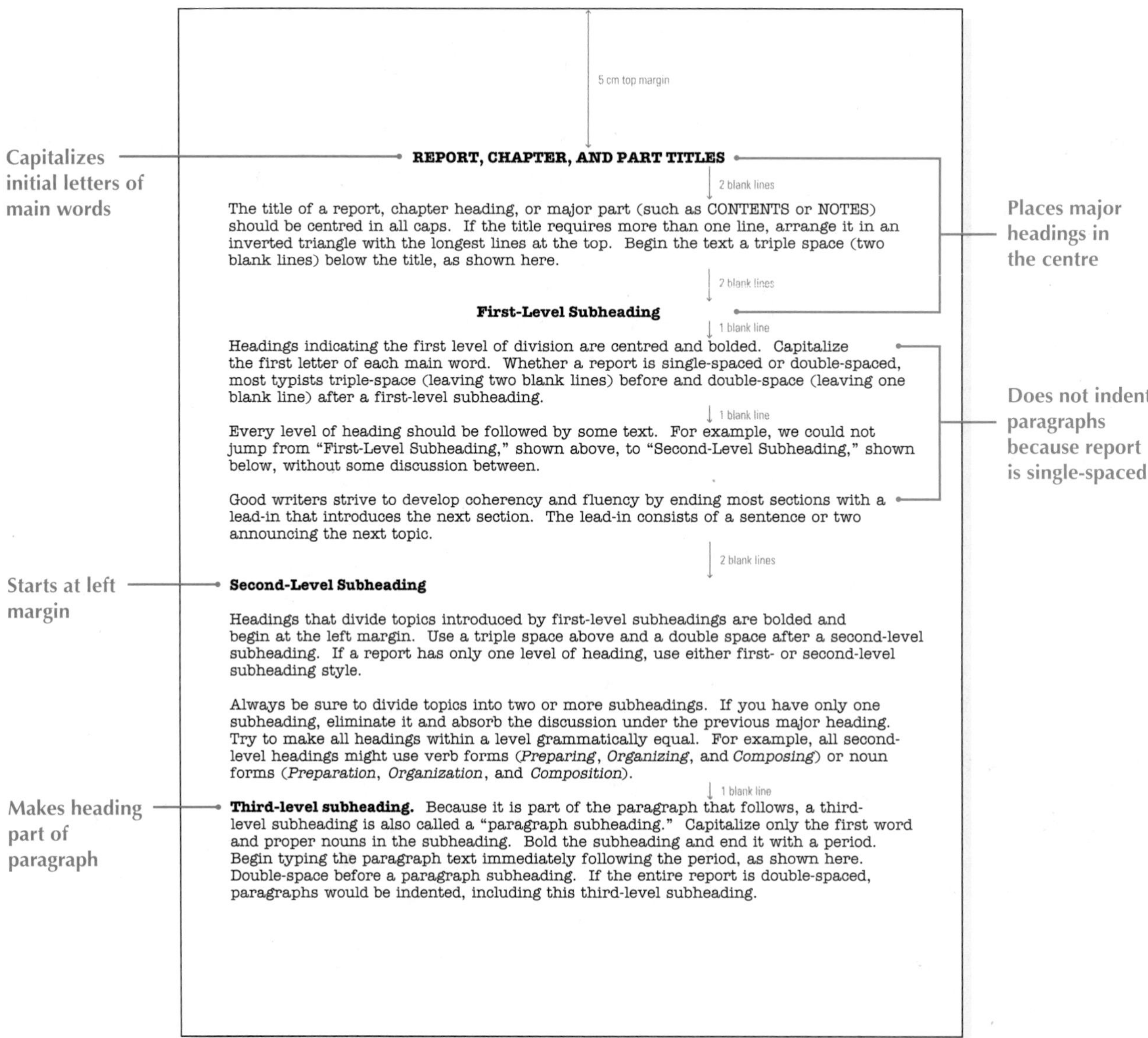

REPORT, CHAPTER, AND PART TITLES

The title of a report, chapter heading, or major part (such as CONTENTS or NOTES) should be centred in all caps. If the title requires more than one line, arrange it in an inverted triangle with the longest lines at the top. Begin the text a triple space (two blank lines) below the title, as shown here.

First-Level Subheading

Headings indicating the first level of division are centred and bolded. Capitalize the first letter of each main word. Whether a report is single-spaced or double-spaced, most typists triple-space (leaving two blank lines) before and double-space (leaving one blank line) after a first-level subheading.

Every level of heading should be followed by some text. For example, we could not jump from "First-Level Subheading," shown above, to "Second-Level Subheading," shown below, without some discussion between.

Good writers strive to develop coherency and fluency by ending most sections with a lead-in that introduces the next section. The lead-in consists of a sentence or two announcing the next topic.

Second-Level Subheading

Headings that divide topics introduced by first-level subheadings are bolded and begin at the left margin. Use a triple space above and a double space after a second-level subheading. If a report has only one level of heading, use either first- or second-level subheading style.

Always be sure to divide topics into two or more subheadings. If you have only one subheading, eliminate it and absorb the discussion under the previous major heading. Try to make all headings within a level grammatically equal. For example, all second-level headings might use verb forms (*Preparing*, *Organizing*, and *Composing*) or noun forms (*Preparation*, *Organization*, and *Composition*).

Third-level subheading. Because it is part of the paragraph that follows, a third-level subheading is also called a "paragraph subheading." Capitalize only the first word and proper nouns in the subheading. Bold the subheading and end it with a period. Begin typing the paragraph text immediately following the period, as shown here. Double-space before a paragraph subheading. If the entire report is double-spaced, paragraphs would be indented, including this third-level subheading.

Informational reports provide data on periodic and situational activities for readers who do not need to be persuaded.

delivering information to readers who do not have to be persuaded. Informational report readers are usually neutral or receptive.

You can expect to write many informational reports as an entry-level or middle-management employee. Because these reports generally deliver nonsensitive data and thus will not upset the reader, they are organized directly. Often they need little background material or introductory comment because readers are familiar with the topics. Although they're generally conversational and informal, informational reports should not be so casual that the reader struggles to find the important points. Main points must be immediately visible. Headings, lists, bulleted items, and other graphic highlighting, as well as clear organization, enable readers to grasp major ideas immediately.

Periodic (Activity) Reports

Periodic reports keep management informed of operations and activities.

Most businesses—especially larger ones—require periodic reports (sometimes called activity reports) to keep management informed of operations. These recurring reports are written at regular intervals—weekly, monthly, yearly—so that management can monitor and, if necessary, remedy business strategies. Some periodic reports simply contain figures, such as sales volume, number and kind of customer service calls, shipments delivered, accounts payable, and personnel data. More challenging periodic reports require description and discussion of activities. In preparing a narrative description of their activities, employees writing periodic reports usually do the following:

- Summarize regular activities and events performed during the reporting period.
- Describe irregular events deserving the attention of management.
- Highlight special needs and problems.

Managers naturally want to know that routine activities are progressing normally. They're often more interested, though, in what the competition is doing and how operations may be affected by unusual events or problems. In companies with open lines of communication, managers expect to be informed of the bad news along with the good news. The periodic report shown in Figure 13.5 (page 320) uses four categories: (1) activity summary, (2) competition update, (3) product problems and comments, and (4) needs.

Trip, Convention, and Conference Reports

Trip and conference reports identify the event, summarize three to five main points, itemize expenses separately, and express appreciation or suggest action to be taken.

Employees sent on business trips or to conventions and conferences typically must submit reports when they return. Organizations want to know that their money was well spent in funding the travel. These reports inform management about new procedures, equipment, and laws as well as supply information affecting products, operations, and service.

The hardest parts of writing these reports are selecting the most relevant material and organizing it coherently. Generally it's best not to use chronological sequencing (*in the morning we did X, at lunch we heard Y, and in the afternoon we did Z*). Instead, you should focus on three to five topics in which your reader will be interested. These items become the body of the report. Then simply add an introduction and closing, and your report is organized. Here is a general outline for trip, conference, and convention reports:

- Begin by identifying the event (exact date, name, and location) and previewing the topics to be discussed.
- Summarize in the body three to five main points that might benefit the reader.
- Itemize your expenses, if requested, on a separate sheet.
- Close by expressing appreciation, suggesting action to be taken, or synthesizing the value of the trip or event.

Jeff Marchant was recently named employment coordinator in the Human Resources Department of an electronics appliance manufacturer headquartered in Windsor, Ontario. Recognizing his lack of experience in interviewing job applicants, he asked permission to attend a one-day conference on the topic. His boss, Angela Taylor, encouraged Jeff to attend, saying, "We all need to brush up on our interviewing techniques." The conference report shown in Figure 13.6 (page 321) discusses the three topics that the writer felt would be important to the reader.

FIGURE 13.5 ***Periodic (Activity) Report—Memo Format***

1 Prewriting

ANALYZE: The purpose of this report is to inform management of the week's activities, customer reactions, and the rep's needs.

ANTICIPATE: The audience is a manager who wants to be able to pick out the report highlights quickly. His reaction will probably be neutral or positive.

ADAPT: Introduce the report data in a direct, straightforward manner.

2 Writing

RESEARCH: Verify data for the landscape judging test. Collect facts about competitors. Double-check problems and needs.

ORGANIZE: Make lists of items for each of the four report categories. Be sure to distinguish between problems and needs. Emphasize needs.

COMPOSE: Write and print first draft on a computer.

3 Revising

REVISE: Look for ways to eliminate wordiness. For greater emphasis use a bulleted list for *Competition Update* and for *Needs.* Make all items parallel.

PROOFREAD: Run spell checker. Adjust white space around headings.

EVALUATE: Does this report provide significant data in an easy-to-read format?

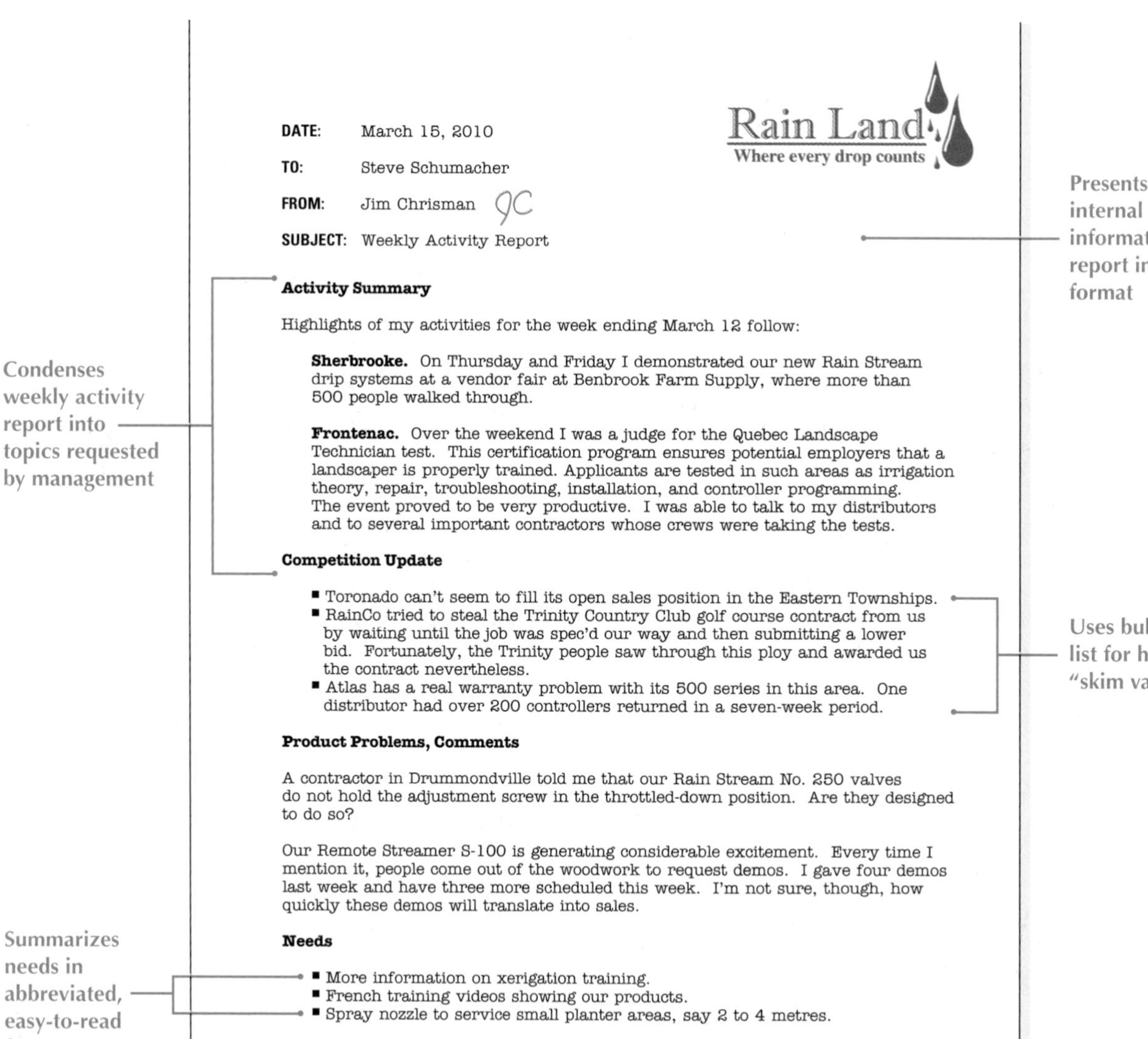

Rain Land
Where every drop counts

DATE: March 15, 2010

TO: Steve Schumacher

FROM: Jim Chrisman *JC*

SUBJECT: Weekly Activity Report

Activity Summary

Highlights of my activities for the week ending March 12 follow:

Sherbrooke. On Thursday and Friday I demonstrated our new Rain Stream drip systems at a vendor fair at Benbrook Farm Supply, where more than 500 people walked through.

Frontenac. Over the weekend I was a judge for the Quebec Landscape Technician test. This certification program ensures potential employers that a landscaper is properly trained. Applicants are tested in such areas as irrigation theory, repair, troubleshooting, installation, and controller programming. The event proved to be very productive. I was able to talk to my distributors and to several important contractors whose crews were taking the tests.

Competition Update

- Toronado can't seem to fill its open sales position in the Eastern Townships.
- RainCo tried to steal the Trinity Country Club golf course contract from us by waiting until the job was spec'd our way and then submitting a lower bid. Fortunately, the Trinity people saw through this ploy and awarded us the contract nevertheless.
- Atlas has a real warranty problem with its 500 series in this area. One distributor had over 200 controllers returned in a seven-week period.

Product Problems, Comments

A contractor in Drummondville told me that our Rain Stream No. 250 valves do not hold the adjustment screw in the throttled-down position. Are they designed to do so?

Our Remote Streamer S-100 is generating considerable excitement. Every time I mention it, people come out of the woodwork to request demos. I gave four demos last week and have three more scheduled this week. I'm not sure, though, how quickly these demos will translate into sales.

Needs

- More information on xerigation training.
- French training videos showing our products.
- Spray nozzle to service small planter areas, say 2 to 4 metres.

Presents internal informational report in memo format
Condenses weekly activity report into topics requested by management
Uses bulleted list for high "skim value"
Summarizes needs in abbreviated, easy-to-read form

FIGURE 13.6 *Conference Report—Memo Format*

Interoffice Memo

DATE: April 22, 2010
TO: Angela Taylor
FROM: Jeff Marchant *JM*
SUBJECT: TRAINING CONFERENCE ON EMPLOYMENT INTERVIEWING

I enjoyed attending the "Interviewing People" training conference sponsored by the National Business Foundation. This one-day meeting, held in Toronto on April 19, provided excellent advice that will help us strengthen our interviewing techniques. Although the conference covered many topics, this report concentrates on three areas: structuring the interview, avoiding common mistakes, and responding to new legislation.

Identifies topic and previews how the report is organized

Structuring the Interview

Job interviews usually have three parts. The opening establishes a friendly rapport with introductions, a few polite questions, and an explanation of the purpose for the interview. The body of the interview consists of questions controlled by the interviewer. The interviewer has three goals: (a) educating the applicant about the job, (b) eliciting information about the applicant's suitability for the job, and (c) promoting goodwill about the organization. In closing, the interviewer should encourage the applicant to ask questions, summarize main points, and indicate what actions will follow.

Sets off major topics with centred headings

Avoiding Common Mistakes

Probably the most interesting and practical part of the conference centred on common mistakes made by interviewers, some of which I summarize here:

1. Not taking notes at each interview. Recording important facts enables you to remember the first candidate as easily as you remember the last—and all those in between.

2. Not testing the candidate's communication skills. To be able to evaluate a candidate's ability to express ideas, ask the individual to explain some technical jargon from his or her current position.

3. Having departing employees conduct the interviews for their replacements. Departing employees may be unreliable as interviewers because they tend to hire candidates not quite as strong as they are.

4. Failing to check references. As many as 15 percent of all résumés may contain falsified data. The best way to check references is to network: ask the person whose name has been given to suggest the name of another person.

Covers facts that will most interest and help reader

Angela Taylor Page 2 April 22, 2010

Responding to New Legislation

Provisions of the Human Rights Code prohibit interviewers from asking candidates—or even their references—about candidates' disabilities. A question we frequently asked ("Do you have any physical limitations that would prevent you from performing the job for which you are applying?") would now break the law. Interviewers must also avoid asking about medical history; prescription drug use; prior workers' compensation claims; work absenteeism due to illness; and past treatment for alcoholism, drug use, or mental illness.

Concludes with offer to share information

Sharing This Information

This conference provided me with valuable training that I would like to share with other department members at a future staff meeting. Let me know when it can be scheduled.

Progress and Interim Reports

Progress and interim reports describe ongoing projects to both internal and external readers.

Continuing projects often require progress or interim reports to describe their status. These reports may be external (advising customers regarding the headway of their projects) or internal (informing management of the status of activities). Progress reports typically follow this pattern of development:

- Specify in the opening the purpose and nature of the project.
- Provide background information if the audience requires filling in.
- Describe the work completed.
- Explain the work currently in progress, including personnel, activities, methods, and locations.
- Anticipate problems and possible remedies.
- Discuss future activities and provide the expected completion date.

Progress reports, such as the one shown in Figure 13.7, include background information to hit the high points of what has been completed, outline what the writer plans to do next, and avoid minute details.

Investigative Reports

Investigative reports provide information without interpretation or recommendations.

Investigative or informational reports deliver data for a specific situation—without offering interpretation or recommendations. These nonrecurring reports are generally arranged in a direct pattern with three segments: introduction, body, and summary. The body—which includes the facts, findings, or discussion—may be organized by time, component, importance, criteria, or convention. What is important is dividing the topic into logical segments, say, three to five areas that are roughly equal and do not overlap.

Whether you are writing a periodic, trip, conference, progress, or investigative report, you'll want to review the suggestions found in the following checklist.

Checklist for Writing Informational Reports

Introduction

✓ **Begin directly.** Identify the report and its purpose.

✓ **Provide a preview.** If the report is over a page long, give the reader a brief overview of its organization.

✓ **Supply background data selectively.** When readers are unfamiliar with the topic, briefly fill in the necessary details.

✓ **Divide the topic.** Strive to group the facts or findings into three to five roughly equal segments that do not overlap.

Body

✓ **Arrange the subtopics logically.** Consider organizing by time, component, importance, criteria, or convention.

Figure 13.7 ***Progress Report—Letter Format***

Tips for Writing Progre ss Reports

- Identify the purpose and nature of the project immediately.
- Supply background information only if the reader must be educated.
- Describe the work completed.
- Discuss the work in progress, including personnel, activities, methods, and locations.
- Identify problems and possible remedies.
- Consider future activities.
- Close by telling the expected date of completion.

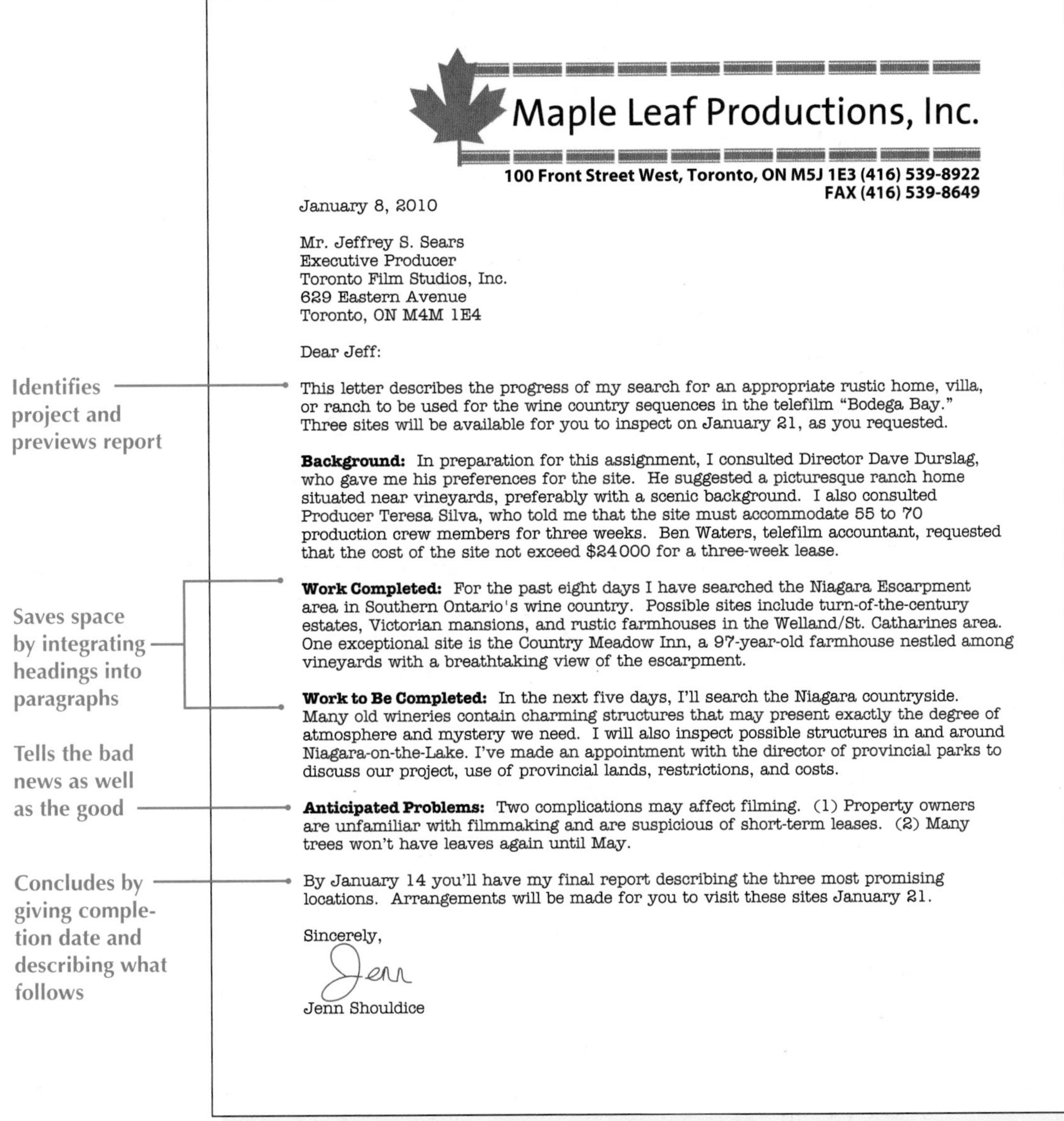

Maple Leaf Productions, Inc.

100 Front Street West, Toronto, ON M5J 1E3 (416) 539-8922
FAX (416) 539-8649

January 8, 2010

Mr. Jeffrey S. Sears
Executive Producer
Toronto Film Studios, Inc.
629 Eastern Avenue
Toronto, ON M4M 1E4

Dear Jeff:

Identifies project and previews report

This letter describes the progress of my search for an appropriate rustic home, villa, or ranch to be used for the wine country sequences in the telefilm "Bodega Bay." Three sites will be available for you to inspect on January 21, as you requested.

Background: In preparation for this assignment, I consulted Director Dave Durslag, who gave me his preferences for the site. He suggested a picturesque ranch home situated near vineyards, preferably with a scenic background. I also consulted Producer Teresa Silva, who told me that the site must accommodate 55 to 70 production crew members for three weeks. Ben Waters, telefilm accountant, requested that the cost of the site not exceed $24 000 for a three-week lease.

Saves space by integrating headings into paragraphs

Work Completed: For the past eight days I have searched the Niagara Escarpment area in Southern Ontario's wine country. Possible sites include turn-of-the-century estates, Victorian mansions, and rustic farmhouses in the Welland/St. Catharines area. One exceptional site is the Country Meadow Inn, a 97-year-old farmhouse nestled among vineyards with a breathtaking view of the escarpment.

Work to Be Completed: In the next five days, I'll search the Niagara countryside. Many old wineries contain charming structures that may present exactly the degree of atmosphere and mystery we need. I will also inspect possible structures in and around Niagara-on-the-Lake. I've made an appointment with the director of provincial parks to discuss our project, use of provincial lands, restrictions, and costs.

Tells the bad news as well as the good

Anticipated Problems: Two complications may affect filming. (1) Property owners are unfamiliar with filmmaking and are suspicious of short-term leases. (2) Many trees won't have leaves again until May.

Concludes by giving completion date and describing what follows

By January 14 you'll have my final report describing the three most promising locations. Arrangements will be made for you to visit these sites January 21.

Sincerely,

Jenn

Jenn Shouldice

- ✓ **Use clear headings.** Supply functional or talking heads (at least one per page) that describe each important section.
- ✓ **Determine degree of formality.** Use an informal, conversational writing style unless the audience expects a more formal tone.
- ✓ **Enhance readability with graphic highlighting.** Make liberal use of bullets, numbered and lettered lists, headings, underlined items, and white space.

Summary/Conclusion

- ✓ **When necessary, summarize the report.** Briefly review the main points and discuss what action will follow.
- ✓ **Offer a concluding thought.** If relevant, express appreciation or describe your willingness to provide further information.

learning objective

5

Writing Short Analytical Reports

Analytical reports present information but emphasize reasoning, conclusions, and recommendations.

Analytical reports differ significantly from informational reports. Although both seek to collect and present data clearly, analytical reports also analyze the data and typically try to persuade the reader to accept the conclusions and act on the recommendations. Informational reports emphasize facts; analytical reports emphasize reasoning and conclusions.

For some readers you may organize analytical reports directly, with the conclusions and recommendations near the beginning. Directness is appropriate when the reader has confidence in the writer, based on either experience or credentials. Front-loading the recommendations also works when the topic is routine or familiar and the reader is supportive.

Directness can backfire, though. If you announce the recommendations too quickly, the reader may immediately object to a single idea. You may have had no suspicion that this idea would trigger a negative reaction. Once the reader is opposed, changing an unfavourable mindset may be difficult or impossible. A reader may also think you have oversimplified or overlooked something significant if you lay out all the recommendations before explaining how you arrived at them. When you must lead the reader through the process of discovering the solution or recommendation, use the indirect method: present conclusions and recommendations last.

Most analytical reports answer questions about specific problems. How can we use a Web site most effectively? Should we close the Bradford plant? Should we buy or lease company cars? How can we improve customer service? Three typical analytical reports answer business questions: justification/recommendation reports, feasibility reports, and yardstick reports. Because these reports all solve problems, the categories are not mutually exclusive. What distinguishes them are their goals and organization.

Justification/recommendation reports follow the direct or indirect pattern depending on the audience and the topic.

Justification/Recommendation Reports

Both managers and employees must occasionally write reports that justify or recommend something, such as buying equipment, changing a procedure, hiring an employee, consolidating departments, or investing funds. These reports may also be called *internal proposals* because their persuasive nature is similar to that of external proposals (presented in Chapter 14). Large organizations sometimes prescribe how these reports should be organized; they use forms with conventional headings. When you are free to select an organizational plan yourself, however, let your audience and topic determine your choice of direct or indirect structure.

Direct Pattern. For nonsensitive topics and recommendations that will be agreeable to readers, you can organize directly according to the following sequence:

The direct pattern is appropriate for justification/recommendation reports on nonsensitive topics and for receptive audiences.

- Identify the problem or need briefly.
- Announce the recommendation, solution, or action concisely and with action verbs.
- Explain more fully the benefits of the recommendation or steps necessary to solve the problem.
- Include a discussion of pros, cons, and costs.
- Conclude with a summary specifying the recommendation and necessary action.

The justification/recommendation report shown in Figure 13.8 on the next page concentrates on four separate benefits of the writer's recommendation.

Indirect Pattern. When a reader may oppose a recommendation or when circumstances suggest caution, don't be in a hurry to reveal your recommendation. Consider using the following sequence for an indirect approach to your recommendations:

The indirect pattern is appropriate for justification/recommendation reports on sensitive topics and for potentially unreceptive audiences.

- Make a general reference to the problem, not to your recommendation, in the subject line.
- Describe the problem or need that your recommendation addresses. Use specific examples, supporting statistics, and authoritative quotes to lend credibility to the seriousness of the problem.
- Discuss alternative solutions, beginning with the least likely to succeed.
- Present the most promising alternative (your recommendation) last.
- Show how the advantages of your recommendation outweigh its disadvantages.
- Summarize your recommendation. If appropriate, specify the action it requires.
- Ask for authorization to proceed if necessary.

The report shown in Figure 13.9 (pp. 327–28) is single-spaced because that is the company's preference. Some companies prefer the readability of double spacing. Be sure to check with your organization for its preference before printing your reports.

Feasibility Reports

Feasibility reports examine the practicality and advisability of following a course of action. They answer this question: Will this plan or proposal work? Feasibility reports typically are internal reports written to advise on matters such as consolidating departments, offering a wellness program to employees, or hiring an outside firm to handle a company's accounting or computing operations. The focus in these reports is on the decision: stopping or proceeding with the proposal. Because your role is not to persuade the reader to accept the decision, you will want to present the decision immediately. In writing feasibility reports, consider these suggestions:

Feasibility reports analyze whether a proposal or plan will work.

- Announce your decision immediately.
- Describe the background and the problem necessitating the proposal.
- Discuss the benefits of the proposal, and describe the problems that may result.

FIGURE 13.8 ***Justification/Recommendation Report: Direct Pattern***

1 Prewriting

ANALYZE: The purpose of this report is to persuade the manager to authorize the purchase and pilot testing of smart tires.

ANTICIPATE: The audience is a manager who is familiar with operations but not with this product. He will probably be receptive to the recommendation.

ADAPT: Present the report data in a direct, straightforward manner.

2 Writing

RESEARCH: Collect data on how smart tires could benefit operations.

ORGANIZE: Discuss the problem briefly. Introduce and justify the recommendation by noting its cost-effectiveness and paperwork benefits. Explain the benefits of smart tires. Describe the action to be taken.

COMPOSE: Write and print the first draft.

3 Revising

REVISE: Revise to break up long paragraphs about benefits. Isolate each benefit in an enumerated list with headings.

PROOFREAD: Double-check all figures. Be sure all headings are parallel.

EVALUATE: Does this report make its request concisely but emphatically? Will the reader see immediately what action is required?

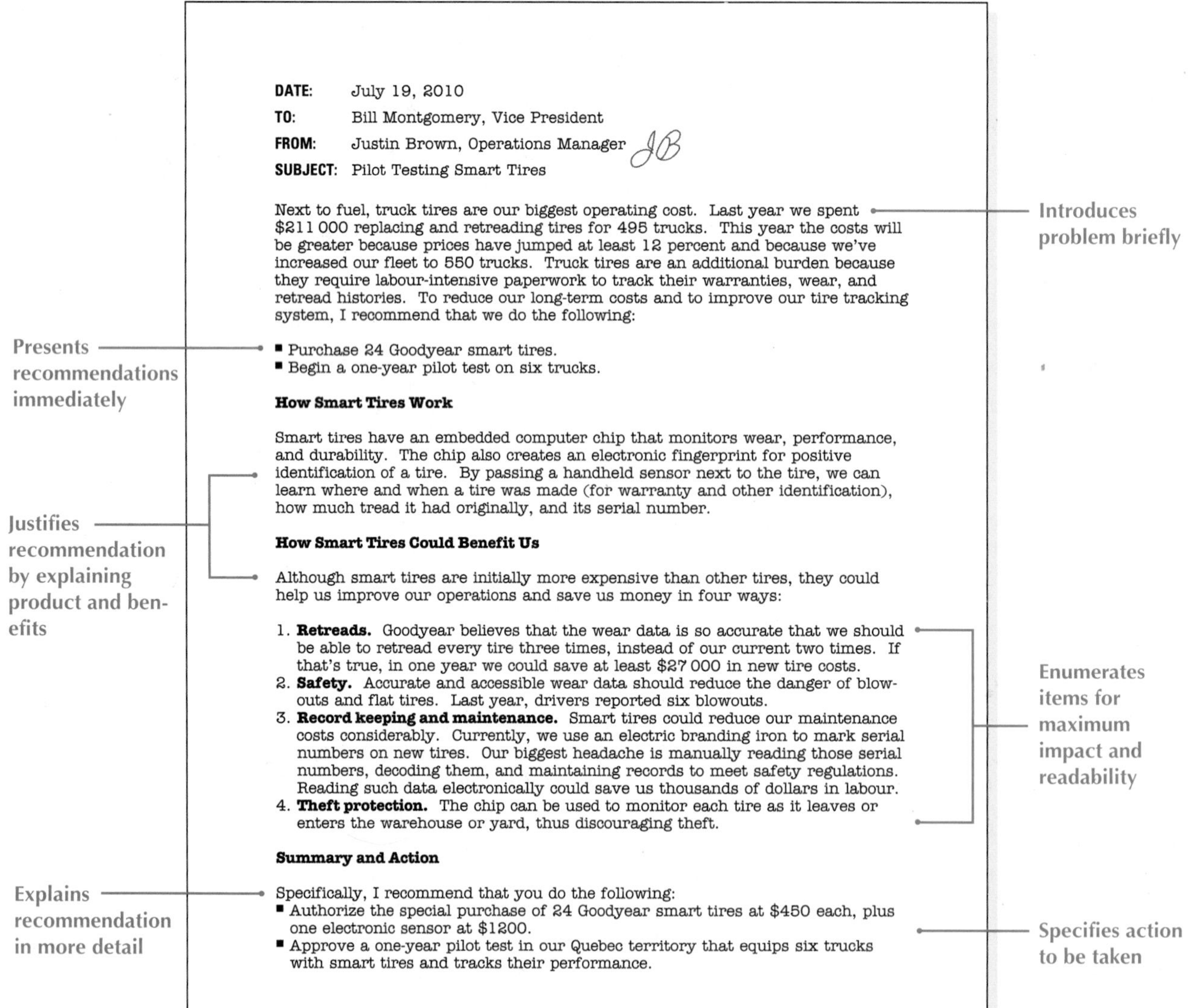

DATE: July 19, 2010
TO: Bill Montgomery, Vice President
FROM: Justin Brown, Operations Manager *JB*
SUBJECT: Pilot Testing Smart Tires

Next to fuel, truck tires are our biggest operating cost. Last year we spent $211 000 replacing and retreading tires for 495 trucks. This year the costs will be greater because prices have jumped at least 12 percent and because we've increased our fleet to 550 trucks. Truck tires are an additional burden because they require labour-intensive paperwork to track their warranties, wear, and retread histories. To reduce our long-term costs and to improve our tire tracking system, I recommend that we do the following:

- Purchase 24 Goodyear smart tires.
- Begin a one-year pilot test on six trucks.

How Smart Tires Work

Smart tires have an embedded computer chip that monitors wear, performance, and durability. The chip also creates an electronic fingerprint for positive identification of a tire. By passing a handheld sensor next to the tire, we can learn where and when a tire was made (for warranty and other identification), how much tread it had originally, and its serial number.

How Smart Tires Could Benefit Us

Although smart tires are initially more expensive than other tires, they could help us improve our operations and save us money in four ways:

1. **Retreads.** Goodyear believes that the wear data is so accurate that we should be able to retread every tire three times, instead of our current two times. If that's true, in one year we could save at least $27 000 in new tire costs.
2. **Safety.** Accurate and accessible wear data should reduce the danger of blow-outs and flat tires. Last year, drivers reported six blowouts.
3. **Record keeping and maintenance.** Smart tires could reduce our maintenance costs considerably. Currently, we use an electric branding iron to mark serial numbers on new tires. Our biggest headache is manually reading those serial numbers, decoding them, and maintaining records to meet safety regulations. Reading such data electronically could save us thousands of dollars in labour.
4. **Theft protection.** The chip can be used to monitor each tire as it leaves or enters the warehouse or yard, thus discouraging theft.

Summary and Action

Specifically, I recommend that you do the following:

- Authorize the special purchase of 24 Goodyear smart tires at $450 each, plus one electronic sensor at $1200.
- Approve a one-year pilot test in our Quebec territory that equips six trucks with smart tires and tracks their performance.

Introduces problem briefly
Presents recommendations immediately
Justifies recommendation by explaining product and benefits
Enumerates items for maximum impact and readability
Explains recommendation in more detail
Specifies action to be taken

FIGURE 13.9 ***Justification/Recommendation Report: Indirect Pattern***

DATE: October 11, 2010

TO: Damon Moore, Director, Human Resources

FROM: Diane Adams, Executive Assistant *DA*

SUBJECT: MEASURES TO HELP EMPLOYEES STOP SMOKING

At your request, I have examined measures that encourage employees to quit smoking. As company records show, approximately 23 percent of our employees still smoke, despite the antismoking and clean-air policies we adopted in 2003. To collect data for this report, I studied professional and government publications; I also inquired at companies and clinics about stop-smoking programs.

This report presents data describing the significance of the problem, three alternative solutions, and a recommendation based on my investigation.

Significance of Problem: Health Care and Productivity Losses

Employees who smoke are costly to any organization. The following statistics show the effects of smoking for workers and for organizations:

- Absenteeism is 40 to 50 percent greater among smoking employees.
- Accidents are two to three times greater among smokers.
- Bronchitis, lung and heart disease, cancer, and early death are more frequent among smokers (Johns, 2007, p. 14).

Although our clean-air policy prohibits smoking in the building, shop, and office, we have done little to encourage employees to stop smoking. Many workers still go outside to smoke at lunch and breaks. Other companies have been far more proactive in their attempts to stop employee smoking. Many companies have found that persuading employees to stop smoking was a decisive factor in reducing their health insurance premiums. Below is a discussion of three common stop-smoking measures tried by other companies, along with a projected cost factor for each.

Alternative 1: Literature and Events

The least expensive and easiest stop-smoking measure involves the distribution of literature, such as "The Ten-Step Plan" from Smokefree Enterprises and government pamphlets citing smoking dangers. Some companies have also sponsored events such as Weedless Wednesday, a one-day occasion intended to develop group spirit in spurring smokers to quit. "Studies show, however," says one expert, "that literature and company-sponsored events have little permanent effect in helping smokers quit" (Riva, 2008, p. 107).

Cost: Negligible

(continued)

Avoids revealing recommendation immediately

Uses headings that combine function and description

Discusses least effective alternative first

Introduces purpose of report, tells method of data collection, and previews organization

Documents data sources for credibility; uses APA style citing author, date, and page number in the text

- Calculate the costs associated with the proposal, if appropriate.
- Show the time frame necessary for implementation of the proposal.

The feasibility report shown in Figure 13.10 (page 329) examines the feasibility of a consultant's plan and provides all necessary information: background, benefits, problems, costs, and time frame.

A typical feasibility report presents the decision, background information, benefits, problems, costs, and a schedule.

Yardstick Reports

Yardstick reports consider alternative solutions to a problem by establishing criteria against which to weigh options.

Yardstick reports examine problems with two or more solutions. To evaluate the best solution, the writer establishes criteria by which to compare the alternatives. The criteria then act as a yardstick against which all the alternatives are measured. This approach is effective when companies establish specifications for equipment

Damon Moore　　Page 2　　October 11, 2010

Alternative 2: Stop-Smoking Programs Outside the Workplace

Local clinics provide treatment programs in classes at their centres. Here in Calgary we have Smokers' Treatment Centre, ACC Motivation Centre, and the New-Choice Program for Stopping Smoking. These behaviour-modification stop-smoking programs are acknowledged to be more effective than literature distribution or incentive programs. However, studies of companies using off-workplace programs show that many employees fail to attend regularly and do not complete the programs.

Cost: $750 per employee, three-month individual program (New-Choice Program)
$500 per employee, three-month group sessions

Highlights costs for easy comparison

Alternative 3: Stop-Smoking Programs at the Workplace

Many clinics offer workplace programs with counsellors meeting employees in company conference rooms. These programs have the advantage of keeping a firm's employees together so that they develop a group spirit and exert pressure on each other to succeed. The most successful programs are on company premises and also on company time. Employees participating in such programs had a 72 percent greater success record than employees attending the same stop-smoking program at an outside clinic (Manley, 2005, p. 35). A disadvantage of this arrangement, of course, is lost work time—amounting to about two hours a week for three months.

Arranges alternatives so that most effective is last

Cost: $500 per employee, three-month program two hours per week release time for three months

Conclusions and Recommendation

Summarizes findings and ends with specific recommendation

Smokers require discipline, counselling, and professional assistance in kicking the nicotine habit, as explained at the University of Manitoba Health System Web site ("How to Quit," 2003). Workplace stop-smoking programs on company time are more effective than literature, incentives, and off-workplace programs. If our goal is to reduce health care costs and lead our employees to healthful lives, we should invest in a workplace stop-smoking program with release time for smokers. Although the program temporarily reduces productivity, we can expect to recapture that loss in lower health care premiums and healthier employees.

Therefore, I recommend that we begin a stop-smoking treatment program on company premises with two hours per week of release time for participants for three months.

Reveals recommendation only after discussing all alternatives

3

References

Lists all references in APA style

Magazine — Johns, K. (2007, May). No smoking in your workplace. *Business Times,* 14–16.

Journal — Manley, D. (2005). Up in smoke: A case study of one company's proactive stance against smoking. *Management Review, 14,* 33–37.

Book — Riva, N. A. (2008). *The last gasp.* New York: Field Publishers.

Web — University of Manitoba Health System (2003, May). *How to quit smoking.* Retrieved August 28, 2006, from http://www.man.umich.edu/1libr/guides/smoking.htm

purchases and then compare each manufacturer's product with the established specs. The yardstick approach is also effective when exact specifications cannot be established.

The real advantage to yardstick reports is that alternatives can be measured consistently using the same criteria. Reports using a yardstick approach typically are organized this way:

FIGURE 13.10 ***Feasibility Report***

DATE: November 11, 2010

TO: Shauna Clay-Taylor, Vice President

FROM: Elizabeth W. Webb, Customer Service Manager *E.W.W.*

SUBJECT: FEASIBILITY OF PROGRESSION SCHEDULE FOR CSRs

The plan calling for a progression schedule for our customer service representatives is workable, and I think it could be fully implemented by April 1. This report discusses the background, benefits, problems, costs, and time frame involved in executing the plan.

Background: Training and Advancement Problems for CSR Reps. Because of the many insurance policies and agents we service, new customer service representatives require eight weeks of intensive training. Even after this thorough introduction, CSRs are overwhelmed. They take about eight more months before feeling competent on the job. Once they reach their potential, they often look for other positions in the company because they see few advancement possibilities in customer service. These problems were submitted to an outside consultant, who suggested a CSR progression schedule.

Benefits of Plan: Career Progression and Incremental Training. The proposed plan sets up a schedule of career progression, including these levels: (1) CSR trainee, (2) CSR Level I, (3) CSR Level II, (4) CSR Level III, (5) Senior CSR, and (6) CSR supervisor. This program, which includes salary increments with each step, provides a career ladder and incentives for increased levels of expertise and achievement. The plan also facilitates training. Instead of overloading a new trainee with an initial eight-week training program, we would train CSRs slowly with a combination of classroom and on-the-job experiences. Each level requires additional training and expertise.

Problems of Plan: Difficulty in Writing Job Descriptions and Initial Confusion. One of the biggest problems will be distinguishing the job duties at each level. However, I believe that, with the help of our consultant, we can sort out the tasks and expertise required at each level. Another problem will be determining appropriate salary differentials. Attached is a tentative schedule showing proposed wages at each level. We expect to encounter confusion and frustration in implementing this program at first, particularly in placing our current CSRs within the structure.

Costs. Implementing the progression schedule involves two direct costs. The first is the salary of a trainer, at about $40 000 a year. The second cost derives from increased salaries of upper-level CSRs, shown on the attached schedule. I believe, however, that the costs involved are within the estimates planned for this project.

Time Frame. Developing job descriptions should take us about three weeks. Preparing a training program will require another three weeks. Once the program is started, I expect a breaking-in period of at least three months. By April 1 the progression schedule will be fully implemented and showing positive results in improved CSR training, service, and retention.

Enclosure

Outlines organization of the report

Reveals decision immediately

Describes problem and background

Evaluates positive and negative aspects of proposal objectively

Presents costs and schedule; omits unnecessary summary

- Begin by describing the problem or need.
- Explain possible solutions and alternatives.
- Establish criteria for comparing the alternatives; tell how the criteria were selected or developed.
- Discuss and evaluate each alternative in terms of the criteria.
- Draw conclusions and make recommendations.

Grids are a useful way to organize and compare data for a yardstick report.

The report shown in Figure 13.11 (pages 330–32) compares three outplacement agencies and recommends one of them.

FIGURE 13.11 ***Yardstick Report***

DATE: April 28, 2010

TO: George O. Dawes, Vice President

FROM: Kelly Linden, Benefits Administrator *KL*

SUBJECT: CHOICE OF OUTPLACEMENT SERVICES

Here is the report you requested April 1 investigating the possibility of CompuTech's use of outplacement services. It discusses the problem of counselling services for discharged staff and establishes criteria for selecting an outplacement agency. It then evaluates three prospective agencies and presents a recommendation based on that evaluation.

Introduces purpose and gives overview of report organization

Problem: Counselling Discharged Staff

Discusses background briefly because readers already know the problem

In an effort to reduce costs and increase competitiveness, CompuTech will begin a program of staff reduction that will involve releasing up to 20 percent of our workforce over the next 12 to 24 months. Many of these employees have been with us for ten or more years, and they are not being released for performance faults. These employees deserve a severance package that includes counselling and assistance in finding new careers.

Uses dual headings, giving function and description

Solution and Alternatives: Outplacement Agencies

Numerous outplacement agencies offer discharged employees counselling and assistance in locating new careers. This assistance minimizes not only the negative feelings related to job loss but also the very real possibility of litigation. Potentially expensive lawsuits have been lodged against some companies by unhappy employees who felt they were unfairly released.

In seeking an outplacement agency, we should find one that offers advice to the sponsoring company as well as to dischargees. Frankly, many of our managers need help in conducting termination sessions. The law now requires certain procedures, especially in releasing employees over forty. CompuTech could unwittingly become liable to lawsuits because our managers are uninformed of these procedures. Here in the metropolitan area, I have located three potential outplacement agencies appropriate to serve our needs: Gray & Associates, Right Access, and Careers Plus.

Announces solution and the alternatives it presents

Establishing Criteria for Selecting Agency

Tells how criteria were selected

In order to choose among the three agencies, I established criteria based on professional articles, discussions with officials at other companies using outplacement agencies, and interviews with agencies. Here are the four groups of criteria I used in evaluating the three agencies:

1. Counselling services—including job search advice, résumé help, crisis management, corporate counselling, and availability of full-time counsellors
2. Administrative and research assistance—including availability of administrative staff, librarian, and personal computers
3. Reputation—based on a telephone survey of former clients and listing with a professional association
4. Costs—for both group programs and executive services

Creates four criteria to use as yardstick in evaluating alternatives

Checklist for Writing Analytical Reports

Introduction

✓ **Identify the purpose of the report.** Explain why the report is being written.

✓ **Preview the organization of the report.** Especially for long reports, explain to the reader how the report will be organized.

Vice President Dawes Page 2 April 28, 2010

Discussion: Evaluating Agencies by Criteria

Each agency was evaluated using the four criteria just described. Data comparing the first three criteria are summarized in Table 1.

Table 1

A COMPARISON OF SERVICES AND REPUTATIONS FOR THREE LOCAL OUTPLACEMENT AGENCIES

	Gray & Associates	Right Access	Careers Plus
Counselling services			
Résumé advice	Yes	Yes	Yes
Crisis management	Yes	No	Yes
Corporate counselling	Yes	No	No
Full-time counsellors	Yes	No	Yes
Administrative, research assistance			
Administrative staff	Yes	Yes	Yes
Librarian, research library	Yes	No	Yes
Personal computers	Yes	No	Yes
Listed by National Association of Career Consultants	Yes	No	Yes
Reputation (telephone survey of former clients)	Excellent	Good	Excellent

Places table close to spot where it is first mentioned

Summarizes complex data in table for easy reading and reference

Counselling Services

All three agencies offered similar basic counselling services with job-search and résumé advice. They differed, however, in three significant areas.

Right Access does not offer crisis management, a service that puts the discharged employee in contact with a counsellor the same day the employee is released. Experts in the field consider this service especially important to help the dischargee begin "bonding" with the counsellor immediately. Immediate counselling also helps the dischargee through the most traumatic moments of one of life's great disappointments and helps him or her learn how to break the news to family members. Crisis management can be instrumental in reducing lawsuits because dischargees immediately begin to focus on career planning instead of concentrating on their pain and need for revenge. Moreover, Right Access does not employ full-time counsellors; it hires part-timers according to demand. Industry authorities advise against using agencies whose staff members are inexperienced and employed on an "as-needed" basis.

Highlights the similarities and differences among the alternatives

In addition, neither Right Access nor Careers Plus offers regular corporate counselling, which I feel is critical in training our managers to conduct terminal interviews. Careers Plus, however, suggested that it could schedule special workshops if desired.

Secretarial and Research Assistance

Both Gray & Associates and Careers Plus offer complete administrative services and personal computers. Dischargees have access to staff and equipment to assist them in their job searches. These agencies also provide research libraries, librarians, and databases of company information to help in securing interviews.

Does not repeat obvious data from table

(continued)

Summarize the conclusions and recommendations for receptive audiences. Use the direct pattern only if you have the confidence of the reader.

Findings

Discuss pros and cons. In recommendation/justification reports evaluate the advantages and disadvantages of each alternative. For unreceptive audiences, consider placing the recommended alternative last.

FIGURE 13.11 ***Yardstick Report (Continued)***

Vice President Dawes — Page 3 — April 28, 2010

Discusses objectively how each agency meets criteria

Reputation

To assess the reputation of each agency, I checked its listing with the National Association of Career Consultants. This is a voluntary organization of outplacement agencies that monitors and polices its members. Gray & Associates and Careers Plus are listed; Right Access is not.

For further evidence I conducted a telephone survey of former agency clients. The three agencies supplied me with names and telephone numbers of companies and individuals they had served. I called four former clients for each agency. Most of the individuals were pleased with the outplacement services they had received. I asked each client the same questions so that I could compare responses.

Costs

All three agencies have two separate fee schedules, summarized in Table 2. The first schedule is for group programs intended for lower-level employees. These include off-site or on-site single-day workshop sessions, and the prices range from $1000 per session (at Right Access) to $1500 per session (at Gray & Associates). An additional fee of $40 to $50 is charged for each participant.

Selects most important data from table to discuss

The second fee schedule covers executive services. This counselling is individual and costs from 10 percent to 18 percent of the dischargee's previous year's salary. Since CompuTech will be forced to release numerous managerial staff members, the executive fee schedule is critical. Table 2 shows fees for a hypothetical case involving a manager who earns $60 000 a year.

Table 2

A COMPARISON OF COSTS FOR THREE AGENCIES

	Gray & Associates	Right Access	Careers Plus
Group programs	$1500/session, $45/participant	$1000/session, $40/participant	$1400/session, $50/participant
Executive services	15% of previous year's salary	10% of previous year's salary	18% of previous year's salary plus $1000 fee
Manager at $60 000/year	$9000	$6000	$11 800

Conclusions and Recommendations

Gives reasons for making recommendation

Although Right Access has the lowest fees, it lacks crisis management, corporate counselling, full-time counsellors, library facilities, and personal computers. Moreover, it is not listed by the National Association of Career Consultants. Therefore, the choice is between Gray & Associates and Careers Plus. Because they have similar services, the deciding factor is costs. Careers Plus would charge nearly $3000 more for counselling a manager than would Gray & Associates. Although Gray & Associates has fewer computers available, all other elements of its services seem good. Therefore, I recommend that CompuTech hire Gray & Associates as an outplacement agency to counsel discharged employees.

Narrows choice to final alternative

- ✓ **Establish criteria to evaluate alternatives.** In yardstick reports, create criteria to use in measuring each alternative consistently.
- ✓ **Support the findings with evidence.** Supply facts, statistics, expert opinion, survey data, and other proof from which you can draw logical conclusions.
- ✓ **Organize the findings for logic and readability.** Arrange the findings around the alternatives or the reasons leading to the conclusion. Use headings, enumerations, lists, tables, and graphics to focus emphasis.

Conclusions/Recommendations

 **Draw reasonable conclusions from the findings.** Develop conclusions that answer the research question. Justify the conclusions with highlights from the findings.

 **Make recommendations, if asked.** For multiple recommendations prepare a list. Use action verbs. Explain needed action.

Summary of Learning Objectives

1 **Use tabulating and statistical techniques to sort and interpret business report data.** Report data are more meaningful when sorted into tables or when analyzed by mean (the arithmetic average), median (the midpoint in a group of figures), and mode (the most frequent response). Range represents a span between the highest and lowest figures. Grids help organize complex data into rows and columns.

2 **Draw meaningful conclusions and make practical report recommendations based on prior logical analysis.** Conclusions tell what the survey data mean—especially in relation to the original report problem. They summarize key findings and may attempt to explain what caused the report problem. They are usually enumerated. In reports that call for recommendations, writers make specific suggestions for actions that can solve the report problem. Recommendations should be feasible and potentially agreeable to the audience. They should all relate to the initial problem. Recommendations may be combined with conclusions.

3 **Organize report data logically and provide cues to aid readers' comprehension.** Reports may be organized in many ways, including by (a) time (establishing a chronology or history of events), (b) component (discussing a problem by geography, division, or product), (c) importance (arranging data from most important to least important, or vice versa), (d) criteria (comparing items by standards), or (e) convention (using an already established grouping). Introductions, transitions, and headings serve as clues to help guide the reader through the text.

4 **Prepare short informational reports.** Periodic, trip, convention, progress, and investigative reports are examples of typical informational reports. Such reports include an introduction that may preview the report purpose and supply background data if necessary. The body of the report is generally divided into three to five segments that may be organized by time, component, importance, criteria, or convention. The body should include clear headings and may use an informal, conversational style unless the audience expects a more formal tone. The summary or conclusion reviews the main points and discusses what action will follow. The conclusion may offer a final thought, express appreciation, or express willingness to provide further information.

5 **Prepare short analytical reports that solve business problems.** Typical analytical reports include justification/recommendation reports, feasibility reports, and yardstick reports. Justification/recommendation reports that are organized directly identify a problem, immediately announce a recommendation or solution, explain and discuss its merits, and summarize the action to

be taken. Justification/recommendation reports that are organized indirectly describe a problem, discuss alternative solutions, prove the superiority of one solution, and ask for authorization to proceed with that solution. Feasibility reports study the advisability of following a course of action. They generally announce the author's proposal immediately. Then they describe the background, advantages and disadvantages, costs, and time frame for implementing the proposal. Yardstick reports compare two or more solutions to a problem by measuring each against a set of established criteria. They usually describe a problem, explain possible solutions, establish criteria for comparing alternatives, evaluate each alternative in terms of the criteria, draw conclusions, and make recommendations. The advantage to yardstick reports is consistency in comparing various alternatives. Most reports serve as a basis for decision making in business.

chapter review

1. What is data tabulation? Provide an original example. Why is tabulation necessary for a researcher who has collected large amounts of data? (Obj. 1)
2. What is cross-tabulation? Give an example. (Obj. 1)
3. Calculate the mean, median, and mode for these figures: 3, 4, 4, 4, 10. (Obj. 1)
4. How can a grid help classify material? (Obj. 1)
5. What are the two most widely read sections of a report? (Obj. 2)
6. How do conclusions differ from recommendations? (Obj. 2)
7. When reports have multiple recommendations, how should they be presented? (Obj. 2)
8. Name five methods for organizing report data. Be prepared to discuss each. (Obj. 3)
9. What three devices can report writers use to prevent readers from getting lost in the text? (Obj. 3)
10. Informational reports typically are organized into what three parts? (Obj. 4)
11. Describe periodic reports and what they generally contain. (Obj. 4)
12. What should a progress report include? (Obj. 4)
13. What sequence should a direct justification/recommendation report follow? (Obj. 5)
14. What are feasibility reports? Are they generally intended for internal or external audiences? (Obj. 5)
15. What is a yardstick report? (Obj. 5)

critical thinking

1. Researchers can draw various conclusions from a set of data. How do you know how to shape conclusions and recommendations? (Obj. 2)
2. Why is audience analysis particularly important in making report recommendations? (Obj. 2)
3. Should all reports be organized so that they follow the sequence of investigation—that is, a description of the initial problem, an analysis of the issues, data collection, data analysis, and conclusions? Why or why not? (Obj. 3)
4. What are the major differences between informational and analytical reports? (Objs. 4 and 5)

activities

13.1 Tabulation and Interpretation of Survey Results (Obj. 1)

CRITICAL THINKING | LISTENING | SPEAKING | TEAM

Your business communication class at North Shore College was asked by the college bookstore manager, Larry Krause, to conduct a survey. Concerned about the environment, Krause wants to learn students' reactions to eliminating plastic bags, of which 45 000 are given away annually by the bookstore. Students answered questions about a number of proposals, resulting in the following raw data:

For major purchases the bookstore should:

	Agree	Undecided	Disagree
1. Continue to provide plastic bags	132	17	411
2. Provide no bags; encourage students to bring their own bags	414	25	121
3. Provide no bags; offer cloth bags at a reduced price (about $3)	357	19	184
4. Give a cloth bag with each major purchase, the cost to be included in registration fees	63	15	482

Your Task. In groups of four or five, do the following:

a. Convert the data into a table with a descriptive title. Arrange the items in a logical sequence.
b. How could these survey data be cross-tabulated? Would cross-tabulation serve any purpose?
c. Given the conditions of this survey, name at least three conclusions that could be drawn from the data.
d. Prepare three to five recommendations to be submitted to Mr. Krause. How could they be implemented?
e. Role-play a meeting in which the recommendations and implementation plan are presented to Mr. Krause. One student plays the role of Mr. Krause; the remaining students play the role of the presenters.

13.2 Evaluating Conclusions (Obj. 2)

E-MAIL

Your Task. Read an in-depth article (800 or more words) in *BusinessWeek, Fortune, Forbes, Canadian Business,* or *Financial Post Magazine.* What conclusions does the author draw? Are the conclusions valid, based on the evidence presented? In an e-mail message to your instructor, summarize the main points in the article and analyze the conclusions. What conclusions would you have drawn from the data?

13.3 Distinguishing Between Conclusions and Recommendations (Obj. 2)

A study of red light violations produced the following findings: Red light traffic violations were responsible for more than 25 000 crashes in several metropolitan areas. Crashes from running red lights decreased by 10 percent in areas using camera programs to cite offenders. Two out of seven local governments studied showed a profit from the programs; the others lost money.[4]

Your Task. Based on the preceding facts, indicate whether the following statements are conclusions or recommendations:

a. Red light violations are dangerous offences.
b. Red light cameras are an effective traffic safety tool.
c. Local governments should be allowed to implement red light camera programs.
d. Although red light camera programs are expensive, they prevent crashes and are, therefore, worthwhile.
e. The city of Centreville should not implement a red light program because of the program's cost.
f. Red light programs are not necessarily profitable for local governments.

13.4 Organizing Data (Obj. 3)

SPEAKING LISTENING

Your Task. In groups of three to five, discuss how the findings in the following reports could be best organized. Consider these methods: time, component, importance, criteria, and convention.

a. A report comparing three locations for a fast-food company's new restaurant. The report presents data on real estate values, construction costs, traffic patterns, competition, provincial taxes, labour availability, and population demographics.
b. A report describing the history of the development of dwarf and spur apple trees, starting with the first genetic dwarfs discovered about 100 years ago and progressing to today's grafted varieties on dwarfing rootstocks.
c. An informational report describing a company's expansion plans in South America, Europe, Australia, and Southeast Asia.
d. An employee performance appraisal submitted annually.

13.5 Evaluating Headings and Titles (Obj. 3)

Your Task. Identify the following report headings and titles as *functional, talking,* or *combination.* Discuss the usefulness and effectiveness of each.

a. Budget
b. Mishandled Baggage Reports Filed by Passengers
c. Upgrades
d. How to Implement Instant Messaging Rules
e. Case History: Focusing on Customer Service

13.6 Writing a Survey: Studying Employee Use of Instant Messaging (Obj. 1)

WEB

Instant messaging (IM) is a popular way to exchange messages in real time. It offers the convenience of telephone conversations and e-mail. Best of all, it allows employees to contact anyone in the world while retaining a written copy of the conversation—without a large telephone bill. But instant messaging is risky for companies. They may lose trade secrets or confidential information over insecure lines. They also may be liable if inappropriate material is exchanged. Moreover, IM opens the door to viruses that can infect a company's entire computer system.

Your boss has just read an article stating that 40 percent of companies now use IM for business and up to 90 percent of employees use IM without their manager's knowledge or authorization. She asks you to prepare a survey of your 48-member staff to learn how many are using IM. She wants to know what type of IM software they have downloaded, how many hours a day they spend on IM, what are the advantages of IM, and so forth. The goal is not to identify those using or abusing IM. Instead, the goal is to learn when, how, and why it is being used so that appropriate policies can be designed.

Your Task. Use the Web to learn more about instant messaging. Then prepare a short employee survey. Include an appropriate introduction that explains the survey and encourages a response. Should you ask for names on the survey? How can you encourage return of the forms? Your instructor may wish to expand this survey into a report by having you produce fictitious survey results, analyze the findings, draw conclusions, and make recommendations.

Rich chapter resources are available on the Web site.

13.7 Progress Report: Checking In (Obj. 4)

E-MAIL

Students writing a long report described in Chapter 14 must keep their instructor informed of their progress.
Your Task. Write a progress report informing your instructor of your work. Briefly describe the project (its purpose, scope, limitations, and methodology), work completed, work yet to be completed, problems encountered, future activities, and expected completion date. Address the e-mail memo report to your instructor.

13.8 Investigative Report: Studying the Journals in Your Field (Obj. 4)

Your campus library has limited funds for the purchase of print journals. As a library intern, you have been assigned the task of examining journals in your field. Your report to the head librarian will help the library decide which journals are most helpful to students.
Your Task. Prepare an informational letter or memo report that identifies three journals in your field. Discuss the format, tone, and readability of each journal. What kinds of articles are presented? Which journals would be most useful to students in your field? Why? Select one article from each journal to critique as part of your report. Address your report to Lisa B. Martin, Head Librarian, College Library, P.O. Box 4230, Toronto, ON M4Y 2Y5. Remember that your goal is to investigate and inform, not necessarily to promote and recommend.

13.9 Investigative Report: Marketing Abroad (Obj. 4)

WEB

You have been asked to prepare a training program for Canadian companies doing business outside the country.
Your Task. Select a country to investigate (preferably one for which your library has *Culturgram* materials). Collect data from *Culturgram* files and from the country's embassy in Ottawa. Interview on-campus international students. Use the Web to discover data about the country. Collect information about formats for written communication, observance of holidays, customary greetings, business ethics, and other topics of interest to businesspeople. Remember that your report should promote business, not tourism. Prepare a memo report addressed to Kelly Johnson, editor for the training program materials.

13.10 Progress Report: Heading Toward That Degree/Diploma (Obj. 4)

You have made an agreement with your parents (or spouse, relative, or significant friend) that you will submit a progress report at this time.
Your Task. Prepare a progress report in letter format. Describe your headway toward your educational goal (such as employment, degree, or certificate). List your specific achievements, and outline what you have left to complete.

13.11 Justification/Recommendation Report: Searching for the Best Philanthropic Project (Obj. 5)

WEB

Great news! MegaTech, the start-up company where you work, has become enormously successful. Now the owner wants to support some kind of philanthropic program. He doesn't have time to check out the possibilities, so he asks you, his assistant, to conduct research and report to him and the board of directors.
Your Task. He wants you to investigate the philanthropic projects at 20 high-profile companies of your choice. Visit their Web sites and study programs such as volunteerism, cause-related marketing, matching funds, charitable donations, and so forth. In a recommendation report, discuss five of the best programs and recommend one that can serve as a philanthropic project model for your company.

13.12 Justification/Recommendation Report: Developing an Organizational E-Mail Policy (Obj. 5)

CRITICAL THINKING | LISTENING | SPEAKING | TEAM | WEB

As a manager in a mid-sized engineering firm, you are aware that members of your department frequently use e-mail and the Internet for private messages, shopping, and games. In addition to the strain on computer facilities, you worry about declining productivity as well as security problems. When you walked by one worker's computer and saw what looked like pornography on the screen, you knew you had to do something. Although workplace privacy is a hot-button issue for unions and employee-rights groups, employers have legitimate reasons for wanting to know what is happening on their computers. A high percentage of lawsuits involve the use and abuse of e-mail. You think that the executive council should establish some kind of e-mail policy. The council is generally receptive to sound suggestions, especially if they are inexpensive. At present no e-mail policy exists, and you fear that the executive council is not fully aware of the dangers. You decide to talk with other managers about the problem and write a justification/recommendation report.
Your Task. In teams discuss the need for an e-mail policy. Using the Web, find information about other firms' use of such policies. Look for examples of companies struggling with lawsuits over e-mail abuse. In your report, should you describe suitable e-mail policies? Should you recommend computer monitoring and surveillance software? Should the

policy cover cell phones, wireless pagers, and instant messaging? Each member of the team should present and support his or her ideas regarding what should be included in the report. Individually or as a team, write a convincing justification/recommendation report to the executive council based on the conclusions you draw from your research and discussion. Decide whether you should be direct or indirect.

13.13 Feasibility Report: International Organization (Obj. 5)

CRITICAL THINKING

To fulfill a senior project in your department, you have been asked to submit a letter report to the dean evaluating the feasibility of starting an organization of international students on campus.

Your Task. Find out how many international students are on your campus, what nations they represent, how one goes about starting an organization, and whether a faculty sponsor is needed. Assume that you conducted an informal survey of international students. Of the 39 who filled out the survey, 31 said they would be interested in joining.

13.14 Feasibility Report: Improving Employee Fitness (Obj. 5)

CRITICAL THINKING

Your company is considering ways to promote employee fitness and morale.

Your Task. Select a possible fitness program that seems reasonable for your company. Consider a softball league, bowling teams, basketball league, lunchtime walks, lunchtime fitness speakers and demos, company-sponsored health club membership, workout room, fitness centre, fitness director, and so on. Assume that your boss has tentatively agreed to one of the programs and has asked you to write a memo report investigating its feasibility.

13.15 Yardstick Report: Evaluating Equipment (Obj. 5)

CRITICAL THINKING

You recently complained to your boss that you were unhappy with a piece of equipment that you use (printer, computer, copier, fax, or the like). After some thought, the boss decided you were right and told you to go shopping.

Your Task. Compare at least three different manufacturers' models and recommend one. Because the company will be purchasing ten or more units and because several managers must approve the purchase, write a careful report documenting your findings. Establish at least five criteria for comparing the models. Submit a memo report to your boss.

13.16 Yardstick Report: Measuring the Alternatives (Obj. 5)

CRITICAL THINKING

Your Task. Consider a problem where you work or in an organization you know. Select a problem with several alternative solutions or courses of action (retaining the present status could be one alternative). Develop criteria that could be used to evaluate each alternative. Write a report measuring each alternative by the yardstick you have created. Recommend a course of action to your boss or to the organization head.

C.L.U.E. review 13

On a separate sheet edit the following sentences to correct faults in grammar, punctuation, spelling, numbers, proofreading, and word use.

1. When conducting research for a report you may face an incredable jumble of data including: printouts, disk files, note cards, copys of articles, inter view notes, questionaire results and statistics.
2. The information in tables are usally easier to read then the same information presented in paragraph.
3. When the Company President and myself use the word average we are refering to the mean which is the arithmetic average.
4. The following 3 statistical terms frequently describe data; Mean, Median and Mode.
5. Readers of business' reports often turn frist to the Conclusions and Reccommendations, therefore these section must be written vary carefully.
6. Informational Reports emphasize facts, Analytical Reports however emphasize reasoning and conclusions.
7. Report Conclusions explain what the problem is, Recommendations tell how to solve it.
8. Frontloading the Recommenddations works when the topic is routine, and when the audience is receptive.
9. In writing most business reports you will genrally organize you're data using 1 of the following 5 methods, time, component, importance, criteria or convention.
10. The Introduction to a report should tell it's purpose and significance, it should also preview the main points.

Rich chapter resources are available on the Web site.

chapter 14

Proposals and Formal Reports

objectives

1 Discuss the general uses and basic components of proposals and grasp their audience and purpose.

2 Discuss formal proposals and how to anticipate a receiver's reaction to your message.

3 Identify the components of typical business plans.

4 Describe the formal report components that precede the introduction as well as elements to include in the introduction and how they further the purpose of your communication.

5 Describe formal report components that follow the introduction and how they further the purpose of your report.

6 Specify tips that aid writers of formal reports as they use their analytic and reflective thinking skills.

springboard *to discussion*

Many companies are realizing the benefits of going green when distributing their annual reports—not only in cost savings but also in social responsibility rewards. For example, in its efforts to "reinforce our commitment to environmental and sustainability leadership," Duke Energy offered an incentive to its shareholders. For every shareholder who opted for electronic delivery of the annual report, the company would donate $1 to the Nature Conservancy. As a result, Duke Energy donated $80 000 to help save trees, energy, and water by offering their shareholders the electronic choice.[1]

learning objective

1

Preparing Formal and Informal Proposals

Proposals are persuasive offers to solve problems, provide services, or sell equipment.

Proposals are written offers to solve problems, provide services, or sell equipment. Some proposals are internal, often taking the form of justification and recommendation reports. You learned about these reports in Chapter 13. Most proposals, however, are external and are a critical means of selling products and services that generate income.

Because proposals are vital to their success, some businesses hire consultants or maintain specialists who do nothing but write proposals. Such proposals typically tell how a problem can be solved, what procedure will be followed, who will do it, how long it will take, and how much it will cost.

Government agencies and many companies use requests for proposals (RFPs) to solicit competitive bids on projects.

Proposals may be divided into two categories: solicited and unsolicited. When firms know exactly what they want, they prepare a request for proposal (RFP) specifying their requirements. Government agencies as well as private businesses use RFPs to solicit competitive bids from vendors. Most proposals are solicited. Enterprising companies looking for work might submit unsolicited proposals. Unsolicited proposals are written when an individual or firm sees a problem to be solved and offers a proposal to do so.

Components of Informal Proposals

Informal proposals may contain an introduction, background information, the proposal, staffing requirements, a budget, and an authorization request.

Informal proposals may be presented in short (two- to four-page) letters. Sometimes called *letter proposals*, they may contain six principal components: introduction, background, proposal, staffing, budget, and authorization request. As you can see in Figure 14.1, both informal and formal proposals contain these six basic parts.

Introduction. Most proposals begin by briefly explaining the reasons for the proposal and by highlighting the writer's qualifications. To make your introduction more persuasive, you need to provide a "hook," such as the following:

- Hint at extraordinary results, with details to be revealed shortly.
- Promise low costs or speedy results.

FIGURE 14.1 ***Components of Formal and Informal Proposals***

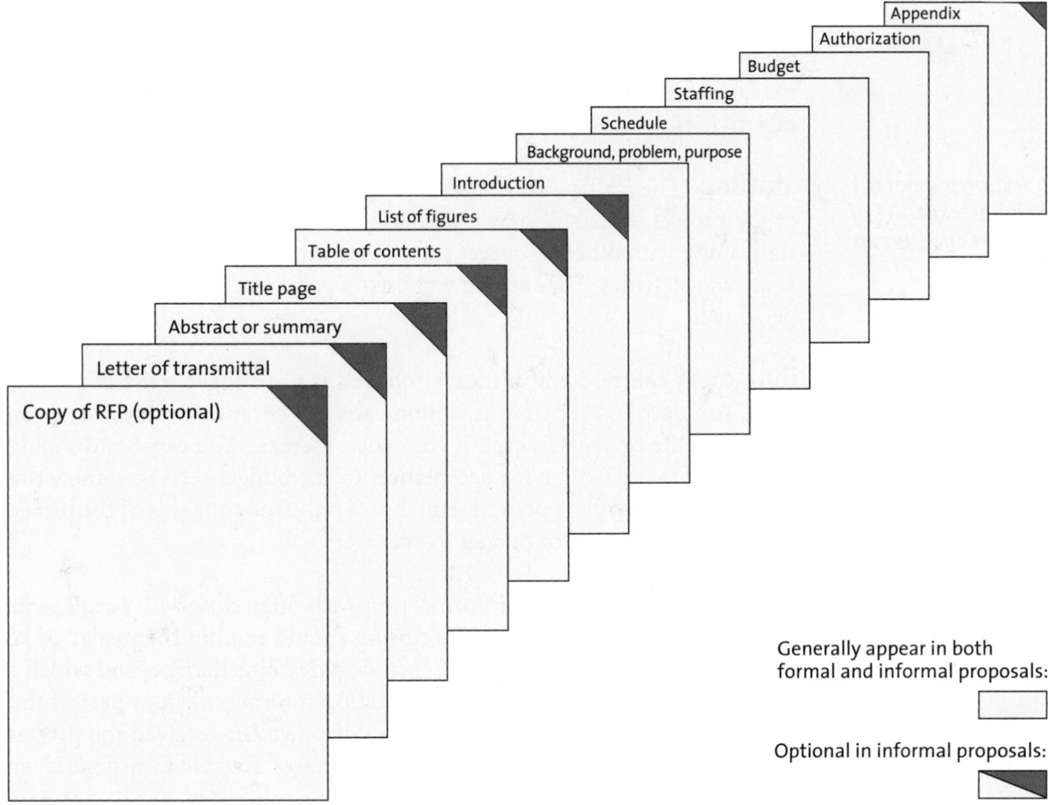

- Mention a remarkable resource (well-known authority, new computer program, well trained staff) available exclusively to you.
- Identify a serious problem (worry item) and promise a solution, to be explained later.
- Specify a key issue or benefit that you feel is the heart of the proposal.

Although writers may know what goes into the proposal introduction, many face writer's block at the beginning. Writer's block can be a big barrier because the writer simply doesn't know how to get started. It is often a good idea to put off writing the proposal introduction until after you have completed other parts. For longer proposals the introduction also describes the scope and limitations of the project, as well as outlining the organization of the material to come.

Background, Problem, Purpose. The background section identifies the problem and discusses the goals or purposes of the project. In an unsolicited proposal your goal is to convince the reader that a problem exists. Thus you must present the problem in detail, discussing such factors as monetary losses, failure to comply with government regulations, or loss of customers. In a solicited proposal your aim is to persuade the reader that you understand the problem completely. Thus, if you are responding to an RFP, this means repeating its language.

In the background section of a proposal, the writer discusses the problem and goals of the project.

The actual proposal section must give enough information to secure the contract but not so much detail that the services are no longer needed.

Proposal, Plan, Schedule. In the proposal section itself, you should discuss your plan for solving the problem. In some proposals this is tricky because you want to disclose enough of your plan to secure the contract without giving away so much information that your services aren't needed. Without specifics, though, your proposal has little chance, so you must decide how much to reveal. Tell what you propose to do and how it will benefit the reader. Remember, too, that a proposal is a sales presentation. Sell your methods, product, and "deliverables"—items that will be left with the client. In this section some writers specify how the project will be managed and how its progress will be audited. Most writers also include a schedule of activities or timetable showing when events will take place.

The staffing section promotes the credentials and expertise of the project leaders and support staff.

Staffing. The staffing section of a proposal describes the credentials and expertise of the project leaders. It may also identify the size and qualifications of the support staff, along with other resources such as computer facilities and special programs for analyzing statistics. The staffing section is a good place to endorse and promote your personnel.

Because a proposal is a legal contract, the budget must be carefully researched.

Budget. A central item in most proposals is the budget, a list of proposed project costs. You need to prepare this section carefully because it represents a contract; you can't raise the price later, even if your costs increase. You can—and should—protect yourself with a deadline for acceptance. In the budget section some writers itemize hours and costs; others present a total sum only. Your analysis of the project will help you decide what kind of budget to prepare.

Authorization Request. Informal proposals often close with a request for approval or authorization. In addition, the closing should remind the reader of key benefits and motivate action. It might also include a deadline date beyond which the offer is invalid. In some organizations authorization to proceed is not part of the proposal. Instead, it is usually discussed after the customer has received the proposal. In this way the customer and the sales account manager are able to negotiate terms before a formal agreement is drawn.

learning objective

2

Special Components of Formal Proposals

Formal proposals differ from informal proposals not in style but in size and format. Formal proposals respond to big projects and may range from 5 to 200 or more pages. To facilitate comprehension and reference, they are organized into many parts, as shown in Figure 14.1. In addition to the six basic components just described, formal proposals may contain some or all of the following front and end parts.

Formal proposals might also contain a copy of the RFP, a letter of transmittal, an abstract, a title page, a table of contents, a list of figures, and an appendix.

Copy of RFP. A copy of the RFP may be included in the opening parts of a formal proposal. Large organizations may have more than one RFP circulating, so identification is necessary.

Letter of Transmittal. A letter of transmittal, usually bound inside formal proposals, addresses the person who is designated to receive the proposal or who will make the final decision. The letter describes how you learned about the problem or confirms that the proposal responds to the enclosed RFP. This persuasive letter briefly presents the major features and benefits of your proposal. Here you should assure the reader that you are authorized to make the bid and mention the time limit for which the bid stands. You may also offer to provide additional information and ask for action, if appropriate.

An abstract summarizes a proposal's highlights for specialists; an executive summary does so for managers.

Abstract or Executive Summary. An abstract is a brief summary (typically one page) of a proposal's highlights that is intended for specialists or for technical readers. An executive summary also reviews the proposal's highlights, but it is written for managers and so should be less technically oriented. Formal proposals may contain one or both summaries. For more information about writing executive summaries or abstracts, use a search engine such as Google.

Title Page. The title page includes the following items, generally in this order: title of proposal, name of client organization, RFP number or other announcement, date of submission, and the authors' names and/or the name of their organization.

Table of Contents. Because most proposals don't contain an index, the table of contents becomes quite important. Tables of contents should include all headings and their beginning page numbers. Items that appear before the contents (copy of RFP, letter of transmittal, abstract, and title page) typically are not listed in the contents. However, any appendixes should be listed.

List of Figures. Proposals with many tables and figures often contain a list of figures. This list includes each figure or table title and its page number. If you have just a few figures or tables, however, you may omit this list.

Appendix. Ancillary material of interest to some readers goes in appendixes. Appendix A might include résumés of the principal investigators or testimonial letters. Appendix B might include examples or a listing of previous projects. Other appendixes could include audit procedures, technical graphics, or professional papers cited in the body of the proposal.

Proposals in the past were always paper-based and delivered by mail or special messenger. Today, however, companies increasingly prefer *online proposals.* Receiving companies may transmit the electronic proposal to all levels of management without ever printing a page, thus appealing to many environmentally conscious organizations.

Well-written proposals win contracts and business for companies and individuals. Many companies depend entirely on proposals to generate their income, so proposal writing is extremely important. The following checklist summarizes important elements to remember in writing proposals.

Checklist for Writing Proposals

Introduction

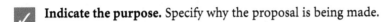

- ✓ **Indicate the purpose.** Specify why the proposal is being made.
- ✓ **Develop a persuasive "hook."** Suggest excellent results, low costs, or exclusive resources. Identify a serious problem or name a key issue or benefit.

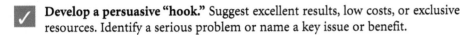

Background, Problem

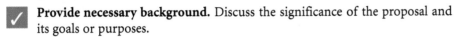

- ✓ **Provide necessary background.** Discuss the significance of the proposal and its goals or purposes.
- ✓ **Introduce the problem.** For unsolicited proposals, convince the reader that a problem exists. For solicited proposals, show that you fully understand the problem and its ramifications.

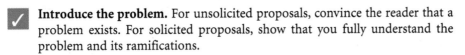

Proposal, Plan

- ✓ **Explain the proposal.** Present your plan for solving the problem or meeting the need.
- ✓ **Discuss plan management and evaluation.** If appropriate, tell how the plan will be implemented and evaluated.
- ✓ **Outline a timetable.** Furnish a schedule showing what will be done and when.

Staffing

- ✓ **Promote the qualifications of your staff.** Explain the specific credentials and expertise of the key personnel for the project.
- ✓ **Mention special resources or equipment.** Show how your support staff and resources are superior to those of the competition.

Budget

- ✓ **Show project costs.** For most projects, itemize costs. Remember, however, that proposals are contracts.
- ✓ **Include a deadline.** Here or in the conclusion present a date beyond which the bid figures are no longer valid.

Authorization

- ✓ **Ask for approval.** Make it easy for the reader to authorize the project (for example, *Sign and return the duplicate copy*).

learning objective

3

Preparing an Effective Business Plan

Another form of proposal is a business plan. Let us say you want to start your own business. Unless you can count on the Bank of Mom and Dad, you will need financial backing such as a bank loan or venture capital supplied by investors. A business plan is critical for securing financial support of any kind. Such a plan also ensures that you have done your homework and know what you are doing in launching your business. It provides you with a detailed road map to chart a course to success.

According to the *Small Business Administration*, most entrepreneurs spend about 400 hours writing a good business plan. The average consultant can do it in about 40 hours.[2] Nevertheless, many budding entrepreneurs prefer to save the cash and do it themselves. Increasingly sophisticated software such as Business Plan Pro, PlanWrite, and Planmagic is available for those who have done their research, assembled the relevant data, and just want formatting help. Free shareware can also be found on the Internet.[3]

Components of Typical Business Plans

If you are serious about starting a business, the importance of a comprehensive, thoughtful business plan cannot be overemphasized. Your business plan is more likely to secure the funds you need if it is carefully written and includes the following elements:

- **Letter of transmittal and/or executive summary with mission statement.** Explain your reason for writing. Provide your name, address, and telephone number, along with contact information for all principals. Include a concise mission statement that describes your business and explains the reasons it will succeed. Because potential investors will be looking for this mission statement, consider highlighting it with a paragraph heading (*Mission statement*) or use bolding or italics. Some consultants say that you should be able to write your mission statement on the back of a business card. Others think that one or two short paragraphs might be more realistic. To give it special treatment, you could make the mission statement a section of its own following the table of contents. Your executive summary should conclude by introducing the parts of the following plan and asking for support.
- **Table of contents.** List the page numbers and topics included in your plan.
- **Company description.** Identify the form of your business (proprietorship, partnership, or corporation) and its business type (merchandising, manufacturing, or service). For existing companies, describe the company's founding, growth, sales, and profit.
- **Product/service description.** In jargon-free language, explain what you are providing, how it will benefit customers, and why it is better than existing products or services. For start-ups, explain why the business will be profitable. Investors aren't always looking for a unique product or service. Instead, they are searching for a concept whose growth potential distinguishes it from other proposals competing for funds.
- **Market analysis.** Discuss market characteristics, trends, projected growth, customer behaviour, complementary products and services, and barriers to entry. Identify your customers and how you will attract, hold, and increase your market share. Discuss the strengths and weaknesses of your direct and indirect competitors.
- **Operations and management.** Explain specifically how you will run your business, including location, equipment, personnel, and management. Highlight experienced and well-trained members of the management team and your advisors. Many investors consider this the most important factor in assessing business potential. Can your management team implement this business plan?
- **Financial analysis.** Outline a realistic start-up budget that includes the costs of legal/professional services, occupancy, licences/permits, equipment, insurance, supplies, advertising/promotions, salaries/wages, accounting, income, and utilities. Also present an operating budget that projects costs for personnel, insurance, rent, depreciation, loan payments, salaries, taxes, repairs, and so on. Explain how much money you have, how much you will need to start up, and how much you will need to stay in business.
- **Appendixes.** Provide necessary extras such as managers' résumés, promotional materials, and product photos.

Sample Business Plans on the Web

Writing a business plan is easier if you can see examples and learn from experts' suggestions. On the Web you will find many sites devoted to business plans. Some sites want to sell you something; others offer free advice. One of the best sites (**www.bplans.com**) does try to sell business plans and software. However, in addition to useful advice and blogs from experts, the site also provides over 100 free samples of business plans ranging from aircraft rental to wedding consultant businesses. These simple but helpful plans, provided by Palo Alto Software, Inc., illustrate diverse business start-ups. In addition, most major financial institutions provide information on their Web sites about how to write business plans. Finally, check provincial and Government of Canada Web sites for helpful business start-up information about financing, marketing, employees, taxes, and legal matters.

learning objective 4

Writing Formal Reports

Formal reports discuss the results of a process of thorough investigation and analysis.

Formal reports are similar to formal proposals in length, organization, and serious tone. Instead of making an offer, however, formal reports represent the end product of thorough investigation and analysis. They present ordered information to decision makers in business, industry, government, and education. In many ways formal reports are extended versions of the analytical business reports presented in Chapter 13. Figure 14.2 shows the components of typical formal reports, their normal sequence, and parts that might be omitted in informal reports.

Introductory Components of Formal Reports

Like proposals, formal reports are divided into many segments to make information comprehensible and accessible.

A number of front and end items lengthen formal reports but enhance their professional tone and serve their multiple audiences. Formal reports may be read by many levels of managers, along with technical specialists and financial consultants. Therefore, breaking a long, formal report into small segments makes its information more accessible and easier to understand for all readers. These segments are discussed here and also illustrated in the model report shown later in Figure 14.3 (which starts on page 352). This analytical report studies the recycling program at West Coast College and makes recommendations for improving its operation.

Cover. Formal reports are usually enclosed in vinyl or heavy paper binders to protect the pages and to give a professional, finished appearance. Some companies have binders imprinted with their name and logo. The title of the report may appear through a cut-out window or may be applied with an adhesive label. Good stationery and office supply stores usually stock an assortment of report binders and labels.

Title Page. A report title page, as illustrated in the Figure 14.3 model report, begins with the name of the report typed in uppercase letters (no underscore and no quotation marks). Next comes *Presented to* (or *Submitted to*) and the name, title, and organization of the individual receiving the report. Lower on the page is *Prepared by* (or *Submitted by*) and the author's name plus any necessary identification. The last item on the title page is the date of submission. All items after the title are typed in a combination of upper- and lowercase letters.

Letter or Memo of Transmittal. Generally written on organization stationery, a letter or memorandum of transmittal introduces a formal report. You will recall that letters are sent to outsiders and memos to insiders. A transmittal letter or memo follows the direct pattern and is usually less formal than the report itself (for example, the letter or memo may use contractions and the first-person pronouns *I* and *we*).

FIGURE 14.2 ***Components of Formal and Informal Reports***

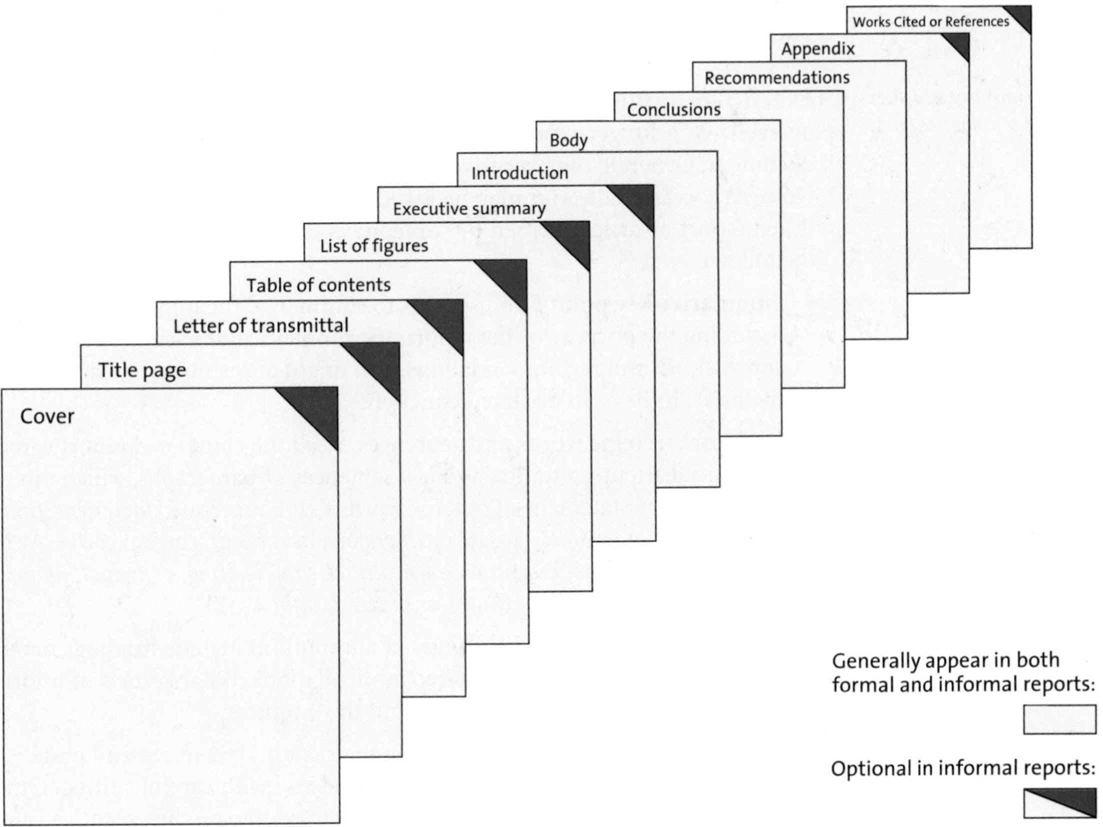

A letter or memo of transmittal gives a personalized overview of a formal report.

The transmittal letter or memo typically (a) announces the topic of the report and tells how it was authorized; (b) briefly describes the project; (c) highlights the report's findings, conclusions, and recommendations, if the reader is expected to be supportive; and (d) closes with appreciation for the assignment, instruction for the reader's follow-up actions, acknowledgment of help from others, or offers of assistance in answering questions. If a report is going to different readers, a special transmittal letter or memo should be prepared for each, anticipating how each reader will use the report.

Table of Contents. The table of contents shows the headings in a report and their page numbers. It gives an overview of the report topics and helps readers locate them. You should wait to prepare the table of contents until after you've completed the report. For short reports you should include all headings. For longer reports you might want to list only first- and second-level headings. Leaders (rows of dots) help guide the eye from the heading to the page number. Items may be indented in outline form or typed flush with the left margin.

List of Figures. For reports with several figures or illustrations, you may wish to include a list of figures to help readers locate them. This list may appear on the same page as the table of contents, space permitting. For each figure or illustration, include a title and page number. Some writers distinguish between tables and all other illustrations, which are called figures. If you make this distinction, you should prepare separate lists of tables and figures. Because the model report in Figure 14.3 has few illustrations, the writer labelled them all "figures," a method that simplifies numbering.

An executive summary supplies an overview of a longer report.

Executive Summary. The purpose of an executive summary is to present an overview of a longer report to people who may not have time to read the entire document. Generally, an executive summary is prepared by the author of the report. However, occasionally you may be asked to write an executive summary of a published report or article written by someone else. In either case you will probably do the following:

- **Summarize key points.** Your goal is to summarize the important points, including the purpose of the report; the problem addressed; and the findings, conclusions, and recommendations. You might also summarize the research methods, if they can be stated concisely.
- **Look for strategic words and sentences.** Read the completed report carefully. Pay special attention to first and last sentences of paragraphs, which often contain summary statements. Look for words that enumerate (*first, next, finally*) and words that express causation (*therefore, as a result, consequently*). Also look for words that signal essentials (*basically, central, leading, principal, major*) and words that contrast ideas (*however, instead, although*).
- **Prepare an outline with headings.** At a minimum include headings for the purpose, findings, and conclusions/recommendations. What kernels of information would your reader want to know about these topics?
- **Fill in your outline.** Some writers use their computers to cut and paste important parts of the text. Then they condense with careful editing. Others find it most efficient to create new sentences as they prepare the executive summary.
- **Begin with the purpose.** The easiest way to begin an executive summary is with the words "The purpose of this report is to . . . ." Experienced writers may be more creative.
- **Follow the report sequence.** Present all your information in the order in which it is found in the report.
- **Eliminate nonessential details.** Include only main points. Don't include anything not in the original report. Use minimal technical language.
- **Control the length.** An executive summary is usually no longer than 10 percent of the original document. Thus, a 100-page report might require a 10-page summary. A 10-page report might need only a 1-page summary—or no summary at all. The executive summary for a long report may also include graphics to adequately highlight main points.

To see a representative executive summary, look at Figure 14.3 (page 355). Although it is only one page long, this executive summary includes headings to help the reader see the main divisions immediately. Let your organization's practices guide you in determining the length and form of an executive summary.

Introduction. Formal reports begin with an introduction that sets the scene and announces the subject. Because they contain many parts serving different purposes, formal reports are somewhat redundant. The same information may be included in the letter of transmittal, the summary, and the introduction. To avoid sounding repetitious, try to present the data slightly differently. However, don't skip the introduction because you've included some of its information elsewhere.

You cannot be sure that your reader saw the information earlier. A good report introduction typically covers the following elements, although not necessarily in this order:

The introduction to a formal report describes the background, explains the purpose, and discusses the significance, scope, and organization of the topic.

- **Background.** Describe events leading up to the problem or need.
- **Problem or purpose.** Explain the report topic and specify the problem or need that motivated the report.
- **Significance.** Tell why the topic is important. You may wish to quote experts or cite newspapers, journals, books, and other secondary sources to establish the importance of the topic.
- **Scope.** Clarify the boundaries of the report, defining what will be included or excluded.
- **Organization.** Orient readers by giving them a road map that previews the structure of the report.

Beyond these minimal introductory elements, consider adding any of the following information that is relevant for your readers:

- **Authorization.** Identify who commissioned the report. If no letter of transmittal is included, also tell why, when, by whom, and for whom the report was written.
- **Literature review.** Summarize what other authors and researchers have published on this topic, especially for academic and scientific reports.
- **Sources and methods.** Describe your secondary sources (periodicals, books, databases). Also explain how you collected primary data, including survey size, sample design, and statistical programs used.
- **Definitions of key terms.** Define words that may be unfamiliar to the audience. Also define terms with special meanings, such as *small business* when it specifically means a business with fewer than 30 employees.

Main Components of Formal Reports

learning objective 5

Body. The principal section in a formal report is the body. It discusses, analyzes, interprets, and evaluates the research findings or solution to the initial problem. This is where you show the evidence that justifies your conclusions. Organize the body into main categories following your original outline or using one of the patterns described earlier (time, component, importance, criteria, or convention).

Although we refer to this section as the body, it does not carry that heading. Instead, it contains clear headings that explain each major section. Headings may be functional or talking. Functional heads (such as *Results of the Survey*, *Analysis of Findings*, or *Discussion*) help readers identify the purpose of the section but don't reveal what's in it. Such headings are useful for routine reports or for sensitive topics that may upset readers. Talking heads (for example, *Recycling Habits of Campus Community*) are more informative and interesting, but they don't help readers see the organization of the report. The model report in Figure 14.3 uses functional heads for organizational sections requiring identification (*Introduction*, *Conclusions*, and *Recommendations*) and talking heads to divide the body.

Conclusions. This important section tells what the findings mean, particularly in terms of solving the original problem. Instead of presenting the conclusions separately, some writers prefer to intermix their conclusions with the analysis of the findings. Other writers place the conclusions before the body so that busy readers can examine the significant information immediately. Still others combine the

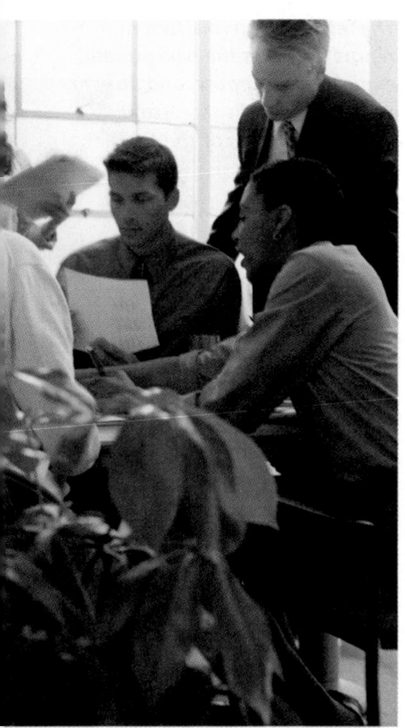

conclusions and recommendations. Most writers, though, present the conclusions after the body because readers expect this structure. In long reports this section may include a summary of the findings. To improve comprehension, you may present the conclusions in a numbered or bulleted list. See Chapter 13 for more suggestions on drawing conclusions.

Recommendations. When asked, you should submit recommendations that make precise suggestions for actions to solve the report problem. Recommendations are most helpful when they are practical and reasonable. Naturally, they should evolve from the findings and conclusions. Do not introduce new information in the conclusions or recommendations. As with conclusions, the position of recommendations is somewhat flexible. They may be combined with conclusions, or they may be presented before the body, especially when the audience is eager and supportive. Generally, though, in formal reports they come last.

Recommendations require an appropriate introductory sentence, such as *The findings and conclusions in this study support the following recommendations.* When making many recommendations, number them and phrase each as a command, such as *Begin an employee fitness program with a workout room available five days a week.* If appropriate, add information describing how to implement each recommendation. Some reports include a timetable describing the who, what, when, where, and how for putting each recommendation into operation. Chapter 13 provides more information about writing recommendations.

Keep in mind the following important piece of business advice: Start with a statement of purpose. If you can't explain your idea in 25 words or less, it's probably not a good idea.

The recommendations section of a formal report offers specific suggestions for solving a problem.

Appendix. Incidental or supporting materials belong in appendixes at the end of a formal report. These materials are relevant to some readers but not to all. Appendixes may include survey forms, copies of other reports, tables of data, computer printouts, and related correspondence. If additional appendixes are necessary, they would be named *Appendix A*, *Appendix B*, and so forth.

The Works Cited or References section section of a formal report identifies sources of ideas mentioned in the report.

Works Cited or References. If you use the MLA (Modern Language Association) referencing format, all citations will be listed alphabetically in the "Works Cited." If you use the APA (American Psychological Association) format, your list is called "References." Regardless of the format, you must include the author, title, publication, date of publication, page number, and other significant data for all ideas or quotations used in your report. For electronic references include the preceding information plus a description of the electronic address or path leading to the citation. Also include the date on which you located the electronic reference. To see electronic and other citations, examine the list of references at the end of Figure 14.3 (page 364). Appendix B of the text contains additional documentation information.

learning objective **6**

Final Writing Tips

Formal reports require careful attention to all phases of the 3-x-3 writing process.

Formal reports are not undertaken lightly. They involve considerable effort in all three phases of writing, beginning with analysis of the problem and anticipation of the audience (as discussed in Chapter 5). Researching the data, organizing it into a logical presentation, and composing the first draft (Chapter 6) make up the second phase of writing. Revising, proofreading, and evaluating (Chapter 7) are completed in the third phase. Although everyone approaches the writing process somewhat differently, the following tips offer advice in problem areas faced by most formal report writers.

- **Allow sufficient time.** The main reason given by writers who are disappointed with their reports is "I just ran out of time." Develop a realistic timetable and stick to it.

- **Finish data collection.** Do not begin writing until you've collected all the data and drawn the primary conclusions. Starting too early often means backtracking. For reports based on survey data, compile the tables and figures first.
- **Work from a good outline.** A big project such as a formal report needs the order and direction provided by a clear outline, even if the outline has to be revised as the project unfolds.
- **Provide a proper writing environment.** You'll need a quiet spot where you can spread out your materials and work without interruption. Formal reports demand blocks of concentration time.
- **Use the features of your computer.** Preparing a report with a word processor enables you to keyboard quickly; revise easily; and check spelling, grammar, and synonyms readily. A word of warning, though: save your document often and print it out occasionally so that you have a hard copy. Take these precautions to guard against the grief caused by lost files, power outages, and computer malfunctions.
- **Write rapidly; revise later.** Some experts advise writers to record their ideas quickly and save revision until after the first draft is completed. They say that quick writing avoids wasted effort spent in polishing sentences or even sections that may be cut later. Moreover, rapid writing encourages fluency and creativity. However, a quick-and-dirty first draft doesn't work for everyone. Many business writers prefer a more deliberate writing style, so consider this advice selectively and experiment to find the method that works best for you.
- **Save difficult sections until later.** If some sections are harder to write than others, save them until you've developed confidence and rhythm by working on easier topics.
- **Be consistent in verb tense.** Use past-tense verbs to describe completed actions. Use present-tense verbs, however, to explain current actions. When citing references, use past-tense verbs. Don't switch back and forth between present- and past-tense verbs in describing related data.
- **Generally avoid *I* and *we*.** To make formal reports seem as objective and credible as possible, most writers omit first-person pronouns. This formal style sometimes results in the overuse of passive-voice verbs. Look for alternative constructions.
- **Let the first draft sit.** After completing the first version, put it aside for a day or two. Return to it with the expectation of revising and improving it. Do not be afraid to make major changes.
- **Revise for clarity, coherence, and conciseness.** Read a printed copy out loud. Do the sentences make sense? Do the ideas flow together naturally? Can wordiness and flabbiness be cut out? Make sure that your writing is so clear that a busy manager does not have to reread any part. See Chapter 7 for specific revision suggestions.
- **Proofread the final copy three times.** First, read a printed copy slowly for word meanings and content. Then read the copy again for spelling, punctuation, grammar, and other mechanical errors. Finally, scan the entire report to check its formatting and consistency (page numbering, indenting, spacing, headings, and so forth).

Smart report writers allow themselves plenty of time, research thoroughly, and draw up a useful outline.

Effective formal reports maintain parallelism in verb tenses, avoid first-person pronouns, and use the active voice.

Putting It All Together

Formal reports in business generally aim to study problems and recommend solutions. Alan Christopher, business school representative to the Student Association (SA) at West Coast College, was given a campus problem to study, resulting in the formal report shown in Figure 14.3.

FIGURE 14.3 ***Model Formal Report With MLA Citation Style***

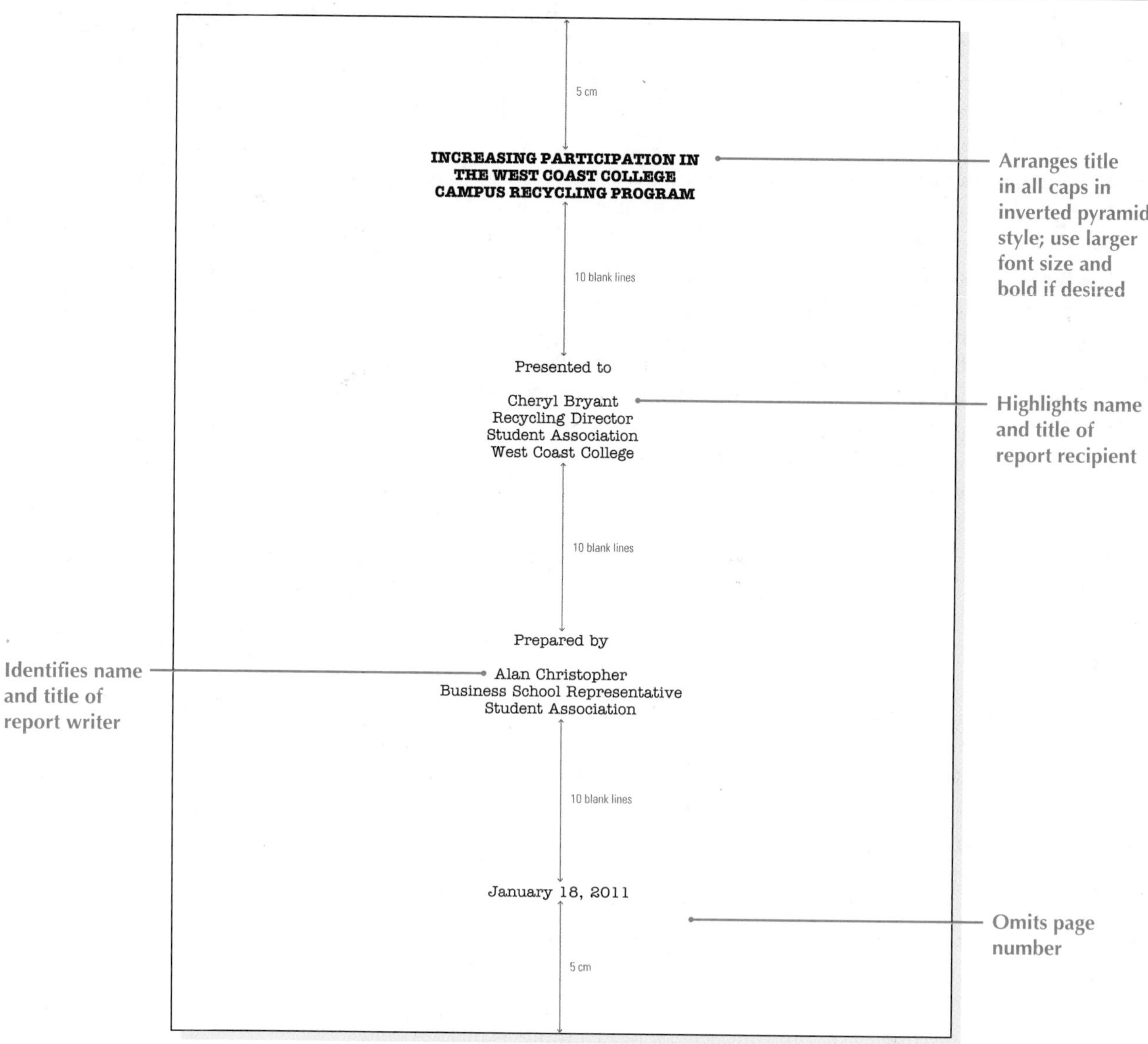

5 cm
INCREASING PARTICIPATION IN
THE WEST COAST COLLEGE
CAMPUS RECYCLING PROGRAM
10 blank lines
Presented to
Cheryl Bryant
Recycling Director
Student Association
West Coast College
10 blank lines
Prepared by
Alan Christopher
Business School Representative
Student Association
10 blank lines
January 18, 2011
5 cm
Arranges title in all caps in inverted pyramid style; use larger font size and bold if desired
Highlights name and title of report recipient
Identifies name and title of report writer
Omits page number

Alan arranges the title page so that the amount of space above the title is equal to the space below the date. If a report is to be bound on the left, move the left margin and centre point 0.5 cm to the right. Notice that no page number appears on the title page, although it is counted as page i.

If you use scalable fonts, word processing capabilities, or a laser printer to enhance your report and title page, be careful to avoid anything unprofessional, such as too many type fonts, oversized print, and inappropriate graphics.

FIGURE 14.3 *Model Formal Report With MLA Citation Style (Continued)*

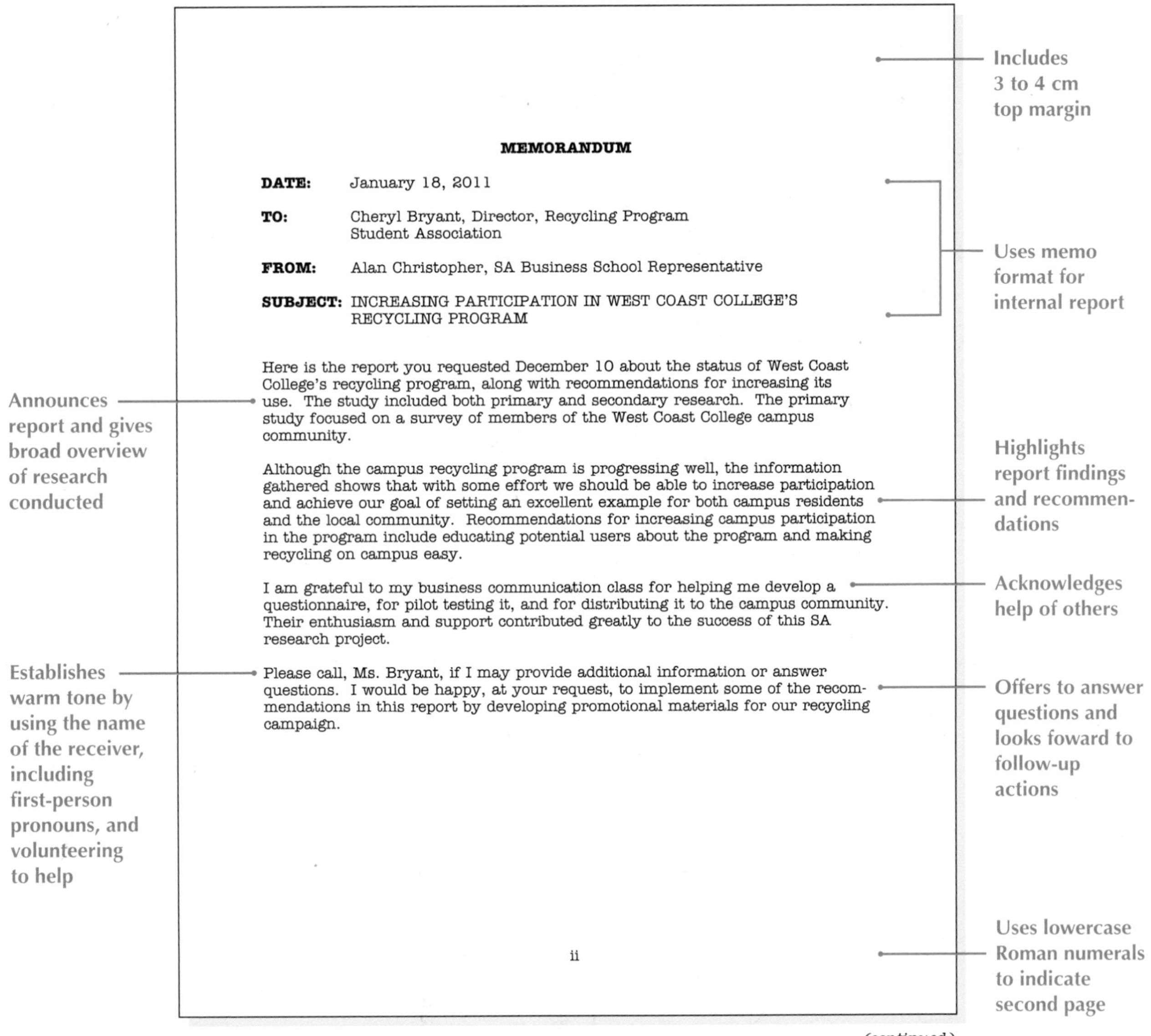

MEMORANDUM

DATE: January 18, 2011

TO: Cheryl Bryant, Director, Recycling Program
Student Association

FROM: Alan Christopher, SA Business School Representative

SUBJECT: INCREASING PARTICIPATION IN WEST COAST COLLEGE'S RECYCLING PROGRAM

Here is the report you requested December 10 about the status of West Coast College's recycling program, along with recommendations for increasing its use. The study included both primary and secondary research. The primary study focused on a survey of members of the West Coast College campus community.

Although the campus recycling program is progressing well, the information gathered shows that with some effort we should be able to increase participation and achieve our goal of setting an excellent example for both campus residents and the local community. Recommendations for increasing campus participation in the program include educating potential users about the program and making recycling on campus easy.

I am grateful to my business communication class for helping me develop a questionnaire, for pilot testing it, and for distributing it to the campus community. Their enthusiasm and support contributed greatly to the success of this SA research project.

Please call, Ms. Bryant, if I may provide additional information or answer questions. I would be happy, at your request, to implement some of the recommendations in this report by developing promotional materials for our recycling campaign.

ii

Includes 3 to 4 cm top margin
Uses memo format for internal report
Announces report and gives broad overview of research conducted
Highlights report findings and recommendations
Acknowledges help of others
Establishes warm tone by using the name of the receiver, including first-person pronouns, and volunteering to help
Offers to answer questions and looks foward to follow-up actions
Uses lowercase Roman numerals to indicate second page

(continued)

Because this report is being submitted within his own organization, Alan uses a memorandum of transmittal. Formal organization reports submitted to outsiders would carry a letter of transmittal printed on company stationery.

The margins for the transmittal should be the same as for the report, about 3 cm on all sides. If a report is to be bound, add an extra 0.5 cm to the left margin. Because the report is single-spaced, the paragraphs are not indented. When a report is double-spaced, paragraphs are indented. A page number is optional.

FIGURE 14.3 ***Model Formal Report With MLA Citation Style (Continued)***

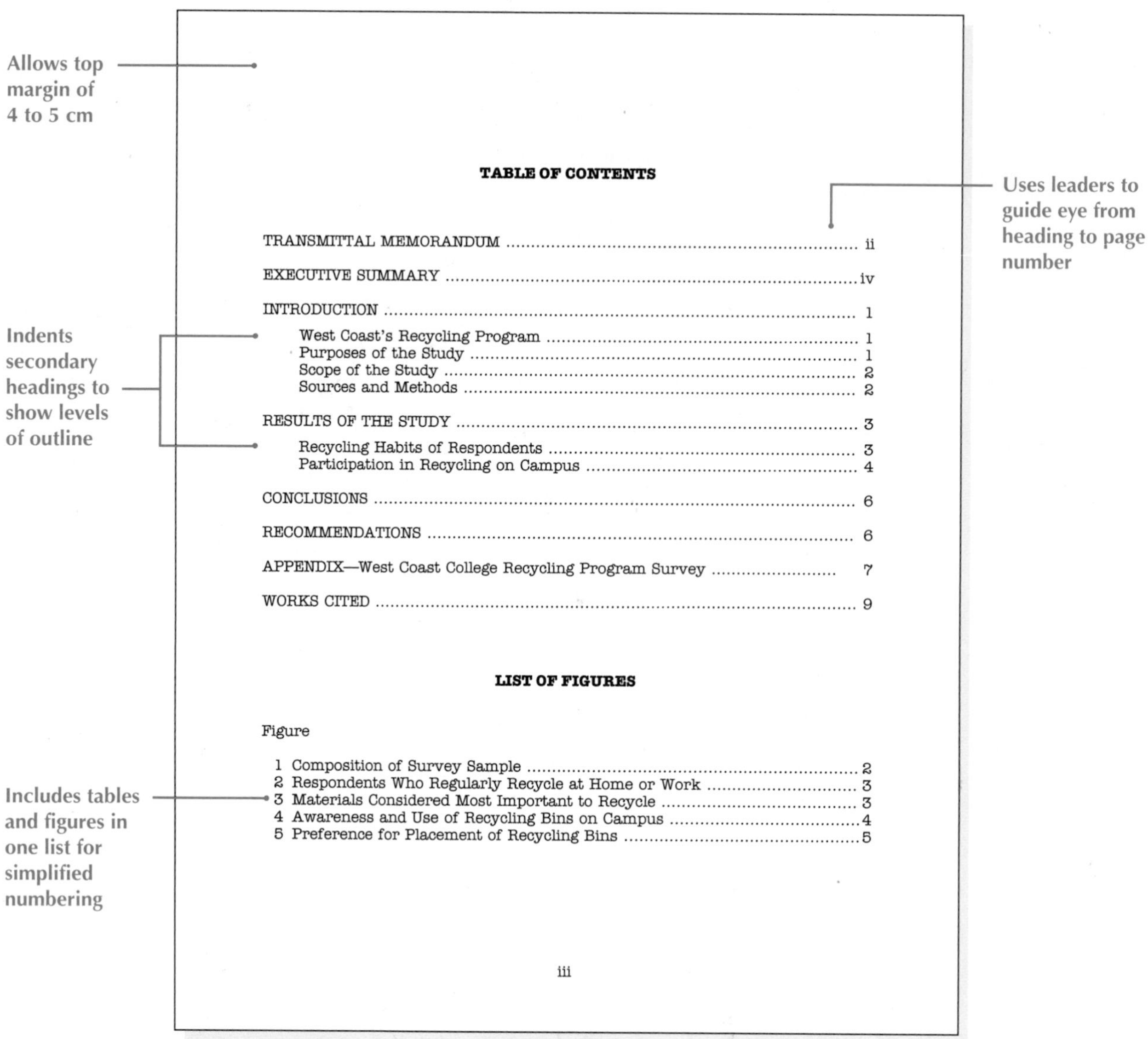

Allows top margin of 4 to 5 cm
Uses leaders to guide eye from heading to page number
Indents secondary headings to show levels of outline
Includes tables and figures in one list for simplified numbering

TABLE OF CONTENTS

TRANSMITTAL MEMORANDUM ii

EXECUTIVE SUMMARY iv

INTRODUCTION 1

- West Coast's Recycling Program 1
- Purposes of the Study 1
- Scope of the Study 2
- Sources and Methods 2

RESULTS OF THE STUDY 3

- Recycling Habits of Respondents 3
- Participation in Recycling on Campus 4

CONCLUSIONS 6

RECOMMENDATIONS 6

APPENDIX—West Coast College Recycling Program Survey 7

WORKS CITED 9

LIST OF FIGURES

Figure

1 Composition of Survey Sample 2
2 Respondents Who Regularly Recycle at Home or Work 3
3 Materials Considered Most Important to Recycle 3
4 Awareness and Use of Recycling Bins on Campus 4
5 Preference for Placement of Recycling Bins 5

iii

Because Alan's table of contents and list of figures are small, he combines them on one page. Notice that he uses all caps for the titles of major report parts and a combination of upper- and lowercase letters for first-level headings. This duplicates the style within the report.

Advanced word processing capabilities enable you to generate a contents page automatically, including leaders and accurate page numbering—no matter how many times you revise!

EXECUTIVE SUMMARY

Purposes of the Report

The purposes of this report are to (1) determine the West Coast College campus community's awareness of the campus recycling program and (2) recommend ways to increase participation. West Coast's recycling program was intended to respond to the increasing problem of waste disposal, to fulfill its social responsibility as an educational institution, and to meet the demands of legislation requiring individuals and organizations to recycle.

A questionnaire survey was conducted to learn about the campus community's recycling habits and to assess participation in the current recycling program. A total of 220 individuals responded to the survey. Since West Coast College's recycling program includes only aluminum, glass, paper, and plastic at this time, these were the only materials considered in this study.

Tells purpose of report and briefly describes survey

Recycling at West Coast

Most survey respondents recognized the importance of recycling and stated that they do recycle aluminum, glass, paper, and plastic on a regular basis either at home or at work. However, most respondents displayed a low level of awareness and use of the on-campus program. Many of the respondents were unfamiliar with the location of the bins around campus and, therefore, had not participated in the recycling program. Other responses indicated that the bins were not conveniently located.

Summarizes findings of survey

The results of this study show that more effort is needed to increase participation in the campus recycling program.

Draws primary conclusion

Recommendations for Increasing Recycling Participation

Based on the findings from our survey of 220 respondents, the researchers make the following recommendations to increase participation in the West Coast College campus recycling program:

1. Relocate the recycling bins for greater visibility
2. Develop incentive programs to gain the participation of individuals and on-campus student groups
3. Train student volunteers to give on-campus presentations explaining the benefits of using the recycling program
4. Increase advertising about the program

Concisely enumerates four recommendations using parallel (balanced) phrasing

iv

Numbers pages that precede the body with lowercase Roman numerals

(continued)

For readers who want a quick picture of the report, the executive summary presents its most important elements. Alan has divided the summary into three sections for increased readability.

Executive summaries focus on the information the reader requires for making a decision related to the issues discussed in the report. The summary may include some or all of the following elements: purpose, scope, research methods, results, conclusions, and recommendations. In jargon-free language, a good executive summary condenses what management needs to know about a problem and its study.

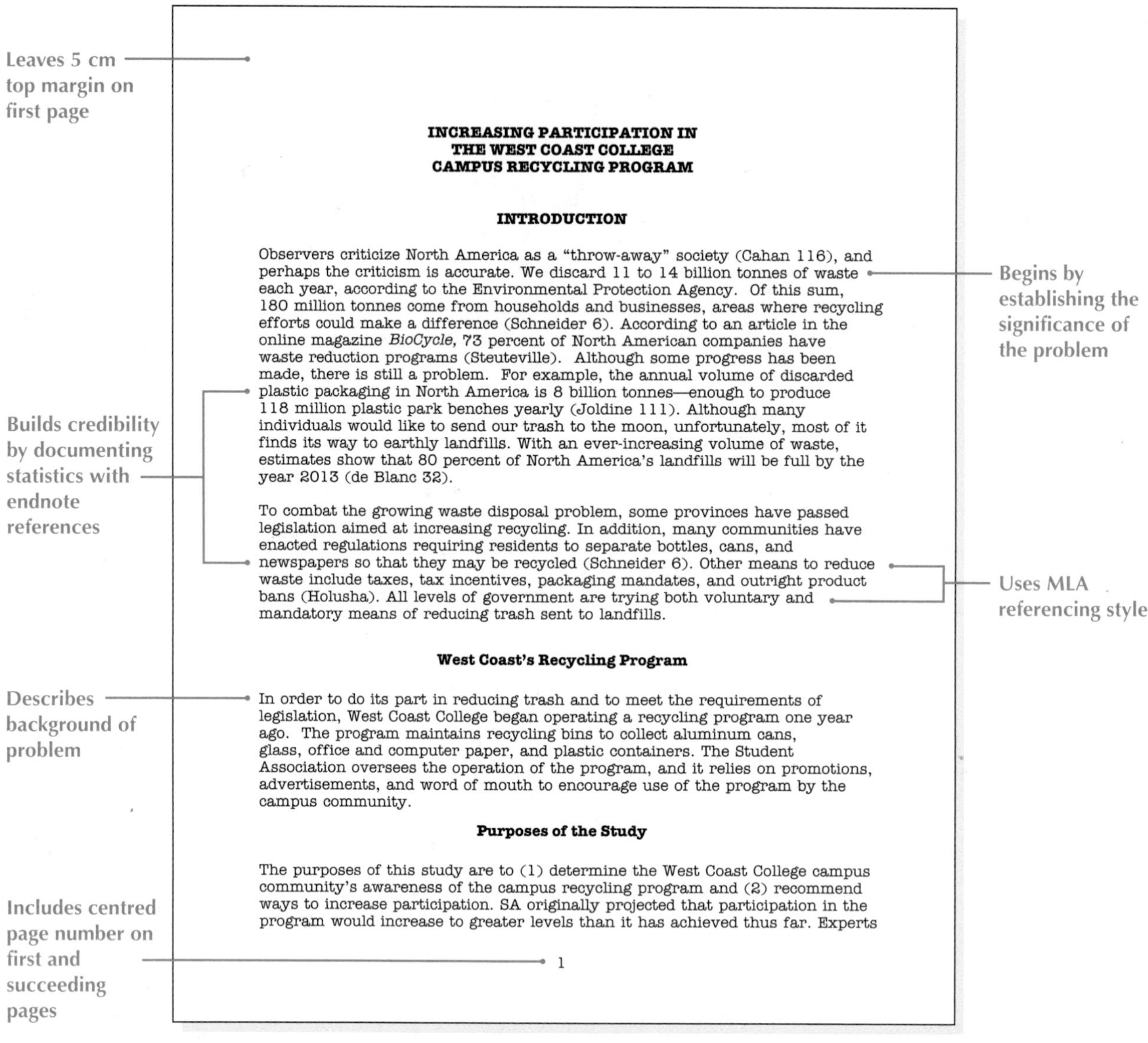

Leaves 5 cm top margin on first page
Begins by establishing the significance of the problem
Builds credibility by documenting statistics with endnote references
Uses MLA referencing style
Describes background of problem
Includes centred page number on first and succeeding pages

INCREASING PARTICIPATION IN THE WEST COAST COLLEGE CAMPUS RECYCLING PROGRAM

INTRODUCTION

Observers criticize North America as a "throw-away" society (Cahan 116), and perhaps the criticism is accurate. We discard 11 to 14 billion tonnes of waste each year, according to the Environmental Protection Agency. Of this sum, 180 million tonnes come from households and businesses, areas where recycling efforts could make a difference (Schneider 6). According to an article in the online magazine *BioCycle,* 73 percent of North American companies have waste reduction programs (Steuteville). Although some progress has been made, there is still a problem. For example, the annual volume of discarded plastic packaging in North America is 8 billion tonnes—enough to produce 118 million plastic park benches yearly (Joldine 111). Although many individuals would like to send our trash to the moon, unfortunately, most of it finds its way to earthly landfills. With an ever-increasing volume of waste, estimates show that 80 percent of North America's landfills will be full by the year 2013 (de Blanc 32).

To combat the growing waste disposal problem, some provinces have passed legislation aimed at increasing recycling. In addition, many communities have enacted regulations requiring residents to separate bottles, cans, and newspapers so that they may be recycled (Schneider 6). Other means to reduce waste include taxes, tax incentives, packaging mandates, and outright product bans (Holusha). All levels of government are trying both voluntary and mandatory means of reducing trash sent to landfills.

West Coast's Recycling Program

In order to do its part in reducing trash and to meet the requirements of legislation, West Coast College began operating a recycling program one year ago. The program maintains recycling bins to collect aluminum cans, glass, office and computer paper, and plastic containers. The Student Association oversees the operation of the program, and it relies on promotions, advertisements, and word of mouth to encourage use of the program by the campus community.

Purposes of the Study

The purposes of this study are to (1) determine the West Coast College campus community's awareness of the campus recycling program and (2) recommend ways to increase participation. SA originally projected that participation in the program would increase to greater levels than it has achieved thus far. Experts

1

The first page of a report generally contains the title printed 5 cm from the top edge. Titles for major parts of a report (such as *Introduction, Results, Conclusion,* and so forth) are centred in all caps. First-level headings are bold and printed with upper- and lowercase letters. Second-level headings begin at the side. For an illustration of heading formats, see Figure 13.4 on page 318.

Notice that Alan's report is single-spaced. Many businesses prefer this space-saving format. However, some organizations prefer double-spacing, especially for preliminary drafts.

Page numbers may be centred 2.5 cm from the bottom of the page or placed 2.5 cm from the upper right corner at the margin.

say that recycling programs generally must operate at least a year before results become apparent (de Blanc 33). The SA program has been in operation one year, yet gains are disappointing. Therefore, SA authorized this study to determine the campus community's awareness and use of the program. Recommendations for increasing participation in the campus recycling program will be made to the SA based on the results of this study.

Scope of the Study

This study investigates potential participants' attitudes toward recycling in general, their awareness of the campus recycling program, their willingness to recycle on campus, and the perceived convenience of the recycling bins. Only aluminum, glass, paper, and plastic are considered in this study, as they are the only materials being recycled on campus at this time. The costs involved in the program were not considered in this study, since a recycling program generally does not begin to pay for itself during the first year. After the first year, the financial benefit is usually realized in reduced disposal costs (Steelman, Desmond, and Johnson 145).

Describes what the study includes and excludes

Sources and Methods

Current business periodicals and newspapers were consulted for background information and to learn how other organizations are encouraging use of in-house recycling programs. In addition, a questionnaire survey (shown in the appendix) of administrators, faculty, staff, and students at West Coast College campus was conducted to learn about this group's recycling habits. In all, a convenience sample of 220 individuals responded to the self-administered survey. The composition of the sample closely resembles the makeup of the campus population. Figure 1 shows the percentage of students, faculty, staff, and administrators who participated in the survey.

Discusses how the study was conducted

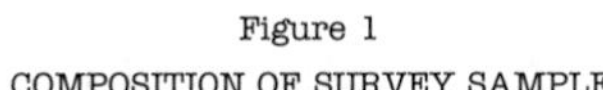

Figure 1

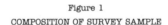

COMPOSITION OF SURVEY SAMPLE

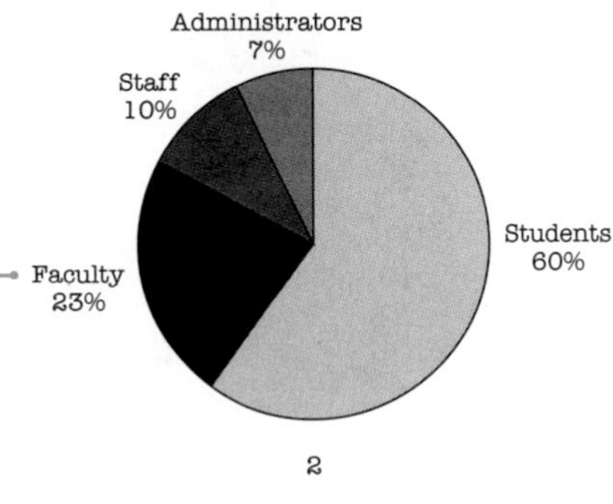

Uses computer-generated pie graph to illustrate makeup of survey

2

(continued)

Because Alan wants this report to be formal in tone, he avoids *I* and *we*. Notice, too, that he uses present-tense verbs to describe his current writing *(this study investigates)*, but past-tense verbs to indicate research completed in the past *(newspapers were consulted)*.

If you use figures or tables, be sure to introduce them in the text. Although it's not always possible, try to place them close to the spot where they are first mentioned. If necessary to save space, you can print the title of a figure at its side.

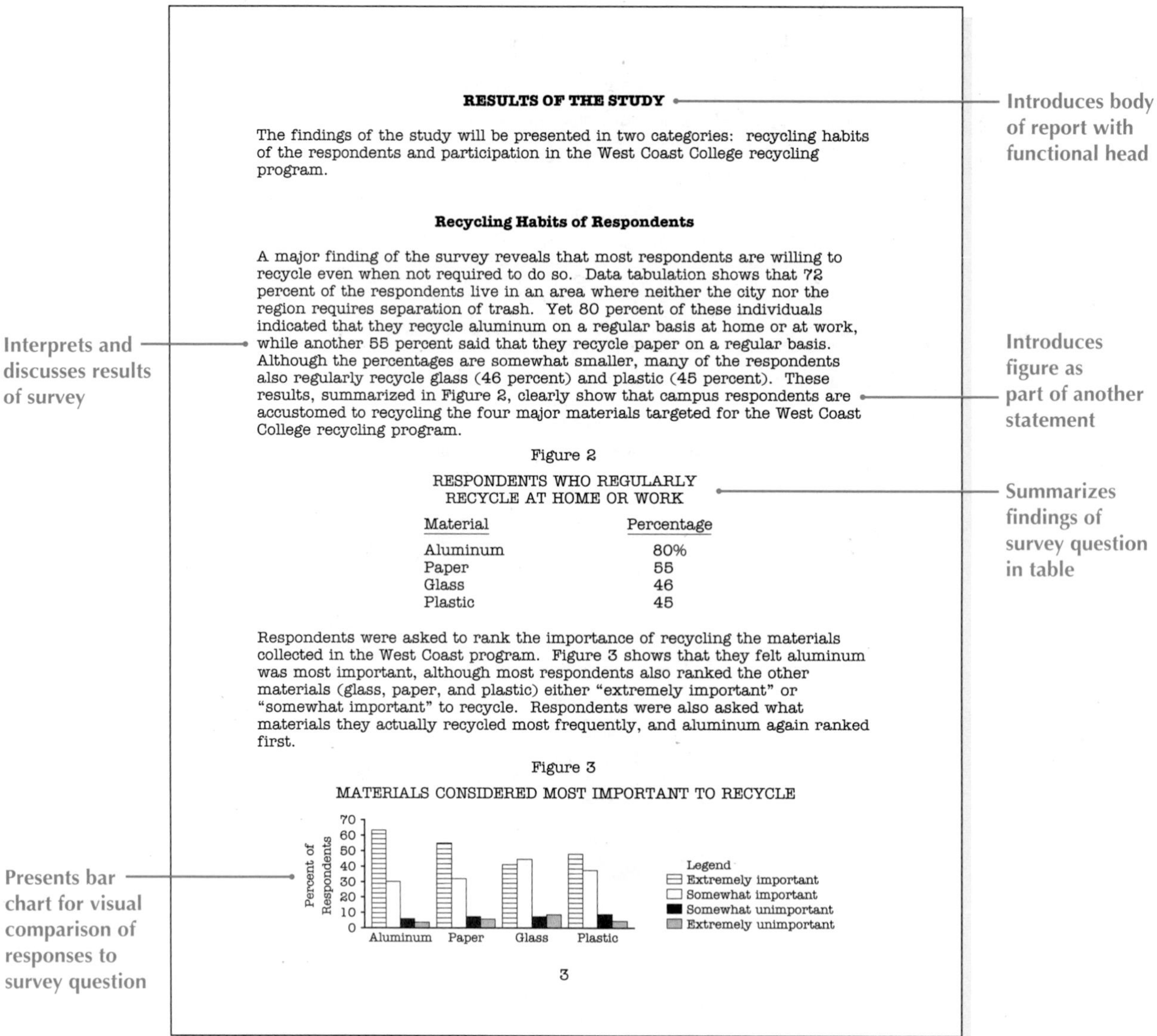

RESULTS OF THE STUDY

The findings of the study will be presented in two categories: recycling habits of the respondents and participation in the West Coast College recycling program.

Recycling Habits of Respondents

A major finding of the survey reveals that most respondents are willing to recycle even when not required to do so. Data tabulation shows that 72 percent of the respondents live in an area where neither the city nor the region requires separation of trash. Yet 80 percent of these individuals indicated that they recycle aluminum on a regular basis at home or at work, while another 55 percent said that they recycle paper on a regular basis. Although the percentages are somewhat smaller, many of the respondents also regularly recycle glass (46 percent) and plastic (45 percent). These results, summarized in Figure 2, clearly show that campus respondents are accustomed to recycling the four major materials targeted for the West Coast College recycling program.

Figure 2

RESPONDENTS WHO REGULARLY RECYCLE AT HOME OR WORK

Material	Percentage
Aluminum	80%
Paper	55
Glass	46
Plastic	45

Respondents were asked to rank the importance of recycling the materials collected in the West Coast program. Figure 3 shows that they felt aluminum was most important, although most respondents also ranked the other materials (glass, paper, and plastic) either "extremely important" or "somewhat important" to recycle. Respondents were also asked what materials they actually recycled most frequently, and aluminum again ranked first.

Figure 3

MATERIALS CONSIDERED MOST IMPORTANT TO RECYCLE

Percent of Respondents
70
60
50
40
30
20
10
0
Aluminum
Paper
Glass
Plastic
Legend
Extremely important
Somewhat important
Somewhat unimportant
Extremely unimportant

3

Introduces body of report with functional head
Interprets and discusses results of survey
Introduces figure as part of another statement
Summarizes findings of survey question in table
Presents bar chart for visual comparison of responses to survey question

Alan selects the most important survey findings to interpret and discuss for readers. Notice that he continues to use present-tense verbs *(the survey reveals* and *these results clearly show)* to discuss the current report.

Because he has few tables and charts, he labels them all as "Figures." Notice that he numbers them consecutively and places the label above each figure. Report writers with a great many tables, charts, and illustrations may prefer to label and number them separately. Tables are labelled as such; everything else is generally called a figure. When tables and figures are labelled separately, tables may be labelled above the table and figures below the figure.

Adds personal interpretation

When asked how likely they would be to go out of their way to deposit an item in a recycling bin, 29 percent of the respondents said "very likely," and 55 percent said "somewhat likely." Thus, respondents showed a willingness—at least on paper—to recycle even if it means making a special effort to locate a recycling bin.

Participation in Recycling on Campus

For any recycling program to be successful, participants must be aware of the location of recycling centres and must be trained to use them (de Blanc 33). Another important ingredient in thriving programs is convenience to users. If recycling centres are difficult for users to reach, these centres will be unsuccessful. To collect data on these topics, the survey included questions assessing awareness and use of the current bins. The survey also investigated reasons for not participating and the perceived convenience of current bin locations.

Introduces more findings and relates them to the report's purpose

Student Awareness and Use of Bins

Two of the most significant questions in the survey asked whether respondents were aware of the SA recycling bins on campus and whether they had used the bins. Responses to both questions were disappointing, as Figure 4 illustrates.

Figure 4

AWARENESS AND USE OF RECYCLING BINS ON CAMPUS

Arranges responses from highest to lowest with "unaware" category placed last

Location	Awareness of bins at this location	Use of bins at this location
Social sciences building	38%	21%
Bookstore	29	12
Administration building	28	12
Computer labs	16	11
Library	15	7
Student centre	9	5
Department offices	6	3
Campus dormitories	5	3
Unaware of any bins; have not used any bins	20	7

Only 38 percent of the respondents, as shown in Figure 4, were aware of the bins located outside the social sciences building. Even fewer were aware of the bins outside the bookstore (29 percent) and outside the administration building (28 percent). Equally dissatisfying, only 21 percent of the respondents had used the most visible recycling bins outside the social sciences

Clarifies and emphasizes meaning of findings

4

(continued)

In discussing the results of the survey, Alan highlights those that have significance for the purpose of the report.

As you type a report, avoid widows and orphans (ending a page with the first line of a paragraph or carrying a single line of a paragraph to a new page). Strive to start and end pages with at least two lines of a paragraph, even if a slightly larger bottom margin results.

building. Other recycling bin locations were even less familiar to the survey respondents and, of course, were little used. These responses plainly show that the majority of the respondents in the West Coast campus community have a low awareness of the recycling program and an even lower record of participation.

Reasons for Not Participating

Respondents offered several reasons for not participating in the campus recycling program. Forty-five percent said that the bins are not convenient to use. Thirty percent said that they did not know where the bins were located. Another 25 percent said that they are not in the habit of recycling. Although many reasons for not participating were listed, the primary one appears to centre on convenience of bin locations.

Location of Recycling Bins

When asked specifically how they would rate the location of the bins currently in use, only 13 percent of the respondents felt that the bins were extremely convenient. Another 35 percent rated the locations as somewhat convenient. Over half the respondents felt that the locations of the bins were either somewhat inconvenient or extremely inconvenient. Recycling bins are currently located outside nearly all the major campus buildings, but respondents clearly considered these locations inconvenient or inadequate.

Discusses results of other survey questions not represented in tables or charts

In indicating where they would like recycling bins placed (see Figure 5), 42 percent of the respondents felt that the most convenient locations would be outside each building on campus. Placing recycling bins near the food service facilities on campus seemed most convenient to another 33 percent of those questioned, while 15 percent stated that they would like to see the bins placed near the vending machines. Ten percent of the individuals responding to the survey did not seem to think that the locations of the bins would matter to them.

Clarifies results of another survey question with textual discussion accompanied by table

Figure 5

PREFERENCE FOR PLACEMENT OF RECYCLING BINS

Outside each building on campus	42%
Near food service facilities	33
Near vending machines	15
Does not matter	10

5

After completing a discussion of the survey results, Alan articulates what he considers the five most important conclusions to be drawn from this survey. Some writers combine the conclusions and recommendations, particularly when they are interrelated. Alan separated them in his study because the survey findings were quite distinct from the recommendations he would make based on them.

Start the conclusions on the same page if more than half a page will be left empty. Otherwise, begin this section on a new page.

Draws conclusions based on survey findings; summarizes previous discussion

CONCLUSIONS

Based on the findings of the recycling survey of members of the West Coast College campus community, the following conclusions are drawn:

1. Most members of the campus community are already recycling at home or at work without being required to do so.
2. Over half of the respondents recycle aluminum and paper on a regular basis; most recycle glass and plastic to some degree.
3. Most of the surveyed individuals expressed a willingness to participate in a recycling program. Many, however, seem unwilling to travel very far to participate; 42 percent would like recycling bins to be located outside every campus building.
4. Awareness and use of the current campus recycling program are low. Only a little over one third of the respondents knew of any recycling in locations on campus, and only one fifth had actually used them.
5. Respondents considered the locations of the campus bins inconvenient. This perceived inconvenience was given as the principal reason for not participating in the campus recycling program.

Lists specific actions to help solve report problem; suggests practical ways to implement recommendations

RECOMMENDATIONS

Supported by the findings and conclusions of this study, the following recommendations are offered in an effort to improve the operations and success of the West Coast recycling program:

1. Increase on-campus awareness and visibility by designing an eye-catching logo that represents the campus recycling program for use in promotions.
2. Enhance comprehension of recycling procedures by training users how to recycle. Use posters to explain the recycling program and to inform users of recycling bin locations. Label each bin clearly as to what materials may be deposited.
3. Add bins in several new locations, particularly in the food service and vending machine areas.
4. Recruit student leaders to promote participation in the recycling program by giving educational talks to classes and other campus groups, informing them of the importance of recycling.
5. Develop an incentive program for student organizations. Offer incentives for meeting recycling goals as determined by SA. On-campus groups—such as sports teams and clubs—could compete in recycling drives designed to raise money for the group, the college, or a charity. Money from the proceeds of the recycling program could be used to fund the incentive program.

6

(continued)

The most important parts of a report are its conclusions and recommendations. To make them especially clear, Alan enumerated each conclusion and recommendation. Notice that each recommendation starts with a verb and is stated in command language for emphasis and readability.

Report recommendations are most helpful to readers when they not only make suggestions to solve the original research problem but also describe specific actions to be taken. Notice that Alan goes beyond merely listing ideas; instead, he provides practical suggestions for ways to implement the recommendations.

Includes copy of survey questionnaire so that report readers can see actual questions

APPENDIX

WEST COAST COLLEGE RECYCLING PROGRAM SURVEY

West Coast College recently implemented a recycling program on campus. Please take a few minutes to answer the following questions so that we can make this program as convenient and helpful as possible for you to use.

Explains why survey is necessary, emphasizing "you" view

1. Please indicate which items you recycle on a regular basis at home or at work. (Check *all* that apply.)
   - ☐ Aluminum
   - ☐ Glass
   - ☐ Paper
   - ☐ Plastic
2. Do you live in an area where the city/region requires separation of trash?
   ☐ Yes ☐ No
3. How important is it to you to recycle each of the following:

	Extremely Important	Somewhat Important	Somewhat Unimportant	Extremely Unimportant
Aluminum				
Glass				
Paper				
Plastic				

Provides range of answers that will be easy to tabulate

4. How likely would it be for you to go out of your way to put something in a recycling bin?

Very Likely	Somewhat Likely	Somewhat Unlikely	Very Unlikely

5. Which of the following items do you recycle *most* often? (Choose *one* item only.)
   - ☐ Aluminum
   - ☐ Glass
   - ☐ Paper
   - ☐ Plastic
   - ☐ Other
6. The following are locations of the recycling bins on campus. (Check *all* those of which you are aware.)
   - ☐ Administration building
   - ☐ Bookstore
   - ☐ Campus dorms
   - ☐ Computer labs
   - ☐ Engineering building
   - ☐ Library
   - ☐ Social sciences building
   - ☐ Student centre
   - ☐ I'm unaware of any of these recycling bins.

7

Alan had space to add the word "Appendix" to the top of the survey questionnaire. If space were not available, he could have typed a separate page with that title on it. If more than one item were included, he would have named them Appendix A, Appendix B, and so on.

Notice that the appendix continues the report pagination.

Figure 14.3 *Model Formal Report With MLA Citation Style (Continued)*

7. Which of the following recycling bins have you actually used? (Check *all* that you have used.)
   - ☐ Administration building
   - ☐ Bookstore
   - ☐ Campus dorms
   - ☐ Computer labs
   - ☐ Engineering building
   - ☐ Library
   - ☐ Social sciences building
   - ☐ Student centre
   - ☐ I've not used any of these recycling bins.
8. If you don't recycle on campus, why don't you participate?
   - ☐ I'm not in the habit of recycling.
   - ☐ I don't know where the bins are.
   - ☐ The bins aren't convenient to me.
   - ☐ Other ________________
9. How do you rate the convenience of the bins' locations?
   - ☐ Extremely convenient
   - ☐ Somewhat convenient
   - ☐ Somewhat inconvenient
   - ☐ Extremely inconvenient
10. Which of the following possible recycling bin locations would be most convenient for you to use? (Check *one* only.)
    - ☐ Outside each building
    - ☐ Near the food service facilities
    - ☐ Near the vending machines
    - ☐ Does not matter
    - ☐ Other ________________
11. Please indicate:
    - ☐ Student
    - ☐ Faculty
    - ☐ Administrator
    - ☐ Staff

COMMENTS:

Thank you for your responses! Please return the questionnaire in the enclosed, stamped envelope to West Coast College, School of Business, Rm. 321. If you have any questions, please call (555) 450-2391.

8

Anticipates responses but also supplies "Other" category

Uses scale questions to capture degrees of feeling

Requests little demographic data to keep survey short

Offers comment section for explanations and remarks

Concludes with appreciation and instructions

(continued)

FIGURE 14.3 *(Continued)*

Works Cited

Cahan, Vicky. "Waste Not, Want Not? Not Necessarily." *BusinessWeek* 17 July 2008: 116. Print.

dē Blanc, Susan. "Paper Recycling: How to Make It Effective." *The Office* Dec. 2007: 32–33. Print.

Freeman, Monique M. Personal interview. 2 Nov. 2010.

Holusha, John. "Mixed Benefits from Recycling." *New York Times.* New York Times, 26 July 2004. Web. 26 Oct. 2010.

Joldine, Lee. *Spirit of the Wolf: The Environment and Canada's Future.* Ed. Jo Davis. Waterloo: Turnaround Decade Ecological Communications, 1998. Print.

Landsburg, Steven E. "Who Shall Inherit the Earth?" *Slate.* Washington Post Co., 1 May 2007. Web. 2 May 2010.

Schneider, Keith. "As Recycling Becomes a Growth Industry, Its Paradoxes Also Multiply." *New York Times* 20 Jan. 2009, sec. 4: 6. Print.

Steelman, James W., Shirley Desmond, and LeGrand Johnson. *Facing Global Limitations.* New York: Rockford Press, 2007. Print.

Steuteville, Robert. "The State of Garbage in America." *BioCycle.* The JG Press, Inc., Apr. 1996. Web. 30 Nov. 2010.

"Top 60 Waste Reduction Tips for Business." *Recycling Council of Ontario.* Recycling Council of Ontario, n.d. Web. 8 July 2010.

9

Magazine

Interview

Online Newspaper

Book—author with an editor

Online Magazine

Newspaper

Book

Online Magazine

World Wide Web

On this page Alan lists all the references cited in the text, as well as others that he examined during his research. (Some authors list only those works cited in the report.) Alan formats his citations following the MLA referencing style. Notice that all entries are arranged alphabetically, that book and periodical titles are italicized, and that the medium of publication is provided. When referring to online items, he italicizes the title of the Web site and provides the date of publication (if available; if not, he uses *n.d.*), as well as the date on which he accessed the electronic reference.

Most word processing software today automatically updates citation references within the text and prints a complete list for you. For more information about documentation styles, see Appendix B.

The campus recycling program, under the direction of Cheryl Bryant and supported by the SA, was not attracting the anticipated level of participation. As the campus recycling program began its second year of operation, Cheryl and the SA wondered whether campus community members were sufficiently aware of the program. They also wondered how participation could be increased. Alan volunteered to investigate the problem because of his strong support for environmental causes. He also needed to conduct a research project for one of his business courses, and he had definite ideas for improving the campus SA recycling program.

Alan's report illustrates many of the points discussed in this chapter. Although it is a good example of typical report format and style, it should not be viewed as the only way to present a report. Wide variation exists in reports.

The following checklist summarizes the report process and report components in one handy list.

Checklist for Preparing Formal Reports

Report Process

✓ **Analyze the report problem and purpose.** Develop a problem question (*How is e-mail affecting productivity and security at MegaTech?*) and a purpose statement (*The purpose of this report is to investigate the use of e-mail at MegaTech and recommend policies and procedures that enhance company productivity and security*).

✓ **Anticipate the audience and issues.** Consider primary and secondary audiences. What do they already know? What do they need to know? Divide the major problem into subproblems for investigation.

✓ **Prepare a work plan.** Include problem and purpose statements, as well as a description of the sources and methods of collecting data. Prepare a tentative project outline and a work schedule with anticipated dates of completion for all segments of the project.

✓ **Collect data.** Begin by searching secondary sources (electronic databases, books, magazines, journals, newspapers) for information on your topic. Then, if necessary, gather primary data by surveying, interviewing, observing, and experimenting.

✓ **Document data sources.** Prepare note cards or separate sheets of paper citing all references (author, date, source, page, and quotation). Select a documentation format and use it consistently.

✓ **Interpret and organize the data.** Arrange the collected information in tables, grids, or outlines to help you visualize relationships and interpret meanings. Organize the data into an outline (Chapter 6).

✓ **Prepare graphics.** Make tables, charts, graphs, and illustrations—but only if they serve a function. Use graphics to help clarify, condense, simplify, or emphasize your data.

✓ **Compose the first draft.** At a computer, write the first draft from your outline. Use appropriate headings as well as transitional expressions (such as *however*, *on the contrary*, and *in addition*) to guide the reader through the report.

- ✓ **Revise and proofread.** Revise to eliminate wordiness, ambiguity, and redundancy. Look for ways to improve readability, such as bulleted or numbered lists. Proofread three times for (a) word and content meaning, (b) grammar and mechanical errors, and (c) formatting.

- ✓ **Evaluate the product.** Examine the final report. Will it achieve its purpose? Encourage feedback so that you can learn how to improve future reports.

Report Components

- ✓ **Title page.** Balance the following lines on the title page: (a) name of the report (in all caps); (b) name, title, and organization of the individual receiving the report; (c) author's name, title, and organization; and (d) date submitted.

- ✓ **Letter of transmittal.** Announce the report topic and explain who authorized it. Briefly describe the project and preview the conclusions, if the reader is supportive. Close by expressing appreciation for the assignment, suggesting follow-up actions, acknowledging the help of others, or offering to answer questions.

- ✓ **Table of contents.** Show the beginning page number where each report heading appears in the report. Using your word processing software, connect the page numbers and headings with leaders (spaced dots). In MS Word, for example, pull down the **Format** menu and go to **Tabs.**

- ✓ **List of illustrations.** Include a list of tables, illustrations, or figures showing the title of the item and its page number. If space permits, put these lists on the same page with the table of contents.

- ✓ **Executive summary.** Summarize the report purpose, findings, conclusions, and recommendations. Gauge the length of the summary by the length of the report and by your organization's practices.

- ✓ **Introduction.** Explain the problem motivating the report; describe its background and significance. Clarify the scope and limitations of the report. Optional items include a review of relevant literature and a description of data sources, methods, and key terms. Close by previewing the report's organization.

- ✓ **Body.** Discuss, analyze, and interpret the research findings or the proposed solution to the problem. Arrange the findings in logical segments following your outline. Use clear, descriptive headings.

- ✓ **Conclusions and recommendations.** Explain what the findings mean in relation to the original problem. If requested, make enumerated recommendations that suggest actions for solving the problem.

- ✓ **Appendix.** Include items of interest to some, but not all, readers, such as a data questionnaire or computer printouts. Add graphics that are not discussed directly in the text.

- ✓ **Works Cited or References.** If footnotes are not provided in the text, list all references in a section called "Works Cited" or "References."

Summary of Learning Objectives

1 **Discuss the general uses and basic components of proposals and grasp their audience and purpose.** Most informal proposals contain the following: (a) a persuasive introduction that explains the purpose of the proposal and qualifies the writer; (b) background material identifying the problem and project goals; (c) a proposal, plan, or schedule outlining the project; (d) a section describing staff qualifications; (e) a budget showing expected costs; and (f) a request for approval or authorization.

2 **Discuss formal proposals and how to anticipate a receiver's reaction to your message.** Beyond the six components generally contained in informal proposals, formal proposals may include these additional parts: (a) copy of the RFP (request for proposal), (b) letter of transmittal, (c) executive summary, (d) title page, (e) table of contents, (f) list of illustrations, and (g) appendix.

3 **Identify the components of typical business plans.** Business plans help entrepreneurs secure start-up funding and also provide a road map to follow as a business develops. Typical business plans include the following: letter of transmittal or executive summary, table of contents, company description, product or service description, market analysis, description of operations and management, financial analysis, and appendixes. For start-up businesses seeking financial backing, the product/service description as well as the operations and management analyses are particularly important. They must promote growth potential and promise a management team capable of implementing the business plan.

4 **Describe the formal report components that precede the introduction as well as elements to include in the introduction and how they further the purpose of your communication.** Formal reports may include these beginning components: (a) vinyl or heavy paper cover, (b) title page, (c) letter of transmittal, (d) table of contents, (e) list of illustrations, and (f) executive summary. The introduction to a formal report sets the scene by discussing some or all of the following topics: background material, problem or purpose, significance of the topic, scope and organization of the report, authorization, review of relevant literature, sources and methods, and definitions of key terms.

5 **Describe formal report components that follow the introduction and how they further the purpose of your report.** The body of a report discusses, analyzes, interprets, and evaluates the research findings or solution to a problem. The conclusion tells what the findings mean and how they relate to the report's purpose. The recommendations tell how to solve the report problem. The last portions of a formal report are the appendix and references.

6 **Specify tips that aid writers of formal reports as they use their analytic and reflective thinking skills.** Before writing, develop a realistic timetable and collect all necessary data. During the writing process, work from a good outline, work in a quiet place, and use a computer. Also, try to write rapidly, revising later. While writing, use verb tenses consistently and avoid *I* and *we*. A few days after completing the first draft, revise to improve clarity, coherence, and conciseness. Proofread the final copy three times.

chapter review

1. What is a proposal? (Obj. 1)
2. What is the difference between solicited and unsolicited proposals? (Obj. 1)
3. What are the six principal components in an informal letter proposal? (Obj. 1)
4. How is a formal proposal different from an informal proposal? (Obj. 2)
5. Why does an entrepreneur need to write a business plan? (Obj. 3)
6. Name eight components of typical business plans. (Obj. 3)
7. What should a business plan mission statement include and how long should it be? (Obj. 3)
8. Why are formal reports written in business? Give an original example of a business-related formal report. (Obj. 4)
9. What is a table of contents, and when should it be written? (Obj. 4)
10. What should be included in the executive summary of a formal report? (Obj. 4)
11. What should be included in the introduction to a formal report? (Obj. 4)
12. What should the writer strive to do in the body of a formal report? (Obj. 5)
13. What is the purpose of a bibliography? (Obj. 5)
14. In your view, what are six of the most important tips for the writer of a formal report? Explain each of your choices. (Obj. 6)
15. What are first-person pronouns, and why do most writers of formal reports avoid them? (Obj. 6)

critical thinking

1. Why are proposals important to many businesses? (Obj. 1)
2. Compare and contrast proposals and business plans. (Objs. 1–3)
3. How do formal reports differ from informal reports? (Objs. 4–6)
4. Discuss the three phases of the writing process in relation to formal reports. What activities take place in each phase? (Objs. 4–6)

activities

14.1 Proposals: Comparing Real Proposals (Objs. 1 and 2)

WEB

Many new companies with services or products to offer would like to land corporate or government contracts. But they are intimidated by the proposal (RFP) process. You have been asked for help by a friend who has started her own designer uniform company. Her goal is to offer her colourful yet functional uniforms to hospitals and clinics. Before writing a proposal, however, she wants to see examples and learn more about the process.

Your Task. Use the Web to find at least two examples of business proposals. Don't waste time on sites that want to sell templates or books. Find actual examples. Then prepare a memo to your friend in which you do the following:

a. Identify two sites with sample business proposals.
b. Outline the parts of each proposal.
c. Compare the strengths and weaknesses of each proposal.
d. Draw conclusions. What can you and your friend learn from these examples?

14.2 Proposals: SportsMed Solicits Your Proposal (Obj. 1)

CRITICAL THINKING | LISTENING | SPEAKING | TEAM

In many areas, sports medicine is increasingly popular. A new medical clinic, SportsMed Institute, is opening its doors in your community. A friend recommended your small business to the administrator of the clinic, and you received a letter asking you to provide information about your service. The new medical clinic specializes in sports medicine, physical therapy, and cardiac rehabilitation services. It is interested in retaining your company rather than hiring its own employees to perform the service your company offers.

Your Task. Working in teams, first decide what service you will offer. It could be landscaping, uniform supply, laundry of uniforms, general cleaning, computerized no-paper filing systems, online medical supplies, patient transportation, supplemental hospice care, temporary office support, or food service. As a team, develop a letter proposal outlining your plan, staffing, and budget. Use persuasion to show why contracting your services is better than hiring in-house employees. In the proposal letter, request a meeting with the administrative board. In addition to a written proposal, you may be expected to make an oral presentation that includes visual aids and/or handouts. Send your proposal to Dr. Daryl Kerr, Director, SportsMed Institute. Supply a local address.

Rich chapter resources are available on the Web site.

14.3 Business Plans: Can Your Team Write a Winning Plan? (Obj. 3)

CRITICAL THINKING | LISTENING | SPEAKING | TEAM | WEB

Business plans at many schools are more than classroom writing exercises. They have won regional, national, and worldwide prizes. Although some contests are part of MBA programs, other contests are available for undergraduates.

As part of a business plan project, you and your team are challenged to come up with an idea for a new business or service. For example, you might want to offer a lunch service with fresh sandwiches or salads delivered to office workers' desks. You might propose building a better Web site for an organization. You might want to start a document preparation business that offers production, editing, and printing services. You might have a terrific idea for an existing business to expand with a new product or service.

Your Task. Working in teams, explore entrepreneurial ventures based on your experience and expertise. Conduct team meetings to decide on a product or service, develop a work plan, assign responsibilities, and create a schedule. Your goal is to write a business plan proposal that will convince potential investors (sometimes your own management) that you have an excellent business idea and that you can pull it off. Check out sample business plans on the Web. The two "deliverables" from your project will be your written business plan plus an oral presentation. Your written report should include a cover, transmittal document (letter or memo), title page, table of contents, executive summary, proposal (including introduction, body, and conclusion), appendix items, optional glossary, and sources. In the body of the proposal, be sure to explain your mission and vision, the market, your marketing strategy, operations, and financials. Address your business plan proposal to your instructor.

14.4 Formal Reports: Intercultural Communication (Objs. 4–6)

TEAM

North American businesses are expanding into foreign markets with manufacturing plants, sales offices, and branch offices abroad. Most North Americans, however, have little knowledge of or experience with people from other cultures. To prepare for participation in the global marketplace, you are to collect information for a report focused on an Asian, Latin American, or European country where English is not regularly spoken. Before selecting the country, though, consult your campus international student program for volunteers who are willing to be interviewed. Your instructor may make advance arrangements with international student volunteers.

Your Task. In teams of three to five, collect information about your target country from the library and other sources. Then invite an international student representing your target country to be interviewed by your group. As you conduct primary and secondary research, investigate the topics listed in Figure 14.4 (page 370). Confirm what you learned in your secondary research by talking with your interviewee. When you complete your research, write a report for the CEO of your company (make up a name and company). Assume that your company plans to expand its operations abroad. Your report should advise the company's executives of the social customs, family life, attitudes, religions, education, and values in the target country. Remember that your company's interests are business-oriented; don't dwell on tourist information. Write your report individually or in teams.

14.5 Executive Summary: Reviewing Articles (Objs. 5 and 6)

WEB

Many managers and executives are too rushed to read long journal articles, but they are eager to stay current in their careers. Assume your boss has asked you to help him stay abreast of research in his field. He asks you to submit to him one executive summary every month on an article of interest.

Your Task. In your field of study, select a professional journal, such as the *Journal of Management*. Using ProQuest, Factiva, EBSCO, or some other database, look for articles in your target journal. Select an article that is at least five pages long and is interesting to you. Write an executive summary in a memo format. Include an introduction that might begin with *As you requested, I am submitting this executive summary of. . . .* Identify the author, article name, journal, and date of publication. Explain what the author intended to do in the study or article. Summarize three or four of the most important findings of the study or article. Use descriptive rather than functional headings. Summarize any recommendations made. Your boss would also like a concluding statement indicating your reaction to the article. Address your memo to Matthew R. Ferranto.

14.6 Unsolicited Proposal: Thwarting Residence Room Thievery (Objs. 1 and 2)

CONSUMER | CRITICAL THINKING | TEAM

As an enterprising college student, you recognized a problem as soon as you arrived on campus. Residence rooms filled with pricey digital equipment were very attractive to thieves. Some students move in with more than $3 000 worth of gear, including laptop computers, flat-screen TVs, digital cameras, MP3 players, video game consoles, PDAs, and DVD players. You solved the problem by buying an extra-large steel footlocker to lock away your valuables. However, shipping the footlocker was expensive (nearly $100), and you had to wait for it to arrive from a catalogue company. Your idea is to propose to the student organization (SO) that it allow you to offer these steel footlockers to students at a reduced price and with campus delivery. Your footlocker, which you found

FIGURE 14.4 *Intercultural Interview Topics and Questions*

Social Customs

1. How do people react to strangers? Friendly? Hostile? Reserved?
2. How do people greet each other?
3. What are appropriate manners when you enter a room? Bow? Nod? Shake hands with everyone?
4. How are names used for introductions? Is it appropriate to inquire about one's occupation or family?
5. What are the attitudes toward touching?
6. How does one express appreciation for an invitation to another's home? Bring a gift? Send flowers? Write a thank-you note? Are any gifts taboo?
7. Are there any customs related to how or where one sits?
8. Are any facial expressions or gestures considered rude?
9. How close do people stand when talking?
10. What is the attitude toward punctuality in social situations? in business situations?
11. What are acceptable eye-contact patterns?
12. What gestures indicate agreement? disagreement?

Family Life

1. What is the basic unit of social organization? Basic family? Extended family?
2. Do women work outside of the home? In what occupations?

Housing, Clothing, and Food

1. Are there differences in the kinds of housing used by different social groups? differences in location? differences in furnishings?
2. What occasions require special clothing?
3. Are some types of clothing considered taboo?
4. What is appropriate business attire for men? for women?
5. How many times a day do people eat?
6. What types of places, food, and drink are appropriate for business entertainment? Where is the seat of honour at a table?

Class Structure

1. Into what classes is society organized?
2. Do racial, religious, or economic factors determine social status?
3. Are there any minority groups? What is their social standing?

Political Patterns

1. Are there any immediate threats to the political survival of the country?
2. How is political power manifested?
3. What channels are used for expression of popular opinion?
4. What information media are important?
5. Is it appropriate to talk politics in social situations?

Religion and Folk Beliefs

1. To which religious groups do people belong? Is one predominant?
2. Do religious beliefs influence daily activities?
3. Which places have sacred value? Which objects? Which events?
4. How do religious holidays affect business activities?

Economic Institutions

1. What are the country's principal products?
2. Are workers organized in unions?
3. How are businesses owned? By family units? By large public corporations? By the government?
4. What is the standard work schedule?
5. Is it appropriate to do business by telephone? by computer?
6. How has technology affected business procedures?
7. Is participatory management used?
8. Are there any customs related to exchanging business cards?
9. How is status shown in an organization? Private office? Secretary? Furniture?
10. Are businesspeople expected to socialize before conducting business?

Value Systems

1. Is competitiveness or cooperation more prized?
2. Is thrift or enjoyment of the moment more valued?
3. Is politeness more important than factual honesty?
4. What are the attitudes toward education?
5. Do women own or manage businesses? If so, how are they treated?
6. What are your people's perceptions of Canadians? Do Canadians offend you? What has been hardest for you to adjust to in Canada? How could Canadians make this adjustment easier for you?

Rich chapter resources are available on the Web site.

by searching the Web, is extremely durable and serves double duty as a coffee table, nightstand, or card table. It comes with a smooth interior liner and two compartments.

Your Task. Working individually or with a team, imagine that you have made arrangements with a manufacturer to act as an intermediary selling footlockers on your campus at a reduced price. Consult the Web for manufacturers and make up your own figures. But how can you get the SO's permission to proceed? Give that organization a cut? Use your imagination in deciding how this plan might work on a college campus. Then prepare an unsolicited proposal to your SO. Outline the problem and your goals of protecting students' valuables and providing convenience. Check the Web for statistics regarding on-campus burglaries. Such figures should help you develop one or more persuasive "hooks." Then explain your proposal, project possible sales, discuss a timetable, and describe your staffing. Submit your proposal to Toni Bell, President, Student Organization.

C.L.U.E. review 14

On a separate sheet edit the following sentences to correct faults in grammar, punctuation, spelling, numbers, proofreading, and word use.

1. The format and organization of a proposal is important, if a writer want it to be taken serious.
2. Proposals are writen offers to do the following solve problems, provide services or sell equippment.
3. Our Vice-President and Manager worked to-gether to prepare 2 RFPs, that solicit competitive bids.
4. Just between you and I we work very hard to develop a "hook" to capture a readers attention.
5. If a proposal is to long and it's Budget is vague it will not succede in it's goal.
6. A important item in most Proposals, is the Budget which is a list of project cost.
7. If a proposal is sent to the President or I it should definitly explain the specific credentials and expertise of key personal for the project.
8. Dr Ryan Williams and him wanted to start there own business therefore they wrote a business plan, that included a detailed market analysis.
9. Mary Morley who is a member of our research and development department wondered whether her formal report would be presented at the May 15th meeting?
10. If you're report is complex be sure to proof-read it 3 times.

unit 5

Presentations

chapter 15

Speaking With Confidence

chapter 16

Employment Communication

chapter 15

Speaking With Confidence

objectives

1 Discuss two important first steps in preparing effective oral presentations.

2 Explain the major elements in organizing the content of a presentation, including the introduction, body, and conclusion.

3 Identify techniques for gaining audience rapport, including using effective imagery, providing verbal signposts, and sending appropriate nonverbal messages.

4 Discuss designing and using effective visual aids, handouts, and multimedia presentation materials and using presentation technology competently.

5 Specify delivery techniques for use before, during, and after a presentation, and apply reflective thinking skills.

6 Explain effective techniques for adapting oral presentations to cross-cultural audiences.

7 List techniques for improving telephone and voice mail skills to project a positive image.

springboard *to discussion*

There is a new way to deliver PowerPoint presentations called *pecha-kucha,* which is Japanese for the sound of conversation, like chit-chat. Created in Japan, this strategy has only two rules. The slideshow must have 20 slides that last 20 seconds each, for a total of 6 minutes and 40 seconds. When the time is up, the presenter sits down and the next person presents.[1]

learning objective

1

Preparing Effective Oral Presentations

Many businesspeople must make presentations as part of their careers.

At some point everyone in business has to sell an idea, and such persuasion is often done in person. Many future businesspeople fail to take advantage of opportunities in university or college to develop their speaking skills. However, such skills often play an important role in a successful career. Speaking skills are useful at every career stage. You might, for example, have to make a sales pitch before customers or speak to a professional gathering. You might need to describe your company's expansion plans to your banker, or you might need to persuade management to support your proposed marketing strategy. This chapter prepares you to use speaking skills in making oral presentations and in using the telephone, voice mail, and conferencing to advantage.

For any presentation, you can reduce your fears and lay the foundation for a professional performance by focusing on five areas: preparation, organization, audience rapport, visual aids, and delivery.

Knowing Your Purpose

Preparing for an oral presentation means identifying the purpose and knowing the audience.

The most important part of your preparation is deciding what you want to accomplish. Whether your goal is to persuade or to inform, you must have a clear idea of where you are going. At the end of your presentation, what do you want your listeners to remember or do?

Eric Evans, a loan officer at Dominion Trust, faced such questions as he planned a talk for a class in small business management. Eric's former business professor had asked him to return to campus and give the class advice about borrowing money from banks in order to start new businesses. Because Eric knew so much about this topic, he found it difficult to extract a specific purpose statement for his presentation. After much thought he narrowed his purpose to this: *To inform potential entrepreneurs about three important factors that loan officers consider before granting start-up loans to launch small businesses.* His entire presentation focused on ensuring that the class members understood and remembered three principal ideas.

Knowing Your Audience

A second key element in preparation is analyzing your audience, anticipating its reactions, and making appropriate adaptations. Audiences may fall into one of the following four categories: friendly, neutral, uninterested, or hostile. By anticipating your audience, you have a better idea of how to organize your presentation. A friendly audience, for example, will respond to humour and personal experiences. A neutral audience requires an even, controlled delivery style. The talk would probably be filled with facts, statistics, and expert opinions. An uninterested audience that is forced to attend requires a brief presentation. Such an audience might respond best to humour, cartoons, colourful visuals, and startling statistics. A hostile audience demands a calm, controlled delivery style with objective data and expert opinion.

Other elements, such as age, gender, education, experience, and the size of the audience will also affect your style and message content. Analyze the following questions to help you determine your organizational pattern, delivery style, and supporting material.

Audience analysis issues include size, age, gender, experience, attitude, and expectations.

- *How will this topic appeal to this audience?*
- *How can I relate this information to my listeners' needs?*
- *How can I earn respect so that they accept my message?*
- *What would be most effective in making my point? Facts? Statistics? Personal experiences? Expert opinion? Humour? Cartoons? Graphic illustrations? Demonstrations? Case histories? Analogies?*
- *What measures must I take to ensure that this audience remembers my main points?*

If you've agreed to speak to an audience with which you are unfamiliar, ask for the names of a half-dozen people who will be in the audience. Contact them and learn about their backgrounds and expectations for the presentation. This information can help you answer questions about what they want to hear and how deeply you should explore the subject. You'll want to thank these people when you start your speech. Doing this kind of homework will impress the audience.

Organizing the Content for a Powerful Impact

learning objective 2

Once you have determined your purpose and analyzed the audience, you are ready to collect information and organize it logically. Good organization and conscious repetition are the two most powerful keys to audience comprehension and retention. In fact, many speech experts recommend the following, admittedly repetitious, but effective plan:

- **Step 1:** Tell them what you are going to say.
- **Step 2:** Say it.
- **Step 3:** Tell them what you've just said.

Capturing Attention in the Introduction

How many times have you heard a speaker begin with *It's a pleasure to be here* or *I'm honoured to be asked to speak*? Boring openings such as these get speakers off to a dull start. Avoid such banalities by striving to accomplish three goals in the introduction to your presentation:

- Capture listeners' attention and get them involved.
- Identify yourself and establish your credibility.
- Preview your main points.

If you are able to appeal to listeners and involve them in your presentation right from the start, you are more likely to hold their attention until the finish. Consider some of the same techniques that you use to open sales letters: a question, a startling

Attention-grabbing openers include questions, startling facts, jokes, anecdotes, and quotations.

fact, a joke, a story, or a quotation. Some speakers achieve involvement by opening with a question or command that requires audience members to raise their hands or stand up. Additional techniques to gain and keep audience attention are presented in the accompanying Career Coach box.

To establish your credibility, you need to describe your position, knowledge, or experience—whatever qualifies you to speak. Try also to connect with your audience. Listeners are particularly drawn to speakers who reveal something of themselves and identify with them.

After capturing attention and establishing yourself, you'll want to preview the main points of your topic, perhaps with a visual aid. You may wish to put off actually writing your introduction, however, until after you have organized the rest of the presentation and crystallized your principal ideas.

Take a look at Eric Evans' introduction, shown in Figure 15.1 (page 380), to see how he integrated all the elements necessary for a good opening.

Organizing the Body

The best oral presentations focus on a few key ideas.

The biggest problem with most oral presentations is a failure to focus on a few principal ideas. Thus, the body of your short presentation (20 or fewer minutes) should include a limited number of main points, say, two to four. Develop each main point with adequate, but not excessive, explanation and details. Too many details can obscure the main message, so keep your presentation simple and logical. Remember, listeners have no pages to leaf back through should they become confused.

When Eric Evans began planning his presentation, he realized immediately that he could talk for hours on his topic. He also knew that listeners are not good at separating major and minor points. Thus, instead of submerging his listeners in a sea of information, he sorted out a few main ideas. In the banking industry, loan officers generally ask the following three questions of each applicant for a small business loan: (1) Are you ready to "hit the ground running" in starting your business? (2) Have you done your homework? and (3) Have you made realistic projections of potential sales, cash flow, and equity investment? These questions would become his main points, but Eric wanted to streamline them further so that his audience would be sure to remember them. He capsulized the questions in three words: *experience*, *preparation*, and *projection*. As you can see in Figure 15.1, Eric prepared a sentence outline showing these three main ideas. Each is supported by examples and explanations.

How to organize and sequence main ideas may not be immediately obvious when you begin working on a presentation. The following methods, which review and amplify those discussed in Chapter 13, provide many possible strategies and examples to help you organize a presentation:

Main ideas can be organized according to chronology, geography/space, topic/function/conventional grouping, comparison/contrast, journalism pattern, value/size, importance, problem/solution, simple/complex, and best case/worst case.

- **Chronology.** Example: A presentation describing the history of a problem, organized from the first sign of trouble to the present.
- **Geography/space.** Example: A presentation about the changing diversity of the workforce, organized by regions in the country (East Coast, West Coast, and so forth).
- **Topic/function/conventional grouping.** Example: A report discussing mishandled airline baggage, organized by names of airlines.
- **Comparison/contrast (pro/con).** Example: A report comparing organic farming methods with those of modern industrial farming.
- **Journalism pattern.** Example: A report describing how identity thieves can ruin your good name. Organized by *who, what, when, where, why,* and *how*.

career coach

Nine Techniques for Gaining and Keeping Audience Attention

Experienced speakers know how to capture the attention of an audience and how to maintain that attention during a presentation. Here are nine proven techniques.

- **A promise.** Begin with a promise that keeps the audience expectant (for example, *By the end of this presentation I will have shown you how you can increase your sales by 50 percent*).
- **Drama.** Open by telling an emotionally moving story or by describing a serious problem that involves the audience. Throughout your talk include other dramatic elements, such as a long pause after a key statement. Change your vocal tone or pitch. Professionals use high-intensity emotions such as anger, joy, sadness, and excitement.
- **Eye contact.** As you begin, command attention by surveying the entire audience to take in all listeners. Take two to five seconds to make eye contact with as many people as possible.
- **Movement.** Leave the lectern area whenever possible. Walk around the conference table or between the aisles of your audience. Try to move toward your audience, especially at the beginning and end of your talk.
- **Questions.** Keep listeners active and involved with rhetorical questions. Ask for a show of hands to get each listener thinking. The response will also give you a quick gauge of audience attention.
- **Demonstrations.** Include a member of the audience in a demonstration (for example, *I'm going to show you exactly how to implement our four-step customer courtesy process, but I need a volunteer from the audience to help me*).
- **Samples/gimmicks.** If you are promoting a product, consider using items to toss out to the audience or to award as prizes to volunteer participants. You can also pass around product samples or promotional literature. Be careful, though, to maintain control.
- **Visuals.** Give your audience something to look at besides yourself. Use a variety of visual aids in a single session. Also consider writing the concerns expressed by your listeners on a flipchart or on the board as you go along.
- **Self-interest.** Review your entire presentation to ensure that it meets the critical *What's in it for me?* audience test. Remember that people are most interested in things that benefit them.

- **Value/size.** Example: A report describing fluctuations in housing costs, organized by prices of homes.
- **Importance.** Example: A report describing five reasons that a company should move its headquarters to a specific city, organized from the most important reason to the least important.
- **Problem/solution.** Example: A company faces a problem such as declining sales. A solution such as reducing the staff is offered.
- **Simple/complex.** Example: A report explaining genetic modification of plants such as corn, organized from simple seed production to complex gene introduction.
- **Best case/worst case.** Example: A report analyzing whether two companies should merge, organized by the best-case result (improved market share, profitability, and employee morale) opposed to the worst-case result (devalued stock, lost market share, employee malaise).

FIGURE 15.1 ***Oral Presentation Outline***

1 Prewriting

ANALYZE: The purpose of this report is to inform listeners of three critical elements in securing business loans.

ANTICIPATE: The audience members are aspiring businesspeople who are probably unfamiliar with loan operations.

ADAPT: Because the audience will be receptive but uninformed, explain terms and provide examples. Repeat the main ideas to ensure comprehension.

2 Writing

RESEARCH: Analyze previous loan applications; interview other loan officers. Gather critical data.

ORGANIZE: Group the data into three major categories. Support with statistics, details, and examples. Plan visual aids.

COMPOSE: Prepare a sentence outline. Consider using presentation software to outline your talk.

3 Revising

REVISE: Develop transitions between topics. Prepare note cards or speaker's notes.

PRACTISE: Rehearse the entire talk and time it. Practise enunciating words and projecting your voice. Practise using your visual aids. Develop natural hand motions.

EVALUATE: Tape-record or videotape a practice session to evaluate your movements, voice tone, enunciation, and timing.

What Makes a Loan Officer Say "Yes"?

I. INTRODUCTION

Captures attention — A. How many of you expect one day to start your own businesses? How many of you have all the cash available to capitalize that business when you start?

Involves audience — B. Like you, nearly every entrepreneur needs cash to open a business, and I promise you that by the end of this talk you will have inside information on how to make a loan application that will be successful.

Identifies speaker — C. As a loan officer at Dominion Trust, which specializes in small-business loans, I make decisions on requests from entrepreneurs like you applying for start-up money.

Transition: Your professor invited me here today to tell you how you can improve your chances of getting a loan from us or from any other lender. I have suggestions in three areas: experience, preparation, and projection. — Previews three main points

II. BODY

Establishes main points

A. First, let's consider experience. You must show that you can hit the ground running.
   1. Demonstrate what experience you have in your proposed business.
   2. Include your résumé when you submit your business plan.
   3. If you have little experience, tell us whom you would hire to supply the skills that you lack.

Transition: In addition to experience, loan officers will want to see that you have researched your venture thoroughly.

B. My second suggestion, then, involves preparation. Have you done your homework?
   1. Talk to local businesspeople, especially those in related fields.
   2. Conduct traffic counts or other studies to estimate potential sales.
   3. Analyze the strengths and weaknesses of the competition.

Transition: Now that we've discussed preparation, we're ready for my final suggestion.

C. My last tip is the most important one. It involves making a realistic projection of your potential sales, cash flow, and equity.
   1. Present detailed monthly cash-flow projections for the first year.
   2. Describe *What-if* scenarios indicating both good and bad possibilities.
   3. Indicate that you intend to supply at least 25 percent of the initial capital yourself.

Transition: The three major points I've just outlined cover critical points in obtaining start-up loans. Let me review them for you.

Develops coherence with planned transitions

III. CONCLUSION

Summarizes main points — A. Loan officers are most likely to say "yes" to your loan application if you do three things: (1) prove that you can hit the ground running when your business opens; (2) demonstrate that you've researched your proposed business seriously; and (3) project a realistic picture of your sales, cash flow, and equity.

B. Experience, preparation, and projection, then, are the three keys to launching your business with the necessary start-up capital so that you can concentrate on where your customers, not your funds, are coming from. — Provides final focus

In the presentation shown in Figure 15.1, Eric arranged the main points by importance, placing the most important point last, where it would have maximum effect. When organizing any presentation, prepare a little more material than you think you will actually need. Wise speakers always have something useful in reserve such as an extra handout, transparency, or idea—just in case they finish early. At the same time, most speakers go about 25 percent over the allotted time, in spite of their practice runs at home in front of the mirror. If your speaking time is limited, as it usually is in your classes, aim for less than the limit when rehearsing, so that you don't take time away from the next presenters.

Summarizing in the Conclusion

Nervous speakers often rush to wrap up their presentations because they can't wait to flee the stage. But listeners will remember the conclusion more than any other part of a speech. That's why you should spend some time to make it most effective. Strive to achieve three goals:

Effective conclusions summarize main points and allow the speaker to exit gracefully.

- Summarize the main themes of the presentation.
- Leave the audience with a specific and memorable "take-away"
- Include a statement that allows you to leave the podium gracefully.

Some speakers end limply with comments such as *I guess that's about all I have to say*. This leaves bewildered audience members wondering whether they should continue listening. Skilled speakers alert the audience that they are finishing. They use phrases such as *In conclusion*, *As I end this presentation*, or *It's time for me to sum up*. Then they proceed immediately to the conclusion. Audiences become justifiably irritated with a speaker who announces the conclusion but then digresses with one more story or talks on for ten more minutes.

A straightforward summary should review major points and focus on what you want the listeners to do, think, or remember. Notice how Eric Evans, in the conclusion shown in Figure 15.1, summarized his three main points and provided a final focus for listeners. In your conclusion you might want to use an anecdote, an inspiring quotation, or a statement that ties in the opener and offers a new insight. Whatever you choose, be sure to include a closing thought that indicates you are finished.

Building Audience Rapport Like a Pro

learning objective

3

Good speakers are adept at building audience rapport. They form a bond with the audience; they entertain as well as inform. How do they do it? Based on observations of successful and unsuccessful speakers, we learn that the good ones use a number of verbal and nonverbal techniques to connect with the audience. Some of their helpful techniques include providing effective imagery, supplying verbal signposts, and using body language strategically.

Effective Imagery

You'll lose your audience quickly if your talk is filled with abstractions, generalities, and dry facts. To enliven your presentation and enhance comprehension, try using some of following techniques. However, beware of exaggeration or distortion. Keep your imagery realistic and credible.

- **Analogies.** A comparison of similar traits between dissimilar things can be effective in explaining and drawing connections.

Use analogies, metaphors, similes, personal anecdotes, personalized statistics, and worst- and best-case scenarios instead of dry facts.

- **Metaphors.** Comparison between otherwise dissimilar things without using the words *like* or *as* results in a metaphor.
- **Similes.** A comparison that includes the words *like* or *as* is a simile.
- **Personal anecdotes.** Nothing connects you faster or better with your audience than a good personal story.
- **Personalized statistics.** Although often misused, statistics stay with people—particularly when they relate directly to the audience.
- **Worst- and best-case scenarios.** Hearing the worst that could happen can be effective in driving home a point.

Verbal Signposts

Knowledgeable speakers provide verbal signposts to indicate when they are previewing, summarizing, or switching directions.

Speakers must remember that listeners, unlike readers of a report, cannot control the rate of presentation or flip back through pages to review main points. As a result, listeners get lost easily. Knowledgeable speakers help the audience recognize the organization and main points in an oral message with verbal signposts. They keep listeners on track by including helpful previews, summaries, and transitions, such as these:

- **Previewing**

  The next segment of my talk presents three reasons for . . .

  Let's now consider the causes of . . .

- **Summarizing**

  Let me review with you the major problems I've just discussed . . .

  You see, then, that the most significant factors are . . .

- **Switching directions**

  Thus far we've talked solely about . . . ; now let's move to . . .

  I've argued that . . . and . . . , but an alternative view holds that . . .

You can further improve any oral presentation by including appropriate transitional expressions such as *first, second, next, then, therefore, moreover, on the other hand, on the contrary,* and *in conclusion*. These expressions build coherence, lend emphasis, and tell listeners where you are headed. Notice in Eric Evans's outline, in Figure 15.1, the specific transitional elements designed to help listeners recognize each new principal point.

Nonverbal Messages

A speaker's appearance, movement, and speech affect the success of a presentation.

Although what you say is most important, the nonverbal messages you send can also have a potent effect on how well your message is received. How you look, how you move, and how you speak can make or break your presentation. The following suggestions focus on nonverbal tips to ensure that your verbal message is well received.

- **Look terrific.** Like it or not, you will be judged by your appearance. For everything but small in-house presentations, be sure you dress professionally. A good tip is to dress at least as well as the best-dressed person in the audience.
- **Animate your body.** Be enthusiastic and let your body show it. Emphasize ideas to enhance points about size, number, and direction. Use a variety of gestures, but don't consciously plan them in advance.

- **Punctuate your words.** You can keep your audience interested by varying your tone, volume, pitch, and pace. Use pauses before and after important points. Allow the audience to take in your ideas.
- **Speak extemporaneously.** Do not read from notes or a manuscript; speak freely. Use your presentation slides to guide your talk. You will come across as more competent and enthusiastic if you are not glued to your notes or manuscript. Use note cards or a paper outline only if presenting without an electronic slideshow.
- **Get out from behind the podium.** Avoid planting yourself behind the podium. Movement makes you look natural and comfortable. You might pick a few places in the room to walk to. Even if you must stay close to your visual aids, make a point of leaving them occasionally so that the audience can see your whole body.
- **Vary your facial expression.** Begin with a smile, but change your expressions to correspond with the thoughts you are voicing. You can shake your head to show disagreement, roll your eyes to show disdain, look heavenward for guidance, or wrinkle your brow to show concern or dismay. To see how speakers convey meaning without words, mute the sound on your TV and watch the facial expressions of a talk show personality.

Planning Visual Aids, Handouts, and Multimedia Presentations

learning objective

4

Before you make a business presentation, consider this wise proverb: "Tell me, I forget. Show me, I remember. Involve me, I understand." Your goals as a speaker are to make listeners understand, remember, and act on your ideas. To get them interested and involved, include effective visual aids. Some experts say that we acquire 85 percent of all our knowledge visually. Therefore, an oral presentation that incorporates visual aids is far more likely to be understood and retained than one lacking visual enhancement.

Visual aids clarify points, improve comprehension, and aid retention.

Good visual aids serve many purposes. They emphasize and clarify main points, thus improving comprehension and retention. They increase audience interest, and they make the presenter appear more professional, better prepared, and more persuasive. Furthermore, research shows that the use of visual aids actually shortens meetings.[2] Visual aids are particularly helpful for inexperienced speakers because the audience concentrates on the aid rather than on the speaker. Good visuals also serve to jog the memory of a speaker, thus improving self-confidence, poise, and delivery.

Types of Visual Aids

Fortunately for today's speakers, many forms of visual media are available to enhance a presentation. Figure 15.2 (page 384) describes the pros and cons of a number of visual aids that can guide you in selecting the best visual aid for any speaking occasion. Three of the most popular visuals are multimedia slides, overhead transparencies, and handouts.

Multimedia Slides. With today's excellent software programs—such as Microsoft PowerPoint, Apple Keynote, Lotus Freelance Graphics, Corel Presentations, and Adobe Presenter or Adobe Ovation—you can create dynamic, colourful presentations with your PC. The output from these programs is generally shown on a computer monitor, a TV monitor, an LCD (liquid crystal display) panel, or a screen. With

FIGURE 15.2 ***Pros and Cons of Visual Aid Options***

Medium	Pros	Cons
Multimedia slides	Create professional appearance with many colour, art, graphic, and font options. Easy to use and transport via removable disk, Web download, or e-mail attachment. Inexpensive to update.	Present potential incompatibility issues. Require costly projection equipment and practice for smooth delivery. Tempt user to include razzle-dazzle features that may fail to add value.
Transparencies	Give professional appearance with little practice. Easy to (1) prepare, (2) update and maintain, (3) locate reliable equipment, and (4) limit information shown at one time.	Appear to some as an outdated presentation method. Hold speaker captive to the machine. Provide poor reproduction of photos and some graphics.
Handouts	Encourage audience participation. Easy to maintain and update. Enhance recall because audience keeps reference material.	Increase risk of unauthorized duplication of speaker's material. Can be difficult to transport. May cause speaker to lose audience's attention.
Flipcharts or whiteboards	Provide inexpensive option available at most sites. Easy to (1) create, (2) modify or customize on the spot, (3) record comments from the audience, and (4) combine with more high-tech visuals in the same presentation.	Require graphics talent. Difficult for larger audiences to see. Prepared flipcharts are cumbersome to transport and easily worn with use.
Video	Give an accurate representation of the content; strong indication of forethought and preparation.	Create potential for compatibility issues related to computer video formats. Expensive to create and update.
Objects for demonstration	Offer a realistic reinforcement of message content. Increase audience participation with close observation.	Lead to extra work and expense in transporting and replacing worn objects. Limited use with larger audiences.

a little expertise and advanced equipment, you can create a multimedia presentation that includes stereo sound, videos, and hyperlinks, as described shortly in the discussion of multimedia presentations.

Overhead Transparencies. Student and professional speakers alike still rely on the overhead projector for many reasons. Most meeting areas are equipped with projectors and screens. Moreover, acetate transparencies for the overhead are inexpensive, easily prepared on a computer or copier, and simple to use. Because rooms need not be darkened, a speaker using transparencies can maintain eye contact with the audience. Many experienced speakers create overhead slides in addition to their electronic slides as a backup plan in the case of malfunctioning presentation technology. A word of caution, though: stand to the side of the projector so that you don't obstruct the audience's view.

Handouts. You can enhance and complement your presentations by distributing pictures, outlines, brochures, articles, charts, summaries, or other supplements. Speakers who use presentation software often prepare a set of their slides along with notes to hand out to viewers. Timing the distribution of any handout, though, is tricky. If given out during a presentation, your handouts tend to distract the audience, causing you to lose control. Thus it's probably best to discuss most of the handouts during the presentation but delay distributing them until after you finish.

To maintain control, distribute handouts after you finish speaking.

Designing a Multimedia Presentation

Few corporate types or entrepreneurs could do without the razzle-dazzle of colourful images to make their point. Electronic slideshows, using PowerPoint in particular, have become a staple of business presentations. However, overuse or misuse may be the downside of the ever-present multimedia slideshow. Over the two decades of the software program's existence, millions of poorly created and badly delivered PowerPoint presentations have tarnished PowerPoint's reputation as an effective communication tool. Tools are helpful only when used properly.

PowerPoint has become the business standard for presenting, defending, and selling ideas.

Applying the 3-x-3 Writing Process to Create a Visually Appealing PowerPoint Presentation

Some presenters prefer to create their slides first and then develop the narrative around their slides. Others prefer to prepare their content first and then create the visual component. The risk associated with the first approach is that you may be tempted to spend too much time making your slides look good and not enough time preparing your content. Remember that great-looking slides can never compensate for thin content. The following discussion reviews the three phases of the writing process and shows how they help you develop a visually appealing PowerPoint presentation. In the prewriting phase you analyze, anticipate, and adapt. In the second phase you research, organize, and compose. In the third phase you revise, edit, and evaluate.

Critics say that PowerPoint is too regimented and distracts attention from the speaker.

Analyzing the Situation. Making the best content and design choices for your slides depends greatly on your analysis of the presentation situation. Will your slides be used during a live presentation? Will they be part of a self-running presentation such as in a store kiosk? Will they be saved on a server so that those with Internet access can watch the presentation at their convenience? Will they be sent as a PowerPoint show or a PDF document—also sometimes called a "deck"—to a client instead of a hard copy?

Anticipating Your Audience. Think about how you can design your presentation to get the most positive response from your audience. Audiences respond, for example, to the colours you use. Primary ideas are generally best conveyed with bold colours such as blue, green, and purple. Because the messages that colours convey can vary from culture to culture, colours must be chosen carefully. In North America, blue is the colour of credibility, tranquility, conservatism, and trust. Therefore, it is the background for many business presentations. Green relates to interaction, growth, money, and stability; it can work well as a background or an accent colour. Purple can also be used as a background or accent colour. It conveys spirituality, royalty, dreams, and humour.[3]

Just as you anticipate audience members' reactions to colour, you can usually anticipate their reaction to special effects. Using animation and sound effects—flying objects, swirling text, clashing cymbals, and the like—only because they are available is not a good idea. Special effects distract your audience, drawing attention away from your main points. You should add animation features only if doing so helps convey your message or adds interest to the content. When your audience members leave, they should be commenting on the ideas you conveyed, not the cool swivels and sound effects.

Follow the 6-x-6 rule and select background and text colours based on the brightness of the room.

Adapting Text and Colour Selections. Adapt the amount of text on your slide to how your audience will use the slides. As a general guideline, most graphic designers encourage the 6-x-6 rule: "six bullets per screen, max; six words per bullet, max."[4] You may find, however, that breaking this rule is sometimes necessary, particularly when your audience will be viewing the presentation on their own, with no speaker assistance.

Adapt the colours based on where the presentation will be given. Use light text on a dark background for presentations in darkened rooms. Use dark text on a light background for computer presentations in lighted rooms. Avoid using a dark font on a dark background, such as red text on dark blue. Likewise, avoid using a light font on a light background, such as white text on pale blue. Dark on dark or light on light results in low contrast, making the slides difficult to read.

Researching Your PowerPoint Options. If you need to present a complicated idea, you will have to learn more about PowerPoint in order to determine the best way to clarify and simplify its visual presentation. Besides using online tutorials and studying books on the subject, when you view other people's presentations, be on the lookout for fresh ways to illustrate your content more effectively. Chances are you will learn the most from fellow students and team members who have truly mastered the software.

Organizing Your Slides. When you prepare your slides, translate the major headings in your presentation outline into titles for slides. Then build bullet points using short phrases. In Chapter 7 you learned to improve readability by using graphic highlighting techniques including bullets, numbers, and headings. In preparing a PowerPoint presentation, you will use those same techniques.

The slides you create to accompany your spoken ideas can be organized with visual elements that will help your audience understand and remember what you want to communicate. Let's say, for example, that you have three points in your presentation. You can create a blueprint slide that captures the three points in a visually appealing way, and then you can use that slide several times throughout your presentation. Near the beginning, the blueprint slide provides an overview of your points. Later, it will provide transitions as you move from point to point; you can direct your audience's attention by highlighting the next point you will be talking about. Finally, the blueprint slide can be used near the end to provide a review of your key points.

Composing Your Slideshow. All presentation programs require you to (a) select or create a template that will serve as the background for your presentation and (b) make each individual slide by selecting a layout that best conveys your message. When you craft your template, you can use one of those provided with the program, download one from your choice of many Web sites, or even create one from scratch.

Novice and even advanced users choose existing templates because they are designed by professionals, who know how to combine harmonious colours, borders, and fonts for pleasing visual effects. If you prefer, you can alter existing templates so they better suit your needs. Adding a corporate logo, adjusting the colour scheme to better match the colours on your organization's Web site, or selecting a different font are just some of the ways you can customize existing templates.

Be careful, though, of what one expert labels "visual clichés."[5] Overused templates and even clip art that ship with PowerPoint can weary viewers who have seen them repeatedly in presentations. Instead of using a standard template, key "PowerPoint template" into Google or your favourite search engine. You will see hundreds of template options available as free downloads. Unless your employer requires that presentations all have the same look, your audience will most likely appreciate fresh templates that complement the purpose of your presentation and provide visual variety.

Overused templates and clip art produce "visual clichés" that bore audiences.

PowerPoint comes with the **AutoContent Wizard** feature, which can help you through the process of creating a slideshow. The Wizard provides outlines for a variety of types of presentations. Relying only on the Wizard, however, generally leads to text-heavy presentations that lack visual elements. Nevertheless, it's a good start for a PowerPoint novice. You can choose from the layout options in PowerPoint, or you can create a layout from scratch by adding your own elements to each slide.

When team members are working together to prepare a slide presentation, be sure that each member is using the same template. That way when they merge their individual sections into one presentation file, no one will be surprised at how the slides look. To maintain a consistent look throughout the presentation, only one team member should be in charge of making colour, font, or other global formatting changes to the slide and title masters. Team members should be encouraged to follow the global formatting established by the master slides. In addition, team members should understand that making global changes only one time, using the master slides, is a definite plus. It prevents the hassles associated with changing many individual slides.

In selecting the best layout for each slide, you again can choose from the layout options that are part of your presentation program, or you can create a layout from scratch by adding your own elements to each slide. You can alter layouts by repositioning, resizing, or changing the fonts for the placeholders where your title, bulleted list, organization chart, video clip, photograph, or other elements will appear. You can experiment with graphic elements that will enhance your presentation by making your slides visually more appealing and memorable.

Try to avoid long, boring bulleted lists. Ensure that your lists are parallel, and use graphics to add interest and illustrate the points. You may use stock photos that you can download from the Web for personal and school use without penalty, or consider taking your own pictures if you own a digital camera.

There are many ways to add variety and pizzazz to your slides. PowerPoint provides a **Diagram Gallery** with six choices for arranging information. You can also animate each item in the diagram. Occasionally, try to convert pure text and bullet points to diagrams, charts, or other images to add punch to your slideshow. These will keep your audience interested and help them retain the information you are presenting.

You can add pizzazz to your slides by animating some items and using diagrams from the Diagram Gallery.

During the composition stage many users fall into the trap of excessive formatting and programming. They waste valuable time fine-tuning their slides and do not spend enough time on what they are going to say and how they will say it. To avoid this trap, set a limit for how much time you will spend making your slides visually appealing. Your time limit will be based on how many "bells and whistles" that (a) your audience expects and (b) your content requires to make it understandable.

Remember that neither every point nor every thought requires a visual. In fact, it is smart to switch off the slides occasionally and direct the focus to yourself. Darkening the screen while you discuss a point, tell a story, give an example, or involve the audience will add variety to your presentation.

Create a slide only if it accomplishes at least one of the following purposes:

- Generates interest in what you are saying and helps the audience follow your ideas
- Highlights points you want your audience to remember
- Introduces or reviews your key points
- Provides a transition from one point to the next
- Illustrates and simplifies complex ideas

Revising, Proofreading, and Evaluating Your Slideshow. Use PowerPoint's **Slide Sorter View** to rearrange, insert, and delete slides during the revision process. This is the time when you will focus on making your presentation as clear as possible. If you are listing items, be sure that you use parallel grammatical form. As you are reviewing, check carefully to find spelling, grammar, punctuation, and other errors. Use PowerPoint's spell checker, but don't rely on it without careful proofing, preferably from a printed copy of the slideshow. Nothing is as embarrassing as projecting errors on a huge screen in front of an audience. Also check for consistency in how you capitalize and punctuate points throughout the presentation.

The final stage in applying the 3-x-3 process to developing a PowerPoint presentation involves evaluation. Consider whether you have done all you can to use the tools PowerPoint provides to communicate your message in a visually appealing way. In addition, test your slides on the equipment and in the room you will be using during your presentation. Do the colours you selected work in this setting? Are the font styles and sizes readable from the back of the room? Figure 15.3 shows examples of the slides that incorporate what you have learned in the discussion. The creator of the presentation varied the slide design to break the monotony of bulleted or numbered lists. Images and animated diagrams add interest and appeal to the slides.

Eight Steps to Making a Powerful Multimedia Presentation

For a powerful presentation, first write the text and then work on templates, font styles, and colours.

We have now discussed many suggestions for making effective PowerPoint presentations, but you may still be wondering how to put it all together. Here is a step-by-step process for creating a powerful multimedia presentation:

1. **Start with the text.** The text is the foundation of your presentation. Express your ideas using words that are clear, concise, and understandable. Once the entire content of your presentation is in place you are ready to begin adding colour and all the other elements that will make your slides visually appealing.
2. **Select background and fonts.** Select a template that will provide consistent font styles, font sizes, and a background for your slides. You can create your own template or use one included with PowerPoint. You cannot go wrong with selecting a basic template design with an easy-to-read font such as Times New Roman or Arial. As a general rule, use no more than two font styles in your presentation. The point size should be between 24 and 36. Title fonts should be larger than text font. The more you use PowerPoint and find out what works and does not work, the more you can experiment with bolder, more innovative background and font options that effectively convey your message.
3. **Choose images that help communicate your message.** Images such as clip art, photographs, and maps should complement the text. Never use an image that is not immediately relevant. Some people consider clip art amateurish, so photographs are often preferable. In addition, clip art is available to any user, so it tends to become stale fast.

FIGURE 15.3 ***Varying PowerPoint Slides for Multimedia Presentations***

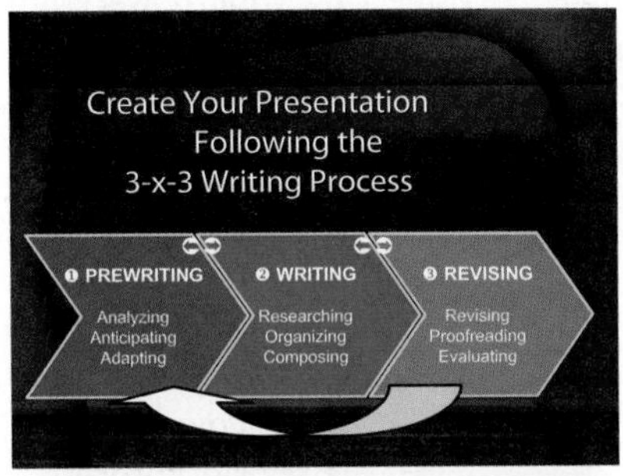

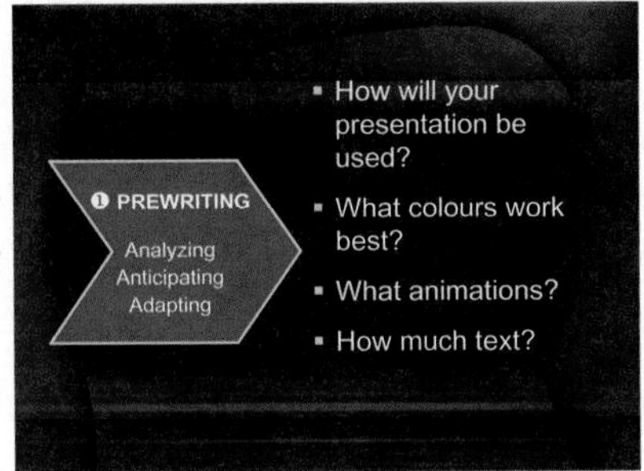

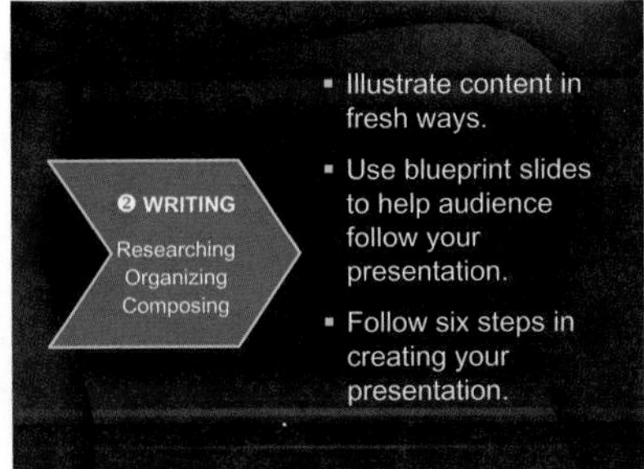

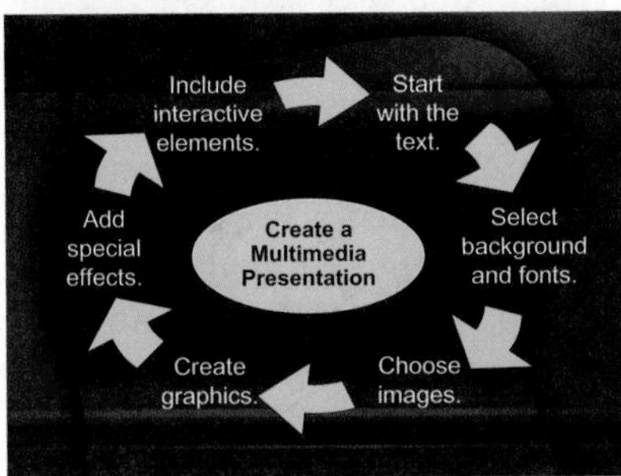

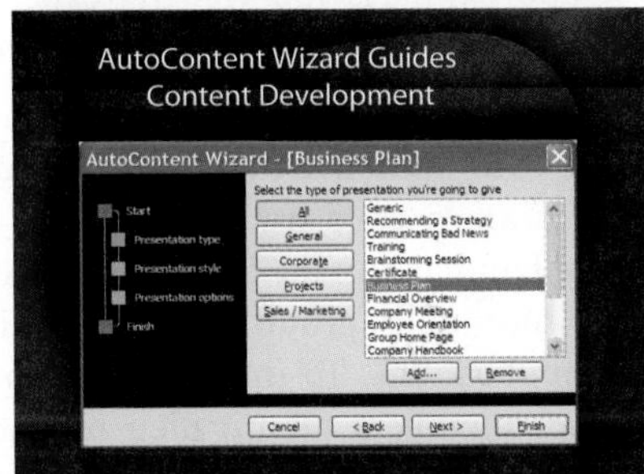

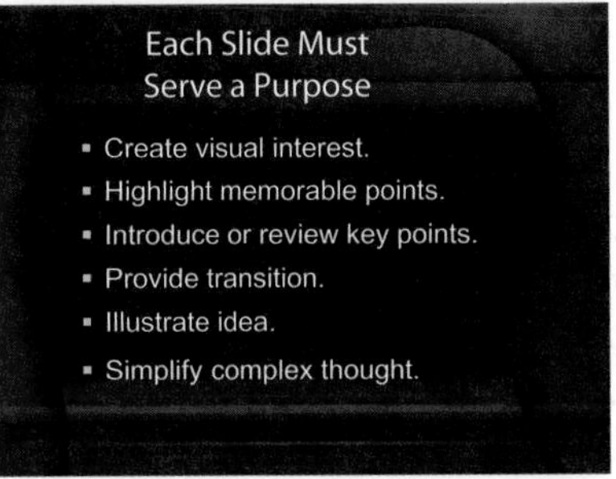

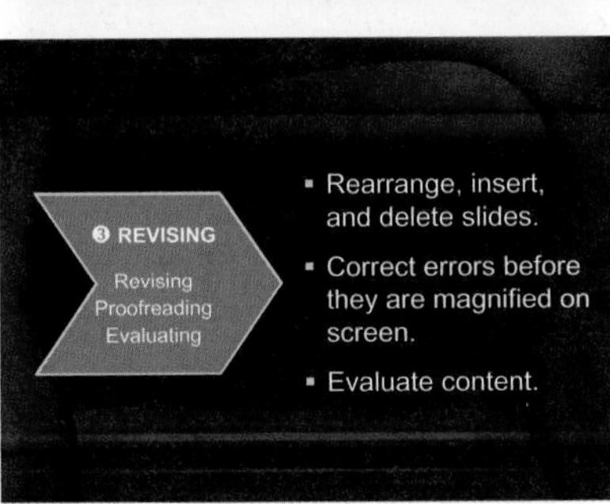

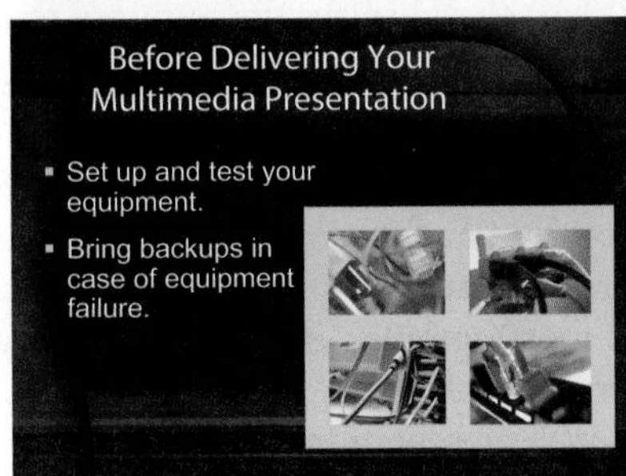

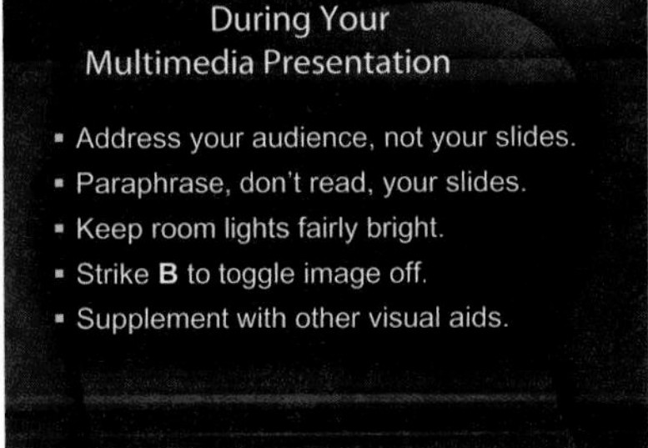

4. **Create graphics.** PowerPoint includes a variety of tools to help you simplify complex information or transform a boring bulleted list into a visually appealing graphic. You can use PowerPoint's **Draw** and **AutoShapes** tools to create a timeline or a flowchart. All of the tools require practice before you can create effective graphics. Remember that graphics should be easy to understand without overloading your audience with unnecessary details or too much text. In fact, put such details in handouts rather than clutter your slides with them.

Learn to simplify complex information in visually appealing graphics.

5. **Add special effects.** To keep your audience focused on what you are discussing, use PowerPoint's **Custom Animation** feature to control when objects or text appear on the screen. Animate points in a bulleted list to appear one at a time, for example, or in a radial diagram to appear as each is discussed. Keep in mind that the first thing your audience sees on every slide should describe the slide's content. With motion paths and other animation options, you can move objects to different positions on the slide; to minimize clutter, you can dim or remove them once they have served their purpose.

   In addition, as you move from slide to slide in a presentation, you can select transition effects such as *wipe down.* The animation and transition options range from subtle to flashy—choose them with care so that the visual delivery of your presentation does not distract from the content of your message.

6. **Create hyperlinks to approximate the Web browsing experience.** Make your presentation more interactive and intriguing by connecting your PowerPoint presentation, via hyperlinks, to other sources that provide content to enhance your presentation. You can hyperlink to (a) other slides within the presentation or in other PowerPoint files; (b) other programs that will open a second window displaying items such as spreadsheets, documents, or videos; and (c) if you have an Internet connection, Web sites.

   Once you have finished discussing the hyperlinked source or watching a video that opened in a second window, you close that window and your hyperlinked PowerPoint slide is once more on view. In this way you can break up the monotony of typical linear PowerPoint presentations. Instead, your hyperlinked show approximates the viewing experience of a Web user who enters a site through a main page or portal and then navigates at will to reach second- and third-level pages.

7. **Engage your audience by asking for interaction.** When audience response and feedback are needed, interactive tools are useful. Audience response systems may be familiar to you from game shows, but they are also used for surveys and opinion polls, group decision making, voting, quizzes and tests, and many other applications. To interact with your audience, present polling questions. Audience members submit their individual or team responses using handheld devices read by a PowerPoint add-in program. The audience immediately sees a bar chart that displays the response results.[6]

Internet options for slide presentations range from posting slides online to conducting a live Web conference with slides, narration, and speaker control.

8. **Move your presentation to the Internet.** You have a range of alternatives, from simple to complex, for moving your multimedia presentation to the Internet or to your company's intranet. The simplest option is posting your slides online for others to access. Even if you are giving a face-to-face presentation, attendees appreciate these *electronic handouts* because they don't have to lug them home. The most complex option for moving your multimedia presentation to the Internet involves a Web conference or broadcast.

   Web presentations with slides, narration, and speaker control have emerged as a way for anyone who has access to the Internet to attend your presentation without leaving the office. For example, you could initiate a meeting via a conference call, narrate using a telephone, and have participants see your slides from the browsers on their computers. If you prefer, you could skip the narration and provide a prerecorded presentation. Web-based presentations have many applications, including providing access to updated training or sales data whenever needed.[7]

   Some businesses convert their PowerPoint presentations to PDF documents or send PowerPoint shows (file extension: *.pps), which open directly in **Slide Show View,** ready to run. Both types of documents are suitable for e-mailing. Among their advantages, they start immediately, can't be easily changed, and typically result in smaller, less memory-intensive files.

Avoiding Being Upstaged by Your Multimedia Presentation

In addition to using multimedia technology to enhance and enrich your message, following are some tips for performing like a professional and keeping the audience engaged.

- Know your material.
- As you show new elements on the slide, allow the audience time to absorb the information, then paraphrase and elaborate on what the listeners have seen. Do not insult your audience's intelligence by reading verbatim from a slide.

- Leave the lights as bright as you can. Make sure the audience can see your face and eyes.
- Use a radio remote control (not infrared) so you can stand near the screen rather than remain tethered to your computer. Radio remotes will allow you to be up to 15 metres away from your laptop.
- Maintain a connection with the audience by using a laser pointer to highlight slide items to discuss. Be aware, however, that a laser point dancing in a shaky hand may make you appear nervous. Steady your hand.
- Don't leave a slide on the screen when you are no longer discussing it. In Slide Show, View Show mode, strike B on the keyboard to turn the screen image on or off by blackening it. Pushing W will turn the screen white.

To avoid making PowerPoint the main event, a speaker should look at the audience, not at the screen; leave the lights on; and use other visualization techniques.

Some presenters allow their PowerPoint slides to steal their thunder. One expert urges speakers to "use their PowerPresence in preference to their PowerPoint."[8] Although multimedia presentations supply terrific sizzle, they cannot replace the steak. In developing a presentation, don't expect your slides to carry the show. You can avoid being upstaged by not relying totally on your slides. Help the audience visualize your points by using other techniques. Drawing a diagram on a whiteboard or flipchart can be more engaging than showing slide after slide of static drawings. Demonstrating or displaying real objects or props provides a welcome relief from slides. Remember that your slides should be used only to help your audience understand the message and to add interest. Your audience came to see and hear *you.*

Polishing Your Delivery and Following Up

learning objective

5

Once you've organized your presentation and prepared visuals, you are ready to practise delivering it. You'll feel more confident and appear more professional if you know more about various delivery methods and techniques to use before, during, and after your presentation.

Delivery Methods

Inexperienced speakers often feel that they must memorize an entire presentation to be effective. Unless you are an experienced performer, however, you will sound wooden and unnatural. What's more, forgetting your place can be disastrous! That's why we don't recommend memorizing an entire oral presentation. However, memorizing significant parts—the introduction, the conclusion, and perhaps a meaningful quotation—can be dramatic and impressive.

If memorizing won't work, is reading from a manuscript your best plan? Definitely not! Reading to an audience is boring and ineffective. Because reading suggests that you don't know your topic very well, the audience loses confidence in your expertise. Reading also prevents you from maintaining eye contact. You can't see audience reactions; consequently, you can't benefit from feedback.

Extemporaneous delivery results in more convincing presentations than those that are memorized or read.

Neither memorizing nor reading creates very convincing presentations. The best plan by far is to present extemporaneously, especially when you are displaying an electronic slideshow such as PowerPoint. Extemporaneous delivery means speaking freely, generally without notes, after preparation and rehearsing. It means that in your talk you comment on the electronic slideshow you have prepared and rehearsed several times. Remember, PowerPoint and other presentation software have replaced traditional outlines and notes. Reading notes or a manuscript in addition to PowerPoint slides will damage your credibility.

career coach

How to Avoid Stage Fright

Ever get nervous before making a presentation? Everyone does! And it's not all in your head, either. When you face something threatening or challenging, your body reacts in what psychologists call the fight-or-flight response. This response provides your body with increased energy to deal with threatening situations. It also creates those sensations—dry mouth, sweaty hands, increased heartbeat, and stomach butterflies—that we associate with stage fright. The fight-or-flight response arouses your body for action—in this case, making a presentation.

Because everyone feels some form of apprehension before speaking, it's impossible to eliminate the physiological symptoms altogether. You can, however, reduce their effects with the following techniques:

- **Breathe deeply.** Use deep breathing to ease your fight-or-flight symptoms. Inhale to a count of ten, hold the breath to a count of ten, and exhale to a count of ten. Concentrate on your counting and your breathing; both activities reduce your stress.
- **Convert your fear.** Don't view your sweaty palms and dry mouth as evidence of fear. Interpret them as symptoms of exuberance, excitement, and enthusiasm to share your ideas.
- **Know your topic.** Feel confident about your topic. Select a topic that you know well and that is relevant to your audience.
- **Use positive self-talk.** Remind yourself that you know your topic and are prepared. Tell yourself that the audience is on your side—because it is!
- **Shift the spotlight to your visuals.** At least some of the time the audience will be focusing on your slides, transparencies, handouts, or whatever you have prepared—and not totally on you.
- **Ignore any stumbles.** Don't apologize or confess your nervousness. If you keep going, the audience will forget any mistakes quickly.
- **Feel proud when you finish.** You'll be surprised how good you feel when you finish. Take pride in what you've accomplished, and your audience will reward you with applause and congratulations. Your body, of course, will call off the fight-or-flight response and return to normal!

If you give a talk without PowerPoint, however, you may use note cards or an outline containing key sentences and major ideas, but beware of reading from a script. By preparing and then practising with your notes, you can talk to your audience in a conversational manner. Your notes should be neither entire paragraphs nor single words. Instead, they should contain a complete sentence or two to introduce each major idea. Below the topic sentence(s), outline subpoints and illustrations. Note cards will keep you on track and prompt your memory, but only if you have rehearsed the presentation thoroughly.

Delivery Techniques

Stage fright is both natural and controllable.

Nearly everyone experiences some degree of stage fright when speaking before a group. "If you hear someone say he or she isn't nervous before a speech, you are talking either to a liar or a very boring speaker," says corporate speech consultant Dianna Booher.[9] Being afraid is quite natural and results from actual physiological changes occurring in your body. Faced with a frightening situation, your body responds with the fight-or-flight response, which is discussed more fully in the accompanying Career Coach box. You can learn to control and reduce stage fright, as well as to incorporate techniques for effective speaking, by using the following strategies and techniques before, during, and after your presentation.

Before Your Presentation

- **Prepare thoroughly.** One of the most effective strategies for reducing stage fright is knowing your subject thoroughly. Research your topic diligently and prepare a careful sentence outline. Those who try to "wing it" usually suffer the worst butterflies—and make the worst presentations.
- **Rehearse repeatedly.** When you rehearse, practise your entire presentation, not just the first half. Place your outline sentences on separate cards. You may also wish to include transitional sentences to help you move to the next topic. Use these cards as you practise, and include your visual aids in your rehearsal. Rehearse alone or before friends and family. Also try rehearsing on audio- or videotape so that you can evaluate your effectiveness.
- **Time yourself.** Most audiences tend to get restless during longer talks. Thus, try to complete your presentation in no more than 20 minutes. Set a timer during your rehearsal to measure your speaking time.
- **Check the room.** If you are using a computer, a projector, or sound equipment, be certain they are operational. Check electrical outlets and the position of the viewing screen. Ensure that the seating arrangement is appropriate to your needs.
- **Greet members of the audience.** Try to make contact with a few members of the audience when you enter the room, while you are waiting to be introduced, or when you walk to the podium. Your body language should convey friendliness, confidence, and enjoyment.
- **Practise stress reduction.** If you feel tension and fear while you are waiting for your turn to speak, use stress-reduction techniques such as deep breathing. Additional techniques to help you conquer stage fright are presented in the Career Coach box on the preceding page.

During Your Presentation

- **Begin with a pause.** When you first approach the audience, take a moment to adjust your notes and make yourself comfortable. Establish your control of the situation.
- **Present your first sentence from memory.** By memorizing your opening, you can immediately establish rapport with the audience through eye contact. You'll also sound confident and knowledgeable.
- **Maintain eye contact.** If the size of the audience overwhelms you, pick out two individuals on the right and two on the left. Talk directly to these people. But don't ignore listeners in the back of the room.

Eye contact, a moderate tone of voice, and natural movements enhance a presentation.

- **Control your voice and vocabulary.** This means speaking in moderate tones but loudly enough to be heard. Eliminate verbal static, such as *ah, er, you know,* and *um.* Silence is preferable to meaningless fillers when you are thinking about your next idea.
- **Put the brakes on.** Many novice speakers talk too rapidly, displaying their nervousness and making it very difficult for audience members to understand their ideas. Slow down and listen to what you are saying.
- **Move naturally.** If you have a lectern, don't remain glued to it. Move about casually and naturally. Avoid fidgeting with your notes, your clothing, or items in your pockets. Do not roll up your sleeves or put your hands in your pockets. Learn to use your body to express a point.

- **Use visual aids effectively.** You should discuss and interpret each visual aid for the audience. Move aside as you describe it so that it can be seen fully. Use a pointer if necessary, but steady your hand if it is shaking.
- **Avoid digressions.** Stick to your outline and notes. Don't suddenly include clever little anecdotes or digressions that occur to you on the spot. If it's not part of your rehearsed material, leave it out so that you can finish on time. Remember, too, that your audience may not be as enthralled with your topic as you are.
- **Summarize your main points.** Conclude your presentation by reiterating your main points or by emphasizing what you want the audience to think or do. Once you have announced your conclusion, proceed to it directly.

After Your Presentation

The time to answer questions, distribute handouts, and reiterate main points is after a presentation.

- **Distribute handouts.** If you prepared handouts with data the audience will need, pass them out when you finish.
- **Encourage questions.** If the situation permits a question-and-answer period, announce it at the beginning of your presentation. Then, when you finish, ask for questions. Set a time limit for questions and answers.
- **Repeat questions.** Although the speaker may hear the question, audience members often do not. Begin each answer with a repetition of the question. This also gives you thinking time. Then direct your answer to the entire audience.
- **Reinforce your main points.** You can use your answers to restate your primary ideas (*I'm glad you brought that up because it gives me a chance to elaborate on . . .*). In answering questions, avoid becoming defensive or debating the questioner.
- **Keep control.** Don't allow one individual to take over. Keep the entire audience involved.
- **Avoid *Yes, but* answers.** The word *but* immediately cancels any preceding message. Try replacing it with *and*. For example, *Yes, X has been tried. And Y works even better because . . .*
- **End with a summary and appreciation.** To signal the end of the session before you take the last question, say something like *We have time for just one more question.* As you answer the last question, try to work it into a summary of your main points. Then express appreciation to the audience for the opportunity to talk with them.

learning objective

6

Adapting to International and Cross-Cultural Audiences

Addressing cross-cultural audiences requires a speaker to consider audience expectations and cultural conventions.

Every good speaker adapts to the audience, and cross-cultural presentations call for special adjustments and sensitivity. When working with an interpreter or speaking before individuals whose English is limited, you'll need to be very careful about your language and choose simple English, avoid jargon and idioms, use short sentences, and pause frequently.

Beyond these basic language adaptations, however, more fundamental sensitivity is often necessary. In organizing a presentation for a cross-cultural audience, you may need to anticipate and adapt to different speaking conventions, values, and nonverbal behaviour. You may also need to contend with limited language skills and a certain reluctance to voice opinions openly.

In addressing cross-cultural audiences, anticipate expectations and perceptions that may differ significantly from what you may consider normal. Remember, for example, that the North American emphasis on getting to the point quickly is not equally prized across the globe. Therefore, think twice about delivering your main idea up front. Many people (notably those in Japanese, Latin American, and Arabic cultures) consider such directness to be brash and inappropriate. Remember that others may not share our cultural emphasis on straightforwardness.[10]

Also consider breaking your presentation into short, discrete segments and developing each topic separately, encouraging discussion periods after each. Such organization enables participants to ask questions and digest what has been presented. This technique is especially effective in cultures where people communicate in "loops." In the Middle East, for example, Arab speakers "mix circuitous, irrelevant (by North American standards) conversations with short dashes of information that go directly to the point." Presenters who are patient, tolerant, and "mature" (in the eyes of the audience) will make the sale or win the contract.[11]

Match your presentation to the expectations of your audience. In Germany, for instance, successful presentations tend to be dense with facts and precise statistics. North Americans might say "around 30 percent" while a German presenter might say "30.4271 percent." Similarly, constant smiling is not as valued in Europe as it is in North America. Many Europeans distrust a speaker who is making jokes, smiling, or laughing in a business presentation. Their expectation is for a rational—that is, serious—fact-based delivery.

Remember, too, that some cultures prefer greater formality than North Americans exercise. Instead of using first names, use only honorifics *(Mr.* or *Ms.*) and last names, as well as academic or business titles such as *Doctor* or *Director*. Writing on a flipchart or transparency seems natural and spontaneous in this country. Abroad, though, such informal techniques may suggest that the speaker does not value the audience enough to prepare proper visual aids in advance.[12]

Although you may have to exercise greater caution with culturally diverse audiences, you still want to use visual aids to help communicate your message. Find out from your international contact whether you can present in English or if you need an interpreter. In many countries listeners are too polite to speak up when they don't understand you.

To ensure clarity and show courtesy, provide handouts in both English and the target language. Never use numbers without projecting or writing them out for all to see. If possible, say numbers in both languages, but only if you can pronounce the target language well enough to avoid embarrassment. Distribute translated handouts summarizing your important information when you finish.

Whether you are speaking to familiar or cross-cultural audiences, your presentation requires attention to content and strategy. The following checklist summarizes suggestions for preparing, organizing, and illustrating oral presentations.

Checklist for Preparing and Organizing Oral Presentations

Getting Ready to Speak

 **Identify your purpose.** Decide what you want your audience to believe, remember, or do when you finish. Aim all parts of your talk toward this purpose.

- **Analyze the audience.** Consider how to adapt your message (its organization, appeals, and examples) to your audience's knowledge and needs.

Organizing the Introduction

- **Get the audience involved.** Capture the audience's attention by opening with a promise, story, startling fact, question, quote, relevant problem, or self-effacing joke.
- **Establish yourself.** Demonstrate your credibility by identifying your position, expertise, knowledge, or qualifications.
- **Preview your main points.** Introduce your topic and summarize its principal parts.

Organizing the Body

- **Develop two to four main points.** Streamline your topic so that you can concentrate on its major issues.
- **Arrange the points logically.** Sequence your points chronologically, from most important to least important, by comparison and contrast, or by some other strategy.
- **Prepare transitions.** Between each major point, write bridge statements that connect the previous item to the next one. Use transitional expressions as verbal signposts (*first, second, then, however, consequently, on the contrary*, and so forth).
- **Have extra material ready.** Be prepared with more information and visuals in case you have additional time to fill.

Organizing the Conclusion

- **Review your main points.** Emphasize your main ideas in your closing so that your audience will remember them.
- **Provide a final focus.** Tell how your listeners can use this information, why you have spoken, or what you want them to do.

Designing Visual Aids

- **Select your medium carefully.** Consider the pros and cons of each alternative.
- **Highlight main ideas.** Use visual aids to illustrate major concepts only. Keep them brief and simple.
- **Use aids skillfully.** Talk to the audience, not to the visuals. Paraphrase their contents.

Developing Multimedia Presentations

- **Learn to use your software program.** Study template and slide layout designs to see how you can adapt them to your purposes.

- ✓ **Select colours based on the light level in the room.** Consider how mixing light and dark fonts and backgrounds affects their visibility.
- ✓ **Use bulleted points for major ideas.** Make sure your points are all parallel and observe the 6-x-6 rule.
- ✓ **Include multimedia options that will help you convey your message.**
- ✓ **Make speaker's notes.** Jot down the narrative supporting each slide and use these notes to practise your presentation.
- ✓ **Maintain control.** Don't let your slides upstage you. Engage your audience by using additional techniques to help them visualize your points.

Improving Telephone and Voice Mail Skills

learning objective 7

One form of business presentation involves presenting yourself on the telephone, a skill that is still very important in today's workplace. Despite the heavy reliance on e-mail, the telephone is still an extremely important piece of equipment in offices. With the addition of today's wireless technology, it doesn't matter whether you are in or out of the office—you can always be reached by phone. This section focuses on traditional telephone techniques and voice mail, both opportunities for making a good impression. As a business communicator, you can be more productive, efficient, and professional by following some simple suggestions.

Telephones and voice mail should promote goodwill and increase productivity.

Making Telephone Calls Efficiently

Before making a telephone call, decide whether the intended call is really necessary. Could you find the information yourself? If you wait a while, will the problem resolve itself? Perhaps your message could be delivered more efficiently by some other means. Some companies have found that telephone calls are often less important than the work they interrupted. Alternatives to telephone calls include instant messaging, e-mail, memos, or calls to automated voice mail systems. If you must make a telephone call, consider using the following suggestions to make it fully productive.

Making productive telephone calls means planning an agenda, identifying the purpose, being courteous and cheerful, and avoiding rambling.

- **Plan a mini-agenda.** Have you ever been embarrassed when you had to make a second telephone call because you forgot an important item the first time? Before placing a call, jot down notes regarding all the topics you need to discuss. Following an agenda guarantees not only a complete call but also a quick one. You'll be less likely to wander from the business at hand while rummaging through your mind trying to remember everything.
- **Use a three-point introduction.** When placing a call, immediately (a) name the person you are calling, (b) identify yourself and your affiliation, and (c) give a brief explanation of your reason for calling
- **Be brisk if you are rushed.** For business calls when your time is limited, avoid questions such as *How are you?* Instead, say, *Lisa, I knew you'd be the only one who could answer these two questions for me.* Another efficient strategy is to set a "contract" with the caller: *Look, Lisa, I have only ten minutes, but I really wanted to get back to you.*

- **Be cheerful and accurate.** Let your voice show the same kind of animation that you radiate when you greet people in person. In your mind, try to envision the individual answering the telephone. A smile can certainly affect the tone of your voice, so smile at that person. Keep your voice and throat relaxed by keeping your head straight. Don't squeeze the phone between your shoulder and your ear. Moreover, be accurate about what you say. *Hang on a second; I'll be right back* is rarely true. It's better to say *It may take me two or three minutes to get that information. Would you prefer to hold or have me call you back?*
- **Bring it to a close.** The responsibility for ending a call lies with the caller. This is sometimes difficult to do if the other person rambles on. You may need to use suggestive closing language, such as *I've certainly enjoyed talking with you. I've learned what I needed to know, and now I can proceed with my work.*
- **Avoid telephone tag.** If you call someone who's not in, ask when it would be best for you to call again. State that you will call at a specific time—and do it. If you ask a person to call you, give a time when you can be reached—and then be sure you are in at that time.
- **Leave complete voice mail messages.** Remember that there's no rush when you leave a voice mail message. Always enunciate clearly. And be sure to provide a complete message, including your name, telephone number, and the time and date of your call. Explain your purpose so that the receiver can be ready with the required information when returning your call.

Receiving Telephone Calls Professionally

Receiving telephone calls productively means identifying yourself, being responsive, acting helpful, and taking accurate messages.

With a little forethought you can project a professional image and make your telephone a productive, efficient work tool. Developing good telephone manners and techniques will reflect well on you and also on your organization.

- **Identify yourself immediately.** In answering your telephone or someone else's, provide your name, title or affiliation, and, possibly, a greeting. For example, *Larry Lopez, Proteus Software. How may I help you?* Force yourself to speak clearly and slowly. Remember that the caller may be unfamiliar with what you are saying and fail to recognize slurred syllables.
- **Be responsive and helpful.** If you are in a support role, be sympathetic to callers' needs. Instead of *I don't know*, try *That's a good question; let me investigate.* Instead of *We can't do that*, try *That's a tough one; let's see what we can do.* Avoid *no* at the beginning of a sentence; it sounds especially abrasive and displeasing because it suggests total rejection.
- **Practise telephone confidentiality.** When answering calls for others, be courteous and helpful, but don't give out confidential information. Better to say *She's away from her desk* or *He's out of the office* than to report a colleague's exact whereabouts.
- **Take messages carefully.** Few things are as frustrating as receiving a potentially important phone message that is illegible. Repeat the spelling of names and verify telephone numbers. Write messages legibly and record their time and date. Promise to give the messages to intended recipients, but don't guarantee return calls.
- **Explain what you're doing when transferring calls.** Give a reason for transferring, and identify the extension to which you are directing the call in case the caller is disconnected.

Making the Best Use of Voice Mail

Because telephone calls can be disruptive, many businesspeople are making extensive use of voice mail to intercept and screen incoming calls. Voice mail links a telephone system to a computer that digitizes and stores incoming messages. Some systems also provide functions such as automated attendant menus, allowing callers to reach any associated extension by pushing specific buttons.

Voice mail eliminates telephone tag, inaccurate message taking, and time-zone barriers; it also allows communicators to focus on essentials.

Voice mail is quite efficient for message storage. Because as many as half of all business calls require no discussion or feedback, the messaging capabilities of voice mail can mean huge savings for businesses. Incoming information is delivered without interrupting potential receivers and without all the niceties that most two-way conversations require. Stripped of superfluous chit-chat, voice mail messages allow communicators to focus on essentials. Voice mail also eliminates telephone tag, inaccurate message taking, and time-zone barriers.

However, voice mail should not be overused. Individuals who screen all incoming calls cause irritation, resentment, and needless telephone tag. Here are some ways to make voice mail work most effectively for you:

- **Announce your voice mail.** If you rely principally on a voice mail message system, identify it on your business stationery and cards. Then, when people call, they will be ready to leave a message.
- **Prepare a warm and informative greeting.** Make your mechanical greeting sound warm and inviting, both in tone and content. Identify yourself and your organization so that callers know they have reached the right number. Thank the caller and briefly explain that you are unavailable. Invite the caller to leave a message or, if appropriate, to call back.
- **Test your message.** Call your number and assess your message. Does it sound inviting? sincere? understandable? Are you pleased with your tone? If not, says one consultant, have someone else, perhaps a professional, record a message for you.

Summary of Learning Objectives

1 **Discuss two important first steps in preparing effective oral presentations.** First, identify what your purpose is and what you want the audience to believe or do, so that you can aim the entire presentation toward your goal. Second, know your audience so that you can adjust your message and style to its knowledge and needs.

2 **Explain the major elements in organizing the content of a presentation, including the introduction, body, and conclusion.** The introduction of a good presentation should capture the listener's attention, identify the speaker, establish credibility, and preview the main points. The body should discuss two to four main points, with appropriate explanations, details, and verbal signposts to guide listeners. The conclusion should review the main points, provide a final focus, and allow the speaker to leave the podium gracefully.

3 **Identify techniques for gaining audience rapport, including using effective imagery, providing verbal signposts, and sending appropriate nonverbal messages.** You can improve audience rapport by using effective imagery, including analogies, metaphors, similes, personal anecdotes, statistics, and best-case/worst-case scenarios. Rapport is also gained by including verbal signposts that tell the audience when you are previewing, summarizing, and

switching directions. Nonverbal messages have a powerful effect on the way your message is received. You should look terrific, animate your movements, punctuate your words, get out from behind the podium, and vary your facial expressions.

4 **Discuss designing and using effective visual aids, handouts, and multimedia presentation materials and using presentation technology competently.** Use simple, easily understood visual aids to emphasize and clarify main points. Choose multimedia slides, transparencies, flipcharts, or other visuals. Generally, it is best to distribute handouts after a presentation. Speakers employing a program such as PowerPoint use templates, layout designs, and bullet points to produce effective slides. A presentation may be enhanced with slide transitions, sound, animation, video elements, and other multimedia effects. Speaker's notes and handouts may be generated from slides.

5 **Specify delivery techniques for use before, during, and after a presentation, and apply reflective thinking skills.** Before your talk prepare a sentence outline on note cards or speaker's notes and rehearse repeatedly. Check the room, lectern, and equipment. During the presentation consider beginning with a pause and presenting your first sentence from memory. Speak freely and extemporaneously, commenting on your slides but using no other notes. Make eye contact, control your voice, speak and move naturally, and avoid digressions. After your talk distribute handouts and answer questions. End gracefully and express appreciation.

6 **Explain effective techniques for adapting oral presentations to cross-cultural audiences.** In presentations before groups whose English is limited, speak slowly, use simple English, avoid jargon and idioms, and opt for short sentences. Consider building up to your main idea rather than announcing it immediately. Also consider breaking the presentation into short segments to allow participants to ask questions and digest small parts separately. Beware of appearing too spontaneous and informal. Use visual aids to help communicate your message, but also distribute translated handouts summarizing the most important information.

7 **List techniques for improving telephone and voice mail skills to project a positive image.** You can improve your telephone calls by planning a mini-agenda and using a three-point introduction (name, affiliation, and purpose). Be cheerful and responsive, and use closing language to end a conversation. Avoid telephone tag by leaving complete messages. In answering calls, identify yourself immediately, avoid giving out confidential information when answering for others, and take careful messages. For your own message prepare a warm and informative greeting and tell when you will be available. Evaluate your message by calling your own number.

chapter review

1. In preparing an oral presentation, you can reduce your fears and lay a foundation for a professional performance by focusing on what five areas? (Obj. 1)
2. In the introduction of an oral presentation, you can establish your credibility by using what two methods? (Obj. 2)
3. For a 20-minute presentation, how many main points should be developed? (Obj. 2)
4. Which part of a speech—the introduction, body, or conclusion—will listeners most remember? (Obj. 2)
5. List six techniques for creating effective imagery in a presentation. Be prepared to discuss each. (Obj. 3)
6. Name three ways for a speaker to use verbal signposts in a presentation. Illustrate each. (Obj. 3)
7. Why are visual aids particularly useful for inexperienced speakers? (Obj. 4)
8. Why are transparencies a favourite visual aid? (Obj. 4)
9. Name specific advantages and disadvantages of multimedia presentation software. (Obj. 4)
10. How is the 6-x-6 rule applied in preparing bulleted points? (Obj. 4)
11. What delivery method is most effective for speakers? (Obj. 5)
12. Why should speakers deliver the first sentence from memory? (Obj. 5)
13. How might presentations before international or cross-cultural audiences be altered to be most effective? (Obj. 6)
14. What is a three-point introduction for a telephone call? (Obj. 7)

critical thinking

1. Why is it necessary to repeat key points in an oral presentation? (Objs. 2 and 5)
2. How can a speaker make the most effective use of visual aids? (Obj. 4)
3. How can speakers prevent multimedia presentation software from stealing their thunder? (Obj. 4)
4. Discuss effective techniques for reducing stage fright. (Obj. 5)

activities

15.1 Critiquing a Speech (Objs. 1–4)

Your Task. Search online or at your library for a speech that has been delivered by a significant businessperson or a well-known political figure. Write a memo report to your instructor critiquing the speech in terms of the following:

a. Effectiveness of the introduction, body, and conclusion
b. Evidence of effective overall organization
c. Use of verbal signposts to create coherence
d. Emphasis of two to four main points
e. Effectiveness of supporting facts (use of examples, statistics, quotations, and so forth)

15.2 Knowing Your Audience (Objs. 1–2)

Your Task. Select a recent issue of *Fortune, Canadian Business, BusinessWeek*, or another periodical related to your field and approved by your instructor. Based on your analysis of your classmates, select an article that will appeal to them and that you can relate to their needs. Submit to your instructor a one-page summary that includes the following: (a) author, article title, source, issue date, and page reference; (b) a one-paragraph article summary; (c) a description of why you believe the article will appeal to your classmates; and (d) a summary of how you can relate the article to their needs.

15.3 Overcoming Stage Fright (Obj. 5)

What makes you most nervous when making a presentation before class? Being tongue-tied? Fearing all eyes are on you? Messing up? Forgetting your ideas and looking silly?
Your Task. Discuss the previous questions as a class. Then, in groups of three or four, talk about ways to overcome these fears. Your instructor may ask you to write a memo (individual or collective) summarizing your suggestions, or you may break out of your small groups and report your best ideas to the entire class.

15.4 Outlining an Oral Presentation (Objs. 1 and 2)

One of the hardest parts of preparing an oral presentation is developing the outline.
Your Task. Select an oral presentation topic from the list in Activity 15.5 or suggest an original topic. Prepare an outline for your presentation using the following format.

Title	
Purpose	
	I. INTRODUCTION
Gain attention of audience	A.
Involve audience	B.
Establish credibility	C.
Preview main points	D.
Transition	
	II. BODY
Main point	A.
Illustrate, clarify, contrast	1.
	2.
	3.
Transition	
Main point	B.
Illustrate, clarify, contrast	1.
	2.
	3.
Transition	
Main point	C.
Illustrate, clarify, contrast	1.
	2.
	3.
Transition	
	III. CONCLUSION
Summarize main points	A.
Provide final focus	B.
Encourage questions	C.

15.5 Choosing a Topic for an Oral Presentation (Objs. 1–5)

Your Task. Select a topic from the following list or from topics provided by your instructor. Prepare a five- to ten-minute oral presentation. Consider yourself an expert who has been called in to explain some aspect of the topic before a group of interested people. Because your time is limited, prepare a concise yet forceful presentation with effective visual aids.

a. What are the top five career opportunities for your college major? Consider job growth, compensation, and benefits. What kind of academic and other experience is typically required to apply for each?

b. What franchise would offer the best investment opportunity for an entrepreneur in your area?

c. How should a job candidate dress for an interview?

d. Are internships worth the effort?

e. What would you need to know if you were deciding whether to go to the next Olympics?

f. What do the personal assistants for celebrities do, and how does one become a personal assistant? (Investigate the Association of Celebrity Personal Assistants.)

g. Can a small or mid-sized company reduce its telephone costs by using Internet phone service?

h. What scams are identified on Industry Canada's Competition Bureau Web site (**http://www.cb-bc.gc.ca**), and how can consumers avoid falling for them?

i. How are businesses and conservationists working together to protect the world's dwindling tropical forests?

j. Should employees be able to use computers in a work environment for anything other than work-related business?

15.6 Improving Telephone Skills by Role-Playing (Obj. 7)

Your Task. Your instructor will divide the class into pairs. For each scenario, take a moment to read and rehearse your role silently. Then play the role with your partner. If time permits, repeat the scenarios, changing roles.

Partner 1

a. You are the personnel manager of Datatronics, Inc. Call Elizabeth Franklin, office manager at Computers Plus. Inquire about a job applicant, Chelsea Chavez, who listed Ms. Franklin as a reference.

b. Call Ms. Franklin again the following day to inquire about the same job applicant, Chelsea Chavez. Ms. Franklin answers today, but she talks on and on, describing the applicant in great detail. Tactfully close the conversation.

Partner 2

a. You are the receptionist for Computers Plus. The caller asks for Elizabeth Franklin, who is home sick today. You don't know when she will be able to return. Answer the call appropriately.

b. You are now Ms. Franklin, office manager. Describe Chelsea Chavez, an imaginary employee. Think of someone with whom you've worked. Include many details, such as her ability to work with others, her appearance, her skills at computing, her schooling, her ambition, and so forth.

C.L.U.E. review 15

On a separate sheet edit the following sentences to correct faults in grammar, punctuation, spelling, and word use.

1. Even though he was President of the company Mr Thomas dreaded the 2 or 3 presentations he made everyyear.
2. The companies CGA asked my colleague and I to explain the principle ways we planned to finance it's thirty year mortgage?
3. My team and I are greatful to be able to give a twenty minute presentation however we can emphasize only 3 or 4 major point.
4. The Introduction to a presentation should accomplish 3 goals (a) Capture attention, (b) Establish credibility and (c) Preview main points.
5. Travis wondered whether focusing on what you want the audience to remember, and summarizing you're main points was equally important in the Conclusion?
6. Speakers must remember that there listeners unlike readers' can not controll the rate of presentation, or flip back thorough pages to review main points.
7. Most novice speakers talk to rapidly, however they can learn to speak more slow, and listen to what they are saying.
8. When speakers first approach the audience they should take a moment to adjust there notes, and make yourself comfortable.
9. One West coast company found that, telephone interruptions consumed about eighteen percent of staff members workdays.
10. Good telephone manners reflect on you and you're company however to few employees are trained proper.

chapter 16

Employment Communication

objectives

1 Prepare for employment by identifying your interests, evaluating your assets, recognizing the changing nature of jobs, choosing a career path, and studying traditional and electronic job-search techniques.

2 Compare and contrast chronological, functional, and combination résumés.

3 Organize, format, and produce a customized résumé.

4 Describe techniques that optimize a résumé for today's technologies, including preparing a scannable résumé, an online résumé, and an e-portfolio.

5 Write a customized cover letter to accompany a résumé.

6 Write effective employment follow-up letters and other messages.

7 Evaluate successful job interview strategies.

springboard *to discussion*

Be careful what you post on Facebook! Many recruiters and hiring managers use the Internet as a tool to evaluate the fit of a potential candidate.[1] Making a good impression on the job hunt may include managing your digital reputation. Half (50 percent) of advertising and marketing executives recently polled said they search online for information about prospective hires at least some of the time. Among those, 14 percent have decided not to hire someone based on their findings.[2]

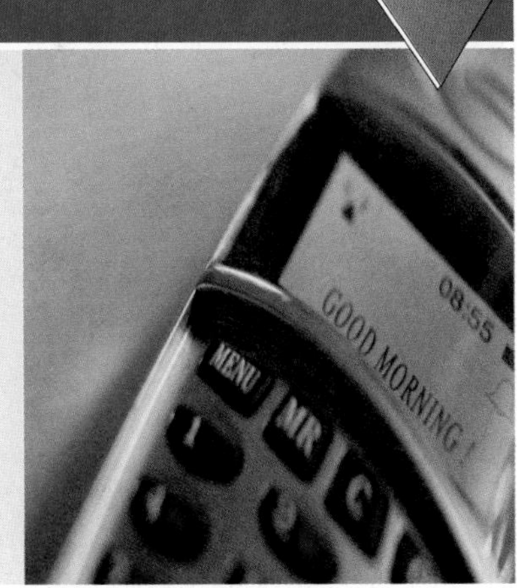

Preparing for Employment

learning objective 1

The Internet has definitely changed the way we look for jobs today, and it has made job searching easier but also more challenging. Because hundreds and perhaps thousands of candidates may be applying for an advertised position, you must do everything possible to be noticed and to outshine the competition. You must also look beyond the Internet.

The better prepared you are, the more confident you will feel during your search. This chapter provides many tips for writing dynamite résumés and cover letters, as well as suggestions for successful interviewing.

Finding a satisfying career means learning about yourself, the job market, and the employment process.

You may think that the first step in finding a job is writing a résumé. Wrong! The job-search process actually begins long before you are ready to prepare your résumé. Regardless of the kind of employment you seek, you must invest time and effort getting ready. You can't hope to find the position of your dreams without (a) knowing yourself, (b) knowing the job market, and (c) knowing the employment process.

One of the first things you should do is obtain career information and choose a specific job objective. At the same time, you should be studying the job market and becoming aware of significant changes in the workplace and hiring techniques. You will want to understand how to use the latest Web resources in your job search. Finally, you'll need to design a résumé and cover letter that can be customized for small businesses as well as for larger organizations that may be using résumé-scanning programs. Following these steps, summarized in Figure 16.1 (page 407) and described in this chapter, gives you a master plan for landing a job you really want.

Identifying Your Interests

Answer specific questions to help yourself choose a career.

The employment process begins with introspection. This means looking inside yourself to analyze what you like and dislike so that you can make good employment choices. Career counsellors charge large sums for helping individuals learn about themselves. You can do the same kind of self-examination—without spending a dime. For guidance in choosing a field that eventually proves to be satisfying, answer the following questions. If you have already chosen a field, think carefully about how your answers relate to that choice.

- *Do you enjoy working with people, data, or things?*
- *Would you like to work for someone else or be your own boss?*

- *How important are salary, benefits, technology support, and job stability?*
- *How important are working environment, colleagues, and job stimulation?*
- *Would you rather work for a large or small company?*
- *Must you work in a specific city, geographical area, or climate?*
- *Are you looking for security, travel opportunities, money, power, or prestige?*
- *How would you describe the perfect job, boss, and coworkers?*

Evaluating Your Qualifications

Decide what qualifications you possess and how you can prove you have them.

In addition to your interests, assess your qualifications. Employers today want to know what assets you have to offer them. Your responses to the following questions will target your thinking as well as prepare a foundation for your résumé. Remember, though, that employers seek more than empty assurances; they will want proof of your qualifications.

- *What computer skills can you offer?* Employers are often interested in specific software programs.
- *What other skills have you acquired in school, on the job, or through activities?* How can you demonstrate these skills?
- *Do you work well with people? Do you enjoy teamwork?* What proof can you offer? Consider extracurricular activities, clubs, class projects, and jobs.
- *Are you a leader, self-starter, or manager?* What evidence can you offer?
- *Do you speak, write, or understand another language?*
- *Do you learn quickly? Are you creative?* How can you demonstrate these characteristics?
- *Do you communicate well in speech and in writing?* How can you verify these talents?

Recognizing the Changing Nature of Jobs

People feel less job security after the downsizing and outsourcing of jobs.

As you learned in Chapter 1, the nature of the workplace is changing. One of the most significant changes involves the concept of the job. Following the downsizing of corporations and the outsourcing of jobs in recent years, companies are employing fewer people in permanent positions.

Jobs are becoming more flexible and less permanent.

Other forms of employment are replacing traditional jobs. In many companies teams complete special projects and then disband. Work may also be outsourced to a group that's not even part of an organization. Because new technologies can spring up overnight, making today's skills obsolete, employers are less willing to hire people into jobs with narrow descriptions. Instead, they are hiring contingency employees who work temporarily and then leave. What's more, big companies are no longer the main employers. People work for smaller companies, or they are starting their own businesses. In fact, more than 78 percent of businesses in Canada have fewer than five employees,[3] and self-employment is growing rapidly. According to a Statistics Canada manager, almost one in five workers is self-employed.[4]

What do these changes mean for you? For one thing, you should probably forget about a lifelong career with a single company. Don't count on regular pay raises, promotions, and a comfortable retirement income. You should also become keenly aware that a career that relies on yesterday's skills is headed for trouble. You're going to need updated, marketable skills that serve you well as you move from job to job.

Figure 16.1 ***The Employment Search***

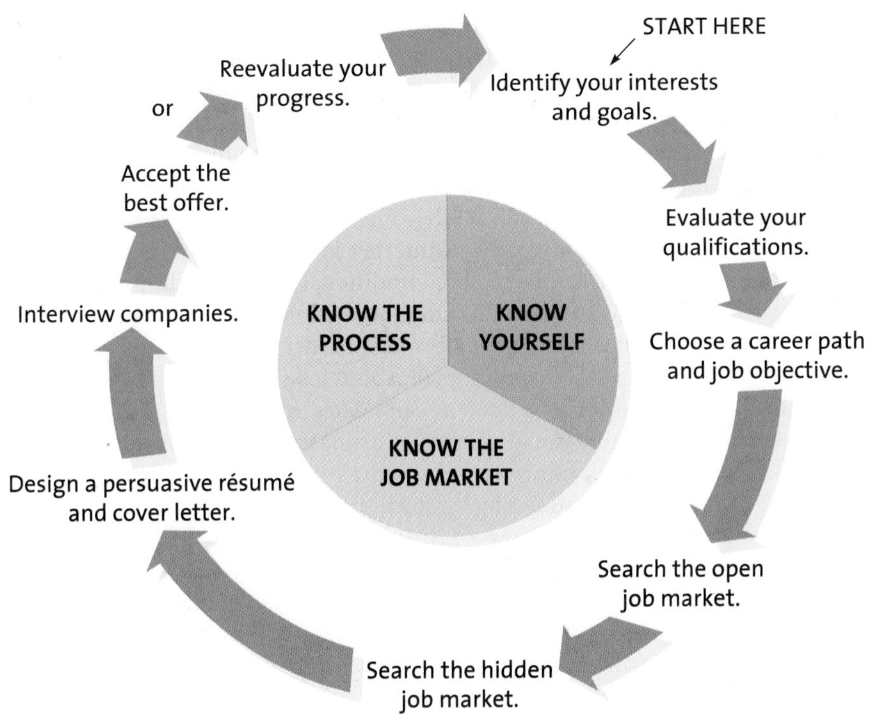

Upgrading your skills and retraining yourself constantly is the best career strategy for the twenty-first century. People who learn quickly and adapt to change will always be in demand, even in a climate of surging change.[5]

Choosing a Career Path

The employment picture today is much different from that of a decade or two ago. By the time you are 30, you can expect to have had five to seven jobs. The average employee will have worked at 12 to 15 jobs over the course of a career, staying an average of 3.6 years at each job.[6] Although you may be changing jobs in the future (especially before your reach 40), you still need to train for a specific career area now. In choosing an area, you'll make the best decisions when you can match your interests and qualifications with the requirements and rewards of specific careers. Where can you find the best career data? Here are some suggestions:

Career information can be obtained at campus career centres and libraries, from the Internet, in classified ads, and from professional organizations.

- Visit your campus career centre.
- Search the Web.
- Use your library.
- Take a summer job, internship, or part-time position in your field.
- Interview someone in your chosen field.
- Volunteer with a nonprofit organization.
- Monitor the classified ads.
- Join professional organizations in your field.

Summer and part-time jobs and internships are good opportunities to learn about different careers.

Searching for a Job Electronically

Job boards list many jobs, but finding a job requires more work than merely clicking a mouse.

Many jobs are posted on the Internet, but most hiring is still done through personal contact.

Searching for a job today is vastly different as a result of the Internet. In the past, a job seeker browsed the local classified ads, found a likely sounding job listing, prepared an elegant résumé on bond paper, and sent it out by mail. All that has changed with the advent of the Internet. The challenge today is realizing how to use the Internet to your advantage. Like other job seekers, you can combine both electronic and traditional job-search tactics to land the job of your dreams.

Searching for a job electronically has become a common, but not always fruitful, approach. With all the publicity given to Internet job boards, you might think that electronic job searching has totally replaced traditional methods. Although Web sites such as Workopolis (**www.workopolis.com**) and Monster (**www.monster.ca**) list thousands of jobs, actually landing a job is much harder than just clicking a mouse.

Both recruiters and job seekers complain about job boards. Corporate recruiters say that the big job boards bring a flood of candidates, many of whom are not suited for the listed jobs. Job candidates grumble that listings are frequently out of date and fail to produce leads. Applicants worry about the privacy of information posted at big boards. Most important, studies have shown that the percentage of hires resulting from job boards is astonishingly low—1.4 percent at Monster.com, 0.39 percent at HotJobs.com, and 0.27 percent at CareerBuilder.com.[7]

Job boards are valuable tools for gathering job search information such as résumé, interviewing, and salary tips. They also serve as a jumping-off point in most searches. They can inform you about the kinds of jobs that are available and the skill sets required. Following are the most common sites:[8]

- Workpolis.com
- Monster.ca
- Working.com
- Jobshark.ca
- HotJobs.ca
- Human Resources and Social Development Canada (**www.hrsdc.gc.ca**)

Beyond the Big Job Boards. Disillusioned job seekers increasingly turn their backs on job boards but not on electronic job-searching tactics. Skilled candidates know how to use their computers to search for jobs at corporate, association, and niche Web sites.

Candidates are doing less pavement pounding and more keyboard pounding in searching for jobs today. Experts say that one-third of all new hires now come through the Internet, and the majority of those leads come from the company's own Web site. Including a referral from a company employee helps to send your résumé to the top of the pile.

Photo: © Rubberball Productions/Getty Images

Searching for a Job Using Traditional Techniques

Finding the perfect job requires an early start and a determined effort. Whether you use traditional or online job-search techniques, you should be prepared to launch an aggressive campaign. Moreover, you can't start too early. Traditional job-search techniques, such as those described here, continue to be critical in landing jobs.

- Check classified ads in local and national newspapers.
- Check announcements in publications of professional organizations.
- Contact companies in which you're interested, even if you know of no current opening.
- Attend career fairs.
- Ask for advice from your professors.
- Develop your own network of contacts.

The Customized Résumé

learning objective 2

After using both online and traditional resources to learn about the employment market and to develop job leads, you'll focus on writing a customized résumé. This means you will prepare a special résumé for every position you want. The competition is so stiff today that you cannot get by with a generic, all-purpose résumé. Although you can start with a basic résumé, you should customize it to fit each company and position if you want your résumé to stand out from the crowd. Include many keywords that describe the skills, traits, tasks, and job titles associated with your targeted job.

The Internet has made it so easy to apply that recruiters are swamped with applications. As a job seeker, you have about five seconds to catch the recruiter's eye—if your résumé is even read by a person. Many companies use computer scanning technologies to weed out unqualified candidates.[9] Your goal is to make your résumé fit the targeted position and stand out. Such a résumé does more than merely list your qualifications. It packages your assets into a convincing advertisement that sells you for a specific job.

The goal of a résumé is winning an interview. Even if you are not in the job market at this moment, preparing a résumé now has advantages. Having a current résumé makes you look well organized and professional should an unexpected employment opportunity arise. Moreover, preparing a résumé early can help you recognize weak areas and give you time to bolster them. It is a good idea to keep your résumé up-to-date. You never know when an opportunity may come along.

Winning an interview is the goal of a customized résumé.

Choosing a Résumé Style

Your qualifications and career goal will help you choose from among three résumé styles: chronological, functional, and combination.

Chronological. The most popular résumé format is the chronological résumé, shown in Figure 16.2 on the next page. It lists your work history job by job, starting with the most recent position. Recruiters often favour the chronological style because such résumés quickly reveal a candidate's education and experience record. Recruiters are familiar with the chronological résumé, and as many as 85 percent of employers prefer to see a candidate's résumé in this format.[10] The chronological style works well for candidates who have less experience in their field of employment and for those who show steady career growth, but it is less appropriate for people who have changed jobs frequently or who have gaps in their employment records. For college students and others who lack extensive experience, the functional résumé format may be preferable.

Chronological résumés focus on job history, with most recent positions listed first.

Functional. The functional résumé, shown in Figure 16.3 (page 411), focuses attention on a candidate's skills rather than on past employment. Like a chronological résumé, the functional résumé begins with the candidate's name, address, telephone number, job objective, and education. Instead of listing jobs, though, the functional résumé groups skills and accomplishments in special categories, such as *Supervisory and Management Skills* or *Retailing and Marketing Experience.* This résumé style highlights accomplishments and can deemphasize a negative employment history. People who are changing careers or who do not have steady employment histories may prefer the functional résumé. Recent graduates with little or no employment experience often find the functional résumé useful. Older job seekers who want to downplay a long job history and job hunters who are afraid of appearing overquali-

Because functional résumés focus on skills, they may be more advisable for graduates with little experience.

FIGURE 16.2 ***Chronological Résumé***

1 Prewriting

ANALYZE: The purpose is to respond to a job advertisement and win an interview.

ANTICIPATE: The reader probably sees many résumés and will skim this one quickly. He or she will be indifferent and must be persuaded to read on.

ADAPT: Emphasize the specific skills that the targeted advertisement mentions.

2 Writing

RESEARCH: Investigate the targeted company and its needs. Find the name of the person who will be receiving this résumé

ORGANIZE: Make lists of all accomplishments and skills. Select those items most appropriate for the targeted job.

COMPOSE: Experiment with formats to achieve readability, emphasis, and attractiveness.

3 Revising

REVISE: Use present-tense verbs to describe current experience. Bullet experience items. Check for parallel phrasing. Adjust spacing for best effect.

PROOFREAD: Be sure to run your spell checker. Read for meaning. Have a friend proofread and critique your draft.

EVALUATE: Will this résumé impress a recruiter in 30 seconds? Will it prompt an invitation to an interview?

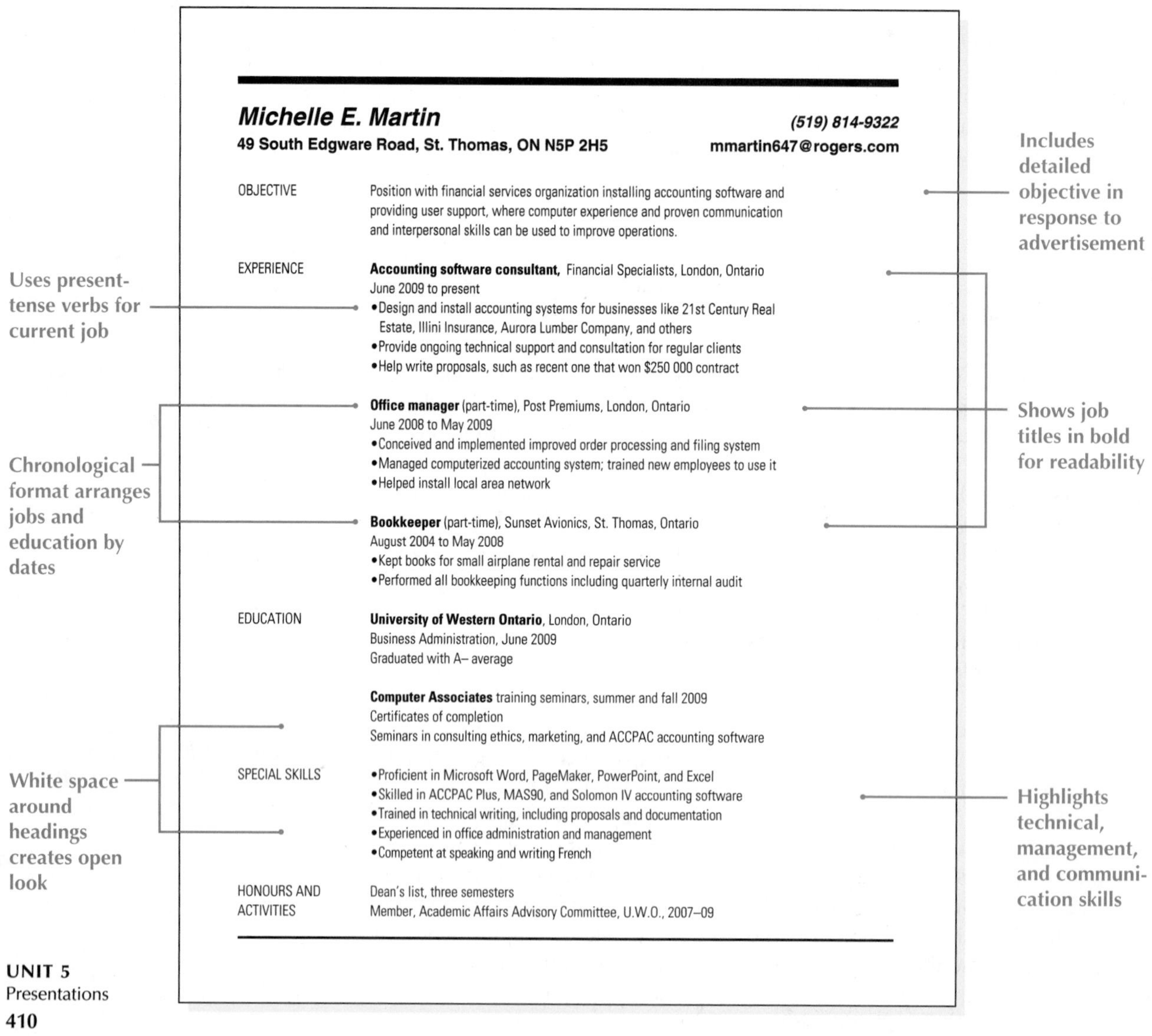

Michelle E. Martin — ***(519) 814-9322***

49 South Edgware Road, St. Thomas, ON N5P 2H5 — **mmartin647@rogers.com**

OBJECTIVE

Position with financial services organization installing accounting software and providing user support, where computer experience and proven communication and interpersonal skills can be used to improve operations.

EXPERIENCE

Accounting software consultant, Financial Specialists, London, Ontario
June 2009 to present
- Design and install accounting systems for businesses like 21st Century Real Estate, Illini Insurance, Aurora Lumber Company, and others
- Provide ongoing technical support and consultation for regular clients
- Help write proposals, such as recent one that won $250 000 contract

Office manager (part-time), Post Premiums, London, Ontario
June 2008 to May 2009
- Conceived and implemented improved order processing and filing system
- Managed computerized accounting system; trained new employees to use it
- Helped install local area network

Bookkeeper (part-time), Sunset Avionics, St. Thomas, Ontario
August 2004 to May 2008
- Kept books for small airplane rental and repair service
- Performed all bookkeeping functions including quarterly internal audit

EDUCATION

University of Western Ontario, London, Ontario
Business Administration, June 2009
Graduated with A– average

Computer Associates training seminars, summer and fall 2009
Certificates of completion
Seminars in consulting ethics, marketing, and ACCPAC accounting software

SPECIAL SKILLS

- Proficient in Microsoft Word, PageMaker, PowerPoint, and Excel
- Skilled in ACCPAC Plus, MAS90, and Solomon IV accounting software
- Trained in technical writing, including proposals and documentation
- Experienced in office administration and management
- Competent at speaking and writing French

HONOURS AND ACTIVITIES

Dean's list, three semesters
Member, Academic Affairs Advisory Committee, U.W.O., 2007–09

Includes detailed objective in response to advertisement
Uses present-tense verbs for current job
Shows job titles in bold for readability
Chronological format arranges jobs and education by dates
White space around headings creates open look
Highlights technical, management, and communication skills

FIGURE 16.3 *Functional Résumé*

Recent graduate Kevin Touhy chose this functional format to de-emphasize his meagre work experience and emphasize his potential in sales and marketing. This version of his résumé is more generic than one targeted for a specific position. Yet, it emphasizes his strong points with specific achievements and includes an employment section to satisfy recruiters.

The functional format presents ability-focused topics. It illustrates what the job seeker can do for the employer instead of narrating a history of previous jobs. Although recruiters prefer chronological résumés, the functional format is a good choice for new graduates, career changers, and those with employment gaps.

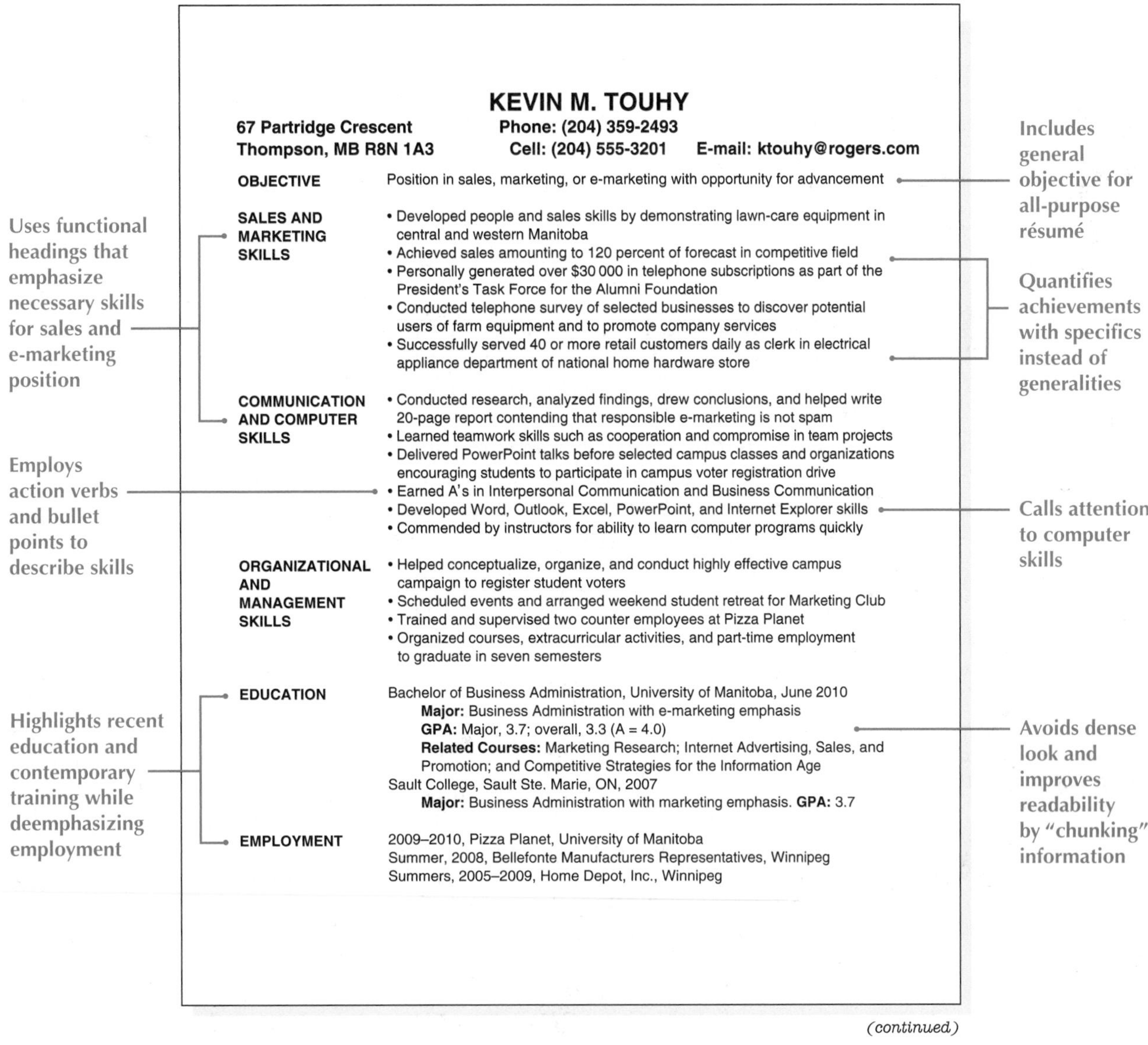

KEVIN M. TOUHY

67 Partridge Crescent **Phone: (204) 359-2493**
Thompson, MB R8N 1A3 **Cell: (204) 555-3201** **E-mail: ktouhy@rogers.com**

OBJECTIVE Position in sales, marketing, or e-marketing with opportunity for advancement

SALES AND MARKETING SKILLS

- Developed people and sales skills by demonstrating lawn-care equipment in central and western Manitoba
- Achieved sales amounting to 120 percent of forecast in competitive field
- Personally generated over $30 000 in telephone subscriptions as part of the President's Task Force for the Alumni Foundation
- Conducted telephone survey of selected businesses to discover potential users of farm equipment and to promote company services
- Successfully served 40 or more retail customers daily as clerk in electrical appliance department of national home hardware store

COMMUNICATION AND COMPUTER SKILLS

- Conducted research, analyzed findings, drew conclusions, and helped write 20-page report contending that responsible e-marketing is not spam
- Learned teamwork skills such as cooperation and compromise in team projects
- Delivered PowerPoint talks before selected campus classes and organizations encouraging students to participate in campus voter registration drive
- Earned A's in Interpersonal Communication and Business Communication
- Developed Word, Outlook, Excel, PowerPoint, and Internet Explorer skills
- Commended by instructors for ability to learn computer programs quickly

ORGANIZATIONAL AND MANAGEMENT SKILLS

- Helped conceptualize, organize, and conduct highly effective campus campaign to register student voters
- Scheduled events and arranged weekend student retreat for Marketing Club
- Trained and supervised two counter employees at Pizza Planet
- Organized courses, extracurricular activities, and part-time employment to graduate in seven semesters

EDUCATION

Bachelor of Business Administration, University of Manitoba, June 2010
Major: Business Administration with e-marketing emphasis
GPA: Major, 3.7; overall, 3.3 (A = 4.0)
Related Courses: Marketing Research; Internet Advertising, Sales, and Promotion; and Competitive Strategies for the Information Age
Sault College, Sault Ste. Marie, ON, 2007
Major: Business Administration with marketing emphasis. **GPA:** 3.7

EMPLOYMENT

2009–2010, Pizza Planet, University of Manitoba
Summer, 2008, Bellefonte Manufacturers Representatives, Winnipeg
Summers, 2005–2009, Home Depot, Inc., Winnipeg

Uses functional headings that emphasize necessary skills for sales and e-marketing position
Employs action verbs and bullet points to describe skills
Highlights recent education and contemporary training while deemphasizing employment
Includes general objective for all-purpose résumé
Quantifies achievements with specifics instead of generalities
Calls attention to computer skills
Avoids dense look and improves readability by "chunking" information

(continued)

FIGURE 16.3 ***Functional Résumé (Continued)***

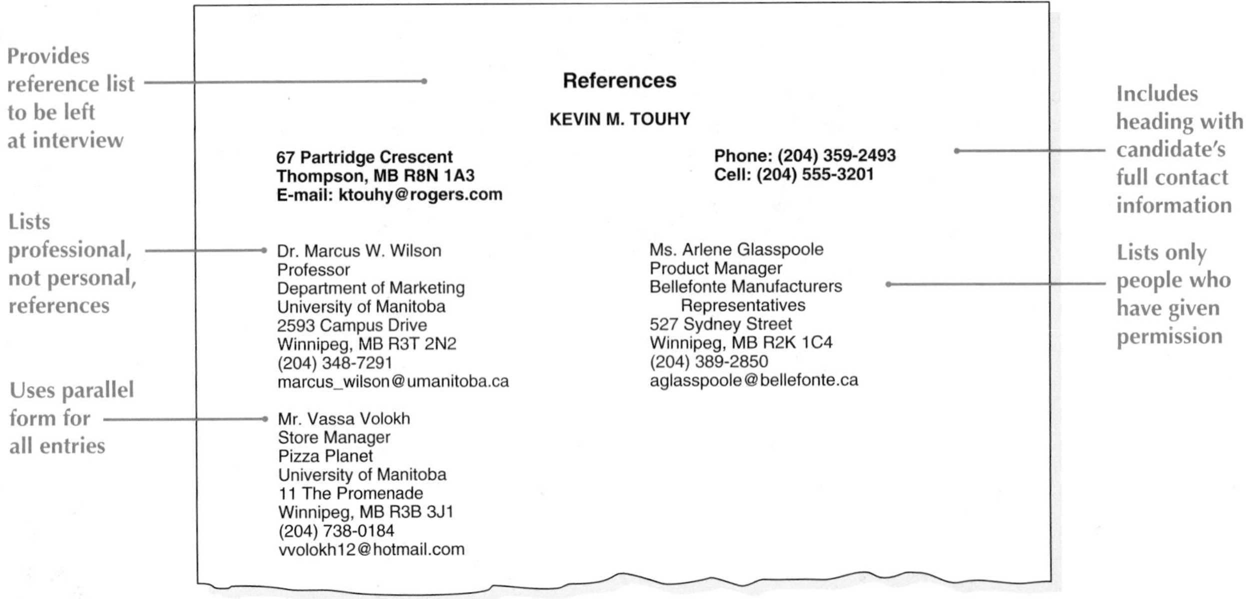

fied may also prefer the functional format. Be aware, though, that job boards may insist on the chronological format. In addition, some recruiters are suspicious of functional résumés, thinking the candidate is hiding something.

Provides reference list to be left at interview
Lists professional, not personal, references
Uses parallel form for all entries
Includes heading with candidate's full contact information
Lists only people who have given permission
References
KEVIN M. TOUHY
67 Partridge Crescent
Thompson, MB R8N 1A3
E-mail: ktouhy@rogers.com
Phone: (204) 359-2493
Cell: (204) 555-3201
Dr. Marcus W. Wilson
Professor
Department of Marketing
University of Manitoba
2593 Campus Drive
Winnipeg, MB R3T 2N2
(204) 348-7291
marcus_wilson@umanitoba.ca
Ms. Arlene Glasspoole
Product Manager
Bellefonte Manufacturers Representatives
527 Sydney Street
Winnipeg, MB R2K 1C4
(204) 389-2850
aglasspoole@bellefonte.ca
Mr. Vassa Volokh
Store Manager
Pizza Planet
University of Manitoba
11 The Promenade
Winnipeg, MB R3B 3J1
(204) 738-0184
vvolokh12@hotmail.com

Combination résumés present capabilities along with a complete job history.

Combination. The combination résumé style, shown in Figure 16.4, draws on the best features of the chronological and functional résumés. Sometimes called the *chrono-functional* résumé, this format emphasizes a candidate's capabilities while also including a complete job history. For recent graduates the combination résumé is a good choice because it enables them to profile what they can do for a prospective employer. If the writer has a specific job in mind, the items should be targeted to that job description.

Deciding on Its Length

Recruiters may say they prefer one-page résumés, but many choose to interview those with longer résumés.

Experts simply do not agree on how long a résumé should be. Conventional wisdom has always held that recruiters prefer one-page résumés. A carefully controlled study of 570 recruiters revealed that they *claimed* they preferred one-page résumés. However, the recruiters actually *chose* to interview the applicants with two-page résumés.[11] Recruiters who are serious about candidates often prefer a full picture with the kind of details that can be provided in a two-page résumé. On the other hand, recruiters are said to be extremely busy and to prefer concise résumés.

Perhaps the best advice is to make your résumé as long as needed to sell your skills to recruiters and hiring managers. Individuals with more experience will naturally have longer résumés. Those with fewer than ten years of experience, those making a major career change, and those who have had only one or two employers will likely have one-page résumés. Those with ten years or more of related experience may have two-page resumes. Finally, some senior-level managers and executives with a lengthy history of major accomplishments might have résumés that are three pages or longer.[12]

FIGURE 16.4 *Combination Résumé*

Because Casey wanted to highlight her skills and capabilites along with her experience, she combined the best features of functional and traditional résumés. She used the tables feature of her word processing program to help her format. Casey's résumé required part of a second page because she included references, a practice preferred by employers in her region who say it saves time.

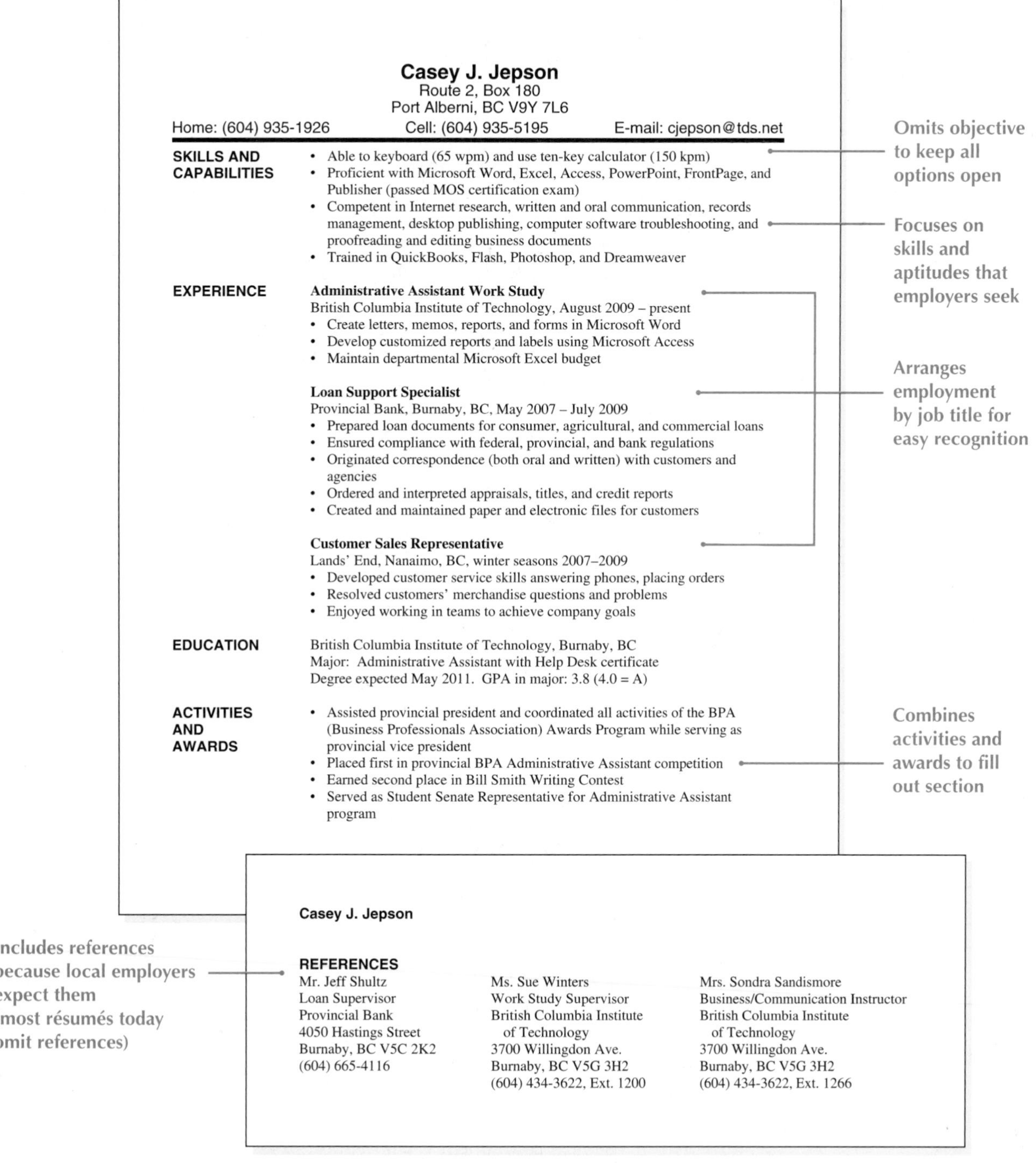

Casey J. Jepson
Route 2, Box 180
Port Alberni, BC V9Y 7L6

Home: (604) 935-1926 Cell: (604) 935-5195 E-mail: cjepson@tds.net

SKILLS AND CAPABILITIES

- Able to keyboard (65 wpm) and use ten-key calculator (150 kpm)
- Proficient with Microsoft Word, Excel, Access, PowerPoint, FrontPage, and Publisher (passed MOS certification exam)
- Competent in Internet research, written and oral communication, records management, desktop publishing, computer software troubleshooting, and proofreading and editing business documents
- Trained in QuickBooks, Flash, Photoshop, and Dreamweaver

EXPERIENCE

Administrative Assistant Work Study
British Columbia Institute of Technology, August 2009 – present
- Create letters, memos, reports, and forms in Microsoft Word
- Develop customized reports and labels using Microsoft Access
- Maintain departmental Microsoft Excel budget

Loan Support Specialist
Provincial Bank, Burnaby, BC, May 2007 – July 2009
- Prepared loan documents for consumer, agricultural, and commercial loans
- Ensured compliance with federal, provincial, and bank regulations
- Originated correspondence (both oral and written) with customers and agencies
- Ordered and interpreted appraisals, titles, and credit reports
- Created and maintained paper and electronic files for customers

Customer Sales Representative
Lands' End, Nanaimo, BC, winter seasons 2007–2009
- Developed customer service skills answering phones, placing orders
- Resolved customers' merchandise questions and problems
- Enjoyed working in teams to achieve company goals

EDUCATION

British Columbia Institute of Technology, Burnaby, BC
Major: Administrative Assistant with Help Desk certificate
Degree expected May 2011. GPA in major: 3.8 (4.0 = A)

ACTIVITIES AND AWARDS

- Assisted provincial president and coordinated all activities of the BPA (Business Professionals Association) Awards Program while serving as provincial vice president
- Placed first in provincial BPA Administrative Assistant competition
- Earned second place in Bill Smith Writing Contest
- Served as Student Senate Representative for Administrative Assistant program

Casey J. Jepson

REFERENCES

Mr. Jeff Shultz	Ms. Sue Winters	Mrs. Sondra Sandismore
Loan Supervisor	Work Study Supervisor	Business/Communication Instructor
Provincial Bank	British Columbia Institute of Technology	British Columbia Institute of Technology
4050 Hastings Street	3700 Willingdon Ave.	3700 Willingdon Ave.
Burnaby, BC V5C 2K2	Burnaby, BC V5G 3H2	Burnaby, BC V5G 3H2
(604) 665-4116	(604) 434-3622, Ext. 1200	(604) 434-3622, Ext. 1266

Omits objective to keep all options open
Focuses on skills and aptitudes that employers seek
Arranges employment by job title for easy recognition
Combines activities and awards to fill out section
Includes references because local employers expect them (most résumés today omit references)

learning objective

3

Arranging the Parts

The parts of résumés should be arranged with the most important qualifications first.

Although résumés have standard categories, their arrangement and content should be strategically planned. A customized résumé emphasize skills and achievements to aim at a particular job or company. It shows a candidate's most important qualifications first and deemphasizes any weaknesses. In organizing your qualifications and information, try to create as few headings as possible; more than six generally looks cluttered. No two résumés are ever exactly alike, but most writers consider including all or some of these items: main heading, career objective, education, experience, capabilities and skills, awards and activities, and references.

Main Heading. Your résumé should always begin with your name. Following your name, list your contact information, including your complete address, area code and phone number, and e-mail address. If possible, include a number where messages may be left for you. The outgoing message at this number should be in your voice, it should mention your full name, and it should be concise and professional. Keep the main heading as uncluttered and simple as possible. Format your name so that it stands out on the page. Don't include the word *résumé*; it's like putting the word *letter* above correspondence.

For your e-mail address, be sure it sounds professional instead of something like *toosexy4you@hotmail.com* or *sixpackguy@yahoo.com.* Also be sure that you are using a personal e-mail address. Putting your work e-mail address on your résumé announces to prospective employers that you are using your current employers' resources to look for a job.

Career objectives are most appropriate for specific, targeted openings; they may limit a broader job search.

Career Objective. Opinion is divided about the effect of including a career objective on a résumé. Recruiters think such statements indicate that a candidate has made a commitment to a career and is sure about what he or she wants to do. Career objectives, of course, make the recruiter's life easier by quickly classifying the résumé. Such declarations, however, can also disqualify a candidate if the stated objective doesn't match a company's job description.[13] A well-written objective—customized for the job opening—can add value to the résumé.

Be careful that your career objective doesn't downplay your talents. For example, some consultants warn against using the term *entry-level* in your objective, as it emphasizes lack of experience or shows poor self-confidence. If you choose to omit the career objective, be sure to discuss your objectives and goals in your cover letter.

Summary of Qualifications. A summary of qualifications can help save the time of recruiters and hiring managers by making your résumé easier to read and ensuring that your most impressive qualifications are not overlooked by a recruiter, who skims résumés quickly. A well-written summary motivates the recruiter to read further.

A summary of qualifications should include three to eight bulleted statements that prove you are the ideal candidate for the position. When formulating these statements, consider your experience in the field, your education, your unique skills, awards you may have won, certifications, and any other accomplishments that you want to highlight. Include numbers wherever possible. Target the most important qualifications an employer will be looking for in the person hired for this position.

Education. The next component is your education—if it is more noteworthy than your work experience. In this section you should include the name and location of schools, dates of attendance, major fields of study, and degrees received. By the way, once you have pursued post-secondary education, you don't need to list high school information on your résumé. Your grade-point average and/or class ranking are important to prospective employers. One way to enhance your GPA is to calculate it for your major courses only (for example, *3.6 in major*). It is not unethical to showcase your GPA in your major—as long as you clearly indicate what you are doing.

The education section shows degrees and GPA but does not list all courses a job applicant has taken.

Under *Education* you might be tempted to list all the courses you have taken, but such a list makes for very dull reading. Refer only to courses if you can relate them to the position sought. When relevant, include certificates earned, seminars attended, workshops completed, and honours earned. If your education is incomplete, include such statements as *B.Sc. degree expected 06/11* or *80 units completed in 120-unit program*. Title this section *Education*, *Academic Preparation*, or *Professional Training*.

Work Experience or Employment History. When your work experience is significant and relevant to the position sought, this information should appear before education. List your most recent employment first and work backwards, including only those jobs that you think will help you win the targeted position. A job application form may demand a full employment history, but your résumé may be selective. Be aware, though, that time gaps in your employment history will probably be questioned in the interview. For each position show the following:

The work experience section of a résumé should list specifics and quantify achievements.

- Employer's name, city, and province
- Dates of employment (month and year)
- Most important job title
- Significant duties, activities, accomplishments, and promotions

Describe your employment achievements concisely but concretely. Avoid generalities such as *Worked with customers*. Be more specific, with statements such as *Served 40 or more retail customers a day*, *Successfully resolved problems about custom stationery orders*, or *Acted as intermediary among customers, printers, and suppliers*. If possible, quantify your accomplishments, such as *Conducted study of equipment needs of 100 small businesses in Halifax*, *Personally generated orders for sales of $90 000 annually*, *Keyboarded all the production models for a 250-page employee procedures manual*, or *Assisted editor in layout, design, and news writing for 12 issues of division newsletter*.

Your employment achievements and job duties will be easier to read if you place them in a bulleted list. When writing these bullet points, don't try to list every single thing you have done on the job; instead, customize your information so that it relates to the target job. Make sure your list of job duties shows what you have to contribute and how you are qualified for the position you are applying for. Do not make your bullet points complete sentences and avoid using personal pronouns (*I, me, my*).

Highlight and quantify your achievements in bullet points that are not complete sentences.

In addition to technical skills, employers seek individuals with communication, management, and interpersonal capabilities. This means you'll want to select work experiences and achievements that illustrate your initiative, dependability, responsibility, resourcefulness, and leadership. Employers also want people who can work together in teams. Thus, include statements like *Collaborated with interdepartmental task force in developing ten-page handbook for temporary workers* and *Headed student government team that conducted most successful fundraiser in campus history*.

Statements describing your work experience can be made forceful and customized by using action verbs, such as those shown in Figure 16.5 (page 416) and illustrated in Figure 16.6 (page 417). Starting each of your bullet points with an action verb will help ensure that your bulleted lists are parallel.

FIGURE 16.5 ***Strengthen Your Résumé With Action Verbs***

constructed	encouraged	facilitated	organized	resolved	spearheaded
converted	engineered	improved	originated	restructured	spurred
designed	established	increased	overhauled	reviewed	strengthened
directed	expanded	introduced	pioneered	revitalized	targeted
enabled	expedited	managed	reduced	screened	transformed

Emphasize the skills and aptitudes that recommend you for a specific position.

Capabilities and Skills. Recruiters want to know specifically what you can do for their company. Therefore, list your special skills, such as *Proficient in preparing federal, provincial, and local payroll tax returns as well as franchise and personal property tax returns.* Include your ability to use the Internet, software programs, office equipment, and communication technology tools. If you speak a foreign language or use sign language, include it on your résumé. Describe proficiencies you have acquired through training and experience, such as *Certified in computer graphics and Web design through an intensive 350-hour classroom program.* Use expressions such as *competent in, skilled in, proficient with, experienced in,* and *ability to*; for example, *Competent in writing, editing, and proofreading reports, tables, letters, memos, manuscripts and business forms.*

You will also want to highlight exceptional aptitudes, such as working well under stress, learning computer programs quickly, and interacting with customers. If possible, provide details and evidence that back up your assertions; for example, *Mastered PhotoShop in 25 hours with little instruction.* Search for examples of your writing, speaking, management, organizational, and interpersonal skills—particularly those talents that are relevant to your targeted job. For recent graduates, this section can be used to give recruiters evidence of your potential. Instead of *Capabilities,* the section might be called *Skills and Abilities.*

Awards, honours, and activities are appropriate for the résumé.

Awards, Honours, and Activities. If you have three or more awards or honours, highlight them by listing them under a separate heading. If not, put them with activities. Include awards, scholarships (financial and other), fellowships, honours, recognition, commendations, and certificates. Be sure to identify items clearly. Your reader may be unfamiliar, for example, with Greek organizations, honours, and awards; tell what they mean. Instead of saying *Recipient of Star Award,* give more details: *Recipient of Star Award, given by Mount Allison University to outstanding graduates who combine academic excellence and extracurricular activities.*

It is also appropriate to include college, community, and professional activities. Employers are interested in evidence that you are a well-rounded person. This section provides an opportunity to demonstrate leadership and interpersonal skills. Strive to use action statements. For example, instead of saying *Treasurer of business club,* explain more fully: *Collected dues, kept financial records, and paid bills while serving as treasurer of 35-member business management club.*

Omit personal data not related to job qualifications.

Personal Data. Today's résumés omit personal data such as birth date, marital status, height, weight, national origin, health, and religious affiliation. Such information doesn't relate to genuine occupational qualifications, and recruiters are legally barred from asking for such information. Some job seekers do, however, include hobbies or interests (such as skiing or photography) that might grab the recruiter's attention or serve as conversation starters. Naturally you shouldn't mention dan-

FIGURE 16.6 *Use Action Verbs in Statements That Quantify Achievements*

Identified weaknesses in internships and researched five alternative programs

Reduced delivery delays by an average of three days per order

Streamlined filing system, thus eliminating 400-item backlog

Organized holiday awards program for 1200 attendees and 140 workers

Designed three pages in HTML for company Web site

Represented 2500 students on committee involving university policies and procedures

Calculated shipping charges for overseas deliveries and recommended most economical rates

Managed 24-station computer network linking data in three departments

Distributed and **explained** voter registration forms to over 500 prospective voters

Praised by top management for enthusiastic teamwork and achievement

Secured national recognition from Communities in Bloom Foundation for tree project

gerous pastimes (such as bungee jumping or sports car racing) or time-consuming interests. But you should indicate your willingness to travel or to relocate, since many companies will be interested.

References. Listing references on a résumé takes up valuable space. Moreover, references are not normally instrumental in securing an interview—few companies check them before the interview. Instead, recruiters prefer that you bring to the interview a list of individuals willing to discuss your qualifications. Ask three to five instructors, your current employer or previous employers, colleagues, or subordinates, and other professional contacts whether they would be willing to answer inquiries regarding your qualifications for employment. Be sure, however, to provide them with an opportunity to refuse. No reference is better than a negative one.

References are unnecessary for the résumé, but they should be available for the interview.

Do not include personal or character references such as friends, family, or neighbours, because recruiters rarely consult them. Companies are more interested in the opinions of objective individuals who know how you perform professionally and academically. One final note: most recruiters see little reason for including the statement *References available upon request.*

Optimizing Your Résumé for Today's Technologies

learning objective

4

Thus far we've aimed our résumé advice at human readers. However, the first reader of your résumé may well be a computer. Hiring organizations today use a variety of methods to process incoming résumés. Some organizations still welcome traditional print-based résumés that may include attractive formatting. Larger organizations, however, must deal with thousands of incoming résumés. Increasingly they are putting those résumés directly into searchable databases. So that you can optimize your chances, you may need three versions of your résumé: (a) a traditional print-based résumé, (b) a scannable résumé, and (c) a plain-text résumé for e-mailing or online posting. This does not mean that you have to write different résumés; you are merely preparing different versions of your traditional résumé.

Because résumés are increasingly becoming part of searchable databases, you may need three versions.

Designing a Traditional Print-Based Résumé

A traditional print-based résumé is attractive, readable, and outlined with headings in an orderly, uncluttered format.

Print-based résumés (also called *presentation résumés*) are attractively formatted to maximize readability. You can create a professional-looking résumé by using your word processing program to highlight your qualifications. The examples in this chapter provide ideas for simple layouts that are easily duplicated. You can also examine template résumés for styling ideas. Their inflexibility, however, leads to frustration as you try to force your skills and experience into a predetermined template sequence. What's more, recruiters who read hundreds of résumés can usually spot a template-based résumé. Instead, create your own original résumé that fits your unique qualifications.

Your print-based résumé should use an outline format with headings and bulleted points to present information in an orderly, uncluttered format. An attractive print-based résumé is necessary (a) when you are competing for a job that does not require electronic submission, (b) to present in addition to an electronic submission, and (c) to bring with you to job interviews. Even if a résumé is submitted electronically, nearly every job candidate will want to have an attractive traditional résumé handy for human readers.

Preparing a Scannable Résumé

Applicant-tracking software scans incoming résumés searching for keywords.

A scannable résumé is one that is meant to be printed on plain white paper and scanned by a computer. These systems scan an incoming résumé with optical character recognition (OCR), looking for keywords. The most sophisticated programs enable recruiters and hiring managers to search for keywords, rank résumés based on the number of "hits," and generate reports. Information from your résumé is stored, usually from six months to a year.

Before sending your résumé, find out whether the recipient uses scanning software. If you can't tell from the job announcement, call the company to ask whether it scans résumés electronically. If you don't get a clear answer and you have even the slightest suspicion that your résumé might be read electronically, you'll be smart to prepare a plain, scannable version.

Scannable résumés use plain formatting, a large font, quality printing, and white space.

Tips for Maximizing Scannability. A scannable résumé must sacrifice many of the graphic enhancements you might have used to dress up your traditional print résumé. To maximize scannability,

- **Avoid unusual typefaces, underlining, and italics.** Moreover, don't use borders, shading, or other graphics to highlight text. These features don't scan well. Most applicant-tracking programs, however, can accurately read bold print, solid bullets, and asterisks.
- **Use 10- to 14-point type.** Because touching letters or unusual fonts are likely to be misread, using a large, well-known font such as 12-point Times Roman or Arial is the safest. This may mean that your résumé will require two pages. After printing, inspect your résumé to see whether any letters touch—especially in your name.
- **Use smooth white paper, black ink, and quality printing.** Avoid coloured or textured paper, and use a high-quality laser or ink-jet printer.
- **Be sure that your name is the first line on the page.** Don't use fancy layouts that may confuse a scanner. Reports generated by applicant-tracking software usually assume that the first line of a résumé contains the applicant's name.
- **List each phone number on its own line.** Your land line and cell phone numbers should appear on separate lines to improve recognition.

FIGURE 16.7 ***Interpersonal Keywords Most Requested by Employers Using Résumé-Scanning Software****

Ability to delegate	Creative	Leadership	Self-accountable
Ability to implement	Customer-oriented	Multitasking	Self-managing
Ability to plan	Detail minded	Open communication	Setting priorities
Ability to train	Ethical	Open minded	Supportive
Accurate	Flexible	Oral communication	Takes initiative
Adaptable	Follow instructions	Organizational skills	Team building
Aggressive worker	Follow through	Persuasive	Team player
Analytical ability	Follow up	Problem solving	Tenacious
Assertive	High energy	Public speaking	Willing to travel
Communication skills	Industrious	Results-oriented	
Competitive	Innovative	Safety conscious	

*Reported by Resumix, a leading producer of résumé-scanning software.

Source: Joyce Lain Kennedy and Thomas J. Morrow, *Electronic Résumé Revolution* (New York: John Wiley & Sons), 70. Reprinted by permission of John Wiley & Sons, Inc.

- **Provide white space.** To ensure separation of words and categories, leave plenty of white space. For example, instead of using parentheses to enclose a telephone area code, insert blank spaces, such as *519 799 2415*. Leave blank lines around headings.
- **Avoid double columns.** When listing job duties, skills, computer programs, and so forth, don't tabulate items into two- or three-column lists. Scanners read across and may convert tables into nonsensical output.
- **Don't fold or staple your résumé.** Send it in a large envelope so that you can avoid folds. Words that appear on folds may not be scanned correctly.

Scanners produce "hits" when they recognize targeted keywords, such as nouns describing skills, traits, tasks, and job titles.

Tips for Maximizing Hits. In addition to paying attention to the physical appearance of your résumé, you must also be concerned with keywords that produce "hits," or recognition by the scanner. To maximize hits,

- **Focus on specific keywords.** Study carefully any advertisements and job descriptions for the position you want. Select keywords that describe skills, traits, tasks, and job titles. Because interpersonal traits are often requested by employers, consult Figure 16.7. It shows the most frequently requested interpersonal traits as reported by Resumix, a pioneer in résumé-scanning software.
- **Incorporate words from the advertisement or job description.** Describe your experience, education, and qualifications in terms associated with the job advertisement or job description for this position.
- **Use typical headings.** Include expected categories such as *Objective*, *Summary of Qualifications*, *Education*, *Work Experience*, *Skills*, and *Accomplishments*. Scanning software looks for such headings.
- **Use accurate names.** Spell out complete names of schools, degrees/diplomas, and dates.
- **Be careful of abbreviations.** Minimize unfamiliar abbreviations, but maximize easily recognized abbreviations—especially those within your field, such as *CAD*, *COBRA*, or *JIT*. When in doubt, though, spell it out! Computers are addled less by whole words.

- **Describe interpersonal traits and attitudes.** Hiring managers look for keywords and phrases such as *time management skills, dependability, high energy, leadership, sense of responsibility,* and *team player.*
- **Use more than one page if necessary.** Computers can easily handle more than one page, so include as much as necessary to describe your qualifications and maximize hits.

Preparing an Online (Plain-Text) Résumé for E-Mailing

Employers prefer online résumés because these plain-text documents are immediately searchable and avoid viruses and software incompatibilities.

An *online* or *plain-text* résumé (also be called an *ASCII résumé*) is an electronic version suitable for e-mailing or pasting into online résumé-bank submission forms. Employers prefer plain-text résumés because they avoid possible e-mail viruses and word processing incompatibilities. Usually embedded within an e-mail message, a plain-text résumé is immediately searchable. You should prepare a plain-text résumé if you want to use the fastest and most reliable way to contact potential employers. To create an online (plain-text) résumé, follow these suggestions:

- **Observe all the tips for a scannable résumé.** An online résumé requires the same attention to content, formatting, and keywords as that recommended for a scannable résumé.
- **Reformat with shorter lines.** Many e-mail programs wrap lines longer than 65 characters. To avoid having your résumé look as if a chain saw has attacked it, use a short line length.
- **Think about using keyboard characters to enhance format.** In addition to using capital letters and asterisks, you might use spaced equal signs (= = =) and tildes (~ ~ ~) to create separating lines to highlight résumé categories.
- **Move all text to the left.** Do not centre items; start all text at the left margin. Remove tabs.
- **Save your résumé in plain text (.txt) or rich text format (.rtf).** Saving your résumé in one of these formats will ensure that it can be read when pasted into an e-mail message. After saving your résumé, send it to yourself. Check to see whether any non-ASCII characters appear; they may show up as question marks, square blocks, or other odd characters. Make any necessary changes.

When sending a plain-text résumé to an employer, be sure that your subject line clearly describes the purpose of your message.

Creating an E-Portfolio

An e-portfolio offers links to examples of a job candidate's performance, talents, and accomplishments in digitized form.

As the workplace becomes increasingly digitized, you have yet another way to display your qualifications to prospective employers—the digitized *e-portfolio.* Resourceful job candidates in other fields—particularly writers, models, artists, and graphic artists—have created print portfolios to illustrate their qualifications and achievements. Now business and professional job candidates are using electronic portfolios to show off their talents.

An e-portfolio is a collection of digitized materials that provides viewers with a snapshot of a candidate's performance, talents, and accomplishments. It may include a copy of your résumé, reference letters, special achievements, awards, certificates, work samples, a complete list of your courses, thank-you letters, and anything else that touts your accomplishments. An advanced portfolio might include links to electronic copies of your artwork, film projects, blueprints, and photographs of classwork that might otherwise be difficult to share with potential employers. Moreover, you can include impressive effects such as colour, animation, sound, and graphics.

E-portfolios are generally presented at Web sites, where they are available around the clock to employers. Some colleges and universities not only make Web site space available for student e-portfolios but also provide instruction and resources for scanning photos, digitizing images, and preparing graphics. E-portfolios may also be burned onto CDs and DVDs to mail to prospective employers.

Job candidates generally offer e-portfolios at Web sites, but they may also burn them onto CDs or DVDs.

E-portfolios have many advantages. At Web sites they can be viewed whenever convenient for an employer. Let's say you are talking on the phone with an employer in another city who wants to see a copy of your résumé. You can simply refer the employer to the Web address where your résumé resides. E-portfolios can also be seen by many individuals in an organization without circulating a paper copy. But the real reason for preparing an e-portfolio is that it shows off your talents and qualifications more thoroughly than a print résumé does.

Applying the Final Touches to Your Résumé

Because your résumé is probably the most important message you will ever write, you'll revise it many times. With so much information in concentrated form and with so much riding on its outcome, your résumé demands careful polishing, proofreading, and critiquing.

In addition to being well written, a résumé must be carefully formatted and meticulously proofread.

As you revise, be certain to verify all the facts, particularly those involving your previous employment and education. Don't be caught in a mistake, or worse, distortion of previous jobs and dates of employment. These items likely will be checked, and the consequences of puffing up a résumé with deception or flat-out lies are simply not worth the risk. Other ethical traps you'll want to avoid are described in the Ethical Insights box on the next page.

Polishing. While you continue revising, look for other ways to improve your résumé. For example, consider consolidating headings. By condensing your information under as few headings as possible, you'll produce a clean, professional-looking document. Study other résumés for valuable formatting ideas. Ask yourself what graphic highlighting techniques you can use to improve readability: capitalization, underlining, indenting, or bulleting. Experiment with headings and styles to achieve a pleasing, easy-to-read message. Moreover, look for ways to eliminate wordiness. For example, instead of *Supervised two employees who worked at the counter*, try *Supervised two counter employees*. Review Chapter 6 for more tips on writing concisely.

In addition to making your résumé concise, make sure that you haven't included any of the following information, which doesn't belong on a résumé.

- Any basis for discrimination (age, marital status, gender, national origin, religion, race, number of children, disability)
- A photograph
- Reasons for leaving previous job
- The word *résumé*
- Social insurance number
- Salary history or requirements
- High school information
- References
- Full addresses of schools or employers (include city and province only)

ethical insights

Are Inflated Résumés Worth the Risk?

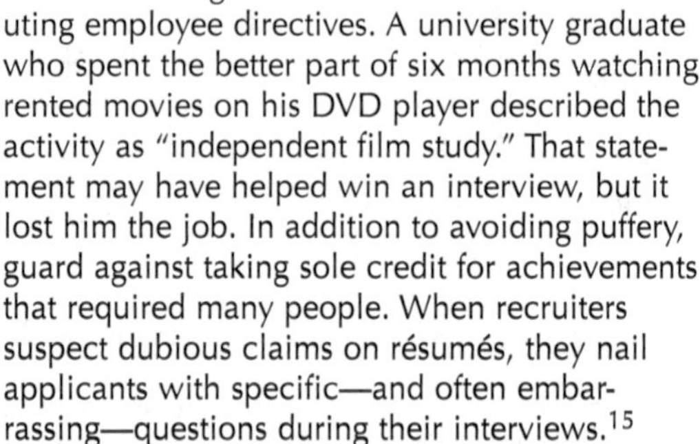

A résumé is expected to showcase a candidate's strengths and minimize weaknesses. For this reason, recruiters expect a certain degree of self-promotion. Some résumé writers, however, step over the line that separates honest self-marketing from deceptive half-truths and flat-out lies. Distorting facts on a résumé is unethical; lying is illegal. Most important, either practice can destroy a career.

Given the competitive job market, it might be tempting to puff up your résumé. You wouldn't be alone in telling fibs or outright whoppers. One study found that 44 percent of applicants lied about their work histories, 23 percent fabricated licences or credentials, and 41 percent falsified their educational backgrounds.[14] Although recruiters can't check everything, most will verify previous employment and education before hiring candidates. Over half will require official transcripts.

After hiring, the checking process may continue. If hiring officials find a discrepancy in a GPA or prior experience and the error is an honest mistake, they meet with the new hire to hear an explanation. If the discrepancy wasn't a mistake, they fire the person immediately. No job seeker wants to be in the unhappy position of explaining résumé errors or defending misrepresentation. Avoiding the following common problems can keep you off the hot seat:

- **Inflated education, grades, or honours.** Some job candidates claim diplomas or degrees from colleges or universities when in fact they merely attended classes. Others increase their grade-point averages or claim fictitious honours. Any such dishonest reporting is grounds for dismissal when discovered.
- **Enhanced job titles.** Wishing to elevate their status, some applicants misrepresent their titles. For example, one technician called himself a programmer when he had actually programmed only one project for his boss. A mail clerk who assumed added responsibilities conferred upon herself the title of supervisor. Even when the description seems accurate, it's unethical to list any title not officially granted.
- **Puffed-up accomplishments.** Some job seekers inflate their employment experience or achievements. One clerk, eager to make her photocopying duties sound more important, said that she assisted the vice president in communicating and distributing employee directives. A university graduate who spent the better part of six months watching rented movies on his DVD player described the activity as "independent film study." That statement may have helped win an interview, but it lost him the job. In addition to avoiding puffery, guard against taking sole credit for achievements that required many people. When recruiters suspect dubious claims on résumés, they nail applicants with specific—and often embarrassing—questions during their interviews.[15]
- **Altered employment dates.** Some candidates extend the dates of employment to hide unimpressive jobs or to cover up periods of unemployment and illness. Let's say that several years ago Cindy was unemployed for 14 months between working for Company A and being hired by Company B. To make her employment history look better, she adds seven months to her tenure with Company A and seven months to Company B. Now her employment history has no gaps, but her résumé is dishonest and represents a potential landmine for her.

The employment process can easily lure you into ethical traps such as those described in Chapter 1. Beware of these specific temptations:

- **The relative-filth trap:** *A little fudging on my GPA is nothing compared with the degrees that some people buy in degree mills.*
- **The rationalization trap:** *I deserve to call myself "manager" because that's what I really did.*
- **The self-deception trap:** *Giving myself a certificate from the institute is okay because I really intended to finish the program, but I got sick.*

Falling into these ethical traps risks your entire employment future. If your honest qualifications aren't good enough to get you the job you want, start working now to improve them.

Above all, make your print-based résumé look professional. Avoid anything humorous or "cute," such as a help-wanted poster with your name or picture on it. Eliminate the personal pronoun *I*. The abbreviated, objective style of a résumé precludes the use of personal pronouns. Use good-quality paper in a professional colour such as white, off-white, or light grey. Print your résumé using a first-rate laser or ink-jet printer. Be prepared with a résumé for people to read as well as one for a computer to read.

Proofreading. After revising, you must proofread, proofread, and proofread again for spelling, mechanics, content, and format. Then have a knowledgeable friend or relative proofread it yet again. This is one document that must be perfect. Because the job market is so competitive, one typo, misspelled word, or grammatical error could eliminate you from consideration.

Because résumés must be perfect, they should be proofread many times.

By now you may be thinking that you'd like to hire someone to write your résumé. Don't! First, you know yourself better than anyone else could know you. Second, you'll end up with either a generic or a one-time résumé. A generic résumé in today's highly competitive job market will lose out to a targeted résumé nine times out of ten. Equally useless is a one-time résumé aimed at a single job. What if you don't get that job? Because you will need to revise your résumé many times as you seek a variety of jobs, be prepared to write (and rewrite) it yourself.

Submitting. If you are responding to a job advertisement, be sure to read the listing carefully to make sure you know how the employer wants you to submit your résumé. Not following the prospective employer's instructions can eliminate you from consideration before your résumé is even reviewed. Employers will probably ask you to submit your résumé in one of the following ways:

- **Word document.** Many employers still ask candidates to send their résumés and cover letters by surface mail. They may also allow applicants to attach their résumés to e-mail messages as MS Word documents, despite the fear of viruses.
- **Online (plain-text) ASCII document.** As discussed earlier, many employers expect applicants to submit résumés and cover letters as plain-text documents. This format is widely used for posting to an online job board or for sending by e-mail. Plain-text résumés may be embedded within or attached to e-mail messages.
- **PDF document.** From a safety perspective, many employers prefer PDF (portable document format) files. A PDF résumé will look exactly like the original and cannot be altered. Newer computers come with Adobe Acrobat Reader for easy reading. Converting your résumé to a PDF file requires Adobe software.
- **Company database.** Some organizations prefer that you complete an online form with your résumé information. This enables them to plug your data into their formats for rapid searching. You might be able to cut and paste your information into the form.
- **Fax.** Although still a popular way of sending résumés, faxing presents problems in blurring and lost information. If you must fax your résumé, use at least a 12-point font to improve readability.

As you prepare to write your current résumé, consult the following checklist to review the job-search process and important résumé-writing techniques.

Checklist for Writing a Customized Résumé

Preparation

- ✓ **Research the job market.** Learn about available jobs, common qualifications, and potential employers. The best résumés are targeted for specific jobs with specific companies.

- ✓ **Analyze your strengths.** Determine what aspects of your education, experience, and personal characteristics will be assets to prospective employers.

- ✓ **Study models.** Look at other résumés for formatting and element placement ideas. Experiment with headings and styles to achieve an artistic, readable product.

Headings and Objectives

- ✓ **Identify yourself.** List your name, address(es), and telephone numbers.

- ✓ **Include a career objective for a targeted job.** If this résumé is intended for a specific job, include a statement tailored to it (*Objective: Cost accounting position in the petroleum industry*).

Education

- ✓ **Name your degree/diploma, date of graduation, and institution.** Emphasize your education if your experience is limited.

- ✓ **List your major and GPA.** Give information about your studies, but don't inventory all your courses.

Work Experience

- ✓ **Itemize your jobs.** Start with your most recent job. Give the employer's name and city, dates of employment (month, year), and most significant job title.

- ✓ **Describe your experience.** Use action verbs to summarize achievements and skills relevant to your targeted job.

- ✓ **Promote your "soft" skills.** Give evidence of communication, management, and interpersonal talents. Employers want more than empty assurances; try to quantify your skills and accomplishments (*Developed teamwork skills while collaborating with six-member task force in producing 20-page mission statement*).

Special Skills, Achievements, and Awards

- ✓ **Highlight your computer skills.** Remember that nearly all employers seek employees who are proficient in using the Internet, e-mail, word processing, databases, spreadsheets, and presentation programs.

- ✓ **Show that you are a well-rounded individual.** List awards, experiences, and extracurricular activities—particularly if they demonstrate leadership, teamwork, reliability, loyalty, industry, initiative, efficiency, and self-sufficiency.

Final Tips

- ✓ **Look for ways to condense your data.** Omit all street addresses except your own. Consolidate your headings. Study models and experiment with formats to find the most readable and efficient groupings.

- ✓ **Double-check for parallel phrasing.** Be sure that all entries have balanced construction, such as similar verb forms (*organized files, trained assistants, scheduled events*).

- ✓ **Make your résumé computer-friendly.** If there's a chance your résumé will be read by a computer, be sure to remove graphics and emphasize keywords.

- ✓ **Consider omitting references.** Have a list of references available for the interview, but don't include them or refer to them unless you have a specific reason to do so.

- ✓ **Project professionalism and quality.** Avoid personal pronouns and humour. Use quality paper and a high-performance printer.

- ✓ **Proofread, proofread, proofread.** Make this document perfect by proofreading at least three times. Ask a friend to check it too.

The Customized Cover Letter

learning objective 5

Cover letters introduce résumés, relate writer strengths to reader benefits, and seek an interview.

Job candidates often labour over their résumés but treat the cover letter as an afterthought. This critical mistake could destroy a job search. Even if an advertisement doesn't request one, be sure to distinguish your application with a customized cover letter (also called a *letter of application*). It has three purposes: (a) introducing the résumé, (b) highlighting your strengths in terms of benefits to the reader, and (c) gaining an interview.

Recruiting professionals disagree about how long to make a cover letter. Many prefer short letters with no more than three paragraphs. Others desire longer letters that supply more information, thus giving them a better opportunity to evaluate a candidate's qualifications. These recruiters argue that hiring and training new employees is expensive and time-consuming; therefore, they welcome extra data to guide them in making the best choice the first time. Follow your judgment in writing a brief or a longer cover letter. If you feel, for example, that you need space to explain in more detail what you can do for a prospective employer, do so.

Regardless of its length, a cover letter should have three primary parts: (a) an opening that introduces the message and identifies the position, (b) a body that sells the candidate, and (c) a closing that requests an interview and motivates action.

Introduce Your Message

The opener of a cover letter gains attention by addressing the receiver by name.

Your cover letter will be more appealing, and will more likely be read, if it begins by addressing the reader by name. Rather than sending it to "Hiring Manager" or "Human Resources Department," try to identify the name of the appropriate individual. Call the organization for the name of the person in charge of hiring for the position. Be sure to get the correct spelling and the complete address of your contact.

How you open your cover letter depends largely on whether the application is solicited or unsolicited. If an employment position has been announced and applicants are being solicited, you can use a direct approach. If you do not know whether a position is open and you are prospecting for a job, use an indirect approach. Whether direct or indirect, the opening should motivate the receiver to continue reading. Strive for openings that are more imaginative than *Please consider this letter an application for the position of . . . .*

Openings for Solicited Jobs. Here are some of the best techniques to open a cover letter for a job that has been announced:

- **Refer to the name of an employee in the company.** Remember that employers always hope to hire known quantities rather than complete strangers:

  At the suggestion of Ms. Jennifer Larson of your Human Resources Department, I submit my qualifications for the position of staffing coordinator.

- **Refer to the source of your information precisely.** If you are answering an advertisement, include the exact position advertised and the name and date of the publication. For large organizations it's also wise to mention the section of the newspaper where the ad appeared:

  From your company's Web site, I learned about your need for a sales representative for the eastern Ontario region. I am very interested in this position and believe that my education and experience are appropriate for the opening.

- **Refer to the job title and describe how your qualifications fit the requirements.** Hiring officers are looking for a match between an applicant's credentials and the job needs:

  Because of my specialized training in computerized accounting at the University of Regina, I feel confident that I have the qualifications you described in your advertisement for a cost accountant trainee.

Openers for unsolicited jobs show interest in and knowledge of the company, as well as spotlighting reader benefits.

Openings for Unsolicited Jobs. If you are unsure whether a position actually exists, you may wish to use a more customized opening. Since your goal is to convince this person to read on, try one of the following techniques:

- **Demonstrate interest in and knowledge of the reader's business.** Show the hiring officer that you have done your research and that this organization is more than a mere name to you:

  Because Signa HealthNet, Inc., is organizing a new information management team for its recently established group insurance division, could you use the services of a well-trained information systems graduate who seeks to become a professional systems analyst?

- **Show how your special talents and background will benefit the company.** Personnel directors need to be convinced that you can do something for them:

  Could your rapidly expanding publications division use the services of an editorial assistant who offers exceptional language skills, an honours degree from the University of Prince Edward Island, and two years' experience in producing a campus literary publication?

In applying for an advertised job, Alysha Cummings wrote the solicited cover letter shown in Figure 16.8 (page 428). Notice that her opening identifies the position and the newspaper completely so that the reader knows exactly what advertisement Alysha means.

Sell Your Strengths in the Body

The body of a cover letter promotes the candidate's qualifications for the targeted job.

Once you have captured the attention of the reader and identified your purpose in the letter opening, you should use the body of the letter to promote your qualifications for this position. If you are responding to an advertisement, you'll want to explain how your preparation and experience fill the stated requirements. If you are prospecting for a job, you may not know the exact requirements. Your employment research and knowledge of your field, however, should give you a reasonably good idea of what is expected for this position.

It's also important to stress reader benefits. In other words, you should describe your strong points in relation to the needs of the employer. Hiring officers want you to tell them what you can do for their organization. This is more important than telling what courses you took in college or what duties you performed on your previous jobs. Instead of *I have completed courses in business communication, report writing, and technical writing*, try this:

> Courses in business communication, report writing, and technical writing have helped me develop the research and writing skills required of your technical writers.

Choose your strongest qualifications and show how they fit the targeted job. And remember, students with little experience are better off spotlighting their education and its practical applications, as these candidates did:

> Because you seek an architect's apprentice with proven ability, I submit a drawing of mine that won second place in the Sinclair College drafting contest last year.

> Composing e-mail messages, business letters, memos, and reports in my communication and microcomputer application courses helped me develop the writing, language, proofreading, and computer skills mentioned in your ad for an administrative assistant.

Employers seek employees who are team players, take responsibility, show initiative, and learn easily.

In the body of your letter, you may choose to discuss relevant personal traits. Employers are looking for candidates who, among other things, are team players, take responsibility, show initiative, and learn easily. Notice how the following paragraph uses action verbs to paint a picture of a promising candidate:

> In addition to developing technical and academic skills at Dalhousie University, I have gained interpersonal, leadership, and organizational skills. As vice president of the business students' organization, I helped organize and supervise two successful fundraising events. These activities involved conceptualizing the tasks, motivating others to help, scheduling work sessions, and coordinating the efforts of 35 diverse students in reaching our goal. I enjoyed my success with these activities and look forward to applying such experience in your management trainee program.

Finally, in this section or the next, you should refer the reader to your résumé. Do so directly or as part of another statement, as shown here:

> Please refer to the attached résumé for additional information regarding my education, experience, and references.

FIGURE 16.8 ***Solicited Cover Letter***

Creates own stationery

Addresses proper person by name and title

Relates writer's experiences to job requirements

Refers reader to résumé

Identifies specific ad and job title

Discusses experience

Discusses schooling

Asks for interview and repeats main qualifications

Alysha Cummings

8011 Davies Road NW, Edmonton, AB T6E 4Z6

May 23, 2010

Ms. Sandra Kaladjian
Manager, Human Resources
Premier Enterprises
57 Bedford Drive NE
Calgary, AB T3K 1L2

Dear Ms. Kaladjian:

Your advertisement for an assistant product manager, appearing May 22 in Section C of the *Calgary Herald,* immediately caught my attention because my education and training closely parallel your needs.

According to your advertisement, the job includes "assisting in the coordination of a wide range of marketing programs as well as analyzing sales results and tracking marketing budgets." A recent internship at Ventana Corporation introduced me to similar tasks. I assisted the marketing manager in analyzing the promotion, budget, and overall sales success of two products Ventana was evaluating. My ten-page report examined the nature of the current market, the products' life cycles, and the company's sales/profit return. In addition to this research, I helped formulate a product merchandising plan and answered consumers' questions at a local trade show. This brief but challenging introduction to product management convinced me that I could be successful and happy in a marketing career.

Intensive course work in marketing and management, as well as proficiency in computer spreadsheets and databases, has given me the kind of marketing and computing training that Premier demands in a product manager. Moreover, I have had some retail sales experience and have been active in campus organizations. I'm confident that my academic preparation, my marketing experience, and my ability to work well with others qualify me for this position.

After you have examined the enclosed résumé for details of my qualifications, I would be happy to answer questions. Please call me to arrange an interview at your convenience so that we may discuss how my marketing, computing, and interpersonal skills could contribute to Premier Enterprises.

Sincerely,

Alysha Cummings

Alysha Cummings

Enclosure

The body of a cover letter can be expanded or contracted depending on how long you want your letter to be. As noted earlier, experts are divided on length. If you prefer a shorter cover letter, reduce the size of the body.

The closing of a cover letter requests an interview and makes it easy to respond.

Request an Interview in the Closing

After presenting your case, you should conclude by asking for an interview. Don't ask for the job. To do so would be presumptuous and naive. In requesting an interview, you might suggest reader benefits or review your strongest points. Sound sincere and appreciative. Remember to make it easy for the reader to agree

FIGURE 16.9 ***E-Mail Cover Letter***

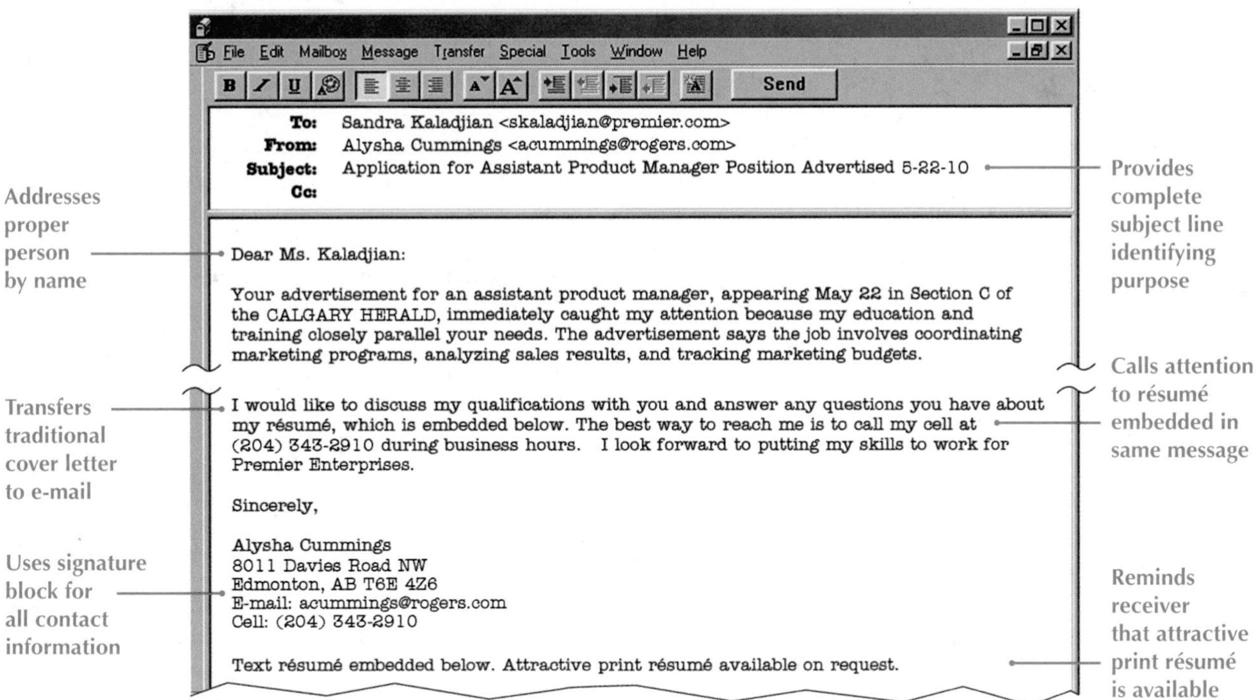
File Edit Mailbox Message Transfer Special Tools Window Help

Send

To: Sandra Kaladjian <skaladjian@premier.com>
From: Alysha Cummings <acummings@rogers.com>
Subject: Application for Assistant Product Manager Position Advertised 5-22-10
Cc:

Dear Ms. Kaladjian:

Your advertisement for an assistant product manager, appearing May 22 in Section C of the CALGARY HERALD, immediately caught my attention because my education and training closely parallel your needs. The advertisement says the job involves coordinating marketing programs, analyzing sales results, and tracking marketing budgets.

I would like to discuss my qualifications with you and answer any questions you have about my résumé, which is embedded below. The best way to reach me is to call my cell at (204) 343-2910 during business hours. I look forward to putting my skills to work for Premier Enterprises.

Sincerely,

Alysha Cummings
8011 Davies Road NW
Edmonton, AB T6E 4Z6
E-mail: acummings@rogers.com
Cell: (204) 343-2910

Text résumé embedded below. Attractive print résumé available on request.

Addresses proper person by name
Transfers traditional cover letter to e-mail
Uses signature block for all contact information
Provides complete subject line identifying purpose
Calls attention to résumé embedded in same message
Reminds receiver that attractive print résumé is available

by supplying your telephone number and the best times to call you. And keep in mind that some hiring officers prefer that you take the initiative to call them. Here are possible endings:

> This brief description of my qualifications and the additional information on my résumé demonstrate my genuine desire to put my skills in accounting to work for you. Please call me at (416) 488-2291 before 10 a.m. or after 3 p.m. to arrange an interview.
>
> Next week, after you have examined the attached résumé, I will call you to discuss the possibility of arranging an interview.

Sending Your Cover Letter

Serious job candidates will send a professional cover letter even if a résumé is submitted online, by e-mail, or by fax.

Many applicants using technology make the mistake of not including cover letters with their résumés submitted by e-mail or by fax. A résumé that arrives without a cover letter makes the receiver wonder what it is and why it was sent. Recruiters want you to introduce yourself, and they also are eager to see some evidence that you can write. Some candidates either skip the cover letter or think they can get by with one-line cover letters such as this: *Please see attached résumé, and thanks for your consideration.*

If you are serious about landing the job, take the time to prepare a professional cover letter. You may use the same cover letter you would send by surface mail, but shorten it a bit. As illustrated in Figure 16.9, an inside address is unnecessary for an e-mail recipient. Also, move your return address from the top of the letter to just below your name. Include your e-mail address and phone number. Remove tabs, bullets, underlining, and italics that might be problematic in e-mail messages. If you are submitting your résumé by fax, send the same cover letter you would send by surface mail. If you are submitting your résumé as a PDF file, do the same for your cover letter.

Final Tips

As you revise your cover letter, notice how many sentences begin with *I*. Although it's impossible to talk about yourself without using *I*, you can reduce "I" domination with this writing technique. Make activities and outcomes, not yourself, the subjects of sentences. For example, rather than *I took classes in business communication and computer applications*, say *Classes in business communication and computer applications prepared me to ....* Instead of *I enjoyed helping customers*, say *Helping customers was a real pleasure.*

A cover letter should look professional and suggest quality.

Like the résumé, your cover letter must look professional and suggest quality. This means using a traditional letter style, such as block or modified block. Also, be sure to print it on the same quality paper as your résumé. As with your résumé, proofread it several times yourself; then have a friend read it for content and mechanics. Don't rely on spell check to find all the errors. The following checklist provides a quick summary of suggestions to review when you compose and proofread your cover letter.

Checklist for Writing a Customized Cover Letter

Opening

- ✓ **Use the receiver's name.** Whenever possible, address the proper individual by name.
- ✓ **Identify your information source, if appropriate.** In responding to an advertisement, specify the position advertised as well as the date and publication name. If someone referred you, name that person.
- ✓ **Gain the reader's attention.** Use one of these techniques: (a) tell how your qualifications fit the job specifications, (b) show knowledge of the reader's business, (c) describe how your special talents will be an asset to the company, or (d) use an original and relevant expression.

Body

- ✓ **Describe what you can do for the reader.** Demonstrate how your background and training fill the job requirements.
- ✓ **Highlight your strengths.** Summarize your principal assets of education, experience, and special skills. Avoid repeating specific data from your résumé.
- ✓ **Refer to your résumé.** In this section or the closing, direct the reader to the attached résumé. Do so directly or incidentally as part of another statement.

Closing

- ✓ **Ask for an interview.** Also consider reviewing your strongest points or suggesting how your assets will benefit the company.

 **Make it easy to respond.** Tell when you can be reached during office hours or announce when you will call the reader. Note that some recruiters prefer that you call them.

E-Mailing

 **Include a cover letter with your résumé.** Send the same letter that might go by land mail but remove the formatting.

 **Put your contact information in the signature area.** Move your return address from the top of the letter to the signature block. Include your phone number and e-mail address.

Follow-up Letters and Other Employment Documents

learning objective

6

To secure good letters of recommendation, find willing people and provide ample data about yourself.

Although the résumé and cover letter are your major tasks, other important letters and documents are often required during the employment process. You may need to make requests, write follow-up letters, or fill out employment applications. Because each of these tasks reveals something about you and your communication skills, you'll want to put your best foot forward. These documents often subtly influence company officials to extend an interview or offer a job.

Reference Request

A reference request is most effective if it provides a description of the position, its requirements, and the recommendation deadline.

Most employers expect job candidates at some point to submit names of individuals who are willing to discuss the candidates' qualifications. Before you list anyone as a reference, however, be sure to ask permission. Try to do this in person. Ask an instructor, for example, if he or she would be willing and has the time to act as your recommender. If you detect any sign of reluctance, don't force the issue. Your goal is to find willing individuals who think well of you.

Application or Résumé Follow-up Letter

A résumé follow-up letter jogs the recruiter's memory, demonstrates your serious interest, and allows you to emphasize your qualifications and add new information.

If your résumé or application generates no response within a reasonable time, you may decide to send a short follow-up letter like the one shown here. Doing so (a) jogs the memory of the personnel officer, (2) demonstrates your serious interest, and (3) allows you to emphasize your qualifications or add new information.

> Dear Ms. Farmer:
>
> Please know that I am still interested in becoming an administrative support specialist with Quad, Inc.
>
> Since I submitted an application [or résumé] in May, I have completed my schooling and have been employed as a summer replacement for office workers in several downtown offices. This experience has honed my word processing and communication skills. It has also introduced me to a wide range of office procedures.
>
> Please keep my application in your active file and let me know when I may put my formal training, technical skills, and practical experience to work for you.

Open by reminding the reader of your interest.

Review your strengths or add new qualifications.

Close positively; avoid accusations that make the reader defensive.

Interview Follow-up Letter

Sending a thank-you letter after an interview reveals good manners and enthusiasm for the job.

After a job interview you should always send a brief letter of thanks. This courtesy sets you apart from other applicants, most of whom will not bother. Your letter also reminds the interviewer of your visit as well as suggesting your good manners and genuine enthusiasm for the job. Follow-up letters are most effective if sent immediately after the interview. In your letter refer to the date of the interview, the exact job title for which you were interviewed, and specific topics discussed. Avoid worn-out phrases such as *Thank you for taking the time to interview me.* Be careful, too, about overusing *I*, especially to begin sentences. Most important, show that you really want the job and that you are qualified for it. Notice how the interview follow-up letter in Figure 16.10 conveys enthusiasm and confidence.

Rejection Follow-up Letter

Following up after a job rejection indicates persistence and may lead to a position.

If you didn't get the job and you think it was perfect for you, don't give up. Employment specialists encourage applicants to respond to a rejection. The candidate who was offered the position may decline, or other positions may open up. In a rejection follow-up letter, it's okay to admit you're disappointed. Be sure to add, however, that you're still interested and will contact them again in a month in case a job opens up. Then follow through for a couple of months—but don't overdo it. You should be professional and persistent, but not a pest. Here's an example of an effective rejection follow-up letter:

Subordinate your disappointment to your appreciation at being notified promptly and courteously.

> Dear Mr. O'Neal:
>
> Although I'm disappointed that someone else was selected for your accounting position, I appreciate your promptness and courtesy in notifying me.

Emphasize your continuing interest. Express confidence in meeting the job requirements.

> Because I firmly believe that I have the technical and interpersonal skills needed to work in your fast-paced environment, I hope you will keep my résumé in your active file. My desire to become a productive member of your Trillium staff remains strong.

Refer to specifics of your interview. If possible, tell how you are improving your skills.

> I enjoyed our interview, and I especially appreciate the time you and Mr. Samson spent describing your company's expansion into international markets. To enhance my qualifications, I've enrolled in a course in international accounting at the University of New Brunswick.

Take the initiative; tell when you will call for an update.

> Should you have an opening for which I am qualified, you may reach me at (506) 719-3901. In the meantime, I will call you in a month to discuss employment possibilities.

Application Forms

Employment application forms, whether on paper or online, require accurate information carefully inserted.

Some organizations require job candidates to fill out job application forms instead of submitting résumés. This practice permits them to gather and store standardized data about each applicant. Whether the application is on paper or online, follow the directions carefully and provide accurate information. The following suggestions can help you be prepared:

- Carry a card summarizing those vital statistics not included on your résumé. If you are asked to fill out an application form in an employer's office, you will need a handy reference to the following data: graduation dates; beginning and ending dates of all employment; salary history; full names, titles, and present work addresses of former supervisors; and full names, occupational titles, occupational addresses, and telephone numbers of persons who have agreed to serve as references.

FIGURE 16.10 ***Interview Follow-up Letter***

Mentions the interview date and specific position

Highlights specific skills for the job

Shows appreciation, good manners, as well as perseverance—traits that recruiters value

Personalizes the message by referring to topics discussed in the interview

Reminds reader of interpersonal skills as well as his enthusiasm and eagerness for this job

2250 Tupper Street
Thunder Bay, ON P7A 4A5

May 26, 2010

Mr. Eric C. Nielson
Comstock Images & Technology
245 Maitland Street
London, ON N6B 2Y2

Dear Mr. Nielson:

Talking with you Thursday, May 25, about the graphic designer position was both informative and interesting.

Thanks for describing the position in such detail and for introducing me to Ms. Ouchi, the senior designer. Her current project designing the annual report in four colours on a Macintosh sounds fascinating as well as quite challenging.

Now that I've learned in greater detail the specific tasks of your graphic designers, I'm more than ever convinced that my computer and creative skills can make a genuine contribution to your graphic productions. My training in Macintosh design and layout suggests that I could be immediately productive on your staff.

You will find me an enthusiastic and hard-working member of any team effort. I'm eager to join the graphics staff at your London headquarters, and I look forward to hearing from you soon.

Cordially,

Christopher D. Wiley

Christopher D. Wiley

- Look over all the questions before starting. Fill out the form neatly, using blue or black ink. Many career counsellors recommend printing your responses; cursive handwriting can be difficult to read.
- Answer all questions. Write *Not applicable or N/A* if appropriate.
- Use accurate spelling, grammar, and punctuation.
- If asked for the position desired, give a specific job title or type of position. Don't say *Anything* or *Open.* These answers make you look unfocused; moreover, they make it difficult for employers to know what you are qualified for or interested in.
- Be prepared for a salary question. Unless you know what comparable employees are earning in the company, the best strategy is to suggest a salary range or to write in *Negotiable* or *Open.*
- Look over the application before submitting to make sure it is complete and that you have followed all instructions. Sign and date the application.

learning objective 7

Interviewing for Employment

Job interviews, for most of us, are intimidating; no one enjoys being judged and, possibly, rejected. You can overcome your fear of the interview process by knowing how it works and how to prepare for it.

Trained recruiters generally structure the interview into three separate activities: (a) establishing a cordial relationship, (b) eliciting information about the candidate, and (c) giving information about the job and company. During the interview its participants have opposing goals. The interviewer tries to uncover any negative information that would eliminate a candidate. The candidate, of course, tries to minimize faults and emphasize strengths to avoid being eliminated. You can become a more skilful player in the interview game if you know what to do before, during, and after the interview.

Before the Interview

Prior to an interview, applicants should research the organization and plan answers to potential questions.

- **Research the organization.** One of the most important steps in effective interviewing is gathering detailed information about a prospective employer. Never enter an interview cold. Recruiters are impressed by candidates who have done their homework. Visit the library or search the Web for information and articles about the target company or its field, service, or product. Visit the company's Web site and read everything. Call the company to request annual reports, catalogues, or brochures. Ask about the organization and possibly the interviewer. Learn something about the company's mission and goals, size, number of employees, customers, competitors, culture, management structure and names of leaders, reputation in the community, financial condition, future plans, strengths, and weaknesses.

  Analyze the company's advertising, including sales and marketing brochures. Talking with company employees is always a good idea, if you can manage it. They are probably the best source of inside information.

  Weblogs, or blogs, are also good sources for company research. Many employees maintain both formal and informal blogs where they share anecdotes and information about their employers. You can use these blogs to learn about a company's culture, its current happenings, and its future plans.
- **Learn about the position.** Obtain as much specific information as possible. What are the functions of an individual in this position? What is the typical salary range? What career paths are generally open to this individual? What did the last person in this position do right or wrong? Learning about the duties and responsibilities of the position will help you practise your best response strategies.
- **Plan to sell yourself.** Identify three to five of your major selling points regarding skills, training, personal characteristics, and specialized experience. Memorize them; then, in the interview, be certain to find a place to insert them.
- **Prepare answers to possible questions.** Imagine the kinds of questions you may be asked and work out sample answers. Although you can't anticipate precise questions, you can expect to be asked about your education, skills, experience, and availability. The accompanying Career Coach box shows some of the most common questions and suggests responses.
- **Prepare success stories.** To feel confident and able to sell your qualifications, prepare and practise success stories. These stories are specific examples of your education and work-related experience that demonstrate your qualifications and achievements.

- **Arrive early.** Get to the interview five or ten minutes early. If you are unfamiliar with the area where the interview is to be held, you might visit it before the scheduled day. Locate the building, parking facilities, and office. Time yourself.
- **Dress appropriately.** What you wear to a job interview still matters. Even if some employees in the organization dress casually, you should look qualified, competent, and successful. Avoid loud colours; strive for a coordinated, natural appearance. Favourite "power" colours for interviews are grey and dark blue. Cover tattoos and conceal body piercings; these can be a turnoff for many interviewers. Don't overdo jewellery, and make sure that your clothes are clean, pressed, odour-free, and lint-free. Shoes should be polished and scuff-free (forget about flip-flops). To summarize, ensure that what you wear projects professionalism and shows your respect for the interview situation.

During the Interview

- **Establish the relationship.** Shake hands firmly. Don't be afraid to offer your hand first. Address the interviewer formally (*Hello, Mrs. Jones*). Allow the interviewer to put you at ease with small talk.
- **Act confident but natural.** Establish and maintain eye contact, but don't get into a staring contest. Sit up straight, facing the interviewer. Don't cross your arms and legs at the same time. Don't manipulate objects such as a pencil or keys during the interview. Try to remain natural and at ease.

During an interview, applicants should act confident, focus on their strengths, and sell themselves.

- **Don't criticize.** Avoid making negative comments about previous employers, instructors, or others. Such criticism may be taken to indicate a negative personality. Employers are not eager to hire complainers. Moreover, such criticism may suggest that you would do the same in this organization.
- **Stay focused on your strengths.** Be prepared to answer questions such as those shown in the Career Coach box on the next page. If the interviewer asks a question that does not help you promote your strongest qualifications, answer briefly. Alternatively, try to turn your response into a positive selling point.

Interviewers tend to ask key questions similar to those in the Career Coach box.

- **Find out about the job early.** Because your time will be short, try to learn all you can about the target job early in the interview. Ask about its responsibilities and the kinds of people who have done well in the position before. Inquiring about the company's culture will help you decide if your personality fits with this organization.
- **Prepare for behavioural questions.** Instead of traditional interview questions, you may be asked to tell stories. The interviewer may say, "Describe a time when . . ." or "Give me an example of. . . ." To respond effectively, learn to use the storytelling or STAR technique. Ask yourself what the Situation or Task was, what Action you took, and what the Results were.[16] Practise using this method to recall specific examples of your skills and accomplishments. Examples of behavioural questions: (1) *Tell me about a problem you solved in a unique way*; (2) *Describe a time when you had to analyze information and make a recommendation*; (3) *Give me an example of a time when you were under stress to meet several deadlines.* To be fully prepared, develop a coherent and articulate STAR narrative for every bullet point on your résumé.
- **Prepare for salary questions.** Remember that nearly all salaries are negotiable, depending on your qualifications. Knowing the typical salary range for the target position helps. The recruiter can tell you the salary ranges—but you will have to ask. If you have little experience, you will probably be offered a salary

career coach

Looking Good When You Answer Key Interview Questions

Interviewers want to learn about your job experiences, skills, and education so that they can evaluate who you are and decide how you might perform on the job. You can be prepared for the questions in most interviews by studying the following typical questions and strategies for answering them successfully.

- **Why do you want to work for us?** Questions like this illustrate why you must research an organization thoroughly before the interview. Go to the company's Web site, read its annual report, conduct library research, ask friends, and read the company's advertisements and other printed materials to gather data. Describe your desire to work for this organization not only from your perspective but also from its point of view. What have you to offer?
- **Why should we hire you?** This is an opportunity for you to sell your strong points in relation to this specific position. Describe your skills, academic preparation, and relevant experience. If you have little experience, don't apologize—the interviewer has read your résumé. Emphasize strengths as demonstrated in your education, such as initiative and persistence in completing assignments, ability to learn quickly, self-sufficiency, and excellent attendance. One career expert said that the best answer he ever heard to this question was "I meet deadlines, pay attention to details, can multitask, and always make my boss look good."
- **What can you tell me about yourself?** Your first response should be to ask what aspect of your job skills and people skills you should focus on. Use this chance to promote yourself. Stick to professional or business-related strengths; avoid personal or humorous references. Be ready with at least three success stories illustrating characteristics important to this job. Demonstrate responsibility you have been given; describe how you contributed as a team player. Focus your answer on an area of your résumé.
- **What are your strongest (or weakest) personal qualities?** Stress your strengths, such as *I believe I am conscientious, reliable, tolerant, patient, and thorough*. Add examples that illustrate these qualities: *My supervisor said that my research was exceptionally thorough*. If pressed for a weakness, you might disguise a strength as a weakness: *Perhaps my greatest fault is being too painstaking with details*, or *I am impatient when tasks are not completed on time*. Don't admit weaknesses, not even to sound human. You'll be hired for your strengths, not your weaknesses.

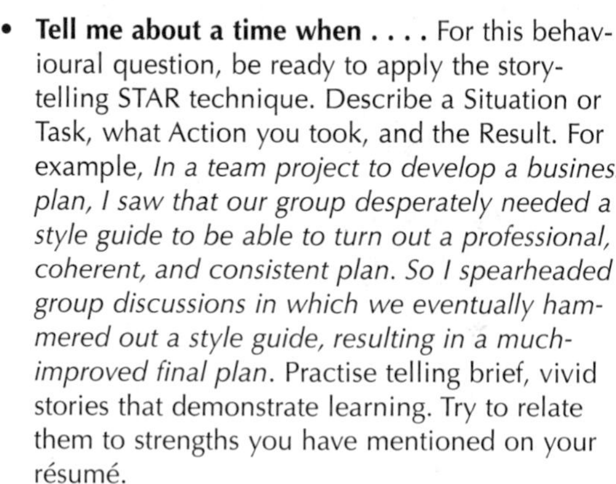

- **Tell me about a time when . . . .** For this behavioural question, be ready to apply the storytelling STAR technique. Describe a Situation or Task, what Action you took, and the Result. For example, *In a team project to develop a business plan, I saw that our group desperately needed a style guide to be able to turn out a professional, coherent, and consistent plan. So I spearheaded group discussions in which we eventually hammered out a style guide, resulting in a much-improved final plan*. Practise telling brief, vivid stories that demonstrate learning. Try to relate them to strengths you have mentioned on your résumé.
- **What do you expect to be doing ten years from now?** Formulate a realistic plan with respect to your present age and situation. One possible response is *Still learning and taking on new challenges*. The important thing is to be prepared for this question.
- **Do you prefer working with others or by yourself?** This question can be tricky. Provide a middle-of-the-road answer that not only suggests your interpersonal qualities but also reflects an ability to make independent decisions and work without supervision.
- **What kinds of people irritate you?** Avoid letting yourself fall into the trap of sounding overly critical. One possible response is *I've always gotten along well with others, but I confess that I can be irritated by complainers who don't accept responsibility*.
- **Have you ever changed your major during your education? Why?** This is another tricky question. Don't admit weaknesses or failures. In explaining changes, suggest career potential and new aspirations awakened by your expanding education, experience, or maturity.
- **Give me an example of a problem you solved and what your role was.** This is a good time to employ the STAR strategy! Tell a concise story

explaining the situation or task, what you did, and the result. For example, *When I was at Ace Products, we continually had a problem of excessive back orders. After analyzing the situation, I discovered that orders went through many unnecessary steps. I suggested that we eliminate much paperwork. As a result, we reduced back orders by 30 percent.* Go on to emphasize what you learned and how you can apply that learning to this job. Practise your success stories in advance so that you will be ready.

- **Tell me about your most rewarding or disappointing work (or school) experiences.** Focus on positive experiences such as technical and interpersonal skills you acquired. Avoid negative or unhappy topics. Never criticize former employers. If you worked for an ungrateful, penny-pinching slave driver in a dead-end position, say that you learned all you could from that job. Move the conversation to the prospective position and what attracts you to it.
- **Have you established any new goals lately?** Watch out here. If you reveal new goals, you may inadvertently admit deficiencies. Instead of *I've resolved to finally learn something about graphic design,* try *Although I'm familiar with simple graphics programs, I decided to get serious about graphic design by mastering Adobe Photoshop and Illustrator.*
- **What are your long- and short-term goals?** Suggest realistic goals that you have consciously worked out before the interview. Know what you want to do with your future. To admit to an interviewer that you're not sure what you want to do is a sign of immaturity, weakness, and indecision.
- **Tell me about a time when you influenced someone to accept your ideas.** The recruiter is interested in your leadership and teamwork skills. You might respond, *I've learned to appreciate the fact that the way you present an idea is just as important as the idea itself. When trying to influence people, I put myself in their shoes and find some way to frame my idea from their perspective. I remember when I . . . .*
- **Do you have any questions?** Always be ready with questions, such as these: *Why is the position open? What are the initial duties? What training is available? How did you [the interviewer] get started with the company? What trends do you see in the company's future?*

somewhere between the low point and the midpoint in the range. With more experience you can negotiate for a higher figure. A word of caution, though: one personnel manager warns that candidates who emphasize money are suspect because they may leave if offered a few thousand dollars more elsewhere.

- **Be ready for inappropriate questions.** If you are asked a question that you think is illegal, politely ask the interviewer how that question is related to this job. Ask the purpose of the question. Perhaps valid reasons exist that are not obvious.
- **Ask your own questions.** Often the interviewer concludes an interview with "Do you have any questions about the position?" The worst thing you can do is say "No," which suggests that you are not interested in the position. Instead, ask questions that will help you gain information and will impress the interviewer with your thoughtfulness and interest in the position. Remember that the interview is a two-way street. You must be happy with the prospect of working for this organization. Inquire about career paths, orientation or training for new employees, or the company's promotion policies. Have a list of relevant questions prepared.
- **Conclude positively.** Summarize your strongest qualifications, show your enthusiasm for obtaining the position, and thank the interviewer for a constructive interview. Be sure you understand the next step in the employment process. Ask the interviewer for a business card, which will provide you with the information you need to write a thank-you letter. Shake the interviewer's hand

with confidence, and acknowledge anyone else you see on the way out. Leaving the interview gracefully and demonstrating enthusiasm will leave a lasting impression on those responsible for making the final hiring decision.

After the Interview

Keeping notes of the meeting helps candidates remember what happened.

- **Make notes on the interview.** While the events are fresh in your mind, jot down the key points—good and bad.
- **Write a thank-you letter.** Immediately write a letter thanking the interviewer for a pleasant and enlightening discussion. Be sure to spell his or her name correctly.

Summary of Learning Objectives

1 **Prepare for employment by identifying your interests, evaluating your assets, recognizing the changing nature of jobs, choosing a career path, and studying traditional and electronic job-search techniques.** The employment process begins with an analysis of your likes and your qualifications. Because the nature of jobs is changing, your future work may include flexible work assignments, multiple employers, and constant retraining. You can learn more about career opportunities through your campus career centre, the Web, your library, internships, part-time jobs, interviews, classified ads, and professional organizations. Traditional job-search techniques range from newspaper ads to developing your own network of friends and relatives. Electronic job-search techniques include visiting Internet job sites and company Web sites.

2 **Compare and contrast chronological, functional, and combination résumés.** Chronological résumés, listing work and education by dates, rank highest with recruiters. Functional résumés, highlighting skills instead of jobs, appeal to people changing careers or those with negative employment histories. Functional résumés are also effective for recent graduates who have little work experience. Combination résumés, including a complete job history along with skill areas, are increasingly popular.

3 **Organize, format, and produce a customized résumé.** Target your résumé for a specific job. Study models to arrange most effectively your main heading, career objective (optional), summary of qualifications (optional), education, work experience, capabilities, awards and activities, personal data (optional), and references (optional). Use action verbs to show how your assets will help the target organization.

4 **Describe techniques that optimize a résumé for today's technologies, including preparing a scannable résumé, an online résumé, and an e-portfolio.** In addition to a print-based traditional résumé, candidates should consider preparing a scannable résumé that limits formatting and emphasizes keywords. Keywords are nouns that an employer might use to describe a position and its requirements. Online résumés (also called ASCII, plain-text, or electronic résumés) are stripped of all formatting and prepared as a text file so that they may be embedded in e-mail messages. An e-portfolio is a collection of digitized materials that illustrate a candidate's performance, talents, and accomplishments. E-portfolios may be posted at Web sites or burned onto CDs.

5 **Write a customized cover letter to accompany a résumé.** Gain attention in the opening by addressing the receiver by name and mentioning the job or a person who referred you. Build interest in the body by stressing your strengths in relation to the stated requirements. Explain what you can do for the targeted company. Refer to your résumé, request an interview, and make it easy for the receiver to reach you. If you send your cover letter by e-mail, shorten it a bit and include complete contact information in the signature block. Remove tabs, bullets, underlining, and italics, which could be problematic in e-mail.

6 **Write effective employment follow-up letters and other messages.** Follow up all your employment activities with appropriate messages. After submitting your résumé, after an interview—even after being rejected—follow up with letters that express your appreciation and continuing interest.

7 **Evaluate successful job interview strategies.** Learn about the job and the organization. Prepare answers to possible questions and be ready with success stories. Act confident and natural. Be prepared with STAR narratives so that you can answer behavioural questions. Be ready to ask or answer salary questions. Have a list of your own questions, summarize your key strengths, and stay focused on your strong points. Afterwards, send a thank-you letter.

chapter review

1. Name at least five questions that you should ask yourself to identify your employment qualifications. (Obj. 1)
2. List five sources of career information. (Obj. 1)
3. How are most jobs likely to be found? Internet job boards? Corporate Web sites? Classified ads? Employment agencies? Professional organizations? Networking? (Obj. 1)
4. What is the goal of a résumé? (Obj. 2)
5. What is a chronological résumé, and what are its advantages and disadvantages? (Obj. 2)
6. What is a functional résumé, and what are its advantages and disadvantages? (Obj. 2)
7. Describe a summary of qualifications, and explain why it is increasingly popular on résumés. (Obj. 3)
8. In addition to technical skills, what traits and capabilities are employers seeking? (Obj. 3)
9. To optimize your résumé for today's technologies, how many versions of your résumé should you expect to make? What are they? (Obj. 4)
10. What changes must be made in a typical résumé to make it effective for computer scanning? (Obj. 4)
11. What are the three purposes of a cover letter? (Obj. 5)
12. What information goes in the body of a cover letter? (Obj. 5)
13. Other than a cover letter, what other kinds of documents might you need to write in the employment process? (Obj. 6)
14. What information should a candidate gather in preparing for a job interview? (Obj. 7)
15. How are behavioural interview questions different from traditional questions? Give an example that would be appropriate for your career field. (Obj. 7)

critical thinking

1. How has the concept of the job changed, and how will it affect your employment search? (Obj. 1)
2. How is a résumé different from a company employment application? (Objs. 1 and 2)
3. Some job candidates think that applying for unsolicited jobs can be more fruitful than applying for advertised openings. Discuss the advantages and disadvantages of letters that prospect for jobs. (Obj. 5)
4. How do the interviewer and interviewee play opposing roles during job interviews? What strategies should the interviewee prepare in advance? (Obj. 7)

activities

16.1 Document for Analysis: Résumé (Objs. 2 and 3)

One effective way to improve your writing skills is to critique and edit the résumé of someone else.

Your Task. Analyze the following poorly organized résumé. Discuss its weaknesses. Your instructor may ask you to revise sections of this résumé before showing you an improved version.

Wendy Lee Cox
9 Franklin Terrace
Timmins, Ontario
Phone: (d) (705) 834-4583 (n) (705) 594-2985
E-mail: wendycox22@aol.com

Seeking to be hired at Mead Products as an intern in Accounting

SKILLS: Accounting, Internet, Windows XP, Excel, PowerPoint, Freelance Graphics

EDUCATION
Now working on diploma in Business Administration. Major, Management and Accounting; GPA is 3.5. Expect to graduate in June 2011.

EXPERIENCE
Assistant Accountant, 2006 to present. March and McLennan, Inc., Bookkeeping/Tax Service, Timmins. I keep accounting records for several small businesses accurately. I prepare 150 to 200 individual income tax returns each year. At the same time for Hill and Hill Truck Line I maintain accurate and up-to-date A/R records. And I prepare payroll records for 16 employees at three other firms.

Peterson Controls Inc., Timmins. Data Processing Internship, 2009 to present. I design and maintain spreadsheets and also process weekly and monthly information for production uptime and downtime. I prepare graphs to illustrate uptime and downtime data.

Rich chapter resources are available on the Web site. 

Timmins Country Club. Accounts Payable Internship, 2009 to 2009. Took care of accounts payable including filing system for the club. Responsible for processing monthly adjusting entries for general ledger. Worked closely with treasurer to give the Board budget/disbursement figures regularly.

Northern College, Timmins. I marketed the VITA program to Northern students and organized volunteers and supplies. Official title: Coordinator of Volunteer Income Tax Assistance Project. I did this for three years.

COMMUNITY SERVICE: Canadian Cancer Society, Central Park High School; All Souls Unitarian Church, assistant director of Children's Choir

16.2 Document for Analysis: Cover Letter (Obj. 5)

The following cover letter was written by Wendy Cox to accompany her résumé (see Activity 16.1).

Your Task. Analyze each section of the following cover letter written by Wendy and discuss its weaknesses. Your instructor may ask you to revise this letter before showing you an improved version.

Dear Human Resources Director:

Please consider this letter as an application for the position of intern that I saw at your Web site. Although I am working part time and trying to finish my diploma program, I think an internship at your industry-leading firm would be beneficial and would certainly look good on my résumé.

I have been studying accounting at Northern College for four years. I have taken courses in business law, statistics, finance, management, and marketing, but I am most interested in my accounting courses. I am especially interested in forensic accounting.

I have been a student volunteer for VITA, in addition to my course work during the tax season. I liked VITA because it is a project to help individuals in the community prepare their income tax returns, and I learned a lot from this experience. I also worked at Marsh and McLennan learning to keep the books for many small business firms. I should mention that I have had another internship, which was at Peterson Controls. I worked with graphs and spreadsheets, but I am more interested in forensics accounting.

I am a competent, accurate, well-organized person who gets along pretty well with others. I feel that I have a strong foundation in accounting as a result of my course work and my experience. I hope you will agree that, along with my personal qualities and my desire to succeed, I qualify for the internship, which begins March 1, with your company.

Sincerely,

16.3 Identifying Your Employment Interests (Obj. 1)

Your Task. In an e-mail or a memo addressed to your instructor, answer the questions in the section "Identifying Your Interests" at the beginning of the chapter. Draw a conclusion from your answers. What kind of career, company, position, and location seem to fit your self-analysis?

16.4 Evaluating Your Qualifications (Objs. 1–3)

Your Task. Prepare four worksheets that inventory your qualifications in these areas: employment, education, capabilities and skills, and honours and activities. Use active verbs when appropriate.

a. **Employment.** Begin with your most recent job or internship. For each position list the following information: employer, job title, dates of employment, and three to five duties, activities, or accomplishments. Emphasize activities related to your job goal. Strive to quantify your achievements.
b. **Education.** List degrees/diplomas, certificates, and training accomplishments. Include courses, seminars, or skills that are relevant to your job goal. Calculate your grade-point average in your major.
c. **Capabilities and skills.** List all capabilities and skills that recommend you for the job you seek. Use words like *skilled, competent, trained, experienced,* and *ability to.* Also list five or more qualities or interpersonal skills necessary for a successful individual in your chosen field. Write action statements demonstrating that you possess some of these qualities. Empty assurances aren't good enough; try to show evidence (*Developed teamwork skills by working with a committee of eight to produce a . . .*).
d. **Awards, honours, and activities.** Explain any awards so that the reader will understand them. List campus, community, and professional activities that suggest you are a well-rounded individual or possess traits relevant to your target job.

16.5 Choosing a Career Path (Obj. 1)

WEB

Many people know amazingly little about the work done in various occupations and the training requirements.

Your Task. To learn more about various occupations, use the National Occupation Classification prepared by Human Resources and Social Development Canada in collaboration with Statistics Canada. Go to **www.hrsdc.gc.ca** and click on "Career Planning" and then on "National Occupational Classification." Find the description of a position for which you could apply in two to five years. Learn about what workers do on the job, working conditions, training and education needed, earnings, and expected job prospects. Print the pages that describe employment in the area in which you are interested. If your instructor directs, attach these copies to the cover letter you will write in Activity 16.10.

16.6 Locating Salary Information (Obj. 1)

WEB

What salary can you expect in your chosen career?

Your Task. Visit Service Canada's Labour Market Information Service at **www.labourmarketinformation.ca** to locate wage and salary information for your geographic area and occupational title. Base your selections on the kind of employment you are seeking now or will be seeking after you graduate. Bring a printout of your occupation report to class. Be prepared to discuss your report during a class discussion and to submit your printout to your instructor.

16.7 Searching the Job Market (Obj. 1)

Where are the jobs? Even though you may not be in the market at the moment, become familiar with the kinds of available positions, because job awareness should become an important part of your education.

Your Task. Clip or print a job advertisement or announcement from (a) the classified section of a newspaper, (b) a job board on the Web, (c) a company Web site, or (d) a professional association listing. Select an advertisement or announcement describing the kind of employment you are seeking now or plan to seek when you graduate. Save this advertisement or announcement to attach to the résumé you will write in Activity 16.9.

16.8 Posting a Résumé on the Web (Obj. 4)

WEB

Learn about the procedure for posting résumés at job boards on the Web.

Your Task. Prepare a list of at least three Web sites where you could post your résumé. Describe the procedure involved in posting a résumé and the advantages for each site.

16.9 Writing Your Résumé (Objs. 2 and 3)

Your Task. Using the data you developed in Activity 16.4, write your résumé. Aim it at a full-time job, part-time position, or internship. Attach a job listing for a specific position (from Activity 16.7). Also prepare a list of references. Revise your résumé until it is perfect.

16.10 Preparing Your Cover Letter (Obj. 5)

Your Task. Write a cover letter introducing your résumé. Again, revise until it is perfect.

16.11 Following up After Submitting Your Résumé (Obj. 6)

Your Task. A month has passed since you sent your résumé and cover letter in response to a job advertisement. Write a follow-up letter that doesn't offend the reader or damage your chances of employment.

16.12 Following up After an Interview (Obj. 6)

Your Task. Assume you were interviewed for the position you seek. Write a follow-up thank-you letter.

16.13 Requesting a Reference (Obj. 6)

Your Task. Your favourite professor has agreed to recommend you. Write to the professor and request that he or she send a letter of recommendation to a company where you are applying for a job. Provide data about the job description and about yourself so that the professor can target its content.

Rich chapter resources are available on the Web site.

16.14 Developing Skill With Behavioural Interview Questions (Obj. 7)

LISTENING | SPEAKING | WEB

Behavioural interview questions are increasingly popular, and they take a little work before you can answer them easily.
Your Task. Use your favourite search engine to locate lists of behavioural questions on the Web. Select five skill areas such as communication, teamwork, and decision making. For each skill area find three behavioural questions that you think would be effective in an interview. In pairs of two students, role-play interviewer and interviewee, alternating with your listed questions. Your goal is to answer effectively in one or two minutes. Remember to use the STAR method when answering.

16.15 Answering Questions in a Virtual Interview (Obj. 7)

WEB

Two Web sites offer excellent interview advice. At **http://interview.monster.com** you can improve your interviewing skills in snappy virtual interviews. You'll find questions, answers, and explanations for interviews in job fields ranging from administrative support to human resources to technology. At **http://www.wetfeet.com/advice/interviewing.asp** you can learn how to answer résumé-based questions and handle pre-interview jitters, as well as see dozens of articles filled with helpful tips.
Your Task. Visit one or both of the targeted Web sites. If the URLs have been changed, use your favourite search engine to locate "Monster Interviews" and "WetFeet Interviews."

16.16 Writing a Rejection Follow-up Letter (Obj. 6)

Assume you didn't get the job. Although someone else was selected, you hope that other jobs may become available.
Your Task. Write a follow-up letter that keeps the door open.

16.17 Swapping Résumés (Obj. 2)

A terrific way to get ideas for improving your résumé is seeing how other students have developed their résumés.
Your Task. Bring your completed résumé to class. Attach a plain cover sheet with your name at the top. In small groups exchange your résumés. On the cover sheet, each reviewer should provide at least two supportive comments and one suggestion for improvement. Reviewers should sign their names with their comments.

C.L.U.E. review 16

On a separate sheet, edit the following sentences to correct faults in grammar, punctuation, numbers, spelling, proofreading, and word use.

1. The employment process begins with introspection which is a word that mean looking inside yourself to analyse what you like and dislike.
2. You cant hope to find the job of your dreams' without first: (1) Knowing yourself; (2) knowing the job market and (3) know the employment process.
3. Candidates complain about Job Boards, because fewer then one point four percent of the candidates are actually hired.
4. With over forty thousand job boards and employment web sites deluging the internet its hard to know where to start looking.
5. Preparing a résumé while you are still in school, help you recognize week qualifications, and give you 2 or 3 years in which to bolster it.
6. Recruiters like to see Career Objectives on résumés, however it may restrict a candidates chances.
7. Todays résumés omit personel data such as birth date, martial status, hite, weigt and religious affiliation.
8. I wonder how many companys now use applicant tracking software to scan candidates résumés and search for keywords?
9. In the latest issue of BusinessWeek did you see the article titled Should you use a career objective on your résumé.
10. Before going to a job interview you should research the following, company size, number of employees, competitors, reputation, strengths and weakness.

appendix A

Competent Language Usage Essentials (C.L.U.E.)

A Business Communicator's Guide

In the business world, people are often judged by the way they speak and write. Using the language competently can mean the difference between individual success and failure. Often a speaker sounds accomplished, but when that same individual puts ideas in print, errors in language usage destroy his or her credibility.

What C.L.U.E. Is

This appendix provides a condensed guide to competency in language usage essentials (C.L.U.E.). Fifty-four guidelines review sentence structure, grammar, usage, punctuation, capitalization, number style, and the use of abbreviations. These guidelines focus on the most frequently used—and abused—language elements. Presented from a business communicator's perspective, the guidelines also include realistic tips for application. Frequent checkpoint exercises enable you to try out your skills immediately. In addition to the 54 language guides in this appendix, you'll find a list of 165 frequently misspelled words plus a quick review of selected confusing words.

The concentrated materials in this guide help novice business communicators focus on the major areas of language use. The guide is not meant to teach or review *all* the principles of English grammar and punctuation. It focuses on a limited number of language guidelines and troublesome words. Your objective should be mastery of these language principles and words, which represent a majority of the problems typically encountered by business writers.

How to Use C.L.U.E.

Your instructor may give you the short C.L.U.E. language diagnostic test (located in the Instructor's Manual) to help you assess your competency. This test will give you an idea of your language competence. After taking the diagnostic test, read and work your way through the 54 guidelines. Concentrate on areas where you are weak. Memorize the spelling list and definitions for the confusing words located at the end of this appendix.

Within these C.L.U.E. materials, you will find two kinds of exercises for your practice. (1) *Checkpoints*, located in this appendix, focus on a small group of language guidelines. Use them to test your comprehension as you complete each section. (2) *Review exercises*, located at the end of each text chapter, cover all guidelines, spelling words, and confusing words. Use the review exercises to reinforce your language skills at the same time you are learning about the processes and products of business communication. As you complete the review exercises, you may wish to use the standard proofreading marks shown on the inside front cover.

Many students want all the help they can get in improving their language skills. For additional assistance with grammar and language fundamentals, try these resources:

- 

CengageNOW! (www.ilrn.com) is an **online learning and homework assessment program** created in concert with the text to present a seamless, integrated learning tool. Students can improve their grades and save study time with CengageNOW! It isn't just reading—it provides a **customized study plan** that lets students **master what they need to know without spending time on what they already know.** The study plan provides a road map to interactive exercises, videos, an e-book, and other resources that help students master the subject.
- **Reference Books.** More comprehensive treatment of grammar and punctuation guidelines can be found in Clark and Clark's *A Handbook for Office Professionals* ISBN 978-0-324-66239-9; Jack Finnbogason and Al Valleau's *A Canadian Writer's Pocket Guide,* ISBN 978-0-17-640627-1; Joanne Buckley's *Checkmate: A Writing Reference for Canadians,* ISBN 978-0-17-610361-3; and *The Harbrace Handbook for Canadians* by John Hodges and Andrew Stubbs, ISBN 978-0-17-622509-4.

Guidelines: Competent Language Usage Essentials

Sentence Structure

GUIDE 1: Express ideas in complete sentences. You can recognize a complete sentence because it (a) includes a subject (a noun or pronoun that interacts with a verb), (b) includes a verb (a word expressing action or describing a condition), and (c) makes sense (comes to a closure). A complete sentence is an independent clause. One of the most serious errors a writer can make is punctuating a fragment as if it were a complete sentence. A fragment is a broken-off part of a sentence.

Fragment	**Improved**
Because 90 percent of all business transactions involve written messages. Good writing skills are critical.	Because 90 percent of all business transactions involve written messages, good writing skills are critical.
The recruiter requested a writing sample. Even though the candidate seemed to communicate well.	The recruiter requested a writing sample, even though the candidate seemed to communicate well.

Tip. Fragments often can be identified by the words that introduce them—words such as *although, as, because, even, except, for example, if, instead of, since, so, such as,* *that, which,* and *when*. These words introduce dependent clauses. Make sure such clauses are always connected to independent clauses.

DEPENDENT CLAUSE — INDEPENDENT CLAUSE

Since she became supervisor, she has had to write more memos and reports.

GUIDE 2: Avoid run-on (fused) sentences. A sentence with two independent clauses must be joined by a coordinating conjunction (*and, or, nor, but*) or by a semicolon (;). Without a conjunction or a semicolon, a run-on sentence results.

Run-on	**Improved**
Robin visited resorts of the rich and the famous he also dropped in on luxury spas.	Robin visited resorts of the rich and famous, and he also dropped in on luxury spas.
	Robin visited resorts of the rich and famous; he also dropped in on luxury spas.

GUIDE 3: Avoid comma-splice sentences. A comma splice results when a writer joins (splices together) two independent clauses without using a coordinating conjunction (*and, or, nor, but*).

Comma Splice	**Improved**
Disney World operates in Orlando, EuroDisney serves Paris.	Disney World operates in Orlando; EuroDisney serves Paris.
	Disney World operates in Orlando, and EuroDisney serves Paris.
Visitors wanted a resort vacation, however they were disappointed.	Visitors wanted a resort vacation; however, they were disappointed.

Tip. In joining independent clauses, beware of using a comma and words such as *consequently, furthermore, however, therefore, then, thus,* and so on. These conjunctive adverbs require semicolons.

✓ *Checkpoint*

Revise the following to rectify sentence fragments, comma splices, and run-ons.

1. Although it began as a side business for Disney. Destination weddings now represent a major income source.
2. About 2000 weddings are held yearly. Which is twice the number just ten years ago.
3. Weddings may take place in less than one hour, however the cost may be as much as $5000.
4. Limousines line up outside Disney's wedding pavilion, they are scheduled in two-hour intervals.
5. Most couples prefer a traditional wedding, others request a fantasy experience.

For all the Checkpoint sentences, compare your responses with the answers at the end of Appendix A, beginning on page A-22.

Grammar

Verb Tense

GUIDE 4: Use present tense, past tense, and past participle verb forms correctly.

Present Tense (Today I ______)	**Past Tense** (Yesterday I _____)	**Past Participle** (I have _____)
am	was	been
begin	began	begun
break	broke	broken
bring	brought	brought
choose	chose	chosen
come	came	come
do	did	done
give	gave	given
go	went	gone
know	knew	known
pay	paid	paid
see	saw	seen
steal	stole	stolen
take	took	taken
write	wrote	written

The package *came* yesterday, and Kevin *knew* what it contained.

If I *had seen* the shipper's bill, I *would have paid* it immediately.

I *know* the answer now; I wish I *had known* it yesterday.

Tip. Probably the most frequent mistake in tenses results from substituting the past participle form for the past tense. Notice that the past participle requires auxiliary verbs such as *has, had, have, would have,* and *could have.*

Faulty	**Correct**
When he *come* over last night, he *brung* pizza.	When he *came* over last night, he *brought* pizza.
If he *had came* earlier, we *could have saw* the video.	If he *had come* earlier, we *could have seen* the video.

Verb Mood

GUIDE 5: Use the subjunctive mood to express hypothetical (untrue) ideas. The most frequent misuse of the subjunctive mood involves using *was* instead of *were* in clauses introduced by *if* and *as though* or containing *wish.*

If I *were* (not *was*) you, I would take a business writing course.

Sometimes I wish I *were* (not *was*) the manager of this department.

He acts as though he *were* (not *was*) in charge of this department.

Tip. If the statement could possibly be true, use *was.*

If I *was* to blame, I accept the consequences.

✓ Checkpoint

Correct faults in verb tenses and mood.

6. If I was you, I would have went to the 10 o'clock meeting.
7. The manager could have wrote a better report if he had began earlier.
8. When the vice president seen the report, he immediately come to my office.
9. I wish the vice president was in your shoes for just one day.
10. If the manager had knew all that we do, I'm sure he would have gave us better reviews.

Verb Voice

For a discussion of active- and passive-voice verbs, see pages 123–124 in Chapter 6.

Verb Agreement

GUIDE 6: Make subjects agree with verbs despite intervening phrases and clauses. Become a detective in locating *true* subjects. Don't be deceived by prepositional phrases and parenthetic words that often disguise the true subject.

> Our study of annual budgets, five-year plans, and sales proposals *is* (not *are*) progressing on schedule. (The true subject is *study*.)
>
> The budgeted item, despite additions proposed yesterday, *remains* (not *remain*) as submitted. (The true subject is *item*.)
>
> A vendor's evaluation of the prospects for a sale, together with plans for follow-up action, *is* (not *are*) what we need. (The true subject is *evaluation*.)

Tip. Subjects are nouns or pronouns that control verbs. To find subjects, cross out prepositional phrases beginning with words such as *about, at, by, for, from, of,* and *to*. Subjects of verbs are not found in prepositional phrases. Also, don't be tricked by expressions introduced by *together with, in addition to,* and *along with*.

GUIDE 7: Subjects joined by* and *require plural verbs. Watch for true subjects joined by the conjunction *and*. They require plural verbs.

> The CEO and one of his assistants *have* (not *has*) ordered a limo.
>
> Considerable time and money *were* (not *was*) spent on remodelling.
>
> Exercising in the gym and jogging every day *are* (not *is*) how he keeps fit.

GUIDE 8: Subjects joined by* or *or* nor *may require singular or plural verbs. The verb should agree with the closest subject.

> Either the software or the printer *is* (not *are*) causing the glitch. (The verb is controlled by the closer subject, *printer*.)
>
> Neither Montreal nor Calgary *has* (not *have*) a chance of winning. (The verb is controlled by *Calgary*.)

Tip. In joining singular and plural subjects with *or* or *nor*, place the plural subject closer to the verb. Then the plural verb sounds natural. For example, *Either the manufacturer or the distributors are responsible.*

GUIDE 9: Use singular verbs for most indefinite pronouns. The following pronouns all take singular verbs: *anyone*, *anybody*, *anything*, *each*, *either*, *every*, *everyone*, *everybody*, *everything*, *neither*, *nobody*, *nothing*, *someone*, *somebody*, and *something*.

Everyone in both offices *was* (not *were*) given a bonus.

Each of the employees *is* (not *are*) being interviewed.

GUIDE 10: Use singular or plural verbs for collective nouns, depending on whether the members of the group are operating as a unit or individually. Words such as *faculty*, *administration*, *class*, *crowd*, and *committee* are considered *collective* nouns. If the members of the collective are acting as a unit, treat them as singular subjects. If they are acting individually, it's usually better to add the word *members* and use a plural verb.

Correct
The Finance Committee *is* working harmoniously. (*Committee* is singular because its action is unified.)

The Planning Committee *are* having difficulty agreeing. (*Committee* is plural because its members are acting individually.)

Improved
The Planning Committee members *are* having difficulty agreeing. (Add the word *members* if a plural meaning is intended.)

Tip. In North America, collective nouns are generally considered singular. In Britain these collective nouns are generally considered plural.

✓ Checkpoint

Correct the errors in subject–verb agreement.

11. The agency's time and talent was spent trying to develop a blockbuster ad campaign.
12. Your e-mail message, along with both of its attachments, were not delivered to my computer.
13. Each of the Fortune 500 companies are being sent a survey regarding women in management.
14. A full list of names and addresses are necessary before we can begin.
15. Either the judge or the lawyer have asked for a recess.

Pronoun Case

GUIDE 11: Learn the three cases of pronouns and how each is used. Pronouns are substitutes for nouns. Every business writer must know the following pronoun cases.

Nominative or Subjective Case	Objective Case	Possessive Case
Used for subjects of verbs and subject complements	Used for objects of prepositions and objects of verbs	Used to show possession
I	me	my, mine
we	us	our, ours
you	you	your, yours
he	him	his
she	her	her, hers
it	it	its
they	them	their, theirs
who, whoever	whom, whomever	whose

GUIDE 12: Use nominative case pronouns as subjects of verbs and as complements. Complements are words that follow linking verbs (such as *am*, *is*, *are*, *was*, *were*, *be*, *being*, and *been*) and rename the words to which they refer.

She and *I* (not *her* and *me*) are looking for entry-level jobs. (Use nominative case pronouns as the subjects of the verb phrase *are looking*.)

We hope that Marci and *he* (not *him*) will be hired. (Use a nominative case pronoun as the subject of the verb phrase *will be hired*.)

It must have been *she* (not *her*) who called last night. (Use a nominative case pronoun as a subject complement.)

Tip. If you feel awkward using nominative pronouns after linking verbs, rephrase the sentence to avoid the dilemma. Instead of *It is she who is the boss*, say *She is the boss*.

GUIDE 13: Use objective case pronouns as objects of prepositions and verbs.

Send the e-mail to *her* and *me* (not *she* and *I*). (The pronouns *her* and *me* are objects of the preposition *to*.)

The CEO appointed Rick and *him* (not *he*) to the committee. (The pronoun *him* is the object of the verb *appointed*.)

Tip. When a pronoun appears in combination with a noun or another pronoun, ignore the extra noun or pronoun and its conjunction. Then the case of the pronoun becomes more obvious.

Jason asked Jennifer and *me* (not *I*) to lunch. (Ignore *Jennifer and*.)

The waiter brought hamburgers to Jason and *me* (not *I*). (Ignore *Jason and*.)

Tip. Be especially alert to the following prepositions: *except*, *between*, *but*, and *like*. Be sure to use objective pronouns as their objects.

Just between you and *me* (not *I*), that mineral water comes from the tap.

Everyone except Robert and *him* (not *he*) responded to the invitation.

GUIDE 14: Use possessive pronouns to show ownership. Possessive pronouns (such as *hers*, *yours*, *whose*, *ours*, *theirs*, and *its*) require no apostrophes.

All reports except *yours* (not *your's*) have to be rewritten.

The apartment and *its* (not *it's*) contents are *hers* (not *her's*) until June.

Tip. Don't confuse possessive pronouns and contractions. Contractions are shortened forms of subject–verb phrases (such as *it's* for *it is*, *there's* for *there is*, *who's* for *who is*, and *they're* for *they are*).

✓ Checkpoint

Correct errors in pronoun case.

16. My partner and me have looked at many apartments, but your's has the best location.

17. We thought the car was her's, but it's licence plate doesn't match.

18. Just between you and I, do you think there printer is working?

19. Theres not much the boss or me can do if its broken, but its condition should have been reported to him or I earlier.

20. We received several applications, but your's and her's were missing.

GUIDE 15: Use pronouns ending in self *only when they refer to previously mentioned nouns or pronouns.*

The president *himself* ate all the M&Ms.

Send the package to Mike or *me* (not *myself*).

Tip. Trying to sound less egocentric, some radio and TV announcers incorrectly substitute *myself* when they should use *I*. For example, "Jerry and *myself* (should be *I*) are cohosting the telethon."

GUIDE 16: Use* who *or* whoever *for nominative case constructions and* whom *or* whomever *for objective case constructions. In determining the correct choice, it's helpful to substitute *he* for *who* or *whoever* and *him* for *whom* or *whomever*.

For *whom* was this software ordered? (The software was ordered for *him*.)

Who did you say called? (You did say *he* called?)

Give the supplies to *whoever* asked for them. (In this sentence the clause *whoever asked for them* functions as the object of the preposition *to*. Within the clause, *whoever* is the subject of the verb *asked*. Again, try substituting *he*: *he asked for them*.)

✓ Checkpoint

Correct any errors in the use of *self*-ending pronouns and *who/whom*.

21. The boss herself is willing to call whoever we decide to honour.

22. Who have you asked to develop ads for our new products?

23. I have a pizza for whomever placed the telephone order.

24. The meeting is set for Wednesday; however, Matt and myself cannot attend.

25. Incident reports must be submitted by whomever experiences a personnel problem.

Pronoun Reference

GUIDE 17: Make pronouns agree in number and gender with the words to which they refer (their antecedents). When the gender of the antecedent is obvious, pronoun references are simple.

> One of the boys lost *his* (not *their*) new tennis shoes. (The singular pronoun *his* refers to the singular *One*.)
>
> Each of the female nurses was escorted to *her car* (not *their cars*). (The singular pronoun *her* and singular noun *car* are necessary because they refer to the singular subject *Each*.)
>
> Somebody on the girls' team left *her* (not *their*) headlights on.

When the gender of the antecedent could be male or female, sensitive writers today have a number of options.

Faulty	**Improved**
Every employee should receive *their* cheque Friday. (The plural pronoun *their* does not agree with its singular antecedent *employee*.)	All employees should receive *their* cheques Friday. (Make the subject plural so that the plural pronoun *their* is acceptable. This option is preferred by many writers today.)
	All employees should receive cheques Friday. (Omit the possessive pronoun entirely.)
	Every employee should receive *a* cheque Friday. (Substitute *a* for a pronoun.)
	Every employee should receive *his or her* cheque Friday. (Use the combination *his or her*. However, this option is wordy and should be avoided.)

GUIDE 18: Be sure that pronouns such as* it, which, this, *and* that *refer to clear antecedents. Vague pronouns confuse the reader because they have no clear single antecedent. The most troublesome are *it, which, this,* and *that.* Replace vague pronouns with concrete nouns, or provide these pronouns with clear antecedents.

Faulty	**Improved**
Our office recycles as much paper as possible because it helps the environment. (Does *it* refer to *paper, recycling,* or *office*?)	Our office recycles as much paper as possible because such efforts help the environment. (Replace *it* with *such efforts*.)
The disadvantages of local area networks can offset their advantages. That merits further evaluation. (What merits evaluation: advantages, disadvantages, or offsetting of one by the other?)	The disadvantages of local area networks can offset their advantages. That fact merits further evaluation. (*Fact* supplies a concrete noun for the vague pronoun *that*.)

Faulty

Negotiators announced an expanded health care plan, reductions in dental coverage, and a proposal of on-site child care facilities. This caused employee protests. (What exactly caused employee protests?)

Improved

Negotiators announced an expanded health care plan, reductions in dental coverage, and a proposal of on-site child care facilities. *This* reduction in dental coverage caused employee protests. (The pronoun *This* now has a clear reference.)

Tip. Whenever you use the words *this, that, these,* and *those* by themselves, a red flag should pop up. These words are dangerous when they stand alone. Inexperienced writers often use them to refer to an entire previous idea, rather than to a specific antecedent, as shown in the preceding example. You can usually solve the problem by adding another idea to the pronoun (such as *this reduction*).

✓ Checkpoint

Correct the faulty and vague pronoun references in the following sentences. Numerous remedies exist.

26. Every employee must wear their picture identification badge.

27. Flexible working hours may mean slower career advancement, but it appeals to many workers.

28. Any renter must pay his rent by the first of the month.

29. Someone in this office reported that his computer had a virus.

30. Obtaining agreement on job standards, listening to coworkers, and encouraging employee suggestions all helped to open lines of communication. This is particularly important in team projects.

Adjectives and Adverbs

GUIDE 19: Use adverbs, not adjectives, to describe or limit the action of verbs.

Andrew said he did *well* (not *good*) on the exam.

After its tune-up, the engine is running *smoothly* (not *smooth*).

Don't take the manager's criticism *personally* (not *personal*).

She finished her homework *more quickly* (not *quicker*) than expected.

GUIDE 20: Hyphenate two or more adjectives that are joined to create a compound modifier before a noun.

Follow the *step-by-step* instructions to construct the *low-cost* bookshelves.

A *well-designed* keyboard is part of this *state-of-the-art* equipment.

Tip. Don't confuse adverbs ending in *-ly* with compound adjectives: *newly enacted* law and *highly regarded* CEO would not be hyphenated.

Checkpoint

Correct any problems in the use of pronouns, adjectives, and adverbs.

31. My manager and me could not resist the once in a lifetime opportunity.
32. Because John and him finished their task so quick, they made a fast trip to the recently opened snack bar.
33. If I do good on the exam, I qualify for many part time jobs and a few full time positions.
34. The vice president told him and I not to take the announcement personal.
35. In the not too distant future, we may enjoy more practical uses of robots.

Punctuation

GUIDE 21: Use commas to separate three or more items (words, phrases, or short clauses) in a series.

Downward communication delivers job instructions, procedures, and appraisals.

In preparing your résumé, try to keep it brief, make it easy to read, and include only job-related information.

The new ice cream flavours include cookie dough, chocolate raspberry truffle, cappuccino, and almond amaretto.

Tip. Some professional writers omit the comma before *and*. However, most business writers prefer to retain that comma because it prevents misreading the last two items as one item. Notice in the previous example how the final two ice cream flavours could have been misread if the comma had been omitted.

GUIDE 22: Use commas to separate introductory clauses and certain phrases from independent clauses. This guideline describes the comma most often omitted by business writers. Sentences that open with dependent clauses (often introduced by words such as *since, when, if, as, although,* and *because*) require commas to separate them from the main idea. The comma helps readers recognize where the introduction ends and the big idea begins. Introductory phrases of more than five words or phrases containing verbal elements also require commas.

If you recognize introductory clauses, you will have no trouble placing the comma. (A comma separates the introductory dependent clause from the main clause.)

When you have mastered this rule, half the battle with commas will be won.

As expected, additional explanations are necessary. (Use a comma even if the introductory clause omits the understood subject: *As we expected.*)

In the spring of last year, we opened our franchise. (Use a comma after a phrase containing five or more words.)

Having considered several alternatives, we decided to invest. (Use a comma after an introductory verbal phrase.)

To invest, we needed $100 000. (Use a comma after an introductory verbal phrase, regardless of its length.)

Tip. Short introductory prepositional phrases (four or fewer words) require no commas. Don't clutter your writing with unnecessary commas after introductory phrases such as *by 2010, in the fall,* or *at this time.*

GUIDE 23: Use a comma before the coordinating conjunction in a compound sentence. The most common coordinating conjunctions are *and, or, nor,* and *but*. Occasionally *for, yet,* and *so* may also function as coordinating conjunctions. When coordinating conjunctions join two independent clauses, commas are needed.

The investment sounded too good to be true, *and* many investors were dubious. (Use a comma before the coordinating conjunction *and* in a compound sentence.)

Niagara Falls is the honeymoon capital of the world, *but* some newlyweds prefer to go to more exotic destinations.

Tip. Before inserting a comma, test the two clauses. Can each of them stand alone as a complete sentence? If either is incomplete, skip the comma.

Promoters said the investment offer was for a limited time and couldn't be extended even one day. (Omit a comma before *and* because the second part of the sentence is not a complete independent clause.)

Lease payments are based largely on your down payment and on the value of the car at the end of the lease. (Omit a comma before *and* because the second half of the sentence is not a complete clause.)

✓ Checkpoint

Add appropriate commas.

36. Before she enrolled in this class Erin used to sprinkle her writing with commas semicolons and dashes.

37. After studying punctuation she learned to use commas more carefully and to reduce her reliance on dashes.

38. At this time Erin is engaged in a serious yoga program but she also finds time to enlighten her mind.

39. Next fall Erin may enroll in communication and merchandising or she may work for a semester to earn money.

40. When she completes her junior year she plans to apply for an internship in Montreal Edmonton or Toronto.

GUIDE 24: Use commas appropriately in dates, addresses, geographical names, degrees, and long numbers.

September 30, 1963, is his birthday. (For dates use commas before and after the year.)

Send the application to James Kirby, 3405 120th Ave. N.W., Edmonton, AB T5W 1M3, as soon as possible. (For addresses use commas to separate all units except the two-letter province abbreviation and the postal code.)

Lisa expects to move from Calgary, Alberta, to Sarnia, Ontario, next fall. (For geographical areas use commas to enclose the second element.)

Karen Munson, CGA, and Richard B. Larsen, Ph.D., were the speakers. (For professional designations and academic degrees following names, use commas to enclose each item.)

The latest census figures show the city's population to be 342 000. (In figures over four digits, use a space to separate every three digits, counting from the right.)

GUIDE 25: Use commas to set off internal sentence interrupters. Sentence interrupters may be verbal phrases, dependent clauses, contrasting elements, or parenthetical expressions (also called transitional phrases). These interrupters often provide information that is not grammatically essential.

> Medical researchers, working steadily for 18 months, developed a new cancer therapy. (Use commas to set off an interrupting verbal phrase.)
>
> The new therapy, which applies a genetically engineered virus, raises hopes among cancer specialists. (Use commas to set off nonessential dependent clauses.)
>
> Dr. James C. Morrison, who is one of the researchers, made the announcement. (Use commas to set off nonessential dependent clauses.)
>
> It was Dr. Morrison, not Dr. Arturo, who led the team effort. (Use commas to set off a contrasting element.)
>
> This new therapy, by the way, was developed from a herpes virus. (Use commas to set off a parenthetical expression.)

Tip. Parenthetical (transitional) expressions are helpful words that guide the reader from one thought to the next. Here are typical parenthetical expressions that require commas:

as a matter of fact	in addition	of course
as a result	in the meantime	on the other hand
consequently	nevertheless	therefore
for example		

Tip. Always use *two* commas to set off an interrupter, unless it begins or ends a sentence.

✓ Checkpoint

Insert necessary commas.

41. James listed 222 George Henry Blvd. Toronto ON M2J 1E6 as his forwarding address.

42. This report is not however one that must be classified.

43. Employment of paralegals which is expected to increase 32 percent next year is growing rapidly because of the expanding legal services industry.

44. The contract was signed May 15 2010 and remains in effect until May 15 2015.

45. As a matter of fact the average North American drinks enough coffee to require 12 pounds of coffee beans annually.

GUIDE 26: Avoid unnecessary commas. Do not use commas between sentence elements that belong together. Don't automatically insert commas before every *and* or at points where your voice might drop if you were saying the sentence out loud.

> **Faulty**
> Growth will be spurred by the increasing complexity of business operations, and by large employment gains in trade and services. (A comma unnecessarily precedes *and*.)

Faulty

All students with high grades, are eligible for the honour society. (A comma unnecessarily separates the subject and verb.)

One of the reasons for the success of the business honour society is, that it is very active. (A comma unnecessarily separates the verb and its complement.)

Our honour society has, at this time, over 50 members. (Commas unnecessarily separate a prepositional phrase from the sentence.)

✓ *Checkpoint*

Remove unnecessary commas. Add necessary ones.

46. Car companies promote leasing because it brings customers back into their showrooms sooner, and gives dealers a steady supply of late-model used cars.

47. When shopping for a car you may be offered a fantastic leasing deal.

48. The trouble with many leases is, that the value of the car at the end of the lease may be less than expected.

49. We think on the other hand, that you should compare the costs of leasing and buying, and that you should talk to a tax advisor.

50. Many North American automakers are, at this time, offering intriguing lease deals.

Semicolons and Colons

GUIDE 27: Use a semicolon to join closely related independent clauses. Experienced writers use semicolons to show readers that two thoughts are closely associated. If the ideas are not related, they should be expressed as separate sentences. Often, but not always, the second independent clause contains a conjunctive adverb (such as *however, consequently, therefore,* or *furthermore*) to show the relation between the two clauses.

Learning history is easy; learning its lessons is almost impossible.

He was determined to complete his degree; consequently, he studied diligently.

Serena wanted a luxury apartment located near campus; however, she couldn't afford the rent.

Tip. Don't use a semicolon unless each clause is truly independent. Try the sentence test. Omit the semicolon if each clause could not stand alone as a complete sentence.

Faulty	**Improved**
There's no point in speaking; unless you can improve on silence. (The second half of the sentence is a dependent clause. It could not stand alone as a sentence.)	There's no point in speaking unless you can improve on silence.
Although I cannot change the direction of the wind; I can adjust my sails to reach my destination. (The first clause could not stand alone.)	Although I cannot change the direction of the wind, I can adjust my sails to reach my destination.

GUIDE 28: Use a semicolon to separate items in a series when one or more of the items contains internal commas.

Representatives from as far away as Longueuil, Quebec; Vancouver, British Columbia; and Whitehorse, Yukon Territory, attended the conference.

Stories circulated about Henry Ford, founder, Ford Motor Company; Lee Iacocca, former CEO, Chrysler Motor Company; and Kiichiro Toyoda, founder, Toyota Motor Corporation.

GUIDE 29: Use a colon after a complete thought that introduces a list of items. Words such as *these*, *the following*, and *as follows* may introduce the list or they may be implied.

The following cities are on the tour: Toronto, Ottawa, and Winnipeg.

An alternative tour includes several West Coast cities: Calgary, Saskatoon, and Edmonton.

Tip. Be sure that the statement before a colon is grammatically complete. An introductory statement that ends with a preposition (such as *by*, *for*, *at*, and *to*) or a verb (such as *is*, *are*, or *were*) is incomplete. The list following a preposition or a verb actually functions as an object or as a complement to finish the sentence.

Faulty	**Improved**
Three Big Macs were ordered by: Pam, Jim, and Lee. (Do not use a colon after an incomplete statement.)	Three Big Macs were ordered by Pam, Jim, and Lee.
Other items that they ordered were: fries, Cokes, and salads. (Do not use a colon after an incomplete statement)	Other items that they ordered were fries, Cokes, and salads.

GUIDE 30: Use a colon after business letter salutations and to introduce long quotations.

Dear Mr. Duran: Dear Lisa:

The Asian consultant bluntly said: "North Americans tend to be too blabby, too impatient, and too informal for Asian tastes. To succeed in trade with Pacific Rim countries, North Americans must become more willing to adapt to native cultures."

Tip. Use a comma to introduce short quotations. Use a colon to introduce long one-sentence quotations and quotations of two or more sentences.

✓ *Checkpoint*

Add appropriate semicolons and colons.

51. Marco's short-term goal is an entry-level job his long-term goal however is a management position.
52. Speakers included the following professors Rebecca Hilbrink University of Western Ontario Lora Lindsey McGill University and Michael Malone Durham College.
53. The recruiter was looking for three qualities loyalty initiative and enthusiasm.
54. Microsoft seeks experienced individuals however it will hire recent graduates who are skilled.

55. Mississauga is an expanding region therefore many business opportunities are available.

Apostrophe

GUIDE 31: Add an apostrophe plus s *to an ownership word that does not end in an* s *sound.*

We hope to show a profit in one year's time. (Add *'s* because the ownership word *year* does not end in an *s*.)

The company's assets rose in value. (Add *'s* because the ownership word *company* does not end in *s*.)

All the women's votes were counted. (Add *'s* because the ownership word *women* does not end in *s*.)

GUIDE 32: Add only an apostrophe to an ownership word that ends in an s *sound—unless an extra syllable can be pronounced easily.*

Some workers' benefits will cost more. (Add only an apostrophe because the ownership word *workers* ends in an *s*.)

Several months' rent are now due. (Add only an apostrophe because the ownership word *months* ends in an *s*.)

The boss's son got the job. (Add *'s* because an extra syllable can be pronounced easily.)

Tip. To determine whether an ownership word ends in an *'s*, use it in an *of* phrase. For example, *one month's salary* becomes *the salary of one month*. By isolating the ownership word without its apostrophe, you can decide whether it ends in an *s*.

GUIDE 33: Use a possessive pronoun or 's to make a noun possessive when it precedes a gerund, a verb form used as a noun.

We all protested *Laura's* (not *Laura*) smoking.

His (not *Him*) talking on his cell phone angered moviegoers.

I appreciate *your* (not *you*) answering the telephone while I was gone.

✓ *Checkpoint*

Correct any problems with possessives.

56. Both companies executives received huge bonuses, even when employees salaries were falling.

57. In just one weeks time we promise to verify all members names and addresses.

58. The manager and I certainly appreciate you bringing this matter to our CGAs attention.

59. All beneficiaries names must be revealed when insurance companies write policies.

60. Is your sister-in-laws job downtown?

Other Punctuation

GUIDE 34: Use one period to end a statement, command, indirect question, or polite request. Never use two periods.

Matt worked at BioTech, Inc. (Statement. Use only one period.)

Deliver it before 5 p.m. (Command. Use only one period.)

Stacy asked whether she could use the car next weekend. (Indirect question)

Will you please send me an employment application. (Polite request)

Tip. Polite requests often sound like questions. To determine the punctuation, apply the action test. If the request prompts an action, use a period. If it prompts a verbal response, use a question mark.

Faulty	**Improved**
Could you please correct the balance on my next statement? (This polite request prompts an action rather than a verbal response.)	Could you please correct the balance on my next statement.

GUIDE 35: Use a question mark after a direct question and after statements with questions appended.

Are they hiring at BioTech, Inc.?

Most of their training is in-house, isn't it?

GUIDE 36: Use a dash to (a) set off parenthetical elements containing internal commas, (b) emphasize a sentence interruption, or (c) separate an introductory list from a summarizing statement. The dash has legitimate uses. However, some writers use it whenever they know that punctuation is necessary, but they're not sure exactly what. The dash can be very effective, if not misused.

Three top students—Gene Engle, Donna Hersh, and Mika Sato—won awards. (Use dashes to set off elements with internal commas.)

Executives at IBM—despite rampant rumours in the stock market—remained quiet regarding dividend earnings. (Use dashes to emphasize a sentence interruption.)

Japan, Taiwan, and Turkey—these were areas hit by recent earthquakes. (Use a dash to separate an introductory list from a summarizing statement.)

GUIDE 37: Use parentheses to set off nonessential sentence elements, such as explanations, directions, questions, or references.

Researchers find that the office grapevine (see Chapter 1 for more discussion) carries surprisingly accurate information.

Only two dates (February 15 and March 1) are suitable for the meeting.

Tip. Careful writers use parentheses to deemphasize and the dash to emphasize parenthetical information. One expert said, "Dashes shout the news; parentheses whisper it."

GUIDE 38: Use quotation marks to (a) enclose the exact words of a speaker or writer; (b) distinguish words used in a special sense, such as slang; or (c) enclose titles of articles, chapters, or other short works.

"If you make your job important," said the consultant, "it's quite likely to return the favour."

The recruiter said that she was looking for candidates with good communication skills. (Omit quotation marks because the exact words of the speaker are not quoted.)

This office discourages "rad" hair styles and clothing. (Use quotes for slang.)

In *BusinessWeek* I saw an article entitled "Communication for Global Markets." (Use quotation marks around the title of an article; use all caps, underlines, or italics for the name of the publication.)

Tip. Never use quotation marks arbitrarily, as in *Our "spring" sale starts April 1.*

✓ Checkpoint

Add appropriate punctuation.

61. Will you please send your print catalogue as soon as possible
62. (Direct quote) Our Stanley Cup promotion said the CEO will cost nearly $500 000
63. (Deemphasize) Two kinds of batteries see page 16 of the instruction booklet may be used in this camera
64. Tim wondered whether sentences could end with two periods
65. All computers have virus protection don't they

Capitalization

GUIDE 39: Capitalize proper nouns and proper adjectives. Capitalize the *specific* names of persons, places, institutions, buildings, religions, holidays, months, organizations, laws, races, languages, and so forth. Don't capitalize common nouns that make *general* references.

Proper Nouns	**Common Nouns**
Michelle Deluca	the manufacturer's rep
Algonquin Provincial Park	the wilderness park
College of the Rockies	the community college
CN Tower	the downtown building
Environmental Assessment Agency	the federal agency
Persian, Armenian, Hindi	modern foreign languages

Proper Adjectives	
Hispanic markets	Italian dressing
Xerox copy	Japanese executives
Swiss chocolates	Red River economics

GUIDE 40: Capitalize only specific academic courses and degrees.

Professor Donna Howard, Ph.D., will teach Accounting 121 next spring.

James Barker, who holds bachelor's and master's degrees, teaches marketing.

Jessica enrolled in classes in management, English, and business law.

GUIDE 41: Capitalize courtesy, professional, religious, government, family, and business titles when they precede names.

Mr. Jameson, Mrs. Alvarez, and Ms. Robinson (Courtesy titles)
Professor Andrews, Dr. Lee (Professional titles)
Rabbi Cohen, Pastor Williams, Pope John (Religious titles)
Senator Tom Harrison, Mayor Jackson (Government titles)
Uncle Edward, Mother Teresa, Cousin Vinny (Family titles)
Vice President Morris, Budget Director Lopez (Business titles)

Do not capitalize a title when it is followed by an appositive (that is, when the title is followed by a noun that renames or explains it).

Only one professor, Jonathan Marcus, favoured a tuition hike.

Local candidates counted on their premier, Lorne Calvert, to raise funds.

Do not capitalize titles following names unless they are part of an address.

Mark Yoder, president of Yoder Enterprises, hired all employees.

Paula Beech, director of Human Resources, interviewed all candidates.

Send the package to Amanda Harr, Advertising Manager, Cambridge Publishers, 20 Park Plaza, Saint John, NB E2L 1G2.

Generally, do not capitalize a title that replaces a person's name.

Only the prime minister, his chief of staff, and one senator made the trip.

The director of marketing and the sales manager will meet at 1 p.m.

Do not capitalize family titles used with possessive pronouns.

my mother, his father, your cousin

GUIDE 42: Capitalize the principal words in the titles of books, magazines, newspapers, articles, movies, plays, songs, poems, Web sites, and reports. Do not capitalize articles (*a*, *an*, *the*) and prepositions of fewer than four letters (*in*, *to*, *by*, *for*) unless they begin or end the title. The *to* in infinitives (*to run*, *to say*, *to write*) is also not capitalized unless it appears as the first word of a title or subtitle.

I enjoyed the book *A Customer Is More Than a Name*.

Did you read the article titled "Companies in Europe Seek Executives With Multinational Skills" that appeared in *Newsweek*?

We liked the article titled "Advice From a Pro: How to Say It With Pictures."

Check the "Advice and Resources" link at the *CareerBuilder* Web site.

(Note that the titles of books are underlined or italicized but the titles of articles are enclosed in quotation marks.)

GUIDE 43: Capitalize north, south, east, west, *and their derivatives only when they represent specific geographical regions.*

from the Pacific Northwest	heading northwest on the highway
living in the East	east of the city
moving to the West Coast	western Quebec, southern Manitoba

GUIDE 44: Capitalize the names of departments, divisions, or committees within your own organization. Outside your organization capitalize only specific department, division, or committee names.

Lawyers in our Legal Assistance Department met at 2 p.m.

Samsung offers TVs in its Consumer Electronics Division.

We volunteered for the Employee Social Responsibility Committee.

You might send an application to the company's personnel department.

GUIDE 45: Capitalize product names only when they refer to trademarked items. Don't capitalize the common names following manufacturers' names.

Sony portable television	Skippy peanut butter	NordicTrack treadmill
Eveready Energizer battery	Norelco razor	Kodak colour copier
Coca-Cola	Apple computer	Big Mac sandwich

GUIDE 46: Capitalize most nouns followed by numbers or letters (except in page, paragraph, line, and verse references).

Room 14	Exhibit A	Flight 12, Gate 43
Figure 2.1	Plan No.1	Model Z2010

✓ Checkpoint

Capitalize all appropriate words.

66. vice president moore bought a new nokia cell phone before leaving for the east coast.

67. when you come on tuesday, travel west on highway 5 and exit at mt. pleasant street.

68. The director of our human resources department called a meeting of the company's building security committee.

69. our manager and president are flying on air canada flight 34 leaving from gate 32 at halifax stanfield international airport.

70. my father read a businessweek article titled can you build loyalty with bricks and mortar?

Number Usage

GUIDE 47: Use word form to express (a) numbers ten *and under and (b) numbers beginning sentences.* General references to numbers *ten* and under should be expressed in word form. Also use word form for numbers that begin sentences. If the resulting number involves more than two words, however, recast the sentence so that the number does not fall at the beginning.

We answered *six* telephone calls for the *four* sales reps.

Fifteen customers responded to the *three* advertisements today.

A total of 155 cameras were awarded as prizes. (Avoid beginning the sentence with a long number such as *one hundred and fifty-five*.)

GUIDE 48: Use figures to express most references to numbers 11 and over.

Over *150* people from *53* companies attended the two-day workshop.

A 120 mL serving of Haagen-Dazs toffee crunch ice cream contains *300* calories and *19* grams of fat.

GUIDE 49: Use figures to express money, dates, clock time, decimals, and percents.

One item cost only *$1.95*; most, however, were priced between *$10* and *$35*. (Omit the decimals and zeros in even sums of money.)

A meeting is scheduled May 12. (Notice that we do not write *May 12th*.)

Deliveries are made at 10:15 a.m. and again at 4 p.m. (Use lowercase *a.m.* and *p.m.*)

All packages must be ready by 4 o'clock. (Do *not* write 4:00 o'clock.)

When sales dropped *4.7* percent, net income fell *9.8* percent. (Use the word *percent* instead of the symbol %.)

GUIDE 50. Use a combination of words and figures to express sums of 1 million and over. Use words for small fractions.

Orion lost *$62.9 million* in the latest fiscal year on revenues of *$584 million*. (Use a combination of words and figures for sums of 1 million and over.)

Only *one half* of the registered voters turned out. (Use words for small fractions.)

Tip. To ease your memory load, concentrate on the numbers normally expressed in words: numbers *ten* and under, numbers at the beginning of a sentence, and small fractions. Nearly everything else in business is generally written with figures.

✓ Checkpoint

Correct any inappropriate expression of numbers.

71. Although he budgeted fifty dollars, Jake spent 94 dollars and 34 cents for his cell phone.

72. Is the meeting on November 7th or November 14th?

73. We receive UPS deliveries at nine AM and again at four fifteen PM.

74. The company applied for a fifty thousand dollar loan at six %.

75. The Canadian population is close to 33 000 000 and the world population is estimated to be nearly 6 600 000 000.

Abbreviations

Abbreviations should be used only when they are clear and appropriate. Be aware that every field (such as technology and engineering) has its own specialized abbreviations. Therefore, be certain before you use such abbreviations that the receiver of your information is familiar with them.

GUIDE 51: Use abbreviations for titles before and after proper names.

Mr. Peter Mansbridge
Rev. Simon Brownsley
Hon. Diane Finley

Joshua Paul, *Jr.*
Samford Amhas, *M.D.*
Ronny Muntroy, *Ph.D.*

GUIDE 52: Learn when to use periods with abbreviations.

Use a period with conventional abbreviations.

Mrs. Ms. Mr. Dr. Hon. Prof.

Acronyms (shortened forms), which are pronounced as a word, do not have periods.

AIDS scuba laser VIP UNICEF NAFTA

Latin abbreviations have periods.

e.g. i.e. etc. vs.

GUIDE 53: Use abbreviations for familiar institutions, organizations, associations, corporations, and people.

Institutions
UBC UWO WLU CNIB

Organizations and Associations
NDP CIA YMCA CAW CAPIC CMA
OPEC G8 OSSTF NHLPA CHRP CSIS

Corporations
IBM CTW CBC

People
PET FDR LBJ JFK

GUIDE 54: Remember your audience when using abbreviations. If the short form or abbreviation is not well known, spell it out it before using it throughout the discussion.

The CBE (Council of Biology Editors) documentation style is used primarily in the sciences. Consult a reference text for information about how to use CBE documentation.

✓ *Checkpoint*

Correct any inappropriate use of abbreviations.

76. My dr., Samnik Shanban, m.d., has wonderful credentials.

77. To save both money and time, the specialist recommended l.a.s.e.r. surgery.

78. The question was addressed to Prof Antle.

79. You should remember to use a large-sized font when preparing overheads, eg, 24-point or larger.

80. Mrs. Cathrick was n.a. for comment.

Key to C.L.U.E. Checkpoint Exercises in Appendix A

This key shows all corrections. If you marked anything else, double-check the appropriate guideline.

1. Disney, destination

2. yearly, which

3. hour; however,
4. pavilion;
5. wedding;
6. If I *were* you, I would have *gone* . . . .
7. could have *written* . . . had *begun* earlier.
8. vice president *saw* . . . immediately *came*
9. vice president *were*
10. manager had *known* . . . would have *given*
11. talent *were* spent
12. attachments, *was*
13. companies *is*
14. addresses *is*
15. lawyer *has*
16. My partner and *I* . . . . , but *yours*
17. was *hers*, but *its*
18. you and *me* . . . *their* printer
19. *There's* not much the boss or *I* can do if *it's* broken, . . . reported to him or *me* earlier.
20. but *yours* and *hers*
21. *whomever*
22. *Whom* have you asked . . . .
23. for *whoever*
24. Matt and *I*
25. by *whoever*
26. Every employee must wear *a* picture identification badge, OR *All employees* must wear picture identification *badges.*
27. slower career advancement, but *flexible scheduling* appeals to many workers. [*Revise to avoid the vague pronoun* it.]
28. Any renter must pay *the* rent . . . . OR *All renters must pay their rent* . . . .
29. reported that *a* computer . . . OR reported that *his or her* computer . . . .
30. communication. *These techniques are* particularly important [*Revise to avoid the vague pronoun* This.]
31. My manager and *I* could not resist the *once-in-a-lifetime* opportunity.
32. John and *he* finished their task so *quickly*
33. do *well* . . . *part-time* jobs and a few *full-time*
34. told him and *me* . . . *personally.*
35. *not-too-distant* future
36. class, Erin . . . with commas, semicolons,
37. studying punctuation,
38. program,
39. merchandising,

40. junior year, . . . in Montreal, Edmonton,
41. Blvd., Toronto, ON M2J 1E6
42. not, however,
43. paralegals, . . . next year,
44. May 15, 2010, . . . May 15, 2015.
45. fact,
46. sooner [*delete comma*]
47. car,
48. is [*delete comma*]
49. think, on the other hand, . . . buying [*delete comma*]
50. automakers are [*delete comma*] at this time [*delete comma*]
51. entry-level job; his long-term goal, however,
52. professors: Rebecca Hilbrink, University of Western Ontario; Lora Lindsey, McGill University; and Michael Malone, Durham College.
53. qualities: loyalty, initiative,
54. individuals; however,
55. region; therefore,
56. companies' . . . employees'
57. one week's time, . . . members'
58. appreciate *your* . . . CGA's
59. beneficiaries'
60. sister-in-law's
61. possible.
62. "Our Stanley Cup promotion," said the CEO, "will cost nearly $500 000."
63. Two kinds of batteries (see page 16 of the instruction booklet)
64. two periods.
65. protection, don't they?
66. Vice President Moore . . . Nokia . . . East Coast
67. When . . . Tuesday, . . . Highway 5 . . . Mt. Pleasant Street.
68. Human Resources Department . . . Building Security Committee
69. Our . . . Air Canada Flight 34 . . . Gate 32 at Halifax Stanfield International Airport
70. *BusinessWeek* article titled, "Can You Build Loyalty With Bricks and Mortar?"
71. $50 . . . $94.34
72. November 7 or November 14 [*delete* th]
73. 9 a.m. . . . 4:15 p.m. (Note only one period at the end of the sentence.)
74. $50 000 . . . 6 percent.
75. 33 million . . . 6.6 billion

76. doctor … M.D.,

77. laser

78. Professor

79. e.g.

80. not available

Confusing Words

accede:	to agree or consent
exceed:	to go over a limit
accept:	to receive
except:	to exclude; (prep) but
adverse:	opposing; antagonistic
averse:	unwilling; reluctant
advice:	suggestion, opinion
advise:	to counsel or recommend
affect:	to influence
effect:	(n) outcome, result; (v) to bring about, to create
all ready:	prepared
already:	by this time
all right:	satisfactory
alright:	unacceptable variant spelling
altar:	structure for worship
alter:	to change
appraise:	to estimate
apprise:	to inform
ascent:	(n) rising or going up
assent:	(v) to agree or consent
assure:	to promise
ensure:	to make certain
insure:	to protect from loss
capital:	(n) city that is seat of government; wealth of an individual; (adj) chief
capitol:	building that houses U.S. state or national lawmakers
cereal:	breakfast food
serial:	arranged in sequence
cite:	to quote; to summon
site:	location
sight:	a view; to see
coarse:	rough-textured
course:	a route; part of a meal; a unit of learning
complement:	that which completes
compliment:	(n) praise, flattery; (v) to praise or flatter
conscience:	regard for fairness
conscious:	aware
council:	governing body
counsel:	(n) advice, lawyer; (v) to give advice
credible:	believable
creditable:	good enough for praise or esteem; reliable
desert:	arid land; to abandon
dessert:	sweet food
device:	invention or mechanism
devise:	to design or arrange
disburse:	to pay out
disperse:	to scatter widely
elicit:	to draw out
illicit:	unlawful
envelop:	(v) to wrap, surround, or conceal
envelope:	(n) a container for a written message
every day:	each single day
everyday:	ordinary
farther:	a greater distance
further:	additional
formally:	in a formal manner
formerly:	in the past
grate:	(v) to reduce to small particles; to cause irritation; (n) a frame of crossed bars blocking a passage
great:	(adj) large in size; numerous; eminent or distinguished
hole:	an opening
whole:	complete
imply:	to suggest indirectly
infer:	to reach a conclusion
lean:	(v) to rest against; (adj) not fat
lien:	(n) a legal right or claim to property

liable:	legally responsible
libel:	damaging written statement
loose:	not fastened
lose:	to misplace
miner:	person working in a mine
minor:	lesser; a person under age
patience:	calm perseverance
patients:	people receiving medical treatment
personal:	private, individual
personnel:	employees
plaintiff:	(n) one who initiates a lawsuit
plaintive:	(adj) expressive of suffering or woe
populace:	(n) the masses; population of a place
populous:	(adj) densely populated
precede:	to go before
proceed:	to continue
precedence:	priority
precedents:	events used as an example
principal:	(n) capital sum; school official; (adj) chief
principle:	rule of action
stationary:	immovable
stationery:	writing material
than:	conjunction showing comparison
then:	adverb meaning "at that time"
their:	possessive form of they
there:	at that place or point
they're:	contraction of they are
to:	a preposition; the sign of the infinitive
too:	an adverb meaning "also" or "to an excessive extent"
two:	a number
waiver:	abandonment of a claim
waver:	to shake or fluctuate

165 Frequently Misspelled Words

absence
accommodate
achieve
acknowledgment
across
adequate
advisable
analyze
annually
appointment
argument
automatically
bankruptcy
becoming
beneficial
budget
business
calendar
cancelled
catalogue
centre
changeable
column
committee
congratulate
conscience
conscious
consecutive
consensus
consistent
control
convenient
correspondence
courteous
criticize
decision
deductible
defendant
definitely
dependant (n)
dependent (adj)
describe
desirable
destroy
development
disappoint
dissatisfied
division
efficient
embarrass
emphasis
emphasize
employee
envelope
equipped
especially
evidently
exaggerate
excellent
exempt
existence
extraordinary
familiar
fascinate
feasible
February
fibre
fiscal
foreign
forty
fourth
friend
genuine
government
grammar
grateful
guarantee
harass
height
hoping
immediate
incidentally
incredible
independent
indispensable
interrupt
irrelevant
itinerary
judgment
knowledge
legitimate
library
licence (n)
license (v)
maintenance
manageable
manufacturer
mileage
miscellaneous
mortgage
necessary
nevertheless
ninety
ninth
noticeable
occasionally
occurred
offered
omission
omitted
opportunity
opposite
ordinarily
paid
pamphlet
permanent
permitted
pleasant
practical
prevalent
privilege
probably
procedure
profited
prominent
qualify
quantity
questionnaire
receipt
receive
recognize
recommendation
referred
regarding
remittance
representative
restaurant
schedule
secretary
separate
similar
sincerely
software
succeed
sufficient
supervisor
surprise
tenant
therefore
thorough
though
through
truly
undoubtedly
unnecessarily
usable
usage
using
usually
valuable
vigorous (but vigour)
volume
weekday
writing
yield

appendix B

Documentation Formats

For many reasons business writers are careful to properly document report data. Citing sources strengthens a writer's argument, as you learned in Chapter 12. Acknowledging sources also shields writers from charges of plagiarism. Moreover, good references help readers pursue further research.

Before we discuss specific documentation formats, you must understand the difference between *source* notes and *content* notes. Source notes identify quotations, paraphrased passages, and author references. They lead readers to the sources of cited information, and they must follow a consistent format. Content notes, on the other hand, enable writers to add comments, explain information not directly related to the text, or refer readers to other sections of a report. Because content notes are generally infrequent, most writers identify them in the text with a raised asterisk (*). At the bottom of the page, the asterisk is repeated with the content note following. If two content notes appear on one page, a double asterisk identifies the second reference.

Your real concern will be with source notes. These identify quotations or paraphrased ideas in the text, and they direct readers to a complete list of references (a bibliography) at the end of your report. Researchers have struggled for years to develop the perfect documentation system, one that is efficient for the writer and crystal clear to the reader. As a result, many systems exist, each with its advantages. The important thing for you is to adopt one system and use it consistently.

Students frequently ask, "But what documentation system is most used in business?" Actually, no one method dominates. Many businesses have developed their own hybrid systems. These companies generally supply guidelines illustrating their in-house style to employees. Before starting any research project on the job, you will want to inquire about your organization's preferred documentation style. You can also look in the files for examples of previous reports.

References are usually cited in two places: (a) a brief citation appears in the text, and (b) a complete citation appears in a bibliography at the end of the report. The two most common formats for citations and bibliographies are those of the Modern Language Association (MLA) and the American Psychological Association (APA). Each has its own style for textual references and bibliography lists.

Modern Language Association Format

Writers in the humanities frequently use the MLA format, as illustrated in Figure B.1. In parentheses close to the textual reference appears the author's name and page cited. If no author is known, a shortened version of the source title is used. At the end of the report, the writer lists all references alphabetically in a bibliography called "Works Cited." To see a long report illustrating MLA documentation, turn to Figure 14.4 in Chapter 14. For more information consult *MLA Handbook for Writers of Research Papers*, 7th edition (New York: Modern Language Association of America, 2009).

Figure B.1 ***Portions of MLA Text Page and Bibliography***

Peanut butter was first delivered to the world by a St. Louis physician in 1890. As discussed at the Peanut Advisory Board's Web site, peanut butter was originally promoted as a protein substitute for elderly patients ("History"). However, it was the 1905 Universal Exposition in St. Louis that truly launched peanut butter. Since then, annual peanut butter consumption has zoomed to 3.3 pounds a person in the United States (Barrons 46). America's farmers produce 1.6 million tons of peanuts annually, about half of which is used for oil, nuts, and candy. Lisa Gibbons, executive secretary of the Peanut Advisory Board, says that "peanuts in some form are in the top four candies: Snickers, Reese's Peanut Butter Cups, Peanut M&Ms, and Butterfingers" (Meadows 32).

Works Cited

Barrons, Elizabeth Ruth. "A Comparison of Domestic and International Consumption of Legumes." *Journal of Economic Agriculture* 23 (2007): 45–49. Print.

"History of Peanut Butter." *PeanutButterLovers.com.* Peanut Advisory Board, n.d. Web. 19 Jan. 2008.

Meadows, Mark Allen. "Peanut Crop Is Anything but Peanuts at Home and Overseas." *Business Monthly* 30 Sept. 2008: 31–34. Print.

MLA In-Text Format. In-text citations generally appear close to the point where the reference is mentioned or at the end of the sentence, inside the closing period. Follow these guidelines:

- Include the last name of the author(s) and the page number. Do not use a comma: (Smith 310).
- If the author's name is mentioned in the text, cite only the page number in parentheses. Do not include either the word *page* or the abbreviations *p.* or *pp.*
- If no author is known, refer to the document title or a shortened version of it: ("Facts at Fingertips" 102).

MLA Bibliographic Format. The "Works Cited" bibliography lists all references cited in a report. Some writers include all works consulted. A portion of an MLA bibliography is shown in Figure B.1. A more complete list of model references appears in Figure B.2. Following are selected guidelines summarizing important points regarding MLA bibliographic format:

- Use italics for the titles of books, magazines, newspapers, journals, and Web sites. Capitalize all main words.
- Enclose the titles of magazine, newspaper, journal, and Web site articles in quotation marks. Include volume and issue numbers for journals only (including journals on the Web).

FIGURE B.2 ***MLA Bibliography Sample References***

Works Cited

Air Canada. *2008 Annual Report.* Dorval, QC. Print. — Annual report

Atamian, Richard A., and Ellen Ferranto. *Driving Market Forces.* New York: HarperCollins, 2008. Print. — Book, two authors

Berss, Marcia. "Protein Man." *Forbes* 24 Oct. 2008: 65–66. Print. — Magazine article

Cantrell, Mark R. and Hilary Watson. "Violence in Today's Workplace." *Office Review* 10 Jan. 2007: 24–29. PDF file. — Magazine article, online, PDF version

"Globalization Often Means That the Fast Track Leads Overseas." *National Post* 17 June 2009: A10. Print. — Newspaper article, no author

"Information Processing." *Encyclopaedia Britannica.* Encyclopaedia Britannica Inc., 2009. Web. 19 Oct. 2009. — Encyclopedia, online

Lancaster, Hal. "When Taking a Tip From a Job Network, Proceed With Caution." *Globe and Mail* 7 Feb. 2009: B1. Print. — Newspaper article, one author

Lang, Roberta. "Most People Fail to Identify Nonverbal Signs." *New York Times.* New York Times, 2 Mar. 2009. Web. 15 November 2009. — Newspaper article, online

Pinkerton Investigation Services. *The Employer's Guide to Investigation Services.* 3rd ed. Atlanta: Pinkerton Information Center, 2009. Print. — Brochure

Procter & Gamble. Home page. Procter & Gamble, 2008. Web. 28 Nov. 2008. — Entire Internet Site

Rivers, Frank. Personal interview. 16 May 2009. — Interview

"Spam: Eliminate It From the Workplace." *SmartPros Accounting.* SmartPros Ltd., 8 Aug. 2008. Web. 12 Sept. 2008. — Internet document, no author

Statistics Canada. *A Portrait of Persons With Disabilities: Target Groups Project.* Ottawa: Ministry of Industry, Science and Technology, 2004. Print. — Government publication

Wetherbee, James C., Nicholas P. Vitalari, and Andrew Milner. "Key Trends in Systems Development in Europe and North America." *Journal of Global Information Management* 3.2 (2008): 5–20. Print. ["3.2" signifies volume 3, issue 2] — Journal article with volume and issue numbers

Wilson, Craig M. "E-Mail Bill May Fail to Curtail Spamming." *eWeek* 9 July 2008: 49. *InfoTrac College Edition.* Web. 26 Aug. 2008. — Article from online database

Yellin, Mike. "Re: Managing Managers and Cell Phones." Online posting. *Yahoo! Groups: ecommerce.* Yahoo! Inc., 9 Sept 2008. Web. 15 Sept. 2008. — Online forum posting

Note: Although MLA style prescribes double-spacing for the works cited, we show single spacing to conserve space and to represent preferred business usage.

- Indicate the medium of publication for every entry in the works-cited list. For print periodicals (journals, newspapers, magazines), the medium appears after the page numbers. For nonperiodical print publications (such as books and pamphlets), the medium appears after the date of publication; however, if the item being cited is only part of a larger work (e.g., an essay, poem, or short story in an anthology or an introduction, preface, foreword, or afterword in a book), give the inclusive page numbers of the piece you are citing after the publication date, then list the medium of publication. For Web publications, the medium appears between the date of publication and the date of access.
- For Web publications, include a retrieval date. A URL should be included only when the reader probably would not be able to locate the source without it. (If you choose to provide a URL, give the complete address [including *http://*] after the date of access, in angle brackets. If you need to divide the URL over two lines, do so only after the double slashes or a single slash.)

American Psychological Association Format

Popular in the social and physical sciences, the American Psychological Association (APA) documentation style uses parenthetic citations. That is, each author reference is shown in parentheses when cited in the text, as shown in Figure B.3. At the end of the report, all references are listed alphabetically in a bibliography called "References." For more information about APA formats, see the *Publication Manual of the American Psychological Association*, 5th edition (Washington, DC: American Psycho-

FIGURE B.3 ***Portions of APA Text Page and Bibliography***

Peanut butter was first delivered to the world by a St. Louis physician in 1890. As discussed at the Peanut Advisory Board's Web site, peanut butter was originally promoted as a protein substitute for elderly patients (History, n.d.). However, it was the 1905 Universal Exposition in St. Louis that truly launched peanut butter. Since then, annual peanut butter consumption has zoomed to 3.3 pounds a person in the United States (Barrons, 2007, p. 46). America's farmers produce 1.6 million tons of peanuts annually, about half of which is used for oil, nuts, and candy. Lisa Gibbons, executive secretary of the Peanut Advisory Board, says that "peanuts in some form are in the top four candies: Snickers, Reese's Peanut Butter Cups, Peanut M&Ms, and Butterfingers" (Meadows, 2008, p. 32).

References

Barrons, E. (2007). A comparison of domestic and international consumption of legumes. *Journal of Economic Agriculture, 23*(3), 45–49.

History of peanut butter (n.d.). Peanut Advisory Board. Retrieved January 19, 2008, from http://www.peanutbutterlovers.com/History/index.html

Meadows, M. (2008, September 30). Peanut crop is anything but peanuts at home and overseas. *Business Monthly, 14*, 31–34.

logical Association, 2001) or *Concise Rules of APA Style* (Washington, DC: American Psychological Association, 2005).

APA In-Text Format. Within the text, document each specific textual source with a short description in parentheses. Following are selected guidelines summarizing important elements of APA style:

- Include the last name of the author(s), date of publication, and page number: (Jones, 2008, p. 36). Use "n.d." if no date is available.
- If no author is known, refer to the first few words of the reference list entry and the year: (Computer Privacy, 2008, p. 59).
- Omit page numbers for general references, but always include page numbers for direct quotations.

FIGURE B.4 ***Model APA Bibliography Sample References***

References

Air Canada. (2008). *2008 Annual Report.* Dorval, QC.	Annual report
Atamian, R. M., & Ferranto, M. (2008). *Driving market forces.* New York: HarperCollins.	Book, two authors
Berss, M. (2008, October 24). Protein man. *Forbes,* 64–66.	Magazine article
Cantrell, M. R., & Watson, H. (2007, January 10). Violence in today's workplace [Electronic version]. *Office Review,* 24–29.	Magazine article, viewed electronically
Globalization often means that the fast track leads overseas. (2009, June 17). *National Post,* p. A10.	Newspaper article, no author
Information processing (2008). In *Encyclopaedia Britannica.* Retrieved October 19, 2008, from Encyclopaedia Britannica Online: http://britannica.com/eb/article-61669	Encyclopedia, online
Lancaster, H. (2009, February 7). When taking a tip from a job network, proceed with caution. *The Globe and Mail,* p. B1.	Newspaper article, one author
Lang, R. T. (2009, March 2). Most people fail to identify nonverbal signs. *The New York Times.* Retrieved November 15, 2009, from http://www.nytimes.com	Newspaper article, online
Pinkerton Investigation Services. (2009). *The employer's guide to investigation services* (3rd ed.) [Brochure]. Atlanta: Pinkerton Information Center.	Brochure
Procter & Gamble home page (2008) Retrieved November 28, 2008, from http://www.pg.com	Web site
Spam: Eliminate it from the workplace. (2008, August 8). *SmartPros.* Retrieved September 12, 2008, from http://accounting.smartpros.com/	Internet document, no author
Wetherbee, J. C., Vitalari, N. P., & Milner, A. (2008). Key trends in systems development in Europe and North America. *Journal of Global Information Management, 3*(2), 5–20. ["3(2)" signifies volume 3, series or issue 2]	Journal article with volume and issue numbers
Wilson, C. M. (2008, July 9). E-mail bill may fail to curtail spamming. *eWeek.* Retrieved August 26, 2008, from InfoTrac database.	Article from online database
Wilson, G., & Simmons, P. (2008). *Plagiarism: What it is, and how to avoid it.* Retrieved July 4, 2008, from Biology Program Guide 2008/2009 at the University of British Columbia Web site: http://www.zoology.ubc/ca/bpg/plagiarism.htm	World Wide Web document with author and date
Yellin, M. (2008, September 9). Re: Managing managers and cell phones. [Msg 44]. Message posted to http://groups.yahoo.com/groups/ecommerce/message44	Online forum or discussion group

APA Reference Format. List all citations alphabetically in a section called "References." A portion of an APA bibliography is shown in Figure B.3. A more complete list of model references appears in Figure B.4. APA style requires specific capitalization and sequencing guidelines, some of which are summarized here:

- Include an author's name with the last name first, followed by initials: Smith, M. A. First and middle names are not used.
- Show the date of publication in parentheses immediately after the author's name: Smith, M. A. (2009).
- Italicize the titles of books. Use "sentence-style" capitalization. This means that only the first word of a title, proper nouns, and the first word after an internal colon are capitalized.
- Do not italicize or underscore the titles of magazine and journal articles. Use sentence-style capitalization for article titles.
- Italicize the names of magazines and journals. Capitalize the initial letters of all main words.
- In citing online documents, list only the search date and main search site page for URLs that are impractically long and complicated.
- To reference a published article that you viewed only in its electronic form, add in brackets after the article title: [Electronic version]. Use this form only if the electronic version is identical to the published version.
- To reference an online article that you have reason to believe has been changed (that is, the format is different from that of the print version, or page numbers are not indicated), add the date you retrieved the document and the URL. Do not include a period after a URL that appears at the end of a line.

key to C.L.U.E. review exercises

Chapter 1

1. To **succeed** in **today's** high-tech **business world,** you need **highly developed** communication skills.
2. You especially need **writing** and **grammar** skills [delete comma] because **employees** spend **60 percent** of **their** time processing documents.
3. One organization paid **$3000** each for **12 employees** to attend a **one-week workshop** in communication training.
4. My coworker and **I were surprised** to learn that more information has been produced in the last **30** years **than** in the previous **5000** years.
5. If you work in **an** office with open **cubicles, it's** rude to listen to **W**eb **radio,** streaming **audio,** or other multimedia [delete comma] without headphones.
6. When making a **decision,** you should gather **information** [delete comma] and **then** weigh the advantages and **disadvantages** of each alternative.
7. If you are defining ***communication,*** for example, a **principal** element **is** the transmission of information and meaning.
8. **Ms.** Johnson had **three** messages to send **immediately; consequently,** she **chose** e-mail because it was **definitely** the [delete **most**] fastest **communication** channel.
9. **Five** elements that make up your frame of reference are the **following:** **e**xperience, **e**ducation, **c**ulture, **expectations,** and **p**ersonality.
10. Just between you and **me,** I'm sure our company **p**resident thinks that honesty and integrity **are** more important **than increased** profits.

Chapter 2

1. Our **company's** management **council** had **already** decided to **appoint an** investigative **team; however, it** acted **too slowly.**
2. **Organizations** are forming teams for at least **three** good **reasons:** better decisions, [delete **more**] faster response **times,** and **increased** productivity.
3. Most teams go through **four** development **phases:** **f**orming, **s**torming, **n**orming, and **p**erforming.
4. Some group members play dysfunctional **roles,** and they disrupt the **group's** progress toward **its** goal.
5. Successful **self-directed** teams are **autonomous; that is,** they can **hire, fire,** and discipline **their** own **members.**
6. Although we tried to reach a **consensus,** several **m**anagers and even the **vice president** opposed the **whole** proposal.
7. At last **month's** staff **meeting,** the CEO and **he complimented** the **team's** efforts and made **warm,** supportive comments.
8. Rather **than** schedule many **face-to-face meetings,** the team decided to investigate a **$3000 desktop** videoconferencing system.
9. When conflict erupted at our **team's January meeting,** we made a **conscious** effort to confront the **underlying** issues.
10. **Fifty-five** people are expected to attend the **t**raining session on April **15; consequently, she** and I must find a [delete **more**] larger room.

Chapter 3

1. **Everyone** knows how to **listen,** but many of us listen at only **25 percent efficiency**.
2. **It's** wise to avoid arguing or criticizing [delete comma] when listening to a superior.
3. The **four** stages of listening are [delete colon] **p**erception, **i**nterpretation, **evaluation,** and **a**ction.
4. To improve **retention,** you should take notes [delete comma] and rewrite **them immediately** after listening.
5. While waiting for the **speaker's** next **idea,** you should review what **has already been said**.
6. **High status** and self-confidence **are** conveyed by erect posture.
7. On May **12** [delete comma] the company **p**resident awarded bonuses to Tyler and **me; however,** we didn't **receive** our cheques until June **1**.
8. In a poll of nearly **3000 employees,** only **one third** felt that **their companies** valued **their** opinions and **suggestions**.
9. The appearance and mannerisms of a speaker **affect** a **listener's** evaluation of a message.
10. A list of suggestions for improving retention of a **speaker's** ideas **is** found in an article titled **"Best** Listening **Habits,"** which appeared in ***Fortune***.

Chapter 4

1. The **p**resident of MainStreet Enterprises, along with other executives of local **companies, is** considering **overseas** sales.
2. International business was **already** common among big **companies; however,** even small **businesses** are now seeking global markets.
3. **Three** different employees asked the **s**upervisor and **me** whether we should give gifts to our Chinese business **guests.**
4. Gifts for the children of an **A**rab are **welcome; however,** gifts for an **Arab's** wife are not **advisable**.
5. In **L**atin **A**merica **knives** are not proper **gifts;** they signify cutting off **a** relationship.
6. When it opened **its $120 million** plant in **Beijing,** Motorola had to offer housing **to** attract **quality** applicants.
7. On May **12 an** article titled **"The Chinese Puzzle,"** which appeared in the magazine ***Workforce Management,*** described the **difficulties** of managing **employees worldwide.**
8. We invited **75** employees to hear the **cross-cultural** talk that begins at **4 p.m.** [Delete one period]
9. Although **C**anada's **two** official languages are **F**rench **and E**nglish, [delete colon and replace with comma] it is unofficially a land of many languages.
10. Transparency **I**nternational's **2005 I**nternational **G**lobal **P**erceptions **I**ndex **ranks I**celand as the most ethical nation.

Chapter 5

1. In this class my friend and I learned that business writing should be [delete colon] **p**urposeful, **economical,** and **r**eader-**o**riented.
2. **Five** or **six** members of our team will **probably** attend the **writers' workshop; therefore,** be sure they **receive** notices.
3. If I **were you,** I would learn the following **three** parts of the writing **process: prewriting, writing,** and revising.
4. **Experts** suggest that you spend **25** percent of your time **planning, 25** percent **writing, 45** percent **revising,** and **5** percent proofreading.
5. Although one of the employees **is** not **available,** we **proceeded** to schedule the meeting at **3** p.m. on **Wednesday,** October **12**.
6. The **vice president** was **surprised** to learn that a **two-day** writing workshop for our **company's** employees would cost **$1200** each.
7. **We're** not asking the seller to **alter its proposal;** we are asking team members to check the **proposal's** figures.
8. **They're** wondering whether a list of all our **customers'** names and addresses **was** inadvertently **released.**
9. As you begin to **write,** you should **analyze** the task [delete comma] and **identify** the purpose.
10. By replacing unfamiliar words with **everyday,** familiar **ones,** you can make **your** audience comprehend your ideas more **quickly**.

Chapter 6

1. When our **m**arketing **m**anager had to write a **20-page report,** she started by collecting information [delete comma] and organizing it.
2. A business **writer's** biggest problem is usually poor **organization,** according to experts.
3. The company **vice president** came to the **p**resident and **me** asking for help with **two** complex but **separate** advertising problems.
4. Because neither of us **was** particularly **creative,** we decided to organize a brainstorming session rather **than** work by **ourselves.**
5. Our **brainstorming** session included [delete colon] Amanda, Rory, **Rashid,** and Cynthia.
6. One of our **principal** goals **was** to create **100** ideas in **30 minutes; however,** we were prepared to meet **for** up to **one** hour.
7. Although we knew the **principles** of **outlining,** we had trouble grouping our ideas into **three** to **five** major headings.
8. Robyn **Clarke's** article titled **"A Better Way to Brainstorm,"** which appeared in the magazine ***Black Enterprise,*** was helpful to the **p**resident and **me.**
9. Frontloading a message saves a **reader's time; therefore, it's** worth making the effort to put the main idea first.
10. By learning to distinguish **phrases** from **clauses, you'll** be better able to avoid **three** basic sentence **faults:** the fragment, the **run-on sentence,** and the comma splice.

Chapter 7

1. My manager **told** my colleague and **me** that we had to be more **conscious** of our proofreading because our reports had **too** many errors.
2. Readers want to scan messages **quickly; therefore,** we should use **everyday** language and be concise.
3. Even in **Europe,** company executives are **disappointed** by messages that are **too** long **and too** difficult to read.
4. One **manager's** report contained so many **redundancies** that **its** main **principles of** requesting **p**rovincial and **f**ederal funding **were** lost.
5. **Your** writing will sound **fresher** [or, less preferably, **more fresh**] [delete comma] if you eliminate trite business **phrases** such as "pursuant to **your** request."
6. All **three** of our **company's recruiters**—Angelica Santos, Kirk Adams, and David Toms—**criticized their poorly written** procedures.
7. To help **receivers** anticipate and comprehend ideas **quickly, two** special writing techniques **are helpful: parallelism,** which involves balanced **writing,** and **bulleting,** which **makes** important points more visible.
8. When I **proofread an** important **document,** I **always** work with a buddy [delete comma] and read from a printed copy.
9. Read a message once for word **meanings;** read it again for **grammar** and mechanics.
10. **It's almost** impossible to improve **one's** communication skills **alone; therefore, everyone** should take advantage of this educational **opportunity.**

Chapter 8

1. More **than 90** percent of **companies** now use **e-mail; therefore,** employees must become more **knowledgeable** about **its** dangers.
2. Most e-mails and memos **deliver straightforward** information that is not sensitive [delete comma] and **requires** little persuasion.
3. If I **were you,** I would check all **incoming e-mails** and attachments that **were** sent to you and **him.**
4. Memos typically contain **four necessary parts:** subject line, opening, **body,** and action closing.
5. Fear of inappropriate e-mail use [delete comma] and the need to boost productivity [delete comma] **have** spurred **employee-monitoring** programs.
6. When you respond **to an** e-mail **message,** you should not **automatically** return the **sender's** message.
7. **Wasn't** it **Dr.** Rivers and **Ms.** Johnson who **always** wrote **their** e-mails in all **capital letters?**
8. A list of the **names** and **addresses** of e-mail recipients **was** sent using the "bcc" function.
9. Our **Information Technology Department,** which was **formerly** in **Room 35,** has moved **its** offices to **Room** 5.

10. The ***Evening News Press,*** our local **newspaper,** featured as its **principal** article a story entitled [delete comma] "Cyber-Slacking **Is K**illing **P**roductivity!"

Chapter 9

1. Business letters, despite the enormous popularity of e-**mail,** must still be **written** when a **permanent** record is **necessary**.
2. If you follow a writing **process,** organizing the content and composing the first draft **are** easier.
3. Chelsea acts as if she **were** the only person who ever received a **compliment** about **her** business **writing.**
4. **Chelsea's letter,** which she sent to the manager and **me,** was distinguished by **three characteristics:** clear content, a **tone of** goodwill, and correct form.
5. Davonne **Jordan, who** I think is our **newly appointed vice president,** wants everyone in the **c**ompany to beware of computer viruses.
6. When the **office m**anager writes business letters or **memos,** he **always** ends **them** with the same "Do not hesitate" phrase.
7. The manager and **I** realized an item was missing from the April **1** shipment; **consequently,** we sent a claim letter for **$131.**
8. After our supervisor and **she** returned from **their** meeting at **2 p.m.,** we were able to sort the **customers'** names and addresses more **quickly**.
9. If you must write an order **letter,** be sure to **include** [delete colon] the **quantity, order number, description, unit price, tax, shipping,** and total costs.
10. Matthew enclosed a cheque for **$200; however,** he worried that it was insufficient to regain the confidence of the customer.

Chapter 10

1. Persuasion requires learning about **your** audience [delete comma] and **analyzing** why **it** might resist your goal.
2. An **especially** effective **argument** includes **two indispensable elements:** a reasonable request [delete comma] and a **well-presented** line of reasoning.
3. If **your** goal **was** to persuade a lending institution to give you **$50 000,** you would probably use rational **appeals.**
4. Our **p**resident and **s**enior **s**ales **m**anager decided to send a sales letter to all current **customers; therefore,** they analyzed the product, **purpose,** and audience.
5. **Their** sales letter focuses on the following **four parts:** (1) **gaining** the **audience's attention,** (2) convincing **it** that the purpose is **worthy,** (3) **o**vercoming **resistance,** and (4) **m**otivating action.
6. Experts agree that one of the biggest mistakes in persuasive **requests is** the failure to **anticipate** [delete comma] and **offset** audience resistance.
7. Because the **m**anager and **he built** interest with **easy-to-read** facts and **figures, their** letter will **undoubtedly succeed.**
8. A claim letter is a form of **complaint; consequently, it's** wise to use the indirect strategy.
9. Anger and emotion **are** not effective in **persuasion,** but many writers **cannot control their tempers.**
10. Our latest press **release,** which was written in our **C**orporate **C**ommunication **Department,** announces the opening of **three C**anadian **offices.**

Chapter 11

1. Bad news is **generally disappointing; however,** the negative feelings can be reduced.
2. **Two** ways to reduce the **disappointment** of bad news **are to** [delete colon] (1) give reasons first [delete comma] and (2) reveal the news sensitively.
3. When delivering bad **news, it's** important that you make sure the **receiver** understands and **accepts** it.
4. The indirect pattern consists of **four parts:** buffer, reasons, bad news, and closing.
5. Although the indirect pattern is not **appropriate** for every **situation,** it is **usually** better **than** a blunt announcement of bad news.
6. On June **1** our company **p**resident and **vice president** revealed a **$4 million** drop in **profits,** which was bad news for **everyone.**
7. Because of declining profits and **rising h**ealth **costs,** the **d**irector of our Human Resources Department announced **an** increase in each **employee's** contribution to **h**ealth **b**enefits.
8. Most of us prefer to be let down **gently** [delete comma] when **we're** being refused **something;**

that's why the **reasons-before-refusal** pattern is effective.

9. When a **well-known t**ire company recalled **hundreds** of thousands of **tires, its p**resident issued **an** apology to the public [delete comma] and all injured **customers.**
10. If I **were you,** I would begin the **bad-news** message with a **compliment,** not a blunt rejection.

Chapter 12

1. Reports are a fact of life in **Canadian business; consequently, business writers** must learn to prepare **them.**
2. Although reports vary in **length, content, form,** and formality **level,** they all have **one** purpose.
3. The primary purpose of reports [delete comma] **is** to answer questions and solve problems **systematically.**
4. Letter reports **usually** have side margins of **2.5 to 3.5** centimetres.
5. The format of a report is determined by **its** [delete colon] **length, topic, audience,** and purpose.
6. The CEO and **manager,** who had **gone** to a conference in the **West,** delivered a report to Jeff and **me** when they returned.
7. If **your** report is authorized by **someone,** be sure to review **its work plan** with **that person** before **proceeding.**
8. Ilia was **offered $500** to finish **Max's report,** but she said it was "**too** little and **too** late."
9. To search the **Internet,** you need a browser such as **M**icrosoft **I**nternet **E**xplorer.
10. If you wish to illustrate report **data,** you may **choose** from among the following visual **aids:** tables, charts, **graphs,** and pictures.

Chapter 13

1. When conducting research for a **report,** you may face an **incredible** jumble of data including [delete colon] printouts, disk files, note cards, **copies** of articles, **interview** notes, **questionnaire results,** and statistics.
2. The information in tables **is usually** easier to read **than** the same information presented in **paragraphs.**
3. When the **c**ompany **p**resident and **I** use the word ***average,*** we are **referring** to the **mean,** which is the arithmetic average.
4. The following **three** statistical terms frequently describe **data: m**ean, **median,** and **m**ode.
5. Readers of **business** [delete apostrophe] reports often turn **first** to the **c**onclusions and **recommendations; therefore,** these **sections** must be written **very** carefully.
6. Informational **re**ports emphasize facts**; a**nalytical reports, **however**, emphasize reasoning and conclusions.
7. Report **c**onclusions explain what the problem **is; r**ecommendations tell how to solve it.
8. Frontloading the **recommendations** works when the topic is **routine** [delete comma] and when the audience is receptive.
9. In writing most business **reports,** you will **generally** organize **your** data using **one** of the following **five methods:** time, component, importance, **criteria,** or convention.
10. The **i**ntroduction to a report should tell **its** purpose and **significance;** it should also preview the main points.

Chapter 14

1. The format and organization of a proposal **are** important [delete comma] if a writer **wants** it to be taken **seriously.**
2. Proposals are **written** offers to do the **following:** solve problems, provide **services,** or sell **equipment.**
3. Our **vice president** and **m**anager worked **together** to prepare **two** RFPs [delete comma] that solicit competitive bids.
4. Just between you and **me,** we **worked** very hard to develop a "hook" to capture a **reader's** attention.
5. If a proposal is **too** long and **its b**udget is **vague,** it will not **succeed** in **its** goal.
6. **An** important item in most **p**roposals [delete comma] is the **budget,** which is a list of project **costs.**
7. If a proposal is sent to the **p**resident or **me,** it should **definitely** explain the specific credentials and expertise of key **personnel** for the project.

8. **Dr.** Ryan Williams and **he** wanted to start **their** own **business; therefore,** they wrote a business plan [delete comma] that included a detailed market analysis.

9. Mary **Morley,** who is a member of our Research and Development **Department,** wondered whether her formal report would be presented at the May **15** **meeting.**

10. If **your** report is **complex,** be sure to **proofread** it **three** times.

Chapter 15

1. Even though he was president of the **company, Mr.** Thomas dreaded the **two** or **three** presentations he made **every year**.
2. The **company's** CGA asked my colleague and **me** to explain the **principal** ways we planned to finance **its** **30-year mortgage.**
3. My team and I are **grateful** to be able to give a **20-minute presentation; however,** we can emphasize only **three** or **four** major **points**.
4. The introduction to a presentation should accomplish **three goals:** (a) capture attention, (b) establish **credibility,** and (c) preview main points.
5. Travis wondered whether focusing on what you want the audience to remember [delete comma] and summarizing **your** main points **were** equally important in the **conclusion.**
6. Speakers must remember that **their listeners,** unlike **readers, cannot control** the rate of presentation [delete comma] or flip back **through** pages to review main points.
7. Most novice speakers talk **too rapidly; however,** they can learn to speak more **slowly** [delete comma] and listen to what they are saying.
8. When speakers first approach the **audience,** they should take a moment to adjust **their** notes [delete comma] and make **themselves** comfortable.
9. One West Coast company found that [delete comma] telephone interruptions consumed about **18** percent of staff **members'** workdays.
10. Good telephone manners reflect on you and **your** **company; however, too** few employees are trained **properly**.

Chapter 16

1. The employment process begins with **introspection,** which is a word that **means** looking inside yourself to **analyze** what you like and dislike.
2. You **can't** hope to find the job of your **dreams** without first [delete colon] (1) knowing **yourself,** (2) knowing the job **market,** and (3) **knowing** the employment process.
3. Candidates complain about job boards [delete comma] because fewer **than 1.4** percent of the candidates are actually hired.
4. With over **40 000** job boards and employment Web sites deluging the **Internet, it's** hard to know where to start looking.
5. Preparing a résumé while you are still in school [delete comma] **helps** you recognize **weak** qualifications [delete comma] and **gives** you **two** or **three** years in which to bolster **them.**
6. Recruiters like to see career objectives on **résumés; however, they** may restrict a **candidate's** chances.
7. **Today's** résumés omit **personal** data such as **birthdate**, **marital** status, **height, weight,** and religious affiliation.
8. I wonder how many **companies** now use **applicant-tracking** software to scan **candidates'** résumés and search for **keywords.**
9. In the latest issue of ***BusinessWeek,*** did you see the article titled **"Should** You Use a Career Objective on Your **Résumé?"**
10. Before going to a job **interview,** you should research the **following:** company size, number of employees, competitors, reputation, **strengths,** and **weaknesses.**

notes

Chapter 1

1. Todd Bishop, "Time to Fight Infomania," *National Post*, 26 September 2007, WK6.
2. Thomas W. Malone, *The Future of Work* (Cambridge: Harvard Business School Press, 2004), 32.
3. Max Messmer, "Enhancing Your Writing Skills," *Strategic Finance*, January 2001, 8; "The Challenges Facing Workers in the Future," *HR Focus*, August 1999, 6.
4. Dwight Cunningham, "The Downside of Technology," *Chicago Tribune Internet Edition*, 2 January 2000; "Wired to the Desk," *Fortune*, Summer 1999, 164.
5. Roman Habtu, "Me 55 and Older: Work or Retire?" *Perspectives on Labour and Income* (Ottawa: Statistics Canada), Spring 2003, vol. 15, no. 1, 47.
6. Based on information from "D-Code Testimonials," available at <http://www.d-code.com/generations.html>, accessed 10 May 2008; "Young Newspaper Readers: Social Activists, Party Animals . . . or Both?—D-Code Survey Shatters Common Myths About Youth Readership," *Canada NewsWire*, 17 January 2006; Barbara Richter, "X,Y, Boom! Generations at Work," *Voice*, Summer 2006, vol. 8, no. 4, 14–17; MayoClinic.com, "Workplace Generation Gap: Understand Differences Among Colleagues," 6 July 2005, available at <http://www.mayoclinic.com/health/working-life/WL00045>, accessed 9 January 2006;
7. G. A. Marken, "New Approach to Moving up the Corporate Ladder," *Public Relations Quarterly*, Winter 1996, 47.
8. Jerry Sullivan, Naoki Karmeda, and Tatsuo Nobu, "Bypassing in Managerial Communication," *Business Horizons*, January/February 1991, 72.
9. M. Messmer, "Enhancing Your Writing Skills," *Strategic Finance*, January 2001, 8. See also B. Staples, "The Fine Art of Getting It Down on Paper, Fast," *The New York Times*, 15 May 2005, WK13(L).
10. Dennis K. Berman, "Online Laundry: Government Posts Enron's E-Mail; Amid Power-Market Minutiae, Many Personal Items," *Wall Street Journal*, 6 October 2003, A1.
11. James D. Sewell and Alexandria Sheriff, "Handling the Stress of the Electronic World," *Technology Watch*, January/February 2005, vol. 56, no. 1, 34.
12. Ronald R. Sims et al., *The Challenge of Front-Line Management: Flattened Organizations in the New Economy* (Westport, CT: Quorum, 2001), 10.
13. Lisa A. Burke and Jessica Morris Wise, "The Effective Care, Handling, and Pruning of the Office Grapevine," *Business Horizons*, May/June 2003, 71.
14. "Who Told You That?" *Wall Street Journal*, 23 May 1985, 33.
15. Stephanie Zimmermann, Beverly Davenport, and John W. Haas, "A Communication Metamyth in the Workplace: The Assumption That More Is Better," *Journal of Business Communication*, April 1996, 185–204.
16. Bob Nelson, "How to Energize Everyone in the Company," *Bottom Line/Business*, October 1997, 3.
17. "The Values Added Banker Brings Ethics to Investing," *National Post*, 4 March 2000, E4.
18. "Do Your Reps' Writing Skills Need a Refresher?" *Customer Contact Management Report*, February 2002, 7.

Chapter 2

1. Jennifer Rivkin, "Why You Need a Wiki," *Profit*, March 2006, vol. 25, no. 1, 59.
2. Patricia Buhler, "Managing in the 90s: Creating Flexibility in Today's Workplace," *Supervision*, January 1996, 24–26.
3. Based on Cheryl Hamilton with Cordell Parker, *Communicating for Results*, 6e (Belmont, CA: Wadsworth, 2000), 279; Barton H. Hamilton, Jack A. Nickerson, and Hideo Owan, "Team Incentives and Worker Heterogeneity: An Empirical Analysis of the Impact of Teams on Productivity and Participation," *Journal of Political Economy*, June 2003, 465; and Harvey Robbins and Michael Finley, *Why Teams Don't Work: What Went Wrong and How to Make It Right* (Princeton, NJ: Peterson's/Pacesetter Books, 1995), 11–12.
4. Frank Mueller, Stephen Procter, and David Buchanan, "Teamworking in Its Context(s): Antecedents, Nature and Dimensions," *Human Relations*, November 2000, 1387.
5. James R. DiSanza and Nancy J. Legge, *Business and Professional Communication* (Boston: Allyn and Bacon, 2000), 98.
6. Jessica Lipnack and Jeffrey Stamps, *Virtual Teams: People Working across Boundaries With Technology*, 2e (New York: John Wiley & Sons, 2000), 18.
7. Jean H. Miculka, *Speaking for Success* (Cincinnati: South-Western, 1999), 127.
8. I. L. Janis, *Groupthink: Psychological Studies on Policy Decisions and Fiascoes* (Boston: Houghton Mifflin, 1982). See also Shaila M. Miranda and Carol Saunders, "Group Support Systems: An Organization

Development Intervention to Combat Groupthink," *Public Administration Quarterly*, Summer 1995, 193–216.

9. Allen C. Amason, Wayne A. Hochwarter, Kenneth R. Thompson, and Allison W. Harrison, "Conflict: An Important Dimension in Successful Management Teams," *Organizational Dynamics*, Autumn 1995, 1.
10. Charles Parnell, "Teamwork: Not a New Idea, But It's Transforming the Workplace," *Executive Speeches*, December 1997/January 1998, 35–40.
11. Jon R. Katzenbach and Douglas K. Smith, *The Wisdom of Teams: Creating the High-Performance Organization* (New York: HarperCollins, 1993), 45.
12. Jon Hanke, "Presenting as a Team," *Presentations*, January 1998, 74–82.
13. Hal Lancaster, "Learning Some Ways to Make Meetings Slightly Less Awful," *Wall Street Journal*, 26 May 1998, B1.
14. John C. Bruening, "There's Good News about Meetings," *Managing Office Technology*, July 1996, 24–25.
15. J. Keith Cook, "Try These Eight Guidelines for More Effective Meetings," *Communication Briefings* Bonus Item, April 1995, 8a. See also Morey Stettner, "How to Manage a Corporate Motormouth," *Investor's Business Daily*, 8 October 1998, A1.
16. Eli Mina, "Meeting Minutes: Should You Record Meeting Minutes Verbatim?" *Office Pro*, June/July 2001, 4.
17. M. Egan, "Meetings can Make or Break Your Career," *Insurance Advocate*, 13 March 2006, 117–24.

Chapter 3

1. Misty Harris, "Canadians Keeping Their Hands to Themselves," *CanWest News*, 27 September 2005, 1.
2. "To Compete A PEO Must Be a Listening Organization," 1999, available at <www.devaindustries.com/articles/ListeningPEO.htm>, accessed 20 March 2003.
3. Harvey Robbins and Michael Finley, *Why Teams Don't Work* (Princeton, NJ: Peterson's/Pacesetter Books, 1995), 123.
4. Conference Board of Canada, "Employability Skills 2000+," available at <www.conferenceboard.ca/nbec>, accessed 20 March 2003.
5. Tom W. Harris, "Listen Carefully," *Nation's Business*, June 1989, 78.
6. L. K. Steil, L. I. Barker, and K. W. Watson, *Effective Listening: Key to Your Success* (Reading, MA: Addison-Wesley, 1983); J. A. Harris, "Hear What's Really Being Said," *Management–Auckland*, August 1998, 18.
7. Eric H. Nelson and Jan Gypen, "The Subordinate's Predicament," *Harvard Business Review*, September/October 1979, 133.
8. International Listening Association, "Listening Factoids," available at <http://www.listen.org/pages/factoids.html>, accessed 16 January 2004.
9. Michael Render, "Better Listening Makes for a Better Marketing Message," *Marketing News*, 11 September 2000, 22–23.
10. International Listening Association, "Listening Factoids."
11. James Butcher, "Dominic O'Brien: Master Mnemonist," *The Lancet*, 2 September 2000, 836.
12. Julia T. Wolf, *Gendered Lives: Communication, Gender, and Culture*, 5e (Belmont, CA: Wadsworth, 2003); Kristin J. Anderson and Campbell Leaper, "Meta-analyses of Gender Effects on Conversational Interruption: Who, What, When, Where, and How," *Sex Roles: A Journal of Research*, August 1998, 225–53; and M. Booth-Butterfield, "She Hears: What They Hear and Why," *Personnel Journal*, vol. 44, 1984, 39.
13. L. P. Stewart and A. D. Stewart, *Communication Between the Sexes: Sex Differences and Sex Role Stereotypes* (Scottsdale, AZ: Gorsuch Scarisbrick, 1990).
14. Jayne Tear, "They Just Don't Understand Gender Dynamics," *Wall Street Journal*, 20 November 1995, A12; Alan Wolfe, "Talking From 9 to 5: How Women's and Men's Conversational Styles Affect Who Gets Heard, Who Gets Credit and What Gets Done at Work," *New Republic*, 12 December 1994.
15. J. Burgoon, D. Coker, and R. Coker, "Communication Explanations," *Human Communication Research*, 12, 1986, 463–94.
16. Ray Birdwhistel, *Kinesics and Context* (Philadelphia: University of Pennsylvania Press, 1970).
17. R. Osterman, "Casual Loses Its Cool in Business: More Employers Are Trying to Tighten up Workplace Clothing Standards", *Sacramento Bee*, retrieved from InfoTrac database, 15 December 2006; "Business Casual: Out of Style?" *HR Focus*, May 2005, 9, retrieved from InfoTrac College Edition database, 15 December 2006.
18. H. Wilkie, "Professional Presence," *Canadian Manager*, Fall 2003, 14; L. Kaplan-Leiserson, "Casual Dress/Back to Business Attire," *Training & Development*, November 2000, 38–39.
19. M. M. Kennedy, "Is Business Casual Here to Stay?" *Executive Female*, September/October 1997, 31.
20. N. Wood and T. Benitez, "Does the Suit Fit?" *Incentive*, April 2003, 31.
21. "Business Casual: Out of Style?" 9; L. Egodigwe, "Here Come the Suits," *Black Enterprise*, March 2003, 59, retrieved from InfoTrac database, 15 December 2006; C. Summerson, "The Suit Is Back in Business," *BusinessWeek*, 18 November 2002, 130.
22. "Not Listening Is an American Thing," *HighGain Inc. Newsletter*, available at <http://www.highgain.com/newsletter/back-issues/e-news/06-00/hg-enews-06-00.html>, accessed 17 January 2001.
23. "What's the Universal Hand Sign for 'I Goofed'?" *Santa Barbara News-Press*, 16 December 1996, D2.
24. James Calvert Scott, "Business Casual Dress: Workplace Boon or Boondoggle?" part 2, *Instructional Strategies*, December 1999, 5.

Chapter 4

1. Lauren McKeon, "Insider," *Canadian Business*, 18 February 2008, 96.
2. I. Rowley, "Japan: Wal-Mart's Looking for a Partner—Again; Slow Sales Indicate the Retailer's Style Isn't Catching on With Local Consumers," *BusinessWeek Online*, 14 September 2006, retrieved from InfoTrac College Edition database, 10 January 2007.
3. E. S. Browning, "In Pursuit of the Elusive Euroconsumer," *Wall Street Journal*, 23 April 1992, B1.

4. Shona Crabtree, "Cultural Differences," *Eagle-Tribune*, available at <http://www.eagletribune.com/news/stories/19990530/BU-001.htm>, accessed 13 February 2001.
5. Mary O'Hara-Devereaux and Robert Johansen, *GlobalWork: Bridging Distance, Culture and Time* (San Francisco: Jossey-Bass, 1994), 245.
6. Guo-Ming Chen and William J. Starosta, *Foundations of Intercultural Communication* (Boston: Allyn and Bacon, 1998), 40.
7. Iris Varner and Linda Beamer, *Intercultural Communication in the Global Workplace* (Boston: McGraw-Hill Irwin, 2001), 18.
8. Edward T. Hall and Mildred Reed Hall, *Understanding Cultural Differences* (Yarmouth, ME: Intercultural Press, 1987), 183–84.
9. Kathleen K. Reardon, *Where Minds Meet* (Belmont, CA: Wadsworth, 1987), 199.
10. Vivan C. Sheer and Ling Chen, "Successful Sino-Western Business Negotiation: Participants' Accounts of National and Professional Cultures," *Journal of Business Communication*, January 2003, 62; Vivienne Luk, Mumtaz Patel, and Kathryn White, "Personal Attributes of American and Chinese Business Associates," *Bulletin of the Association for Business Communication*, December 1990, 67.
11. Cynthia Gallois and Victor Callan, *Communication and Culture* (New York: John Wiley Sons, 1997), 24.
12. Susan S. Jarvis, "Preparing Employees to Work South of the Border," *Personnel*, June 1990, 763.
13. Gallois and Callan, *Communication and Culture*, 29.
14. Lennie Copeland and Lewis Griggs, *Going International: How to Make Friends and Deal Effectively in the Global Marketplace* (New York: Random House, 1985), 94.
15. Copeland and Griggs, 108.
16. N. Singh and A. Pereira, *The Culturally Customized Web Site* (Burlington, MA: Elsevier Butterworth-Heinemann, 2005), 139–48.
17. Ibid.
18. Copeland and Griggs, 12.
19. Nicholas Keung, "Learning the Signs of Communication," *Toronto Star*, 22 May 1999, L1–L2.
20. Lillian H. Chaney and Jeanette S. Martin, *Intercultural Business Communication* (Englewood Cliffs, NJ: Prentice Hall, 1995), 67.
21. Gretchen Weber, "English Rules," *Workforce Management*, May 2004, 47–50.
22. Roger Axtell, *Do's and Taboos Around the World*, 2e (New York: Wiley, 1990), 71.
23. L. H. Chaney and J. S. Martin, *Intercultural Business Communication*, 2e (Upper Saddle River, NJ: Prentice Hall, 2000), 83.
24. Robert McGarvey, "Foreign Exchange," *USAir Magazine*, June 1992, 64.
25. "The Way We'll Be," *Toronto Star*, 23 March 2005, A1.
26. Graham Lowe, "Revamp HR Policies to Retain Older Workers," *Canadian HR Reporter*, 8 November 2004, vol. 17, no. 19, 17.
27. Carter Hammett, "Companies Win Through Team Building," *The Toronto Sun Career Connection*, available at <www.canoe.ca/CareerConnectionNews/030213_teambuilding.html>, accessed 12 February 2003.
28. Rae Andre, "Diversity Stress as Morality Stress," *Journal of Business Ethics*, June 1995, 489–96.
29. Genevieve Capowski, "Managing Diversity," *Management Review*, June 1996, 16.
30. Joel Makower, "Managing Diversity in the Workplace," *Business and Society Review*, Winter 1995, 48–54.
31. George Simons and Darlene Dunham, "Making Inclusion Happen," *Managing Diversity*, December 1995, available at <http://www.jalmc.org/mk-incl.htm>, accessed 9 August 1996.
32. Bill Saporito, "Can Wal-Mart Get Any Bigger?" *Time*, 13 January 2003, 38.
33. Ken Cottrill, "The World According to Hollywood," *Traffic World*, 6 November 2000, 15.
34. Somporn Thapanachai, "Awareness Narrows Cross-cultural Gap in Thai Management Training Courses," *Bangkok Post*, 6 October 2003.
35. Conference Board of Canada, "Towards Maximizing the Talents of Visible Minorities: Potential, Performance, and Organizational Practices," publication 608-04, available at <http://www.conferenceboard.ca/MTVM/608-04MaxTalentsBooklet.pdf>.

Chapter 5

1. "RadioShack Lays Off Employees Via E-Mail," *USA Today*, 30 August 2006, available at <http://www.usatoday.com/tech/news/2006-08-30-radioshack-email-layoffs_x.htm> .
2. Ronald R. Sims, John G. Veres III, Katherine A. Jackson, and Carolyn L. Facteau, *The Challenge of Front-Line Management* (Westport, CT: Quorum Books, 2001), 89.
3. Mark Bacon, quoted in "Business Writing: One-on-One Speaks Best to the Masses," *Training*, April 1988, 95. See also Elizabeth Danziger, "Communicate Up," *Journal of Accountancy*, February 1998, 67.
4. For more information see Marilyn Schwartz, *Guidelines for Bias-Free Writing* (Bloomington: Indiana University Press, 1994).
5. Leslie Matthies, as described in Carl Heyel, "Policy and Procedure Manuals," in *The Handbook of Executive Communication* (Homewood, IL: Dow Jones-Irwin, 1986), 212.
6. "Effect of Product Liability Laws on Small Business: An Introduction to International Exposure Through a Comparison of U.S. and Canadian Law," *Journal of Small Business Management*, 7 January 1998, 72.
7. Lewis N. Klar, "Torts," *Canadian Encyclopedic Digest*, 1998, Electric Library Canada, accessed 9 June 1997.
8. Lisa Jenner, "Develop Communication and Training With Literacy in Mind," *HR Focus*, March 1994, 14.
9. Minister of Public Works and Government Services and WWLIA, "Misleading Advertising under the Federal Competition Act," 1996, available at <http://wwlia.org/ca-compl.htm>, accessed 18 April 2000.
10. Ibid.
11. Kristin R. Woolever, "Corporate Language and the Law: Avoiding Liability in Corporate Communications," *IEE Transactions on Professional Communication*, 2 June 1990, 95–98.

12. Lisa Jenner, "Employment-at-Will Liability: How Protected Are You?" *HR Focus*, March 1994, 11.
13. Judy E. Pickens, "Communication—Terms of Equality: A Guide to Bias-Free Language," *Personnel Journal*, August 1985, 5.

Chapter 6

1. Based on Marketwire, "RedFlag-Deals.com: Canadians Remain Loyal to Canadian Retailers for Online Shopping Reveals Annual Survey" and "RedFlagDeals.com Launches Boxing Day Sales Early!" 19 December 2007, 1.
2. Adrian Furnham, "The Brainstorming Myth," *Business Strategy Review*, Winter 2000, 21–28.
3. Dean Rieck, "AH HA! Running a Productive Brainstorming Session," *Direct Marketing*, November 1999, 78.
4. Kimberly Paterson, "The Writing Process," *Rough Notes*, April 1998, 59–60.
5. Based on information from <http://www.gapinc.com>, accessed 4 March 2004.
6. Dianna Booher, "Develop the First Draft Quickly," *E-Writing* (New York: Pocket Books, 2001), 126; Andrew Fluegelman and Jeremy Joan Hewes, "The Word Processor and the Writing Process," in *Strategies for Business and Technical Writing*, 4e, ed. Kevin J. Harty (San Diego: Harcourt Brace Jovanovich, 1989), 43. See also Lynn Quitman Troyka, *Simon & Schuster Handbook for Writers*, 4e (Upper Saddle River, NJ: Prentice Hall, 1996), 49.
7. Robert W. Goddard, "Communication: Use Language Effectively," *Personnel Journal*, April 1989, 32.
8. Frederick Crews, *The Random House Handbook*, 4e (New York: Random House, 1991), 152.
9. "Creating the Right Environment," *National Post* joint venture supplement with Conference Board of Canada, 27 April 1999, CB1, CB3.

Chapter 7

1. Francine Kopun, "Oxford Dictionary Recognizes Austin Powers: Shagadelic Joins Truthiness as One of the Few Oxford English Entries Traceable to a Person", *Toronto Star*, 14 December 2007, available at <http://www.thestar.com/printArticle/285575>, accessed 15 February 2008.
2. Peter Elbow, *Writing With Power: Techniques for Mastering the Writing Process* (Oxford: Oxford University Press, 1998), 30.
3. A. A. Milne, *Pooh's Little Instruction Book* (New York: Penguin Putnam, 1995).
4. William Power and Michael Siconolfi, "Memo to: Mr. Ball, RE: Your Messages, Sir: They're Weird," *Wall Street Journal*, 30 November 1990, 1; Ralph Brown, "Add Some Informal Polish to Your Writing," *Management*, March 1998, 12.
5. Dianna Booher, *E-Writing* (New York: Pocket Books, 2001), 148.

Chapter 8

1. "Workers Suffering From 'Email Stress,'" *Evening Standard*, 13 August 2007, available at <http://www.thisislondon.co.uk/news/article-23408089-details/Workers+suffering+from+'email+stress'/article.do>, accessed 12 March 2008.
2. Ipsos-Reid, "Canadians' Love Affair With Email Continues," 30 October 2001, available at <www.angusreid.com/media/dsp_displaypr.prnt.cfm?ID_to_view=1345>, accessed 18 June 2003.
3. From Todd Humber, "No Second Chances for First Impressions," *Canadian HR Reporter*, 13 August 2008, vol. 20, no. 14, 22; Denise Balkisson, "Victimology," *Toronto Life*, March 2008, available at <http://www.torontolife.com/features/victimology/>, accessed 15 March 2008.
4. John Fielden, "Clear Writing Is Not Enough," *Management Review*, April 1989, 51.
5. Sandra Swanson, "Beware: Employee Monitoring Is on the Rise," *Information Week*, 20 August 2001, 57.
6. Based on Maggie Jackson, "Casual Day a Bad Fit?" *Los Angeles Times Careers*, 19 January 1998, 27–28.
7. Based on Lisa M. Bee and Gerald L. Maatman, Jr., "E-Mail Abuse Leaves Firms Exposed," *National Underwriter*, 26 January 2004, 27.
8. Gustavo Capdevila, "Information: Summit to Act on Junk E-mail 'Epidemic,'" *Global Information Network*, 7 July 2004, 1.

Chapter 9

1. Cassandra Szklarski, "Experts Bemoan Decline of Handwriting in Age of Keyboards, Gadgets," Canadian Press NewsWire, 8 November 2006.
2. Max Messmer, "Enhancing Your Writing Skills," *Strategic Finance*, January 2001, 8–10.
3. Dennis Chambers, *Writing to Get Action* (Bristol, VT: Velocity Business Publishing, 1998), 12.
4. Steven N. Spertz and Glenda S. Spertz, *The Rule of Law: Canadian Business Law*, 2e (Toronto: Copp Clark, 1995), 289.
5. Gary L. Clark, Peter F. Kaminski, and David R. Rink, "Consumer Complaints: Advice on How Companies Should Respond Based on an Empirical Study," *Journal of Services Marketing*, Winter 1992, 41–50.
6. Robert Klara, "Press 1 to Gripe," *Restaurant Business*, 15 May 1998, 96–102.
7. Marcia Mascolini, "Another Look at Teaching the External Negative Message," *Bulletin of the Association of Business Communication*, June 1994, 46; Robert J. Aalberts and Lorraine A. Krajewski, "Claim and Adjustment Letters," *Bulletin of the Association for Business Communication*, September 1987, 2.
8. Pamela Gilbert, "Two Words That Can Help a Business Thrive," *Wall Street Journal*, 30 December 1996, A12.
9. Margaret H. Caddell, "Is Letter Writing Dead?" *OfficePro*, November/December 2003, 22.
10. J. Fallows, "Enough Keyword Searches. Just Answer My Question", *New York Times*, 12 June 2005, BU3.
11. Based on "McDonald's USA Introduces New Packaging," available at <http://www.mcdonalds.com/usa/good/environment/packaging.html>, accessed 27 May 2004; Elizabeth Crowley, "EarthShell Saw Big Macs and Big Bucks—Got Big Woes: Environmentally Safe Sandwich Containers for McDonald's

Haven't Been Easy to Make," *Wall Street Journal*, 10 April 2001; Frank Edward Allen, "McDonald's to Reduce Waste in Plan Developed With Environmental Group," *Wall Street Journal*, 17 April 1991, B1; Martha T. Moore, "McDonald's Trashes Sandwich Boxes," *USA Today*, 2 November 1990, 1; Michael Parrish, "McDonald's to Do Away With Foam Packages," *Los Angeles Times*, 2 November 1990, 1; and Mark Hamstra, "McD Supersizes Efforts to Cut Down on Costs," *Nation's Restaurant News*, 29 June 1998, 1, 60.

Chapter 10

1. Joanne Sasvari, "Reward Programs a Two-Way Street," *National Post* Travel and Loyalty supplement, 19 September 2007, IS2.
2. "Shoppers Seek the Hardcore," *Toronto Star*, 19 September 2007, B5.
3. K. E. Fracaro, "Managing by Persuasion," *Contract Management*, August 2004, vol. 44, no. 8, 4, retrieved from InfoTrac College Edition database, 28 December 2006.
4. Elaine Tyson, "Direct Mail Success Strategies," *Circulation Management*, 1 February 2004.
5. Kevin McLaughlin, "Words of Wisdom," *Entrepreneur*, October 1990, 101. See also Linda Wastphal, "Empathy in Sales Letters," *Direct Marketing*, October 2001, 55.
6. "EarthShell Corporation and Hood Packaging Corporation Sign Definitive Agreement for Food Service Wraps," *Canadian Corporate News*, 10 February 2004.

Chapter 11

1. ePolicy Institute, "2004 Survey on Workplace E-Mail and IM Reveals Unmanaged Risks," available at <http://www.epolicyinstitute.com/survey/>, accessed 14 July 2004.
2. Jeff Mowatt, "Breaking Bad News to Customers," *Agency Sales*, February 2002, 30; Elizabeth M. Dorn, "Case Method Instruction in the Business Writing Classroom," *Business Communication Quarterly*, March 1999, 51–52.
3. Mimi Browning, "Work Dilemma: Delivering Bad News a Good Way," *Government Computer News*, 24 November 2003, 41; Mowatt, "Breaking Bad News."
4. Browning, "Work Dilemma"; Bob Lewis, "To Be an Effective Leader, You Need to Perfect the Art of Delivering Bad News," *InfoWorld*, 13 September 1999, 124.
5. Jeanette W. Gilsdorf, "Metacommunication Effects on International Business Negotiating in China," *Business Communication Quarterly*, June 1997, 27.
6. Browning, "Work Dilemma," 41; Lewis, "To Be an Effective Leader," 124.
7. Danylo Hawaleshka, "The Cups Runneth Over," *Macleans.ca*, accessed 1 May 2006; Bill Mah, "Roll-up-the-Rim Litter Rolls Out Criticism of Tim Hortons: Critics Suggest Using Scratch Cards in Promo," *Edmonton Journal*, 1 March 2005, available at <http://global.factiva.com>.
8. Based on "SUV Surprise," *Wall Street Journal*, 15 June 2004, W7.
9. Jordana Mishory, "Don't Shoot the Messenger: How to Deliver Bad News and Still Keep Customers Satisfied," *Sales and Marketing Management*, June 2004, 16.
10. Tom Cahill, "Bear Stearns Tells Employees Dress Up—Dot Com Is Over," *Bloomberg News Service*, 17 September 2002; "Bear Stearns Reinstates Formal Dress Code," *Reuters Business Report*, 21 September 2002; "Dress Codes: 'Business Conservative' Is Making a Comeback," *HR Briefing*, 1 March 2003, 7.

Chapter 12

1. "Vision Critical On-line Panels: A New Tool for Customizing Customer Insight," available at <www.visioncritical.com/presentation/VC_online_panels111406.pdf>, accessed 7 May 2008.
2. L. Little, "Using a Multiple Search," *Wall Street Journal*, 7 March 2006, D1, retrieved from Factiva database, 23 November 2006.
3. Mike Brennan and Judith Holdershaw, "The Effect of Question Tone and Form on Responses to Open-Ended Questions: Further Data," *Marketing Bulletin*, 1999, 57–64.
4. Barton Goldsmith, "The Awesome Power of Asking the Right Questions," *OfficeSolutions*, June 2002, 52; Gerald W. Bracey, "Research-Question Authority," *Phi Delta Kappan*, November 2001, 191.
5. Daphne A. Jameson, "The Ethics of Plagiarism: How Genre Affects Writers' Use of Source Materials," *Bulletin of the Association for Business Communication*, June 1993, 18.
6. Indiana University Writing Tutorial Services, "Plagiarism: What It Is and How to Recognize and Avoid It," available at <http://www.indiana.edu/~wts/pamphlets/plagiarism.shtml>, accessed 27 July 2004.
7. D. Brady, "*!#?@ the E-Mail. Can We Talk?" *BusinessWeek*, 4 December 2006, 109.

Chapter 13

1. Mark Stevenson, "Global Gourmet," *Canadian Business*, July 1993, vol. 66, no. 7, 22–33, retrieved from CBCA business database (document ID: 998669), 7 May 2008.
2. "Loblaw Builds on Legacy of Community Involvement and Environmental Responsibility With Release of First Corporate Social Responsibility Report," *Canada NewsWire*, 30 April 2008, Retrieved from CBCA current events database (document ID: 1470662761), 7 May 2008.
3. Charlene Marmer Solomon, "Marriott's Family Matters," *Personnel Journal*, October 1991, 40–42; Jennifer Laabs, "They Want More Support—Inside and Outside of Work," *Workforce*, November 1998, 54–56.
4. "Red Light Camera Reform," *WestWays*, May/June 2003, 19.

Chapter 14

1. "Duke Energy Donates $80 000 to the Nature Conservancy for Shareholders Choosing Paperless Delivery of Annual Report," *Canada NewsWire*, 3 April 2006, 1, retrieved from CBCA current events database (document ID: 1249183421), 6 May 2008.
2. MasterPlans: Professional Business Plan Writers, "Rapid Development Cycle," n.d., available at <http://www .masterplans.com>, accessed 12 July2007.

3. Marcia Layton Turner, "Guide to Business Plan Consultants: Hiring Help Is the Next Best Thing to Writing Your Plan Yourself," *Work.com*, available at <http://www.work.com/business-plan-consultants-880>, accessed 3 July 2007.

Chapter 15

1. Roberto Rocha, "Rock Your PowerPoint Presentations. Holy Triad of Pitches: Be Brief, Be Brilliant, Be Gone," *National Post*, 9 January 2008, FP5.
2. Wharton Applied Research Center, "A Study of the Effects of the Use of Overhead Transparencies on Business Meetings, Final Report," cited in "Short, Snappy Guide to Meaningful Presentations," *Working Woman*, June 1991, 73.
3. Dianna Booher, *Speak With Confidence: Powerful Presentations That Inform, Inspire, and Persuade* (New York: McGraw-Hill Professional 2003), 126. For more detailed information on the use of colour in presentations, go to <http://www.indezine.com/ideas/prescolors.html>.
4. S. Bates, *Speak Like a CEO: Secrets for Commanding Attention and Getting Results* (New York: McGraw-Hill Professional 2005), 113.
5. "How to Avoid the 7 Deadly Sins of PowerPoint," *Yearbook of Experts News Release Wire*, 30 July 2004, retrieved from LexisNexis Academic database, 11 October 2004.
6. For more information, go to <http://www.turningtechnologies.com>, <http://www.audienceresponse.com>, or <http://www.optiontechnologies.com>.
7. Robert J. Boeri, "Fear of Flying? Or the Mail? Try the Web Conferencing Cure," *Emedia Magazine*, March 2002, 49.
8. John Ellwood, "Less PowerPoint, More Powerful Points," *The Times* (London), 4 August 2004, 6.
9. Booher, *Speak With Confidence*, 14; Dianna Booher, *Executive's Portfolio of Model Speeches for All Occasions* (Englewood Cliffs, NJ: Prentice Hall, 1991), 259.
10. Peter Schneider, "Scenes From a Marriage: Observations on the Daimler-Chrysler Merger From a German Living in America," *New York Times Magazine*, 12 August 2001, 47.
11. Ronald E. Dulek, John S. Fielden, and John S. Hill, "International Communication: An Executive Primer," *Business Horizons*, January/February 1991, 23. See also Susan J. Marks, "Nurturing Global Workplace Connections," *Workforce*, September 2001, 76ff.
12. Dulek, Fielden, and Hill, "International Communication," 22.

Chapter 16

1. "Your Profile on Social Sites Can Make or Break Your Job Opportunities," *National Post*, 19 September 2007, WK3.
2. "Survey: Half of Employers Search Online for Information about Potential Hires," *Canada NewsWire*, 4 October 2007, 1, available at <http://www.proquest.com/>.
3. "Small Business Sentinel," *National Post*, 4 March 2000, E3.
4. "Financial Outlook," *Maclean's*, 22 March 1999, 37.
5. Brian O'Connell, *The Career Survival Guide* (New York: McGraw-Hill, 2003), 11–12.
6. Anne Kates Smith, "Charting Your Own Course," *U.S. News & World Report*, 6 November 2000, 57.
7. Lorraine Farquharson, "Technology Special Report: The Best Way to Find a Job," *Wall Street Journal*, 15 September 2003, R8.
8. Mark Swartz, "Internet Job Boards Are Tricky," *The Spectator* (Hamilton), 11 May 2005, 34.
9. P. Korkki, "So Easy to Apply, So Hard to Be Noticed," *New York Times*, 1 July 2007, BU YT16.
10. "Résumé Styles: Chronological Versus Functional? Best-Selling Author Richard H. Beatty Joins in the Résumé Discussion," *Internet Wire*, 5 November 2002.
11. Elizabeth Blackburn-Brockman and Kelly Belanger, "One Page or Two? A National Study of CPA Recruiters' Preferences for Résumé Length," *Journal of Business Communication*, January 2001, 29–57.
12. K. Isaacs, "How to Decide on Resume Length," available at <http://www.resumepower.com/resume-length.html>, accessed 21 July 2007.
13. Katharine Hansen, "Should You Use a Career Objective on Your Résumé?" *Quintessential Careers*, available at <http://www.quintcareers.com/resume_objectives.html>, accessed 5 October 2004; Robert Half, "Some Résumé Objectives Do More Harm Than Good," *CareerJournal.com*, available at <http://www.careerjournal.com/jobhunting/résumés/19971231-half3.html>, accessed 5 October 2004.
14. Roland E. Kidwell, Jr., "'Small' Lies, Big Trouble: The Unfortunate Consequences of Résumé Padding From Janet Cooke to George O'Leary," *Journal of Business Ethics*, May 2004, 175.
15. Joan E. Rigdon, "Deceptive Resumes Can Be Door-Openers But Can Become an Employee's Undoing," *Wall Street Journal*, 17 June 1992, B1. See also Barbara Solomon, "Too Good to Be True?" *Management Review*, April 1998, 28.
16. Daisy Wright, "Tell Stories, Get Hired," *OfficePro*, August/September 2004, 32–33.

acknowledgments

Chapter 1

pp. 7–8 Figure 1.2 based on Chickowski, E. (2006, January 9). "Phones Offer More Than Call Option; E-Mail, Text Messaging, Ability to Play Music Among Bells, Whistles." *San Diego Business Journal*, p. 17; Quittner, J. (2006, September 4). "Wikis Offer Quick Way to Collaborate; Software Acts Like Intranet, Letting Widely Scattered Staffers Pool Knowledge." *Crain's New York Business*, 34; "Blogs, Podcasts Pushed as Enterprise Tools." (2006, January 12). *Information Week;* Brandon, J. (2006, June 6). "Reworking the office: How Will You Be Working—One, Five, Twenty Years Down the Road." *PC Magazine*, 97; "Open Source VoIP Takes a Few Steps Forward." (2006, November 7). *Information Week;* Tricker, J. (2005, September). "Office Design trends: Bring on the Boomerang-Shaped Table." *Indiana Business Magazine*, 4; Mirel, D. "Wide Open Spaces: Cubicle-Ridden Offices Transition to More Open-Offices Formats, a Result of Advanced Mobile Technology and Innovative Office Design." (2006, May–June). *Journal of Property Management*, 30; Held, S. (2006, September). Office Tech Update: From 'Print and Distribute' to 'Distribute and Print.'" *Indiana Business Magazine*, 64; Gardyasz, J. (2006, April 24). "CustomerVision Bringing Wikis to Business." *Business Record* (Des Moines), 3; "The Future of Tech." (2005, June 20). *BusinessWeek*, 81; Mann, A. (2006, November 1). "Enterprise Content Now Encompassing Wikis, Blogs, Podcasts and More." *Network World;* Klein, K. E. (2006, August 21). "A Company Blog Keeps People Connected." (2006, August 21). *BusinessWeek Online*. Retrieved November 12, 2006, from InfoTrac College Edition database; Brynko, B. (2006, March). "Top Ten Technology Trends." *Information Today*, 1; Totty, M. (2005, September 12). "Prime Time for Videoconferences." *The New York Times*, p. R6; and Hof, R. H. (2006, June 19). "Web 2.0: The New Guy at Work." *BusinessWeek*, 58.

p. 17 Tech Talk box based on Susan Kousek, "Writing E-Mail That Saves Your and Recipients' Time," *Writing Techniques*, January 2004, 3; Kevin Maney, "How the Big Names Tame E-Mail," *USA Today*, 24 July 2003, A1; Elizabeth Weinstein, "Help! I'm Drowning in E-Mail!" *The Wall Street Journal*, 10 January 2002, B1; and "Ten Tips for Managing E-Mail," *The Office Professional*, February 2004, 1.

Chapter 2

p. 29 Tech Talk [virtual teams] based on Gordon, J. (2005, June). "Do Your Virtual Teams Deliver Only Virtual Performance?" *Training*, 20; Brown-Johnston, N. (2005, January–February). "Virtual Teamwork: Smart Business Leaders are Building High-Performance Virtual Teams." *Detroiter*, 55; "Managing Virtual Teams." (2004, March 16). *Info-Tech Advisor Newsletter*; Snyder, B. (2003, May). "Teams That Span Time Zones Face New Work Rules." *Stanford Business Magazine*. Retrieved April 15, 2007, from http://www.gsb.stanford.edu/news/bmag/sbsm0305/feature_virtual_teams.shtml; Loudin, K. H. (2003, June). "Building Bridges: Virtual Teamwork in the 21st Century." *Contract Management;* and Armstrong, D. (2000, March). "Building Teams Across Borders." *Executive Excellence*, 10.

p. 30 Discussion of Tuckman's model based on Robbins, H. A., & Finley, M. (1995). *Why Teams Don't Work*. Princeton, NJ: Peterson's/Pacesetter Books, Chapter 22.

p. 31 Figure 2.1. Portions reprinted with permission of Peterson's, a division of International Thomson Publishing, FAX 800-730-2215. Adapted from *Why Teams Don't Work* © 1995 by Harvey A. Robbins and Michael Finley.

pp. 31–32 Discussion of conflict and groupthink based on Peggy L. McNamra, "Conflict Resolution Strategies," *OfficePro*, August/September 2003, 25; W. H. Weiss, "Building and Managing Teams," *SuperVision*, November 2002, 19; Stephanie Reynolds, "Managing Conflict Through a Team Intervention and Training Strategy," *Employee Relations Today*, Winter 1998, 57–64; Odette Pollar, "Sticking Together," *Successful Meetings*, January 1997, 87–90; Kathleen M. Eisenhardt, "How Management Teams Can Have a Good Fight," *Harvard Business Review*, July/August 1997, 77–85; Erich Brockmann, "Removing the Paradox of Conflict from Group Decisions," *Academy of Management Executives*, May 1996, 61–62 and StevenA. Beebe & John T. Masterson, *Communicating in Small Groups* (New York: Longman 1999), 198-200.

pp. 35–37 Discussion of team-based presentations based in part on Jon Hanke, "Presenting as a Team," *Presentations*, January 1998, 74–82; Frank Jossi, "Putting It All Together: Creating Presentations as a Team," *Presentations*, July 1996, 18–26; Jon Rosen, "10 Ways to Make Your Next Team Presentation a Winner," *Presentations*, August 1997, 31.

pp. 37–42 Discussion on meetings based on Phyllis Davis, "Meeting Know How," *Women in Business*, March/April 2003, 27; Jay Antony, "The Good Meeting," *Harvard Business Review*, April 2003, 126; Hal Lancaster, "Learning Some Ways to Make Meetings Slightly Less Awful," *The Wall Street Journal*, 26 May 1998, B1; and Melinda Ligos, "Why Your Meetings Are a Total Bore," *Sales & Marketing Management*, May 1998, 84.

pp. 42–44 Discussion on collaboration tools based in part on Bulkeley, W. M. (2006, September 28). "Better Virtual Meetings." *The Wall Street Journal*, p. B1.; Crockett, R. O. (2007, February 26). "The 21st Century Meeting." *BusinessWeek*, 72; Delio, M. (2005, March 28). "Enterprise Collaboration With Blogs and Wikis." *InfoWorld*, 5. Retrieved December 6, 2006, from InfoTrac College Edition database.

Chapter 3

pp. 51–53 Tips for workplace listening based on Tom D. Lewis and Gerald Graham, "7 Tips for Effective Listening," *The Internal Auditor*, August 2003, 23; Liz Hughes, "How to Be a Good Listener," *Women in Business*, September/October 2002, 17; Shari Caudron, "Listen Up!" *Workforce*, August 1999, 25–27; Hal Lancaster, "It's Time to Stop Promoting Yourself and Start Listening," *The Wall Street Journal*, 10 June 1997, B1; "Good Ideas Go Unheard," *Management Review*, February 1998, 7; Morey Stettner, "Angry? Slow Down and Listen to Others," *Investor's Business Daily*, 19 January 1998, A1; and John W. Haas and Christa L. Arnold, "An Examination of the Role of Listening in Judgments of Communication," *Journal of Business Communication*, April 1995, 123–139.

p. 52 Listening to Superiors based on Valerie Priscilla Goby and Justus Helen Lewis, "The Key Role of Listening in Business: A Study of the Singapore Insurance Industry," *Business Communication Quarterly*, June 2000, 411; Lynn O. Cooper, "Listening Competency in the Workplace: A Model for Training," *Business Communication Quarterly*, December 1997, 75–84; and Michael C. Dennis, "Effective Communication Will Make Your Job Easier, *Business Credit*, June 1995, 45.

p. 52 Listening to Colleagues and Teammates based on Patrice M. Johnson and Kittie W. Watson, "Managing Interpersonal and Team Conflict: Listening Strategies," appearing in *Listening in Everyday Life*, edited by Michael Purdy and Deborah Borisoff (New York: University Press of America, 1997), Chapter 5; Max E. Douglas, "Creating Distress in the Workplace: A Supervisor's Role, *Supervision*, October 1996, 6–9; Robert McGarvey, "Now Hear This: Lend Your Employees an Ear—and Boost Productivity," *Entrepreneur*, June 1996, 87; Brian Tracy, "Effective Communication," *Executive Excellence*, October 1998, 13; Stuart Silverstein, "But Do They Listen? Companies Making an Effort to Build Skill," *Los Angeles Times*, 19 July 1998, D5; and Andrew Wolvin and Carolyn Gwynn Coakley, *Listening*, 5e (New York: McGraw-Hill, 1996), Chapters 5 and 8.

p. 52 Listening to Customers based on Nick Langley, "Looking After the Customers," *Computer Weekly*, 2 November 2000, 100; Jeff Caplan, "Golden Age Customer Service Returns," *Direct Marketing*, July 2000, 60; Rosemary P. Ramsey and Ravipreet S. Sohi, "Listening to Your Customers: The Impact of Perceived Salesperson Listening Behavior on Relationship Outcomes," *Journal of the Academy of Marketing Science*, Spring 1997, 127–137; Daniel Pedersen, "Dissing Customers: Why the Service Is Missing From America's Service Economy," *Newsweek*, 23 June 1997, 56; Michael Render, "Better Listening Makes for a Better Marketing Message," *Marketing News*, 11 September 2000, 22–23; Lynn Thomas, "Listening: So What's in It for Me?" *Rough Notes*, December 1998, 631.

p. 53 Figure 3.1 based on Lynn Thomas, "Listening: So What's in It for Me?" *Rough Notes*, December 1998, 63–43.

Chapter 4

p. 73 Figure 3.1 based on Chaney, L. H., & Martin, J. S. (2000). *Intercultural Business Communication*, 2e. Upper Saddle River, NJ: Prentice Hall, Chapter 5; J. Chung's analysis appearing in Chen, G. M., & Starosta, W. J. *Foundations of Intercultural Communication.* Boston: Allyn and Bacon, 1998, 51; and O'Hara-Devereaux, M., & Johansen, R. (1994). *Globalwork: Bridging Distance, Culture, and Time.* San Francisco: Jossey-Bass, p. 55.

p. 75 Tech Talk box based on Bob Tedeschi, "To Reach Internet Users Overseas, More American Web Sites Are Speaking Their Language, Even Mandarin," *The New York Times*, 12 January 2004, C6; Martin J. Spethman, "Web Site Globalization," *World Trade*, November 2003, 56; Steve Alexander, "Learn the Politics of Going Global," *Computerworld*, 1 January 2001, S8–S10; Sari Kalin, "The Importance of Being Multiculturally Correct," *Computer World*, 6 October 1997, G16–17; and Laura Morelli, "Writing for a Global Audience on the Web," *Marketing News*, 17 August 1998, 16.

Chapter 5

pp. 104–106 Information on Adapting to Legal Responsibilities based in part on Robert J. Walter and Gradley J. Sleeper, "Employee Recruitment and Retention: When Company Inducements Trigger Liability," *Review of Business*, Spring, 2002, 17; Pamela J. Cordier, "Essentials of Good Safety Communications," *Pulp & Paper*, May 2003, 25; and Kristin R. Woolever's "Corporate Language and the Law: Avoiding Liability in Corporate Communications," *IEE Transactions on Professional Communication*, 2 June 1990, 95–98.

Chapter 8

p. 225 Using E-Mail Smartly and Safely is based on Mary Munter, Priscilla S. Rogers, and Jone Rymer, "Business E-Mail: Guidelines for Users," *Business Communication Quarterly*, March 2003, 26; "E-Mail Acceptable Use: An Enforceable Policy," *Info-Tech Advisor Newsletter*, 30 September 2003; Kevin Maney, "How the Big Names Tame E-Mail," *USA Today*, 24 July 2003, 1A; "Email: The DNA of Office Crimes," *Electric Perspectives*, September/October, 2003, 4; Liz Hughes, "E-Mail Etiquette:

Think Before You Send," *Women in Business*, July/August 2003, 29; Elizabeth Weinstein, "Help! I'm Drowning in E-Mail!" *The Wall Street Journal*, 10 January 2002, B1; Lauren Gibbons Paul, "How to Tame the E-Mail Beast," *CIO*, 15 October 2001, 84; Dale Bowen and Bryan Gold, "Policies and Education Solve E-Mail Woes," *American City & County*, May 2001, 8.

Chapter 9

p. 185 Logo courtesy of Booster Juice.

pp. 198-201 Discussion of claim and adjustment letters based on Moshe Davidow, "Organizational Responses to Customer Complaints: What Works and What Doesn't," *Journal of Service Research*, February 2003, p. 26; Michael W. Michelson Jr., "Turning Complaints Into Cash," *The American Salesman*, December 2003, 22; Jeffrey R. Torp, "In Person, by Phone, by Mail, or Online: Managing Customer Complaints," *ABA Bank Compliance*, March/April 2003, 10; Chulmin Kim, Sounghie Kim, Subin Im, and Shanghoon Shin, "The Effect of Attitude and Perception on Consumer Complaint Intentions," *The Journal of Consumer Marketing 20*, 2003, 352; Michelle Andrews and Jodie Kirshner, "Cancel Me! Really! I Mean It!," *U.S. News & World Report*, 25 August 2003, 58; Kevin Lawrence, "How to Profit From Customer Complaints: Turning Problems Into Opportunities," *Canadian Manager*, Fall 2000, 25; Jeffrey J. Roth, "When the Customer's Got a Beef," *ABA Banking Journal*, July 1998, 24–29; Geoffrey Brewer, "The Customer Stops Here," *Sales & Marketing Management*, March 1998, 30–36; Bill Knapp, "Communication Breakdown," *World Wastes*, February 1998, 16; and Stephen S. Tax, Stephen W. Brown, and Murali Chandrashekaran, "Customer Evaluations of Service Complaint Experiences: Implications for Relationship Marketing," *Journal of Marketing*, April 1998, 60–76.

Chapter 10

pp. 216–217 Effective Persuasion Techniques based on Hoar, R. (2005, March 1). "Be More Persuasive." *Management Today*, 56; Venter, D. (2006). "Negotiation Persuasion." Retrieved June 29, 2006, from http://www.calumcoburn.co.uk/articles/articles-persuasion.html; Muir, G. (2006). "*All Presenting Is Persuasive.*" *Link&Learn eNewsletter*. Retrieved June 29, 2006, from http://www.linkageinc.com/company/news_events/link_learn/enewsletter/archive/2006/01; "Master the Art of Persuasion to Boost Your Managerial Effectiveness." (2006, February). *Payroll Manager's Report*, 15; Cialdini, R. B. (2002, April). "The Science and Practice of Persuasion." *Cornell Hotel & Restaurant Administration Quarterly*, 40; and Francaro, K. E. (2004, August). "Managing by Persuasion." *Contract Management*, 4.

pp. 228–232 Planning and Composing Effective Sales Messages partly based on Benady, D. (2006, August 17). "From Search Box to Letterbox." *Marketing Week*, 33; Magill, K. (2006, August 1). "E-Mail Creative: What Works and What Doesn't." *Multichannel Merchant*, *2*(8), 21–22. Retrieved February 25, 2007, from Business Source Premier (EBSCO) database; and Zarwan, J. (2006, August 1). "Direct Mail Delivers." *American Printer*, *123*(8), 52–53. Retrieved February 25, 2007, from Business Source Premier (EBSCO) database.

Chapter 12

p. 288 Figure 11.9 based on Sullivan, D. (2006, August 21). "ComScore Media Metrix Search Engine Ratings." Retrieved June 28, 2007, from http://searchenginewatch.com/reports/article.php/2156431. During 2005 and 2006, AOL Search has lost percentage points, as did MSN, albeit less significantly than AOL. Yahoo has been hovering at around the 30 percent mark, while Google's popularity continues to rise.

Chapter 13

p. 309 Caption based on "Canadian Vehicle Survey," Transport Canada <www.tc.gc.ca/pol/en/aca/cvs/menu.htm>.

Chapter 14

p. 370 Figure 14.4 based on Sydel Sokuvitz and Amiso M. George, "Teaching Culture: The Challenges and Opportunities of International Public Relations," *Business Communication Quarterly*, June 2003, 97; Anthony C. Koh, "Teaching Understanding Cultural Differences for Business in an Internet-Based Economy," *Journal of Teaching in International Business, 15* (2), 2003, 27; and Karen S. Sterkel, "Integrating Intercultural Communication and Report Writing in the Communication Class," *The Bulletin of the Association for Business Communication*, September 1988, 14–16.

Chapter 15

p. 379 Career Coach box based on Dianna Booher, "Selling Your Ideas," *Executive Excellence*, May 2004, 27; Sandra Gittlen, "The Public Side of You," *Network World*, 26 July 2004, 61; Hal Lancaster, "Practice and Coaching Can Help You Improve Um, Y'Know, Speeches," *The Wall Street Journal*, 9 January 1996, B1; and Bert Decker, "Successful Presentations: Simple and Practical," *HR Focus*, February 1992, 19.

p. 381 Discussion of effective imagery based on Ellyn Spragins, "In a Manner of Speaking," *Fortune Small Business*, June 2003, 18; Jeff Olson, *Giving Great Presentations* (Bristol, VT: Velocity Business Publishing, 1997), 32–37; Kevin Daley, "Using the Right Evidence for Effective Presentations," *Communication Briefings*, April 1997, 8a; and Patricia Calderon, "Anatomy of a Great Presentation," *Windows Magazine*, June 1998, 2031.

p. 384 Figure 15.2 based on Dianna Booher, *Speak With Confidence* (New York: McGraw-Hill Professional, 2003), 131–143; U.S. Department of Labor, "Presenting Effective Presentations With Visual Aids" <http://www.osha.gov/doc/outreachtraining/htmlfiles/traintec.html> (Retrieved 11 October 2004); and Shay McConnon, *Presenting With Power* (Oxford: How To Books, Ltd., 2002), 38–43.

p. 385 Discussion of multimedia presentations partially based on Bill Howard, "Showtime Follies: The PowerPoint Road Show Presentation Lives On, Despite Maltreatment of the Art Form by Occasionally Clueless Presenters," *PC Magazine*, 13 July 2004, 81; Stephen Porter, "Punch Up Your PowerPoint," *Staging Rental Operations*, 1 May 2004, 3; Linda Bird, "15 Top PowerPoint Tips," *PC Magazine* (30 December 2003), 71; and Greg Jaffe, "What's Your Point, Lieutenant? Please Just Cut to the Pie Charts," *The Wall Street Journal*, 26 April 2000, A1.

Chapter 16

p. 408 Searching for a Job Electronically based on Lorraine Farquaharson, "Technology (A Special Report); The Best Way To . . . Find a Job," *The Wall Street Journal*, 15 September 2003, R8; Kris Maher and Rachel Emma Silverman, "Your Career Matters: Online Job Sites Yield Few Jobs, Users Complain," *The Wall Street Journal*, 2 January 2002, A7; Elisabeth Goodrich and Michelle George, "Employer-Backed Job Site Lets Companies Avoid Monster," *InformationWeek*, 25 February 2002, 24.

p. 417 Optimizing Your Résumé for Today's Technologies based on Anne Fisher, "How to Ruin an Online Job Hunt," *Fortune*, 28 June 2004, 43; Michelle Conlin, "The Résumé Doctor Is In," *Business Week*, 14 July 2003, 116; Frequently Asked Questions, Quintessential Resumes & Cover Letters <http://www.resumesandcoverletters.com/services_prices.html> (Retrieved 26 September 2004); and "How to Write a Scannable Résumé," University of Kentucky Career Center <http:www.uky.edu/CareerCenter/scanhowto.html> (Retrieved 28 September 2004)

index

A

Abbreviations, A-21–A-22
Abstract, 342
Abusive language, 244
Academic documentation, vs. business documentation, 295
Accede, exceed, A-26
Accept, except, A-26
Access, electronic, for formal research methods, 112–113
Access cards, 316
Action stage in listening, 54
Action verbs, 417
Active voice, managing, 123
Activity reports, 319
Adaptation
- audience, 217
- direct request letter, 191
- justification/recommendation report, 326
- of message to audience, 98–104
- in writing process, 98

Adjectives, A-10–A-11
Adjustment letters, 198–199, 201
- apology, 200
- goals, 199, 207
- language of, 200
- persuasive, 225

Adverbs, A-10–A-11
Adverse, averse, A-26
Advice, advise, A-26
Affect, effect, A-26
Age, avoiding bias, 101
Agreement
- on procedures, 33
- on purpose, 33

All ready, already, A-26
All right, alright, A-26
Alphanumeric outlines, 116–117
Altar, alter, A-26
American Press Institute, 123
American Psychological Association (APA), 298, 350, B-1, B-4
- bibliography sample references, B-5
- in-text format, B-4
- reference format, B-5

Analysis
- business letters, 188
- financial, 345
- market, 345
- in writing process, 95–97

Analytical reports, 118, 333
- checklist, 330–333
- in memo format, 276
- writing short, 324–333

Anticipation, in writing process, 97–98
APA. *See* American Psychological Association (APA)
Apology letters, 200
Appearance
- of business documents, 60, 63
- of people, 60–62
- in workplace, 62

Appendix, in report, 343
Application follow-up letter, 431
Application forms, 432
Appraise, apprise, A-26
Appreciation, showing, 190
ASAP (as soon as possible), 79
Ascent, assent, A-26
ASCII document, online, 423
Assure, ensure, insure, A-26
Audience
- adapting to, 217
- analysis, and report organization, 273
- intercultural, 77–78
- international and cross-cultural, 394–397
- profiling, 97
- receptive, 119
- techniques for gaining and keeping attention of, 379
- unreceptive, 120
- workplace, 82

Audience rapport
- how best speakers build, 381–383
- techniques for gaining, 399

Audioconferencing, 43
Authorization request, 342
AutoContent Wizard feature, for presentation, 387

B

Baby boomers, 9
Bad news letters. *See* Negative messages
Bar charts, 300
Barriers
- listening process and, 53–55, 63
- mental, 53
- physical, 53

bcc (blind carbon copy), 161
Bias, avoiding
- age, 101
- disability, 101
- gender, 100–101
- racial or ethnic, 101

Bias-free language, 100
Bibliography, 350. *See also* Documentation
Blank space, 142
Blind carbon copy, 161
Block style for business letters, 188–189
Blogs, 8, 44, 97
Body, in e-mail and memos, 158
Body language. *See* Nonverbal communication
Bold type, 142
Books, finding, for research, 285
Boolean searches, 289
Brainstorming, 113
- for brochure, 114

Buffers for opening, 246
Bulleted lists, using, for quick comprehension, 141
Business communication, functions of, 14
Business communicators, goals of ethical, 19, 143
Business databases, 288
Business documents
- academic documentation vs., 295
- appearance of, 60

Business letters
- analyzing, 188
- characteristics of good letter, 183–186
- as confidential, 183

conveying formality and sensitivity, 184
delivering persuasive, well-considered messages, 184
formatting, 189
necessity of, 183
as permanent record, 183
requests for information or action, 188–190
structure and characteristics of, 186, 206
Business messages, 120
Business organizations, 81
Business outlines, components of, 118
Business plans, components of, 344–345, 367
Business reports
3-x-3 writing process, 302
basics, 302
Business writers, Web search tools for, 288
Business writing
basics of, 92, 106
goal of, 92, 136
Bypassing, 11–12, 21

C

Capital, capitol, A-26
Capitalization, 142, A-18–A-20
Carbon copy, 161
Card catalogues, 285
Career Coach
audience attention, 379
avoiding stage fright, 392
casual apparel in workplace, 61
interview questions, 436
multi-generational workforce, 9
Careless language, 245
Casual apparel, perils of, 61
Cc (carbon copy), 161
Cell phones, 43
Cereal, serial, A-26
Channels of communication
choosing best, 96
e-mail as channel of choice, 154
formal, 16
informal, 18
selecting, 96
Charts
bar, 300
flow, 301
line, 300
organization, 301
pie, 300
Checklist
for composing sentences and paragraphs, 128–129
for customized cover letter, 430
for customized résumé, 424
for e-mail messages and memos, 173
for preparing and organizing oral presentations, 395–397
for preparing formal reports, 365–366
for productive meetings, 41
for writing analytical reports, 330–333
for writing direct requests, 194
for writing goodwill messages, 205
for writing informational reports, 322
for writing positive reply letters, 201
for writing proposals, 343
Chrono-functional résumé, 412
Chronological résumé, 410
Citation formats, 298
Cite, site, sight, A-26
Claim letters, 227
body of, 193
denying claims, 256–257
direct, 195
Claims, delaying, 191, 194
Clarity, revising for, 136
Clauses and phrases, 122
Closings. *See* Conclusions
Cluster diagrams, 116
Coarse, course, A-26
Coherence, transitional expressions to build, 128
Coherent paragraphs, 127
Collaborate, ability to, 34
Collaborative documents, technology to edit and revise, 96
Collaborative technology, usefulness of, 42, 46
Colons, A-14–A-16
Combination résumé, 412–413
Commas, A-11–A-13
Comma splice, A-3
Comments, inserting, in Word, 96
Communication, 16
business, 14
channels, choosing, 97
checklist for improving, 80
clear, 19
in digital groups, 29
emphasis on instant, 14–16
examining, 10
innovative, 5–6
intercultural, 69–70, 77
in new world of work, 9
nonverbal, 57–58
oral, 15
in organizations, 13–16
process of, 10–12, 21
style of, 74
written, 15
Communication skills
importance of, 20–21
strengthening, 20–21
Communication technology
evolving nature of, 286–290
nature of, 303
use of, 33
Communicators, 78
Company database, 423
Company intranets, 7
Company policy, 247
Competent Language Usage Essentials (C.L.U.E.)
abbreviations, A-21–A-22
capitalization, A-18–A-20
grammar, A-4–A-8
number usage, A-20–A-21
punctuation, A-11–A-14
sentence structure, A-2–A-3
Complaint letters, 225, 227, 235
Complement, compliment, A-26
Complex documents, proofreading, 145–146
Composing
sentences and paragraphs, checklist for, 128–129
short paragraphs for readability, 128
in writing process, 121
Compound prepositions, reducing, 139
Computer programs, 145
Conciseness, revising for, 137
Conclusions
drawing, 310–314
in e-mail and memos, 159–160, 174
of formal reports, 349–350
for writing analytical reports, 333
for writing informational reports, 322
Conference reports, 319, 321
Conferences
voice, 8, 43
Web, 8, 43
Conflict
ability to confront, 33
six-step procedure for dealing with, 31
Congratulatory messages, answering, 206
Conscience, conscious, A-26
Consumer protection, 199
Consumer reports, 309
Consumers, 81
Context (cultural dimension), 73
Conversational tone, revising for, 137
Cooling-off period, 136
Copy, carbon/courtesy, 161
Copyright laws, 19
Correlations, 309
Council, counsel, A-26

Courteous tone, 102
Courtesy copy, 161
Cover letter, customized, 425–431
Cover letter, solicited, 428
Credible, creditable, A-26
Credit
giving, for ideas, 20
refusing, 256–257
Credit denials, 258
Critical listening, 52
Critical thinking, learning, 6
Cross-cultural audience, adapting to, 394–395
Cross-tabulated data, 308
Cultural gap, bridging, 76–77
Cultures
basis of self-identity and community, 72
characteristics of, 71, 83
comparing low- and high-context, 73
definition of, 83
dimensions of, 73, 83
as dynamic, 72
as inherently logical, 72
learning, 71
understanding, 71
visible and invisible in, 72
Customer reply letter, 197
Customers, disappointed, dealing with, 253–254

D

Dangling modifier, 124
Dashes, A-17
Data
analyzing, for conclusions, 311
categories of, 284
documenting, 295
illustrating, 298
interpreting, 308–310
as lists/alphanumeric/decimal outlines, 129
organization of, 114, 314
primary sources, 303
tabulating and analyzing, 308
Database, 285
commercial, 287
Data.com, 254
Decimal outline, 117
Decoding, 11
Defamation, 244
Delivery methods, 391–392
Dependent clauses, 122
Desert, dessert, A-26
Device, devise, A-26
Digital formats, of reports, 278
Digital groups, communication in, 29
Direct claims, 191, 207
concluding, 194
explaining and justifying, 193
opening, 192
Direct-mail letters, to promote services and products, 184
Direct-mail sales letters, 228
Directness, revising for, 139–140
Direct opening, 119
in business letters, 186
Direct organizational pattern, 120, 325
Direct paragraph plan, 125
Direct reply letters, 196–198
adjustments, 198–201
arrange information logically, 198
closing, 200–201
emphasizing positive in, 198
opening, 196, 199
reasons for, 199
Direct writing, 127
Disability bias, avoiding, 101
Disburse, disperse, A-26
Discriminative listening, 52
Distractions, 13, 55
Diverse workforce, 6
Diversity. *See also* Cultures; Intercultural communication, importance of
dividends of, 81
divisiveness of, 81
Documentation
in academic world, 295
in business, 295, 303
completing, 96
learning, 296
purposes of, 295
Donation request, refusing, 250
Dovetailing sentences, 127
Downward communication flow, 16–17
Drafting, paragraphs, 125

E

E-commerce, 6
Editing tools, 96
Effective business plan, preparing, 344
Effective teams, 32
Electronic databases, 285
Electronic handouts, 390
Electronic indexes, 285
Electronic notetaking, 296
Electronic presentations, 7
Electronic research data, managing, 290
Elicit, illicit, A-26
E-mail, 97, 142
adaptation, 157
analysis, 157
anticipation, 157
bad and good, 167
as business letters, 183
composition, 157
confirmation, 173, 175
content, tone, and correctness in, 165
cover letter, 429
evaluation, 157
formatting, 159
function of, 156
information and procedure, 168–169, 175
informative, 160
managing, 17
for online collaboration, 42
online résumé for, 420
organization, 157
proofreading, 157
reply, 175
request, 171
research, 157
revision, 157
skill in writing, 156
structure and format of, 158, 174
writing confirmation, 172
E-mail practices, smart, 164–166
Emotional interference, 21
Empathy, 76, 99
Employment, interviewing for, 434–438
Employment search, 407
career path, 407
interests, 405
nature of jobs, 406
preparing for, 405–408
qualifications, 406
using traditional techniques, 408–409
Empty words, purging, 139
Encoding, 11
Envelop, envelope, A-26
E-portfolios
advantages, 421
creating, 420
Ethical business communicators, goals of, 19–20
Ethical responsibility, acceptance of, 34
Ethnic bias, avoiding, 101
Ethnocentrism
avoiding, 76
effects of, 83
Evaluation, 136
in listening process, 54
in writing process, 146
Every day, everyday, A-26
Executive summary, 342, 347
Eye contact, message from, 59

F

Face-to-face conversation, 97
Face-to-face group meeting, 97
Facial expression, message from, 59

Facts
identifying, in conversation, 55
opinions versus, 19, 55
Familiar words, 103
Farther, further, A-26
Fax, best use of, 97
Feasibility reports, 325, 329
Feedback to sender, 12
Fillers, removing, 138
Flesch-Kincaid Index, 142
Flow charts, 301
Fog Index, 142
Follow-up letters, 439
and employment documents, 431
Formal channels, 16
Formality, in different cultures, 74
Formally, formerly, A-26
Formal proposals, 367
appendix, 343
components of, 341–342
executive summary, 342
list of figures, 343
table of contents, 343
title page, 343
Formal reports, 349
appendix of, 350
body of, 349
components of, 346–347, 367
conclusions of, 349
cover, 346
example of, 352–364
executive summary, 348
final writing tips, 350–367
introduction, 348
letter/memo of transmittal, 346–347
list of figures, 347
recommendations of, 350
table of contents, 347
tips, 350–351
title page, 346
works cited/references, 350
writing, 346–350
Formats, 278
for alphanumeric outline, 117
for decimal outline, 117
digital, 278
letter, 278
manuscript, 278
memo, 278
outlining, 117
toolbar, 96
Forms, printed, 278
Frames of reference, differing, 12
Frontloading, 186
advantages of, 120
Functional résumé, 411–412

G

Gap recruiting brochure, 117
GATT. *See* General Agreement on Tariffs and Trade (GATT)
Gender, aware of differences, 56
Gender bias, avoiding, 100
General Agreement on Tariffs and Trade (GATT), 69
Generalizations, 72–73
Generation X, 9
Generation Y, 9
Gestures, 77
posture and, 59
Glass ceiling, 81
Globalization, of markets, 4–5, 69–70
Global village, 69, 286
Good-guy syndrome, 245
Goodwill messages, 202–206
checklist for, 205
response to, 204
sympathy, 204
thank-you letter, 202–204
Goodwill tone, in business letter, 188
Google, 287
Grammar, 144
Grammar-checking software, 145
Grapevine, 18
Graphics and objectives, matching, 298
Graphic techniques, improving readability with, 142
Grate, great, A-26
Grids, 309
Group decisions, 32
Groups, 122
and teams, 28, 45
Groupthink, 45
avoiding, 32
Groupware, 42
Guide words, 161

H

Handheld wireless devices, 7
Handouts, 384
designing, 400
planning, 383–385
Headings, 140, 317
identifying, 162
for visual impact, 142
Hole, whole, A-26
Horizontal flow of communication, 18
Human resources information, 106
Hyperlinks, 390

I

Ideas
to build coherence, 127
emphasizing, 123
for Old Navy/Gap recruiting brochure, 115
organizing, into patterns, 118–121
sustaining key, 127
tips for activating, 116
Illustrations, 301
Imply, infer, A-26
Incident reports, 172
Inclusive language, 19–20
Independent clauses, 122
Indirect opening, 119
in business letters, 186
Indirect paragraph plan, to explain and persuade, 126
Indirect organizational pattern, 120, 325
Individualism, 73
Inflated résumés, 422
Informal channels, 18
Informal proposals
authorization request, 342
background, problem, purpose of, 341
budget, 342
components of, 340–341
introduction, 340
proposal, plan, schedule of, 341–342
staffing, 342
Informal reports, components of, 347
Informal research, 113
Information
collecting, 36
distributing advance, for meeting, 38
Informational reports, 118
in letter format, 274
Information mobility, 287
Instant messaging (IM), 43, 97, 101
Intercultural audiences, written messages for, 79
Intercultural communication, importance of, 69–70, 83
Intercultural environments, improving written messages in, 84
Intercultural proficiency
achieving, 76
checklist for improving, 80
Internal communication, 14
Internal proposals, 324
Internal request, refusing, 251
International audience, adapting to, 394
Internet, 70
-based business, 6
tips and techniques for search in, 287–288
and Web, 286
Interpretation stage, in listening, 54, 56
Interview follow-up letter, 432–433

Interviews, 294
    before, 434
    during, 435–436
Intimate zone, 60
Intranets, company, 7
Introduction, capturing attention in, 377
Investigative reports, 322
Investment information, 105
Invitations, declining, 251–252
Italics, 142
"I/we" view, cultivating, 99

J

Jargon, 103
Job boards, 408
Job refusals, 260
Jobs
    collecting information and generating ideas on, 114
    openings for solicited, 426
    openings for unsolicited, 426
Journals, 285
Justification reports, 324
    direct pattern, 326
    indirect pattern, 327

K

KISS formula, 137

L

Lag time, 56
Language
    for adjustment letters, 200
    careless, 245
    inclusive, 19–20
    simplifying, 103
Language skills, 13. *See also* Competent Language Usage Essentials (C.L.U.E.)
Leadership, shared, 34
Lead-ins, long, deleting, 138
Lean, lien, A-26
Legal responsibilities, adapting communication to, 104–106
Letter of application, 425
Letters, 97, 118
    adjustments, 207
    apologize, 200
    business (*see* Business letters)
    claim, 191, 227
    complaint, 227
    formats, 188, 278
    information or action request, 194
    and memos, 120
    order, 190–191
    proposals, 340
    with requests, 201, 207
    reports, tips for, 274
    routine, 183
    structure of requests and responses, 187
Liable, libel, A-27
Line charts, advantage of, 300
Listening
    barriers, 53–55
    checklist, 57
    to colleagues and teammates, 52
    critical, 52
    to customers, 52
    discriminative, 52
    importance of, 63
    improving workplace listening, 55–57
    keys for improving skills in, 55–57
    poor listening habits, 51
    process, and barriers, 63
    to superiors, 52
    types of workplace, 52–53, 63
    in work place, 51–53
Lists
    and bullets, 140
    to organize ideas, 115
Logical development, in claim letter, 225
Loose, lose, A-27

M

Magazines, 285
Mailed questionnaires, disadvantages of, 291
Main sentence, 125
Manuscript formats, 278
Maps, 301
Marketing information, 105
Markets, globalization of, 69–70
Maybe, avoiding, 313
Mean, 309
Meaningful paragraphs, 129
Median, 309
Meetings
    agenda for, 39
    ending and following up, 41
    handling conflict in, 41
    participating actively and productively in, 40
    planning and participating in, 37–42
    problem solving, 38
    purpose, 38
"Melting pot" approach, 70
Memo formats, 278
Memos, 97, 118, 170
    confirmation, writing, 172
    formatting hard-copy, 161–163
    parts of, 158
    structuring, 158
Mental barriers to listening, 53
Messages
    channels of transmission, 11
    checklist, 104
    concise, 146
    decoding, 11
    efficient, 137
    goodwill, 202–207
    idea in, 11
    to intercultural audiences, 77
    kinds of, 120
    oral, 78
    written, 79
Metasearch engines, 288
Metastatic carcinomas, 103
Miner, minor, A-27
Misplaced modifiers, 128
Misspelled words, A-28
MLA (Modern Language Association), 350. *See also* Modern Language Association (MLA)
Mode, 309
Modern Language Association (MLA), 298, B-1–B-4
    bibliographic format, B-2
    bibliography sample references, B-3
    in-text format, B-2
Modifiers, dangling and misplaced, 124–125
Multi-generational workforce, understanding, 9
Multimedia presentations
    adapting text and colour selections, 386
    analyzing situation, 385
    anticipating audience, 385
    composing slideshow, 386
    designing, 385, 400
    developing, 396
    organizing slides, 386
    planning, 383–385
    researching PowerPoint options, 386
    steps to making, 388

N

NAFTA. *See* North American Free Trade Agreement (NAFTA)
Names and numbers, 144
Negative expressions, 102
Negative messages
    3-x-3 writing process, 244
    announcing to employees, 261
    avoiding legal problems, 244
    buffering the opening, 246
    checklist, 252, 258, 260

closing pleasantly, 248
cushioning bad news, 247
delivering customers, 253–258
delivering personally, 259
delivering workplace, 259–260
direct pattern, 243–244
follow-up message, 255
four-part indirect pattern for, 243
goals in communicating, 242
indirect pattern, 243
within organizations, 259
in other cultures, 262
presenting reasons, 247
refusing requests, 249–253
strategies for delivering, 242–246
techniques for delivering, 246, 263
Netiquette, 165
News releases, 234
Noise, 11
Nonverbal communication, 57, 77
checklist, 62
forms of, 58, 63
functions of, 58, 63
techniques for improving, 64, 83
Nonverbal messages, 11, 57–58, 382
Norming, phase in team development, 30
North American Free Trade Agreement (NAFTA), 69–70
Notes, to ensure retention, 56
Notetaking
electronic, 296
manual, 296
Noun phrases, avoiding, 140
Numbered lists, using, for quick comprehension, 141
Number usage, A-20–A-21

O

Objectivity in communication, 19
Obstacles, overcoming, 13
Ombudsman programs, 18
Online catalogues, 285
Online collaboration, e-mail for, 42
Online résumé, for e-mailing, 420
Open-access business information, 288
Openings
in e-mail and memos, 158, 173
for solicited jobs, 426
for unsolicited jobs, 426
Opinions
facts and, 55
labelling, 19
Oral communication, 15
disadvantages of, 15
improving, 83
Oral messages, 78
Oral presentations
computers for, 121
effective, 399
knowing your audience, 376
knowing your purpose, 376
organizing body, 378
outline for, 380
preparing effective, 376
techniques for adapting, 400
Order letters, 190–191
Organizational communication, forms of, 15
Organizational patterns, for informational and analytical reports, 315
Organization charts, 301
Organizations
communication in, 13–16
flow of communication in, 16–18
progressive, 4–5
structure, changing, 4–5
Organizing ideas, direct and indirect patterns for, 129
Outlines, 114–115
Outlining formats, 117

P

Pamphlets, 285
Paragraph plans, classic, 130
Paragraphs
coherence, 127
drafting meaningful, 125
in pivoting plan, 126
techniques for composing meaningful, 130
Parallelism, 140–141
Paraphrasing, to increase understanding, 56
Paraphrasing, plagiarizing and, 297
Parentheses, A-17
Participants, selecting, for meeting, 38
Passive voice, managing, 123
Patience, patients, A-27, 76, 83
Patterns
organizing ideas into, 118–121
for receptive audiences, 119
PDF (portable digital format) document, 272, 423
Peer-to-peer tools, for online communication, 5
Perception, stage in listening, 53
Performing, phase in team development, 30
Periodicals, 285
Periodic reports, 319
memo format, 320
Personal data, 416
Personal digital assistants (PDAs), 287
Personal, personnel, A-27
Personal zone, 60
Persuasion techniques, effective, 216–217
Persuasive action, request for, 224
Persuasive claims, writing, 225
Persuasive favour, request for, 223
Persuasive memo, 226
Persuasive messages, 216
3-x-3 writing process, 217–218, 234
building interest, 220
checklist, 228
components of, 218–221, 234
definition of, 216
ethical, 221
favours and actions, 222
four-part indirect pattern for, 218
gaining attention, 219–220
motivating action, 220–221
within organizations, 222–225, 235
purpose of, 217
reducing resistance, 220
researching and organizing data, 218
sales messages, 228
strategies for, 216
techniques for crafting successful, 221
writing successful, 222–228
Persuasive press releases
basic elements in, 235
developing, 234
Phone calls, best use of, 97
Phone conferencing, 43
Phones, video, 8
Photographs, in reports, 301
Phrases, clauses and, 122
Physical distractions, as barriers to communication, 21
Pie charts, 300
Plagiarizing and paraphrasing, 297
Plain English, 19
Plaintiff, plaintive, A-27
Podcasts, 8
Populace, populous, A-27
Positive words, 247
Posture, and gestures, 59
Powerful impact, organizing content for, 377
PowerPoint presentation, 3-x-3 writing process for, 385
Precede, proceed, A-27
Precedence, precedents, A-27
Precise words, 103
Prejudices, 72
Prepositions, reducing compound, 139
Presence technology, and communication, 8

Presentations, 376–397
electronic, 7
mulitmedia, 385–391
team-based written/oral, organizing, 35–37
Primary data, 284
Principal, principle, A-27
Print-based résumé, designing traditional, 418
Printed forms, 278
Printers, multifunctional, 7
Print indexes, 285
Print resources, 284
Problems, handling, with orders, 254–256
Progress reports, 322
letter format, 323
Pronouns
case, A-6–A-7
first-person, use of, in business messages, 137
reference, A-9–A-10
and paragraph coherence, 127
Proofreading, 136
complex documents, 145–146
first draft, 186
résumés, 423
routine documents, 144–145
in writing process, 144
Proposals, 97, 118
formal, 340
informal, 340
letter, 340
Prototypes, 72
Pseudolistening, 53
Public zone, 60
Punctuality, 75
Punctuation, A-10, 144
apostrophes, A-16
commas, A-11–A-14
dashes, A-17
parentheses, A-17
periods, A-18
question marks, A-17
quotation marks, A-18
semicolons and colons, A-14–A-16
Purpose, identifying, 95

Q

Question marks, A-17
Questions
for audience profiling, 98
clarifying, 56

R

Racial bias, avoiding, 101
Range, 309
Raw data, analyzing, 309
Readability
composing short paragraphs for, 128
formulas, 143
improving, with graphic techniques, 142
measuring, 142
revising for, 140
Reader cues, providing, 315–316
Receiver benefits, 11
spotlighting, 99
Receptive audiences, direct pattern for, 119
Recommendation reports, 313–314, 324
Redundancies, eliminating, 138
Reference request, 431
Rejection follow-up letter, 432
Remembering, factors for effective, 54
Reply letter, to customer request, 185
Report data
gathering and selecting, 284
organizing, 333
Reports, 97
3-x-3 writing process, 278–282
analytical reports, 273, 275, 324–333
analyzing problem and purpose, 279
anticipating audience and issues, 280
basics of, 272–278
conclusions and recommendations, 312
direct pattern, 273
elements in introducing, 316
formats of, 278
functions, 273
with graphics, 303
incident, 172
incorporating graphics in, 301–302
informational reports, 273
justification/recommendation, 324
levels of headings in, 318
ordering information logically, 314–315
organizational patterns, 273
periodic, 319
progress and interim, 322
recommendations, preparing, 311
sources, 282–286, 291–295
to-file, 172
work plan, 282
writing formal, 346–350
writing informational, 317–324
writing styles, 277
Reports, yardstick, 327
Request for proposal (RFP), 340
Request letter, direct, 191
Requests
clarifying, in business letters, 189
making, for information, 169
replying to, 170–172, 185
structure for, 187
Research
definition of, 112
formal, 112
habits, developing, 296
informal, 113
observation and experimentation, 294–295
in writing process, 112–114
Résumé, 438
with action verbs, 416
applying final touches to, 421
arranging parts, 414
checklist for, 424
inflated, 422
optimizing, for technology, 417, 421
polishing, 421
proofreading, 423
in rich text format, 420
submitting, 423
Résumé follow-up letter, 431
Résumé-scanning software, 419
Résumé style
choosing, 409
chronological, 409
combination, 412
functional, 409
Retention, enhancing, 54
Revising messages, checklist for, 143
Revision
for clarity, 136
for conciseness, 137
goals of, 143
for readability, 140
techniques, 146–147
in writing process, 136–137
Robert's Rules of Order, 39
Routine documents, proofreading, 144–145
Routine letters, 183

S

Safety messages, 105
Sales letters, 233
traditional, 228
Sales messages
3-x-3 writing process to, 229
adapting audience, 229
analyzing the product and purpose, 229
building interest, 230
checklist, 232
composing outstanding, 235
crafting, 229

gaining attention, 230
motivating action, 231–232
putting it together, 232
reducing resistance, 231
Sample business plans, on Web, 345–346
Saving face, 76
Scannable résumé, preparing, 418
Scratch lists, 114–115
Search engines, 288
Search, manual, for formal research, 113
Search tools, identifying, 287
Secondary data, 284
Self-directed teams, 45
self-ending pronouns, A-10
Semicolons, A-14–A-16
Sender, in communication process, 10
Sentence
fragments, A-2
run-on, A-3
structure, A-2–A-3
Sentences
basic elements, 122
creating effective, 122
kinds of, 125
preferring short, 123
supporting sentence, 125
Sexist language, 100
Signature block, in e-mail and memos, 161
Silence, to show tolerance, 77
Slander, 244
Social interaction, space zones for, 60
Social zone, 60
Space zones, for social interaction, 60
Spell checker software, 145
Sprint writing, 122
Stage fright, avoiding, 392
Stationary, stationery, A-27
Stereotypes versus prototypes, 72–73
Storming, phase in team development, 30
Style checkers, 145
Subject directories, 288
Subject line, in e-mail and memos, 158, 173
Subject–verb agreement, A-6, 122
Survey data, as tables, 310
Surveys
advantages of, 291
preparing, 293
Sympathy messages, 205

T

Tables, 308
making, 299
numerical datas in, 309
TEAM concept, 33
Team-based management, expanded, 5
Team-based written/oral presentations
organizing, 35–37
techniques for, 45
Team development
phases of, 30
understanding, 30–33
Team failure, problems, symptoms and solutions, 31
Team presentation, editing, rehearsing, and evaluating, 37
Team reports, organizing, writing, and revising, 36
Teams
characteristics of successful, 33–35, 45
effectiveness, developing, 34
groups and, 28, 45
working with, 94
Teamwork skills, strengthening, 44
Technology
advances in, 70
for editing and revising collaborative documents, 96
presence, 8
Teleconferences, 43, 97
Telephone and voice mail skills, improving, 397, 400
Telephone calls
making, 397
receiving, 398
Territory, 60
Thank-you letter, 203
Than, then, A-27
Their, there, they're, A-27
Time, ordering data by, 314–315
Tips
for activating ideas, 115
for converting raw data, 310
for formal reports, 367
for formatting hard-copy memos, 163
for making outlines, 117
for maximizing scannability, 418
for memo reports, 276
for writing claim letters, 227
for writing conclusions, 312
for writing progress reports, 323
for writing recommendations, 313
To-file reports, 172
Tolerance, 76, 83
Tone
importance of, in persuasion messages, 217
moderate, in claim letter, 225
To, too, two, A-27
Track changes, 96
Traditionalists, 9
Transitional expressions, A-13, 127
to build coherence, 128
connections with, 127
Transitions, 316
Transmittal, letter of, 342
Trip reports, 319
Trite business phrases, dumping, 140

U

Underlining, 142
Unprocessed data, 308
Unreceptive audiences, indirect pattern for, 120
Upward flow of communication, 17–18

V

Verbs
active or passive, 124
agreement, A-5–A-6
mood, A-4–A-5
subjects and, 122
tense, A-4
voice, A-5
Verbal data, 309
Verbal signposts, 382
Vertical lists, for improving readability, 142
Videoconference, 43, 97
Video phones, 8
Vigour, revising for, 139–140
Virtual communities, 286
Virtual teams, formation of, 29
Visual aids
designing, 400
planning, 383–385
types of, 383
Visual impact, headings for, 142
Voice conference, 8, 43
Voice mail, 97, 399
Voice over Internet Protocol (VoIP), 7
Voice recognition software, 7
VoIP. *See* Voice over Internet Protocol (VoIP)

W

Waiver, waver, A-27
Web, 75
and internet, 286
sample business plans on, 345
Web conference, 8, 43
Weblogs, for online communication, 5
Web pages, computers for, 121
Web search tools, for business writers, 288
Web sources, evaluating, 289–291
Web, to sell products, 70
Wikipedia, 286
Wikis, 8, 44, 97
Wireless devices, handheld, 7

Words
- confusing, A-26–A-27
- misspelled, A-28
- purging empty, 139

Work environments, changes in, 6
Workforce
- diverse, 6
- intercultural, 70
- multi-generational, 9

Workforce diversity, capitalizing on, 80–83
Workplace
- audiences, tips for improving communication among, 82
- changes in, 4–9
- groups and teams in, 28–29
- listening in, 51–53
- listening, techniques for improving, 63
- manners, demonstration of, 34
- positive nonverbal signals in, 62

Work plan, for formal report, 283
Work teams, 81
World Wide Web, 70, 75, 286
Writing process
- adaptation phase, 98–104
- altered, 106
- analysis phase, 95–97
- anticipation phase, 97–98
- approaching, 92–93
- composing, 121
- for effective e-mail messages and memos, 156
- evaluation in, 146
- organizing, 114–118
- proofreading, 144
- research, 112–114
- revision, 136–137

Writing request
- and reply e-mail messages/ memos, 169

Writing style, 277
Written communication, 15–16
Written messages, 79
- computers for, 121
- drawbacks of, 16

Y

Yardstick reports, 327
- advantage to, 328

"You" view, cultivating, 99

Z

Zones, space, 60